READINGS IN MANAGEMENT

An Organizational Perspective

READINGS IN MANAGEMENT

An Organizational Perspective

CARL R. ANDERSON
MARTIN J. GANNON

University of Maryland

LITTLE, BROWN AND COMPANY
Boston   Toronto

PREFACE
An Overview of the Management Profession

In a recent address to the Eastern Academy of Management, Clarence Walton, the president of the Catholic University of America, predicted that management will become the focus of the liberal arts education.[1] One of the basic premises of his statement is the need to integrate fields of knowledge such as sociology, psychology, engineering, anthropology, and biology into the broader discipline that we today call management, accomplishing goals that require the inputs of a group of people in a coordinated fashion.

Walton's statement reflects the marked change in the way the academician and the practitioner view the practice of management. Management writers, even through the 1960s, had rarely thought about their profession as an integrated body of knowledge. Early writers such as Fayol and Taylor relied primarily on practical experience or training in a specialized discipline (such as engineering) for development of their skills or "principles" of management. Others specialized in one or more of the classic disciplines, as Max Weber did in economics and sociology. With the publication of the results of the Hawthorne studies, specialists in the "behavioral" fields of psychology and sociology dominated the management scene for several years. More recently, however, management specialists have found that they need to have knowledge of all these subjects and to apply sound principles from each according to a logical framework.

The cornerstone of the study of management, then, is the organization and integration of this rather diverse body of knowledge. This book of readings parallels the integrated organizational perspective that Martin Gannon has developed in his recent work.[2] According to this perspective, there are four dimensions within which managerial activities take place: organization design, planning and control, behavioral processes, and decision making. Although each manager will typically be involved in activities only within one or two dimensions at a time, each must understand the importance of these dimensions and how they relate to one another.

Organization design is the construction of the most stable characteristics of the organization, including tasks, physical relationships among people, the flow of work, and authority. Typical problems in organization design include determining the proper number of subordinates that each manager should supervise, the amount of authority that should be placed in each organizational position, the formal system of communication between units, and the procedures for handling employee grievances.

[1] Distinguished Lecture, Eastern Academy of Management, The George Washington University, Washington, D.C., 1976.
[2] Martin Gannon, *Management: An Organizational Perspective* (Boston: Little, Brown, 1977).

The second dimension, a system for *guiding and monitoring organizational activities,* primarily involves planning and control. That is, the organization must rationally guide its activities by developing a plan or a set of plans that provides a blueprint for its future. In conjunction with its planning activities, the organization must develop *control systems* that will effectively monitor significant deviations from these courses of action.

The third basic dimension of management involves the *behavioral processes* that occur in organizations. These processes involve the employee's reactions to his or her job, including job satisfaction and task motivation, the relationship between leaders and subordinates, and the relationships among individuals within groups.

Finally, decision making is a problem-solving activity that comes into play when managers feel that the gap between *what is* and *what should be* is too great. After managers make decisions, they analyze the performance of organizational members, organizational subsystems, and the entire organization (separately or together). If they decide that changes are warranted, the managers initiate them within the dimensions of organization design, planning and control, and behavioral processes.

The readings in the following chapters serve two basic educational purposes. Each chapter presents normative discussions that summarize the current state of knowledge *within* each dimension of management. The *integration* of these dimensions is then examined in order to aid the student of management in formulating sound decision frameworks. In order to make "ideal" decisions, a manager needs both kinds of knowledge; he needs to know the relevant material from specialized disciplines, and he needs to know how to integrate and apply this diverse material. Readings have been selected according to these two criteria.

Following the format of Gannon's book, the readings have been arranged in terms of the four dimensions of management; and there is one additional section, on managerial careers, entrepreneurship, and the problems that managers will face in the future. Each section is preceded by a short discussion of its underlying themes and of each article to provide the student with some guidelines concerning the purpose of the chapter and reasons for inclusion of these particular articles. To further facilitate the use of this book, we have provided a readings cross-reference matrix (see pp. 429–433) that shows how the articles correspond to chapters in seventeen selected management textbooks.

We would like to give special thanks to the authors, researchers, and publishers who granted permission to reprint these selections. Specific recognition is given to the authors in the introduction to each chapter.

CONTENTS

III BEHAVIOR IN ORGANIZATIONS

Section A: Motivation   168

Section B: Leadership   194

Section C: Group Behavior   239

Section D: Communication   275

IV MANAGERIAL DECISION MAKING

READINGS IN MANAGEMENT

An Organizational Perspective

V MANAGERIAL CAREERS AND ORIENTATIONS

Section A: Entrepreneurship   334

Section B: The Individual and His Career   377

Section C: The Current and Future State of Management   381

ORGANIZATION
DESIGN

I

■ The construction of the most stable characteristics of the organization is an essential first step in understanding the role of the modern manager. The following two groups of readings are focused on the design of organizations. Section A, Organizational Models, is concerned with theoretical and descriptive statements of the ways various management writers view the concept of organization. Section B, Technology and Environmental Uncertainty, examines one important influence on the design of the organization, the external environment — especially the task environment in which the firm operates.

Section A:
Organizational
Models

Models of organizations are important since "the model which a manager holds normally determines his perception of the organizational world about him. It leads to certain assumptions about people and certain interpretations of events he encounters. The underlying model serves as an unconscious guide to each manager's behavior. He acts as he thinks."[1] Thus the model of organization that a manager holds ultimately affects the success or failure of the organization through its effect on the day-to-day activities of the manager.

The four readings in this section are intended to provide a broad, though not comprehensive, selection of viewpoints on models of organization. The first selection by Max Weber presents the classic bureaucratic model in the words of its creator. The effect of this formulation on the present world is so pronounced that it hardly needs emphasis. A key point in Weber's model is that authority in the organization lies with the "supreme chief." Further, the bureaucracy ideally functions according to the ten criteria that Weber set forth in the early part of this century. Although Weber draws on the military for many examples, he did not intend this model to apply only to the military. In Weber's words, "this type of organization is in principle applicable . . . in profit making businesses or in charitable organizations, or in any other types of private enterprises."

In the second reading, Warren Bennis examines the dysfunctional consequences of the bureaucratic model and explores some changing conditions that may make Weber's classic formulation obsolete. Bennis points out that bureaucracy leads to conformity and "groupthink," does not allow for personal growth and development, and converts people into the "organization man" stereotype. To support his argument, Bennis includes an interesting selection from Weber's later writings in which Weber himself condemns the bureaucratic model.

Why does bureaucracy yield these dysfunctional consequences? Bennis postulates that the underlying assumptions of the bureaucratic model are inadequate. He believes the human element should receive more emphasis,

[1] K. Davis, "Evolving Models of Organizational Behavior," *Academy of Management Journal,* March 1968, pp. 27–38.

and that the model should take into consideration the influence of the external environment on the organization. As an alternative to the bureaucratic model, Bennis proposes the "organic-adaptive" model, which better meets the changing environmental conditions he outlines. A comparison of these first two articles can generate an interesting discussion on the applicability of bureaucracy in today's world; is there still a place for bureaucracy?

In the third selection, Peter Drucker presents a descriptive rather than theoretical view of the problems of design, structure, and organizational models. As he states,

> organization structures are becoming increasingly short lived and unstable. Few managers seem to realize that the right organization structure is not performance itself but rather a prerequisite of performance. The wrong structure is indeed a guarantee of nonperformance; it produces friction and frustration, puts the spotlight on the wrong issues, and makes mountains out of trivia.

Two additional models of organization are then discussed, the administrative model of Fayol and the federal decentralization model of General Motors. According to Drucker, if they fit the environmental conditions they are still applicable, but they fit "increasingly fewer situations" for the following reasons:

1. Today's businesses are not manufacturing institutions, but have their emphasis on outside services and nonbusiness service institutions.
2. Today's businesses are not single-product firms; they have great complexity and diversity.
3. Many companies are now multinational.
4. Information handling has become a major organizational problem.
5. The basic organizational problem today concerns not manual production workers but knowledge work and knowledge workers.
6. Businesses are increasingly entrepreneurial rather than managerial organizations.

As a solution to these changing conditions, Drucker discusses three new design principles, team organization, simulated decentralization, and systems structure. Drucker agrees with Bennis that any structure must incorporate both task and personal elements.

The first three selections in this section have presented some remarkable contrasts in organizational models. Let us examine just one dimension: organizational design. Weber's bureaucratic model is largely centered on task and efficiency; Bennis concentrates on the personal dimension and proposes the elimination of many standard bureaucratic characteristics; Drucker focuses on new organization designs, which draw on the experience of past successful models, and he proposes changes or modifications in these basic structures. The last selection by Galbraith draws on all of these models in the design of "matrix" structures. Matrix structures combine departmentation by function (separate departments for engineering, marketing, industrial relations, and so forth) and departmentation by product. The product manager has the overall responsibility for the completion of projects; the functional managers lend employees to the product manager to complete the projects, and they exercise technical authority over their completion.

These views of organization design are certainly not all-inclusive. But they do present some major historical trends and controversies in the field. One conclusion might be, as Drucker has stated, "there is no one final answer." The next group of readings examines one major reason why this is so.

MAX WEBER

Legal Authority: The Pure Type with Employment of a Bureaucratic Administrative Staff

The purest type of exercise of legal authority is that which employs a bureaucratic administrative staff. Only the supreme chief of the organization occupies his position of authority by virtue of appropriation, of election, or of having been designated for the succession. But even *his* authority consists in a sphere of legal 'competence.' The whole administrative staff under the supreme authority then consists, in the purest type, of individual officials who are appointed and function according to the following criteria: [9]

(1) They are personally free and subject to authority only with respect to their impersonal official obligations.

(2) They are organized in a clearly defined hierarchy of offices.

(3) Each office has a clearly defined sphere of competence in the legal sense.

(4) The office is filled by a free contractual relationship. Thus, in principle, there is free selection.

(5) Candidates are selected on the basis of technical qualifications. In the most rational case, this is tested by examination or guaranteed by diplomas certifying technical training, or both. They are *appointed*, not elected.

(6) They are remunerated by fixed salaries in money, for the most part with a right to pensions. Only under certain circumstances does the employing authority, especially in private organizations, have a

[9] This characterization applies to the 'monocratic' as opposed to the 'collegial' type, which will be discussed below.

Reprinted with permission of Macmillan Publishing Co., Inc. from pp. 333–336 of *The Theory of Social and Economic Organizations* by Max Weber. Copyright 1954 by Talcott Parsons.

right to terminate the appointment, but the official is always free to resign. The salary scale is primarily graded according to rank in the hierarchy; but in addition to this criterion, the responsibility of the position and the requirements of the incumbent's social status may be taken into account.[10]

(7) The office is treated as the sole, or at least the primary, occupation of the incumbent.

(8) It constitutes a career. There is a system of 'promotion' according to seniority or to achievement, or both. Promotion is dependent on the judgment of superiors.

(9) The official works entirely separated from ownership of the means of administration and without appropriation of his position.

(10) He is subject to strict and systematic discipline and control in the conduct of the office.

This type of organization is in principle applicable with equal facility to a wide variety of different fields. It may be applied in profit-making business or in charitable organizations, or in any number of other types of private enterprises serving ideal or material ends. It is equally applicable to political and to religious organizations. With varying degrees of approximation to a pure type, its historical existence can be demonstrated in all these fields.

1. For example, this type of bureaucracy is found in private clinics, as well as in endowed hospitals or the hospitals maintained by religious orders. Bureaucratic organization has played a major role in the Catholic Church. It is well illustrated by the administrative role of the priesthood [11] in the modern church, which has expropriated almost all of the old church benefices, which were in former days to a large extent subject to private appropriation. It is also illustrated by the conception of the universal Episcopate, which is thought of as formally constituting a universal legal competence in religious matters. Similarly, the doctrine of Papal infallibility is thought of as in fact involving a universal competence, but only one which functions 'ex cathedra' in the sphere of the office, thus implying the typical distinction between the sphere of office and that of the private affairs of the incumbent. The same phenomena are found in the large-scale capitalistic enterprise; and the larger it is, the greater their role. And this is not less true of political parties, which will be discussed separately. Finally, the modern army is essentially a bureau-

[10] See below, chap. iv.
[11] *Kaplanokratie.*

cratic organization administered by that peculiar type of military functionary, the 'officer.'

2. Bureaucratic authority is carried out in its purest form where it is most clearly dominated by the principle of appointment. There is no such thing as a hierarchy of elected officials in the same sense as there is a hierarchical organization of appointed officials. In the first place, election makes it impossible to attain a stringency of discipline even approaching that in the appointed type. For it is open to a subordinate official to compete for elective honours on the same terms as his superiors, and his prospects are not dependent on the superior's judgment.[12]

3. Appointment by free contract, which makes free selection possible, is essential to modern bureaucracy. Where there is a hierarchical organization with impersonal spheres of competence, but occupied by unfree officials—like slaves or dependents, who, however, function in a formally bureaucratic manner—the term 'patrimonial bureaucracy' will be used.

4. The role of technical qualifications in bureaucratic organizations is continually increasing. Even an official in a party or a trade-union organization is in need of specialized knowledge, though it is usually of an empirical character, developed by experience, rather than by formal training. In the modern state, the only 'offices' for which no technical qualifications are required are those of ministers and presidents. This only goes to prove that they are 'officials' only in a formal sense, and not substantively, as is true of the managing director or president of a large business corporation. There is no question but that the 'position' of the capitalistic entrepreneur is as definitely appropriated as is that of a monarch. Thus at the top of a bureaucratic organization, there is necessarily an element which is at least not purely bureaucratic. The category of bureaucracy is one applying only to the exercise of control by means of a particular kind of administrative staff.

5. The bureaucratic official normally receives a fixed salary. By contrast, sources of income which are privately appropriated will be called 'benefices.'[13] Bureaucratic salaries are also normally paid in money. Though this is not essential to the concept of bureaucracy, it is the arrangement which best fits the pure type. Payments in kind are apt to have the character of benefices, and the receipt of a benefice normally implies the appropriation of opportunities for earnings and of positions. There are, however, gradual transitions in this field with many intermediate

---

[12] On elective officials, see below, sec. 14.

[13] *Pfründen*. On this concept, see below, sec. 7.—ED.

types. Appropriation by virtue of leasing or sale of offices or the pledge of income from office are phenomena foreign to the pure type of bureaucracy.

6. 'Offices' which do not constitute the incumbent's principal occupation, in particular 'honorary' offices, belong in other categories, which will be discussed later.[14] The typical 'bureaucratic' official occupies the office as his principal occupation.

7. With respect to the separation of the official from ownership of the means of administration, the situation is essentially the same in the field of public administration and in private bureaucratic organizations, such as the large-scale capitalistic enterprise.

8. Collegial bodies will be discussed separately below.[15] At the present time they are rapidly decreasing in importance in favour of types of organization which are in fact, and for the most part formally as well, subject to the authority of a single head. For instance, the collegial 'governments' in Prussia have long since given way to the monocratic 'district president.'[16] The decisive factor in this development has been the need for rapid, clear decisions, free of the necessity of compromise between different opinions and also free of shifting majorities.

9. The modern army officer is a type of appointed official who is clearly marked off by certain class distinctions. This will be discussed elsewhere.[17] In this respect such officers differ radically from elected military leaders, from charismatic condottieri,[18] from the type of officers who recruit and lead mercenary armies as a capitalistic enterprise, and, finally, from the incumbents of commissions which have been purchased.[19] There may be gradual transitions between these types. The patrimonial 'retainer,' who is separated from the means of carrying out his function, and the proprietor of a mercenary army for capitalistic purposes have, along with the private capitalistic entrepreneur, been pioneers in the organization of the modern type of bureaucracy. This will be discussed in detail below.[20]

[14] See below, sec. 14.

[15] See sec. 15.

[16] *Regierungs präsident.*

[17] See chap. iv. As has already been remarked, chap. iv was left incomplete and the part which is available contains no discussion of this subject.—Ed.

[18] See sec. 10.

[19] See sec. 8.

[20] The parts of Weber's work included in this translation contain only fragmentary discussions of military organization. It was a subject in which Weber was greatly interested and to which he attributed great importance for social phenomena generally. This factor is one on which, for the ancient world, he laid great stress in his important study, *Agrarverhältnisse im Altertum.* Though at various points in the rest of *Wirtschaft und Gesellschaft* the subject comes up, it is probable that he intended to treat it systematically but that this was never done.—Ed.

Beyond Bureaucracy

Will organization men fit the new organizations?

WARREN BENNIS

Most of us spend all of our working day and a great deal of our non-working day in a unique and extremely durable social arrangement called "bureaucracy." I use the term "bureaucracy" descriptively, not as an epithet about those "guys in Washington" or as a metaphor *a la* Kafka's *Castle* which conjures up an image of red tape, or faceless and despairing masses standing in endless lines. Bureaucracy, as I shall use the term here, is a social invention, perfected during the industrial revolution to organize and direct the activities of the business firm.

It is my premise that the bureaucratic form of organization is becoming less and less effective; that it is hopelessly out of joint with contemporary realities; that new shapes, patterns, and models are emerging which promise drastic changes in the conduct of the corporation and of managerial practices in general. In the next 25 to 50 years we should witness, and participate in, the end of bureaucracy and the rise of new social systems better suited to twentieth century demands of industrialization. (Sociological evolutionists substantially agree that 25 to 50 years from now most people in the world will live in industrialized societies.)

Corsica, according to Gibbon, is much easier to deplore than to describe. The same holds true for bureaucracy. Basically, bureaucracy is a social invention which relies exclusively on the power to influence through rules, reason, and law. Max Weber, the German sociologist who developed the theory of bureaucracy around the turn of the century, once described bureaucracy as a social machine:

> Bureaucracy is like a modern judge who is a vending machine into which the pleadings are inserted together with the fee and which then disgorges the judgment together with its reasons mechanically derived from the code.

The bureaucratic "machine model" Weber outlined was developed as a reaction against the personal subjugation, nepotism, cruelty, emotional vicissitudes, and capricious judgment which passed for managerial practices in the early days of the industrial revolution. The true hope for man, it was thought, lay in his ability to rationalize, calculate, to use his head as well as his hands and heart. Thus, in the bureaucratic system social roles were institutionalized and reinforced by legal tradition rather than by the "cult of personality"; rationality and predictability were sought for in order to eliminate chaos and unanticipated consequences; emphasis was placed on technical competence rather than

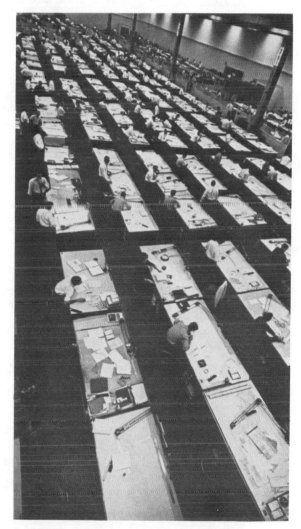

"It is horrible to think that the world could one day be filled with nothing but those little cogs, little men clinging to little jobs and striving towards bigger ones." (Max Weber)

arbitrary or "iron whims." These are oversimplifications, to be sure, but contemporary analysts of organizations would tend to agree with them. In fact, there is a general consensus that the anatomy of bureaucracy consists of the following "organs":

■ a division of labor based on functional specialization.
■ a well-defined hierarchy of authority.
■ a system of rules covering the rights and duties of employees.
■ a system of procedures for dealing with work situations.
■ impersonality of interpersonal relations.
■ promotion and selection based on technical competence.

It does not take great critical imagination to detect the flaws and problems in the bureaucratic model. We have all *experienced* them:

■ bosses without (and underlings with) technical competence.
■ arbitrary and zany rules.
■ an underworld (or informal) organization which subverts or even replaces the formal apparatus.
■ confusion and conflict among roles.
■ cruel treatment of subordinates based not on rational or legal grounds but upon inhumanity.

The tremendous range of unanticipated consequences provides a gold mine of material for comics like Charlie Chaplin and Jacques Tati who capture with a smile or a shrug the absurdity of authority systems based on pseudologic and inappropriate rules.

Almost everybody, including many observers of organizational behavior, approaches bureaucracy with a chip on his shoulder. It has been attacked for many reasons: for theoretical confusion and contradictions; for moral and ethical reasons; on practical grounds such as its inefficiency; for methodological weaknesses; for containing too many implicit values and for containing too few. I have recently catalogued the criticisms of bureaucracy and they outnumber and outdo the ninety-five theses tacked on the church door at Wittenberg in attacking another bureaucracy. A small sample of these:

(1) Bureaucracy does not adequately allow for personal growth and the development of mature personalities.
(2) It develops conformity and "group-think."
(3) It does not take into account the "informal organization" and the emergent and unanticipated problems.
(4) Its systems of control and authority are hopelessly outdated.
(5) It has no adequate juridical process.
(6) It does not possess adequate means for resolving differences and conflicts between ranks, and most particularly, between functional groups.
(7) Communication (and innovative ideas) are thwarted or distorted due to hierarchical divisions.
(8) The full human resources of bureaucracy are not being utilized due to mistrust, fear of reprisals, etc.
(9) It cannot assimilate the influx of new technology or scientists entering the organization.

(10) It modifies personality structure so that people become and reflect the dull, gray, conditioned "organization man."

Max Weber, the developer of the theory of bureaucracy, came around to condemn the apparatus he helped immortalize. While he felt that bureaucracy was inescapable, he also thought it might strangle the spirit of capitalism or the entrepreneurial attitude, a theme which Schumpeter later developed. And in a debate on bureaucracy Weber once said, more in sorrow than in anger:

> It is horrible to think that the world could one day be filled with nothing but those little cogs, little men clinging to little jobs and striving towards bigger ones—a state of affairs which is to be seen once more, as in the Egyptian records, playing an ever-increasing part in the spirit of our present administrative system, and especially of its offspring, the students. This passion for bureaucracy . . . is enough to drive one to despair. It is as if in politics . . . we were deliberately to become men who need 'order' and nothing but order, who become nervous and cowardly if for one moment this order wavers, and helpless if they are torn away from their total incorporation in it. That the world should know no men but these: it is such an evolution that we are already caught up in, and the great question is therefore not how we can promote and hasten it, but what can we oppose to this machinery in order to keep a portion of mankind free from this parcelling-out of the soul, from this supreme mastery of the bureaucratic way of life.

In what ways has bureaucracy been modified over the years in order to cope more successfully with the problems that beset it? Before answering that, we have to say something about the nature of organizations, *all* organizations, from mass production leviathans all the way to service industries such as the university or hospital. Organizations are primarily complex, goal-seeking units. In order to survive they must also accomplish the secondary tasks of (1) maintaining their internal system and co-ordinating the "human side of enterprise"—a process of mutual compliance here called *reciprocity*—and (2) adapting to and shaping the external environment—here called *adaptability*. These two organizational dilemmas can help us to organize the pivotal ways in which the bureaucratic mechanism has been altered—and found wanting.

Reciprocity primarily covers the processes which can mediate conflict between the goals of management and the individual goals of the workers. Over the past several decades a number of interesting theoretical and practical resolutions have been made which truly allow for conflict and mediation of interest. They revise, if not transform, the very nature of the bureaucratic mechanism by explicit recognition of the inescapable tension between individual and organizational goals. These theories can be called, variously, *exchange, group, value, structural, situational*—depending on what variable of the situation one wishes to modify.

The *exchange* theories postulate that wages, incomes, and

services are given to the individual for an equal contribution to the organization in work. If the inducements are not adequate, men may withdraw and work elsewhere. This may be elaborated upon by regarding "payments" to individuals as including motivational units. That is to say, the organization provides a psychological anchor in times of rapid social change and a hedge against personal loss, as well as position, growth and mastery, success experience, and so forth—in exchange for energy, work, commitment.

Management tends to interpret motivation in economic terms. Man is logical; man acts in the manner which serves his self-interest; man is competitive. Elton Mayo and his associates were among the first to see human *affiliation* as a motivating force, to view industrial organization as a *social* system as well as an economic-technical system. A manager, they stated, should be judged in terms of his ability to sustain co-operation. In fact, once a cohesive, primary work group is seen as a motivating force, a managerial elite may become obsolete, and the work group itself becomes the decision maker. This allows decisions to be made at the most relevant point of the organization, where the data are most available.

Before this becomes possible, however, some theorists believe that the impersonal *value* system of bureaucracy must be modified. In this case the manager plays an important role as the instrument of change in interpersonal relations. He must instill values which permit and reinforce the expression of feeling, experimentalism, and norms of individuality, trust, and concern. Management, according to R. R. Blake, is successful insofar as it maximizes a "concern for people"—with "concern for production."

Others believe that a new conception of the *structure* of bureaucracy will create more relevant attitudes towards the function of management than formal role specifications now do. If the organization is seen as organic rather than mechanistic, as adapting spontaneously to its needs, then decisions will be made at the critical point and roles and jobs will devolve on the "natural" organizational incumbent. The shift would probably be from the individual level to cooperative group effort, from delegated to shared responsibility, from centralized to decentralized authority, from obedience to confidence, from antagonistic arbitration to problem-solving. Management centered upon problem-solving, that assumes or relaxes authority according to task demands, has most concerned some theorists who are as much interested in an organization's success and productivity as in its social system.

However, on all sides we find a growing belief that the effectiveness of bureaucracy should be evaluated by human *situation* as well as economic criteria. Social satisfaction and personal growth of employees must be considered as well as the productivity and profit of the organization. The criticism and revisions of the bureaucratic organization tend to concentrate on the internal system and its human components. But although it appears on the surface that the case against bureaucracy has to do with its ethical-moral posture and the social fabric, the real *coup de grace* has come from the environment.

Bureaucracy thrives in a highly competitive, undifferentiated and stable environment, such as the climate of its youth, the Industrial Revolution. A pyramidal structure of authority, with power concentrated in the hands of a few with the knowledge and resources to control an entire enterprise was, and is, an eminently suitable social arrangement for routinized tasks.

However, the environment has changed in just those ways which make the mechanism most problematic. Stability has vanished. As Ellis Johnson said, ". . . the once-reliable constants have now become galloping variables."

The factors accelerating change include:

■ the growth of science, research and development activities, and intellectual technology.

■ the increase of transactions with social institutions (and their importance in conducting the enterprise)—including government, distributors and consumers, shareholders, competitors, raw material and power suppliers, sources of employees (particularly managers), trade unions, and groups within the firms. There is also more interdependence between the economic and other facets of society, leading to greater complications of legislation and public regulation.

■ competition between firms diminishing as their fates intertwine and become positively correlated.

"Work groups will be transient and changing. . . . People will learn to develop quick and intense relationships on the job and to bear the loss of more enduring work relationships."

My argument so far, to summarize quickly, is that the first assault on bureaucracy arose from its incapacity to manage the tension between individual and management goals. However, this conflict is somewhat mediated by the growth of a new ethic of productivity which includes personal growth and/or satisfaction. The second and more major shock to bureaucracy is caused by the scientific and technological revolution. It is the requirement of *adaptability* to the environment which leads to the predicted demise of bureaucracy and to the collapse of management as we know it now.

A forecast falls somewhere between a prediction and a prophecy. It lacks the divine guidance of the latter and the empirical foundation of the former. On thin empirical ice, I want to set forth some of the conditions that will dictate organizational life in the next 25 to 50 years.

■ THE ENVIRONMENT. Those factors already mentioned will continue in force and increase. Rapid technological change and diversification will lead to interpenetration of the government—its legal and economic policies—with business. Partnerships between industry and government (like Telstar) will be typical. And because of the immensity and expense of the projects, there will be fewer identical units competing for the same buyers and sellers. Or, in reverse, imperfect competition leads to an oligopolistic and government-business controlled economy. The three main features of the environment will be (1) interdependence rather than competition, (2) turbulence rather than steadiness, and (3) large scale rather than small enterprises.

■ POPULATION CHARACTERISTICS. We are living in what Peter Drucker calls the "educated society," and I think this is the ·most distinctive characteristic of our times. Within fifteen years, two-thirds of our population living in metropolitan areas will have attended college. Adult education programs, especially the management development courses of such universities as M.I.T., Harvard, and Stanford, are expanding and adding intellectual breadth. All this, of course, is not just "nice," but necessary. For as Secretary of Labor Wirtz has pointed out, computers can do the work of most high school graduates—cheaper and more effectively. Fifty years ago education used to be regarded as "nonwork" and intellectuals on the payroll (and many of the staff) were considered "overhead." Today, the survival of the firm depends, more than ever before, on the proper exploitation of brain power.

One other characteristic of the population which will aid our understanding of organizations of the future is increasing job mobility. The lowered expense and ease of transportation, coupled with the real needs of a dynamic environment, will change drastically the idea of "owning" a job—or "having roots," for that matter. Participants will be shifted from job to job and even employer to employer with much less fuss than we are accustomed to.

■ WORK VALUES. The increased level of education and mobility will change the values we hold about work. People will be more intellectually committed to their jobs and will probably require more involvement, participation, and autonomy in their work. (This turn of events is due to a composite of the following factors: (1) positive correlation between a person's education and his need for autonomy; (2) job mobility places the educated in a position of greater influence in the system; (3) job requirements call for more responsibility and discretion.)

Also, people will tend to be more "other-directed" in their dealings with others. David McClelland's studies suggest that as industrialization increases, "other-directedness" increases; so we will tend to rely more heavily on temporary social arrangements, on our immediate and constantly-changing colleagues.

■ TASKS AND GOALS. The tasks of the firm will be more technical, complicated, and unprogrammed. They will rely more on the intellect than muscle. And they will be too complicated for one person to handle or for individual supervision. Essentially, they will call for the collaboration of specialists in a project or team form of organization.

Similarly there will be a complication of goals. "Increased profits" and "raised productivity" will sound like over-simplifications and cliches. Business will concern itself increasingly with its adaptive or innovative-creative capacity. In addition, *meta*-goals will have to be articulated and developed; that is, supra-goals which shape and provide the foundation for the goal structure. For example, one meta-goal might be a system for detecting new and changing goals; another could be a system for deciding priorities among goals.

Finally, there will be more conflict and contradiction among diverse standards of organizational effectiveness, just as in hospitals and universities today there is conflict between teaching and research. The reason for this is the increased number of professionals involved, who tend to identify as much with the supra-goals of their profession as with those of their immediate employer. University professors can be used as a case in point. More and more of their income comes from outside sources, such as private or public foundations and consultant ·work. They tend not to make good "company men" because they are divided in their loyalty to professional values and organizational demands.

■ ORGANIZATION. The social structure of organizations of the future will have some unique characteristics. The key word will be "temporary"; there will be adaptive, rapidly changing *temporary systems*. These will be "task forces" organized around problems-to-be-solved. The problems will be solved by groups of relative strangers who represent a set of diverse professional skills. The groups will be arranged on organic rather than mechanical models; they will evolve in response to a problem rather than to programmed role expectations. The "executive" thus becomes a co-ordinator or "linking pin" between various task forces. He must be a man who can speak the diverse languages of research, with skills to relay information and to mediate between groups. *People will be differentiated not vertically, according to rank and role, but flexibly and functionally according to skill and professional training.*

Adaptive, problem-solving, temporary systems of diverse specialists, linked together by co-ordinating and task evaluating specialists in an organic flux—this is the organizational form that will gradually replace bureaucracy as we know it. As no catchy phrase comes to mind, let us call this an *organic-adaptive* structure.

As an aside—what will happen to the rest of society, to the manual laborers, to the less educated, to those who desire to work under conditions of high authority, and so forth? Many such jobs will disappear; other jobs will be automated. However, there will be a corresponding growth in the service-type occupations, such as those in the "war on poverty" and the Peace Corps programs. In times of change, where there is a discrepancy between cultures, when industrialization and especially urbanization proceeds rapidly, the market for men with training and skill in human interaction increases. We might guess that approximately 40 percent of the population would be involved in jobs of this nature, 40 percent in technological jobs, with a 20 percent bureaucratic minority.

■ MOTIVATION. Our above discussion of "reciprocity" indicated the shortcomings of bureaucracy in maximizing employee effectiveness. The "organic-adaptive" structure should increase motivation, and thereby effectiveness, because it enhances satisfactions intrinsic to the task. There is a harmony between the educated individual's need for meaningful, satisfactory, and creative tasks and a flexible organizational structure.

Of course, where the reciprocity problem is ameliorated, there are corresponding tensions between the individual's involvement in his professional community and his involvement in his employing organization. Professionals are notoriously "disloyal" to organizational demands.

There will, however, also be reduced commitment to work groups, for these groups, as I have already mentioned, will be transient and changing. While skills in human interaction will become more important, due to the growing needs for collaboration in complex tasks, there will be a concomitant reduction in group cohesiveness. I would predict that in the organic-adaptive system people will have to learn to develop quick and intense relationships on the job, and learn to bear the loss of more enduring work relationships.

In general I do not agree with Clark Kerr, Harold Leavitt, and others in their emphasis on a "New Bohemianism" in which leisure—not work—becomes the emotional-creative sphere of life. They assume a technological slow-down and leveling-off, and a stabilizing of social mobility. This may happen in a society of the distant future. But long before then we will face the challenge of creating the new service-type organizations with an organic-adaptive structure.

Jobs in the next century should become more rather than less involving; man is a problem-solving animal and the tasks of the future guarantee a full agenda of problems. In addition, the adaptive process itself may become captivating to many. At the same time, I think that the future I described is not necessarily a "happy" one. Coping with rapid change, living in the temporary work systems, setting up (in quick-step time) meaningful relations—and then breaking them—all augur social strains and psychological tensions. Learning how to live with ambiguity and to be self-directing will be the task of education and the goal of maturity.

In these new organizations, participants will be called on to use their minds more than at any other time in history. Fantasy, imagination, and creativity will be legitimate in ways that today seem strange. Social structures will no longer be instruments of psychic repression but will increasingly promote play and freedom on behalf of curiosity and thought. I agree with Herbert Marcuse's thesis in *Eros and Civilization* that the necessity of repression and the suffering derived from it, decreases with the maturity of the civilization.

Not only will the problem of adaptability be overcome through the organic-adaptive structure, but the problem we started with, reciprocity, will be resolved. Bureaucracy, with its "surplus repression," was a monumental discovery for harnessing muscle power *via* guilt and instinctual renunciation. In today's world, it is a lifeless crutch that is no longer useful. For we now require structures of freedom to permit the expression of play and imagination and to exploit the new pleasure of work.

Peter F. Drucker

New templates
for today's organizations

Traditional structures are no longer adequate
for today's complex organizations;
new designs are required to serve their needs

Today's businesses are increasingly complex and diverse. In this article, a well-known organization theorist describes new principles of organization design now in use and their applications to today's businesses and institutions. It is his position that not only must the new principles make it possible for organizations to function and perform, but they must also serve the higher goals of human endeavor.

Mr. Drucker has contributed many articles to HBR and has authored several books, including *The Effective Executive* and *The Practice of Management*. The present article is a consolidation of several chapters from his new book, *Management: Tasks, Responsibilities, Practices*, published this year by Harper & Row. Until 1972, Mr. Drucker was professor of management at New York University. He is now Clarke Professor of Social Science at Claremont Graduate School, Claremont, California.

Organization structures are becoming increasingly short-lived and unstable.

The "classical" organization structures of the 1920s and 1930s, which still serve as textbook examples, stood for decades without needing more than an occasional touching up. American Telephone & Telegraph, General Motors, Du-Pont, Unilever, and Sears, Roebuck maintained their organizational concepts, structures, and basic components through several management generations and major changes in the size and scope of the business. Today, however, a company no sooner finishes a major job of reorganizing itself than it starts all over again.

General Electric, for instance, finished a tremendous organization overhaul around 1960, after almost a decade of hard work; since then it has revamped both its structure and its overall strategies at least twice. Similarly, Imperial Chemicals in Great Britain is restructuring an organization design that is barely 10 years old. And the same restlessness and instability afflict organization structures and concepts in the large U.S. commercial banks, in IBM, and in U.S. government agencies. For instance, the Health, Education and Welfare Department has been subjected to a "final" reorganization almost every year in its 20-year history.

To some extent this instability is a result of gross overorganizing. Companies are resorting to reorganization as a kind of miracle drug in lieu of diagnosing their ailments. Every business observer can see dozens of cases where substantial, even massive organization surgery is being misapplied to take care of a fairly minor procedural problem, or—even more often—to avoid facing up to personnel decisions. Equally common is the misuse of reorganization as a substitute for hard thinking on objectives, strategies, and priorities. Few managers seem to recognize that the right organization structure is not performance itself, but rather a prerequisite of performance. The wrong structure is indeed a guarantee of nonperformance; it produces friction and frustration, puts the spotlight on the wrong issues, and makes mountains out of trivia. But "perfect organization" is like "perfect health": the test is the ills it does not have and therefore does not have to cure.

Even if unnecessary organization surgery were not as rampant in our institutions as unnecessary appendectomies, hysterectomies, and tonsillectomies are said to be in our hospitals, there would still be an organization crisis. Twenty years ago many managers had yet to learn that organization design and organization structure deserve attention, thinking, and hard work. Almost everyone accepts this today; indeed, organization studies have been one of the true "growth industries" of the past twenty years. But while a few years ago organization theory had "the answers," today all is confusion.

The crisis is simultaneously a crisis of organization theory and of organization practice. Ironically, what is happening is not at all what organization theorists like Chris Argyris, Warren Bennis, Douglas McGregor (and I myself) have been predicting for at least 10 years: pressures for a more free-form and humanistic organization that provides greater scope for personal fulfillment play almost no part in the present organization crisis. Instead the main causes of instability are *changes in the objective task*, in the kind of business and institution to be organized. This is at the root of the crisis of organization practice.

The organization theorists' traditional answer to "organization crisis"—more organization development—is largely irrelevant to this new problem. Sometimes they seem to be pushing old remedies to cure a disease that no one has heard of before, and that inhibits a totally unfamiliar type of body. The kind of business and institution to be organized today is an enormously different beast from that of 20 years ago.

These changes in the objective task have generated new design principles that do not fit traditional organization concepts. And therein lies the crisis of theory. On the other hand, the past 20 years have also seen the emergence of new understandings of which organization needs require the most attention, and of how to go about the job of analyzing organization needs and designing organization structures. Only when we have an idea of what the new "body" looks like can we begin to treat its ills.

In what follows I compare old models with new realities and describe the new design principles. These principles can be matched to the tasks of modern management as well as to the formal needs of all organizations, independent of their purpose. In exploring these relationships, we can discern a way to avoid the organization crisis that affects so many businesses and institutions.

The early models

Twice in the short history of management we have had the "final answer" to organization problems.

The first time was around 1910 when Henri Fayol, the French industrialist, thought through what were, to him, the universally valid functions of a manufacturing company. (I am using the word "function" in the common, management sense, not in the way Fayol used it to describe administrative concerns.) Of course, at that time the manufacturing business presented the one truly important organization problem.

Then in the early 1920s Alfred P. Sloan, Jr., in organizing General Motors, took the next step. He found "the answer" for organizing a large, multidivisional manufacturing company. The Sloan approach built the individual divisions on the functional structure that Fayol had specified for a manufacturing business, that is, on engineering, manufacturing, selling, and so on; but it organized the business itself by the concept of federal decentralization, that is, on the basis of decentralized authority and centralized control. By the mid-1940s GM's structure had become the model for larger organizations around the world.

Where they fit the realities that confront organization designers and implementers today, the Fayol and Sloan models are still unsurpassed. Fayol's functional organization is still the best way to structure a small business, especially a small manufacturing business. Sloan's federal decentralization is still the best structure for the big, single-product, single-market company like GM. But more and more of the institutional reality that has to be structured and organized does not "fit." Indeed the very assumptions that underlay Sloan's work—and that of Fayol—are not applicable to today's organization challenges.

GM model vs. present realities

There are at least six ways in which the GM structure no longer serves as a model for present organization needs.

1. General Motors is a manufacturing business. Today we face the challenge of organizing the large nonmanufacturing institution. There are not only the large financial businesses and the large retailers, but also, equally, there are worldwide transportation, communications, and customer service companies. The latter, while they may manufacture a product, have their greatest emphasis on outside services (as most computer businesses do). Then there are, of course, all the nonbusiness service institutions, e.g., hospitals, universities, and government agencies. These "nonmanufacturing" institutions are, increasingly, the true center of gravity of any developed economy. They employ the most people, and they both contribute to and take the largest share of the gross national product. They present the fundamental organization problems today.

2. General Motors is essentially a single-product, single-technology, single-market business. Even accounting for the revenues of its large financial and insurance subsidiaries, four fifths of its total revenue are still produced by the automobile. Although Frigidaire and Electromo-

tive are large, important businesses and leaders in the consumer appliance and locomotive markets, respectively, they are but minor parts of GM. Indeed, GM is unique among large companies in being far less diversified today than it was 30 or 40 years ago. Then, in the late 1930s and early 1940s, General Motors had major investments in the chemical industry (Ethyl), in the aircraft industry (North American Aviation), and in earth-moving equipment (Euclid). All three are gone now and have not been replaced by new diversification activities outside the automotive field.

The cars that General Motors produces differ in details, such as size, horsepower, and price, but they are essentially one and the same product. A man who came up the line in, say, the Pontiac Division, will hardly find Chevrolet totally alien—and even Opel in Germany will not hold a great many surprises for him.

By contrast, the typical businesses of today are multiproduct, multitechnology, and multimarket. They may not be conglomerates, but they are diversified. And their central problem is a problem General Motors did not have: the organization of complexity and diversity.

There is, moreover, an even more difficult situation to which the GM pattern cannot be applied: the large single-product, single-technology business that, unlike GM, cannot be subdivided into distinct and yet comparable parts. Typical are the "materials" businesses such as steel and aluminum companies. Here belong, also, the larger transportation businesses, such as railroads, airlines, and the large commercial banks. These businesses are too big for a functional structure; it ceases to be a skeleton and becomes a straitjacket. They are also incapable of being genuinely decentralized; no one part on its own is a genuine "business." Yet as we are shifting from mechanical to process technologies, and from making goods to producing knowledge and services, these large, complex, but integrated businesses are becoming more important than the multidivisional businesses of the 1920s and 1930s.

3. General Motors still sees its international operations as organizationally separate and outside. For 50 years it has been manufacturing and selling overseas, and something like one quarter of its sales are now outside North America. But in its organization structure, in its reporting relationships, and above all in its career ladders,

---

1. For a discussion of these developments, see the epilogue to the new edition of my *Concept of the Corporation* (New York, John Day, 1972).

GM is a U.S. company with foreign subsidiaries. Rather than leaning toward an international, let alone a multinational operation, GM's top management is primarily concerned with the U.S. market, the U.S. economy, the U.S. labor movement, the U.S. government, and so on. This traditional structure and viewpoint of GM's top management may, in large part, explain the substantial failure of GM to take advantage of the rapid expansion and growth of such major non-U.S. automobile markets as Europe, where GM's share has actually been dropping, or Brazil, where GM failed to anticipate a rapidly emerging automobile market.[1]

In contrast, during the last 20 years many other companies have become multinational. For these companies, a great many cultures, countries, markets, and governments are of equal, or at least of major, importance.

4. Because GM is a one-product, one-country company, information handling is not a major organization problem and thus not a major concern. At GM everyone speaks the same language, whether by that we mean the language of the automotive industry or American English. Everyone fully understands what the other one is doing or should be doing, if only because, in all likelihood, he has done a similar job himself. GM can, therefore, be organized according to the logic of the marketplace, and the logic of authority and decision. It need not, in its organization, concern itself a great deal with the logic and flow of information.

By contrast, multiproduct, multitechnology, and multinational companies have to design their organization structure to handle a large flow of information. At the very least they have to make sure that their organization structure does not violate the logic of information. And for this task, GM offers no guidance—GM did not have to tackle the problem.

5. Four out of every five GM employees are either manual production workers or clerks on routine tasks. In other words, GM employs yesterday's rather than today's labor force.

But the basic organization problem today concerns knowledge work and knowledge workers. They are the fastest growing element in every business; in service institutions, they are the core employees.

6. Finally, General Motors has been a "managerial" rather than an "entrepreneurial" business. The strength of the Sloan approach lay in its ability to manage, and manage superbly, what was already there and known.

Today's organizer is challenged by an increasing demand to organize entrepreneurship and innovation. But for this undertaking, the General Motors model offers no guidance.

New design principles

We do not know how to handle these new organization realities or how to satisfy their structural demands. Nevertheless, the organizing task has not waited. To tackle the new realities, we have in the past 20 years improvised ad hoc design solutions to supplement the Fayol and Sloan models. As a result, the organization architect now has available five so-called design principles, i.e., five distinct organization structures. The two traditional ones already mentioned have been known as principles of organization design for many years:

O Henri Fayol's functional structure.
O Alfred P. Sloan's federal decentralization.

Three are new; indeed they are so new that they are not generally known, let alone recognized, as design principles:

O Team organization.
O Simulated decentralization.
O Systems structure.

In team organization, a group—usually a fairly small one—is set up for a specific task rather than for a specific skill or stage in the work process. In the past 20 years we have learned that whereas team design was traditionally considered applicable only to short-lived, transitory, exceptional task-force assignments, it is equally applicable to some permanent needs, especially to the top-management and innovating tasks.

In an organization that is both too big to remain functionally organized and too integrated to be genuinely decentralized, simulated decentralization is often the organization answer. It sets up one function, one stage in the process, or one segment as if it were a distinct business with genuine profit and loss responsibility; it treats accounting fictions, transfer prices, and overhead allocations as if they were realities of the marketplace. For all its difficulties and frictions, simulated decentralization is probably the fastest growing organization design around these days. It is the only one that fits, albeit poorly,

2. This is, for instance, the verdict of organization theorist Harold Koontz, in his well-publicized article, "The Management Theory Jungle," *Journal of the Academy of Management*, December 1965; see also his "Making Sense of Management Theory," HBR July-August 1962, p. 24.

the materials, computer, chemical, and pharmaceutical companies, as well as the big banks; it is also the only design principle suited for the large university, hospital, or government agency.

Finally, in systems structure, team organization and simulated decentralization are combined. The prototype for this design principle was NASA's space program, in which a large number of autonomous units—large government bodies, individual research scientists, profit-seeking businesses, and large universities—worked together, organized and informed by the needs of the situation rather than by logic, and held together by a common goal and a joint top management. The large transnational company, which is a mix of many cultures, governments, businesses, and markets, is the present embodiment of an organization based on the systems concept.

None of the new design principles is easy or trouble-free. Compared to the traditional designs of functionalism and federal decentralization, they are indeed so difficult, complex, and vulnerable that many organization theorists maintain that they are not principles at all, but abominations.[2] And there is no question that wherever the traditional principles can be used, they should be; they are infinitely easier. The traditional principles are, however, far more limited in their scope than the new ones, and when misapplied they can cause even greater problems.

Design logics

Each of the five design principles expresses or embodies a logic that makes that principle the appropriate one to apply when one or another task of management requires a structure. In this discussion we can identify three, or maybe four, logics upon which the five principles are based. For instance, although they do it differently, the functional and team design principles both embody work and task and are thus appropriate designs to consider when faced with work- or task-oriented management problems.

Historically these two design principles have been viewed as antithetical, but actually they are complementary. In the functionally organized structure, the work skills—manufacturing, accounting, and so on—are designed to be static; the work moves from one stage to others. In team structure, the work is conceived as static, with skills moving to meet the requirements of the task. Because of their complementary nature, these two design principles are the only possible choices for dealing with, say, the structure of

knowledge. For if you need a specific task performed and a team effort would do it best, then you need static functions as bases from which persons, and their expertise, can be moved to form a team.

Two other design logics, corresponding to those involving work and task, can also be defined. Simulated decentralization and Sloan's federal decentralization both deal with *results* and *performance*. They are result-focused designs. Unlike functional and team structures, however, they are not complementary; they are not even alternatives. Federal decentralization is an "optimum," simulated decentralization a "lesser evil" to be resorted to only when the stringent requirements of federal decentralization cannot be met.

The last of the available design principles, systems design, is focused on *relationships*, another dimension of management. Because relations are inevitably both more numerous and less clearly definable than either work and task or results, a structure focused on relations will present greater difficulties than either a work-focused or a result-focused design. There are, however, organization problems, as in the true multinational business, in which the very complexity of relationships makes systems design the only appropriate design principle.

This rough classification indicates that at least one additional design principle might yet be developed. *Decision* is as much a dimension of management as are work and task, results and performance, and relations. Yet, so far, we know of no decision-focused design principle of organization structure, but should one ever be developed, it might have wide applicability.[3]

Ideally, an organization should be multiaxial, that is, structured around work and task, *and* results and performance, *and* relationships, *and* decisions. It would function as if it were a biological organism, like the human body with its skeleton and muscles, a number of nervous systems, and with circulatory, digestive, immunological, and respiratory systems, all autonomous yet interdependent. But in social structures we are still limited to designs that express only one primary dimension.

So, in designing organizations, we have to choose among different structures, each stressing a different dimension and each, therefore, with distinct costs, specific and fairly stringent re-

3. Herbert A. Simon and his school have been attempting to develop one—at least this is how I read H.A. Simon's *Administrative Behavior* (New York, Macmillan, 1957) and I.G. March and H.A. Simon's *Organizations* (New York, John Wiley & Sons, 1958).

quirements, and real limitations. There is no risk-free organization structure. And a design that is the best solution for one task may be only one of a number of equally poor alternatives for another task, and just plain wrong for yet a third kind of work.

Major tasks of management

A somewhat different way of viewing the relationships between the design logics and principles is to identify the principal tasks of management that the principles can structure. We have learned that, in a very general analysis, organization design should simultaneously structure and integrate three different kinds of work: (1) the operating task, which is responsible for producing the results of today's business; (2) the innovative task, which creates the company's tomorrow; and (3) the top-management task, which directs, gives vision, and sets the course for the business of both today and tomorrow. No one organization design is adequate to all three kinds of work; every business will need to use several design principles side-by-side.

In addition, each organization structure has certain formal specifications that have nothing to do with the purpose of the structure but are integral parts of the structure itself. Just as a human body can be described as having certain characteristics, regardless of the occupation of its inhabitant, so can an organization structure. Bodies have arms and legs, hands and feet, all related to each other; similarly, organizations are structured to satisfy the need for:

O *Clarity*, as opposed to simplicity. (The Gothic cathedral is not a simple design, but your position inside it is clear; you know where to stand and where to go. A modern office building is exceedingly simple in design, but it is very easy to get lost in one; it is not clear.)

O *Economy* of effort to maintain control and minimize friction.

O *Direction of vision* toward the product rather than the process, the result rather than the effort.

O *Understanding* by each individual of his own task as well as that of the organization as a whole.

O *Decision making* that focuses on the right issues, is action-oriented, and is carried out at the lowest possible level of management.

O *Stability*, as opposed to rigidity, to survive turmoil, and *adaptability* to learn from it.

O *Perpetuation and self-renewal*, which require that an organization be able to produce tomorrow's leaders from within, helping each person develop continuously; the structure must also be open to new ideas.

Even though every institution, and especially every business, is structured in some way around all the dimensions of management, no one design principle is adequate to all their demands and needs. Nor does any one of the five available design principles adequately satisfy all of the formal specifications. The functional principle, for instance, has great clarity and high economy, and it makes it easy to understand one's own task. But even in the small business it tends to direct vision away from results and toward efforts, to obscure the organization's goals, and to sub-optimize decisions. It has high stability but little adaptability. It perpetuates and develops technical and functional skills, that is, middle managers, but it resists new ideas and inhibits top-management development and vision. And every one of the other four principles is similarly both a "good fit" against some formal organization specifications and a "misfit" against others.

One conclusion from this discussion is that organization structures can either be pure or effective, but they are unlikely to be both. Indeed, even the purest structure we know of, Alfred Sloan's GM, was actually mixed. It was not composed just of decentralized divisions, with functional organization within the divisions. It also contained, from the beginning, some sizable simulated decentralization. For instance, Fisher Body had responsibility for all body work but not for any final product. And top management was clearly structured as a team, or rather as a number of interlocking teams.

This does not mean that an organization structure must by necessity be unwieldy or a confused mixture. The tremendous vitality of some older structures—Sears, Roebuck and GM, for instance—shows that a dynamic balance can be achieved. One implication is clear, however, and that is that pure structure *is* likely to end up badly botched. (This tendency may explain the difficulties that both GE and Imperial Chemicals—each trying for pure decentralization—have been experiencing.) Above all, our observations lead us to conclude that organization design is a series of risk-taking decisions rather than a search for the "one best way." And by and large, organization theorists and practitioners have yet to learn this.

Building the new structure

There are a number of important lessons to be learned from the previous discussion and from the experiences of the past 20 years. Some concern new ideas or conclusions we have not recognized before, while others involve rethinking old concepts and relationships that we thought were settled years ago.

The first thing we can conclude is that Fayol and Sloan were right: good organization structures will not just evolve. The only things that evolve by themselves in an organization are disorder, friction, and malperformance. Nor is the right structure—or even the livable one—intuitive, any more than Greek temples or Gothic cathedrals were. Traditions may indicate where the problems and malfunctions are, but they are of little help in finding solutions. Organization design and structure require thinking, analysis, and a systematic approach.

Second, we have learned that designing an organization structure is not the first step, but the last. The first step is to identify and organize the building blocks of organization, that is, the key tasks that have to be encompassed in the final structure and that, in turn, carry the structural load of the final edifice. This is, of course, what Fayol did with his functions of a manufacturing company, when he designed them according to the work to be done.

We now know that building blocks are determined by the kind of contribution they make. And we know that the traditional classification of the contributions, e.g., the staff-and-line concept of conventional U.S. organization theory, is more of a hindrance to understanding than a help.

Designing the building blocks or tasks is, so to speak, the "engineering phase" of organization design. It provides the basic materials. And like all materials, these building blocks have their specific characteristics. They belong in different places and fit together in different ways.

We have also learned that "structure follows strategy." Organization is not mechanical. It is not done by assembly, nor can it be prefabricated. Organization is organic and unique to

4. The fundamental work on this topic, an in-depth study of the design of modern organization in pioneering American companies such as DuPont, General Motors, and Sears, was done by Alfred D. Chandler in his book *Strategy and Structure* (Cambridge, M.I.T. Press, 1962).

each individual business or institution. We realize now that structure is a means for attaining the objectives and goals of an institution. And if a structure is to be effective and sound, we must start with objectives and strategy.[4]

This is perhaps the most fruitful new insight we have in the field of organization. It may sound obvious, and it is. But some of the worst mistakes in organization building have been made by imposing on a living business a mechanistic model of an ideal organization.

Strategy—that is, the answer to the question: "What is our business? What should it be? What will it be?"—determines the purpose of structure. It thereby determines the key tasks or activities in a given business or service institution. Effective structure is the design that makes these key activities function and produce results. In turn the key activities are the load-bearing elements of a functioning structure. Organization design is, or should be, primarily concerned with the key activities; other purposes are secondary.

Some of the new insights into organization design require us to unlearn old ideas. A few of the noisiest and most time-consuming battles in organization theory and practice are pure sham. They pose an either/or dichotomy when the correct answer is "both—in varying proportions."

The first of these sham battles that had better be forgotten is between task-focus and person-focus in job design and organization structure. Structure and job design have to be task-focused. But assignments have to fit both the person and the needs of the situation. There is no point in confusing the two, as the old and tiresome discussion of the nonproblem insists on doing. Work is always objective and impersonal; the job itself is always done by a person.

Somewhat connected with this old controversy is the discussion of hierarchical versus free-form organization.

Traditional organization theory knows only one kind of structure, applicable alike to building blocks and whole buildings. It is the so-called scalar organization, that is, the hierarchical pyramid of superior and subordinates.

Today another—equally doctrinaire—organization theory is becoming fashionable. It maintains that shape and structure are what we want them to be—they are, or should be, free form. Everything—shape, size, and apparently tasks—derive from interpersonal relations. Indeed, it is argued, the purpose of the structure is to make it possible for each person "to do his thing."

It is simply not true, however, that one of these forms represents total regimentation and the other total freedom. The amount of discipline required in both is the same; they only distribute it differently.

Hierarchy does not, as the critics allege, make the person at the top of the pyramid more powerful. On the contrary, the first effect of hierarchical organization is to protect the subordinate against arbitrary authority from above. A scalar or hierarchical organization does this by defining a sphere within which the subordinate has authority, a sphere within which the superior cannot interfere. It protects the subordinate by making it possible for him to say, "This is *my* assigned job." Protection of the subordinate also underlies the scalar principle's insistence that a man have only one superior. Otherwise, the subordinate is likely to find himself caught between conflicting demands, commands, interests, and loyalties. There is a lot of truth in the old proverb, "Better one bad master than two good ones."

At the same time, the hierarchical organization gives the most individual freedom. As long as the incumbent does whatever the assigned duties of his position are, he has done his job. He has no responsibility beyond it.

We hear a lot of talk these days about the individual's right to do his own thing. But the only organization structure in which this is remotely possible is a hierarchical one. It makes the least demands on the individual to subordinate himself to the goals of the organization or to gear his activities into the needs and demands of others.

Teams, by contrast, demand, above all, very great self-discipline from each member. Everybody has to do the team's "thing." Everybody has to take responsibility for the work of the entire team and for its performance. The one thing one cannot do on a team is one's own "thing."

Organization builders (and even organization theorists) will have to learn that sound organization structure needs both (a) a hierarchical structure of authority, and (b) a capacity to organize task forces, teams, and individuals for work on both a permanent and a temporary basis.

The 'one-way' myth

Organization theory and organization practice still assume that there is "one final answer," at least for a particular business or institution. In itself, this belief is a large part of today's organization crisis. It leads to doctrinaire structures that impose one template on everybody and everything—e.g., operating and innovating components; manufacturing and service units; single-product and multimarket businesses. And if any person or process, no matter how insignificant, seems out of place, a total root-and-branch reorganization has to be done to accommodate it.

Maybe there is one right answer—but if so, we do not yet have it. Indeed for certain businesses and institutions, such as a large airline or government agency, we do not even have one poor answer—all we have are a multitude of equally unsatisfactory approaches. But, as remarked before, the organizing task will not wait; it will by necessity continue to be a central preoccupation of managers. Therefore, they had better learn to understand the design principles we already have. They must also learn the formal specifications of organization, and the relationships between the tasks of a business and the structures available to it.

The true lesson of the organization crisis is, however, quite different. It is that the traditional quest for the one right answer—a quest pursued as wholeheartedly by the new "heretics" of free-form organization as by the most orthodox classicists—pursues the wrong quarry. It misconceives an organization as something in itself rather than as a means to an end. But now we can see that liberation and mobilization of human energies—rather than symmetry, harmony, or consistency—are the purpose of organization. Human performance is both its goal and its test.

MATRIX ORGANIZATION DESIGNS

How to combine functional and project forms

JAY R. GALBRAITH

Mr. Galbraith is a faculty member in the Alfred P. Sloan School of Management, M.I.T.

Each form of organizational design has its own set of advantages and disadvantages. If, for example, the functional structure is adopted, projects fall behind; if project organization is chosen, technologies are less well-developed. The matrix design attempts to achieve the benefits of both forms. The history of The Standard Products Co. illustrates the change from the functional form to a pure matrix form. Measures were taken that allowed Standard to achieve high levels of technical sophistication necessary to innovate products and simultaneously get these products to the market quickly to maintain competitive position. Since not all organizations need a pure matrix organization, the author describes the alternatives and lists some factors that help determine the choices.

Each era of management evolves new forms of organization as new problems are encountered. Earlier generations of managers invented the centralized functional form, the line-staff form, and the decentralized product division structure as a response to increasing size and complexity of tasks. The current generation of management has developed two new forms as a response to high technology. The first is the free-form conglomerate; the other is the matrix organization, which was developed primarily in the aerospace industry.

The matrix organization grows out of the organizational choice between project and functional forms, although it is not limited to those bases of the authority structure.[1] Research in the behavioral sciences now permits a detailing of the choices among the alternate intermediate forms between the project and functional extremes. Detailing such a choice is necessary since many businessmen see their organizations facing situations in the 1970's that are similar to those faced by the aerospace firms in the 1960's. As a result, a great many unanswered questions arise concerning the use of the matrix organization. For example, what are the various kinds of matrix designs, what is the difference

1. See John F. Mee, "Matrix Organization," *Business Horizons* (Summer, 1964), p. 70.

22   Reprinted by permission of the author and *Business Horizons* from *Business Horizons,* February 1971, pp. 29–40.

between the designs, how do they work, and how do I choose a design that is appropriate for my organization?

The problem of designing organizations arises from the choices available among alternative bases of the authority structure. The most common alternatives are to group together activities which bear on a common product, common customer, common geographic area, common business function (marketing, engineering, manufacturing, and so on), or common process (forging, stamping, machining, and so on). Each of these bases has various costs and economies associated with it. For example, the functional structure facilitates the acquisition of specialized inputs. It permits the hiring of an electromechanical and an electronics engineer rather than two electrical engineers. It minimizes the number necessary by pooling specialized resources and time sharing them across products or projects. It provides career paths for specialists. Therefore, the organization can hire, utilize, and retain specialists.

These capabilities are necessary if the organization is going to develop high technology products. However, the tasks that the organization must perform require varying amounts of the specialized resources applied in varying sequences. The problem of simultaneously completing all tasks on time, with appropriate quality and while fully utilizing all specialist resources, is all but impossible in the functional structure. It requires either fantastic amounts of information or long lead times for task completion.

The product or project form of organization has exactly the opposite set of benefits and costs. It facilitates coordination among specialties to achieve on-time completion and to meet budget targets. It allows a quick reaction capability to tackle problems that develop in one specialty, thereby reducing the impact on other specialties. However, if the organization has two projects, each requiring one half-time electronics engineer and one half-time electromechanical engineer, the pure

project organization must either hire two electrical engineers—and reduce specialization—or hire four engineers (two electronics and two electromechanical)—and incur duplication costs. In addition, no one is responsible for long-run technical development of the specialties. Thus, each form of organization has its own set of advantages and disadvantages. A similar analysis could be applied to geographically or client-based structures.

The problem is that when one basis of organization is chosen, the benefits of the others are surrendered. If the functional structure is adopted, the technologies are developed but the projects fall behind schedule. If the project organization is chosen, there is better cost and schedule performance but the technologies are not developed as well. In the past, managers made a judgment as to whether technical development or schedule completion was more important and chose the appropriate form.

However, in the 1960's with a space race and missile gap, the aerospace firms were faced with a situation where both technical performance and coordination were important. The result was the matrix design, which attempts to achieve the benefits of both forms. However, the matrix carries some costs of its own. A study of the development of a matrix design is contained in the history of The Standard Products Co., a hypothetical company that has changed its form of organization from a functional structure to a matrix.

A COMPANY CHANGES FORMS

The Standard Products Co. has competed effectively for a number of years by offering a varied line of products that were sold to other organizations. Standard produced and sold its products through a functional organization like the one represented in Figure 1. A moderate number of changes in the product line and production processes were made each

FIGURE 1

Standard's Functional Organization

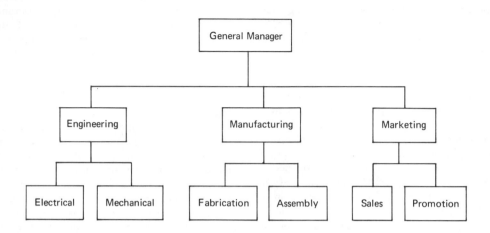

year. Therefore, a major management problem was to coordinate the flow of work from engineering through marketing. The coordination was achieved through several integrating mechanisms:

Rules and procedures—One of the ways to constrain behavior in order to achieve an integrated pattern is to specify rules and procedures. If all personnel follow the rules, the resultant behavior is integrated without having to maintain on-going communication. Rules are used for the most predictable and repetitive activities.

Planning processes—For less repetitive activities, Standard does not specify the procedure to be used but specifies a goal or target to be achieved, and lets the individual choose the procedure appropriate to the goal. Therefore, processes are undertaken to elaborate schedules and budgets. The usefulness of plans and rules is that they reduce the need for on-going communication between specialized subunits.

Hierarchical referral—When situations are encountered for which there are no rules or when problems cause the goals to be exceeded, these situations are referred upward in the hierarchy for resolution. This is the standard management-by-exception principle. This resolves the nonroutine and unpredictable events that all organizations encounter.

Direct contact—In order to prevent top executives from becoming overloaded with problems, as many problems as possible are resolved by the affected managers at low levels by informal contacts. These remove small problems from the upward referral process.

Liaison departments—In some cases, where there is a large volume of contacts between two departments, a liaison department evolves to handle the transactions. This typically occurs between engineering and manufacturing in order to handle engineering changes and design problems.[2]

The Standard Products Co. utilized these mechanisms to integrate the functionally organized specialties. They were effective in the sense that Standard could respond to changes in the market with new products on a timely basis, the new products were completed on schedule and within budget, and the executives had sufficient time to devote to long-range planning.

Matrix Begins Evolution

A few years ago, a significant change occurred in the market for one of Standard's major

2. For a more detailed explanation, see Jay R. Galbraith, *Organization Design* (Reading, Mass.: Addison-Wesley Publishing Co., Inc., 1971).

product lines. A competitor came out with a new design utilizing an entirely new raw material. The initial success caused Standard to react by developing one of their own incorporating the new material. They hired some specialists in the area and began their normal new product introduction activities. However, this time the product began to fall behind schedule, and it appeared that the product would arrive on the market at a time later than planned. In response, the general manager called a meeting to analyze the situation.

Task Force After a briefing, it was obvious to the general manager and the directors of the three functions what was happening. Standard's lack of experience with the new material had caused them to underestimate the number and kinds of problems. The uncertainty led to a deterioration in usefulness of plans and schedules. The problems affected all functions, which meant that informal contacts and liaison processes were cumbersome; therefore, the majority of the problems were referred upward. This led to overloads on the directors of the functions and the general manager, which in turn added to the delays. Thus, the new situation required more decision making and more information processing than the current organization could provide.

The directors of engineering and manufacturing suggested that the cause of the problem was an overly ambitious schedule. More time should have been allowed for the new product; if realistic schedules were set, the current coordination processes would be adequate. They proposed that the schedules be adjusted by adding three to six months to the current due dates, which would allow more time to make the necessary decisions.

The director of marketing objected, reporting that the company would lose a good percentage of the market if the introduction was delayed. A number of big customers were waiting for Standard's version of the new product, and a delay would cost the company some of these customers. The general manager agreed with the marketing director. He proposed that they should not change the schedule to fit their current coordination processes, but that they should introduce some new coordination mechanisms to meet the scheduled due dates.

The group agreed with the general manager's position and began to search for alternative solutions. One of the solution requirements suggested was to reduce the distance between the sources of information and the points of decision. At this point the manufacturing director cautioned them about decentralizing decisions. He reminded them of previous experiences when decisions were made at low levels of the engineering organization. The data the decision makers had were current but they were also local in scope; severe problems in the manufacturing process resulted. When these decisions were centralized, the global perspective prevented these problems from developing. Therefore, they had to increase decision-making power at lower levels without losing the inputs of all affected units. The alternative that met both requirements was a group with representation from all the major departments to enter into joint decisions.

The group was appointed and named the "new product task force." It was to last as long as cross-functional problems occurred on the new product introduction. The group was to meet and solve joint problems within the budget limits set by the general manager and the directors; problems requiring more budget went to the top management group. The purpose was to make as many decisions as possible at low levels with the people most knowledgeable. This should reduce the delays and yet ensure that all the information inputs were considered.

The task force consisted of nine people; three, one from each function, were full-time and the others were part-time. They met at least every other day to discuss and resolve joint problems. Several difficulties caused them to shift membership. First, the engineering representatives were too high in the organization and, therefore, not knowledgeable about the technical alternatives and consequences. They were replaced with lower level people. The opposite occurred with respect to the manufacturing representatives. Quite often they did not have either information or the authority to commit the production organization to joint decisions made by the task force. They were replaced by higher level people. Eventually, the group had both the information and the authority to make good group decisions. The result was effective coordination: coordination = f (authority $\times$ information).

Creation of the task force was the correct solution. Decision delays were reduced, and collective action was achieved by the joint decisions. The product arrived on time, and the task force members returned to their regular duties.

Teams—No sooner had the product been introduced than salesmen began to bring back stories about new competitors. One was introducing a second-generation design based on improvements in the raw material. Since the customers were excited by its potential and the technical people thought it was feasible, Standard started a second-generation redesign across all its product lines. This time, they set up the task force structure in advance and committed themselves to an ambitious schedule.

Again the general manager became concerned. This time the product was not falling behind schedule, but in order to meet target dates the top management was drawn into day-to-day decisions on a continual basis. This was leaving very little time to think about the third-generation product line. Already Standard had to respond twice to changes initiated by others. It was time for a thorough strategy formulation. Indeed, the more rapid the change in technology and markets, the greater

the amount of strategic decision making that is necessary. However, these are the same changes that pull top management into day-to-day decisions. The general manager again called a meeting to discuss and resolve the problem.

The solution requirements to the problem were the same as before. They had to find a way to push a greater number of decisions down to lower levels. At the same time, they had to guarantee that all interdependent subunits would be considered in the decision so that coordination would be maintained. The result was a more extensive use of joint decision making and shared responsibility.

The joint decision making was to take place through a team structure. The teams consisted of representatives of all functions and were formed around major product lines. There were two levels of teams, one at lower levels and another at the middle-management level. Each level had defined discretionary limits; problems that the lower level could not solve were referred to the middle-level team. If the middle level could not solve the problem, it went to top management. A greater number of day-to-day operating problems were thereby solved at lower levels of the hierarchy, freeing top management for long-range decisions.

The teams, unlike the task force, were permanent. New products were regarded as a fact of life, and the teams met on a continual basis to solve recurring interfunctional problems. Task forces were still used to solve temporary problems. In fact, all the coordination mechanisms of rules, plans, upward referral, direct contact, liaison men, and task forces were used, in addition to the teams.

Product Managers   The team structure achieved interfunctional coordination and permitted top management to step out of day-to-day decision making. However, the teams were not uniformly effective. Standard's strategy required the addition of highly skilled, highly educated technical people to continue to innovate and compete in the high technology industry. Sometimes these specialists would dominate a team because of their superior technical knowledge. That is, the team could not distinguish between providing technical information and supplying managerial judgment after all the facts were identified. In addition, the specialists' personalities were different from the personalities of the other team members, which made the problem of conflict resolution much more difficult.[3]

Reports of these problems began to reach the general manager, who realized that a great number of decisions of consequence were being made at lower and middle levels of management. He also knew that they should be made with a general manager's perspective. This depends on having the necessary information and a reasonable balance of power among the joint decision makers. Now the technical people were upsetting the power balance because others could not challenge them on technical matters. As a result, the general manager chose three technically qualified men and made them product managers in charge of the three major product lines.[4] They were to act as chairmen of the product team meetings and generally facilitate the interfunctional decision making.

Since these men had no formal authority, they had to resort to their technical competence and their interpersonal skills in order to be effective. The fact that they reported to the general manager gave them some additional power. These men were successful in bringing the global, general manager perspective lower in the organization to improve the joint decision-making process.

The need for this role was necessitated by the increasing differences in attitudes and goals among the technical, production, and marketing team participants. These differ-

ences are necessary for successful subtask performance but interfere with team collaboration. The product manager allows collaboration without reducing these necessary differences. The cost is the additional overhead for the product management salaries.

Product Management Departments   Standard Products was now successfully following a strategy of new product innovation and introduction. It was leading the industry in changes in technology and products. As the number of new products increased, so did the amount of decision making around product considerations. The frequent needs for tradeoffs across engineering, production, and marketing lines increased the influence of the product managers. It was not that the functional managers lost influence; rather, it was the increase in decisions relating to products.

The increase in the influence of the product managers was revealed in several ways. First, their salaries became substantial. Second, they began to have a greater voice in the budgeting process, starting with approval of functional budgets relating to their products. The next change was an accumulation of staff around the products, which became product departments with considerable influence.

At Standard this came about with the increase in new product introductions. A lack of information developed concerning product costs and revenues for addition, deletion, modification, and pricing decisions. The general manager instituted a new information system that reported costs and revenues by product as well as by function. This gave product managers the need for a staff and a basis for more effective interfunctional collaboration.

In establishing the product departments, the general manager resisted requests from the product managers to reorganize around product divisions. While he agreed with their analysis that better coordination was needed across functions and for more effective product decision making, he was unwilling to take

3. See Paul R. Lawrence and Jay Lorsch, "Differentiation and Integration in Complex Organizations," *Administrative Science Quarterly* (June, 1967).

4. Paul R. Lawrence and Jay Lorsch, "New Management Job: the Integration," *Harvard Business Review* (November-December, 1967).

the chance that this move might reduce specialization in the technical areas or perhaps lose the economies of scale in production. He felt that a modification of the information system to report on a product and a functional basis along with a product staff group would provide the means for more coordination. He still needed the effective technical group to drive the innovative process. The general manager also maintained a climate where collaboration across product lines and functions was encouraged and rewarded.

The Matrix Completed

By now Standard Products was a high technology company; its products were undergoing constant change. The uncertainty brought about by the new technology and the new products required an enormous amount of decision making to plan-replan all the schedules, budgets, designs, and so on. As a result, the number of decisions and the number of consequential decisions made at low levels increased considerably. This brought on two concerns for the general manager and top management.

The first was the old concern for the quality of decisions made at low levels of the organization. The product managers helped solve this at middle and top levels, but their influence did not reach low into the organization where a considerable number of decisions were made jointly. They were not always made in the best interest of the firm as a whole. The product managers again recommended a move to product divisions to give these low-level decisions the proper product orientation.

The director of engineering objected, using the second problem to back up his objection. He said the move to product divisions would reduce the influence of the technical people at a time when they were having morale and turnover problems with these employees. The increase in joint decisions at low levels meant that these technical

people were spending a lot of time in meetings. Their technical input was not always needed, and they preferred to work on technical problems, not product problems. Their dissatisfaction would only be aggravated by a change to product divisions.

The top management group recognized both of these problems. They needed more product orientation at low levels, and they needed to improve the morale of the technical people whose inputs were needed for product innovations. Their solution involved the creation of a new role—that of subproduct manager.[5] The subproduct manager would be chosen from the functional organization and would represent the product line within the function. He would report to both the functional manager and the product manager, thereby creating a dual authority structure. The addition of a reporting relation on the product side increases the amount of product influence at lower levels.

The addition of the subproduct manager was intended to solve the morale problem also. Because he would participate in the product team meetings, the technical people did not need to be present. The subproduct manager would participate on the teams but would call on the technical experts within his department as they were needed. This permitted the functional department to be represented by the subproduct manager, and the technical people to concentrate on strictly technical matters.

Standard Products has now moved to a pure matrix organization as indicated in Figure 2. The pure matrix organization is distinguished from the previous cross-functional forms by two features. *First,* the pure matrix has a dual authority relationship somewhere in the organization. *Second,* there is a power balance between the product management and functional sides. While equal power is an unachievable razor's edge, a

5. Jay Lorsch, "Matrix Organization and Technical Innovations" in Jay Galbraith, ed., *Matrix Organizations: Organization Design for High Technology* (Cambridge, Mass.: The M.I.T. Press, 1971).

FIGURE 2

Standard's Pure Matrix Organization

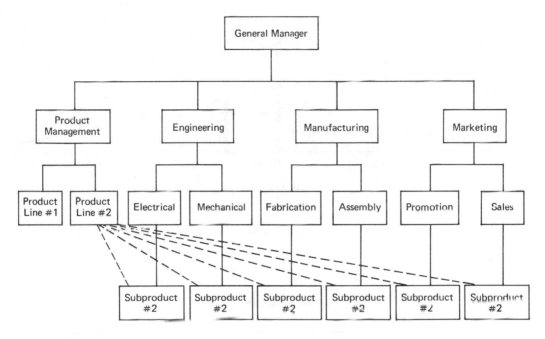

- - - - = Technical authority over the product

———— = Formal authority over the product (in product organization, these relationships may be reversed)

reasonable balance can be obtained through enforced collaboration on budgets, salaries, dual information and reporting systems, and dual authority relations. Such a balance is required because the problems that the organization faces are uncertain and must be solved on their own merits—not on any predetermined power structure.

Thus over a period of time, the Standard Products Co. has changed from a functional organization to a pure matrix organization using dual authority relationships, product management departments, product teams at several levels, and temporary task forces. These additional decision-making mechanisms were added to cope with the change in products and technologies. The changes

caused a good deal of uncertainty concerning resource allocations, budgets, and schedules. In the process of task execution, more was learned about the problem causing a need for rescheduling and rebudgeting. This required the processing of information and the making of decisions.

In order to increase its capacity to make product relevant decisions, Standard lowered the level at which decisions were made. Coordination was achieved by making joint decisions across functions. Product managers and subproduct managers were added to bring a general manager's perspective to bear on the joint decision-making processes. In addition, the information and reporting system was changed in order to provide reports by func-

FIGURE 3

The Range of Alternatives

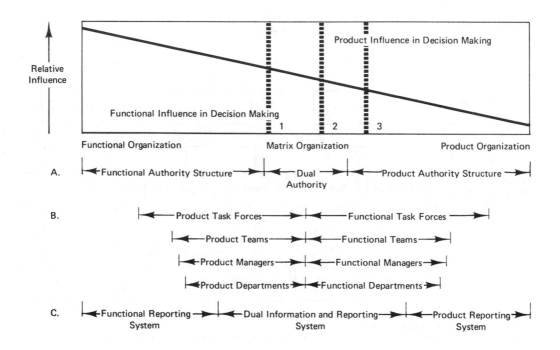

tion and by product. Combined, these measures allowed Standard to achieve the high levels of technical sophistication necessary to innovate products and simultaneously to get these products to the market quickly to maintain competitive position.

HOW DO I CHOOSE A DESIGN?

Not all organizations need a pure matrix organization with a dual authority relationship. Many, however, can benefit from some cross-functional forms to relieve top decision makers from day-to-day operations. If this is so, how does one choose the degree to which his organization should pursue these lateral forms? To begin to answer this question, let

us first lay out the alternatives, then list the choice determining factors.

The choice, shown in Figure 3, is indicated by the wide range of alternatives between a pure functional organization and a pure product organization with the matrix being half-way between. The Standard Products Co. could have evolved into a matrix from a product organization by adding functional teams and managers. Thus there is a continuum of organization designs between the functional and product forms. The design is specified by the choice among the authority structure; integrating mechanisms such as task forces, teams and so on; and by the formal information system. The way these are combined is illustrated in Figure 3. These design variables help regulate the relative distribution of influence between the product and functional considerations in the firm's operations.

The remaining factors determining influence are such things as roles in budget approvals, design changes, location and size of offices, salary, and so on. Thus there is a choice of integrating devices, authority structure, information system, and influence distribution. The factors that determine choice are diversity of the product line, the rate of change of the product line, interdependencies among subunits, level of technology, presence of economies of scale, and organization size.

Product Lines

The greater the diversity among product lines and the greater the rate of change of products in the line the greater the pressure to move toward product structures.[6] When product lines become diverse, it becomes difficult for general managers and functional managers to maintain knowledge in all areas; the amount of information they must handle exceeds their capacity to absorb it. Similarly, the faster the rate of new product introduction, the more unfamiliar are the tasks being performed.

Managers are, therefore, less able to make precise estimates concerning resource allocations, schedules, and priorities. During the process of new product introduction, these same decisions are made repeatedly. The decisions concern trade-offs among engineering, manufacturing, and marketing. This means there must be greater product influence in the decision process. The effect of diversity and change is to create a force to locate the organization farther to the right in Figure 3.

Interdependence

The functional division of labor in organizations creates interdependencies among the specialized subunits. That is, a problem of action in one unit has a direct impact on the goal accomplishment of the other units. Organizations usually devise mechanisms that uncouple the subunits, such as in-process-inventory and order backlogs. The degree to which inventories and backlogs develop is a function of how tight the schedule is. If there is a little slack in the schedule, then the functional departments can resolve their own problems. However, if rapid response to market changes is a basis of competition, then schedules are squeezed and activities run in parallel rather than series.[7] This means that problems in one unit directly affect another. The effect is a greater number of joint decisions involving engineering, manufacturing, and production. A greater need for product influence in these decisions arises due to the tight schedule. Thus the tighter the schedule, the greater the force to move to the right in Figure 3.

Although the tightness of the schedule is the most obvious source of interdependence, tight couplings can arise from reliability requirements and other design specifications. If the specifications require a more precise fit and operation of parts, then the groups designing and manufacturing the parts must also "fit and operate" more closely. This requires more coordination in the form of communication and decision making.

Level of Technology

If tight schedules and new products were the only forces operating, every organization

---

6. For product line diversity, see Alfred Chandler, *Strategy and Structure* (Cambridge, Mass.: The M.I.T. Press, 1962); for product change rate, see Tom Burns and G. M. Stalker, *Management and Innovation* (London: Tavistock Publications, 1958).

7. For a case study of this effect, see Jay Galbraith, "Environmental and Technological Determinants of Organization Design" in Jay Lorsch and Paul R. Lawrence, eds., *Studies in Organization Design* (Homewood, Ill.: Richard D. Irwin, Inc., 1970).

would be organized around product lines. The level of technology or degree to which new technology is being used is a counteracting force. The use of new technologies requires expertise in the technical specialties in engineering, in production engineering, in manufacturing, and market research in marketing. Some of the expertise may be purchased outside the organization.

However, if the expertise is critical to competitive effectiveness, the organization must acquire it internally. If the organization is to make effective use of the expertise, the functional form of organization is superior, as described earlier in the article. Therefore the greater the need for expertise, the greater the force to move to the left in Figure 3.

Economies of Scale and Size

The other factor favoring a functional form is the degree to which expensive equipment in manufacturing, test facilities in engineering, and warehousing facilities in marketing are used in producing and selling the product. (Warehousing introduces another dimension of organization structure, for example, geographical divisions. For our purposes, we will be concerned only with product and function dimensions.) It is usually more expensive to buy small facilities for product divisions than a few large ones for functional departments. The greater the economies of scale, the greater the force to move to the left in Figure 3. Mixed structures are always possible. That is, the capital intensive fabrication operation can organize along functional process lines, and the labor intensive assembly operation can organize along product lines.

The size of the organization is important in that it modifies the effect of expertise and economies of scale. That is, the greater the size of the organization the smaller the costs of lost specialization and lost economies of scale when the product form is adopted. Thus while size by itself has little effect on organization structure, it does moderate the effects of the previously mentioned factors.

The Choice

While research on organizations has not achieved a sophistication that would allow us to compute the results of the above factors and locate a point in Figure 3, we can still make our subjective weightings. In addition, we can locate our present position and make changes in the appropriate directions as product lines, schedules, technologies, and size change during the normal course of business. The framework provides some basis for planning the organization along with planning the strategy and resource allocations.

If the organization's present structure is on the left side of the figure, many of the symptoms occurring in the Standard Products example signal a need for change. To what degree are communication overloads occurring? Are top executives being drawn into day-to-day decisions to the detriment of strategy development? How long does it take to get top level decisions made in order to continue work on new products? If the answers to these questions indicate an overload, then some movement toward a matrix is appropriate. Probably a sequence of moves until the bottlenecks disappear is the best strategy; this will allow for the proper attitudinal and behavioral changes to keep pace.

If the organization is product organized, then movements to the left toward a matrix are more subtle. They must be triggered by monitoring the respective technological environments.

An example from the aerospace industry may help. In the late fifties and early sixties the environment was characterized by the space race and missile gap. In this environment, technical performance and technology development were primary, and most firms adopted organizations characterized by the dotted line at "1" in Figure 9. The functional departments had the greatest influence on the decision-making process. During the McNamara era, they moved to point "2." The environment shifted to incentive contracts, PERT-cost systems, and increased importance of cost and schedule considerations.

Currently, the shift has continued toward point "3." Now the environment is characterized by tight budgets, a cost overrun on the C-5 project, and Proxmire hearings in the Senate. The result is greater influence by the project managers. All these have taken place in response to the changing character of the market. A few firms recently moved back toward point "2" in response to the decreasing size of some firms. The reduction in defense spending has resulted in cutbacks in projects and employment. In order to maintain technical capabilities with reduced size, these firms have formed functional departments under functional managers with line responsibility. These changes show how changes in need for expertise, goals, and size affect the organization design choice.

Many organizations are experiencing pressures that force them to consider various forms of matrix designs. The most common pressure is increased volume of new products. Organizations facing this situation must either adopt some form of matrix organization, change to product forms of organization, or increase the time between start and introduction of the new product process.

For most organizations, the matrix design is the most effective alternative. Managers must be aware of the different kinds of matrix designs and develop some basis for choosing among them.

Section B:
Technology and
Environmental Uncertainty

In Section A, most of the writers pointed to conditions outside the firm, particularly changing conditions, that caused one type of organizational structure to be more suitable than another. The writers in this section examine two of the more important of these external factors, environmental uncertainty and technology.

Many studies have contributed to what we now know of the technological environment's effect on the firm. Several important studies have found that the type of technology is related to specific properties of the organization's structure. Probably the most famous of these is the study by Joan Woodward. She found that several properties of structure, such as the number of levels in the hierarchy and line-to-staff ratios, vary according to the type of technology employed. This type of research has spawned great interest in the technology-structure relationship. In the first selection, Raymond Hunt critically examines much of this literature. One of his conclusions is that "it is not material technology, *per se,* that presents organizational challenges, but the nature of the behavioral and problem-solving tasks confronting those operating the system at its various levels." Hunt goes on to differentiate between performance and problem-solving systems. The problem-solving system seems more applicable to the uncertain environmental situation, whereas the performance system is more like the "classic" models of management developed in response to environmental stability. These conclusions coincide especially with those of Drucker; both authors agree that changes in the environment necessitate structures that differ in several properties from the traditional organizational forms.

In the second reading, Dennis Organ examines one of the human problems of dynamic organization structures. The selection deals with the problem of *how* organizations should interact with their environments, given that the structure should meet the demands of the organization's particular environment. The focus is on the "linking pin" or "boundary agent" that acts as the mediator between the firm and the relevant environment. Individuals do this interacting, not organizations, and Organ outlines methods for analyzing the role demands, role expectations, role conflicts, role stresses, and skills, abilities, and traits needed by people who are to fulfill these boundary roles.

Boundary agents establish linkages in order to reduce the threats of uncertainty posed by dependence on the environment, as discussed previously by Hunt. They obviously need certain skill levels but they also need certain personal attributes or qualities. Boundary agents are caught between the conflicting pressures from outsiders and members of their own organizations. The reader should examine several roles described in the first section in the terms which Organ outlines. For example, an interesting exercise is to analyze the project manager in Galbraith's matrix organization according to the criteria set forth for a boundary agent.

These two readings, when combined, give an interesting picture of the role of technology in the design of organizations. Undoubtedly it plays a major role as Hunt's literature review suggests. On the other hand, Organ emphasizes the inherent human problems that occur in any structure or design and that must be overcome for successful organizational functioning.

Technology and Organization[1]

RAYMOND G. HUNT[*]

In order to solve practical problems of organizational design, it is necessary initially to understand the many differences between types of organizations and the reasons that these differences exist. The fact that these aspects have not been considered until the mid-1960's is reflected by the independence of developments in organizational design and theory until this time.[2] However, recent progress in comparative analysis of organizations, together with integrative theory building, gives promise of altering this state of affairs, especially regarding the appreciation of technology as a main basis for differentiating organizational varieties and explaining organizational processes.

These recent developments are the foundation for this paper; first, we will outline the ways in which organizations may be classified, and then we will appraise the current understanding of the relationship between technology and organizational design.

CLASSIFYING ORGANIZATIONS

To be useful, a schema for distinguishing organizations must identify cogent parameters or dimensions that cut across particular cases and provide a basis for ordering those cases, even if it is only on a yes-no basis. Different schemas will be useful for different purposes, but since every organization can be construed as having: (1) a function in society; (2) a pattern of input; (3) a pattern of output; (4) a set of procedures for converting inputs into outputs (something to which we shall apply the term "throughput"[3]); and (5) a pattern according to which it is put together, it follows that any organization could be classified on any or all of these bases. Indeed, allowing for some mixed cases and some ambiguous ones, examples of all five kinds of classification can be found.

*Professor of Psychology, co-editor of Current Perspectives in Social Psychology and a co-author of Nurses, Patients, and Social Systems.

[1]Preparation of this paper was assisted by NASA Grant NGR 33-015-061.

[2]R. M. Cyert and J. G. March, "Organizational Design," In Eds., W. W. Cooper, H. J. Leavitt and M. W. Shelly, New Perspectives in Organization Research (New York: Wiley, 1964), Chapter 29, p. 558.

[3]In this usage we are following the example of D. Katz and R. Kahn, The Social Psychology of Organizations (New York: Wiley, 1966).

36 Reprinted by permission of the author and Academy of Management Journal from Academy of Management Journal, September 1970, pp. 235–252.

Classification by Social Function

In Chapter 5 of their remarkable book, Katz and Kahn[4] present a "typology" of organizations based on "first-order" and "second-order factors." First-order factors describe "genotypic functions" that differentiate among all kinds of organizational systems and subsystems. Thus, in Katz and Kahn's typology there are productive or economic organizations (e.g., factories); maintenance organizations (e.g., those, like schools, specialized to socialize people); adaptive organizations (e.g., research labs); and managerial or political organizations. These first-order distinctions have to do principally with the part played by the organization in the larger society; thus, they can claim kinship with Parsons' social function criteria.[5] With regard to actual organizations, of course, these categories are not mutually exclusive. A particular organization could fall into more than one class: A T & T may be mainly an economic organization, but in its research labs it contains adaptive organizations.

Defined by its contributions to the larger social system, an organization's social function, unlike the other four of its facets, has to do with its *relations* with the society as a whole, not just with its own characteristics. Talking of an organization's social functions is to treat It (the organization) not so much as an integral system, but as a subsystem of a larger system. One might therefore infer that this essentially *exogenous* criterion for classification is different from and independent of the others. Katz and Kahn obviously think so with their distinction between first- and second-order factors (see also Pugh, footnote 10).[6] To be sure, an organization's social function is likely to influence its perceived social value which, in turn, may affect its access to societal resources, including technological ones which may help shape its other characteristics. But any such linkages depend entirely on the organization's embeddedness in the larger societal system. In any event, these linkages are complex and clearly not direct.

For very general purposes, classification by social function can be helpful. However, the variability within functional types is too great for them to afford much analytic power.[7] Katz and Kahn are aware of this, of course, as their positing of second-order factors implies. These second-order factors have more to do with input, output, or conversion methods (throughput), or else with design features.

---

[4]*Ibid.*

[5]T. Parsons, *Structure and Process in Modern Societies* (Glencoe, Ill.: Free Press, 1960).

[6]D. Katz and R. Kahn, *Social Psychology*, "Dimension of Organization Structure," *Administrative Science Quarterly* 13 (1968), pp. 65-105.

[7]See, C. A. Perrow, "A Framework for the Comparative Analysis of Organizations," *American Sociological Review* (1967), 32, pp. 195-208.

Classification by Form or Pattern

Pattern denotes the discernable "phenomenology" or anatomy of an organization—its characteristics or properties *qua* organization. This aspect of organizations we shall herein reference by the term "structure," or, when construed in a purposive sense, "design."

With its functional traditions, American scholarship has tended to pay more attention to operational than to structural properties of organization.[8] To be sure, structure is only revealed in the functions of organizations,[9] but structure there is nevertheless. We mean by it the varied patterns of interaction, intended or otherwise, that characterize an organization. To the degree these patterns are codified or standardized, we can speak of the organization as being formal. And "formal organizational structure" can be defined in terms of prescriptions regarding lines of authority, divisions of labor, and allocations of resources[10] that often can be found memorialized in such things as organization charts, job descriptions, and budgetary formulae. Such pointers are far from infallible guides to organizational reality, but even so it is essential to recognize that the nature of the formal organization has much to do with limiting and shaping organizational life (including whatever "informal" processes may be spawned therein). Moreover, the idea of formal structure is fundamental to rational organization design.

Our concept of structure in substance and in spirit approximates Anthony's idea of "system" as distinct from "process."[11] The latter has to do with the actual events and decisions that transpire within the organization, whereas the former represents the formal and informal framework within which these are done—the "formula," as it were, according to which the organization's tasks are specified, interrelated, performed, and controlled. Obviously this formula can be either explicit or not explicit.

As for the use of structural criteria for classifying organizations, it has long been traditional[12] to distinguish three basic forms of organization design: (1) line organization, (2) functional organization, and (3) line-staff organization. In line organizations everybody does essentially the same kind of work under the more or less immediate authority of a "man at the top." Some degree of internal specialization may lead to departmentalization of line organizations, but this does not necessarily change their fundamentals.

---

[8]See, R. G. Hunt, "Review of Systems of Organization" by E. J. Miller and A. K. Rice, *Administrative Science Quarterly,* 1968, 13, pp. 360-362.

[9]D. Katz and R. Kahn, *Social Psychology,* Chapter 1.

[10]See, D. S. Pugh, *et al., "Dimensions";* W. F. Whyte, *Organizational Behavior: Theory and Application* (Homewood, Ill.: Irwin-Dorsey, 1969).

[11]R. N. Anthony, *Planning and Control Systems* (Cambridge, Mass.: Harvard University Press, 1965).

[12]See J. Woodward, *Industrial Organization: Theory and Practice* (London: Oxford University Press, 1965).

Pure functional organizations are scarce, apparently because they are based on the sensible but hard to implement idea that since it is difficult to combine all necessary managerial-supervisory skills in single individuals, it is wise to organize around functions—skills, activities, etc. —rather than people. The desire to include functional specialists within an organization while retaining unity of command is the basis for the widespread "compromise" development of line-staff organizations wherein supporting specialists work through particular line managers.

It is obviously possible to combine these models in various ways and mention might be made of such special cases as project organizations (which, in a sense, are temporary, special-purpose, line organizations) and matrix organizations (which are meldings of project and functional models calculated to satisfy institutional needs for permanence). Furthermore, other structural classifications are possible. Pugh, *et al;* stress a multidimensional characterization built around performance regulation, centralization of authority, and the degree to which operations are controlled by line management rather than by impersonal records and procedures generated from staff offices.[13] Burns and Stalker's well known distinction between "organic" and "mechanistic" management patterns is another somewhat similar example.[14] Organic organizations are characterized by less formalized definitions of jobs, by more stress on flexibility and adaptability, and by communication networks involving more consultation than command. Mechanistic organizations are more rigidly specialized functionally, and in general, define an opposite pole on an organic-mechanistic continuum. Finally, of course, distinctions between bureaucratic and nonbureaucratic organizations exemplify the classificatory use of structural or design criteria.[15]

Classification by Output

Classifying organizations according to their output is a common practice that may involve one of two emphases. One, the kind or type of output (i.e., the product), is a standard basis for defining industries (e.g., automobile, motion pictures, etc.) and is too familiar to require further comment. But, output can also be viewed from the standpoint of the quantity or volume of whatever it is that is produced. For example, Woodward, although she thought of it more as a direct expression of technology, used to good effect classification of industrial firms as unit, small-batch, large-batch, and mass production.[16] The immediate meaning of unit, batch, and

[13]D. S. Pugh, *et al.,* "Dimensions."

[14]T. Burns and G. M. Stalker, *The Management of Innovation* (London: Tavistock Publications, 1961).

[15]See, e.g., D. Katz and R. Kahn, *Social Psychology,* Ch. 5; N. P. Mouzelis, *Organization and Bureaucracy* (Chicago: Aldine, 1967); W. F. Whyte, "Organizational Behavior," Ch. 1; W. Bennis, "Beyond Bureaucracy," *Transaction* (1965), 2, pp. 31-35.

[16]J. Woodward, *Industrial Organization.*

mass production is plain: it describes a scale of production quantities ranging from one of a kind through a few to very many.

W. F. Whyte makes use of these same distinctions, but only as sub-categories within a broader, more heterogeneous system of classes.[17] Whyte's primary breakdown of organizations into "office, service, manu-facturing, and continuous process" varieties clearly employs criteria other than output. Indeed it makes use of just about all criteria save social function. Office and service classes, for instance, appear to be distinguish-able on the basis of the nature of their outputs, but they (and surely manu-facturing and continuous processing) are classifications that also make use of other bases for categorization, notably throughout processes and, possibly, input as well.

Classification by Input

Distinctions between organizations based on input rest on contrasts regarding the raw materials on which the system works. The possibilities here are at least as numerous as the vast number offered to classifications based on output. One input distinction that has received special attention in the literature, however, is that between organizations (such as prisons, schools, employment agencies) that deal mainly with people and those organizations that operate chiefly on things, objects, hardware, or the like. Erving Goffman has provided some especially exotic discussions of "people-processing" systems, and the topic is capable of generating more than a little emotion. It is doubtless that such systems differ from others, if for no other reason than because their raw materials are "re-active" instead of passive. In fact, this reactivity can itself be made a basis for a distinction between organizations by focusing on the form of feedback controlling the system's operations. We shall illustrate this in the next section.

In the meantime, take notice of Thompson and Bates' use of a "ratio of mechanization to professionalization" to distinguish organizations.[19] By this they mean the extent to which technology is represented in human or nonhuman resources. But whether this is truly a classification based on input is questionable for, if Thompson and Bates stress the *locus* of tech-nology, the notions of mechanization and professionalization seem to link the distinction closely to technology itself.

Classification by Throughput

Conversion processes or throughput are the various things done, with or without tools and machines, to transform inputs into outputs. The term

---

[17]W. F. Whyte, "Organizational Behavior."

[18]E. Goffman, *Asylums* (Garden City, N. Y.: Doubleday Anchor, 1961).

[19]J. D. Thompson, and F. L. Bates, "Technology, Organization, and Administration," *Administrative Science Quarterly* (1957), 2, pp. 325-342.

"technology" is usually applied to these processes.[20] Our own definition of technology encompasses the three facets of technology (1) operations, (2) materials, and (3) knowledge, differentiated by Hickson et al.,[21] and includes the sequencing of activities involved in the conversion process, thereby including what Whyte, among others, refers to as "work flow."[22]

A straightforward throughput classification might be exemplified by J. D. Thompson's distinction between long-linked, mediating, and intensive technologies.[23] The first of these includes conversion processes (like those found in automobile assembly plants) involving serially interdependent operations, standard products, and constant, repetitive work rates. Mediating technologies link clients who "are or wish to be interdependent (as banks link depositors and lenders)." These, too, commonly employ standardization along with bureaucratic formats. Intensive technologies are those involving application of a variety of techniques to the change of some specific object, in which actual operations are determined by feedback from the object itself. This is clearly a "custom technology," and includes such examples as hospitals, schools, research projects, and tailor shops. Obviously a single organization might include within itself multiple technologies.

We have already mentioned that Whyte's classification of organizations included an admixture of output and throughput criteria; the same was true of Woodward's classification. Along with other categories defined by output, both Whyte and Woodward include in their schemas a "continuous process" category (e.g., a fully automated oil refinery) that indexes technology rather than output.[24]

It must be evident that input and output systems, as well as throughput systems, can be described in terms of the processes or technologies by which they are implemented. That is, the operations by which inputs—raw materials—are introduced into a system describe a technology, and the same is true on the output (product) side. This fact, plus the other consideration that conversion processes in an organization must be relative to the input and output to and from the system (e.g., knowledge of the raw materials and product specifications) strongly suggest that the input-conversion-output cycle represents a single basic technological sequence or organizational substrate. Thus, the crucial consideration may not be the particular properties of the inputs or the outputs per se, but

---

[20]For a useful discussion of definitional issues, see D. J. Hickson, D. S. Pugh, and D. C. Pheysey, "Operations Technology and Organization Structure: An Empirical Reappraisal," *Administrative Science Quarterly* (1969), 14, pp. 378-397.

[21]*Ibid.*

[22]W. F. Whyte, "Organizational Behavior."

[23]J. D. Thompson, *Organizations in Action* (New York: McGraw-Hill, 1967).

[24]W. F. Whyte, "Organizational Behavior"; Woodward, *Industrial Organization.* Notice might be taken of Hickson, et al.'s incorporation of this category, along with unit production, mass production, and the others, into a throughput scale of "production continuity" (see Hickson, et al., "Operations Technology").

the technologies according to which they are accomplished.[25] In any case, it seems clear that input, output, and technology (throughput) are inextricably joined. Taken together they constitute the basic *endogenous* operaional properties of organizations and, when actualized, collectively describe what Anthony calls organizational "process" (or function) as distinguished from structure (system).[26]

There is, of course, nothing in these unifying assertions to preclude variation in technological manifestations at different points in the process cycle. Input and conversion operations might be highly routinized, for example, but output methods (e.g., marketing) might be quite nonroutine.[27] And certainly nothing prevents separate analyses of respective technological features of input, output, or conversion subsystems. The point here is that input and output criteria for classifying organizations may be structurally significant only insofar as they indirectly index technological phenomena.

Another thing that may have been evident in our exposition is the difficulty one has treating technology or process without making reference to structural or design aspects of the organization (see, e.g., the allusion to bureaucratic formats in the presentation above of Thompson's "mediating" technology). This is no accident of discursive formats. Indeed, we have taken notice of Anthony's proposition that system (structure) represents the formulae for organizational processes (input-throughput-output).[28] Certainly the two dimensions are intimately entwined, even if the nature and degree of that intimacy may not yet be altogether clear; furthermore, they are both technologies. Conversion processes, or, more generally, modes of production, constitute what Olsen has called "material technologies." He has described modes of organization as "social technologies."[29] Thus, from Anthony's perspective, exploring relations between "technology" and "organization" resolves itself into an analysis of relations between system and process. From Olsen's standpoint, this amounts to tracing the linkages between material and social technologies. We should hardly be surprised to find a good deal of interdependence in these relationships. Indeed, the expectation is implicit in the now common characterization of organizations as sociotechnical systems. In a manner of speaking, then, describing relations between technology and organi-

---

[25]For a related discussion with different conclusions see Hickson, *et al., Ibid.,* p. 380.

[26]R. N. Anthony, "Planning and Control."

[27]Distinctions could be drawn, but throughout this discussion we shall use the basic terms "routine" (or "routinized") and "program" ("programmed") more or less interchangably to mean the extent to which an organization's tasks can and have been specified and prescribed—formalized. Programming performance (as, to take an extreme example, in a robot) is difficult when tasks are vague, variable, or complicated, but the process can be generally regarded (with neither approval nor disapproval) as a broad organizational means of reducing operational uncertainty by eliminating operator discretion.

[28]Anthony, "Planning and Control."

[29]M. E. Olsen, *The Process of Social Organization* (New York: Holt, Rinehart, Winston, 1968).

zational forms amounts to an extended definition of the meaning of the concept of the sociotechnical system. With that observation, a more explicit overview of technology and organizational patterns is in order.

TECHNOLOGY AND ORGANIZATION DESIGN

Beginning at least with Veblen and Marx, material technology has been regularly proposed as a major influence on organizational phenomena. Indications of its broad significance can be found in Toynbee's demonstration of changing forms of English social organization as new industrial technologies emerged during the 18th and 19th Centuries. Margaret Mead has provided vivid portrayals of interrelations between technological advances and social patterns.[30] More recently, Dubin[31] has nominated technology as the single most important determinant of work behavior and Mouzelis[32] has spoken at length of the determining effect of technological structures and processes on organizational interaction. Stinchcombe, too, in context with his discussion of "motives for organizing," mentions technology among the basic variables affecting organizing capacity,[33] and Olsen lists material technology as one of four primary factors underlying forms of social organization (the other three are the natural environment, population, and the human being).[34] Finally, in his excellent review of comparative studies, Udy points out two basic "casual mechanisms" that shape organizations. One operates via people to affect structures, and the other is *ecological* and deals with how activity is limited and channeled.[35] Together with the "social setting," which we are disregarding here, technology can be construed as imposing ecological limits on organizational properties.

In somewhat the same way, social technology can be looked upon as constraining material technology, as in the case of cultural or organizational resistance to change[36] or as in the extent to which a system is attuned to the receipt of inputs regarding new material technologies. Burns and Stalker, to cite a pertinent instance, found that firms adapting successfully to the electronics industry were characterized by a more global task model and a different communication process for innovative information than were the less successful ones. In the adaptive firms, technological or market information was introduced to reprogram routine operations, thus enhancing flexibility in a technologically changing environment.[37]

[30]A. Toynbee, *The Industrial Revolution* (Boston: Beason, 1956); M. Mead, (ed.) *Cultural Patterns and Technological Change* (New York: New American Library, 1955).
[31]R. Dubin, *The World of Work* (Englewood Cliffs: Prentice Hall, 1958).
[32]N. P. Mouzelis, *Organization and Bureaucracy.*
[33]A. L. Stinchcombe, "Social Structure and Organization," ed., J. G. March, *Handbook of Organizations* (Chicago: Rand McNally, 1965. pp. 142-194).
[34]M. E. Olsen, *Social Organization.*
[35]S. H. Udy, "The Comparative Analysis of Organizations," ed., J. G. March, "Handbook of Organizations," pp. 678-710.
[36]See, e.g., M. Mead, "Cultural Patterns" for illustrations of such cultural disinclinations.
[37]T. Burns and G. M. Stalker, "Management of Innovation."

To undergird these contentions, a significant empirical literature has now emerged relating technology to various organizational matters. The most noteworthy examples are probably Woodward's seminal studies.[38] Her work and other relevant investigations have been well reviewed by Perrow, J. D. Thompson, and Hickson, *et al.*, so there is no need for repetition here.[39] It will be sufficient to observe that, although the nature, degree, and conditions of its effect remain controversial,[40] technology has been shown to affect structure, to shape interaction, and to influence the personal characteristics of organizational members.[41]

Yet, as late as 1964, W. R. Scott felt constrained to mark the infrequency with which technological variables had been built into theory.[42] The reasons for this seem to reside partly in a preoccupation of organizational scholars with nonstructural human relations or "informal" processes[43] and partly from the fact that, although technological phenomena were widely recognized and sometimes even categorized, until recently there literally were no technological *variables* to build into theory.[44] Perhaps what is most important in the technology-organization literature of the past few years, therefore, aside from empirical explication, is that it has begun to give form to conceptualizations of managable technological variables or dimensions. Prominent in this connection have been the work of Bell, Harvey, Perrow, Whyte, and Pugh and Hickson.

The Technology Variable

It will be recalled from our earlier discussion that productive as it was empirically, the technology varible was ambiguous in Woodward's classification scheme. She regarded her entire scheme as a direct index of technology, even as a scale of technological complexity ranging from unit to mass to process modes of production. Harvey, however, has quite reasonably pointed out that the complexity scale could equally well be the reverse.[45] And Woodward's own findings that unit production and continuous process organizations tended to exhibit many common characteristics that contrasted sharply with other kinds of organizations, could

---

[38]J. Woodward, *Industrial Organization.*

[39]C. A. Perrow, "Framework for Comparative Analysis"; J. D. Thompson, "Organizations in Action"; D. S. Hickson, *et al.*, "Operations Technology."

[40]Illumination of the controversy can perhaps best be found in Hickson, *et al.*, "Operations Technology."

[41]One example of this last point, which is here mentioned only incidentally, may be found in R. Biauner's studies of alientation e.g., *Alienation and Freedom* (Chicago: University of Chicago Press, 1964).

[42]W. R. Scott, "Theory of Organizations," ed., R. E. L. Faris, *Handbook of Modern Sociology* (Chicago: Rand McNally, 1964), pp. 485-530.

[43]See N. P. Mouzelis, *Organization and Bureaucracy,* for further discussion of this point.

[44]W. F. Whyte, "Organzational Behavior," (Chapter 3).

[45]E. Harvey, "Technology and the Structure of Organizations," *American Sociological Review* (1968), 33, pp. 247-259.

imply a "circular" interpretation of the technological dimension underlying her classification.

The precise mechanisms linking technologies with organizational forms are still problematical in the literature, but, as a generality, the critical technological element to which organizational structure must respond seems best conceptualized as *complexity*. This is something that unit production organizations, for instance, may have in at least as long a supply as their continuous process counterparts—a moment's reflection on the many esoteric one-of-a-kind products produced under the American space program vindicates that assertion. To state it simply, this view of correlation between organization and technology signifies that the concrete manifestations of technology are less important than the essential complexity underlying them. Having said that, however, it is necessary to acknowledge immediately that complexity is an elusive concept that takes many forms.

Bell, for instance, has dealt explicitly with the matter of complexity and structure in his study of spans of control (ratios of personnel to supervisors) in a large hospital.[46] He defined complexity as:

(a) The degree of predictability of work demands;

(b) The discretion provided for in a position; and

(c) The responsibility of the job-holder (construed as the time lapse between decision and its supervisory review or assessment).

Bell then showed that as complexity increased with regard to either subordinates' or supervisors' roles, the span of control decreased.

Harvey, using Woodward's work as a point of departure, prefers to speak of a complexity dimension ranging from technical diffuseness ("made to orderness") to specificity.[47] He argues that one needs to take account not only of the *form* of technology (as Woodward tried to do), but also of the amount of "changefulness" *within* a form. As he puts it: A unit production firm might produce the same thing most of the time and thus be "specific." Or, it might vary its outputs and be "diffuse." Harvey postulated that whether the organization is specific or diffuse, it will have differential implications for its structural characteristics. He conceived three "sociotechnical types" (marriages of technology and internal organizational structure): (1) diffuse, (2) intermediate, and (3) specific (defined in terms of frequency of product change) and showed that when compared with specific types, diffuse types had fewer specialized subunits, fewer levels of authority, a lower ratio of managers and supervisors to total personnel, and a lessened degree of performance program specification.

[46]G. D. Bell, "Determinants of Span of Control," *American Journal of Sociology* (1967), 73, pp. 90-101.

[47]E. Harvey, "Technology and the Structure."

Drawing mainly on the work of Woodward, Harvey, and Bell, together with his own experience, Whyte has gone about the detailed application of technological concepts to analysis of that basic organizational element, the span of control, asking what factors are responsible for its variations. He concludes that there are five factors:

(1) The complexity (in Bell's sense) of the job for the supervisor and subordinate;

(2) The visibility of results from performing the work;

(3) The interdependence and need for coordination among tasks;

(4) The degree to which interdependent activities require human rather than mechanical control; and

(5) The kinds of personnel required by the technology.[48]

Probably the most searching attempts at conceptualizing technology and relating it to organizational processes can be found in Perrow's work with his contingent, two-dimensional model that elaborates a distinction between routine and nonroutine technologies.[49] Perrow's emphasis is on classifying technologies regarding the frequency with which exceptional cases[50] are encountered and with reference to the nature of the search process (for solutions) that ensues when exceptions (problems) do occur. Using this general model, he relates task-structure to analogous control/coordination processes involving variations in individual or group discretion and the nature of the feedback mechanisms controlling performance (i.e., their degree of "programing"). Perrow also distinguishes three functional areas in management: (1) design and planning, (2) technical control and support of product, and (3) the supervision of production and marketing, each of which he ties in with the technological and task dimensions described. Finally, in a tentative way, Perrow undertakes to relate nontask-related (i.e., informal) interaction to the basic model.

In a later paper, Perrow refined his basic model and extended it to connect with the psychological processes of its human operatives.[51] He stresses a kind of "cognitive" conception of technology working as a system of cues (that may vary in clarity), which signal the initiation of performance routines (that also may vary in their degree of explicit "programming") and involve provision for handling exceptions that may be

---

[48]W. F. Whyte, "Organizational Behavior."

[49]C. A. Perrow, "Framework for Comparative Analysis."

[50]I.e., tasks, decisions, etc. not covered, or perceived to be covered, by existing performance programs. Such exceptions define problems for which organizational solutions must be sought if the system is to function, or at least if it is to function smoothly.

[51]C. A. Perrow, "Technology and Structural Changes in Business Firms" (Paper presented at First World Congress, International Industrial Relations Assn, Geneva, September 1967).

procedurally more or less routinized. The notable feature of this construction is that regardless of how complicated or elaborate, a system may be viewed as technologically routine to the extent that:

(1) The signals that initiate its processes are unambiguous;

(2) The performance processes so cued are programed; and

(3) When faced with exceptions not covered by regular performance routines, search processes and problem-solving methods are programed.

The properties of technology emphasized by other writers (e.g. Harvey's "changefulness" or Whyte's "human" vs "mechanical" control) can probably be treated in Perrow's formulation as either sources of cognitive complexity (exceptions) or as proxies for it.

Perrow's cognitive constructions rather closely parallel the much more general cybernetic model of human problem-solving due to Miller, Galanter, and Pribram.[52] These authors construe individual performance in relation to a cognitive Test-Operate-Test-Exit (TOTE) model which is based on the notion of "plan." A plan is defined as any hierarchical process controlling the sequence in which a set of operations is performed. They discuss a variety of ways that plans may differ (communicability, source, detail, flexibility, etc.) and also discuss plans for searching and solving, distinguishing between systematic and heuristic varieties.

Very briefly, their idea is that people have images of reality and an array of plans for dealing with it. As information in the form of environmental signals flows into a human performance system, it is "tested" for fit with existing plans which then may be put into operation. Results of action are appraised via feedback from the performance, and the system moves on either to another performance segment or, if a problem has arisen, to a more or less standardized search routine. Of course, the system could cycle into a search routine immediately if the initial "test" yielded no suitable performance program. From Miller, Galanter, and Pribram's presentation it is evident that when a search plan exists one may not even be aware of it, although it is necessary to perceive the exception—it is the function of the TOTE unit to guarantee that. Thus, regardless of how complicated it may be materially, at the behavioral level, technology can be defined in terms of an ordered set of skills or habits that differ mainly in their degree of routinization, integration, or mechanization. Complicated material technologies may be more difficult to program and they may place greater demands on human resources, but be that as it may, what counts operationally is behavioral routinization. We may say, then, that technological complexity is a function of the frequency with which problems (exceptions) confront organizational operations and the practical difficulty and degree of individual discretion or judgment required in resolving or finding solutions to them.

[52]G. A. Miller, E. Galanter, and K. H. Pribram, *Plans and the Structure of Behavior* (New York: Holt, Rinehart, Winston, 1960).

Performance vs Problem-Solving System

It may be concluded from the foregoing that it is not material technology, *per se,* that presents organizational challenges, but the nature of the behavioral and problem-solving tasks confronting those operating the system at all its various levels. The extent to which an organization's task systems can be programmed and operational uncertainty thereby eliminated seem to be the critical circumstances. However, no performance program can anticipate every contingency; exceptions will occur. Even if it can be reduced, operational uncertainty cannot be totally eliminated. Consequently, as Perrow has maintained, the decisive structural determinants are apt to be associated with the handling of exceptions to task programs. The frequency of such exceptions, of course, will not be unrelated to material technology, but it still may not parallel it closely—very complicated material technologies may, for instance, be highly programmed. But, in any event, the more crucial consideration would seem to be the importance of exceptions to the viability of the organization and how these exceptions can be handled by it.

If paradoxical, then, it seems nevertheless reasonable to assume that the more a system depends upon its performance programs to control its outputs, the more seriously it must view exceptions to their application or breakdowns in their operation and, hence, the more it must be geared to deal with them if and when they occur. If problem-solving processes are routinized along with task performance, one could expect a different kind of organization from the one that would result when they are not. In an unpublished paper, Perrow has presented some data consistent with such an expectation.[53]

If this is sensible, a potential basis for the similarity found by Woodward between unit production and process organizations is discoverable via the simple expedient of conceiving, somewhat after the fashion of Burns and Stalker,[54] of two quite different kinds of organization: one geared chiefly to performance (as in a mass production factory or a modern bank) and the other one geared to problem-solving (as in a hospital or a design and development enterprise). In a unit production firm, the system deals almost entirely with exceptions, and its problem-solving modes are likely to be unroutinized, especially if it is technologically diffuse.[55] In automated continuous process organizations, whether exceptions are frequent or not, they will be critical when they occur so that such systems, too, are likely to be structured as problem-solving or trouble-shooting affairs. Thus, both unit production organizations (at any rate diffuse ones involved with complicated material technologies) and continuous process varieties are likely

---

[53]C. A. Perrow, Working Paper on Technology and Structure (University of Wisconsin, 1970), mimeo.

[54]T. Burns and G. M. Stalker, "Management of Innovation."

[55]For data regarding this point, see E. Harvey, "Technology and Structure."

to be similarly structured—as organic problem-solving systems. Other operations, facing fewer exceptions and less vitally affected by ones that occur or are equipped with simple routines for solving the problems that ensue from them, are likely to be differently structured—as mechanistic performance systems. We shall not now go into the matter further, but it does seem likely that over the long run firms may tend to organize more and more as performance systems, whether or not it is good for them to do so.[56]

Organization-Level Analysis of Technology and Structure

So far we have talked of relations between technology and structure mostly at the so-called level of the organization, treating the system largely as a unitary entity. Yet, we have mentioned the frequent internal technological diversity of organizations—a fact that confronts organization-level analyses with thorny problems. In addition to complicating life, it prompts serious questions about suitable units of system analysis, for there is no inherent reason to expect technologically diverse organizations to be any less diverse structurally. Therefore, assessments of technology-structure correlations might profit from being based on homogeneous organizational subsystems instead of "forcing" aggregated total systems into statistically defined "types." Or, a system-level alternative might be to devise suitable indexes of technological diversity for use either as independent variables or as "test factors."

To illustrate the force of this point: it is possible that one reason Hickson, et al. found stronger relations between organizational size and structure than between technology and structure (leaving aside their definition of technology), is that size may well be correlated with diversity.[57] Small unit production firms (missing from Hickson, et al.'s research) are likely to be technologically more homogeneous (in the cognitive sense described above) than are very large firms (which were heavily represented in the Hickson, et al. investigation). While no evidence exists bearing on the matter, actually, Hickson, et al.'s attempts to reconcile their findings with Woodward's are not too different from the present thesis. In any event, the issue is one which deserves attention in future research.

Designing Organizational Structures

The design of an organization refers to the composition of its structure; moreover, "design" implies a purposive formulation legitimized by an organization's formal authority.[58] Certainly, presumptions of organiza

---

[56]Pertinent discussions of processes of bureaucratization can be found in N. P. Mouzelis, *Organization and Bureaucracy*, and in M. E. Olsen, "Social Organization," Ch. 17.

[57]D. J. Hickson, et al, "Operations Technology."

[58]See C. J. Haberstroh, "Organization Design and Systems Analysis", ed., J. G. March, *Handbook of Organizations*, pp. 1171-1213.

tional rationality implicit in the idea of design connote a sense of organizational construction which is neatly adapted by managerial plan to the objectives and circumstances (technological or other) of a particular organization, adaptations optimized by careful analyses and the systematic application of "principles" of organization and management theory. Yet curiously enough, in her extensive studies, Woodward found firms, both successful and unsuccessful, to vary markedly in "organization consciousness." Even among firms "in which production systems were basically the same," considerable differences could be found regarding the extent to which they tried "to rationalize their production, in their awareness of technical developments, and in their use of techniques such as work study, methods engineering, and operations research."[59]

Woodward was led to the view that conscious organizational planning rarely is based on technical considerations; that it amounts mostly to implicit recognition of technologically constrained situational demands; and that it represents the institutionalization of prevailing organizational realities. Woodward did find process-type firms to be successful a little more often than any other kind, but, by and large she discovered that successful firms were mostly those organizations which were *typical* of their technological types. Successful large-batch firms, for instance, tended to be mechanistic (in Burns and Stalker's sense), whereas other successful firms tended to be organic. And, the same organizational characteristic associated with success among large-batch firms—formalization of roles—augured failure among process types. But, in Woodward's studies, the organizational designing was so "unconsicous" that most managers were not even aware of how their organizations compared structurally with others.

Findings like Woodward's suggest that planning is either absent (which it often surely is) or that it is more apparent than real (coming to little more than formalization of what already is). Undoubtedly, much ostensible organizational analysis and design does represent a sort of managerial doodling instigated by external affiliations,[60] motivated by managers' desires to display virtuousity, or motivated by their needs to "keep up with the Joneses." This analysis and design may also depend heavily upon having time to think about such things—on organizational "slack," as Perrow put it.[61] Furthermore, Blau, Scott, and V. A. Thompson have suggested that organizational elaboration often arises simply from desires on the part of those in power either to evade unpleasant tasks or to bolster the prevailing status structure,[62] or from some other consideration (e.g. empire-building) quite extraneous to technical requirements of organizational tasks.

[59]J. Woodward, *Industrial Organization*, p. 42.
[60]See *Ibid.*, p. 21.
[61]C. A. Perrow, "Comparative Analysis."
[62]P. Blau and W. R. Scott, *Formal Organizations* (San Francisco: Chandler, 1962); V. A. Thompson, *Modern Organization* (New York: Knopf, 1961).

Still, Woodward found too, that "organic" firms tended as a group to be low in organization-consciousness, thus implying that these things may not depend altogether on managerial caprice. And, while organization-consciousness was not always a mark of "mechanistic" orientations —organization charts sometimes poorly reflected what actually happened in the firm—consciousness did not seem to be altogether random regarding technology. In short, some technologies seem to prompt more concern with design than others. It follows that they would, from arguments like Udy's; that the salience of technology as an influence upon structure will decrease with its flexibility and that mechanization of technology will enhance the salience of group structure[63]—a proposition fully consistent with Cyert and March's assertion that questions of organizational design are meaningful only when alternative modes of performance exist.[64]

These issues have been well reviewed by J. D. Thompson who offers an array of propositions relating technology to organizational operations and thence to rational organizational design.[65] His book nicely illustrates both how operations depend on technology and how various principles of organizational design implicitly assume sustaining technologies. The latter is a matter of overarching significance highlighted by Woodward's finding that success was associated with "textbook" management applications only among large-batch concerns;[66] this suggests the conclusion that management theory has been largely based on this technological model, without this fact having been understood. If that is true, application of standard managerial precepts in other technological contexts is likely to yield less than salutary consequences. Miller and Rice have made this point, commenting that classical theories of organization drew mainly on experience in industries representing only a narrow technological range.[67] They add that their own experiences support Woodward's implication that the models and principles derived do not fit either process or unit production industries. Hickson, et al. have also argued the relativity of design precepts to technological environments, though they appear to believe this is because technology is relevant mostly at "shop-floor levels" and, therefore, chiefly in small organizations "where nothing is far removed from the workflow itself."[68]

In any case, it follows, as Perrow also has said,[69] that there can probably be no "one best" organizational structure or managerial orientation —not participative management, not bureaucracy, not any single fashionable methodology. In this regard, one might call to mind Fiedler's persua-

[63]S. H. Udy, "Analysis of Organizations."

[64]R. M. Cyert and J. G. March, "Organization Design."

[65]J. D. Thompson, "Organizations in Actions."

[66]J. Woodward, Industrial Organization.

[67]E. J. Miller and A. K. Rice, Systems of Organization (London: Tavistock Publications, 1967).

[68]D. J. Hickson, et al, "Operations Technology," p. 396.

[69]C. A. Perrow, "Comparative Analysis."

sive arguments that effective leadership entails an adaption of "style" to organizational context.[70] In the same way, organizational success depends fundamentally upon meshing design (social technology) with the material technology out of which emerge the organization's tasks. It may be, as Woodward's work suggests, that organizations tend as a "natural" process to shape themselves into at least a loose match of technologies, but that does not mean that management design activity is irrelevant or that management ought to become passive and desist from efforts to plan and enhance operational effectiveness.[71] What follows is only that it must acknowledge the technological imperative.[72] Social and material technology be mutually adapted in system designs. Admittedly, until more adequately differentiated social technological models become available from comparative studies this will be hard to do. But, who ever said management was easy?

CONCLUDING OBSERVATIONS

We have distinguished between two fundamentally different models for organization—performance and problem-solving. Analogous in conception to Burns and Stalker's mechanistic and organic management models, this distinction has the virtue of making management methods the means to ends—e.g. problem-solving—rather than inherently good or bad things. In any event, we have also suggested that most management theories pertain to performance models, not to problem-solving models of organization, but that, for various reasons, organizations tend to evolve toward performance models; i.e., they endeavor to increase routinization. It may be, as Olsen says, that such tendencies arise from the organization's continual efforts to rationalize its functioning in order to achieve its goals more effectively,[73] but nevertheless there are many times when such movement is premature and disfunctional. Consequently, it will sometimes require deliberate managerial effort to resist such evolution when it would compromise the flexibility and creativity of the system and defeat effective goal achievement.

Probably nowhere is this maxim more applicable than in research and development environments (whether in industry, universities, or whereever). Decentralized, organically operated project organizations have been effective vehicles for accomplishing goals in such contexts, but the moral of our story, paradoxically perhaps, is that centralized authority may be necessary to preserve their adaptive integrity in the face of "natural" forces

---

[70]F. E. Fiedler, *A Theory of Leadership Effectiveness* (New York: McGraw Hill, 1967).

[71]I am indebted to John D. Senger for pointing out the possible analogy between this "natural" process and Darwinian evolution of form and its attendant costs. Managerial manipulation of organizational forms then might be considered an attempt to reduce the costs of evolutionary development, even if it might not always succeed.

[72]See Hickson, "Operations Technology."

[73]M. E. Olsen, *Social Organization,* pp. 300-301.

toward bureaucratization. Udy, for instance, hypothesized that technological "complexity" stimulates concerns for coordination that tend to lead toward elaboration and formalization of administration.[74] Furthermore, the generation of inflexibility occasioned by predilections toward "empire building" within projects and by dispositions to assimilate project organizations to functional (or administrative) divisions are familiar experiences in research and develoment environments.[75]

Finally, we should close by commenting that nothing in the foregoing should be interpreted to preclude various kinds of performance or information programming. Nor should it foreclose use of searching methods for systems analysis; the basic message is that these things must be employed in the service of a fundamental problem-solving model of organization. In brief, they should be means to ends and not devices for transforming the organizational design or for reducing it to some tepid least common denominator. One unforunate (or fortunate, depending on your view) consequence of this policy, of course, it that it leaves the organization in a condition of heavy dependence on the commitment and competence of the people who run it—or at least those who manage it.

SUMMARY

Various means of classifying organizations are reviewed and the relevance of technology to the structure of organization is discussed. Developments in the operationalization of technological variables are traced, and the implications for purposive organizational planning considered. Emphasis is placed on a "cognitive" interpretation of technological complexity and on the role of uncertainty as a basic constraint upon organizational design. Two basically distinct organizational models are differentiated: one is oriented toward problem-solving and the other toward performance. It is concluded that most management theories pertain to the latter and not the former, and various consequences of that judgment are considered.

---

[74] S. H. Udy, "Analysis of Organizations."

[75] See C. J. Haberstroh, "Organization Design," pp. 1208-1209 for a brief discussion of these issues.

DENNIS W. ORGAN

LINKING PINS BETWEEN ORGANIZATIONS AND ENVIRONMENT

Individuals do the interacting

The author is a faculty member in the area of personnel and organizational behavior at Indiana University.

The need for organizations to adapt to their environments is the subject of considerable discussion. Often ignored is the fact that adaptation is achieved only through the behavior of individuals acting as boundary agents. The nature of the boundary agent's role appears to be quite different from that of internal organization roles. Effective boundary agent performance calls for a rather distinct profile of individual skills, traits, and values. The "ideal" person will be able to manipulate words and symbols, have a good memory, be both flexible and extroverted, and possess economic and political values. Selection and placement techniques should not ignore the implications of social role dynamics for finding the best boundary agents.

Management circles in recent years have returned again and again to the environment theme with the regularity of a Greek chorus. The term is used to mean different things by different people, and sometimes it is not clear if it really means anything at all. Nevertheless, it is perhaps reasonable to assume that most people who use the word with reference to organizations have in mind something like the definition suggested by Churchman: the environment of an organization is composed of those agencies or forces that affect the performance of the organization, but over which the organization has little or no direct control.[1]

The development and popularization of open systems theory and its application to organization and management have undoubtedly contributed greatly to the environmental theme, at least in academic writings. The recent attention given to ecology in the mass media has perhaps generalized the popular concern over environment beyond that of physical environment to broad classes of external constraints and forces. However, underlying the pervasive emphasis of management practitioners on organizations' environments is, most likely, simply a heightened awareness of the complex interdependence among elements of modern society.

Thus, more than ever before, leaders of organizations realize their dependence upon other organizations and other parts of society for the recruitment of new members; acquisition of raw materials, technology, knowledge, and money; the disposal of finished products (whether they be goods and services, or, in the case of universities, trained and educated personnel); and, perhaps most important, the legitimacy and social support attached to the organization's existence and objectives.

1. C. W. Churchman, *The Systems Approach* (New York: Dell Publishing Co., 1968), p. 36.

Reprinted by permission of the author and *Business Horizons* from *Business Horizons,* December 1971, pp. 73–80.

Furthermore, it is acknowledged that the environments of many organizations are maelstroms of accelerating change, or, in the apt words of Emery and Trist, "turbulent fields."[2] Consequently, there is a growing suspicion that the more relevant criterion of organizational effectiveness is not, as it used to be, that of efficiency, but rather that of adaptability to changes in the environment.

ROLE OF THE "BOUNDARY AGENT"

This increased awareness of organizational dependency on other elements of the social matrix has, in turn, suggested the strategic importance of interaction with the environment. To the extent that organizations depend on other organizations for survival and growth, they must establish linkages, or mechanisms of some kind, with those organizations in order to reduce the threats of uncertainty posed by dependence. Ultimately, of course, such linkages take the form of organizational roles, acted out by "boundary agents" who fill these roles. It is not really organizations that interact—it is people. It is such roles as those of salesman, purchasing agent, labor negotiator, credit manager, liaison personnel, lobbyist, and so forth that constitute the interorganizational linkages.

More important, it is through the behavior of these boundary agents that the organization adapts (or fails to adapt) to changes in the environment. It is through the reports of boundary agents that other organization members acquire their knowledge, perceptions, and evaluations of organization environments. It is through the vigilance of boundary agents that the organization is able to monitor and screen important happenings in the environment. To use a very strained analogy, it is the organization's boundary agents that

function as sensory organs for the organization.

Given the strategic importance of the functions performed by these linkages (roles), one must presume that leaders of organizations would have considerable interest in the type of person who is best suited for these roles. The question is no idle one, because, as will be shown, there is evidence that these roles are qualitatively different from those that are largely internal to the organization.

The evidence suggests that the positions considered here are best manned by persons with rather distinctive profiles of abilities, traits, and values. Kahn and his associates, who have made significant contributions to the study of these positions, have called them boundary positions.[3] Obviously, specific kinds of boundary positions (such as purchasing agent or industrial relations spokesman) require job-specific knowledge and skills. However, to the extent that they share the feature of important transactions with outsiders, they seem to share also the need for certain personal attributes of individuals in those positions.

NATURE OF BOUNDARY POSITIONS

Role Conflict

Kahn and his associates have gathered evidence that documents the distinctive nature of boundary positions. First of all, people in such positions are susceptible to a high degree of role conflict—that is, they frequently get caught in the cross fire between people who expect different things of them.

This is not too surprising, since the boundary agent has to maintain interaction with, and owes allegiance to, two different

---

2. F. E. Emery and E. L. Trist, "The Causal Texture of Organizational Environments," *Human Relations,* XVIII (August, 1968), pp. 20-26.

3. R. L. Kahn, D. Wolfe, R. Quinn, J. D. Snoek, and R. Rosenthal, "System Boundaries," in *Organizational Stress* (New York: John Wiley & Sons, Inc., 1964), pp. 99-124.

kinds of people: those constituents in his own organization plus those agents representing other constituencies on whom his organization depends. The management spokesman in collective bargaining must contend not only with the expectations and pressures of his management colleagues, but also with those of the union spokesmen. The manager of the foreign subsidiary must take into account both the directives issuing from U.S. headquarters and those from the government and pressure groups in the host country. The industrial salesman must balance customer demands for quality, price, and custom-made features against his constituents' needs for unit profit, balanced production lines, low set-up cost, and so forth.

In short, the boundary agent has to grapple with at least two different—sometimes contradictory—sets of goals, values, and beliefs. Therefore, the performance of the boundary agent is likely to be a key variable in the prevention, mitigation, and resolution of interorganizational conflict. If he is skillful in the judicious bending to pressures, compromising between conflicting demands, and balancing off some issues against others, he may be able to ward off serious conflict between organizations. On the other hand, if he is impulsive, rigid, or insensitive to others' beliefs and values, he may engender conflict even where it is not inherent in relationships between organizations.

Perhaps less obvious is the finding that the boundary agent frequently gets caught in cross fires even among his own constituents. He is likely to find that his constituents have varying, biased conceptions of his role. The credit officer's role may be viewed by financial people as that of minimizing losses due to bad debts (calling for a stringent credit policy), while marketing managers conceive his task to be that of facilitating the growth of sales and new customers (using flexible, lenient credit procedures). Strauss conducted a study of purchasing agents and found that different departments (such as engineering,

production scheduling, and manufacturing) tried to impose their own goals on the purchasing agent's office.[4]

The point is that large organizations seldom have explicit, concrete over-all goals; rather, each specialized department has its own goal because different functional divisions or sections are evaluated by different criteria. Therefore, any important transaction between the boundary agent and the environment will have differential effects on the "track records" of various departments. Thus, the boundary agent will often find himself caught in the middle between conflicting expectations of his own organizational kinsmen.

Lack of Authority

Second, the boundary agent, by virtue of the fact that he has to interact with outsiders, must operate in situations where he does not have formal authority. He cannot solve his problems by "pulling rank" on persons who owe no allegiance to his organization. He must, therefore, use other and more subtle means of influence. He may be able to use expertise as power, as in the case of industrial salesmen who have encyclopedic technical knowledge about customers' products and the constraints imposed by their production methods.

In many cases, however, he must use the power of friendship or even the tactic of ingratiation. In short, he must be able to increase his attractiveness as a person to outsiders, even if it involves such acts as gently deriding his own organization, projecting an image of himself as an understanding ally of outsiders, making concessions to their beliefs and values, compromising on "principles," and "talking their language."

4. G. Strauss, "Tactics of Lateral Relationship: the Purchasing Agent," *Administrative Science Quarterly* (No. 7, 1962), pp. 161-86.

Unfortunately, it is precisely these tactics that his constituents may frown upon, if they are aware of them, even though they are of strategic value to the boundary agent for securing more substantive benefits for his organization. Such tactics may be interpreted by his constituents as reflecting disloyalty.

It should also be pointed out that the boundary agent often has to use these same informal methods of influence (such as friendship power or ingratiation) with his constituents. For example, the field salesman is adversely affected by low product quality, but he probably has no direct authority over quality control personnel.

Of course, informal modes of influence are often used also by persons in internal organization positions. Few organization officials use formal authority exclusively; certainly most officers would at least prefer to avoid the explicit invocation of the authority of their office, and much important communication is lateral rather than vertical. Still, a common ingredient of all intra-organizational interactions is the implicit obligation of all participants to follow standard procedures, policies, and traditions. This backdrop is lacking in typical interchanges between boundary agents and the environment.

The boundary agent's job is made doubly difficult simply because of his greater exposure to the organization's environment. Because of his frequent interaction with outsiders and his susceptibility to being influenced by them, his constituents may withhold their trust and support, granting him only a narrow range of discretion and decision making.

Agent of Change

Because the boundary agent has to listen to outsiders' criticisms and attempt to view his own organization through outsiders' eyes, he is apt to feel more keenly than his constit-

---

"The boundary agent in a sense becomes an activist broker . . . ."

---

uents the defects in his organization and the need for change. The advocacy of change then initiates protracted struggles with organization officials who simply do not see the organization from the vantage point of the boundary agent and defend the status quo.

These struggles may generate further suspicions about the boundary agent's commitment to the organization's values and objectives. The boundary agent in a sense becomes an activist broker between the viewpoints, criticisms, values, and information of outsiders, on the one hand, and the values, objectives, policies, and attitudes of his constituents. Not only must he represent the organization to its environment, but he must also represent the environment to his constituents.

The preceding considerations produce an over-all picture of the nature of boundary agents' jobs. These persons are often caught between conflicting pressures, both between constituents and outsiders and even among constituents. They often have to become agents of organizational change by modifying the beliefs and attitudes of constituents. They have to represent the organization—with all of its faults—to outsiders, and they have to negotiate the resolution of conflicts of interest. Their jobs are further complicated by their lack of authority over important persons, an inevitable violation of the classic principle that authority must be sufficient to carry out responsibility.[5]

The need to modify constituents' attitudes, to enhance and maintain their support and trust so as to preserve ample discretion for his own decision making, coupled with the need to make himself

---

5. Kahn and others, *Organizational Stress*, p. 106.

attractive to outsiders, puts the boundary agent in the position of having to be two-faced and to lead something of a double life.

THE BOUNDARY AGENT'S PROFILE

Given a description of the nature of boundary positions, can we draw any tentative conclusions about the kind of persons who should fill such positions? That is, what type of person—in terms of his abilities, traits, and values—would probably be most effective in this role for attaining substantive benefits for his organization and avoiding needless conflicts with important other parties? What type of person would experience greater job satisfaction and less strain in these positions?

General Abilities and Intelligence

Probably more important than any measure of over-all intelligence are the verbal and memory skills of the boundary agent. The boundary agent must represent the norms and values of his organization to outsiders in a way that does not offend or alienate them. Therefore, he must "watch his language." He must avoid the use of words that have unpleasant emotional connotations for other parties. The manager of the overseas subsidiary is perhaps well-advised not to use the word "capitalism" indiscriminately in certain underdeveloped nations because of the term's historic connotations. The bargaining spokesman for management, in negotiation with union officials, uses such terms as "management prerogatives" with some risk.

Legislative lobbyists probably do not get very far if their active vocabulary is confined to such emotional symbols as "free enterprise," "corporate sovereignty," or "bureaucratic flunkies." The choice of relatively sterile, even awkward, terminology is less likely to conjure up specters of demons and ideological straw men that only impede the process of communication and negotiation.

The boundary agent must also be sensitive to the values of the parties with whom he deals, and those values are probably manifested in their selective use of certain words and phrases. He must be careful that semantics does not inflate the true differences of interests. He must be able to decode the positions taken by other parties and then encode them into the customary verbal repertoire of his own constituents; in a sense, he must be bilingual, at least with regard to the connotative dimensions of words.

Especially important, he can ingratiate himself with outsiders if he is sensitive to the symbols and words they use, and judiciously uses these words in his dealings with outside parties. Walton and McKersie tell of a labor official who was able to win the favor of high-ranking management people with the use of such business-like language as "the policy of our organization" and "the decisions of our executive board."[6] This technique can also act as a cue to outsiders that the boundary agent understands, and appreciates the reasons for, their positions.

The above requirements place a premium on facility in manipulating words and symbols. Note that it is not vocabulary size that is important, although that may help, but a type of verbal skill represented by sensitivity to the connotations of words and the subtleties of semantics.

Good memory is important because it increases the potential of the boundary agent for ingratiating. A mind that holds onto otherwise trivial facts, dates, names, and so on about people can be used to project the impression that he is really interested in those people. We assume that people with average memories remember only those things they understand, like, or are interested in. Thus, the boundary agent who readily recalls isolated details about an outsider's place of birth, accomplishments, previous occupations,

---

6. R. E. Walton and R. B. McKersie, *A Behavioral Theory of Labor Negotiations* (New York: McGraw-Hill Book Company, 1965), pp. 226-27.

public statements, and so on has an advantage in establishing a viable relationship with that outsider. The outsider, for his part, feels subtle obligations to reciprocate in some way that may be of importance to the boundary agent's task.

Personality Traits

It would seem that the boundary agent must be, above all, a person of flexibility, as opposed to ridigity. The rigid person strives for consistency in thought and behavior, has a distaste for ambiguity, commits himself strongly to beliefs and values, and tends to structure his behavior according to internally programmed rules rather than external situational factors.

These characteristics might be desirable for organizational members in many internal positions, but they would probably be dysfunctional for boundary role performance. The rigid person might easily allow his internally programmed rules to warp his perception of trends in the organization's environment, imputing structure to those trends where structure or certainty do not exist. He might forego long-run organizational benefits for the sake of abstract principles.

The flexible person would find it easier to vary his behavior according to the audience, the situation, or the issues. He would likely concede minor principles if the substantive outcomes were worth it. His thinking would be guided more by the criteria of feasibility and opportunity than by the norms and traditions of his constituency.

Unfortunately, these same characteristics may cause his constituents to view him as "wishy-washy" and deficient in his commitment to the organization. They may, therefore, deny him the support and discretion he needs for transactions with outsiders. This dilemma almost inevitably leads the effective boundary agent to be a little two-faced; he must be flexible when carrying out his job at the boundary (when interacting with outsiders and assessing environmental trends), yet he must project an image of staunch commitment and steadfastness before his constituents in order to preserve the flexibility of action which he needs.

The boundary agent is also likely to be more effective if he is more of an extrovert than an introvert. The extrovert, according to Kahn and his associates, is "extremely responsive to changes in external stimuli" and enjoys the company of other people. For this reason, the extrovert would probably be more skillful at establishing and using friendship power with outsiders, and he would probably be more sensitive to outsiders' norms and values. The introvert, on the other hand, has difficulty maintaining interpersonal relationships under conditions of stress and tends to be unrealistic in his assessments of external constraints on his behavior.

Values

Here the Allport-Vernon-Lindzey framework of six basic value categories theoretical, economic, aesthetic, social, political, and religious—will serve as a basis for discussion. (The social and theoretical values will not be included because they yield less obvious predictions than the other four.) Economic and political values would seem to be desirable for the boundary agent. Economic values reflect a pragmatic style of thought and behavior, and a preference for solutions that work, even if they are not logical, elegant, internally consistent, or even unqualifiedly ethical if considered out of context. The person with strong political values would have the habit of forecasting the effects of his statements and behavior on the attitudes of outsiders, as well as his own constituents. He would appreciate the importance of personal and group persuasion as substitutes for formal authority and rigidly specified rules and obligations.

Macaulcy, in his study of noncontractual relationships between business organizations, found that such officials as financial officers and controllers desired written contracts with buyers and vendors, while industrial salesmen and purchasing agents preferred the flexible give-and-take of informal understanding.[7]

On the other hand, a person with strong aesthetic or religious values might balk at using ingratiation as an influence tactic or shrink from the concession of principles that might be necessary in order to effect substantive benefits for the organization. Such a person might also be repelled by the "hypocrisy" required of the boundary agent as he moves from one audience to another.

It may seem to the reader that an unnecessarily dark portrait has been drawn of the "ideal" boundary agent—that what is called for is a person without convictions, courage, or principles. But that is not the case. It is simply suggested here that the boundary agent, because of his concern for the organization's dependence on other agencies and the larger set of forces and constraints within which the organization exists, must necessarily evaluate his behavior within a larger framework than is true of internal organization members. Organizational morality, if that term must be used, must have a much more relativistic dimension, as Machiavellian as that may sound.

The reader may also respond with the query, "Are not the personal attributes suggested here simply desirable qualities for *any* organizational member? Wouldn't these traits be able to predict superior individual performance in any position?"

To some extent, the answer to the above question is "yes." For example, a number of studies have demonstrated a positive correlation between various measures of verbal ability and managerial performance.[8]

However, it is difficult to imagine how extroversion or political values would be essential for the job effectiveness of a cost accountant or production engineer. Furthermore, the position taken in this article is that the attributes discussed—even though some of them are perhaps desirable for people in a variety of organizational offices—are of greater importance for the performance of the boundary agent.

A SOCIAL ROLE ORIENTATION IN SELECTION AND PLACEMENT

Essentially, what is at issue here is the need for a social role orientation for the analysis of organizational positions and the placement of persons in those positions. Boundary positions constitute only one class of organization offices along the social-psychological role dimension, and even this one class could perhaps be further divided. Division might be based, for example, on the importance of the interaction with outsiders, the degree of conflict with outsiders, whether the outside party is dealt with in a one-shot episode or in a continuing relationship, the degree of status or authority the boundary agent has among his own constituents by virtue of his position, or by the percentage of working time that must be allocated to dealing with outside parties.

For the most part, the development and use of selection and placement techniques have ignored the implications of social role dynamics for individual attributes. Yet, if a unifying framework for the prediction of managerial performance is to emerge, there must be more emphasis on the social roles inherent in various kinds of organizational positions. For the manager's role is largely defined by the different groups of persons he must interact with, the congruence and/or conflict among those persons' expectations of him, and the need for "shifting gears" in his behavioral style as he confronts different social situations. The variations in managerial

---

7. S. Macauley, "Non-contractual Relations in Business: a Preliminary Study," *American Sociological Review,* XXVIII, pp. 55-67.

8. See, for example, J. P. Campbell, M. D. Dunnette, E. E. Lawler, III, and K. E. Weick, Jr., *Managerial Behavior, Performance, and Effectiveness* (New York: McGraw-Hill Book Company, 1970), p. 130, 181-88.

social roles, it would seem, call for corresponding variations in the abilities, personality traits, and values among the people needed to carry out those roles.

Furthermore, if the role analysis of an organizational position seems to call for certain individual attributes, one can specify how those attributes would be reflected in biographical data. If, as has been argued, boundary agents should have above-average memory and verbal skills, political and economic values, and a personality profile marked by extroversion and flexibility, then one can go a bit further and suggest how these would be manifested in a person's previous life experience. One would, for example, look for numerous college courses and good marks in the humanities, social sciences, or other disciplines rich in verbal content. Such a finding would probably reflect a sensitivity to semantics, a good memory for the trivia that help make impressive essay exam answers, and an ability and willingness to use "buzz" words for ingratiation purposes.

Another relevant biographical item would be membership in numerous social organizations of a nonideological character,

reflecting extroversion, political values, the use of friendship power, and practice in ingratiation. On the other hand, one would hope to find that the person is not a member of organizations demanding ideological purity. Membership in these groups might indicate rigidity in thought and behavior. In fact, the use of biographical items such as these could lead to an operational program to test the validity of the arguments put forth here.

We have heard much about the importance of organizational environments and related issues of how different departments and divisions should be structured to match the demands of their particular environments. We should not forget that organizations, as such, do not interact with the environment.

Individuals do the interacting, and they do it within a greater or less detailed framework of role demands, role expectations, role conflicts, and resultant role stress. What is needed now is a program for identifying persons with the requisite skills and attributes which enable them to cope with the problems confronting the organization boundary agent.

GUIDING AND MONITORING
THE ORGANIZATION

II

■ In order to guide organizational activities one must have rational guide-lines for attaining the goals of the organization. Then it is possible to monitor significant deviations from these guidelines. Part II is divided into three sections. Section A is concerned with planning, Section B with control, and Section C with planned and systematic change.

Section A:
Planning

Planning reflects *today's* activities in order to reach a desired state. This definition differs, at least conceptually, from those that stress mere prediction (forecasting) or more vague definitions such as "thinking about what is to be done and how to do it."

The readings selected for the planning section reinforce this definition. In the first selection, W. David Gardner presents an extremely interesting (and frightening) description of the failure of the computer division of RCA. Project Intercept represented one of the biggest planning failures in the history of American enterprise (500 million dollars). Planning failure is undoubtedly at the core of this disaster, but the reader should also examine the case in terms of areas highlighted in other sections of this text. For example, there are outstanding instances of communication breakdown, and rich detail is provided of the roles of various types of leaders in a major corporation.

The second selection, from *Industry Week*, focuses on the key elements of a successful management by objectives program. MBO is designed to specify a series of activities aimed at a future goal, and thus directly coincides with the above definition of planning. Over the years a chief complaint about MBO systems is that they are used only in certain management positions, for example, staff work. As the article states, "performance goals are needed in every position where performance and results directly and vitally affect the contribution of the man to the organization." In other words, planning is essential for every managerial position. A useful exercise is to cast the RCA situation in an MBO framework, highlighting responsibilities and key objectives for each of the major participants in the project. Many substantial improvements in the RCA planning scheme can be obtained in this way, if only with the benefit of hindsight.

The third article, by David Cleland and William King, makes a case for a formal planning body in an organization that has as its major function long-range planning. This article draws on material presented in Part I of the text. Cleland and King base much of their argument for a formal planning team on the complexity of the environment and changing environmental conditions, which necessitate long-range planning in order to remain competitive. As a basic framework for the planning function, they suggest a matrix structure, which reduces disciplinary parochialism, provides for checks and balances, and enhances personal involvement and innovation.

The final planning selection, by M. Scott Myers, explores the role of planning for effective systems management, an area that has become a key part of the modern managerial function. According to Myers, an effective planning system tends to meet certain needs of the people whose job is influenced by it. For example, employees understand and agree with the purpose of the planning system; they know how to use it; they are in control of it and can influence its revision; and they receive timely feedback from it. Myers provides an excellent example of a system that meets these criteria, the Texas Instruments job-posting system.

Curtain Act at RCA

W. David Gardner

Early in 1970, the RCA computer people who attended the Marketing Achievement Club meeting in San Francisco realized that something was happening to them and to their computer division — something good. They were a part of a new era — the L. Edwin Donegan, Jr., era — and to just about everyone at the meeting in San Francisco's mammoth Masonic Temple that seemed to be a very good thing indeed.

Donegan was enjoying a meteoric rise at RCA, having just been appointed vice president and general manager of the division after only a year there. Here was a man who was clearly different from the conservative, old-shoe type of managers who had been running the computer division in recent years. Donegan's Irish good looks and enormous vitality were in sharp contrast to the folksy and plodding manner of the former chief of the computer operation, James Bradburn, who, although he didn't know it at that time, would gradually be eased out of the computer operation by RCA corporate management while Donegan would be eased in.

Donegan wasted no time in putting his stamp on the division and he started with the meeting of the Marketing Achievement Club, membership in which is meant to be a reward for sales achievement during the previous year. Gone were the RCA homemade aspects of the meeting and in their place was a slick and smooth production with a stress on visuals. Under the old RCA regime, the emphasis had been on individual recognition and communication among the sales people, while Donegan used the meeting primarily as a motivational vehicle. "Donegan really fired them up," said one ex-RCA man who attended. "Particularly the young salesmen. When they arrived at the meeting they were proud that they made the club, but when they left they left feeling they were going to do three times better."

There were, however, a few men at the meeting who had silent reservations about ex-IBMer Donegan's first Marketing Achievement Club meeting. To them, the meeting was somewhat more extravagant than they were accustomed to and this caught their eye. For instance, the consultant who worked on the meeting was paid a fee of more than $100,000 and attendance at the meeting was puffed up to about 1,000 people at an increase in cost by bringing in large numbers of non-sales types. The result was that RCA's Computer Division seemed to have grown larger very rapidly.

But more important, the atmosphere of the meeting had changed sharply. It didn't seem to be a meeting of RCA's Marketing Achievement Club at all; but rather, considering the slick production, a meeting of IBM's 100 Per Cent Club. In this regard, the San Francisco meeting would prove to be a microcosm of the problems that would help lead to disaster in September of 1971 when RCA would pull out of the computer business entirely, in disgrace. Donegan would attempt to transform RCA's Computer Division into an IBM with an almost missionary zeal. If IBM had done anything — anything at all — then the same thing was often good enough for RCA. When he was at IBM, for example, Donegan had attended a meeting of the 100 Per Cent Club at the very same Masonic Temple. Likewise, in the next two years, Donegan would pick as the sites of RCA's Marketing Achievement Club meetings locations where IBM had held its meetings for its 100 Per Cent Club — the Broadmoor in Colorado Springs and the Fountainebleau in Miami Beach.

Donegan joined RCA in January of 1969. An RCA press release announcing his appointment by the then chief of computer marketing, Edwin S. McCollister, stated that Donegan, who was just past 40, would be responsible for "all field and home office sales department functions, and will make his headquarters at the computer division's home office in Cherry Hill, N.J." RCA documents on file with the Securities and Exchange Commission indicate that Donegan received a basic annual salary of $75,000, but that figure presumably was inflated by bonuses. It is not entirely clear why McCollister hired a new marketing leader, but the best explanation seems to be that McCollister was tiring of his job after nearly a decade in RCA marketing and he hired Donegan with the idea that the latter would be his replacement. McCollister no doubt was thinking the changing of the marketing guard would take place over a period of years. However, within a year, not only would Donegan overtake McCollister, but he would take over the entire Computer Systems Division and be on his way to a corporate vice presidency. And in another year, Donegan would be under consideration for the presidency of the entire RCA Corp., which, with annual sales of more than $3 billion, ranked as one of the 25 largest corporations in the U.S.

McCollister was a steady, deliberate type, who quietly compiled an impressive marketing record — during his reign annual computer division revenues went from $14 million in 1960 to $237 million in 1969. He lacked Donegan's glamour and charisma perhaps, but he was decisive and he had a good common touch. As Donegan's star rose at RCA, McCollister was to suffer a fate similar to that met by some other old-line RCA employees. McCollister found that he became something of an unperson, moved aside by Donegan and the IBM team he was assembling. Nevertheless, McCollister fared better than some other old-time RCA men, who were simply sacked.

During the 1960s — during the era of Bradburn and McCollister and of A. L. Malcarney, the former group executive vice president — RCA had been taken virtually from the ground up in computers to the point where it had a solid base in the industry. Although RCA went full scale into the commercial electronic data processing field relatively late — in 1958 — it had managed a few technological coups. The RCA 501 was the industry's first completely transistorized system and the Spectra 70 product line was the first major commercial system to use integrated circuits. By and large, though, RCA tended to follow IBM's lead by fitting under the pricing umbrella of the Computer Colossus with relatively unexciting equipment. In spite of slight edp profits in 1964 and 1965, RCA's computer operation never settled into a profitable enterprise, largely because of the capital that was constantly plowed back into the rapidly growing business.

When Donegan arrived at RCA in January of 1969 he carried an impressive curriculum vitae with him. In 18 years at IBM he had moved rapidly up the ladder, starting at the bottom as a marketing representative in the Data Processing Division and, with several stops along the way, working his way up to vice president of the Service Bureau Corp. Bigger things were said to have been slated for Donegan at IBM, but he was impatient and ambitious and when the RCA offer came, he jumped. During his first year at RCA, an all-time high was set in the amount of business booked. True, McCollister was still heading RCA marketing, but the gains were in no small part due to Donegan, whose Irish wit, charm and vitality quickly won him supporters — and RCA orders. Donegan's supporters, and he had many from the start, began using words like charismatic and aggressive to describe him. Also, Bradburn and McCollister were very pleased with the way their new marketing man was working out. But there were indications that Donegan seemed to be uneasy about the quaint RCA way of doing things. To him, IBM's way was still the only way and in August of 1969 he began what would eventually turn into a wholesale raid on IBM: he hired Joseph W. Rooney to head up RCA's home office sales department at Cherry Hill.

While Donegan was consolidating his position at Cherry Hill, he was also rapidly making a name for himself at 30 Rockefeller Plaza, RCA's corporate headquarters. When he joined RCA, Donegan kept his home in Greenwich, Connecticut, and he made it a point to visit corporate often.

At 30 Rockefeller Plaza, Donegan found a valuable patron in Chase Morsey, Jr., who also lived in Greenwich. Morsey was the power behind the RCA throne, the throne being represented by chief executive officer Robert W. Sarnoff. Morsey's official title was executive vice president, operations staff, and in reality Morsey was the No. 2 man in influence at RCA while he held that post during 1969, 1970 and the first six months of 1971 — the period during which the computer operation was taken from modest lift-off, to soaring promise, and, finally, to crashing fiasco. Morsey's credentials for his high position in a technology company like RCA were slightly unusual — he had worked at the Ford Motor Co. for 16 years, rising to general marketing manager of the Ford Division, and most immediately before his joining RCA, he owned and operated a Ford agency in Arizona. Like Donegan's training and background at IBM, Morsey's training and background at Ford would contribute to the thinking that led to the coming disaster in the RCA computer operation.

Morsey's rise at RCA was so rapid that it was only natural perhaps that corporate gossips quickly began referring to him as RCA's executive suite Rasputin. Robert Sarnoff and Morsey had ascended to power in the late 1960s and they brought with them all the *right* academic credentials and the hip new management buzz words and practices. They represented a departure from the old hard-nosed common sense and deliberate style of the RCA of David Sarnoff, the electronics pioneer who had propelled the company into a position of world leadership in electronics. There was something of the country club and the jet set in Robert Sarnoff and Morsey, and Donegan fit easily into their style.

On the other hand, Bradburn didn't fit. He was a Christian Scientist; he wouldn't take a drink; no one was ever known to have accused him of possessing charm. The inevitable happened: Sarnoff and Morsey forced a Donegan promotion on Bradburn, who was said to have quietly resisted. Bradburn, of course, lost. Donegan was made vice president and general manager of Computer Systems Jan. 1, 1970, and Bradburn retained his old title, but lost a great deal of his power. The skids were greased under him. In December of 1970, Bradburn "resigned from RCA because of pressing personal requirements," according to the official company version. RCA insiders, however, say that Bradburn was fired abruptly by Sarnoff. Whatever the circumstances of his leaving, it must have been a difficult experience for Bradburn, who had done a creditable job in building up the computer operation and who enjoyed a good reputation in the industry. (It was expensive for Sarnoff to get rid of Bradburn: SEC records indicate RCA agreed to pay Bradburn about $230,000 when he left.)

In January, 1971, RCA formed a new organization called RCA Computer Systems with Donegan heading it up as corporate vice president and general manager. Donegan quickly began surrounding himself with IBMers. One exception in the group was an old-line RCA manufacturing vice president, John Lenox, but he was soon fired by Donegan.

Although the change in management took place over a few months, it nevertheless was extremely sudden for a high technology business like the computer industry. Coupled with the massive injection of new IBM blood into RCA, the suddenness of the management change would prove to be more than the RCA organism could tolerate and both factors would contribute to the eventual loss of control of the computer operation. Part of the explanation for the sudden shift in management direction seems to be explained, at least in part, by Robert Sarnoff's background. For a decade, Sarnoff had been running RCA's broadcasting affiliate, the National Broadcasting Company, and sudden wholesale management changes in broadcasting are common occurrences.

Donegan proved to be as good a salesman at 30 Rockefeller Plaza selling his ideas on the computer operations as he was out in the field selling computers. RCA had always aspired to becoming No. 2 behind IBM in the computer industry, but during 1970 the drive to become No. 2 took on a new urgency and a new credibility as well, largely because Sarnoff and Donegan made such a public flap over the issue. In March of 1971, for instance, Robert Sarnoff would tell RCA stockholders the following:

"Our highest priorities today are the establishment of a profitable computer business and capture of the domestic industry's No. 2 position. RCA has made a greater investment in this effort than in any prior venture in its history, and we are convinced that the returns will be substantial.

"This investment has already resulted in a more rapid growth rate for RCA than for the domestic industry as a whole . . ."

During this period Chase Morsey seems to have become particularly interested in share of market and RCA targeted 10% of the U.S. commercial edp market as a goal. There are many at RCA who believed that Morsey's automotive background in Detroit — where there is something of a fetish over share of market — was an important factor in RCA wanting to grow so rapidly, even at the cost of profitability. Morsey was instrumental in commissioning a $100,000 marketing report by the Arthur D. Little, Inc., which, in large part, advised RCA on how to go about increasing market share.

However, there can be a danger in growing too rapidly in the computer business, because so much of the equipment is leased rather than sold outright. In a leasing environment, of course, revenues are delayed, but the manufacturer must still bear the full expense of the equipment at the start. Sarnoff once put his finger on this problem: "It's a funny kind of business. You can be so successful and wait so long for a return."

But how do you become No. 2 if you only have 3 or 4% of the edp business? How do you get that critical mass of 10%? Why, you take it out of IBM's hide, that's how. Or, that's how Donegan felt. "We have two options if we want to get 10% of the market," Donegan once explained. "We can get a little out of the hide of each of the other Dwarfs, or we can get it out of IBM's hide. It's easier for us to get after IBM."

In this sense, Donegan resembled Napoleon licking his chops before Waterloo. No one, of course, takes anything out of IBM's hide; it's the other way around and one can only wonder precisely what Donegan was doing during his 18 years at IBM that led him to think otherwise. Before long, Donegan would watch new IBM machines and pricing tactics throw the RCA computer operation from a state of self-inflicted confusion into a full-scale rout.

Still, Donegan persevered. Internally at RCA, his program became known as "Intercept," the idea being that RCA would introduce a new family of computers that would intercept IBM customers and bring them over to RCA. But where would RCA get a new line of computers? At that time, 1970, a new line was under development, internally called NTS (for New Technology Series), but wouldn't be ready for announcement until around the first of 1972. Donegan thought that was too far in the future, so he decided to take the existing Spectra machines, put new skins around them, soup up their memories, and, in effect, reintroduce the Spectra line with a great deal of fanfare and hoopla.

The "new" family was introduced in September of 1970 and consisted of four machines, which the company called the RCA Series 2, 3, 6 and 7, although its internal code name — FS (for Follow Spectra) — was a more appropriate and accurate appellation. The 2 corresponded to the Spectra 70/45, and the 3 with the Spectra 70/46. The 2 and 3 were essentially cost-reduced versions of the 45 and 46 with new skins, new memory interfaces and other unimportant changes. The 6 corresponded to the 70/60, and the 7 to the 70/61. The 6 was basically the same machine as the 70/60 with a new skin. The 7 did replace a translation table memory with a content-addressable memory, but, for all practical purposes, both the 6 and the 7 were just price cuts of the Spectra 70/60 and 70/61.

"The point I'd like to stress," said Joseph W. Rooney, Donegan's computer marketing chief when the new series was unveiled, "is that in just about every case, RCA's new series of computers offers, or will offer, the IBM user a very attractive alternative to upgrading his system to either a larger System/360 computer, or a System/370 series computer." That was the crux of the strategy for the RCA series.

At the same time, Donegan described a new marketing concept which he called "guaranteed conversion." The main thrust of the guaranteed conversion plan was that the customer and RCA would agree to a program for converting the customers from IBM equipment (the plan was restricted to IBM users) and if RCA failed to perform as specified, then RCA would pay a substantial monetary penalty to the user. Donegan claimed that guaranteed conversion was "one of the most significant business policy innovations in the history of the computer industry" and RCA embarked upon a massive merchandising and sales campaign to lure users to take advantage of the plan. The plan flopped; over the next several months, the guaranteed conversion plan attracted no more than four takers.

The "Intercept" strategy was planned with detailed knowledge of plans of IBM's 370 line, of which just two machines — the Model 370/155 and the 165 — had been announced when the RCA Series was publicly unveiled. Since so many RCAers had come over from IBM, RCA had a good handle on the specifications and marketing strategy on the 145, the 135 and the 125. The 145 and the 135 had not been announced at the time of RCA's announcement and the 125 still had not been announced by IBM at this writing. Donegan simply priced the RCA Series low enough to make it a more attractive customer buy than what he expected the entire 370 line would offer. He conceded that the RCA equipment couldn't compete in speed, so the key was what Donegan regarded as memory advantages and pricing that the RCA equipment had over the 370 and 360 lines.

"But what about the 145 that is rumored to be very close to announcement?" said Rooney at the unveiling of the RCA Series. "Well, we've studied the question and we have the answer." Rooney's "answer" was that RCA had already come to "certain conclusions" about the 145 and that RCA's pricing of its new machines was an alternative to customers who would consider buying a 145. One week later, IBM announced the 145, but it wasn't the same machine RCA had on its competitive analysis charts. The 145 had a larger memory and a lower price tag than RCA had anticipated.

So much, then, for RCA's competitive stance against the 145. Against the 145, sales of RCA's 6 and 7 were negligible.

RCA made a big fuss about what it termed the success of the new line, claiming that the RCA Series had quickly attracted more orders than the company had expected for the remainder of the year. At first, this was said to have been accomplished in three days, but later the time frame was changed to three weeks. This marked the start of great confusion over RCA's way of logging order bookings under the Donegan regime.

Some three weeks after the announcement of the new line, Donegan triumphantly proclaimed that "33% of the new orders represent customers coming to RCA for the first time." He didn't say so, but that also meant 67% *weren't* coming to RCA for the first time. The 67% represented existing RCA customers and that hinted at great problems, because it meant that the new machines could be chiefly impacting RCA equipment rather than IBM equipment.

In general, RCA enjoyed a good press on the new family but Donegan was particularly sensitive to criticism of his new series. For instance, when *Datamation* observed that RCA had simply "reintroduced the Spectra" and that RCA would have to sell 360 technology against 370 technology, Donegan complained to the publication about those observations and other statements that he regarded as slurs.

Many at RCA — particularly some old-line employees — had expressed fears about the RCA Series impacting the company's existing customer base. The safe way, they argued, would be to wait for the NTS Series, but Donegan would have none of that. The NTS Series consisted of five machines, possibly six, ranging in specifications from a relatively small machine with about one-half the capability of the IBM 360/50 to a big computer with a capability in the range of the IBM 195. The line was scheduled for introduction from September of 1971 to January of 1972 with deliveries slated to begin in the third and fourth quarters of 1972. Steady production runs were to begin in early 1973.

The NTS line was to have embodied several new and unique technological features, which led the RCA people working on it — there were as many as 150 engineers committed to the program at one point — to feel that the series would offer real, rather than imagined, advantages over the 360 and 370 line. The whole line was to be based on virtual memory[1] and a virtual memory operating system was being prepared. The line was to utilize a fair degree of medium-scale integration throughout and the specs called for use of advanced circuitry, such as transistor-transistor logic, emitter-coupled logic, and custom RCA high speed circuits. In addition, the RCA engineers were concentrating on what they regarded as an innovation that would permit the freeing of input/output channels more than previously had been possible with the concurrent result that more of the cpu would be free for computational purposes. There are indications that two or three of the machines — on the low end — were being developed by Siemens, RCA's licensee in Germany. Because of U.S. antitrust regulations, the two firms had to work at arm's length, but it is known that there was at least some loose cooperation between the two.

[1] Virtual memory employs a memory mapping technique that permits the user-programmer to be unconcerned about the relationship of the addresses he uses and the physical addresses assigned in the computer system.

The NTS program was slowed down for a number of reasons. First, Donegan moved the engineering group from the large machine — called the NTS 1000 — over to work on his RCA Series. Second, Donegan moved the RCA designing and engineering leaders aside to make way for a new flow of IBM people, who lost valuable time while they settled into their jobs and while they instituted IBM development practices, which tended to confuse old-line RCA people. These practices included involvement of marketing people during the design and development stage. In addition, there are indications that Siemens' leadership was becoming increasingly skeptical about Donegan with one result being that Siemens was becoming more independent of RCA. For one thing, Siemens did not introduce the entire RCA Series in Europe. The West German industrial giant felt the new line would primarily impact its existing Spectra base rather than pick up enough new business to make it worthwhile to introduce.

As far as financial matters at RCA were concerned, Donegan remained true to form: he was upset that RCA's computer operation didn't do its accounting the way IBM did its accounting. (IBM uses the conservative operating method while RCA used an accounting combination that utilized both the financing and operating methods.) When Donegan hacked his way through the computer operation's financial thicket (and there are those who believe it took him an inordinately long time to slice through), when he hacked through all the installment purchase contracts, third party sales agreements, in-house sales to RCA, when he finally came to the proverbial bottom line, he found that RCA's computer operation was not in the neat financial shape he had assumed it to be in. In addition, the IBMers who joined RCA were generally unhappy with what they regarded as the computer operation's liberal accounting methods. On the other hand, the pre-Donegan RCA financial people regarded the operation's bookkeeping as about average for the non-IBM segment of the computer industry. Whatever the situation, Donegan was unhappy about it and in late 1970 he removed David Campbell as controller. There was endless internal debate on the accounting practices of the computer unit, but this debate would become academic during late 1970 and 1971 as Donegan and his chief financial advisor, W. William Acker, would begin to lose their grip on finances.

On the corporate level, the computer operation was also taking its financial toll and this problem, coupled with other financial pressures, was placing the RCA Corp. in an uncomfortable financial squeeze. In early 1971, the situation was this: operating earnings had been dropping and the corporation was increasingly resorting to long term financing. The company was stepping up short term borrowing, and it was evident that it would soon need more long term financing, primarily to keep the computer operation growing. In addition, common equity was dropping to about 40% of total capitalization and pretax coverage of fixed charges had dropped in 1970 to slightly more than a troubling three times earnings. Small wonder, then, that there were nervous men in corporate finance.

In early 1971, RCA's top financial man, Howard L. Letts, executive vice president, finance, "retired" unexpectedly, but that was just one signal that all was not well in corporate finance. Many felt that Sarnoff had pushed Letts into early retirement and not long thereafter, Sarnoff's favorite, Chase Morsey, was named to the financial post.

It should be made clear here that RCA was in sound financial condition at the time and still is. The point is that things were clearly deteriorating, and one of the biggest problems was caused by the computer operation in general and by the acceleration of leased edp equipment in particular. It is one of the great ironies of the computer industry that the better you do, the worse off you can be financially. Because the industry is largely a lease and rental business, companies that grow rapidly — and RCA was one — are required to make massive capital outlays, but since much of the equipment is leased, they must wait long periods to get their money back. During late 1970 and early 1971, a feeling began growing at RCA that massive cash inputs into the computer business — the most popular figure bandied about as the investment necessary was $500 million — could be justified, if the computer operation's losses could be stemmed. In 1970 the loss was $10 million on revenues of $257 million and there were great hopes that the computer operation was approaching break-even.

In late 1970, the computer operation put together its first business plan for 1971 and it was quickly apparent that the Donegan team anticipated 1971 would be a bumper year for the Computer Systems Division. The 1971 business plan estimated revenues of $323 million — up from $257 million in 1970 — and a break-even or near break-even in the profit and loss column. Furthermore, the computer operation's long-range plan called for profits of $12 million in 1972, $25 million in 1973 and $50 million in 1974. If the plan's projections were reliable, then Donegan would turn the operation around in 1971. He would be the hero of the computer industry.

There were several management and financial fingers in the pie, including those of pre-Donegan personnel from the Bradburn era, but the first business plan was essentially the creation of Donegan and his financial staff, which was led by William Acker.

No one likes to tell the boss bad news, but there seemed to be a particularly great reluctance among the people surrounding Donegan to bear bad tidings to him and, as some of his critics maintain, he tended to surround himself with organization men who were not used to challenging the boss. Devil's advocates were not popular with Donegan. At any rate, there was bad news aplenty and it took Donegan an unusually long time to get the unhappy message that 1971 would not be the year of the Great Turnaround. The new controller of the computer unit, Carmen Ferraioli, had the final responsibility for accepting the business plan and Ferraioli did not accept the plan, because, it was said, he felt it was overly optimistic.

The computer operation immediately set to work drawing up a new plan but by now the Donegan team had begun to lose its grip on finance and planning. The computer operation worked without a budget from Jan. 1 into April and until then an air of uncertainty hung over the computer operation. When the second plan was presented in April it was strikingly different from the first plan: instead of $323 million, revenues were estimated at $261 million, and instead of break-even, a loss of $36 million was predicted.

One of the purposes of efficient financial controls between corporate and various line operations of course, is that they act as an early warning system for problems in line units. RCA had always maintained adequate efforts in financial operations. However, just as the computer operation began having serious problems, the relationship between corporate and the computer operation's financial units began breaking down; one result was that many problems in the line operation went unnoticed by corporate. That is hardly surprising, perhaps, because during the computer operation's crucial months from late 1970 to September of 1971 the computer operation had three different controllers and Acker, Donegan's top financial man, had sparse financial background, having been primarily a marketing type at IBM. (Donegan, too, never claimed much expertise for himself in the financial area.) At the corporate level, the top financial post was vacated suddenly in 1971 when Howard Letts left as vice president of finance.

"RCA is the first non-IBM computer company running under IBMers." Donegan boasted in late 1970. "We have an 18 to 19 year average in the business, the bulk with IBM . . . We're on the way to a marketing organization as good as IBM's."

In order to build his own organization in the likeness of IBM, Donegan first had to repudiate what had been done by the RCA regime before him. To make way for the new stream of IBM people, there was a wholesale replacement of top RCA people. As soon as Bradburn was fired, one of Donegan's first official acts as chief of the computer operation was to fire Joseph Stefan as general manager of the Magnetics Products Division and N. Richard Miller as general manager of the Graphic Systems Division. H. H. Jones was removed as vice president of finance of the RCA Information Systems Group (another man lost from a key financial post) and named general manager of Magnetics Products. On and on the housecleaning went, spreading through all units of the computer operation. In the field, Donegan installed new regional managers in all of RCA's five regions and 27 new regional managers in 34 marketing districts. A whole new layer of IBMers took over product development. Manufacturing remained relatively stable, although Donegan fired the top manufacturing man, John Lenox.

"When high level people came in from IBM, we were just informed that they were coming," said one former RCA computer personnel officer. "On the lower levels, the personnel office got the message to hire IBM guys, too. Anytime we got someone from IBM, he had an advantage to begin with." The personnel man estimated that 18 of the top 25 jobs at the Marlboro headquarters had been taken over by ex-IBMers. Besides Joseph Rooney in marketing and William Acker in finance, Donegan hired Orville Wright away from IBM to serve initially as vice president of government marketing and, later, as president of the new Systems Development Division. The IBM men hired IBM men and those IBM men, in turn, hired more IBM men.

Along with the IBM people came IBM procedures — and heavy new expenses.

From marketing practices and ranking systems on personal performance to a massive reorganization of product development, the RCA computer organization was being patterned after IBM. Employees were ranked according to ability a la IBM — 1, 2, 3, 4, 5. An IBM-inspired attrition control program — aimed at determining why people left RCA — was instituted. There was a "Speak Up" program patterned after IBM's in which employees could make known their problems and complaints to higher-ups in RCA. There were new task forces, and new study groups, and new management and development programs — all based on the way IBM did it. There were attempts to book orders along the line of the strict IBM way versus the looser RCA manner, and this overlap created enough confusion so that no one was ever quite certain precisely what the real number of bookings were and how solid orders were.

Orville Wright, who had done a bang-up marketing job in Washington, tripling sales in RCA's office there, was named to head up the new Systems Development Division, which, once again, was based on IBM's System Development Division. "At first, nobody complained about all the IBM people," said the personnel man. "The old-time RCAers felt the IBM people and their practices were necessary for us to move ahead. But the IBM way of doing things was shoved down our throats and people began resenting it. As time went on, as it became apparent there wasn't any real progress being made, then the RCAers began resenting the IBMers, too."

In the end, the problem was fairly simple: IBM, with annual revenues of $7.5 billion in 1970, could afford its highly structured apparatus while RCA's computer operation, with revenues of less than $260 million, just couldn't.

No one, of course, can blame IBM for Donegan's zeal in attempting to remake RCA into a mini-IBM. But IBM presented RCA with another serious problem in the form of stiff competition, something Robert Sarnoff referred to obliquely when the final collapse came as "the severe pressures generated by a uniquely entrenched competition."

In attempting to fight IBM head-on, and stressing compatibility with IBM, RCA always made itself vulnerable to the Goliath's competitive moves. Because of confusion generated by the new way in which Donegan was booking orders, there was no accurate breakdown on bookings for the RCA Series, but a rough estimate would look like this: of some 225 systems ordered, the overwhelming majority were 2s, perhaps more than 150. There were no more than 20 orders for the 3 while the 6 picked up perhaps 25 orders and the 7 no more than 10. Announced one week after the RCA Series, the IBM 370/145 — cheaper than expected and with its larger-than-anticipated memory — virtually blocked sales of the 6 and 7 to all but existing RCA customers. When the 135 was announced, in March of 1971, new sales of the 2 dried up. But the crowning blows — the Nagasaki and Hiroshima — were IBM's peripherals price cuts in May, 1971, which put IBM on a par and often below RCA's charges for complete systems. New RCA orders dwindled to a trickle and many old orders turned to water.

The chief result, then, of the RCA Series was to impact the existing RCA equipment base and, because of this, the line was a disaster. Computer people no doubt will debate for years whether this happened primarily because of an overly aggressive IBM or a miscalculating RCA.

In June, the situation was clearly deteriorating further. It was becoming apparent within RCA that the RCA Series was impacting RCA equipment. At the same time, expenses in the computer operation were mounting and it seemed that every time there was a new budget estimate the loss was upped. The loss figure reportedly rose between April and June from $36 million to the low $40 millions.

Donegan, however, charged forward. In late June he presided over groundbreaking ceremonies for a new $16 million headquarters at Marlboro — a move that many regarded as an unnecessary extravagance in view of the tightening financial squeeze. The story that made the rounds at the time was that Anthony Conrad, who was then preparing to take over as RCA's new president, had opposed the $16 million building project, but that Donegan had obtained approval for it from Robert Sarnoff. At groundbreaking ceremonies for the $16 million building program, Donegan said: "RCA remains committed to play a major role in the computer industry in this decade."

A month later — just three days before the cost-conscious Anthony Conrad would take over as RCA's president and chief operating officer — Donegan announced the establishment of an expensive new computer operation in the United Kingdom (headed by former IBMers, naturally). RCA had been displaying sensitivity to criticism that it had no edp computer business in the booming European market and the new U.K. operation was the start of a master plan that envisioned the establishment of an RCA computer operation throughout the Continent. True, RCA had no operation of its own in Europe, but its arrangement with Siemens had been a highly profitable one for RCA with annual sales averaging about $40 million and profits on that of about $15 million. Furthermore, the cost for RCA to build up a European operation of its own would be astronomical and, given the tight financial status of things at home, would surely act as a drain on the computer operation for years to come.

On Aug. 10, Anthony Conrad, RCA's new president, arrived in Marlboro with his corporate staff in tow for a full dress review of the computer operation. Conrad had developed a reputation at RCA for being a tough profit-and-loss man, but he was also respected for his fairness. His arrival at Marlboro was preceded by some minor trepidation on the part of the Marlboro people. Already, there had been some key changes made in financial operations. Carmen Ferraioli had resigned as controller of the computer operation to take another job and Julius Koppelman had taken his place. Koppelman was taking over some duties from Donegan's top financial man, William Acker. And Chase Morsey was now — on Aug. 10 — the top financial man at the RCA Corp., having been appointed executive vice president of finance and planning just over a month before. Morsey attended the Marlboro meeting, too.

The meeting elicited a rather grim picture of the computer operation. (At that time, losses of the entire RCA Computer Systems Div. had been escalated to between $63 and $80 million for 1971. The total loss estimates also included figures from RCA's Graphic Systems, Memory Products, and Magnetic Products Divisions, which totaled some 15% of the computer business.) One man who attended the meeting quoted Conrad as saying at the conclusion: "Well, it's not a pretty picture, but at last we have the real picture." When Conrad and his staff left, the Marlboro people had the impression that Conrad felt he had gotten to the bottom of the situation, but that the situation could be handled. At that, Donegan and his team went back to work, attempting to whip the computer operation into line, assuming that they had the full support of corporate to push ahead in the coming years.

The next significant contact between corporate and the computer operation occurred on Sept. 17. Early that Friday morning Donegan was summoned to 30 Rockefeller Plaza from Marlboro. Donegan is reported to have regarded it as just a routine meeting, but shortly after he arrived at corporate headquarters, he was told news he couldn't believe: RCA had decided to pull out of the computer business. Actually, the decision had been made before the board of directors' special meeting and a press release announcing the board's unanimous approval had been prepared beforehand. Donegan did not attend the board meeting.

Several weeks later, in his only recorded public statement (other than the press handout) on the decision, to a United Press International reporter in London, Sarnoff would say: "I've been asked why I made the decision when I made it. In July we said we had no intention of getting out of the computer business and yet in September we were getting out. What had happened in between?

"Well, we had several studies under way and it became apparent as losses mounted that the industry itself was changing, including the problem of uniquely entrenched competition. Finally I came to the conclusion that in view of everything we could not afford the price of staying in it. I made the final decision on Thursday afternoon and I called a board meeting for Friday. A decision like that is a little like getting married or divorced — it couldn't be made sooner, it couldn't be made later, I take full responsibility for it."

The decision was a blow to Sarnoff, both to him personally and to his image, which he values highly. Robert Sarnoff had been living in the shadow of David Sarnoff and the son had been attempting without much avail to shake the image of the boss's son ever since he took over as RCA's chief executive officer in 1968. Robert Sarnoff had intensified an aggressive RCA acquisition program during the height of the conglomerate rage, and when Wall Street soured on conglomerates some of that disillusion rubbed off on RCA, which had been transformed from an electronics-based company into a broader based quasi-conglomerate. In addition, Robert Sarnoff had hoped that computers would bring to him and RCA what color television had brought to his father and RCA — profits and prestige.

One of Robert Sarnoff's acquisitions was Coronet Industries, which is a highly successful carpeting firm. The deal which brought Coronet into RCA gave the carpeting company's head, Martin B. Seretean, nearly 1.5 million shares of RCA stock, more than 15 times the amount of stock owned by Robert Sarnoff, thus giving Seretean a certain clout on the RCA board of directors because he was the firm's largest single stockholder. Seretean has the reputation of being a hard driving incisive businessman — a man who will not tolerate fumbling and indecision. Seretean, along with other RCA directors, Stephen M. DuBrul, Jr., of Lehman Bros. and Donald A. Petrie of Lazard Freres & Co., is said to have become a critic of the computer operation. Of the decision to pull out of the computer business, Seretean points out that the directors' decision was unanimous and says simply, "I think the decision was a sound one."

(Some observers believe that Sarnoff's decision to promote Anthony Conrad to RCA president and chief operating officer and, in fact, to downgrade his own position somewhat, was an attempt to placate his critics on the board. When Conrad was named president, incidentally, many of Donegan's supporters were stunned that their man didn't get the post. Donegan — and others — were under consideration for the RCA presidency early in 1971.)

Donegan also found that during the summer of 1971 he lost one of his most powerful supporters, Chase Morsey, who had turned against the computer operation. Sarnoff, then, was in the uncomfortable position of presiding over a computer operation that was beginning to give all the appearances of going out of control while a group on the board of directors and at corporate was demanding that he do something about it. Sarnoff did do something; he pulled the whole temple down.

The stunning thing is that RCA decided to scuttle its computer business without consulting anyone in the computer operation to see if it couldn't be saved, or at least to see if sections of it couldn't be salvaged for RCA. The rest of the story is well known. Donegan quickly teamed up with Mohawk Data Science Corp. in an attempt to keep the computer operation going pretty much as it had been, but RCA top management rejected the effort and sold its customer base to Univac. MDS said it offered more than Univac and after the MDS offer was rejected by RCA, many RCA computer people complained bitterly that RCA had rejected the MDS offer because RCA management would have lost face if MDS succeeded with the computer operation where RCA had failed. RCA management, which went into a shell of silence about the computer operation after Sept. 17, never offered a full explanation of why the MDS offer was rejected.

RCA's decision to get out of the general purpose computer business had massive consequences — as a result, nearly 8000 people (not counting those who went to Univac) lost their jobs and more than 500 customers with about $1 billion of equipment were confused about their future. In all, RCA got a $490 million pretax write-off, and that was about twice the size of the largest previous bust in the history of U.S. business — the $250 million write-off Ford Motor Co. got for bombing with the Edsel. On the other hand, Wall Street's reaction to the RCA decision was generally good and RCA stock rose on the news that the firm was getting out of the computer business.

The decision was also a blow to the remainder of the computer industry. Because RCA stressed compatibility with IBM equipment, IBM might be expected by some to pick up most of the RCA customers sooner or later. That, of course, will be a plus for IBM, which may be able to add two or three percent of market share to its business, but there could be a minus involved for IBM: the whole incident raises nagging questions of antitrust and monopoly for the company that is generally conceded to have 70% of the computer business. Indeed, shortly after RCA's demise, James Guzy, Memorex's executive vice president, blamed IBM for driving RCA out of business. Also important is the psychological blow dealt the rest of the industry. Many computer users are wary of dealing with anyone but IBM and the clumsy exit of RCA will only tend to make users think twice about doing business with anyone but IBM.

If RCA computer users were upset about the way RCA abruptly left the business, then they should have talked to RCA's employees. The users would have felt better if only because the employees felt worse. In Marlboro, as at other RCA locations across the country, people were laid off in large groups and now only a small cadre is left. Now, as this is written, the Marlboro facility has an eerie atmosphere to it. The inside work areas are nearly silent and nearly empty while outside there is manic activity on the headquarters building, which is an unhappy and constant reminder of the waste of it all. When the workmen look inside the building, now and then they see someone in the nearly-deserted interior. They may even catch a glimpse of L. Edwin Donegan, who still walks the building, but not in the manner of the director of a 10,000-man strong company, but in a quiet and slow step, like Hamlet's ghost. And though it's all over now, there are many who still insist, and, indeed, who will insist until the day they go to their graves, that corporate never gave the computer operation a fair chance.

"If you only knew how close we were to making it," says one of these. "We were so close, so close."

How to manage by objectives

INDUSTRY WEEK

Stated objectives don't necessarily lead to sound decisions. To be useful to management, objectives must be measurable, specific, tangible, and under the effective control or influence of those setting the goals.

MANY OF OUR "OBJECTIVES" are no more than light at the end of the tunnel. Bringing "a just and lasting peace to Southeast Asia" or "cleaning up the environment" are examples of phrases that may spur activity, but do little to tell us where we want to go, how we are going to get there, and how we will know when we have arrived.

The parallel for managers is this: most companies believe they are managing by objectives. But many objectives are platitudes such as, "We will maximize our profits" or, "We will improve our market penetration." Even quantified objectives such as, "We will increase our return on investment from 20 to 23%," contain a vital flaw; if you don't make it, you don't know why.

"If you don't know why you failed to reach the target," says Herbert E. Geissler, management consultant in the Cleveland office of McKinsey & Co., "you don't know what to do differently next year. And, the likelihood of not making this objective is further increased, if managers have put some stretch in their goals—which they should—for objectives should always be just beyond the reach of the manager, far enough so he stretches for the objective but not so far he doesn't bother trying."

Dr. George S. Odiorne, author of the book *Management by Objectives*, describes the process as one "whereby the superior and subordinate managers of an organization jointly identify its common goals, define each individual's major areas of responsibility in terms of the results expected of him, and use these measures as guides for operating the unit and assessing the contribution of each of its members."

Contrasted with management by objectives, or ends, is management by controls, or means. Managers who practice management by objectives think and speak in terms of results. Those who practice management by controls think and speak in terms of what people are doing.

The interesting paradox of many organizations is that increasing management by control can easily result from an effort to fulfill objectives. To such managers, Charles L. Hughes, author of the award-winning book, *Goal Setting*, suggests that "if they would think not so much about the doing of a task as about the final outcome, they would be taking advantage of supervisory tactics which would allow them to profit from self-control on the part of their employees."

Mr. Hughes continues, "A goal is an end, a result, not just a task or function to be performed. The identification of meaningful goals both for

Reprinted by permission of *Industry Week* from *Industry Week*, June 8, 1970, pp. **81** 40–45.

the organization and the individual that will effectively influence and support each other is essential to effective performance on the part of the organization and its members alike."

Goal characteristics

Time out for a quiz. The 20 most common errors in setting goals are shown in Fig. 1, based on a study of 1,100 managers reported by Dr. Odiorne. Mr. Geissler says that most companies, in setting objectives, go through a pattern that starts with objectives so nebulous that they hamper the ability to perform, let alone to measure. Next time around, they start putting numbers on the objectives, such as increasing return on investment from 20 to 23%, but the numbers don't tell them how to get from where they are to where they want to go.

A year or two farther down the road, says Mr. Geissler, the company learns to develop subobjectives: the action steps needed to move the organization toward its objectives. Then, in the next steps, understanding and using the objectives become part of the management process in terms of exploding specific objectives into discrete steps and actions that individual managers have to execute by a specific date.

Learning to manage by objectives may be something like learning to ride a bicycle—just reading about it doesn't develop the process. "Objectives are evolved through trial and error," says Mr. Geissler. "If companies make them a meaningful part of the management process, actually set their objectives down in writing and try to monitor results along the way, they will learn what the deficiencies are, but it takes time."

Top down or bottom up

Where do objectives originate, at the top or at the bottom? Mr. Hughes points out that major business objectives can be set only by people who are in a position to understand the broad, long range implications of forecast trends and strategies to meet the company's requirements.

Dr. Odiorne describes top management measures of organizational performance as necessary to define the boundaries within which subordinates can legitimately propose goals. Once these boundaries are known, individual goals and bud-

FIG. 1

Where goals go astray . . .

Common errors managers make in setting goals, based on a survey of 1,100 managers, are reported by Dr. George S. Odiorne:

Doesn't clarify common objectives for the whole unit.

Sets goals too low to challenge the individual subordinate.

Doesn't use prior results as a basis for using intrinsic creativity to find new and unusual combinations.

Doesn't clearly shape his unit's common objectives to fit those of the larger unit of which he is a part.

Overloads individuals with patently inappropriate or impossible goals.

Fails to cluster responsibilities in the most appropriate positions.

Allows two or more individuals to believe themselves responsible for doing exactly the same things when he knows having one man responsible is better.

Stresses methods of working rather than clarifying individual areas of responsibility.

Emphasizes tacitly that it is pleasing him rather than achieving the job objective which counts.

Makes no policies as guides to action, but waits for results and then issues ad hoc judgments in correction.

Doesn't probe to discover what program his subordinate proposes to follow to achieve his goals but accepts every goal uncritically without a plan for its successful achievement.

Is too reluctant to add his own (or higher management's) known needs to the programs of his subordinates.

Ignores the very real obstacles that are likely to hinder the subordinate in achieving his goals, including the numerous emergency or routine duties which consume time.

Ignores the new goals or ideas proposed by his subordinates and imposes only those which he deems suitable.

Doesn't think through and act upon what he must do to help his subordinates succeed.

Fails to set intermediate target dates by which to measure his subordinates' progress toward their goals.

Doesn't introduce new ideas from outside the organization nor does he permit or encourage subordinates to do so, thereby freezing the status quo.

Fails to permit his subordinates to seize targets of opportunity in lieu of stated objectives that are less important.

Is rigid about not scrapping previously agreed-upon goals that have subsequently proved unfeasible, irrelevant or impossible.

Doesn't reinforce successful behavior when goals are achieved, or correct unsuccessful behavior when they are missed.

FIG. 2

Setting goals to measure the unmeasurable . . .

1 It is often necessary to devise measurements of present levels in order to be able to estimate or calculate change from this level.

2 The most reliable measures are the real time or raw data in which the physical objects involved comprise the measures to be used (dollars of sales, tone of output, number of home runs hit).

3 When raw data can't be used, an index or ratio is the next most accurate measure. This is a batting average, a percentage, a fraction, or a ratio.

4 If neither of the above two can be used, a scale may be constructed. Such scales may rate "from one to ten," a nominal rating against a checklist of adjectives such as "excellent, fair, poor" or one which describes "better than or worse than" some arbitrary scale. These are useful but less precise than the above.

5 Verbal scales are the least precise but can be extremely useful in identifying present levels and noting real change. Verbs such as "directs, checks, and reports" are indicative of actions to be taken.

6 General descriptions are the least useful, but still have value in establishing benchmarks for change. "A clear, cloudless fall day" is obviously not the same as a "cloudy, foggy misty day" and the two descriptions could be used to state conditions as they exist and conditions as they should be.

7 The statements of measurement should be directed more toward results than toward activity. (Much activity may prove impossible to state in specific terms, whereas results of that activity can be stated.)

8 In stating results sought or defining present levels, effort should be made to find indicative, tangible levels and convert verbal or general descriptions into such tangible scales, ratios or raw measures where possible.

9 If you can't count it, measure it, or describe it, you probably don't know what you want and often can forget about it as a goal.

gets should be solicited and to the extent possible should be used to adapt to organization goals.

"The establishment of measures of organization performance should precede goal-setting meetings between managers and subordinates. These measures of organization performance delineate the areas of decision of both parties in the joint goal-setting process," says Dr. Odiorne.

Mr. Geissler agrees that "the top of the house has to determine where they want to go, how they want to get there, when they want to get there, and what resources they have available to get them there. These basic parameters have to be communicated downward so that the down-the-line managers can then outline how they think they can achieve these things."

But he suggests that this must then form the basis for a dialog over a period of time. "Without a continuing dialog rather than a series of edicts zinging back and forth, you'll never get meaningful objectives. The man at the top isn't familiar enough with the specifics to say, 'Here are the five things we have to do'—he can only provide broad directions. The manager down the line lacks the overview to choose the broad objectives but he is expert on the detail. So it takes a continuing dialog between top, middle, and line managers to make them work as a really effective team."

Mr. Geissler describes the dialog concept as relatively new in the area of planning. "In the past, it was generally thought you went through a very mechanistic procedure in which you analyzed your operating environment and isolated the opportunities that were most attractive. Once you had figured out what opportunities you wished to capitalize on, you outlined what it would take to do the job in terms of steps and resources. Then you exploded that into programs, timetables, budgets, and so forth to do it.

"Where that breaks down," says Mr. Geissler, "is in not permitting feedback of knowledge between the various levels of the operating organization."

In his view, objective-setting and action programming are a continuous process. "To do that, you have to have frequent face to face discussions, not dog and pony shows in which the division manager comes in and puts on a glowing presentation for one day, lays out so much detail that nobody can understand it, and gets a rubber stamp approval because he wore the president out," Mr. Geissler comments with a smile.

"Modern objectives setting involves the division

manager sitting down with the president and talking through basic parameters such as what are the issues that are going to dictate the future of this piece of the business, what are the major problems that you see in the future, and why are they major to you. While you get some chaff with the seed," admits Mr. Geissler, "the process builds understanding between the two men as to what's important in that piece of the business. And once that step is taken you've isolated the issues both in terms of opportunities and of problems."

The division manager is then prepared to go back and meet with his own staff people to discuss how they can capitalize on the opportunities and solve the problems. Various alternatives can be considered together with the resource requirements for each to develop practicality and feasibility trade-offs.

"The division manager again can meet with the president in a relatively informal discussion. The division manager outlines the ways in which he can capitalize the opportunities and lick the problems in a way that permits the president to consider what resources he can apply and what resources he may wish to juggle throughout the business.

"The dialog process enhances understanding and mutual respect, and brings increased credibility both for the objectives and for the entire planning process," believes Mr. Geissler. "And, if the division manager builds his own dialogs among marketing, manufacturing, engineering, and others, he can achieve the same thing."

Kinds of objectives

Dr. Odiorne believes that performance goals are needed in every position where performance and results directly and vitally affect the contribution of the man to the organization. He points out that almost without exception, the application of time study techniques to managerial work has failed. "If the job being studied lends itself to measurement of repetitive cycles of work performed, it probably isn't supervisory work to begin with," says Dr. Odiorne. "Increased effort doesn't necessarily produce better results; selective choices of effort are more important."

On this basis, he believes goals fall into three basic categories: regular or routine objectives, problem solving objectives, and innovative or improvement objectives.

Regular or routine objectives he characterizes

as statements of ordinary requirements which are necessary for the survival of the firm. Often they are covered by the job description as the purpose and duties of the position and thus as a charter to perform certain duties attached to it. But he points out that management by objectives can enlarge the job description in two ways: first, all such duties are reviewed annually and changes noted in writing with mutual agreement on those duties as a result; second, measures are established specifying when those routine duties are well done.

Problem solving objectives most often are performed by staff department groups. Industrial engineers, cost accountants, quality control men, pro-

---

"A goal is an end . . . not just a task or function to be performed."

---

duction planners, and other such specialists find most of their objectives in the areas of problem solving, says Dr. Odiorne. The importance of stating problems in these areas as objectives lies in the fact that they are specified with some precision, the causes of the variance from standards are determined, and a solution is developed and applied.

Innovative or improvement objectives differ from the first two in being action decisions rather than reaction decisions. The innovative category of objectives starts with the assumption that even the perfect completion of routine objectives isn't good enough, says Dr. Odiorne, and that problem solving is merely a necessary step in keeping that regular level of objective at the regular level.

Objectives for change

For that reason, innovative or improvement objectives are most essential to company growth, are of a higher order than the others, and are rarest in occurrence. These are the objectives most vulnerable to platitudes.

"Simply having an objective doesn't lead to sound decisions," says Dr. Odiorne. "The objective must be stated in terms which lend themselves to measurement of results. Indeed, the reason for establishing an objective is to permit its use in measurement later on."

Objectives must also be specific, tangible, and under the effective control or influence of those setting the goals. "To some," he notes, "these limits bar the establishment of objectives, for at first glance many areas seem to be incapable of being precisely defined." But he suggests approaches to measuring the unmeasurable in Fig. 2.

Because of the measurement aspect and interfunctional familiarity with the organization, many companies assign the planning function to accounting. "Many outstanding accountants function well in a planning role," agrees Mr. Geissler, "but by nature most accountants are oriented to the past rather than to the future." For that reason, he suggests that while the quantification of performance and the monitoring and measurement of results may be carried out by accountants, marketing men are the logical ones to handle planning.

"The marketing man is the one who has been given the staff responsibility for determining which products are best suited to the needs of the customers and what it takes to get those products to the customer at a price the company can make a profit on," says Mr. Geissler. "This makes him the logical individual to spearhead the planning function, the pulling together of information to

"Objectives are evolved through trial and error."

set objectives, to lay out strategies, to build the programs to carry out those strategies. He will act as the catalyst between all of the functions in carrying out the planning exercise.

"Business strategy is related to a specific market line or product of most companies. It is an extension of the overall business objectives, but it is the next level of detail," explains Mr. Geissler. "The overall company might wish to grow in sales and earnings per share of a given amount. The product/marketing manager's first task is to lay out the strategy within his business segment to support that corporate objective. He has to make sure his product is the right product for the market, that it is focused in the right market seg-

ments, that it is getting to the customer in the most effective manner, that manufacturing is supporting this effort with the right quality as well as reliable delivery and competitive delivery times, that engineering is designing a product that has relatively low cost.

"Over the longer pull," says Mr. Geissler, "the product/marketing manager is responsible for new product developments, for changes in the manufacturing processes to permit economies and hence better pricing, for predicting future price levels, for determining the service to be provided to the customer, for pulling together all the actions needed to support that market segment. He has to take the broad corporate objectives and figure out what targets he must hit and the actions needed to hit those targets."

Mr. Geissler suggests that in the typical corporation there would be several of these men, each directing a specific area of the enterprise, their combined and individual efforts contributing to and supporting the corporate objectives.

How many objectives?

It is very hard for a man to work on more than three or four major objectives at one time, believes Mr. Geissler. But he notes that some companies have a dozen objectives on the basis that if a man hits a third of them, management will be happy. "The problem," suggests Mr. Geissler, "is that he may hit the wrong third. It is better practice to have a focused effort and move in sequence; hit the most important third this year, the next third the year after."

Another point Mr. Geissler makes is that objectives can be conflicting. "Inventory levels are a good example," he says. "The financial manager has the objective of keeping the investment in the company to a minimum so that for a given amount of profit you have a good rate of return. The sales department wants to have inventory levels up to reduce the possibility of a stock-out and a dissatisfied customer.

"Conflicts like this become a trading off situation," says Mr. Geissler, "where a price tag must be put on the merits of each of these objectives. What is the cost of a stock-out? What is the cost of holding inventory? Where they balance out is the inventory level."

Similar trade-offs are involved in setting corporate objectives, Mr. Geissler observes. "You must eventually start balancing out the merits of increasing market share against the possible threat of competitive retaliation and price cutting; or the profit value of an extra share point versus the profit value of an extra price point. This is the science of management, quantifying things that have been determined by but feel over the years.

Corporate goals vary

"Different businesses of necessity have different objectives. If a company is like E. I. du Pont de Nemours & Co., one of the major goals has to be return on investment because it has so much of it.' If a company is interested in going the conglomerate route, it has to maximize earnings per share growth. Other companies just like to maximize volume," says Mr. Geissler.

He also notes that corporate objectives are surprisingly personal, reflecting the nature and character of the chief executive and involving the kind of business he wants to run. But he adds, "In setting corporate objectives, what you are doing through the dialog process is determining what is feasible and most desirable in terms of the capabilities and potentialities of the various areas of the corporation combined."

He illustrates with increasing return on investment. "Return on investment is specific, profits divided by assets, but highly complex," says Mr. Geissler. "Profit, for example, is a function of sales levels, cost levels, price levels, and product mix. Assets also get broken down into a number of pieces.

"To get at improving return on investment, each of these pieces should be broken down into specific objectives, both short term and long term.

The next level of management must be involved in a dialog to set objectives for the components that end up as return on investment even though they are tied together at the corporate level."

The degree of improvement has to be cut and fit in order to meet the overall goal and often involves an iterative process in which some managers will try to set easy targets and be told they're not enough, says Mr. Geissler.

"Trade-offs again come into play," he says, "concerning such questions as: 'Should a greater effort be placed on increasing sales or on reducing costs?' Usually it is easier to reduce costs than to increase sales, but the marginal income on sales is typically two to three times that of the percentage improvement you can get in costs. The trade-off may thus depend on the point in time. If the chief executive needs profits in a hurry, he's better off with cost reduction; if he wants to build a viable business, he's better off building sales.

"And this is why," adds Mr. Geissler, "objectives of necessity change from time to time—because the environment the company operates in is always shifting."

Numerical fairy tales

Most budgeting and profit planning tend to be numerical fairy tales, observes Mr. Geissler, and most managers are adept at playing the numbers game. But unless the numbers are supported by discrete actions to be carried out by specific individuals by a specified time, it's unlikely that the numbers will come true.

"That's the big shortcoming, the usual pitfall. And yet you have to do that kind of planning successfully before you can do the more esoteric but more important kinds like strategic planning," concludes Mr. Geissler.

Organizing for Long-Range Planning

Future organization strategies are vital to organizational survival, yet the classical approach does not provide the needed focus. A matrix form of organization clearly shows promise.

DAVID I. CLELAND AND WILLIAM R. KING

Both authors are faculty members at the University of Pittsburgh. David I. Cleland is in systems management and William R. King is in the area of business administration.

Nearly every text dealing with long-range planning, almost as an afterthought, devotes a section near the end of the book to "Organization for Planning." In such sections, much is made of line versus staff and whether the long-range planning staff should be at the corporate level, division level, or both, on the organization chart. Little in the way of a creative approach to the long-range planning process is put forth and few documented cases of innovative planning organizations are available.[1]

Of course, the concept of a planning organization is itself not well understood in any context other than that of a professional planning staff. Most organizations operate as though strategic planning was simply another aspect of the manager's job, or alternatively, as though only top management and professional planners should have anything of substance to do with strategic planning for the overall organization. These two concepts, either alone or in combination, presume that strategic planning should be done within the framework of the existing traditional bureaucratic organization.

STRATEGIC PLANNING ORGANIZATION

Modern organizations are too complex for either of these simplistic approaches. If the organization is to be opportunistic, adapt to change, and influence the future—all of the things that planners constantly promise as benefits of comprehensive organizational strategic planning—it must not be bound to either the practices or the organizational structures of the past. There is a wealth of "hard-nosed" evidence to support this pontifical statement.

First, some of the main thrusts of change in our industrial society serve to remind us that strategic planning is inescapable if the organization is to survive—protracted product development cycles, accelerating product obsolescence, rapid state-of-the-art proliferation, changing social values, increasing demand of people for more participation in the decision process, and growing organizational complexity and interdependency.

Second, coincident with these changes has come the recognition that good ideas for the

1. The authors use the term "long-range" or "strategic planning" to denote that planning dealing with the next and subsequent generations of products and services.

Reprinted by permission of the authors and *Business Horizons* from *Business Horizons,* August 1974, pp. 25–32.

> " . . . strategic planning is a job to be performed by managers—not for them. . . . professional planners are not the doers of planning in this model; rather, they are the facilitators."

future are not the special prerogative of top managers or professional planners. Yet many organizations continue to operate with a multilayered chain of command where many people can say no but few can say yes. Such an organization stifles the generation of ideas and complicates the process of bringing them to fruition.

Yet innovative ideas may be the life blood of the organization's future, and constitute the basic building blocks of the planning system. If those ideas are truly new, they may be lost in the bureaucratic milieu. If, for instance, new products and markets that are not simply extensions of existing products and markets are to be developed, effective ways of generating ideas, evaluating those ideas, and developing them to fruition must be found.

In order for strategic planning to accomplish this, the planning effort must be supported with the skills and knowledge that exist at organizational interfaces at all levels. In most organizations, these interfaces are "cracks" through which good ideas are lost. The goal of a strategic planning system should be to convert ideas into organizational assets to be used in creating the organizations' future.

BASIC TENETS OF THE APPROACH

Several tenets form the basis for the planning organizational structure which we describe in this article. These tenets, together with their consequent organizational structure and planning process, have been applied with success

in a number of business and public organizations. However, such limited testing and evaluation does not guarantee their universal worth.

Managers Are the Planners

The first tenet of the planning organizational approach to be presented is that *modern participative management is appropriate to the formalized strategic planning process of the organization* as well as to the planning aspects of the individual manager's job. Thus, the inference can be drawn from this basic assumption that *strategic planning is a job to be performed by managers—not for them.* However critical the role of the professional planning staff is to an effective strategic planning process, professional planners are not the doers of planning in this model; rather, they are the facilitators.

The doers of strategic planning are managers—both top managers and lower-level line managers—thereby ensuring that the people who will be charged with implementing the plans are those who have generated the goals and developed and approved the plans.

Fulfilling Management Needs

Another basic tenet of the planning organization approach is that there are unique needs inherent in the strategic planning processes and in the role of the line manager as an active participant in overall organizational planning. These needs are those which cannot readily be met by the existing organization with its reliance on bureaucratic forms and procedures.

These needs have a variety of natures— from substantive and objective to psychological and subjective. At the objective level, for instance, are informational needs. True organizational strategic planning requires that the planner-manager be provided with an understanding of information concerning the likely future environment in which the organization will operate. Such information for the overall organization is not normally supplied to the line manager. If it is, it is provided in a written summary that is an inadequate form for conveying real in-depth understanding and acceptance. Thus, in the traditional organization, even if the line manager is involved in overall organizational planning, he is not often supplied with adequate information to permit him to operate effectively and to have confidence in the credibility of strategic decisions.

The psychological constraints of the bureaucratic organization also serve to inhibit effective planning, thus creating a planning need to be served by an alternative organization. For instance, the purview of a lower-level manager is necessarily restricted by his day-to-day activities as well as by his formal job description. When he becomes involved in higher-level interorganizational decision making, he is treading on the traditional ground of others who are higher in the organization. These territorial imperatives and their resulting impact on the people in the organization can be of great consequence to effective planning and to effective continued operation of the organization.

Authorities, Roles, and Information

A third tenet which forms the basis for the approach suggested here is that *an organizational structure for strategic planning is largely prescribed by sets of two kinds:*

Definitions of the authorities, responsibilities, and roles of planning participants

Definitions of the data bases available to planning participants and the nature of the data flows among participants.

Thus, while the specification of the existing formal and informal organization is important to the determination of the kind of

The Cyclical Planning Process

planning that can be done, the nature of the process which can be used, and the content of the plans which are formulated for any particular organization, it is assumed here that a planning organization—defined in terms of authorities, responsibilities, roles, and information—can be superimposed on the existing organization to effect better planning. To understand the impact of these authority, role, and information sets, the strategic planning process itself first needs to be examined.

THE PLANNING PROCESS

The general nature of the planning process which is presumed here in the specification of a planning organization is one which is common to many industrial and public organizations. However, while the general structure of the process is pervasive, the procedures and policies which govern its operation and the organizational structure which is used to facilitate the process are neither widely used nor understood.

The figure shows a general cyclical planning process involving four key organizational elements—top management, professional planners, financial analysts, and line managers. No specific organizational structure is meant to be implied by the figure. It merely describes a cyclical *process* involving the flow of statements of goals, general strategies, assumptions, planning guidelines, and forecasts from the top-level to lower-level managers, the preparation of plans at the lower level (and their submission back to top management through a planning staff which reviews them for congruence with overall goals), compatibility with other plans, validity, and so on. It presumes a financial staff, which reviews them for financial and budgetary soundness and implications.

Of course, the process is highly abstracted in the figure. The line manager may well have a planning staff of his own to aid him in his preparation of the plans. Indeed, several of these cycles may be "stacked" atop one another to include various lower levels of management in the planning process. However, all of the critical elements of the variety of planning process being dealt with is adequately described by even such an abstraction as the figure.

THE PLANNING ORGANIZATION

While there are a wide variety of planning difficulties created by the bureaucratic organization, perhaps the most serious has to do with the nurturing of new ideas. Innovative ideas are the lifeblood of effective strategic planning for most organizations, since they are the harbingers of potential future strategies. Fortunately, many new ideas are constantly coming to the surface in most dynamic organizations. However, it would be foolhardy to assume that these ideas emerge and flow upward through the chain of command. In addition to the intrinsic stultifying effect of multilayered organizations, there may be conscious attempts on the part of managers to impede the flow of ideas—for indeed, ideas are the stuff of which

change is born, and change is resisted by many who fear obsolescence.

To remedy this, the organizational approach should be adaptive and flexible enough to encourage and facilitate the emergence and development of ideas from any source within the organization, since it is clear that the generation of good ideas is not the sole province of these managers who occupy top positions in the organizational hierarchy. In Japan, a nation with economic growth that surpasses ours, economic success is attributed "to the assistance and joint effort of others."[2]

The Japanese business and government culture reflects this group concern by following a decision-making technique whereby decisions are made by groups in accordance with a free consensus. In such an approach, the flows of authority and responsibility depart radically from the so-called chain of command to reflect a high degree of participation. The value of such participation is borne out by Howard F. Van Zandt's statement, "whereas in the United States a considerable proportion of management ideas are conceived in the executive suite and imposed from the top down, in Japan the reverse is true. More often than not, proposals start from somewhere down the line."[3]

The Japanese system provides the key to the development of a modern planning organization. Since new products or services do indeed emerge as ideas in an organization, these ideas need to be managed in their life cycle from initial concept through production and distribution in the market place. Emerging ideas are harbingers of future changes, so that by designing a system that permits the management of these ideas, the formulation of strategy in the organization is facilitated. By identifying these emerging

---

2. Howard F. Van Zandt, "How to Negotiate in Japan," *Harvard Business Review* (November-December 1970).
3. Van Zandt, "How to Negotiate in Japan."

ideas, those which show promise can be segregated for further study and analysis. Thus, in managing change in this fashion, the idea is taken as the point of departure for developing a planning organization. The key to that organization is the matrix form.

The Matrix Form

An appropriate model for this role of ideas in the development of future strategy is found in the defense industry where simple, formal theories of organization have been modified by *matrix forms*. In creating the matrix form, unified command and span-of-control concepts have been abandoned. Some of the success in the defense industry can be attributed in part to the management of ideas. To quote Merton J. Peck and Frederic M. Scherer: "The precipitating factor in the decision to begin serious development of a new weapon system is usually one or more technical or scientific ideas."[4]

As these ideas emerge and show promise, a *project manager* (often called a team leader) can be put in charge of the idea; he becomes an entrepreneur, managing the idea across the organization by pulling together a team whose various members have the skills necessary to evaluate the emerging ideas and find answers to the questions:

1. What is the nature of the future business opportunity? What function does it serve?

2. What and when is the need?

3. What is the marketability?

4. What is the competitive situation?

5. What is the organizational capability?

6. What investment is required?

7. What is the influence of political, social, and economic considerations?

8. What specific strategy should be developed to satisfy a market need?

The results of the project team study is forwarded for final study by the body of executive-line officials responsible for selecting future alternative strategies. The composition and operation of these project teams, when coupled with the structural nature of the line organization, provide an adaptive and responsible approach to the development of strategy.

The use of horizontal project management techniques which cut across the vertical functionally-oriented organization serves to create a matrix organization.[5] The use of matrix organizational structure is important both from the standpoint of its effectiveness and the message which it conveys to the rest of the organization—"Innovation is important in this organization—so important that an interdisciplinary-participative 'organization' has been created to manage innovation."

The Matrix Form in Strategic Planning

Of course, the project team approach which is inherent in the matrix organization is not a strategic planning organization itself, even though the ideas that are being managed are related to strategic planning. However, the same concept can be directly applied to the process of strategic planning through project teams who are responsible for the various aspects of strategic planning. For instance, project teams can be organized and held responsible for assisting in the development of alternative strategies in support of overall organizational opportunities, that is, an interdisciplinary, interorganizational project team is pulled together to study a broad market opportunity or one which is charged with

4. Merton J. Peck and Frederic M. Scherer, *The Weapons Acquisition Process: An Economic Analysis* (Boston: Division of Research, Graduate School of Business Administration, Harvard University, 1962), p. 326.

5. See David I. Cleland and William R. King, *Systems Analysis and Project Management* (New York: McGraw-Hill, 1968).

developing a statement of goals for the organization.

The interdisciplinary, interorganizational character of these teams is critical since it ensures that various points of view and experiential bases will be brought to bear. In this way, both disciplinary and organizational parochialism are reduced.

Organizational parochialism is the tendency of a manager to view his organization as the center of affairs in the current period and in a product line which has already been successful—a form of myopia.

Disciplinary parochialism is a similar malady in which the manager still performs (often unknowingly) in a narrow specialized function in which he was educated and in which he won his first kudos. Having attained his credentials in a specialty such as engineering, he never quite forgets that specialty and tends to view that discipline as the most important activity in the organization, rather than practicing his managerial role of integrating the various disciplinary and organizational efforts.

Both of these forms of parochialism serve to inhibit effective planning and both are effectively addressed through the interdisciplinary makeup of planning project teams.

The Line Manager's Role

In line with the basic premise of *participation*, the project teams utilized in the strategic planning effort should be made up of the line managers who are specifically assigned on a full- or part-time basis to the task. If the charge of the project team is a substantial and time-consuming one, the team members may be part-time while the team leader should be temporary, and each should expect to return to his management post after the assignment is completed.

Also, the team can be complemented with full- or part-time staff help. This ensures that sufficient human resources will be available to bring the task to a timely conclusion, while at the same time ensuring that line managers will be collectively responsible for its completion.

Thus, the manager who forms a part of a planning team is a true *participant* in the planning process. His time is formally allocated to it and he must explicitly participate and devote his energy and attention to it.

Moreover, a corollary to the basic premise about participation serves to further integrate the manager into planning. If those who must implement planning should be charged with doing it, then the converse is probably true. This leads directly to a strategy for implementing plans.

The strategy is to charge those who have generated, developed, and nurtured ideas during the planning process with the responsibility for carrying them out after they become an accepted part of the strategic plan. With this simple device, a variety of knowledge and commitment is secured for the plan which no quantity of formal orders or no volume of exhortation could achieve.

The Top Manager's Role

The first role of the manager of the planning organization is the establishment of that unit. If there is any new idea which must come from the top, it is the creation of a radically

new and innovative way of planning. Such an organization should provide for checks and balances and provide a maximum opportunity for participation on the part of those executives who will ultimately be responsible for implementing the decision. In addition, the long-range planning organization should provide an opportunity for widespread participation by technical people at all levels.

In creating this organization, the chief executive must provide the necessary incentives whereby people are rewarded for contributing to the development of future strategy. He should also demonstrate, by his personal involvement, that the continuous development of future strategy is of vital concern in the organization.

A more specific statement related to the top manager's continuing role after the establishment of such an organization is given by John Mee in another context:

> In systems of organization built around a results management concept, management will be considered a human resource, and authority will flow from the desired results of the system rather than from the dictation of one individual. The knowledge, skills and values of individuals will determine their place in the order of subsystems and the total system. Their contributions and their opportunities for achievement and self-realization will be judged by their competence to achieve desired results in systems assignments . . . .[6]

Of course, the development of a long-range sense of direction and purpose for an organization is usually touted as the primary challenge to chief executives. While the problems of controlling current operations is a key responsibility of chief executives, the forces of change in our society clearly challenge the provident executive to devote more time to his role as an organizational strategist.

But the chief executive clearly cannot be a planner in the sense of doing the planning. Obviously, he has limited time. He simply cannot either do or direct the myriad of

studies necessary to build forecasts, test assumptions, and conduct cost-effectiveness studies; an organization must be created to do this for him. His responsibility is developing future organizational strategy centers around the final evaluation and selection of strategic alternatives and the design of a master plan of implementation for those alternatives.

But more important, the chief executive can provide an environment where the development of long-range strategy is a way of life. This requires that he create an organization where there is a continuing assessment of future environmental trends, and a more-or-less continuous effort to develop a range of strategic alternatives for evaluation by the senior executives. If such an environment has been created, the chief executive makes the final choice of strategic alternatives for the organization to pursue.

The selection of these objectives requires the resolution of conflicting views within the executive group. After such strategic objectives have been selected, the chief executive provides for their dissemination to the appropriate level within the organization, and for the design of a program of implementation.

The chief executive, therefore, functions as a "linking pin" among various project teams, planning teams, suborganizations, and executives in this sort of planning organization. He also serves as a balancing force that ensures the emergence and development of ideas which form the organization's future.

The Role of the Staff Planner

The staff planner has four basic functions with regard to the planning process. *First,* he plays a role in the initiation of the process. This role is shared with other staff specialists, who provide informational input to planning, and it is also shared with top management.

Second, the staff planner is the facilitator of the planning process. He schedules all

---

6. Mee, John F., "Speculation About Human Organization in the 21st Century," *Business Horizons* (February 1971), p. 16.

aspects of the process and makes sure that they are carried out.

The *third* major staff planning function is that of review and evaluation. Staff planners review the various plans prepared by line managers, evaluate them for a consistency with each other and with the assumptions and guidelines that have been laid down, and synthesize them into a plan which is then passed on to other staff specialists—financial analysts—and finally to top management for a review. Top management can then move to plan or send them back through the cycle to be redone.

The *fourth* function of the staff planner is consultation. He must be available for consultation with managers during the planning process so that they have access to such items as interpretations of assumptions and forecasts, clarification of planning guidelines, and preliminary evaluation of the feasibility of plans.

The later aspect of this consultative role is of primary importance. While the staff planner performs a review and evaluation function, it is clearly inefficient for the process to become so formal that plans are developed and then rejected on the basis of criteria which could be communicated between staff planner and managerial planner early enough in the planning process to avoid wasted planning effort.

Other Roles

While the roles just defined are critical to the success of the planning organization, there are a wide variety of variations which may prove to be useful. For instance, a council of top executives has been successfully used as a "murder board," which critiques and evaluates the results of the planning teams. An "assistant to" who acts as an alter ego and planning facilitator for the chief executive can also be useful.

In all cases, however, these roles are minor perturbations of the basic planning organiza-

tion structure, that of a matrix organization which is based on a team, each with a temporary lifetime. This horizontal structure is coupled with the mutual structure of the functional organization to provide an adaptive and responsible approach to the development of a strategy, and, through the interdisciplinary and organizational makeup of the teams, provides a checks and balances guard against the pitfalls of parochialism.

The matrix planning organization has many advantages over the traditional way in which planning is done. Among the advantages are these:

- The effect of organizational and disciplinary parochialism is reduced.
- Personal involvement through participation is enhanced; an individual feeling of "belonging" is strengthened.
- A "checks and balances" through consensus decision making is provided.
- An "organization" is created to facilitate innovation, thus complementing the organization designed for efficiency, control, and discipline.
- The chief executive has another "organization" he can draw upon to assist him in developing long-range strategies.

Of course, if project techniques are to be used by an organization to assist in the development of long-range strategies, then the people who will be serving on the project teams (or will be supervising project team efforts) need to be familiarized with project management techniques and concepts. This training is essential simply because bureaucratic organizational structures are still very much a way of life in our society, even though the bureaucratic form of organization is "out of joint with contemporary realities."[7]

If future organizational strategies are vital to the survival of an organization, why not organize the resources in a way that facilitates innovation. Classical organizational approaches do not provide the necessary focus. The use of a matrix form of organization clearly shows promise in the right direction.

7. Bennis, Warren G., "The Coming Death of Bureaucracy," *THINK* (International Business Machines Corporation, 1966).

M. SCOTT MYERS

The Human Factor in Management Systems

SMALL COMPANIES APPROACHING BIG-NESS encounter problems which earlier did not exist or were not as serious. These new problems may be variously manifested as alienation, disloyalty, lack of commitment, high turnover, absenteeism, uncooperativeness, lack of integrity, or deterioration of standards. Solutions for these problems commonly emerge in the form of programs for communication, attitude measurement, merit rating, motivation, recognition, and morale improvement, and are implemented through techniques such as engineered labor standards, piecework incentives, "zero-defects" plans, and paid suggestion systems. These efforts may yield short-term gains, but frequently their ultimate impact is increased alienation and net loss. The inadequacy of these strategies stems from the fact that they are usually dealing with interdependent symptoms of more fundamental causes. When the interdependence of these problems is not recognized, the tendency is to treat them separately.

For example, in Texas Instruments (TI), which grew from 5,000 to 50,000 employees in twelve years, it was not immediately apparent that many of these problems were symptoms of common causes. Management systems specialists noted that systems failures tended to increase with the size of the organization and the complexity of their systems technology. Yet, from an engineering point of view, the hardware and software were not at fault. Many systems designers felt the answer was to "communicate" the

systems better or to put more "teeth" in the procedures.

Similarly, supervisors in all functions encountered changes in turnover and alienation problems that also seemed to correspond with organization size. But from a wages-hours-working conditions point of view, job satisfaction needs seemed to be better satisfied than ever before. Even so, strong reactive behavior of employees occasionally led to capitulatory fattening of benefits and wages.

It is the theme of this paper, then, that both systems designers and supervisors are dealing with symptoms of the same fundamental problem: reaction to what is often felt to be domination by official authority through the media of supervisory practice and management systems. Fortunately or unfortunately, as the case may be, management systems are perceived by and serve as extensions of the managers who direct them. The managers, then, have the same (or greater) motivating, dissatisfying, supporting, or threatening impact as they would have without the systems. Thus, systems themselves, depending on how they are developed, have a primary role of generating the attitudes and perceptions that cause them to succeed or fail.

DIAGNOSING SYSTEMS FAILURES

Systems failures were correctly diagnosed by TI management as human failures. To discover ways of developing more synergistic relationships between systems and the people they influenced, task forces were formed comprised of systems specialists, systems users, and industrial psychologists. The task-force efforts led to a new definition of a management system and conditions for its effectiveness. The TI job-posting system, described herein, exemplifies an evolving system which is effective. It is only one of the examples showing that systems designers achieve their missions better by giving greater emphasis to the human factor in management systems technology.

In trying to determine who some systems fail, TI task force members made eight observations:

1. People at work encounter many systems that do little to bring out their best. Instead, some systems evoke "system-fighting" behavior and encourage the application of ingenuity, effort, and even dishonesty to circumvent them. Time clocks symbolize a restrictive system, and it has become common practice for payroll people to beat the system by lining up at the clock before punching out to pick up a little free time each day. The same employees, when leaving the premises for a special luncheon or appointment, may accidentally-on-purpose forget to punch their cards when leaving and re-entering the plant. Also, consider engineered labor standards as a basis for piecework incentive. They are designed to motivate higher performance, but more characteristically they evoke group pressures to sustain production norms which determine pay rates.

2. Some systems and jobs are designed to fit the lowest level of talent in an organization. The design of a keypunch operator's job, for example, is commonly guided by the directive, "assume that they can't think." Thus, pressures from supervision tend to quash creativity and nonconformity and encourage people to "follow instructions." Creativity among keypunch operators, therefore, is seldom rewarded and may actually provoke admonitions. People hired for increasingly simple jobs are increasingly better-informed, thus widening the disparity between job demands and their competence.

3. System-controlled processes, such as the paced assembly line, though intended to increase efficiency, may have the opposite effect. An ore refinery, for example, geared to process 1,000 tons per day, may enable the refinery operators to "stay busy" when the intake of raw materials drops to 500 tons.

4. Some systems compete to their mutual detriment. In the chemical industry, for example, engineering and operations may inadvertently be placed in conflict by inappropriate criteria of performance. Engineering may be rewarded for constructing processing plants at lower per-square-foot cost, though a greater expenditure might

result in greater efficiency by operations and, hence, greater return on investment to the company.

5. Systems may also interfere with job effectiveness simply because they are tradition, protocol, or authority-based. Performing a filing function in a prescribed manner "because we've always done it that way" or "because I told you to" stifles creativity and motivation, as well as the development of a more efficient system.

6. Similarly, rules sometimes remain in the rule books long after people have learned informal and efficient short cuts which disregard the official rules. Such a situation has double-edged potential for punishment, as people may be admonished for either "violating rules" or "slavish conformity."

7. Some systems perpetuate social stratification by prescribing rules according to job grade. Examples of such systems are compensation plans, time-keeping procedures, paid leave, and other supplemental benefits.

8. Systems may be formal or informal, simple or complex, official or unofficial, but all come into existence because of needs of individuals or groups at some level of the organization. For example, the office check pool (highest poker hand in paycheck serial number) is an informal and unofficial system that forms almost spontaneously, and is perpetuated by a combination of needs that are social (group cohesiveness), financial, diversion, and risk-taking in nature. Management may perceive the check pool as a violation of company rules on gambling, and may try to stop it. Attempts to quash the check pool may be implemented through a system of posted notices, newspaper inserts, public pronouncements, and supervisory instruction, all reinforced by specific or veiled threats of punishment. But, if the need to pertuate the check pool is strong enough, or if the pleasure of circumventing authority is great enough, the pool system goes underground, thereby satisfying rebellion needs provoked by management edict, and perhaps increasing the system's value in satisfying social, diversion, and risk-taking needs.

CONDITIONS FOR EFFECTIVE SYSTEMS

After analyzing the various reasons for a system's success and failure, the task force members concluded that systems users' attitudes and perceptions may be shaped by the style in which the system is administered, as well as by its design and the processes of developing and installing it. Identified as the key factor was whether the system is managed by someone above the user (company-managed system), or by the people who use the system to do their job (user-managed system). This conclusion is illustrated by comparing the behavior of two groups of machine operators toward their respective assembly lines.

One group, in a paper carton factory, was idled for a few hours (with pay) while industrial engineers introduced improvements into their line. The operators clustered near the coke machine,

M. Scott Myers *is Management Research Consultant for Texas Instruments as well as lecturer, consultant and conference leader for business organizations, educational institutions, management associations, and civic groups. He has published extensively in various business journals on the subject of management.*

laughing, drinking cokes, and smoking. When the engineers completed the installation, they briefed the operators on the changes, and asked for questions. Receiving no questions, they assumed the installation completed. But the system actually reduced the line yield and, hence, was less effective than before. The engineered changes had altered role relationships on the line and, even before giving it a fair trial, the operators had conspired, perhaps unconsciously, to make the system fail.

In contrast, a superintendent and foreman in an electronics assembly department involved the operators in planning and balancing their own assembly line and setting their first week's production goals. They achieved their Friday evening goal on Wednesday, and went on to almost double their first week's goal. From an engineering point of view, the electronic assembly line was not as well designed as the paper carton line, but it worked because the operators made it work. It was their system and not one handed down by management.

In other words, *a management system is considered effective* when the people whose job performance is influenced by it:

1. Understand its purpose.
2. Agree with its purpose.
3. Know how to use it.
4. Are in control of it.
5. Can influence its revision.
6. Receive timely feedback from it.

Stated negatively, as a basis for understanding system failure, it may be generalized that *a management system is not effective* when the people whose job performance is influenced by it:

1. Do not understand its purpose.
2. Disagree with its purpose.
3. Do not know how to use it.
4. Feel they are unnecessarily restricted by it.
5. Feel it is hopeless to try to change it.
6. Receive inadequate feedback from it.

In the light of these conditions, consider, for example, the company-managed manpower inventory as an example of an ineffective management system.

A SPECIMEN COMPANY-MANAGED SYSTEM

Manpower inventories are initiated presumably to match employee talent with job opportunity. EDP-based systems are usually used for storage and retrieval of vocational information obtained from personnel records or through a specially designed questionnaire. Cards are keypunched in machine code listing job incumbents' educational achievements, job experience, aspirations, and

other skills or achievements such as foreign language facility, patents, publications, and honors. When the system is installed, job openings are matched against skill and education descriptors, and the records of potential candidates are referred to the hiring supervisor.

Though occasionally useful for locating rare skills, manpower inventories are found in practice to have several fundamental shortcomings. For one, it is futile to try to keep them updated in terms of changing skills, aspirations, and membership in the work force. Second, the sensitivity and accuracy of the system are limited by the translation of personnel data to machine language. Third, qualified candidates are often eliminated by supervisory reluctance to free them for reassignment. Fourth, the system—particularly when managed through characteristic big-company bureaucracy—will seldom give feedback to the members in terms of availability of opportunities, frequency of review, and probability of candidacy. The manpower inventory's impact as a management control system for limiting self-initiated action is perhaps its most harmful characteristic. The system casts employees in conforming, passive, and dependent roles, responding to initiative from management to administer the system and to "find" them when needed. Systems of this type do little to inspire personal initiative in assuming responsibility for effectiveness and growth. Misled by an assumption that paternalistic management has his interests at heart and is looking out for his welfare, he may drift into obsolescence or retirement waiting for management to point the way.

A SPECIMEN USER-MANAGED SYSTEM

Consider for contrast the consequences of a user-managed, or employee-oriented, system. A system is considered as user-managed when it can be actuated by the lowest-level user in the organization. The user actuates the system to satisfy a personal goal, and it is important to him that he knows how to use the system and will incur no risk in doing so. The TI job-posting system is an example of a user-managed staffing system.

The job-posting system came into existence to satisfy the needs of the users who complained about halted careers and opportunities lost to outsiders to whom the recruiting advertisements were directed. Task forces of users, totaling approximately 900 employees from all levels and major functions of the company, participated in the development of the system and in its subsequent revisions.

The TI job-posting system is based on the company philosophy that individuals are responsible for their own development. A philosophy of self-development is a platitude and an excuse for company dereliction if realistic opportunities are not provided to enable members to meet this responsibility. Job posting can be one of the most effective systems for making self-development a realistic expectation.[1]

The system, to support an internal staffing strategy, must give present employees advantages over outsiders. For example, present employees have one-week's opportunity to bid on a job of their choice before outside applicants may be considered. Job requirements are defined in terms of education, skill and experience, job grade, and location. Monthly listings of all job openings are published, distributed, and posted in the company newspaper, and interim openings are posted weekly on bulletin boards.

Any employee can actuate the system by completing a form designating his interest in a posted job, and submitting this job bid to his personnel department. Notification of his supervisor is optional at this point with the bidder.

His bid is screened along with others by personnel and, if not eliminated, is referred to the requesting supervisor who screens, interviews, and selects a candidate (or decides to consider outside applicants). The selected candidate is offered the job by the requesting supervisor and if he accepts it, he notifies his own supervisor that he has accepted the new job. The requesting supervisor initiates the personnel transfer paperwork, and the individual is released to his new job. The releasing supervisor has up to three weeks to post the vacated job and select and train a replacement. In practice, many jobs are filled immediately from a reservoir of qualified bidders on file from previous bids. Hence, several bidders may be released simultaneously for their respective new assignments.

Job posting dramatically converts an employee utilization system into one that assures its success, simply because the user benefits from the use of the system. Individuals in quest of growth, responsibility, and change are far more sensitive and perceptive search mechanisms than the programmed computer which performs the search function for the manpower inventory. More importantly, the individual is now responsible for his own growth opportunities and can initiate self-development actions suggested by job-posting specifications and bidding rejects. Participation in TI's Educational Assistance Program increased approximately 80 percent after the formal job-posting system was installed.

The system synergistically serves the needs of the user and the organization. Talent now finds more complete and positive expression through promotions, transfers, and reassignments. Although increased turnover causes short-term inconvenience, the organization nets long-term gains when high-talent transferees find outlets for their competence inside the organization rather than devoting most of their energy to outside activities or looking for a better job. Job posting also benefits the organization as a system for coping with cutbacks in work force, placing graduates from training programs, upgrading educational assistance participants, and placing persons returning from leave.

Other staffing systems which provide interface with job posting become more user-oriented. Training, for example, is now more often selected by the job incumbent and keyed to his perceptions of opportunity on the work force rather than a management-prescribed program which not always has realistic relationships to job opportunity. Training for training's sake gives way to learning as a means for attaining a personal goal.

Similarly, aptitude testing, long perceived as a mysterious tool of management for selecting and rejecting candidates for jobs and training programs, can become an aid to the individual in helping him understand his strong points and limitations. With the insights offered by aptitude tests, coupled with opportunities identified on posted jobs, he can gauge the scope of his aspirations and remedial learning activities and thus assume greater responsibility for his own self-development.

ROLE OF THE MANAGEMENT-SYSTEM DESIGNER

When people on or off the job encounter difficulty in the pursuit of goals, there is a tendency to blame "the system." For example, problems usually attributed to "the system" are often encountered in making group insurance claims, in changing telephone numbers or in changing a mailing address, in getting a charge-account error corrected, in clearing an expense account, or in getting an accounts receivable balanced Physical aspects of systems are convenient scapegoats at the "customer-complaint desk," and systems' administrators (users) often attribute their own limitations to restrictions imposed by the system. Attempts to remedy a system, of necessity, lead back to the system designer.

The system designer can often defend his applications of software and hardware, and then assert that the system failed only because people misused it. *Within that point of view lies the crux of most management systems problems.*

The system designer is correct in diagnosing systems failures as human failures. But he usually fails to recognize that his responsibility embraces the human factor—that the system designer's role is one of facilitating human processes, and that helpful systems function as extensions of man, not man as an appendage of systems. Furthermore, the system designer often overlooks his responsibility for seeing to it that the system user is adequately trained to administer the system. Systems failures sometimes result from designer permissiveness in allowing the user to divest himself of the responsibility for helping design the system. Because of sheer job pressure, the user sometimes welcomes the staff man's takeover.

Sometimes systems users try to participate in the design of their systems, and the systems designers may appropriately urge them to do so. But the system user frequently encounters the same problem in talking to the systems designer that the foreman sometimes encounters when he tries to talk to the personnel psychologist—in neither case is the staff man's jargon fully understood. The system user may be as confused with the designer's use of terms such as SYSGEN, time-sharing, syntax-directed, bomb-out, and real-time, as the foreman was with the psychologist's use of emotional stability, exophoria, IQ, manic-depressive, and ego-drive. In both cases, it is the staff man's dereliction in failing to adapt his terminology to the boundaries of his customer's language.

A system user can no more divest himself of responsibility for system design than the foreman can delegate the handling of grievances and job instruction to the personnel department. When systems designers and personnel managers permit this type of disengagement, the results almost always are ineffective systems and inept foremen.

QUALIFICATIONS AND SYSTEMS DESIGNERS

Systems designers, recognizing the importance of the users' attitudes to the system's success, have taken the initiative in familiarizing themselves with their users' operations, or have attempted to involve users in developing systems. These cooperative efforts were often discouraged by the job demands of the user or the system designer's jargon. Moreover, it was illustrated in the job-posting system that sensitivity to the human factor—the causes of commitment and alienation—is an essential ingredient for developing and managing effective systems. Thus, it is apparent that systems designers must apply three types of competence in developing workable systems:

1. Technical knowledge of electronic data processing and related technology.

2. Knowledge of the functions or operations to be served by the system, and the proposed system's relation to, and potential impact on, other systems.

3. Sensitivity to the factors evoking human commitment and alienation in the development and administration of management systems.

CONCLUSION

A management system is a process of people interacting to apply resources to achieve goals. Management systems designers tend to place major emphasis on hardware and software (technology), but the primary emphasis must be on the human factor. Computers, machines, buildings, materials, and money lie idle and lifeless in the absence of humans. Hence, all management may be conceived of as the management of human effort. The materiel with which people interact may be organized to facilitate their efforts and to inspire their commitment, or it may be organized in a way that impedes their efforts and evokes their opposition. Hence, it may be generalized that people's attitudes and perceptions are the primary causes of all systems failures, enabling poorly-designed systems to succeed, and causing well-designed systems to fail.

The hardware and software available for facilitating modern management systems have almost unlimited potential, to be exploited or limited by the people who interact with them. People who man the work force also have untapped potential, to be utilized or limited by the systems with which they interact. If synergistic relationships are to exist between people and their systems, human development and systems development must be guided by persons who understand both people and systems, ideally within the same administrative unit.

Thus, formalized and effective management systems cannot be established as the warp and the woof of the organization if systems development is relegated to staff functions. Many organizations try it, just as they try to delegate the planning function to staff groups. Neither will succeed, of course, as planning and control functions are mainstream processes which must be managed by the persons who are to implement them.

REFERENCES

Concepts in this paper, developed through involvement with TI management systems personnel, were strongly influenced by the contributions of A. Graham Sterling and Charles L. Kettler. They are elaborated upon in M. Scott Myers, *Every Employee a Manager*, (McGraw-Hill, 1970).

1. See also Theodore M. Alfred, "Checkers or choice in manpower management," *Harvard Business Review*, (Jan-Feb, 1967), 157-169.

Section B:
Control

Control is the monitoring of plans and the pinpointing of significant deviations from them. Planning and control are opposite sides of the same coin.

In the first selection, Norton Bedford provides background and definitions of control as a general concept and managerial control. According to Bedford, "managerial control is the process of directing a set of persons, equipment, and materials according to an established plan of action toward a specified objective. Essentially, managerial control functions by comparing achieved outcomes with desired outcomes and adjusting operations so that the gap between the two is reduced." Quite obviously, in this definition planning is an essential first step in the process and is followed by control. Further, Bedford recognizes the interrelationships between various aspects of the organization and the control function. For example, he sees motivation as an essential control function (as does Gellerman in the third reading) and organization structure as a "basic instrument of managerial control." Again, integration of managerial and organizational processes is a necessary ingredient for success.

William Sihler discusses "four central and critical factors" of management control systems in an excellent article defining the optimum management control system. The system should be congruent with the goals of the organization. The MBO framework outlined in the previous section directly affects this factor. Also, the control system should be related to the structure of the organization. Additionally, the quantity and quality of the information provided to the manager are crucial in the success of the system. Still, the information must be provided in a timely fashion in order to be of use to the manager. Sihler feels an important function of management planning and control systems is to aid managers in identifying areas where their time can be productively spent and should consume a minimal amount of time in making such identifications. Proper and efficient identification of important areas is an essential aspect of the "management by exception" principle that has become an important part of many modern control systems.

Finally, a reading from Saul Gellerman, "Behavioral Strategies," has been included in this section, although this kind of analysis is usually not associated with control. Gellerman is concerned with two strategies for managing behavior. The first, the cost control approach, focuses on limiting the opportunities for costly behavior (such as absenteeism or featherbedding); the second, the value added approach, does not emphasize restricting or suppressing costly behavior but finding ways of replacing it with more efficient or productive behavior. Under the value added approach, then, cost reduction is largely accomplished by the employees themselves. Gellerman sees several environmental changes that may require the value added approach to be used more often in modern management systems. In essence, Gellerman makes the point that, to be successful in today's world, control systems must take account of the need for self-control as well as for the more formal institutionalized control that is common in most organizations.

Managerial Control

Norton M. Bedford

INTRODUCTION

It seems to be characteristic of man to attempt to control nature and himself so as to adapt the world to his purposes. Through physical science he endeavors to control nature and through social science he seeks to control himself. Although success to date in both areas leaves room for doubt, the development of controls for realizing the benefits of the sciences seems to be the best hope for mankind. Without a means for influencing or controlling the actions or inactions of man and nature, man's fate must rest with the whims of the gods.

Many are the control devices that have been developed over the centuries but increasingly the need for greater control is sensed. In response to this need, there have developed in recent years theoretical and empirical studies of control that have been synthesized in part under the heading of "control theory" and enable rigorous abstract generalized work on the problem. In the context of the foregoing wide scope of the control concept, managerial control represents the application of the concept to the problem of administration. Therefore, to place things in sequential perspective, it seems desirable to seek first an understanding of control concepts and methods and then turn to their application in the area of management.

Definition of Control

In loose terms and restricted to people, control has been defined as the power, the authority, or the influence that one person has to direct the actions of others. In this restricted sense, but in more precise terms, control is any process by which one or more persons direct the behavior of others. Normally, it requires a flow of information and has even been defined as

From Joseph W. McGuire, *Contemporary Management: Issues and Viewpoints,* © 1974, pp. 507–509, 512–514. Reprinted by permission of Prentice-Hall, Inc., Englewood Cliffs, New Jersey.

". . . nothing but the sending of messages which effectively change the behavior of the recipient. . . ."[1]

More broadly, to cover both man and machine, control as a concept may be defined as directing a set of variables toward a preconceived objective. For control to exist there must be something, an activity or a process, to be controlled. But this is not sufficient, for whether the something to be controlled is the actions of a person, a machine, a group of resources, or any process, control cannot be applied unless the way in which the variable components of the process are to be directed has been determined. That is, an objective or goal must be specified for the process, entity, or activity to indicate the way in which it is to be directed. But given a process and specified objectives, a control problem exists.

Control methods involving measurements and information are ways of influencing the variables in the process. If the control methods (also called controls) are capable of influencing the process sufficiently to provide for the achievement of the objective, a controlled structure or system exists. If the control methods are not applied adequately, the system or structure is said to be "out of control."

Normally, there will be a number of ways by which the objective(s) for a process may be attained. The problem of selecting the best way is referred to as the optimal control problem. It requires that some type of performance criterion be established according to which alternative sets of control methods may be ranked. In economic endeavor, cost minimization may be the performance criterion, but conceptually any criterion could be selected.

Control systems, representing different sets of control methods or techniques, may be classified in several ways. They may be deterministic or stochastic depending on the degree of precision with which they control the process. Statistical quality control is a typical stochastic system used in management whereas thermostatic control of building temperature would represent a somewhat deterministic control system. The control systems may be closed (feedback) or open (nonfeedback) depending on the degree to which they are sensitive to the output results. A control system that locks and unlocks a bank vault at specified hours but is insensitive to the varying times that employees need to have access to the vault, so that human interference is needed to adjust the opening and closing times, is an open-loop control system. That is, the control exists independent of the desired opening and closing times. The thermostat that automatically adjusts to changes in the external temperature is the typically cited closed-loop system. Thus an open-loop exists when one or more parts of the operating system are not part of the control system. A closed-loop would exist when all the controls are part of the operating system. A managerial control system might be considered to be of the open-loop variety if policy objectives were subject to change, but closed-loop if policy objectives were not subject to change and the organizational unit operated independent of any non-routine managerial action. Other classifications of control systems are those that distinguish between continuous or discrete signaling with respect to time, be-

[1]Norbert Weiner, *The Human Use of Human Beings* (Boston: Houghton Mifflin Co., 1950), p. 124.

tween process control systems and organizational control systems, and various other distinctions.

In the general sense that control is itself a process that ensures that what "ought" to be done is done, a sense of "oughtness" underlies the control concept. But since "what ought to be done" depends on the situation—the situation ethics notion—control methods may be loose or rigorous, may permit unrestricted objectives to be set or require that objectives be based on human values, and may cover large systems or subsystems.

In the engineering area, the control concept has been defined rather rigorously. Being concerned with feedback control systems, the American Institute of Electrical Engineers defined a feedback control system as a "control which tends to maintain a prescribed relationship of one system variable to another by comparing functions of these variables and using the differences as a means of control."[2] As these control methods, techniques, and principles have been applied to areas outside engineering production processes and machine operations, some of the rigor has been carried forward to systems designed to control social institutions. Evidence of this exists in the use of logical and mathematical tools in dealing with social issues and with the elaborate computer-based information systems now abounding. Included in these tools are linear programming, integer programming, inventory control theory, dynamic programming, statistical measures, and a host of others normally grouped under the heading of management science.

• • •

Relation of Control to Management

Managerial control is the process of directing a set of persons, equipment, and materials according to an established plan of action toward a specified objective. Essentially, managerial control functions by comparing achieved outcomes with desired outcomes and adjusting operations so that the gap between the two is reduced. A part of managerial control involves determining the desired outcomes. To function, managerial control must have a controller (an administrator) who responds to information provided by a feedback procedure. Thus, managerial control includes two functions: The first is motivational in that the system endeavors to prevent variation from desired actions by motivating people to take such actions as to preclude any variation. The second is corrective in that the system seeks to re-establish desired actions if a variation has occurred. The more rapidly corrective feedback information enables the re-establishment of appropriate action, the more the two functions fuse into one. Thus, managerial control encompasses the cycle beginning with an objective on the part of a manager or other person in the organization (X), followed by an effort to influence another person or group (Y) to so act that the objective of X is attained. X may use various means to influence Y, ranging from assigned or assumed authority to logical reasoning to emotional appeal. But whenever X by any means influences Y's actions, X is said to have exercised managerial control.

[2] A.I.E.E. Committee Report, "Proposed Symbols and Terms for Feedback Control Systems," *Electrical Engineering* (1951), p. 909.

The degree of managerial control exercised is the probability that Y will do that which X requests, assuming Y would not otherwise have so acted.

The basic instrument of managerial control is an organizational structure. Fundamentally, every organization is a control system that can be represented by the feedback (closed loop) control schema. Each part of every organization can be similarly depicted. Roberts suggests the following diagrammatic view of the organization or any of its parts as a control system.[7]

In this scheme of things, control is a feedback process involving the reiterative performance of the following steps:

1. A decision or policy for action is made in accordance with some decision model that aims to satisfy desired objectives.
2. Subject to various external and internal disturbances, actions are taken to comply with the decision. This action results in some type of accomplishment.

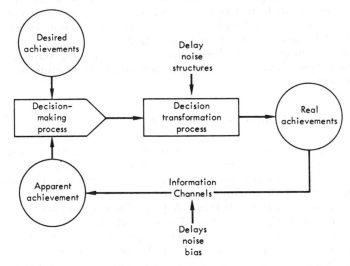

FIGURE 43. Diagrammatic View of the Organization as a Control System

3. The accomplishment success, as perceived by a sensor (observer), and subject to various noise interferences, is reported back to the decision-making apparatus. Typically, the perception is symbolized in terms of measurement and by classification arranged into an effective communication medium for transmission to the decision-making vehicle.
4. The feedback communication, as perceived by the decision maker, is used to evaluate success of past plans and actions.
5. The evaluated comparison and other data are inserted into the decision model and used to develop plans and policies to attain goals.

[7]E. B. Roberts, "Industrial Dynamics and the Design of Management Control Systems," in C. P. Bonini, R. K. Jaedicke, and H. M. Wagner (Eds.), *Management Controls* (New York: McGraw-Hill Book Co., Inc., 1964), p. 103.

The foregoing view of the organization as a control system is very similar to engineering control systems, but the distinction between the two needs to be maintained for a time at least. The engineering conception of control, when it is applied in the human area, assumes the prevalance of a rationalistic human behavior norm in the organization that may not be valid. In an organization in which people are directed, one might expect a change in the way leaders exercise control, from the command viewpoint implied by engineering control to a discussion and persuasion viewpoint to motivate individuals. This human feature of control, wherein the effort is to gain willing cooperation, may, of course, ultimately be included in the engineering conception through worker participation in setting goals and objectives. In any event, the emergence of the human aspects of the control process suggest the opportunity for expanding new kinds of controls to supplement those used in the past. A broadening of the control process seems underway.

Upon analysis, the notion that control is "the directing of a set of variables toward a preconceived objective" implies that managerial control is not so much a method of directing as it is a power to direct and motivate variables toward a preconceived objective. In this larger sense, control is not only an efficiency concept directed to determining the technically optimal movement of a set of variables but also is the power to cause the variables to take action. In the sense of power to direct variables, the notion of an amount of control exists that may be quantified in terms of the number and size of variables to be directed. Thus, the amount of control in an organization could be increased by increasing the activities of an organization. Assuming a management motivation toward more and more power, the tendency will ever be for organizations to expand the control element in the organization. The amount of control may be increased by expanding the number of economic resources of the organization or by directing the organization to other activities in society, such as education, crime prevention, pollution control, and other activities. Inevitably, the desire for control will expand the objectives of business entities, move business into social responsibilities, increase the role of business in society, and thus increase the amount of control in the business entity. This effort to increase the total amount of control of the entity will mobilize all management personnel toward a common objective and thus mitigate the competitive struggle among themselves for a greater portion of the total power of the entity. Each management person can increase his power of control by maintaining his fixed proportion of the control in the entity as the amount of control in the entity increases.

Internally, the amount of control in an organization would be increased by improving the efficiency with which human and other resources are directed toward objectives of the organization. Since this view of control as efficiency methods spans both motivational (before the fact) control and corrective (after the fact) control, management control is a broader notion than engineering control, in which emphasis is on corrective control using the theory of feedback information.

Given a set of objectives and a set of means, the amount of internal control would be measured by the smallness of variations from the most efficient pursuit of the objective. It might also be measured as the negative of the amount of entropy (disorder) in the organization. If entropy is conceived as random action, entropy might be measured as the variation between random action in the organization and the actual actions of the organization. A reduction in entropy would reflect an increase in control. In this context statistical control measures, which are based on the assumption that a certain degree of randomness is to be expected in all actions, are devices for eliminating gross entropy elements only. The ultimate pursuit of control is to eliminate all randomness, and as progress is made in reducing the cost of information and the cost of corrective action, more deterministic and less statistical control methods may be expected.

WILLIAM H. SIHLER

Toward Better Management Control Systems

Four central and critical factors should be considered in building, using, and evaluating a management control system:

- Is the system related to and does it reinforce the objectives of the organization? Is there congruence between the system and the goals; or, is there disharmony and friction?
- Is the system well related to the organizational structure? Does information flow in a way which is acceptable to those who generate and use the data? Is coordination and consolidation of information effective and easy?
- Does the manager receive the information he requires to do his job? Does he get too little information? Too much information? Does it tell him something useful about the activities over which he has control and which he can influence? Does it threaten him with punishment on account of activities for which he has neither responsibility nor authority?
- Is the information provided in time to be of use to the manager?

Each of these points is amplified in the pages that follow.

It is not likely that a control system will be perfect along each parameter, but a serious defect in any one of these four critical areas is sufficient to damage a system that may be well-planned in the other three. For example, enthusiastic and cooperative managers quickly lose interest in a system that does not meet their needs or the needs of others as they see these needs.

The adage is also worth emphasizing that a system is no better than the managers who operate it. No system, however well planned and appropriate, can survive uninformed or intentional

misuse, can thrive if it is ignored, or can overcome misapplication by those not trained in its use. An internal combustion engine, no matter how well designed and carefully manufactured, can quickly be immobilized by a few grains of sugar.

The following discussion tends to focus on the design and implementation of an information system for planning and control. The same principles are relevant to the modification of an existing system and, most importantly, to using an imperfect system. A manager himself may not be able to secure modification of a control system to suit his convenience. If he is aware of the basic elements of system design, however, he can often modify the data he receives or interpret them in ways that make his managerial task easier. The topics presented are therefore relevant to the front-line manager as well as to the staff specialist in information systems.

OBJECTIVES

In a full-employment society, where resources are by definition scarce in the sense that it is not possible to have more of one item without sacrificing another, a common criterion for measuring a system's value is whether it helps allocate resources efficiently. This criterion can be applied in two ways. First, for a given level of physical output, is the cost (resources consumed to produce the output) as small as possible? For programs where the output is not measurable in physical terms such as pounds, feet, or dollars, it is possible but difficult to substitute a subjective measure of "psychic-emotional" benefit.

Second—the converse of the first criterion—for a given level of cost, is the output as high as possible? Given the time spent generating information, is the most relevant and necessary information being provided? Taken together, these are known as the maximum-output, minimum-cost criteria.

Before the managerial planning and control system can be made to support the organization's specific objectives, it is important that the *substantive objectives* themselves are worked out with some degree of clarity and that they are internally consistent. For example, if an organization's major objective is to minimize reporting errors, the control system will be designed differently than if the objective is to serve the customer in the shortest possible time. In the former circumstance, a report might be double checked in several ways by different men before the transaction is reported. In the latter situation, the system will be designed to keep errors in reporting to a minimum within the constraint of the desired speed of service. As many banks have found, it is necessary to tolerate a painful error level in order to avoid the more painful loss of business to a more responsive competitor. (The contrast between the possible objectives and related systems in the banking industry is particularly striking to those who have dealt with European banks.)

Similarly, there should be a high degree of harmony between short- and long-term objectives. One company found that top management's commitment to a compound long-term growth of 15 percent a year was being achieved at a higher cost than necessary as a result of its short-term policy of rewarding plant managers for minimizing excess capacity in plant operations. Although the growth plans were widely known, plant managers attempted to expand piecemeal, buying the smallest possible piece of equipment to do the job. This conflict in *temporal objectives* resulted in the longer-range managerial planning being subverted by the short-range control systems.

When the objectives of a corporation are reasonably coherent and consistent, it is feasible to develop a control system that will reinforce the objectives by measuring the level of accomplishment and its cost.

It is still necessary to be sure that the control system itself is efficient and measures up to the minimum-cost maximum-output criteria. A control system can develop unmoderated growth, expanding apparently for its own sake alone. In an age when computers can consume in an hour paper costing twice or three times as much as the computer's capital cost per hour, the temptation to report everything to everyone must be avoided. If the purpose of a system is the specific control of a detailed subsection of an operation, it should provide detailed operating information to that subsection's management. The same information usually need not be provided to the senior management level. Similarly, it is not necessary that all shift foremen be provided with monthly consolidated profit and loss statements. They are interesting, and such results may eventually have some impact on the particular shift, but this information is not likely to be of much immediate use to a man with responsibility for first-line management. In other words, the differences in the requirements for specific operating control and general overall evaluation and appraisal must be kept in mind when developing a control system.

ORGANIZATION

The relationships between organizational structure and systems for planning and control are rich and complex. The subject greatly exceeds the space that can be devoted to it here. As a result, just a few of the most significant aspects will be mentioned briefly.

Basic Philosophy—A control system usually reflects the basic attitude toward human nature of those who designed it. In many cases, this attitude has become ingrained in the organization, and the control system then reflects this "organizational consciousness." For instance, one "theory" holds that the individual is basically untrustworthy, must be strictly regulated, and is incapable of taking intelligent initiative. The control systems developed under the influence of this approach tend to be overwhelming in their control of the individual. Action in all possible circumstances is prescribed in advance in minute detail. Massive reports are collected to show just what is done minute-by-minute. In part these systems protect the individual who can demonstrate that his actions at all points were in accord with the regulations.

Other theories tend to emphasize the positive aspects of human behavior. They assume that management and employees are basically motivated toward the good of the organization and that the role of a control system should be to provide information necessary to permit the management to control the operations—not for the operations to control the management. Much less information is passed upward through the administrative structure. Although uniform practices may provide for common occurrences and for those areas in which operational uniformity is critical, the basic purpose of the system is to get information necessary for problem-solving to those with the intelligence and skills to solve the problem in the specific circumstances that may arise.

For example, the two different approaches would result in greatly different designs for an information and management control system in a job-order machine shop. The first approach mentioned, the one emphasizing total organization, might develop a scheduling system that concentrated in the production control department all information on machines, skills, manpower, jobs in process, and backlog. From that department, which might utilize high-speed computational equipment to do the scheduling, would come orders assigning men and machines to jobs and specifying all the details of sequence and working time. Reports would be kept to determine whether the schedules had been met. The foreman's job would be one of insuring that the instructions were followed, reporting results and explaining variances, and checking the standard procedures of the control center if the instructions could not be followed.

An alternative approach could be developed on the assumption that the foremen could do the best job of matching the machine capacity and human skills. A system would be designed which generated information needed by the foreman to manage his subdepartment. Foremen might be provided a current listing of jobs coming into the department including the operations required, the expected time of arrival in the subdepartment, and the maximum completion date feasible. The system could also permit the location and expeditious treatment of jobs whose status had suddenly increased. The emphasis throughout would be on providing information to permit management decision, such as assignment of work to specific men or machines, to be made as close to the point of action as possible.

Organizational Structure—Additional major organizational factors which have a bearing on the nature of a control system are the departmental and shift structure and the line-staff arrangements. To be useful, the control system must be designed so that required information both precedes and follows the flow of work through the organization. This permits anticipatory action and post-action appraisal and evaluation.

It is not necessary that all employees and all management know everything. It is essential, however, that a man has the information he needs to make decisions. Similarly, it is important that the information necessary for evaluation be properly organized so that praise is given where deserved and corrective action taken where required.   In the following section, various aspects of these generalities are discussed specifically.

Information Flow—Regarding the flow of information, for example, identification of the causes of defects is critical in maintaining product quality. Rather than have the defects and rejects analyzed by staff quality-control men, some companies have taken a more direct approach. All department heads meet together to review the previous period's defective or problem production. At one iron foundry, senior management from production and production-related staff sections (such as metallurgy) start their day with a conference at the scrap heap. The various rejects are examined, the causes for the defect are jointly determined, and responsibility for correcting the defect is assigned. The face-to-face resolution of the defect issue, usually one of the most acrimonious issues in an organization, eliminates much of the paperwork normally involved in settling this question. It also eliminates a major cause of friction in an operation, friction which can unnecessarily absorb large quantities of management's energy while creating great amounts of ill-feeling between departments and between line and staff management.

An example of information not being provided to the proper sources can be seen in a situation which existed in a ship-repair yard. One set of managers had the responsibility for bidding on jobs, and the bids often had to be made in circumstances that prevented extensive consultation with the yard foremen who would do the work. Further, the items bid on often turned out to be only a portion of the work required. A full assessment could only be made once the ship was in dry dock and the engines had been taken apart. Further work was then negotiated between the contract executives and the ship-owners.

Once work had begun, little effort was made to keep track of shop costs on a current basis so that the foremen would have an idea of the costs incurred on a job. Costs were often not even available upon completion of the job when the final negotiation of price took place. It was frequently long after payment had been received that the yard's management learned whether the job had made a contribution to overhead and profit.

A period of profit difficulty inspired the shipyard's president to put more emphasis on cost control. He discovered that more effective information was essential to achieving his objectives. He therefore began to introduce organizational and system changes designed to make it possible for the contract managers to assume overall responsibility for a given job, including negotiation of the price and control of costs. In addition, shop foremen were also to be given information on current job cost more rapidly—perhaps twice weekly. In any event, it was considered essential to have the costs by the time the final price negotiation was undertaken a few days after the job was completed.

Information and Rewards—The impact of the information system and the reward structure on behavior is a familiar subject. Where the reward system conflicts with the corporate goals, the reward system usually has the stronger impact on the actions of managers and employees.

This reaction is reasonable. Corporate goals are rather vague objectives that should find concrete reinforcement in the reward system. Further, the reward system is the source of the dollars-and-cents in the pay envelope, of the promotion, and of other status privileges such as reserved parking spots.

Thus, where the information system and the reward system are in conflict, serious distortions of action are likely to occur. For example, one company's regulations provided that no shift could take any credit for a job not completed by the end of that shift. Work reports were collected thirty minutes before the end of the shift. No doubt these arrangements made sense in departments where the jobs were small, where one transistor more or less did not amount to a great deal. It was probably also thought that the rule would eliminate the difficult task of allocating credit for partly completed jobs.

On the other hand, in departments where jobs were large and frequently required more than one shift to complete, the distortion was substantial and detrimental. Shift foremen hid work that had been partly completed so they could finish it on their shift the next day and obtain some credit for the time and costs charged to them. Also, very little work was done in the last half hour of each shift. Indeed, after the last task was done that could be fully completed

before the reports were collected, little was accomplished on the shift. Great distrust was created between shifts, reducing cooperation where cooperation is always difficult to develop.

Another serious type of distortion in the information system can be created, for instance, by a manager who insists that his subordinates meet an unrealistic level of performance. When he backs his demands with threats of major punishment, his men are apt to supplement their ability to produce with "creative" reporting in order to show the required results. Creative reporting can take a variety of forms, from outright fraudulent action to generous estimates of key variables where there is reasonable room for uncertainty.

Creative reporting can create many serious problems. One of the most serious is that it undermines the reliability and effectiveness of the information system by making it a less accurate reflection of reality. A variety of internal audits may help eliminate or reduce the creativity; but, by the time the corrections are made, it may be too late to make effective changes in the operations or to maintain confidence in the general information system.

Status Incongruence

The growth of elaborate information systems has tended to increase the problem of status incongruence—situations in which men of lower status are required to tell executives of higher status what to do. Because of the technical requirements of automated data systems, specialists are required to design, implement, and maintain them. These men may be respected by the organization for their technical skill, but they often are considered to have less status than line operating executives who appear to be inferior in terms of pay and education. There is a danger, therefore, that the ideas of the staff, however valid, may not be well received by the line. The problem is compounded if various analytic, diagnostic, and corrective functions are assigned to these technical departments. When lower status groups not only have responsibility for maintaining the system itself but for analyzing operations and for initiating corrective action or innovation, their suggestions are likely at least to be subverted and perhaps rejected outright by operating managers, to the confusion and consternation of the staff.

It is difficult to lay down general rules for more effective staff-line relationships. The information systems aspect is but a recent development in a history of conflicts between line managers and staff specialists of all sorts, including industrial engineers, controllers, personnel specialists, and others who arrive from central office staff positions claiming to know how to reorganize work and improve efficiency. In the information area, one technique which has often been effective is to pair a technical specialist with an executive from the field, giving them joint responsibility for such tasks as working out a new system and for trouble-shooting when difficulties arise with an existing system.

Wherever possible, appropriate status relationships and information processing should be in harmony with information flowing from lower to higher management while action is initiated in reverse. Yet it is important that innovations and suggestions are not stifled in the junior ranks. A positive response to suggestions is obviously an effective attitude for senior management to have.

Control of Data
The problem of data control is linked to most of the organizational factors that have been discussed. The trend toward electronic data processing has had the tendency to concentrate the collection of data in a few data centers, taking away traditional local control of this function. Whereas local management formerly had some control over what information was generated when and could develop special analyses if necessary from the data at hand, now these functions are performed elsewhere according to schedules that may not be the most convenient or effective for local management. Furthermore, local management has lost control over the nature of information it receives. It is now given data, perhaps by departments of lower status, without being directly involved in the analysis of the data or even its processing.

The control of information thus becomes involved in interdepartmental conflict, status problems, and assumptions about human nature. Interdepartmental rivalry can be particularly serious if one department controls and harbors information that another department must have. For example, if the production scheduling department does not provide sufficiently early warning about impending changes, the production departments themselves may not have sufficient flexibility and time to adjust without waste of resources.

Careful thought must be given, in planning and using control and information systems, to insure that the right information gets to the right place

in the organization. It is possible that blocks in the information flow are unintentional—one department may not be aware of another department's needs. The question of what is the "right" information is discussed below.

Excess Information
The preceding comments have suggested some of the dangers of too little information. Although this is perhaps the more common problem, it is also true that too much information can be equally inefficient. Many efforts at "scientific management" have foundered because managers have been unable to make sense of the mass of information that was provided, often in relatively undigested form and in bulky computer printout format. After struggling with the material for a while, field managers conclude that the benefits are not worth the effort. They ignore the elaborate documents and instead concentrate on those few items that are most useful. Their reaction may be one of disillusionment with all data processing.

This reaction is unfortunate and unnecessary. A careful analysis of an executive's needs should also indicate what he does not need. There is a positive benefit in not providing him with relatively useless data, although such data may be kept for background and backup information in the event a special analysis is required.

CRITICAL VARIABLES

An efficient information system generates data relevant to the manager who uses the reports. An important first step in the development of an information system, therefore, is the identification of these critical variables.

The specific nature of the variables changes for different operations. They may be recorded in dollars, hours, weights, in ratio form (such as a productivity measure of units per hour or per dollar), or in any of many other ways. The two common characteristics, however, of all relevant control data are:

1. The data must report on a portion of the operation over which management has some actual control, a portion which management can change or influence.

2. The data must relate to the more-significant rather than to the less-significant aspects of the operation.

Although the reasons may be self-evident why these are the two significant common characteristics for effective control and planning systems, it is worthwhile emphasizing a few of the more important factors. First, considering that the manager should be neither over- nor under-informed, it is essential that the information he receives is relevant. This condition requires that the information is focused on what the manager can manage himself, on what he can control. If the labor force is fixed in size and pay, as in many service organizations, the local manager may want information about productivity, about whether he is using his labor force to produce the maximum revenue or accomplish the most work. His superiors, who have responsibility for overall planning, may find total dollars useful in their jobs. Total dollar cost figures might be relatively useless to the local executive, however.

For reasons of relevance, it is often advisable to avoid cluttering reports for operating managers with a myriad of complex accruals and allocations for costs over which they have no control. A plant manager, who has no direct influence whatever over research expenditures, is not aided if his operating budget and reports carry an allocation for corporate research and development. It is confusing enough when these allocations are separately identified on the budget and control reports. It is particularly confusing when they are integrated into standard costs and cannot be separated or segregated when detailed operations analyses are made.

The second point mentioned relates to the importance of concentrating on the significant rather than on the insignificant aspects within the functions over which the manager has control. In the case of a service industry, the most important measures would be those giving an index of productivity. In the space program, quality control might be the most important factor, the one measured first and in several ways. In other situations, the important variable might be production volume, speed, product mix, or almost any combination of these and other elements. But, whatever the critical variables, the information system should generate data of use in their evaluation and management.

The nature of the information required at each level of management may well differ in most cases. The president of a company may be most concerned with the monthly income statements and ultimately with the financial reports for the entire year. Given his responsibility for overall administration and the need to explain the company's policies and prospects to share-holders and public, these aggregate results are necessary for him to exercise his duties. The same reports may be worthless to the manager of one of the company's plants or to a salesman. Likewise, the reports of value to first- or second-line management may not be of use to senior management. A well-designed system allows for these differences in needs, focusing on the relevant variables for each level of administration.

TIMELINESS

From the manager's point of view, the most relevant information on the most critical variables is worth nothing unless it arrives in time for him to take action based on the information it contains. Trends must be discovered in time for corrective action to be taken or, depending on the circumstances, in time for the managers to capitalize on favorable opportunities. It is easy to see the consternation that sets in among stock market traders when the reports of transactions on the security exchanges begin to run late. A few minutes delay can make the difference between affluence and insolvency. Other examples may be less spectacular. For the shipyard cited earlier, the failure to have cost information available at the time final price negotiations were taking place made it very difficult to know where to resist the pressure to make price concessions. In the same company, financial reports were prepared only once a quarter and were not available until four to six weeks after the quarter ended. In these circumstances, management was in the position of a pilot flying in the clouds under instrument control but whose instruments did not work until he had landed.

In many firms, reports for a month are ready by the middle of the following month. Moreover, it is often possible to obtain reports on critical variables weekly or daily or even more often, as is done in the case of electric generating stations in times of peak demand. Occasionally some educated guesses are required for some entries in order to produce reports promptly, but this action may be preferable to delaying until all information can be collected. For example, the Chesapeake and Ohio Railroad releases a preliminary financial report each January 1 for the previous year and has it in the mail that day.

The temptation, given the need for prompt information, is to push for faster and faster reporting. The controller of a large international oil company recently said that when he came with the company thirty years ago, consolidated financial statements were prepared once a year. During the next twenty years, schedules were advanced to permit consolidated reporting on a quarterly basis. The last ten years have seen the development of monthly reporting, and he looks forward to weekly and even daily reporting within the next ten. Given the need to plan transportation and to balance the various sources of production with the demands of the world-wide marketplace, he could use daily information to good advantage.

Faster reporting does have its costs. In the C&O instance cited, it is primarily the preliminary work and the cost of having the financial and accounting staff show up on New Year's Eve. In other cases, faster reporting can be much more expensive, involving massive redesigning of systems, major investments in data processing equipment, and costs of training and supporting the skilled manpower to run the system. It is therefore essential to ask at each step whether the increase in reporting speed is worth the cost of obtaining that speed. The appraisal of the tradeoffs may be (of necessity) intuitive, one in which the figures and facts are not precise, but it is an evaluation worth making.

The same questions need to be asked, the same tradeoffs need to be made, when any change is contemplated in a management information system. Questions should be asked from time to time about existing systems as well. Changes in business practice, in environmental circumstances, in staffing, and in other relevant factors, may change the nature of information needed by an effective manager. As new systems are put in, old systems providing unnecessary information may be phased out. Some companies, such as the large English store chain of Marks & Spencer, have even gone so far as to eliminate almost all central record keeping. The argument they advance is that the cost of maintaining much of the information is far greater than the benefits derived from knowing what it is.

SUMMARY

Time, not dollars, is often the scarcest resource. This is particularly true of skilled managerial time, a scarce commodity indeed. It is essential that managerial time be spent where it can be most productive. One important function of a good management planning and control system is to help managers identify the areas in which their time can be most productively spent. The system should also consume the minimum amount of managerial time in making such an identification. These characteristics have led to emphasis on the development of systems that meet the criteria discussed in this note and to the resulting technique known as "management by exception." Managers concentrate on those areas that are in difficulty and capitalize on those areas that are going unusually well. The information system should assist in bringing these areas to management's attention and should not obscure them amongst massive quantities of useless data.

The key elements required to permit management by exception are:

1/The provision of information on critical and manageable variables;

2/The dissemination of this information to those who can take actions based on it;

3/The generation of the data in time for it to be of use.

Proper organization of the information system, its harmonious support of the corporate goals, and its congruence with the structure of the organization all contribute to its effectiveness.

It is unrealistic to expect perfection in all aspects. Once a satisfactory system is operating, however, it is useful to identify areas of conflict, areas that tend to interfere with the functioning of the system, so that remedial action can be taken should the conflict be sufficiently severe. Otherwise, it may be most efficient to avoid tinkering with the system and to accept the fact that few things are perfect this side of heaven.

William W. Sihler *is Associate Professor of Business Administration at the University of Virginia. His current interests are in the area of corporate financial management especially capital structure and corporate planning. He has broad experience in management education and consulting.*

SAUL GELLERMAN

Behavioral Strategies

WE ARE CONCERNED HERE with behavior—with what people actually do at work, and the ways in which they do it—as a factor in productivity.

Behavior has been regarded traditionally as a contributor to costs, either as overhead or through behavior-related costs, such as errors, scrappage, and delays. Elaborate strategies have been contrived to control these costs, usually by various restrictions upon behavior (rules, reports, standards, etc.).

To the extent that most organizations have a conscious strategy for managing behavior at all, it is likely to be some variant of this "cost-control" approach. Let it be clearly understood that the term "cost-control" is not used here in its conventional sense of limiting unproductive expenditures, but only to describe methods of **restricting behavior.** An alternative strategy for behavior management is emerging from the behavioral sciences: Instead of merely restricting costly behavior, it seeks to **encourage actions which add to productivity and efficiency.** We can therefore refer to it as a **value-adding** behavioral strategy.

Actually, behavior can add both cost and value to the product or service it affects. Some common forms of costly behavior are inattentiveness, absenteeism, conspiracy to restrict production, featherbedding, and certain forms of turnover and militant unionism. Behavior that can add value includes ingenuity, adaptability, skill acquisition, coopera-

tion, voluntary effort beyond minimum requirements, and loyalty under stressful conditions.

An effective strategy for encouraging behavior that adds value must recognize that any human action (regardless of whether its consequences are costly or valuable) is an extraordinarily subtle phenomenon, with complex determinants which are neither fully understood nor fully controllable. Therefore, an effective value-adding strategy can hardly be a simple set of infinitely repeatable procedures. But it can seek to match at least some of the subtlety it aims to manage with a subtle mixture of its own—a mixture of behavioral research and hardheaded managerial realism. Thus, the purpose of a value-adding strategy in behavior management is to put behavioral research to work as a practical management tool.

The cost-control and value-adding strategies are not mutually exclusive. However, it does appear that cost-control as a strategy for managing behavior has already contributed about all that it can. Further gains in human productivity are more likely to result from a wider application of the value-adding approach, possibly including some replacement of cost-control methods.

Value-adding is hardly a panacea, even if it offers some clear advantages over an exclusive reliance upon cost-control, namely, that it is a constructive alternative to the blind alley represented by attempts to extend the cost-control approach; and, more importantly, that it is based on a growing body of knowledge. In time, therefore, the effectiveness with which this knowledge can be applied will probably increase.

Yet the value-adding strategy is neither easy to implement nor spectacular in its effects, even when it is successfully implemented. All that can be said for it is that it offers a promising avenue to improved productivity, but not many of the other options now open to management can claim even that much. The attraction of a value-adding strategy for behavior management is not so much in the magnitude of its promise as in the access it provides to a relatively untapped source of added productivity.

To capitalize upon untapped human potentialities, managers must master some difficult arts. For example, they must anticipate the consequences to other people's behavior of changes in their own behavior. (This includes managerial methods as well as the personal conduct of managers.) Another requirement of an effective value-adding strategy is that managers distinguish between motivating influences which, regardless of their potential power, are not really susceptible to effective control and motivating influences whose potential power may be less impressive but which can be controlled.

The logic inherent in attempting to capitalize upon the potentialities in behavior, instead of trying only to minimize its costs, leads to a somewhat disconcerting conclusion. This is that a value-adding approach to behavior management requires management itself to change its *raison d'être*. In pursuing this particular avenue to productivity gains, management actually encounters the necessity to revolutionize itself.

Controlling Costs and Adding Values

The cost-control approach to behavior assumes that costly behavior is more significant in its impact than value-adding behavior. Its essential strategy is to limit the opportunities for costly behavior to occur. Some of its more common tactics are stress on personnel selection; designing jobs that are easily learned and require little effort or judgment; measurement and control systems designed to pinpoint deviations from prescribed rules; pressure on managers to operate within budgets that circumscribe their choice of tactics; protracted bargaining; and a willingness to accept costly strikes to avoid presumably costlier settlements.

A corollary to the cost-control approach is a strategy for cost reduction and productivity gains. The underlying assumption is that costly behavior is inevitable. Therefore, to cut costs below the "normal" levels that are achieved by control systems, it is necessary to restrict the availability of assets that can be wasted. Whatever cost reduction is achieved is therefore accomplished largely within the controller's department. Productivity gains are sought primarily from nonbehavioral sources. These include new technologies which reduce manpower requirements and therefore achieve the ultimate in controlling both costly and value-adding behavior—by eliminating them.

The value-adding approach assumes that, under certain conditions, costly behavior can be minimized without the necessity of imposing controls, largely because it is replaced by value-adding behavior. It follows that the essential problem of management is not so much to restrict or suppress costly behavior as to find ways of replacing it. Therefore, the strategy of this approach is to increase opportunities for value-adding behavior to occur. Some of its more common tactics are participative management styles, job enrichment, chains of two-way communication "loops," and programs for employee advancement and development.

These tactics do not lead unfailingly to value-adding behavior, especially when they represent a recent conversion from the cost-control approach. Implementing them effectively requires skills and attitudes which most managers must acquire through experience. In the process of acquiring that experience, some skepticism, clumsiness, and false starts are inevitable. There are undoubtedly many situations (chiefly involving alienated or less-educated groups, or people who find adaptation to any new habits difficult) in which the cost-control approach is more appropriate.

The same line and staff groups are involved in the value-adding approach as in the cost-control approach, but their preoccupations tend to be different. The personnel department's emphasis shifts from administration to research, training, and organization development. The industrial relations department's emphasis shifts from bargaining to serving as a two-way communications channel between negotiations. The line managers' emphasis shifts from policing to planning, expediting, and coaching.

The strategy for cost reduction under the value-adding approach is not to limit resources that might be wasted, but rather to limit wasteful behavior itself. The focus is on eliminating the underlying reasons for slowdowns, carelessness, turnover, etcetera. To increase productivity, the value-adding approach seeks to create conditions which enhance feelings of personal responsibility and pride in accomplishments. Cost reduction is largely accomplished by the employees themselves, as are productivity gains. The staff is freed to concentrate on what the employees should do, instead of being preoccupied with how they do it. The value-adding approach does not dispense with financial control or engineering improvements; instead it removes the financial control or engineering staff from the supervisory support business and places them in the planning and analysis business, where the impact of such improvements is maximized, thus enhancing productivity.

An obsolescing assumption. The notion that behavior contributes primarily to cost rather than to value is not without factual support. Left to their own devices, men will vary widely in the wisdom, energy, and goodwill with which they approach their work. The introduction of assembly line technology early in this century was not based on mere assumption, but on observation: the average working man was not particularly efficient even when he wanted to be, and frequently he didn't even want to be. As products and processes became more complex, the need to prescribe and control behavior was increasingly taken for granted.

It was not only that processes were difficult; people were difficult, too. The goldbrick, the shop lawyer, the malcontent, and the petty pilferer were all real enough. They still are. So was (and is) the tendency of management and labor to look upon each

other as adversaries; so is the gifted employee who departs after acquiring valuable experience and training; and so is the mediocre employee who wouldn't think of leaving but is loudly critical of management.

In brief, people are often viewed quite justifiably as troublesome necessities, and for this reason enormous efforts have gone into making them both less troublesome and less necessary. Thus the principal *raison d'être* for many first-line supervisors is to see to it that employees behave in prescribed ways or at least that they do not behave in proscribed ways. The bulk of their supervisory training may be devoted to arming them for the conflicts that almost inevitably result.

The difficulty with the assumption that most people, left to their own devices, are more likely to create costs than to create value is that history is in the process of invalidating it. Processes have begun during our own lifetimes which are radically changing perceptions and attitudes about work and the institutions in which it is done. Since attitudes and perceptions have a lot to do with determining behavior, it is not surprising that the behavior of people at work is changing, too. Paradoxically, it appears that a good deal of the newer forms of costly behavior are at least indirect results of the failure of management to provide effective channels for value-adding behavior.

The engine that is producing these changes is the sheer availability of ideas. All of the major sources of ideas—education, communications media, and direct contacts between people—have undergone explosive expansion.

Only a little more than a generation ago, a high school graduate was considered an educated man. Currently, about sixty percent of United States high school graduates enter some form of advanced education, and about half of those will proceed at least as far as a bachelor's degree. Advanced education is rapidly becoming the norm, not the exception.

Communications media bring events from halfway around the world flooding instantaneously to our attention. By contrast, during the formative years of the men now in the upper echelons of management, events that occurred outside a circle of a few hundred miles were seldom remarked and rarely affected men's actions.

As for personal contacts, as many as twenty percent of American households may change their address in a given year. Thus the sheer range and variety of contacts with hitherto unfamiliar people (and potentially, at least, with new ideas) to which most Americans are exposed is enormous.

Each year delivers to the labor force young men and women to whom the depression of the 1930's and World War II—the great chastening experiences of the generations which currently command American industry—are only history. The formative years of these young people have been spent in an era of prosperity, nuclear stalemate, the social insurrection, the like of all of which the world has never seen.

Thus the variety and newness of the ideas available to shape the attitudes of working people of all kinds is more than sufficient to invalidate many hitherto unquestioned assumptions about the sources and potentialities of their behavior.

It does not necessarily follow that the cost-creating potentiality of behavior has been lessened or that its value-adding potentiality has increased. Indeed the evidence to date offers scant support for such an optimistic conclusion. It is easy enough to demonstrate that behavior has become so costly that certain jobs and enterprises have had to be abandoned, and that the inexorable rise in labor costs continually threatens to race ahead of productivity gains and thereby render still more jobs and enterprises marginal. The evidence for an optimistic interpretation of the effects of recent history must be sought in subtler, admittedly less certain, sources than economic statistics.

But it is precisely because labor costs have risen, with or without corresponding productivity gains, that the cost-control approach is suspected of having contributed all it can. The various components of this approach (personnel selection, job design, etc.) have shown no signs of improved efficacy for years. Although there are undoubtedly many organizations which are not employing the cost-control approach to behavior as efficiently as they could, it would appear that the state of the art has been advanced about as far as it can be. Barring some unforeseen breakthrough, we are unlikely to generate any more efficiency from limiting opportunities for costly behavior than we have already seen.

Even if the cost-control approach to behavior has actually reached its limits, it could hardly be abandoned. But it obviously needs to be supplemented by compatible approaches whose effects extend beyond those of cost control. The value-adding approach fits this description. Therefore, the question of whether the cost-control approach has run out of steam or simply has not been used adroitly enough need not detain us.

Value-adding behavior. The combined pressures of the marketplace and employee demands for higher compensation show no sign of letting up; if anything, both appear to be on the increase. Therefore, the challenge of increased productivity—producing more, better, and/or less expensive goods and services in relation to the cost of producing them—promises to remain the prime challenge to management. Failure to meet the challenge can only result in inflation or recession, depending on whether the consumer or the producer has to pay for the failure. Any tools that promise to advance productivity beyond current levels demand attention.

The promise emerges from behavioral science analyses of organizations which have consistently outstripped comparable organizations in terms of profit and efficiency. More often than not, the managers of such profit leaders tend to use techniques which have the effect of stimulating value-adding behavior of employees. More often than not, the organizations that lag behind the leaders do not use such techniques or use them perfunctorily. Both types of organizations use cost-control approaches to behavior; the difference is that these are only part of the leaders' managerial repertory while they constitute the lion's share of the laggers' approach to management.

Most value-adding techniques were not invented by behavioral scientists. They are simply what the behavioral scientists discovered when they began to make systematic comparisons of organizations with different productivity records. The fact that value-adding techniques also make sense in terms of what we know about motivation buttresses the belief that value-adding behavior can be stimulated. Although controlled experiments are difficult to bring off in the behavioral field without sacrificing realism, those which have been both reasonably controlled and reasonably realistic indicate that value-adding behavior can indeed be deliberately increased through a variety of managerial techniques.

The principal difficulty with value-adding techniques is not that they are hard to master, but rather that they are hard to believe. To use them effectively requires the abandonment, or at least the suspension, of beliefs so ingrained that they often seem synonymous with common sense. For many managers, the suggestion that, for example, employees can learn to regulate their own activities quite responsibly simply flies in the face of experience. Furthermore, an unconvinced manager is hardly likely to convince an employee with whom he tries an ostensibly value-adding approach. The behavioral scientist has an explanation for this lack of credibility, but even the explanation is a bit demanding intellectually and very demanding emotionally. It is not surprising, therefore, that attempts to date to introduce value-adding approaches to behavior where they have not been used before often proceed haltingly and sometimes disappointingly. How to bridge the credibility gap with regard to value-adding techniques has not yet been satisfactorily solved.

The behavioral scientists' explanation for the disparity between the manager's (or employee's) experience and the implications of the value-adding approach is that experience is not always a reliable guide to truth. That is, we too seldom question our experiences to be certain we understand their meaning. We are likely to select those aspects of our experiences that confirm our beliefs or can be interpreted that way and give them more weight than aspects that do not fit so readily into our preconceptions. Or we may assume that our experiences have covered the range of possibility, or at least most of it, so that events which contradict our assumptions would seem highly improbable or fantastic.

But the most difficult of all the behavioral scientists' explanations is the one which attributes the behavior that we witness to our own assumptions about the capabilities of the person being observed. According to this concept, everyone has a considerably broader repertory of potential behavior than he actually exhibits, and the behavior he does exhibit tends to fit the expectations of the people on whom he depends. Thus, costly behavior can be the result (at least in part) of management's expectations that it will occur. More precisely, costly behavior is in part a reaction to cost-controlling behavior on the part of management: a way of

restoring at least a measure of equitability to the relationship. A man who feels mistrusted and thereby abused will derive some degree of comfort from depriving his abuser of something he presumably wants. That may be why many cost-control techniques are only effective up to a certain point and then begin to yield diminishing returns.

The behavioral scientist is therefore in the position of having discovered some principles which, potentially, could have a profound effect upon productivity. But actually implementing them demands that managers partake of what is, for many of them, a heady brew. The unsolved problem, and perhaps the key to the puzzle, is this: **What enabled the managers to whom value-adding approaches came naturally to react to their experience in ways that made these approaches seem like the logical thing to do?**

Motivational Leverage. The essence of an effective behavioral strategy is motivation, that is, introducing influences which lead to behavioral changes. Effectiveness in this sense demands an awareness of which influences lead to which behavior changes under what circumstances. But the problem is even more complex. An effective behavioral strategy also requires an awareness of the extent to which an influence can actually be introduced, controlled, and maintained at an optimum level. The term "leverage" can be used to describe the extent to which a motivational influence is susceptible to adequate control.

It is important to distinguish between motivational power and motivational leverage. A motivator can be considered "powerful" if it leads to behavior changes which occur promptly rather than slowly, which are sharply different from previous behavior rather than subtly different, and which are relatively lasting rather than only temporary. The distinction between these two aspects of motivators—power and leverage—is important because some of the more powerful behavior-changing influences actually provide very little leverage. As a practical matter, therefore, they are ineffective motivators, irrespective of how powerful they might be in the abstract.

For example, job security and money are both capable of producing marked behavior changes under certain conditions. But these conditions are increasingly rare. They include a sustained high level of unemployment, inadequate alternative employment opportunities, inadequate purchasing power and a substantial degree of personal influence upon increments to income. Years of sustained prosperity in a high-consumption, almost fully employed economy have eroded all of these conditions. Despite some glaring exceptions (which glare because they are exceptions), the bulk of the United States labor force is or soon will be effectively beyond the reach of these two powerful motivators.

This is not to suggest that Americans are oblivious to money or to security, but rather that management can seldom manipulate either on a scale that is sufficient to induce distinct or lasting behavior changes. The major exceptions with regard to money are in "membership" behavior (joining, staying in, or leaving an organization), and in the degree of emphasis given to rewarded rather than unrewarded actions. The major exceptions with regard to security are in occupational groups which face technological displacement or competition from other groups of workers.

However, there is quite a bit of leverage left in some relatively neglected motivators. Whether these are as powerful in the abstract as other motivators of lesser leverage is a question that managers can leave for academicians to ponder. A motivator in hand is worth more than two in the abstract; a moderate increase in productivity that is actually accomplished is worth much more than a dramatic increase that can only be dreamed of.

Behavioral research has uncovered a number of highly leveraged motivators, and a sensible behavioral strategy puts as many of them to work as it can. It makes no more sense to argue the merits of one highly leveraged motivator "against" another (say, job enrichment "versus" participation) than it does to argue whether a baseball team should be capable of hitting "or" fielding. The effects are complementary, not competitive.

Some examples of highly leveraged motivators, in addition to the two just mentioned, are: management "by objectives," communication by dialogue, periodic changes of assignments, and team building. It must be stressed that none of these are universally effective, so that sound behavioral strategy demands a judicious selection based on an intimate awareness of the potentialities of the individuals and groups involved.

Indeed, that "intimate awareness" is one of the most important and least attainable variables in the equation. Neither length of experience nor certainty of conviction offer, in themselves, any assurance that potentialities have been realistically assessed. This is why so much of "organization development" is devoted to teaching people to reveal more of their own repertory of behavior than their jobs normally elicit from them; and to increasing their sensitivity to the breadth of other people's repertories. An organization which can not encourage its members to become more than they have been can not grow; it has no motivational leverage.

Self-revolutionizing management. The assumptions underlying a value-adding strategy for behavioral management are at least partly incompatible with the assumptions underlying the traditional definition of management itself (planning, organizing, and controlling). A value-adding strategy rests on the assumption that most people will invest more effort and ingenuity in their work if it is made more completely **theirs'**—if they can recognize in it a unique and significant contribution of their own. The assumption underlying traditional concepts of management is that planning, organizing, and controlling are each inherently indivisible and demand skills that are inherently scarce. Hence these functions are largely monopolized by management and within management are largely concentrated at higher levels. The contribution that most workers and many lower-level managers make to their work, therefore, is largely to do what someone else has decided they should do. Their own contribution to it is rarely unique or significant. No amount of artistry in "communications" can alter that.

This basic conflict limits the effectiveness of value-adding strategies in a number of ways. It creates resistance, usually in the form of scoffing or simple disbelief. Even when the rationale of value-adding is accepted intellectually, the underlying assumption (that managing must be the sole prerogative of managers, especially of top managers) may seem so self-evident that the commitment to value-adding is made reservedly—and consequently, inadequately. Finally, even when the concept of managerial "indispensability" is not especially cherished and when management is quite prepared to experiment with forms of distributed control, impatience with slow changes or intolerance of errors undermines the opportunity to learn how to implement the new strategy effectively.

The basic problem is that conventional managerial doctrine and behavioral research results imply different kinds of managerial behavior. Unless the doctrine is altered, experiments with various value-adding tactics actually introduce conflict into the system; and that conflict is usually resolved by the rejection of the intruding ideas by the entrenched ideas. Experiments with value-adding tactics are therefore unlikely to result in more than temporary fads unless management is enabled to face and accept their full implications. This basic conflict, rather than any inherent defect in value-adding tactics themselves, is the reason why so many experiments with these tactics tend to run a faddish course.

To seek to capitalize upon the constructive potentialities in behavior is to allow the camel's nose into the tent, because the "tent" has been erected on the premise that those potentialities were negligible. Various value-adding approaches will lead only to marginal or temporary improvements in productivity wherever management is unable or unwilling to alter its concept of what its own role should be. Value-adding methods of behavior management are likely to flourish only when everything else that management does is consistent with them.

The changes that value-adding methods require of management are essentially shifts of emphasis, rather than a wholesale revision of managerial job descriptions. Controlling is massively delegated, freeing time for planning, which becomes more research-based and, as a by-product, more sensitive to the motivational implications in managerial decisions. Decision making itself becomes more a matter of resolving questions on which subordinates cannot reach their own consensus than of making all key decisions for them. Performance reviews are largely based on variances from previously accepted targets rather than on detailed investigations. At middle- and lower-management levels, there is more emphasis on coaching and coordinating; less on measurement and inspection; and still less on completing reports to superiors.

In many ways, management's situation with respect to value-adding strategies is not unlike that of a parent dealing with a son who is emerging from adolescence into manhood. In both instances, the subordinates must prove themselves capable of using increased behavioral options wisely and productively. In both instances, tensions and misunderstandings between superiors and subordinates are perhaps inevitable, so that a generous leavening of goodwill is needed on both sides. And perhaps most important, in both instances, time is on the side of the subordinates. In management's case, its failure to comprehend the way in which time is turning its basic assumptions into irrelevancies can only work to its own detriment.

How, then, can managements be remade so that they not only adapt to changes but, better still, anticipate them and help to shape them? The behavioral sciences offer some clues, but hardly a pat formula. Much remains to be learned. But three approaches appear to have promise:

♦ A selection method which seeks to identify for future leadership opportunities those people who are already attuned to the forces that bring change.

♦ A program of assignment changes which ignores the usual staff-line and functional distinctions and allows men to alter their assignment in phase with the life cycle of the product on which they are working.

♦ Organization development, which is actually a group of practices aimed at improving internal communication.

Taken together, programs of this kind provide tools through which management can in effect manage its own renaissance. They also help to create conditions in which a behavioral strategy can be deliberately selected and implemented with some hope of success. This is a far cry from simply accepting behavior as a nuisance to be restricted or ignored.

In effect, management gives up some of its power to restrict behavior in exchange for a hoped-for increase in value-adding behavior. The exchange involves a calculated risk, but the risk must be viewed in its larger context and measured against the potential rewards.

Section C:
Organization Change
and Development

Readings in this section emphasize organization development (OD), which is the introduction of planned and systematic change into the organization within the dimensions of organization design and behavioral processes. In general, two strategies are employed in OD efforts. The first, sometimes called the structure approach, concentrates on changing the task, or the structure, rules, or policies of the organization. The second strategy focuses on modifying some aspect of the people in the organization. Generally, the most effective change efforts incorporate both structural or task variables and people variables. Readings have been selected to provide insights into those OD programs which use both strategies of change and development.

The first selection, by Paul Lawrence, is one of the most reprinted articles on organization development. Although it was written more than twenty years ago, the ideas it contains are still very applicable to the modern organization. Lawrence's article presents at least two major ideas. The first is that the main source of resistance to change lies in social or "people" factors rather than in the technical aspects of the business. As one solution to this source of resistance, Lawrence critically examines the notion of participation, particularly the famous study completed by Coch and French. He concludes that,

> The significance of these research findings from management's point of view, is that executives and staff experts need not expertness in using the devices of participation but a real understanding, in depth and detail, of the specific social arrangements that will be sustained or threatened by the change or by the way in which it is introduced.

Lawrence's second major idea deals with means of improving the working relationships between staff and line groups in an organization. Lawrence, in reviewing his original article in a 1969 reprint in the *Harvard Business Review*, points out that these problems have probably escalated since the original publication: "The gap that exists in outlook and orientation between specialized groups in industry has increased . . . even as the number of such groups has continued to escalate. These larger gaps have in turn created even more difficult problems of securing effective communication and problem solving between groups." Finally, it is worth noting that resistance to change should always be a warning to management that the system may be "out of control."

The second selection, by Martin Evans, follows the theme begun by Lawrence. Evans indicates that OD programs can fail in three ways: by not tailoring the program to the needs of the organization, by not modeling the appropriate behaviors in the program itself, and by not reordering personnel and reward subsystems. Evans then provides an excellent discussion of the third type of failure. Motivation is cited as most important in fostering beliefs about performance and rewards necessary for the success of the OD effort.

The final two articles in this section deal with more specific techniques of OD, especially interpersonal ones. In "The Fifth Achievement," Robert Blake and Jane Mouton deal with a crucial problem facing our society today. Our society is often described as becoming legalistic; problems are normally solved according to some formal legal structure. As Blake and Mouton point out, legalism is only one of man's four achievements, the others being science, politics, and organizational hierarchy. A fifth achievement, "a sharply increased understanding by every man of the roots of conflict and the human skills of gaining the resolution of differences," is seen as an attractive alternative to the other four. In implementing and explaining the fifth achievement, Blake and Mouton rely on their famous conflict grid, which emphasizes both the task and personal aspects of a conflict. Two concepts essential to successful conflict resolution — conformity and flexibility — are analyzed in terms of the grid. Finally, Blake and Mouton provide several possible applications of the fifth achievement that would have a profound effect on modern trends.

The final article in this section, by V. P. and L. L. Luchsinger, was selected partly because of its current popularity and partly because the authors of this text have had success in analyzing and resolving conflicts through transactional analysis. Although TA has been criticized as "Freud warmed over," it certainly provides a simplified schema for thinking about interpersonal conflict. An interesting comparison can be drawn between the adult-adult transaction state and the 9,9 conflict management style of the conflict grid. Both seem to emphasize a rational problem-solving approach, which is problem- or task-oriented but does not neglect the need for a strong person-oriented emphasis. Finally, in reviewing this section, the reader should keep in mind that the ultimate goal of any OD effort is to improve some aspects that have been found lacking through the control system.

How to Deal with Resistance to Change

Paul R. Lawrence

One of the most baffling and recalcitrant of the problems which business executives face is employee resistance to change. Such resistance may take a number of forms — persistent reduction in output, increase in the number of "quits" and requests for transfer, chronic quarrels, sullen hostility, wildcat or slowdown strikes, and, of course, the expression of a lot of pseudological reasons why the change will not work. Even the more petty forms of this resistance can be troublesome.

All too often when executives encounter resistance to change, they "explain" it by quoting the cliché that "people resist change" and never look further. Yet changes must continually occur in industry. This applies with particular force to the all-important "little" changes that constantly take place — changes in work methods, in routine office procedures, in the location of a machine or a desk, in personnel assignments and job titles.

Not one of these changes makes the headlines, but in total they account for much of our increase in productivity. They are not the spectacular once-in-a-lifetime technological revolutions that involve mass layoffs or the obsolescence of traditional skills, but they are vital to business progress.

Does it follow, therefore, that business management is forever saddled with the onerous job of "forcing" change down the throats of resistant people? My answer is *no*. It is the thesis of this article that people do *not* resist technical change as such and that most of the resistance which does occur is unnecessary. I shall discuss these points, among others:

1. A solution which has become increasingly popular for dealing with resistance to change is to get the people involved to "participate" in making the change. But as a practical matter "participation" as a device is not a good way for management to think about the problem. In fact, it may lead to trouble.
2. The key to the problem is to understand the true nature of resistance. Actually, what employees resist is usually not technical change but social change — the change in their human relationships that generally accompanies technical change.
3. Resistance is usually created because of certain blind spots and attitudes which staff specialists have as a result of their preoccupation with the technical aspects of new ideas.

4. Management can take concrete steps to deal constructively with these staff attitudes. The steps include emphasizing new standards of performance for staff specialists and encouraging them to think in different ways, as well as making use of the fact that signs of resistance can serve as a practical warning signal in directing and timing technological changes.

5. Top executives can also make their own efforts more effective at meetings of staff and operating groups where change is being discussed. They can do this by shifting their attention from the facts of schedules, technical details, work assignments, and so forth, to what the discussion of these items indicates in regard to developing resistance and receptiveness to change.

Let us begin by taking a look at some research into the nature of resistance to change. There are two studies in particular that I should like to discuss. They highlight contrasting ways of interpreting resistance to change and of coping with it in day-to-day administration.

Is Participation Enough?

The first study was conducted by Lester Coch and John R. P. French, Jr. in a clothing factory.[1] It deserves special comment because, it seems to me, it is the most systematic study of the phenomenon of resistance to change that has been made in a factory setting. To describe it briefly:

The two researchers worked with four different groups of factory operators who were being paid on a modified piece-rate basis. For each of these four groups a minor change in the work procedure was installed by a different method, and the results were carefully recorded to see what, if any, problems of resistance occurred. The four experimental groups were roughly matched with respect to efficiency ratings and degree of cohesiveness; in each group the proposed change modified the established work procedure to about the same degree.

The work change was introduced to the first group by what the researchers called a "no-participation" method. This small group of operators was called into a room where some staff people told the members that there was a need for a minor methods change in their work procedures. The staff people then explained the change to the operators in detail, and gave them the reasons for the change. The operators were then sent back to the job with instructions to work in accordance with the new method.

The second group of operators was introduced to the work change by a "participation-through-representation" method — a variation of the approach used with the third and fourth groups which turned out to be of little significance.

The third and fourth groups of operators were both introduced to the work change on a "total-participation" basis. All the operators in these groups met with the staff men concerned. The staff men dramatically demonstrated the need

---

[1] See Lester Coch and John R. P. French, Jr., "Overcoming Resistance to Change," *Human Relations,* Vol. 1, No. 4, 1948, p. 512.

for cost reduction. A general agreement was reached that some savings could be effected. The groups then discussed how existing work methods could be improved and unnecessary operations eliminated. When the new work methods were agreed on, all the operators were trained in the new methods, and all were observed by the time-study men for purposes of establishing a new piece rate on the job.

Research Findings

The researchers reported a marked contrast between the results achieved by the different methods of introducing this change:

No-participation group — The most striking difference was between Group #1, the no-participation group, and Groups #3 and #4, the total-participation groups. The output of Group #1 dropped immediately to about two thirds of its previous output rate. The output rate stayed at about this level throughout the period of 30 days after the change was introduced. The researchers further reported:

"Resistance developed almost immediately after the change occurred. Marked expressions of aggression against management occurred, such as conflict with the methods engineer, . . . hostility toward the supervisor, deliberate restriction of production, and lack of cooperation with the supervisor. There were 17% quits in the first 40 days. Grievances were filed about piece rates; but when the rate was checked, it was found to be a little 'loose.' "

Total-participation groups — In contrast with this record, Groups #3 and #4 showed a smaller initial drop in output and a very rapid recovery not only to the previous production rate but to a rate that exceeded the previous rate. In these groups there were no signs of hostility toward the staff people or toward the supervisors, and there were no quits during the experimental period.

Appraisal of Results

Without going into all the researchers' decisions based on these experiments, it can be fairly stated that they concluded that resistance to methods changes could be overcome by *getting the people involved in the change to participate in making it*.

This was a very useful study, but the results are likely to leave the manager of a factory still bothered by the question, "Where do we go from here?" The trouble centers around that word "participation." It is not a new word. It is seen often in management journals, heard often in management discussions. In fact, the idea that it is a good thing to get employee participation in making changes has become almost axiomatic in management circles.

But participation is not something that can be conjured up or created artificially. You obviously cannot buy it as you would buy a typewriter. You cannot hire industrial engineers and accountants and other staff people who have the ability "to get participation" built into them. It is doubtful how helpful it would be to call in a group of supervisors and staff men and exhort them, "Get in there and start participation."

Participation is a feeling on the part of people, not just the mechanical act of being called in to take part in discussions. Common sense would suggest that people are more likely to respond to the way they are customarily treated — say, as people whose opinions are respected because they themselves are respected for their own worth — rather than by the stratagem of being called to a meeting or being asked some carefully calculated questions. In fact, many supervisors and staff men have had some unhappy experiences with executives who have read about participation and have picked it up as a new psychological gimmick for getting other people to think they "want" to do as they are told — as a sure way to put the sugar coating on a bitter pill.

So there is still the problem of how to get this thing called participation. And, as a matter of fact, the question remains whether participation was the determining factor in the Coch and French experiment or whether there was something of deeper significance underlying it.

Resistance to What?

Now let us take a look at a second series of research findings about resistance to change. . . . While making some research observations in a factory manufacturing electronic products, a colleague and I had an opportunity to observe a number of incidents that for us threw new light on this matter of resistance to change.[2] One incident was particularly illuminating:

We were observing the work of one of the industrial engineers and a production operator who had been assigned to work with the engineer on assembling and testing an experimental product that the engineer was developing. The engineer and the operator were in almost constant daily contact in their work. It was a common occurrence for the engineer to suggest an idea for some modification in a part of the new product; he would then discuss his idea with the operator and ask her to try out the change to see how it worked. It was also a common occurrence for the operator to get an idea as she assembled parts and to pass this idea on to the engineer, who would then consider it and, on occasion, ask the operator to try out the idea and see if it proved useful.

A typical exchange between these two people might run somewhat as follows:

Engineer: "I got to thinking last night about that difficulty we've been having on assembling the x part in the last few days. It occurred to me that we might get

---

[2] For a complete report of the study, see Harriet O. Ronken and Paul R. Lawrence, *Administering Changes: A Case Study of Human Relations in a Factory* (Boston, Division of Research, Harvard Business School, 1952).

around that trouble if we washed the part in a cleaning solution just prior to assembling it."

Operator: "Well, that sounds to me like it's worth trying."

Engineer: "I'll get you some of the right kind of cleaning solution, and why don't you try doing that with about 50 parts and keep track of what happens."

Operator: "Sure, I'll keep track of it and let you know how it works."

With this episode in mind, let us take a look at a second episode involving the same production operator. One day we noticed another engineer approaching the production operator. We knew that this particular engineer had had no previous contact with the production operator. He had been asked to take a look at one specific problem on the new product because of his special technical qualifications. He had decided to make a change in one of the parts of the product to eliminate the problem, and he had prepared some of these parts using his new method. Here is what happened:

He walked up to the production operator with the new parts in his hand and indicated to her by a gesture that he wanted her to try assembling some units using his new part. The operator picked up one of the parts and proceeded to assemble it. We noticed that she did not handle the part with her usual care. After she had assembled the product, she tested it and it failed to pass inspection. She turned to the new engineer and, with a triumphant air, said, "It doesn't work."

The new engineer indicated that she should try another part. She did so, and again it did not work. She then proceeded to assemble units using all the new parts that were available. She handled each of them in an unusually rough manner. None of them worked. Again she turned to the engineer and said that the new parts did not work.

The engineer left, and later the operator, with evident satisfaction commented to the original industrial engineer that the new engineer's ideas were just no good.

Social Change

What can we learn from these episodes? To begin, it will be useful for our purposes to think of change as having both a technical and a social aspect. The *technical* aspect of the change is the making of a measurable modification in the physical routines of the job. The *social* aspect of the change refers to the way those affected by it think it will alter their established relationships in the organization.

We can clarify this distinction by referring to the two foregoing episodes. In both of them, the technical aspects of the changes introduced were virtually identical: the operator was asked to use a slightly changed part in assembling the finished product. By contrast, the social aspects of the changes were quite different.

In the first episode, the interaction between the industrial engineer and the operator tended to sustain the give-and-take kind of relationship that these two people were accustomed to. The operator was used to being treated as a person with some valuable skills and knowledge and some sense of responsibility about her work; when the engineer approached her with his idea, she felt she was being dealt with in the usual way. But, in the second episode, the new engineer was introducing not only a technical change but also a change in the operator's customary way of relating herself to others in the organization. By his brusque manner and by his lack of any explanation, he led the operator to fear that her usual work relationships were being changed. And she just did not like the new way she was being treated.

The results of these two episodes were quite different also. In the first episode there were no symptoms of resistance to change, a very good chance that the experimental change would determine fairly whether a cleaning solution would improve product quality, and a willingness on the part of the operator to accept future changes when the industrial engineer suggested them. In the second episode, however, there were signs of resistance to change (the operator's careless handling of parts and her satisfaction in their failure to work), failure to prove whether the modified part was an improvement or not, and indications that the operator would resist any further changes by the engineer. We might summarize the two contrasting patterns of human behavior in the two episodes in graphic form; see *Exhibit I*.

It is apparent from these two patterns that the variable which determines the result is the *social* aspect of the change. In other words, the operator did not resist the technical change as such but rather the accompanying change in her human relationships.

Exhibit I.   Two contrasting patterns of human behavior

	Change		Results
	Technical aspect	Social aspect	
Episode 1	Clean part prior to assembly	Sustaining the customary work relationship of operator	1. No resistance 2. Useful technical result 3. Readiness for more change
Episode 2	Use new part in assembly	Threatening the customary work relationship of operator	1. Signs of resistance 2. No useful technical result 3. Lack of readiness for more change

Confirmation

This conclusion is based on more than one case. Many other cases in our research project substantiate it. Furthermore, we can find confirmation in the research experience of Coch and French, even though they came out with a different interpretation.

Coch and French tell us in their report that the procedure used with Group #1, i.e., the no-participation group, was the usual one in the factory for introducing work changes. And yet they also tell us something about the customary treatment of the operators in their work life. For example, the company's labor relations policies are progressive, the company and the supervisors place a high value on fair and open dealings with the employees, and the employees are encouraged to take up their problems and grievances with management. Also, the operators are accustomed to measuring the success and failure of themselves as operators against the company's standard output figures.

Now compare these *customary* work relationships with the way the Group #1 operators were treated when they were introduced to this particular work change. There is quite a difference. When the management called them into the room for indoctrination, they were treated as if they had no useful knowledge of their own jobs. In effect, they were told that they were not the skilled and efficient operators they had thought they were, that they were doing the job inefficiently, and that some "outsider" (the staff expert) would now tell them how to do it right. How could they construe this experience *except* as a threatening change in their usual working relationship? It is the story of the second episode in our research case all over again. The results were also the same, with signs of resistance, persistently low output, and so on.

Now consider experimental Groups #3 and #4, i.e., the total participation groups. Coch and French referred to management's approach in their case as a "new" method of introducing change; but, from the point of view of the *operators* it must not have seemed new at all. It was simply a continuation of the way they were ordinarily dealt with in the course of their regular work. And what happened? The results — reception to change, technical improvement, better performance — were much like those reported in the first episode between the operator and the industrial engineer.

So the research data of Coch and French tend to confirm the conclusion that the nature and size of the technical aspect of the change does not determine the presence or absence of resistance nearly so much as does the social aspect of the change.

Roots of Trouble

The significance of these research findings, from management's point of view, is that executives and staff experts need not expertness in using the devices of participation but a real understanding, in depth and detail, of the specific social arrangements that will be sustained or threatened by the change or by the way in which it is introduced.

These observations check with everyday management experience in industry. When we stop to think about it, we know that many changes occur in our factories without a bit of resistance. We know that people who are working closely with one another continually swap ideas about short cuts and minor changes in procedure that are adopted so easily and naturally that we seldom notice them or even think of them as change. The point is that because these people work so closely with one another, they intuitively understand and take account of the existing social arrangements for work and so feel no threat to themselves in such everyday changes.

By contrast, management actions leading to what we commonly label "change" are usually initiated outside the small work group by staff people. These are the changes that we notice and the ones that most frequently bring on symptoms of resistance. By the very nature of their work, most of our staff specialists in industry do not have the intimate contact with operating groups that allows them to acquire an intuitive understanding of the complex social arrangements which their ideas may affect. Neither do our staff specialists always have the day-to-day dealings with operating people that lead them to develop a natural respect for the knowledge and skill of these people. As a result, all too often the men behave in a way that threatens and disrupts the established social relationships. And the tragedy is that so many of these upsets are inadvertent and unnecessary.

Yet industry must have its specialists — not only many kinds of engineering specialists (product, process, maintenance, quality, and safety engineers) but also cost accountants, production schedulers, purchasing agents, and personnel men. Must top management therefore reconcile itself to continual resistance to change, or can it take constructive action to meet the problem?

I believe that our research in various factory situations indicates why resistance to change occurs and what management can do about it. Let us take the "why" factors first.

Self-preoccupation

All too frequently we see staff specialists who bring to their work certain blind spots that get them into trouble when they initiate change with operating people. One such blind spot is "self-preoccupation." The staff man gets so engrossed in the technology of the change he is interested in promoting that he becomes wholly oblivious to different kinds of things that may be bothering people. Here are two examples:

1. In one situation the staff people introduced, with the best of intentions, a technological change which inadvertently deprived a number of skilled operators of much of the satisfaction that they were finding in their work. Among other

things, the change meant that, whereas formerly the output of each operator had been placed beside his work position where it could be viewed and appreciated by him and by others, it was now being carried away immediately from the work position. The workmen did not like this.

The sad part of it was that there was no compelling cost or technical reason why the output could not be placed beside the work position as it had been formerly. But the staff people who had introduced the change were so literal-minded about their ideas that when they heard complaints on the changes from the operators, they could not comprehend what the trouble was. Instead, they began repeating all the logical arguments why the change made sense from a cost standpoint. The final result here was a chronic restriction of output and persistent hostility on the part of the operators.

2. An industrial engineer undertook to introduce some methods changes in one department with the notion firmly in mind that this assignment presented him with an opportunity to "prove" to higher management the value of his function. He became so preoccupied with his personal desire to make a name for his particular techniques that he failed to pay any attention to some fairly obvious and practical considerations which the operating people were calling to his attention but which did not show up in his time-study techniques. As could be expected, resistance quickly developed to all his ideas, and the only "name" that he finally won for his techniques was a black one.

Obviously, in both of these situations the staff specialists involved did not take into account the social aspects of the change they were introducing. For different reasons they got so preoccupied with the technical aspects of the change that they literally could not see or understand what all the fuss was about.

We may sometimes wish that the validity of the technical aspect of the change were the sole determinant of its acceptability. But the fact remains that the social aspect is what determines the presence or absence of resistance. Just as ignoring this fact is the sure way to trouble, so taking advantage of it can lead to positive results. We must not forget that these same social arrangements which at times seem so bothersome are essential for the performance of work. Without a network of established social relationships a factory would be populated with a collection of people who had no idea of how to work with one another in an organized fashion. By working *with* this network instead of *against* it, management's staff representatives can give new technological ideas a better chance of acceptance.

Know-how of Operators Overlooked

Another blind spot of many staff specialists is to the strengths as well as to the weaknesses of firsthand production experience. They do not recognize that the production foreman and the production operator are in their own way specialists themselves — specialists in actual experience with production problems. This point should be obvious, but it is amazing how many staff specialists fail to appreciate the fact that even though they themselves may have a superior knowledge of the technology of the production process involved, the foreman or the operators may have a more practical understanding of how to get daily production out of a group of men and machines.

The experience of the operating people frequently equips them to be of real help to staff specialists on at least two counts: (1) The operating people are often able to spot practical production difficulties in the ideas of the specialists — and iron out those difficulties before it is too late; (2) the operating people are often able to take advantage of their intimate acquaintance with the existing social arrangements for getting work done. If given a chance, they can use this kind of knowledge to help detect those parts of the change that will have undesirable social consequences. The staff experts can then go to work on ways to avoid the trouble area without materially affecting the technical worth of the change.

Further, some staff specialists have yet to learn the truth that, even after the plans for a change have been carefully made, it takes *time* to put the change successfully into production use. Time is necessary even though there may be no resistance to the change itself. The operators must develop the skill needed to use new methods and new equipment efficiently; there are always bugs to be taken out of a new method or piece of equipment even with the best of engineering. When a staff man begins to lose his patience with the amount of time that these steps take, the people he is working with will begin to feel that he is pushing them; *this* amounts to a change in their customary work relationships, and resistance will start building up where there was none before.

The situation is aggravated if the staff man mistakenly accuses the operators of resisting the idea of the change, for there are few things that irritate people more than to be blamed for resisting change when actually they are doing their best to learn a difficult new procedure.

Management Action

Many of the problems of resistance to change arise around certain kinds of *attitudes* that staff men are liable to develop about their jobs and their own ideas for introducing change. Fortunately, management can influence these attitudes and thus deal with the problems at their source.

Broadening Staff Interests

It is fairly common for a staff man to work so hard on one of his ideas for change that he comes to identify himself with it. This is fine for the organization when he is working on the idea by himself or with his immediate colleagues;

the idea becomes "his baby," and the company benefits from his complete devotion to his work.

But when he goes to some group of operating people to introduce a change, his very identification with his ideas tends to make him unreceptive to any suggestions for modification. He just does not feel like letting anyone else tamper with his pet ideas. It is easy to see, of course, how this attitude is interpreted by the operating people as a lack of respect for their suggestions.

This problem of the staff man's extreme identification with his work is one which, to some extent, can only be cured by time. But here are four suggestions for speeding up the process:

1. The manager can often, with wise timing, encourage the staff man's interest in a different project that is just starting.
2. The manager can also, by his "coaching" as well as by example, prod the staff man to develop a healthier respect for the contributions he can receive from operating people; success in this area would, of course, virtually solve the problem.
3. It also helps if the staff man can be guided to recognize that the satisfaction he derives from being productive and creative is the same satisfaction he denies the operating people by his behavior toward them. Experience shows that staff people can sometimes be stimulated by the thought of finding satisfaction in sharing with others in the organization the pleasures of being creative.
4. Sometimes, too, the staff man can be led to see that winning acceptance of his ideas through better understanding and handling of human beings is just as challenging and rewarding as giving birth to an idea.

Using Understandable Terms

One of the problems that must be overcome arises from the fact that the typical staff man is likely to have the attitude that the reasons why he is recommending any given change may be so complicated and specialized that it is impossible to explain them to operating people. It may be true that the operating people would find it next to impossible to understand some of the staff man's analytical techniques, but this does not keep them from coming to the conclusion that the staff specialist is trying to razzle-dazzle them with tricky figures and formulas — insulting their intelligence — if he does not strive to his utmost to translate his ideas into terms understandable to them. The following case illustrates the importance of this point:

A staff specialist was temporarily successful in "selling" a change based on a complicated mathematical formula to a foreman who really did not understand it. The whole thing backfired, however, when the foreman tried to sell it to his operating people. They asked him a couple of sharp questions that he could not answer. His embarrassment about this led him to resent and resist the change so much that eventually the whole proposition fell through. This was unfortunate in terms not only of human relations but also of technological progress in the plant.

There are some very good reasons, both technical and social, why the staff man should be interested in working with the operating people until his recommendations make "sense." (This does not mean that the operating people need to understand the recommendations in quite the same way or in the same detail that the staff man does, but that they should be able to visualize the recommendations in terms of their job experiences.) Failure of the staff man to provide an adequate explanation is likely to mean that a job the operators had formerly performed with understanding and satisfaction will now be performed without understanding and with less satisfaction.

This loss of satisfaction not only concerns the individual involved but also is significant from the standpoint of the company which is trying to get maximum productivity from the operating people. A person who does not have a feeling of comprehension of what he is doing is denied the opportunity to exercise that uniquely human ability — the ability to use informed and intelligent judgment on what he does. If the staff man leaves the operating people with a sense of confusion, they will also be left unhappy and less productive.

Top line and staff executives responsible for the operation should make it a point, therefore, to know how the staff man goes about installing a change. They can do this by asking discerning questions when he reports to them, listening closely to reports of employee reaction, and, if they have the opportunity, actually watching the staff man at work. At times they may have to take such drastic action as insisting that the time of installation of a proposed change be postponed until the operators are ready for it. But, for the most part, straighforward discussions with the staff man in terms of what they think of his approach should help him, over a period of time, to learn what is expected of him in his relationships with operating personnel.

New Look at Resistance

Another attitude that gets staff men into trouble is the *expectation* that all the people involved will resist the change. It is curious but true that the staff man who goes into his job with the conviction that people are going to resist any idea he presents with blind stubbornness is likely to find them responding just the way he thinks they will. The process is clear: whenever he treats the people who are supposed to buy his ideas as if they were bullheaded, he changes the way they are used to being treated; and they *will* be bullheaded in resisting *that* change!

I think that the staff man — and management in general — will do better to look at it this way: When resistance *does* appear, it should not be thought of as something to be *overcome*. Instead, it can best be thought of as a useful red flag — a signal that something is going wrong. To use a rough analogy, signs of resistance in a social organization are useful in the same way that pain is useful to the body as a signal that some bodily functions are getting out of adjustment.

The resistance, like the pain, does not tell what is wrong but only that something *is* wrong. And it makes no more sense to try to overcome such resistance than it does to take a pain killer without diagnosing the bodily ailment. Therefore, when resistance appears, it is time to listen carefully to find out what the trouble is. What is needed is not a long harangue on the logics of the new recommendations but a careful exploration of the difficulty.

It may happen that the problem is some technical imperfection in the change that can be readily corrected. More than likely, it will turn out that the change is threatening and upsetting some of the established social arrangements for doing work. Whether the trouble is easy or difficult to correct, management will at least know what it is dealing with.

New Job Definition

Finally, some staff specialists get themselves in trouble because they assume they have the answer in the thought that people will accept a change when they have participated in making it. For example:

In one plant we visited, an engineer confided to us (obviously because we, as researchers on human relations, were interested in psychological gimmicks!) that he was going to put across a proposed production layout change of his by inserting in it a rather obvious error, which others could then suggest should be corrected. We attended the meeting where this stunt was performed, and superficially it worked. Somebody caught the error, proposed that it be corrected, and our engineer immediately "bought" the suggestion as a very worthwhile one and made the change. The group then seemed to "buy" his entire layout proposal.

It looked like an effective technique — oh, so easy — until later, when we became better acquainted with the people in the plant. Then we found out that many of the engineer's colleagues considered him a phony and did not trust him. The resistance they put up to his ideas was very subtle, yet even more real and difficult for management to deal with.

Participation will never work so long as it is treated as a device to get somebody else to do what you want him to. Real participation is based on respect. And respect is not acquired by just trying it; it is acquired when the staff man faces the reality that he needs the contributions of the operating people.

If the staff man defines his job as not just generating ideas but also getting those ideas into practical operation, he will recognize his real dependence on the contributions of the operating people. He will ask them for ideas and suggestions, not in a backhanded way to get compliance, but in a straightforward way to get some good ideas and avoid some unnecessary mistakes. By this process he will be treating the operating people in such a way that his own behavior will not be perceived as a threat to their customary work relationships. It will be possible to discuss, and accept or reject, the ideas on their own merit.

The staff specialist who looks at the process of introducing change and at resistance to change in the manner outlined in the preceding pages may not be hailed as a genius, but he can be counted on in installing a steady flow of technical changes that will cut costs and improve quality without upsetting the organization.

Role of the Administrator

Now what about the way the top executive goes about his *own* job as it involves the introduction of change and problems of resistance?

One of the most important things he can do, of course, is to deal with staff people in much the same way that he wants them to deal with the operators. He must realize that staff people resist social change, too. (This means, among other things, that he should not prescribe particular rules to them on the basis of this article!)

But most important, I think, is the way the administrator conceives of his job in coordinating the work of the different staff and line groups involved in a change. Does he think of his duties *primarily* as checking up, delegating and following through, applying pressure when performance fails to measure up? Or does he think of them *primarily* as facilitating communication and understanding between people with different points of view — for example, between a staff engineering group and a production group who do not see eye to eye on a change they are both involved in? An analysis of management's actual experience — or, at least, that part of it which has been covered by our research — points to the latter as the more effective concept of administration.

I do not mean that the executive should spend his time with the different people concerned discussing the human problems of change as such. He *should* discuss schedules, technical details, work assignments, and so forth. But he should also be watching closely for the messages that are passing back and forth as people discuss these topics. He will find that people — himself as well as others — are always implicitly asking and making answers to questions like: "How will he accept criticism?" "How much can I afford to tell him?" "Does he really get my point?" "Is he playing games?" The answers to such questions determine the degree of candor and the amount of understanding between the people involved.

When the administrator concerns himself with these problems and acts to facilitate understanding, there will be less logrolling and more sense of common purpose, fewer words and better understanding, less anxiety and more acceptance of criticism, less griping and more attention to specific problems — in short, better performance in putting new ideas for technological change into effect.

Failures in OD Programs—
What Went Wrong?

The failure of organizational development programs may rest in the organization's inability to perceive that the individual's job performance is linked to the satisfaction of his needs.

MARTIN G. EVANS

Martin G. Evans is a faculty member in management studies at the University of Toronto. The article is based on a presentation made at the joint conference of the British Psychological Society, the British Sociological Association, the Ergonomics Research Society, and the Operations Research Society. The author wishes to thank Alan Dale, Ray Loveridge, and Stuart Timperly for their assistance.

Why do many packaged organizational development (OD) programs fail to produce sustained organizational change? Do they in fact fail? The evidence on this is sparse. At a conservative estimate, evaluation results are available for fewer than 10 percent of all OD programs. Some may be evaluated privately for the organizations concerned, but most are not evaluated at all. The literature on evaluation that is available tends to lack the safeguards of a research design which protects against certain alternative explanations of the observed change, such as regression toward the mean, historical change, and maturation of the individuals involved.

In any event, the research that has evaluated the impact of packaged OD programs has resulted in mixed findings. Occasionally, the programs have increased managerial effectiveness, but, more often, little effect on performance coupled with improved job satisfaction is noted among subordinates. What, then, goes wrong? At least three factors inhibit the organization from learning from such programs:

Failure to tailor the program to the needs of the organization. The introduction of such a package is rarely preceded by a diagnosis of the problems of the organization followed by either the search for appropriate programs or by the development of a program specially designed to suit the organization.

Failure to model the appropriate behaviors in the program itself. Most OD packages are explicitly based upon a human resources model of organizational participants. Although an OD package is much more than a new motivational approach, most packages are designed to enhance individual motivation through increased participation and the engagement of the individual's higher order needs of growth and self-esteem. For example, the managerial grid of R. R. Blake and J. S. Mouton is designed to help managers integrate a concern for people and a concern for the task. In operation, however, the program models a concern for the task—that of getting people through the program. Managers are assigned to go participate with little concern for their individual needs.

The failure of the organization to reorder its personnel and reward subsystems. The former should model the appropriate new behaviors and the latter should reinforce the managers who begin to change their behavior.

For the remainder of this article, I will focus on the third set of inhibiting factors. The failure of the organization to consider a change in its personnel and reward policies

Reprinted by permission of the author and *Business Horizons* from *Business Horizons*, April 1974, pp. 18–22.

stems from a misunderstanding of the nature of motivation. In the past, the focus on motivation theory has been on the nature of human needs and a growing awareness of the changing salience of such needs through the economic-social-self actualizing-complex man sequence. The way in which the individual's behavior may be linked to the satisfaction of such needs has been ignored until recently.

A MODEL OF MOTIVATION

A number of writers have developed a model suggesting that motivation to perform is a function of the attractiveness, desirability, or importance of the individual's needs (this has been focused on) and the individual's beliefs as to whether or not high performance will enable him to gain satisfaction from those needs.
Thus:

$$\text{Motivation to perform} = \frac{\text{Need}}{\text{desirability}} \times \frac{\text{Belief that effort}}{\text{leads to reward}}$$

Of course, individuals have more than one need or desired reward, so that a complete understanding of motivation to perform requires a summation of these needs (for example, money, esteem, power, or promotion). It is clear that motivation will be high only when the individual believes that high performance will enable him to satisfy his needs and the needs satisfied by high performance are important to the individual. Conversely, if either beliefs or the importance of needs is low, the motivation will be low. If the individual values money, then money will not motivate him to perform if he works in an organization where salary increments are automatic and based upon seniority rather than being based specifically upon performance.

The elaboration of the model of motivation to include the individual's beliefs about the probability that performance will lead to a reward is an important step. First, there is

growing evidence to suggest that this model is appropriate for individual motivation in organizations because it is a good predictor of job performance and satisfaction. Second, it introduces a set of variables—beliefs about performance-reward links—that are under the influence of the organization. The organization, through its policies and practices, determines the nature of actual performance-reward links. These, in turn, form the basis for individual beliefs about the links. The organization, whether it likes it or not and whether it recognizes it or not, influences these beliefs.

Every time the organization makes a promotion or salary raise decision based upon seniority ("Buggins' turn next" or "lateral arabesque" considerations), the individual's beliefs that performance leads to promotion or a pay raise are weakened, and, consequently, the individual's motivation to perform is lessened. An individual's motivation to perform is likely to be lowered if he sees someone whom he regards as incompetent promoted. His motivation to perform is likely to be raised if he sees someone whom he regards as competent promoted, regardless of whether the individual himself is promoted.

IMPLICATIONS AND LIMITATIONS

Theoretically, most behavioral science OD programs such as job enrichment and the managerial grid should create conditions for strong links between high performance and the individual's own goals. I have reviewed elsewhere the research evidence that suggests the motivation for high performance is enhanced by at least four conditions:

1. The job which provides a challenge and freedom to set one's own standards creates importance for the higher order needs of self-esteem and self-actualization and provides conditions under which the individual who performs well can obtain these rewards.

2. If the individual's manager is both task and person oriented, then person-oriented supervision

implies that the manager can reward the individual in a variety of ways corresponding to the individual's needs and that the supervisor perceives the particular set of needs deemed to be important by each individual; task centeredness implies that such rewards are contingent on performance.

3. If a pay raise is clearly based upon performance, the value of the raise is enhanced when it is linked with performance and is seen as an esteem type reward; when high variations in pay increases occur both between persons and over time for the same person (such variation, of course, being related to performance); and when the individual can choose the form of his pay increase (for example, substitution of the fringe benefits such as a longer holiday, shorter work week, insurance program, or pension).

4. If promotion policies are clearly based upon performance, a promotion is valued as an esteem reward when linked with performance.[1]

Such conditions are strongly emphasized by the OD packages previously mentioned. If each of these programs is properly implemented, certain expectations are aroused in the mind of the participants. These expectations may include involvement in decisions concerning the work the individual does; involvement in decisions about the criteria for performance that will be applied to him and whether or not he (and his peers) have met these criteria; and the building of an organizational climate which shows concern for the individual and which facilitates a free exchange of information.

The problem is that beliefs about path-goal links are based upon history. In the past, it is likely that weak links between high performance and goal attainment have been established, while strong links between goal attainment and such conditions as seniority, keeping one's "nose clean," or not rocking the boat have been established. Consequently, when an OD program is implemented, specific attempts must be made to build strong links between high performance and goal attainment.

Despite their designers' intentions, such programs often have little impact on the

1. M. G. Evans, "Managing the New Managers," *Personnel Administration* (May-June 1971), pp. 31-38.

> "Every time the organization makes a promotion or salary raise decision based upon seniority . . . the individual's belief that performance leads to promotion or a pay raise is weakened, and, consequently, the individual's motivation to perform is lessened."

infrastructure of the organization. Careful attempts are made to implement the program into the work flow and budgeting processes of the organization, but the programs are not implemented into the personnel policies of the organization—into making pay, promotion, or job transfer decisions. The necessary path-goal links between high performance and the individual's goals have not been developed; the old links of survival leading to reward remain; and motivation to perform well stays weak.

APPLICATION TO POLICY

For all managers, but especially for personnel managers, a change in emphasis in their activities is necessary. A. Bowey has pointed out that the compensation policies for lower level employees, for example, can be designed with one or more of several goals in mind: administrative ease, reduction of uncontrolled overtime, individual or group motivation, satisfied unions, optimization of work flow, and facilitation of technological change.

The following is a list of factors which should be considered in the formulation of four managerial policies.

Compensation policy. What should be the nature of remuneration? The possibilities include salary, fringe benefits, and deferred payments such as pensions and stock options. How frequently should changes in remuneration be made? What should be the basis for those changes?

Promotion policy. What should be the performance basis for promotion? What organization members will form the locus of decision making concerning promotions?

Manpower planning policy. What will be the future vacancies in the organization, and what skills will be needed to fill those vacancies? Who are the potential candidates to fill these job openings? Are they available? Who will choose the new employees? Will the new employee need training? Will he be trained on or off the job? Again, at what levels are such decisions made?

Geographic mobility policy. Is mobility necessary for job performance? How much mobility is needed? Who decides what the mobility requirements should be?

Compensation

As far as compensation and its form are concerned, one of the major constraints is the legal position with regard to tax of various forms of compensation. Nevertheless, most organizations, probably for administrative ease, take a system-wide approach; everyone gets the same mix of pay and fringe benefits with some minor differentiation by job level. However, any differentiation is determined by the organization, and there is little effort to tailor the compensation to match the desires of the individual, despite the fact that employees seek individual differences in the mix. If the organization were to introduce the so-called "cafeteria plan" for compensation, the individual would be able to choose among forms of remuneration—straight salary, pension, longer holidays, or medical insurance. The probable result would be that, dollar for dollar, the organization would be distributing desirable, and thus more valuable, rewards to its members, thereby enhancing their motivation.

From an administrative point of view, the complications inherent in individual choice look nightmarish. But the problems can be handled through computerized accounting, payroll and personnel systems, or the contracting of compensation services outside the organization (for example, to banks).

The second problem is the linkage between performance and reward. A prerequisite is an assessment system that is trusted by the individuals concerned. The assessment must be tied to observable behavior and performances rather than to diffuse personality characteristics, and the system must be accepted by—and probably developed by—those who do the assessing and those who are assessed. The use of the criterion development scheme involving the retranslation of expectations method provides a vehicle for the participative development of performance criteria.[2]

In other words, assessment is an important arena for management-group participation. The management by objectives program attempts to do this, but it should probably be widened from a one-to-one basis to a one-to-all procedure. This is essential in the phase of developing desirable criteria upon which performance is to be judged.

Through this process, the organization will help resolve the individual-group performance conflict. Such a process will build systems-wide criteria into the performance criteria for groups and individuals. One criterion will involve the contribution made by the individual to the group, or by the group to the organization. For example, P. R. Lawrence and J. W. Lorsch have shown that successful integrators were rewarded for the job of facilitating the integration and contribution of two groups.

Promotion

The major implication is concerned with the criteria for promotion. If promotion is to be a motivator, it needs to be closely tied to performance and based on criteria that are shared and agreed upon by the people involved. The procedure for criteria development suggested by M. D. Dunnette and described above is appropriate here.

2. M. D. Dunnette, "Managerial Effectiveness: Its Definition and Measurement," *Studies in Personnel Psychology* (October 1970).

"The concern in manpower planning activities and their implementation is organization centered. When decisions are made concerning the human resources available and about the kinds of on- or off-the-job training required to fit people for their managerial positions of the future, little or no account is taken of the individual's own preferences."

The second factor of importance concerns the wishes of the people involved. Are these taken into account? Can an individual refuse a particular promotion without jeopardizing his chances in the future? Is the organization living up to the values implied by its adoption of the OD program and allowing individuals to have some real choice?

Manpower Planning and Mobility

The concern in manpower planning activities and their implementation is organization centered. When decisions are made concerning the human resources available and about the kinds of on- or off-the-job training required to fit people for their managerial positions of the future, little or no account is taken of the individual's own preferences. The fact that he should be an active participant in planning his own career is often neglected. His job assignments and training are based only upon organizational considerations, rather than on an individual basis.

To be consistent with the values implied in OD, the manpower planning function must be expanded so that when the characteristics of the available human resources are gathered, the plans, aspirations, and needs of the individuals concerned must be mapped, as well as their skills, experiences, and potential.

In one OD program monitored by the author, it became clear that the OD activity did not extend to this personnel process.[3]

People did not have a grasp of their potential careers in the organization. New job assignments and their implications were not explained to, or discussed with, the people concerned. Information about job changes and even work location changes were presented as *faits accomplis*. Individuals were well aware of the contrast between the way the organization was treating them and the values implied by the OD training.

What I have suggested is that a major barrier to the effective implementation of an OD program results from its partial application to the task subsystem of the organization and from the failure of the personnel subsystem to implement its activation in a way consistent with the values implied in the OD program. As a result, the necessary beliefs about performance and reward are not established in the minds of the organization's members, who fail to see the value (or payoff) in behaving in the ways described by the program.

Some general suggestions have been made about personnel areas in which alternative policies might be appropriate and congruent with the OD values. With the use of computerized personnel and manpower records, the practical difficulties of implementing a more personalized personnel system can be overcome.

3. S. R. Maxwell and M. G. Evans, "An Evaluation of Organizational Development: Three Phases of the Managerial Grid," *Journal of Business Administration* (Fall 1973).

The Fifth Achievement

ROBERT R. BLAKE

JANE SRYGLEY MOUTON

Recognizing man's four achievements in dealing with differences among men, i.e., science, politics, hierarchy, and law, the authors foresee a fifth achievement by which men will ultimately be able to work out their differences. It will be the establishment of a problem-solving society in which its members can resolve differences through their own insight. Here presented is the Conflict Grid for use in evaluating good or bad ways for ending disputes as a vehicle for creative problem solving in the future and a basis for such a problem-solving society.

A great new challenge to the American way of conducting its national life is taking shape. Conformity with older patterns is breaking down. Yet creative definitions of new patterns are not forthcoming, or at best are coming at a snail's pace. Unless the challenge of finding new patterns that can serve to strengthen society is successfully met, some of the nation's most cherished human values may very well be sacrificed. If we can meet it, however, our deeply embedded beliefs as to the role of men in society may not only be reinforced but may find even richer and more extensive applications in the society of tomorrow.

What is this challenge?

We widely acknowledge the objective of an open and free society based on individual responsibility and self-regulated participation by all in the conduct of national life. That men will differ in the ways they think and act is accepted as both inevitable and desirable. Indeed, this is one hallmark of an open

Robert R. Blake is president, and Jane Srygley Mouton is vice president, Scientific Methods, Incorporated, Austin, Texas.

society. Differences are intrinsically valuable. They provide the rich possibility that alternatives and options will be discovered for better and poorer ways of responding to any particular situation. Preserving the privilege of having and expressing differences increases our chances of finding "best" solutions to the many dilemmas that arise in living. They also add the spice of variety and give zest to human pursuits.

When it is possible for a man to make a choice from among several solutions, and when he can make this choice without infringing upon another man's freedom or requiring his cooperation, there is genuine autonomy. This is real freedom.

But in many situations not every man can have his own personal solution. When cooperation and coordination are required in conducting national life—in government, business, the university, agencies of the community, the home, and so on—differences that arise must find reconciliation. A solution must be agreed upon and embraced which can provide a pattern to which those involved are prepared to conform their behavior. Yet efforts to reconcile differences in order to achieve consensus-based patterns of conduct often only serve to promote difficulties. When disagreements as to sound bases for action can be successfully resolved, freedom can be retained and necessary solutions implemented. Dealing with the many and varied misunderstandings that are inevitable in a society dedicated to preserving the privilege of having and expressing differences is the challenge. As individuals, we find this hard to do. As members of organized groups, we appear to find it even more difficult.

FOUR CLASSICAL SOLUTIONS FOR RESOLVING CONFLICTS

In the conduct of society there are at least four major and different kinds of formal, structural arrangements which we rely on for resolving differences. They are the scientific method; politics; law, with its associated police powers; and organizational hierarchy.

Of undisputed value in finding the objective solution to which agreement can readily be given are the methods of science. A well-designed experiment confirms which of several alternatives is the most valid basis of explanation while simultaneously demonstrating the unacceptability of the remaining explanations.

Our political mechanisms are based on the one-man-one-vote approach to problem solving. This provides for the resolution of differences according to a weighting approach, and the basis is usually that the majority prevail. By this means, decisions can be made and actions taken even though differences may remain. Simply being outvoted, however, does not aid those on the losing side in changing their intellectual and emotional attitudes. While it ensures that a solution is chosen, the fact that it is often on a win-lose or a compromise basis may pose further problems when those who are outvoted resolve to be the winners of the future. Often the underlying disagreements are deepened.

Legal mechanisms apply only in resolving differences when questions of law are involved and other means of reaching agreement usually have met with failure. With application of associated police powers, the use of force is available to back up legal mechanisms when law is violated. But this constitutes a far more severe solution to the problem. The ultimate failure of law which invites the use of military power is in effect a court of last resort.

Within society's formal institutions such as business, government, education, and the family, organizational hierarchy, or rank, can and does permit the resolution of differences. The premise is that when a disagreement arises between any two persons of differing rank, the one of higher rank can impose a solution unilaterally based on his position. In the exercise of authority, suppression may also sacrifice the validity of a solution, since there is no intrinsic basis of truth in the idea that simply because a man is the boss of other men he is ordained with an inherent wisdom. While this arrangement provides a basis for avoiding indecision and impasse, it may and often does have the undesirable consequence of sacrificing the support of those to whom it is applied for the solution of the problem, to say nothing of its adverse effects on future creativity.

These classical solutions to dealing with differences—science, politics, law, and hierarchy—represent real progress in learning to conduct the national life. Where it can be applied, scientific method provides a close to ideal basis for resolving differences. That politics, courts of justice, and organizational hierarchy, though more limited, are necessary is indisputable. But that they are being questioned and increasingly rejected is also indisputable. Even if they were not, none of these alone nor all of them together provide a sound and sufficient basis for the development of a truly problem-solving society.

WHAT IS THE FIFTH ACHIEVEMENT?

There is another essential ingredient. It is a sharply increased understanding by every man of the roots of conflict and the human skills of gaining the resolution of differences. The acquisition of such insight and skill by every man could provide a social foundation for reaching firm and sound understandings on a direct man-to-man basis of the inevitable disagreements that arise in conducting the national life. This kind of deepened skill in the direct resolution of differences could do much to provide a realistic prospect that the antagonisms, cleavages, or injustices real and imagined in society today can be reduced if not eliminated. It offers the promise that the sicknesses of alienation and apathy, the destructive aggressions, and the organization-man mentality can be healed.

The Fifth Achievement, then, is in the establishment of a problem-solving society where differences among men are subject to resolution through insights that permit protagonists themselves to identify and implement solutions to their differences upon the basis of committed agreement. That men ultimately will be able to work out, face to face, their differences is a hoped-for achievement of the future. Extending their capacity to do so could reduce the number of problems brought before the bench or dealt with through hierarchy. At the same time, scientific and political processes could be strengthened if progress were made in this direction. Even more important, it could perhaps lead to the resolution of many conflicts on a local level that block the development of a creative and committed problem-solving community. Success in meeting this challenge in the period ahead is perhaps the surest way to preserve and strengthen the values of a free society while protecting and even strengthening the privilege of having and expressing differences.

HOW TO INCREASE SKILL IN MANAGING CONFLICT

Why do men rely on these other four approaches to conflict settlement while placing lower value on the resolution of differences in a direct, man-to-man way? One explanation for this might be that they do not hold in concert a conceptual basis for analyzing situations of disagreement and their causes. It should be said that conceptual understanding, while necessary for strengthening behavior, is clearly not in itself a sufficient basis for learning the skills of sound resolution of conflict. Personal entrapment from self-deception about one's motivations is too great. Insensitivity about one's behavior and the reactions of others to it is too extensive. To connect a conceptual analysis to one's own behavior and conduct in ways that permit insight and change seems to require something more in the way of personal learning.

Classroom learning methodologies that could enable men to gain insights regarding conflict and acquire skills for resolving it seem to be impoverished. To aid men in acquiring both the conceptual understanding for managing conflict and the skills to see their own reactions in situations of conflict, man-to-man feedback seems to be an essential condition. A variety of situations involving laboratory learning that permit this have been designed (Bach & Wyden, 1969; Blake & Mouton, 1968; Bradford, Gibb, & Benne, 1964; Schein & Bennis, 1965). They set the stage for men to learn to face their differences and find creative and valid solutions to their problems.

Success in mastering this Fifth Achievement will undoubtedly require reconception of the classroom in ways that permit the study of conflict as a set of concepts and the giving and receiving of feedback in ways that enable men to see how to strengthen their own capacities and skills for coping with it directly.

Conceptual Analysis of Conflict   This paper concentrates upon a first step toward this Fifth Achievement by presenting a conceptual basis for analyzing situations of conflict. The Conflict Grid in Figure 1 is a way of identifying basic assumptions when men act in situations where differences are present, whether disagreement is openly expressed or silently present (Blake & Mouton, 1964; Blake, Shepard, & Mouton, 1964).

Whenever a man meets a situation of conflict, he has at least two basic considerations in mind. One of these is the *people* with whom he is in disagreement. Another is *production of results*, or getting a resolution to the disagreement. It is the

FIG. 1.   *The Conflict Grid*

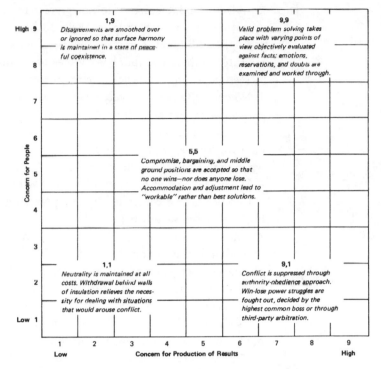

amount and kind of emphasis he places on various combinations of each of these elements that determine his thinking in dealing with conflict.

Basic attitudes toward people and toward results are visualized on nine-point scales. These form the Grid in Figure 1. The nine-point scale representing concern for producing a result provides the horizontal axis for the Grid. The phrase "concern for" does not show results produced but rather denotes the degree of emphasis in his thinking that the man places on getting results. The *1* end represents low concern, and the *9* represents the highest possible concern. The same applies on the vertical or concern-for people axis. Considering the interactions of these two scales, there are 81 possible positions. Each describes an intersection between the two dimensions.

The following pages discuss strategies of managing conflict according to the five basic theories—those appearing at the

four corners and the center of the figure. When these basic styles are understood, one can predict for each how a man
operating under that style is likely to handle conflict. There
are eight additional important theories composed from various
mixtures of these five, but basic issues of conflict resolution can
be seen in dealing with these "pure" theories.

No one style is exclusively characteristic of one man in comparison with another, although one style may be dominant in
a man's actions. Furthermore, even though one may be dominant for a time, it may be abandoned and replaced by another
when the first has been ineffective in achieving resolution.

What are some of the ways of dealing with conflict?

Conflict can be controlled by overpowering it and suppressing one's adversary (9,1 in the lower right corner of the Grid).
An ultimate expression of this is in the extremes of police power and military action. Extracting compliance by authority-
obedience is possible when rank is present. The conflict can be
cut off and suppressed in this way, "Yours not to question
why!" When rank is not available, a win–lose basis expresses
the same set of assumptions. Winning for one's own position
predominates over seeking a valid solution.

Another strategy is to smooth conflict by cajolery, by letting a man know that with a little patience he will find that all
is right (1,9 in the upper left corner). The assumption of sweetness and light often leads to resolution by people's retracting
from previously held positions, preferring personal acceptance
to solution validity. This can promote accord and harmony, but
it sacrifices conviction and insight into differences, while decreasing the likelihood of achieving valid solutions. Staying
out of situations that provoke controversy or turning away
from topics that promote disagreement represents a set of assumptions about how to live in a conflict-free way (1,1 in the
lower left corner). Then one need not be stirred up even though
the issue may need resolution. A man can remain composed if
he does not let himself be drawn into controversy; he avoids it
by remaining neutral. This kind of "see no disagreement, hear
no disagreement, and speak no disagreement" represents a
withdrawal from social responsibility in a world where the reso-

lution of differences is key to finding sound solutions. It is the ultimate in alienation.

A third set of assumptions leads to a middle-of-the-road solution to differences through accommodation and adjustment. Disagreement is settled through bargaining a compromise solution (5,5). The assumptions underlying compromising of one's convictions are at the root of this approach. It means agreeing so as to be agreeable, even to sacrificing sound action; settling for what you can get rather than working to get what is sound in the light of the best available facts and data.

The mental attitude behind the one-man-one-vote approach often leads to the endorsement of positions calculated to get majority support even though this means giving up a solution of deeper validity. The same assumptions often prevail behind the scenes in out-of-court settlements.

Outside the sphere of industrial management, solutions to major political and international problems of recent years provide classic examples of 5,5 splitting. One is the "separate but equal" approach to solving what is seen as the race problem. The cessation of hostilities in Korea by the establishment of the thirty-eighth parallel as a line of demarcation between North and South in the early Fifties is another. This set a precedent for setting up the "Demilitarized Zone" between North and South Vietnam. The Berlin Wall is probably the most significant symbol of the East-West split. The 5,5 attitude is reflected daily by news reporters and commentators who quote "unidentified but high-level sources" or hide their sources by attributing their facts merely to "usually reliable sources."

Under a 9,9 approach, disagreement is valued as an inevitable result of the fact that strong-minded people have convictions about what is right. A man says, "Nothing is sacrosanct. What are the facts? What are the causes? What are the conclusions?" Reservations and emotions that interrupt agreement based on logic and data are confronted through candid discussion of them directly with the person involved in the disagreement. Insight and resolution are possible but involve maturity and real human skill. This approach may be time-consuming in the short run but time-conserving over the long term. It permits men to disagree, to work out their disagreements in the light of facts, and ultimately to understand one another. Such problem-solving constructiveness in conflict situations is the fundamental basis for realizing the Fifth Achievement.

How does effective conflict management interrelate with other social processes of seemingly equal or greater significance in strengthening society? Indeed, it might be maintained that the challenge to society seen today is in nonconformity with its norms, rather than in faulty management of conflict.

In what ways are conflict and conformity interdependent (Blake & Mouton, 1961)? Men in everyday life do conform to the expectations of others and the patterns of their institutions. This readiness to conform reduces conflict and is what permits regularity, order, and predictability. To adhere to common norms provides a basis for organized effort. From conformity with conventionalized social and organizational practices can come a sense of identification, belonging, and *esprit de corps.* On the other hand, failure to conform may stir conflict with one's colleagues and associates so that the nonconformist is rejected. Indeed, anxiety about rejection can be so overwhelming that, for many, conformity becomes an end in itself rather than a means to cooperation through interdependence. Under these circumstances, the capacity to challenge outmoded traditions, precedents, and past practices is lost. With sound ways of approaching and resolving conflict, outmoded patterns can successfully be challenged and upgraded by replacement of them with agreements which themselves can promote problem solving and creativity. In this way, finding new and better ways to accomplish personal, organizational, national, and perhaps even international objectives becomes possible.

Just stimulating people to challenge and contest status quo conformities, however, is likely to do little more than provoke disagreement and controversy, increase polarization, and ultimately end in win-lose, impasse, compromise, or chaos. Yet the status quo requirements must continuously be challenged in a problem-solving and creative way, not in a manner that pits man against man to see who can win or, even worse, in a way that ends in anarchy.

The Conflict Grid is useful in seeing the more subtle connections among conflict and conformity and creative problem solving. Conformity to the 9,1 authority-obedience demands that are involved in hierarchical rank is exemplified by the boss, teacher, or parent who gives the orders to subordinates, students, or children who are expected to obey. The exercise of initiative which produces differences is equivalent to insubordination. Conformity under 9,1 may produce the protocol of surface compliance, but the frustrations of those who are suppressed are often evident. Ways of striking back against the boss, teacher, or parent appear. Such acts may be open ones of resistance and rebellion or disguised ones of sabotage, cheating, or giving agreement without following through. Each of these in a certain sense involves reverse creativity, where ingenuity is exercised in attacking or "beating" the system. It is creativity in resentment of the system, not in support of it.

In another type of conformity, the rules of relationship are, "Don't say anything if you can't say something nice" (1,9). Togetherness, social intimacy, and warmth engendered by yielding one's convictions in the interests of personal acceptance are certainly objectionable solutions in a society where having and expressing differences is relied on as the basis for finding sound courses of action. It can produce a quorum of agreement but smother creative problem solving in sweetness and love. The kind of disagreement that might provoke resentment is avoided. The opportunity for creative problem solving to emerge is absent.

Another kind of conformity relates to adhering to the form and not to the substance of life. Here people conform by going through the motions expected of them, treadmilling through the days, months, and years (1,1). In this way, survival is accomplished by being visible without being seen.

Organization-man conformity (5,5) entails positively embracing the status quo with minimum regard for the soundness of status quo requirements. Yet, even here, as new problems arise, differences appear and disagreements become evident. There are several kinds of 5,5 actions that on shallow examination may give the appearance of approaching problems from an altered, fresh, and original point of view. Pseudo-creativity may be seen when new approaches, even though they constitute only small departures from the outmoded past, are recommended on the basis of their having been tried elsewhere. Under these circumstances a man is forwarding actions taken by others rather than promoting examination of actions on the basis of his own convictions. In this way, he can suggest, while avoiding the challenge or rejection of his own convictions. Deeper examination of 5,5 behavior leads to the conclusion that imitation rather than innovation is the rule.

In other instances, solutions which are proposed as compromise positions can give the impression of "flexibility" in thought. When adjustment and accommodation, backing and filling, twisting and turning, shifting and adapting take place in the spirit of compromise, the motivation behind them is usually to avoid interpersonal emotions resulting from confrontation. Behaving in this manner is a reaction to disagreement, and it means that personal validity is being eroded.

Flexibility is a highly valued component in mature and effective behavior. But is it not contradictory to advocate flexibility on the one hand and to forewarn against compromise on the other? This question is important to clarify.

Flexibility calls for deliberate examination of options and alternatives. It means having back-up tactics that permit swift resolution of unforeseen circumstances, a climate that permits people to move back and forth and in and out from one situation to another, but based on facts, data, and logic of the situation as it unfolds. These are the characteristics of creative problem solving that permit gains to be made as opportunities arrive; that permit opportunities to be created, threats to be anticipated, and risks that result when people fail to react to be reduced.

Thus there are actions to adjust a difference to keep peace and actions to adjust to altered circumstances for better results. It is most important to distinguish between the two kinds. Flexibility for better results is likely to have a stamp of 9,9 on it; "flexibility" to keep peace by avoiding clash of personalities is in the 5,5 area. One is enlivening and promotes creativity. The other leads to the perpetuation of the organization-man mentality of status quo rigidities.

In the final analysis, conformity is to be valued. The problem is to ensure that the thinking of men conforms with sound purposes and premises. Conformity which means adherence to premises of human logic so that decisions reached are furthering growth capacity in sound and fundamental ways is what every individual might be expected to want. It is what man should want in the underpinnings of his daily interactions. It is conformity at this level that promotes the pursuit of creative and innovative solutions. Only when the values of a nation stimulate experimentation and promote a truly constructive attitude toward discovery and innovation is the full potential from creative efforts available as a source of thrust for replacing outmoded status quo conformities with more problem-solving requirements (9,9).

What Men Want— Transnationally

Though varying widely in their ways of *actually* dealing with conflict, studies show that leaders in the United States, Great Britain, the Middle and Far East all indicate that they would *prefer* the 9,9 approach of *open confrontation* as the soundest way of managing situations of conflict, particularly under circumstances where outmoded conformities are under examination (Mouton & Blake, 1970). Though extremely difficult, it appears to be the soundest of several possible choices. This is not to imply that every decision should be made by a leader through calling a meeting or obtaining team agreement. Nor for a crisis situation does it imply that a leader should withhold exercising direction. But a 9,9 foundation of interdependence can build a strong basis for an open, problem-solving society in which men can have and express differences and yet be interrelated in ways that promote the mutual respect, common goals, and trust and understanding they must have to achieve results in ways that lead to personal gratification and maturity.

POSSIBILITIES OF THE FIFTH ACHIEVEMENT FOR STRENGTHENING SOCIETY

This challenge to America, the need for men to learn to confront outmoded status quo requirements and to manage the resultant conflict in such ways as to promote creative problem solving, promises much for the decades ahead, if we can meet and master it.

Consider for a moment the possibility of success in mastering this Fifth Achievement. What might it mean?

1. Enriched family life rather than the steady rise in the divorce rate.

2. Sounder child rearing, evidenced in teen-age youngsters capable of expression and action in dealing in a problem-solving rather than a protest way with adults and the institutions of society who are capable of interacting in an equally sound way.

3. The conversion of academic environments from subject-oriented learning centers to ones that expand the capacity of individuals for contributing creatively to the evolving character of society.

4. The betterment of communities in ways that more fully serve human wants.

5. The more rapid integration of minorities into a more just society, with the reduction and eventual elimination of disenfranchised, alienated segments.

6. Fuller and more creative use of human energies in conducting the organizations that serve society.

7. A greater readiness to support and utilize science for approaching problems when evidence, facts, and data come to have an ever greater value as the bases for gaining insight.

8. A strengthening of politics by readiness to advocate positions on the basis of statesmanlike convictions rather than to adopt positions for political expediency.

9. Reliance on knowledge rather than rank in the resolution of differences and disagreements in organization situations.

10. A stronger basis for mind-meeting agreements rather than resorting to legal actions to force a resolution of disputes.

If erosion of social institutions has not already become too great, all of these aims can perhaps be forwarded over time by our classical institutions for settling conflicts. But surely men capable of resolving their conflicts directly would forward human progress with a dramatic thrust—and on a far more fundamental and therefore enduring basis.

If this Fifth Achievement is to be realized, it is likely that greater use of the behavioral sciences will be essential. For in the behavioral sciences may well lie the key to a more rewarding and progressive society in which men can share and evaluate their differences, learn from them, and use conflict as a stepping stone to the greater progress that is possible when differences can be resolved in a direct, face-to-face way.

Will this challenge be met, or will the cherished freedom of having and expressing differences be sacrificed?

REFERENCES   Bach, G. R., & Wyden, P. *The ultimate enemy.* New York: Morrow, 1969.

Blake, R. R., & Mouton, Jane S. The experimental investigation of interpersonal influence. In A. D. Biderman & H. Zimmer (Eds.), *The manipulation of human behavior.* New York: Wiley, 1961.

Blake, R. R., & Mouton, Jane S. *The managerial grid.* Houston: Gulf, 1964.

Blake, R. R., & Mouton, Jane S. *Corporate excellence through grid organization development: A systems approach.* Houston: Gulf, 1968.

Blake, R. R., Shepard, H. A., & Mouton, Jane S. *Managing intergroup conflict in industry.* Houston: Gulf, 1964.

Bradford, L. P., Gibb, J. R., & Benne, K. D. (Eds.) *T-group theory and laboratory method: Innovation in re-education.* New York: Wiley, 1964.

Mouton, Jane S., & Blake, R. R. Issues in transnational organization development. In B. M. Bass, R. B. Cooper, & J. A. Haas (Eds.), *Managing for task accomplishment.* Lexington, Mass.: D. C. Heath, 1970. Pp. 208-224.

Schein, E. H., & Bennis, W. G. (Eds.) *Personal and organizational change through group methods: The laboratory approach.* New York: Wiley, 1965.

V. P. LUCHSINGER
L. L. LUCHSINGER

Transactional Analysis for Managers, or How to Be More OK with OK Organizations

This important device is a whole lot more than "fun and games" and has made a serious impact on the management profession.

A contribution from current nonfiction literature and psychoanalysis that will have a great impact on the management profession is Transactional Analysis. Introduced over a decade ago by Eric Berne, M.D., Transactional Analysis provides the manager with an analytical tool that can help him understand the most complex phenomena in management — the interactions between manager and employee.

Many managers have already been exposed to the principles of Transactional Analysis. The subject received much publicity in 1964 when the book *Games People Play* by Dr. Berne climbed to the top of the popular reading lists. A more current title on the best seller lists, *I'm OK — You're OK*, by Thomas A. Harris, M.D., explores the subject of Transactional Analysis in greater depth.

A possible reason for the delay in applying the principles of Transactional Analysis to management has been the fascination and popularity of games, perhaps to the extent of faddism. Dr. Berne wrote *Games People Play* in response to requests for more information about games. Games overshadowed the

subject of Transactional Analysis. The more recent book by Dr. Harris is directed at the general public and has not been identified as a manual for managers. Practitioners and scholars of management are looking at the possible contributions of Transactional Analysis to the improved practice of management.

Harris describes Transactional Analysis as a method for examining a transaction between two people "wherein 'I do something to you and you do something back' and determining which part of the multinatured individual is 'coming on.' "[1]

Transactional Analysis (this term will be capitalized when referring to the entire system) can be divided into four component parts: structural analysis, transactional analysis (the analysis of a specific transaction), games analysis, and script analysis. The four areas are briefly described to provide a reference for the language and terms of Transactional Analysis.

Structural Analysis. Structural Analysis is concerned with the "segregation and analysis of the ego states."[2] Berne identified the three ego

V. P. Luchsinger and L. L. Luchsinger are on the faculty at Texas Tech University.

158 V. P. Luchsinger and L. L. Luchsinger, "Transactional Analysis for Managers, or How to Be More OK with OK Organizations," pp. 5–12, *MSU Business Topics*, Spring 1974. Reprinted by permission of the publisher, Division of Research, Graduate School of Business Administration, Michigan State University.

states as the Parent, Adult, and Child. (When referred to as ego states these terms are capitalized.) They are represented in the following diagram and in the literature on Transactional Analysis as P-A-C.

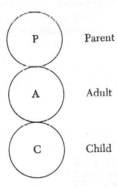

P   Parent

A   Adult

C   Child

The three ego states are not concepts like Freud's id, ego, and superego. They are phenomenological realities, based on real world behavior. Although lines separate the ego states, the lines are not barriers. A healthy person is able to move from ego state to ego state.

The Parent ego state is that body of recordings in the brain that reflects the unquestioned events or imposed external restraints perceived by a person during his early years of life. Characteristics of a person acting in the Parent include being overprotective, distant, dogmatic, indispensible, and upright. Physical and verbal clues that someone is acting in the Parent include the wagging finger to show displeasure, reference to laws and rules, and reliance on ways that were successful in the past. Parent inputs to behavior are taught.

The Adult, assuming the rationality of man, is the information seeker and processor. It functions as a computer processing new data, making decisions, and updating the data in the original recording of the Parent and Child. The Adult is characterized by logical thinking and reasoning. This ego state can be identified by verbal and physical signs which include thoughtful concentration and

factual discussion. Adult inputs to behavior are reasoned.

The Child ego state is the body of data that is recorded in the brain as a result of experiences during the first five years of life. Characteristics of the Child include creativity, conformity, depression, anxiety, dependence, fear, and hate. Physical and verbal clues that a person is acting in the Child are silent compliance, attention seeking, temper tantrums, giggling, and coyness. The Child is also characterized by non-logical and immediate actions which result in immediate satisfaction. Child inputs to behavior are laden with feeling and emotion.

Analysis of Transaction. Analysis of transactions (T.A.) is the technique for examining a transaction or interaction between two people and the ego states involved. Recognizing the ego states of the two people involved in the transaction can help a person communicate and interact more effectively.

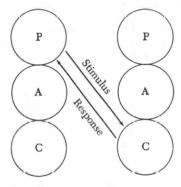

Transactions can be classified as complementary or non-complementary. Transactions are complementary when the lines of communication between the two people are parallel. For example, a person in the Parent state interacting with the Child of another person would be involved in a complementary transaction if the response from the second person originates from the Child and is directed to the Parent. Both are acting in the perceived and expected ego states. Complementary transactions are important because they indicate completed communications or interaction between the two people.

A non-complementary or crossed transaction occurs when the interactions do not have common origination and terminal ego states. The following example shows the stimulus directed from the Adult to the Adult being crossed with a response from the Parent to the Child. In this situation the communication is crossed and ineffective.

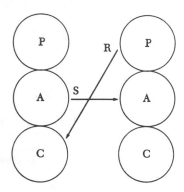

It is possible for the stimulus to originate in any of the three ego states and be directed to any of the three ego states. This produces nine possible types of complementary transactions.

The number of non-complementary transactions varies depending upon how one describes the ego states and the forms of contamination-mixed ego states that might appear in an ego state. At this point we turn the subject of non-complementary transactions back to the psychoanalyst and consider only complementary transactions.

Games Analysis. Berne defines a game as an ongoing series of complementary ulterior transactions progressing to a well-defined, predictable outcome.[3] Games are basically dishonest and self-defeating as the interactions are not honest requests but gambits or moves in a game.

Some of the games managers play include "You're a Professional Now" and "The Man at the Bench." Articles about the games managers play have been written by Ronald J. Burke (1968),[4] Joe Kelly (1968),[5] and Curtis J. Potter (1969).[6] However, a more serious pragmatic approach has been offered by J. V. D. Meininger (1973).[7] The purpose of this article is to avoid the popularity of games and focus upon the analysis of transactions.

Script Analysis. Script analysis is an examination of transactions and interactions to determine the nature of one's life script. It is a method for uncovering early decisions on how life should be lived. When confronted with a situation, a person acts according to his script which is based on what he expects or how he views his life position. In a sense, man's behavior becomes quasi-programed by the script which emerges out of life experience.

Life Positions

Transactional Analysis uses the four following classifications to describe the life positions that a person holds for himself and others:

I'm not OK, You're OK
I'm not OK, You're not OK
I'm OK, You're not OK
I'm OK, You're OK[8]

A person lives his life in one of these life positions. Such a life position or view of himself and others affects how he will interact with them. Only the "I'm OK, You're OK" position is considered healthy.

MANAGER—EMPLOYEE INTERACTION

Managers and employees continually interact with each other. Accepting the idea that the manager initiates most of the interactions and transactions, examples of the nine complementary transactions are used to illustrate manager-employee interactions.

Manager in the Parent Ego State

The manager in the Parent is typified by the "I'm OK, You're not OK" life style. He will be a source of admonitions, rewards, rules, criticisms, and praise. He can be expected to thrive on power and use personal successes or the failures of others as justification for a course of action.

Parent-Parent Transaction

The Parent-Parent transaction can be beneficial in cases where the employee joins forces with the manager and supports the manager. An executive secretary who dictates orders in the absence of the manager provides an excellent example of the cooperative or supportive Parent-Parent transaction. There are disadvantages to this type of transaction. Consider the situation in which the manager and employee are competing for the position of "Best" Parent. In such a situation the employee will promote his own ideas and orders rather than those of the manager.

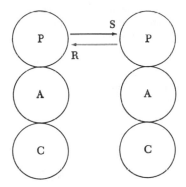

If the manager and employee have opposing recordings in the Parent, they will work against each other.

Another disadvantage can be found when the employee communicates with the manager. In the example below the employee is agreeing with the Parent in the manager without really engaging in a meaningful dialogue.

MANAGER: "An effective maintenance repair program always reduces costs."

EMPLOYEE: "I always say that a stitch in time saves nine."

Both the manager and employee agree on a basic philosophical issue that a maintenance program can save money. No facts were mentioned or introduced in this transaction.

Parent-Adult Transaction

The manager in the Parent ego state will have difficulty with the employee in the Adult ego state. In such transactions the manager will be frustrated because the employee will not perform as directed. The manager may consider the employee an incorrigible smart aleck. The employee will be con-

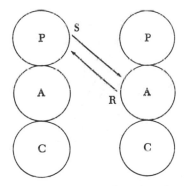

demned for not respecting the voice of authority and experience.

The employee will be frustrated by the manager's failure to act in the Adult.

The dialogue below provides an example of this transaction:

MANAGER: "An effective maintenance repair program always reduces costs."

EMPLOYEE: "The problem is the new supplier. Maintenance and production records show that his parts don't last as do the parts from Acme Company."

The manager, using the standard cliche about effective maintenance, finds himself confronted with facts. In the Parent he is not able to accept this "smart alecky" reply and the idea that his successful method from the past may be wrong. The employee will not be able to accept a slogan in place of facts and records. Due to the mutual frustration, such a relationship will not be productive or long lasting.

Parent-Child Transaction

Perhaps the ideal situation when the manager is in the Parent is for the employee to be in the Child. The manager will find this advantageous in that he will have a loyal and dutiful employee who will respect him and follow his orders.

This ideal situation has disadvantages. The manager may feel that his employees are incapable of assuming responsibility. The manager continually lives with the possibility that someday one or more of the employees in the Child will change from compliance to tantrums.

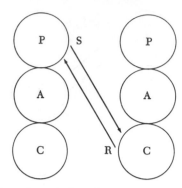

The employee finds such a transaction advantageous in that it eliminates much responsibility and pressure. Acting in the Child prevents much conflict and provides for ease in operation. The employee suffers from this interaction in that he must surrender his Adult. He doesn't think and his job must be routine so he performs only as directed. The example below uses the same stimulus used in the previous example:

MANAGER: "An effective maintenance repair program always reduces costs."
EMPLOYEE: "Yes, sir."

In this transaction there is no meaningful feedback for the manager except that he has a loyal employee who agrees. Although a real problem may exist, the employee finds it easier to perform as directed than to bring the factual information to the attention of the manager.

A closing note on the Parent: The Parent is not the best ego state for the manager to exercise in his daily interactions with employees. The limitations outweigh the advantages. Although it may be useful and required in some situations, it limits effectiveness and denies the use of current facts.

Manager in the Adult Ego State

The manager in the Adult tries to reason out issues, clarifies and informs employees of issues, and has concern for facts, figures, and human needs. His life style generally is the "I'm OK, You're OK" position.

Adult-Parent Transaction

While the manager attempts to use the information he has processed, the employee in the Parent prefers to use cliches and rules of the past. Citing past successes or proven methods, the employee will not favor change or progress even when it is based on facts, figures, and logic.

In such a transaction the employee will try to control and dominate the manager by using the Parent ego state. This transaction style can be effective only on a temporary basis. It can be used to help a new manager understand the rules and guidance under which the employees operate. The employee in the Parent can be accepted for the facts that he can provide.

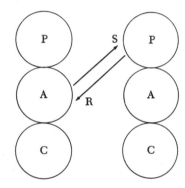

There are many disadvantages to this transaction style. The classic example is the Parent's resentment of the young college graduate in a managerial position. The older and experienced employees who know what is to be done and how to do it do not want the newcomers to change the ways of old. The manager in this situation must remain in the Adult. He must not compete by entering his Parent nor retreat by entering the Child. The manager must remind the employee who is the manager and who is the employee.

The employee in the Parent can create other difficulties for the manager if other employees in the Child recognize and accept the employee in the Parent. The employee in the Parent may have better interaction with the other employees. Acting in the Parent the employee may discount all of the benefits that management attempts to use while introducing change. An employee in the Parent can create hostile feelings toward managers in the Adult.

A typical Adult-Parent transaction is provided below:

MANAGER: "The new supplier's parts will last if we make the adjustments as directed in his technical instructions."

EMPLOYEE: "We never had this problem with the old supplier. You just can't beat the old reliable supplier."

In this example the manager is attempting to communicate with facts and logic. The employee is not concerned with facts or instructions but with past success. Although there may be valid reasons for changing suppliers, the employee in the Parent refuses to accept facts or technical instruction.

Adult-Adult Transaction

An ideal manager-employee relationship exists in the Adult-Adult. Complementary transactions in these states are very effective because both persons are acting in a rational and businesslike manner. Data is processed, decisions are made, and both parties are working toward the solution. Satisfaction is gained from the solution rather than the manager having a dutiful employee or the employee only trying to please her boss.

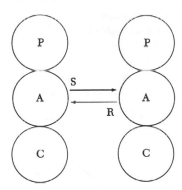

There are some inherent disadvantages to the Adult-Adult transactions. The elimination of the Child can make the transactions dull due to the

lack of stimulation that the Child can provide. The Adult-Adult level may prevent decisions from being reached due to the rational data processing procedures. This may prevent the manager and employee from meeting deadlines. When a decision has to be made but cannot be reached because of lengthy discussions, the manager may have to make the decision in the Parent.

An example of the manager in the Adult directing a stimulus to an employee who responds in the Adult demonstrates the exchange of facts.

MANAGER: "The new supplier's parts will last if we make the adjustments as directed in his technical instructions."

EMPLOYEE: "We found that using his recommended tension level reduced our product acceptance by 6 percent."

Such a transaction, based on facts and figures, may help the manager and the employee identify the real problem. Both the manager and the employee want a solution based on facts.

Adult-Child Transaction

The Adult-Child interaction can be effective if the manager is aware of the ego state of the employee. In such interactions the manager can allow the employee in the Child to be creative.

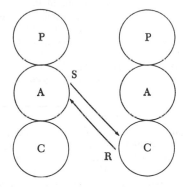

The manager in the Adult often assumes that his employees are also in the Adult. Very often this assumption prevents the manager from recognizing that the employee is in the Child ego state. This creates a situation that will be frustrating to the manager and the employee. The manager will find himself assigning more responsibility than the employee can handle. The manager becomes frustrated when the work is not done and the employee becomes discouraged because he cannot do the work.

Another disadvantage is the irrational responses that an employee in the Child will give to the manager in the Adult. An example is provided.

MANAGER: "The new supplier's parts will last if we make the adjustments as directed in his technical instructions."

EMPLOYEE: "I hate to make that darn adjustment. I get my hands dirty."

In this example we can see the Child rebelling against the factual Adult.

A closing note on the Adult: The Adult is capable of providing efficient analysis of information. The efficiency of the Adult must be increased when it is supported by the strength of the Parent and the creativity of the Child.

Manager in the Child Ego State

The manager in the Child ego state will have very little to contribute in the form of effective management. Although creativity is one of the characteristics of the Child, the role of a manager requires more than just creativity. Creativity alone does not offset the disadvantages of being anxious, fearful, conforming, and acting on whims.

The manager in the Child is defensive. He assumes the basic "I'm not OK, You're OK" life position.

Child-Parent Transaction

An employee acting in the Parent will control the manager in the Child. The Parent will be strong and overbearing on the Child. The manager will yield to the employee. If the Child in the manager objects or does something that is not approved by the employee in the Parent, the manager is punished. The employee holds threats of punishment over the manager. The threats may be of ridicule, loss of popularity, or demotion.

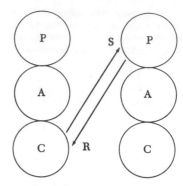

An example of the manager and employee illustrates the Child-Parent transaction.

MANAGER: "I'll show them that we cannot operate with inferior parts. Stop the machines."

EMPLOYEE: "If you stop the machines the men don't get paid. The men will not like you if they stop getting paid."

The manager in the Child state, seeking an immediate solution, decides on an irrational course of action. The employee in the Parent condemns the manager. The Child in the manager might be expected to ask the employee, in the Parent, what to do. This results in the employee making the decisions.

Child-Adult Transaction

Sometimes it is possible for an Adult employee to control the manager in the Child. More often, the

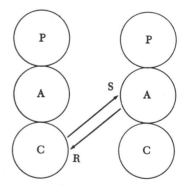

employee will become discouraged by the manager. The manager who makes his decision on whims, fancies, and emotions will pose a threat to the employee who want to interact with the manager in terms of facts. A major disadvantage of this transaction style is that the organization may lose many good employees.

The following example provides an Adult response to a Child stimulus.

MANAGER: "I'll show them that we cannot operate with inferior parts. Stop the machines."

EMPLOYEE: "Stopping the machines will not solve the problem. Our repair and production records should be shown to the purchasing department."

In this example the manager's Child has provided a solution to the problem. The employee, responding in the Adult, attempts to present a solution based on facts.

Child-Child Transaction

The manager in the Child interacting with an employee in the Child will not last very long in an organization that reviews performance. The manager is not capable of leading or directing and the

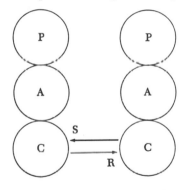

employee is not able to follow. The manager will act on whim and fancy and the employee will be the same. The chances for effective transactions and performance are as great as might be observed with two small children building sand castles. All will go well as long as all is going well.

The effectiveness of the Child-Child transaction can be seen in the example below:

MANAGER: "I'll show them that we cannot operate with inferior parts. Stop the machines."

EMPLOYEE: "Good. We will have a good time with real long coffee breaks."

The manager is taking action that will halt production. In his Child he is having a tantrum. The employee, also in the Child, appreciates the immediate satisfaction.

A closing note on the Child: The manager in the Child ego state may prove to be a liability to the organization. In the Child a person cannot be expected to make decisions or provide the direction and guidance that is expected of a manager.

Hints for Managers

The effective manager should be able to analyze transactions with employees. Transaction Analysis provides him with a theoretical framework within which to examine the interactions with employees. The manager should be able to identify the ego states from which both parties are interacting. A better understanding of himself, employees, and interactions with others will make the manager more comfortable, confident, and effective. He will be aware of ego states and seek the proper ego states when interacting with employees.

Transactional Analysis is a managerial tool. It should help the manager in his daily transactions with employees.

1.   Thomas A. Harris, M.D., *I'm OK — You're OK* (New York: Harper & Row Publishers, Inc., 1967), pp. 12-13.
2.   Eric Berne, *Transactional Analysis in Psychotherapy* (New York: Grove Press, 1961), p. 22.
3.   Eric Berne, M.D., *Games People Play* (New York: Grove Press, 1964), p. 48.
4.   Ronald J. Burke, "Games Managers Play," *Personnel Administration*, September 1968, pp. 52-57.
5.   Joe Kelly, "Executive Defense Mechanisms and Games," *Personnel Administration*, July 1968, pp. 30-35.
6.   Curtis J. Potter, "Games Managers Play," *Supervisory Management*, April 1969, pp. 29-33.
7.   J. V. D. Meininger, *Success through Transactional Analysis* (New York: Grosset & Dunlap, Inc., 1973).
8.   Harris, *I'm OK — You're OK*, p. 43.

BEHAVIOR
IN ORGANIZATIONS

- The first two parts of this text focused on the "objective" characteristics of the firm; the human element was not the key focus of the managerial decision process. However, the human variable was often cited as a crucial part of the decision process, for example, in organizational change and development. This part of the book focuses directly on the behavioral characteristics of the firm, including motivation, leadership, group behavior, and communication. Integration of the behavioral processes with the other dimensions is essential; even though the design, planning, and control processes of the firm are "correct," behavioral problems can lead to ultimate failure.

Section A:
Motivation

Motivation in organizational settings is seen by most management writers as a dual process. On the one hand, motivation depends on inner states such as needs, drives, values, and attitudes that "cause" an individual to behave in a certain manner. Several writers have focused on this side of the motivational coin. Motivation in organizational settings is equally dependent, however, on the conditions that the organization presents to its members. Such factors as opportunity for job autonomy, closeness of supervision, social interaction with the peer group, and type and frequency of communication can lead to higher levels of motivation in some individuals than in others. According to this definition of motivation, then, individual characteristics must "match" the organizational conditions in order to attain the factors associated with a motivated work force, including high productivity, low absenteeism and turnover, and contributions beyond the minimum required to retain employment.

In the first selection, David McClelland illustrates this definition exactly. According to McClelland, "our detailed knowledge of human motives shows that each one leads a person to behave in different ways. The contrast is not between being 'motivated' or 'unmotivated' but between being motivated toward A or toward B." His concept of achievement motivation (n Ach) suggests that a certain segment of our population enjoys challenges. These people seem to take moderate risks, prefer situations in which they have personal responsibility, and seek immediate feedback on their performance. How does an organization "motivate" these people? By providing these kinds of conditions. For example, a supervisor might allow a high achiever a great deal of autonomy and provide him with periodic reports of performance. These characteristics are built into some jobs (such as sales) but they certainly can be provided in others. Finally, in a review of several of his research studies, McClelland demonstrates that nAch can be learned.

The second article, by Charles Greene, focuses on a problem that continues to remain controversial in the motivational literature, the relationship between satisfaction, rewards, and performance. The argument since the beginning of the human relations era has been that job satisfaction leads to increased performance; a happy employee is a productive one. Greene reviews the evidence for this argument but also provides evidence for the antithesis of this statement: high performance leads to job satisfaction. (This may be especially true for high achievers.) Of course, as Greene points out, performance depends on many factors other than motivation, including employee ability, availability of the proper resources, and the type of rewards that are given for performance. The situation is, then, much more complicated than it would first appear, and Greene focuses on the factors that lead to high *effort* on the part of the employee, which seems to be the more logical approach to motivational studies.

The final selection, by Martin Koughan, is one of the most controversial in the entire text; he allows his employees to set their own pay levels. The focus of this article should be the motives of employees and the organizational factors that lead them to use this system wisely. Why, for example, did Larsen take a *cut* in pay when the new program was instituted? Why have profits continued to increase in spite of the increased costs? Although this article does not provide the usual amount of detail that is available in a case study, we included it in order to "motivate" the reader to further thought about the problem.

That Urge to Achieve

David C. McClelland

Most people in this world, psychologically, can be divided into two broad groups. There is that minority which is challenged by opportunity and willing to work hard to achieve something, and the majority which really does not care all that much.

For nearly twenty years now, psychologists have tried to penetrate the mystery of this curious dichotomy. Is the need to achieve (or the absence of it) an accident, is it hereditary, or is it the result of environment? Is it a single, isolatable human motive, or a combination of motives — the desire to accumulate wealth, power, fame? Most important of all, is there some technique that could give this will to achieve to people, even whole societies, who do not now have it?

While we do not yet have complete answers for any of these questions, years of work have given us partial answers to most of them and insights into all of them. There is a distinct human motive, distinguishable from others. It can be found, in fact tested for, in any group.

Let me give you one example. Several years ago, a careful study was made of 450 workers who had been thrown out of work by a plant shutdown in Erie, Pennsylvania. Most of the unemployed workers stayed home for a while and then checked back with the United States Employment Service to see if their old jobs or similar ones were available. But a small minority among them behaved differently: the day they were laid off, they started job-hunting.

They checked both the United States and the Pennsylvania Employment Office; they studied the "Help Wanted" sections of the papers; they checked through their union, their church, and various fraternal organizations; they looked into training courses to learn a new skill; they even left town to look for work, while the majority when questioned said they would not under any circumstances move away from Erie to obtain a job. Obviously the members of that active minority were differently motivated. All the men were more or less in the same situation objectively: they needed work, money, food, shelter, job security. Yet only a minority showed initiative and enterprise in finding what they needed. Why? Psychologists, after years of research, now believe they can answer that question. They have demonstrated that these men possessed in greater degree a specific type of human motivation. For the moment let us refer to this personality characteristic as "Motive A" and review some of the other characteristics of the men who have more of the motive than other men.

Suppose they are confronted by a work situation in which they can set their own goals as to how difficult a task they will undertake. In the psychological laboratory, such a situation is very simply created by asking them to throw rings

170 Reprinted by permission from *Think* Magazine, November–December 1966, pp. 19–32. Published by IBM, copyright 1966 by International Business Machines Corporation.

over a peg from any distance they may choose. Most men throw more or less randomly, standing now close, now far away, but those with Motive A seem to calculate carefully where they are most likely to get a sense of mastery. They stand nearly always at moderate distances, not so close as to make the task ridiculously easy, nor so far away as to make it impossible. They set moderately difficult, but potentially achievable goals for themselves, where they objectively have only about a 1-in-3 chance of succeeding. In other words, they are always setting challenges for themselves, tasks to make them stretch themselves a little.

But they behave like this only if *they* can influence the outcome by performing the work themselves. They prefer not to gamble at all. Say they are given a choice between rolling dice with one in three chances of winning and working on a problem with a one-in-three chance of solving in the time allotted, they choose to work on the problem even though rolling the dice is obviously less work and the odds of winning are the same. They prefer to work at a problem rather than leave the outcome to chance or to others.

Obviously they are concerned with personal achievement rather than with the rewards of success *per se,* since they stand just as much chance of getting those rewards by throwing the dice. This leads to another characteristic the Motive A men show — namely, a strong preference for work situations in which they get concrete feedback on how well they are doing, as one does, say in playing golf, or in being a salesman, but as one does not in teaching, or in personnel counseling. A golfer always knows his score and can compare how well he is doing with par or with his own performance yesterday or last week. A teacher has no such concrete feedback on how well he is doing in "getting across" to his students.

The *n* Ach Men

But why do certain men behave like this? At one level the reply is simple: because they habitually spend their time thinking about doing things better. In fact, psychologists typically measure the strength of Motive A by taking samples of a man's spontaneous thought (such as making up a story about a picture they have been shown) and counting the frequency with which he mentions doing things better. The count is objective and can even be made these days with the help of a computer program for content analysis. It yields what is referred to technically as an individual's *n* Ach score (for "need for Achievement"). It is not difficult to understand why people who think constantly about "doing better" are more apt to do better at job-hunting, to set moderate, achievable goals for themselves, to dislike gambling (because they get no achievement satisfaction from success), and to prefer work situations where they can tell easily whether they are improving or not. But why some people and not others come to think this way is another question. The evidence suggests it is not because they are born that way, but because of special training they get in the home from parents who set moderately high achievement goals but who are warm, encouraging and nonauthoritarian in helping their children reach these goals.

Such detailed knowledge about one motive helps correct a lot of common sense ideas about human motivation. For example, much public policy (and much business policy) is based on the simpleminded notion that people will work harder "if they have to." As a first approximation, the idea isn't totally wrong, but it is only a half-truth. The majority of unemployed workers in Erie "had to" find work as much as those with higher n Ach, but they certainly didn't work as hard at it. Or again, it is frequently assumed that *any* strong motive will lead to doing things better. Wouldn't it be fair to say that most of the Erie workers were just "unmotivated"? But our detailed knowledge of various human motives shows that each one leads a person to behave in *different* ways. The contrast is not between being "motivated" or "unmotivated" but between being motivated toward A or toward B or C, etc.

A simple experiment makes the point nicely: subjects were told that they could choose as a working partner either a close friend or a stranger who was known to be an expert on the problem to be solved. Those with higher n Ach (more "need to achieve") chose the experts over their friends, whereas those with more n Aff (the "need to affiliate with others") chose friends over experts. The latter were not "unmotivated"; their desire to be with someone they liked was simply a stronger motive than their desire to excel at the task. Other such needs have been studied by psychologists. For instance, the need for Power is often confused with the need for Achievement because both may lead to "outstanding" activities. There is a distinct difference. People with a strong need for Power want to command attention, get recognition, and control others. They are more active in political life and tend to busy themselves primarily with controlling the channels of communication both up to the top and down to the people so that they are more "in charge." Those with high n Power are not as concerned with improving their work performance daily as those with high n Ach.

It follows, from what we have been able to learn, that not all "great achievers" score high in n Ach. Many generals, outstanding politicians, great research scientists do not, for instance, because their work requires other personality characteristics, other motives. A general or a politician must be more concerned with power relationships, a research scientist must be able to go for long periods without the immediate feedback the person with high n Ach requires, etc. On the other hand, business executives, particularly if they are in positions of real responsibility or if they are salesmen, tend to score high in n Ach. This is true even in a Communist country like Poland: apparently there, as well as in a private enterprise economy, a manager succeeds if he is concerned about improving all the time, setting moderate goals, keeping track of his or the company's performance, etc.

Motivation and Half-truths

Since careful study has shown that common sense notions about motivation are at best half-truths, it also follows that you cannot trust what people tell you about their motives. After all, they often get their ideas about their own motives from common sense. Thus a general may say he is interested in achievement (because he has obviously achieved), or a businessman that he is interested only in making money (because he has made money), or one of the majority of unemployed in Erie that he desperately wants a job (because he knows he needs one); but a careful check of what each one thinks about and how he spends his time may show that each is concerned about quite different things. It requires special measurement techniques to identify the presence of *n* Ach and other such motives. Thus what people say and believe is not very closely related to these "hidden" motives which seem to affect a person's "style of life" more than his political, religious or social attitudes. Thus *n* Ach produces enterprising men among labor leaders or managers, Republicans or Democrats, Catholics, or Protestants, capitalists or Communists.

Wherever people begin to think often in *n* Ach terms, things begin to move. Men with higher *n* Ach get more raises and are promoted more rapidly, because they keep actively seeking ways to do a better job. Companies with many such men grow faster. In one comparison of two firms in Mexico, it was discovered that all but one of the top executives of a fast-growing firm had higher *n* Ach scores than the highest scoring executive in an equally large but slow-growing firm. Countries with many such rapidly growing firms tend to show above-average rates of economic growth. This appears to be the reason why correlations have regularly been found between the *n* Ach content in popular literature (such as popular songs or stories in children's textbooks) and subsequent rates of national economic growth. A nation which is thinking about doing better all the time (as shown in its popular literature) actually does do better economically speaking. Careful quantitative studies have shown this to be true in Ancient Greece, in Spain in the Middle Ages, in England from 1400–1800, as well as among contemporary nations, whether capitalist or Communist, developed or underdeveloped.

Contrast these two stories for example. Which one contains more *n* Ach? Which one reflects a state of mind which ought to lead to harder striving to improve the way things are?

Excerpt from story A (4th grade reader): "Don't Ever Owe a Man — The world is an illusion. Wife, children, horses and cows are all just ties of fate. They are ephemeral. Each after fulfilling his part in life disappears. So we should not clamour after riches which are not permanent. As long as we live it is wise not to have any attachments and just think of God. We have to spend our lives without trouble, for is it not time that there is an end to grievances? So it is better to live knowing the real state of affairs. Don't get entangled in the meshes of family life."

Excerpt from story B (4th grade reader): "How I Do Like to Learn — I was sent to an accelerated technical high school. I was so happy I cried. Learning is not very easy. In the beginning I couldn't understand what the teacher taught us. I always got a red cross mark on my papers. The boy sitting next to me was very enthusiastic and also an outstanding student. When he found I couldn't do the problems he offered to show me how he had done them. I could not copy his work. I must learn through my own reasoning. I gave his paper back and explained I had to do it myself. Sometimes I worked on a problem until midnight. If I couldn't finish, I started early in the morning. The red cross marks on my work were getting less common. I conquered my difficulties. My marks rose. I graduated and went on to college."

Most readers would agree, without any special knowledge of the n Ach coding system, that the second story shows more concern with improvement than the first, which comes from a contemporary reader used in Indian public schools. In fact the latter has a certain Horatio Alger quality that is reminiscent of our own McGuffey readers of several generations ago. It appears today in the textbooks of Communist China. It should not, therefore come as a surprise if a nation like Communist China, obsessed as it is with improvement, tended in the long run to outproduce a nation like India, which appears to be more fatalistic.

The n Ach level is obviously important for statesmen to watch and in many instances to try to do something about, particularly if a nation's economy is lagging. Take Britain, for example. A generation ago (around 1925) it ranked fifth among 25 countries where children's readers were scored for n Ach — and its economy was doing well. By 1950 the n Ach level had dropped to 27th out of 39 countries — well below the world average — and today, its leaders are feeling the severe economic effects of this loss in the spirit of enterprise.

Economics and n Ach

If psychologists can detect n Ach levels in individuals or nations, particularly before their effects are widespread, can't the knowledge somehow be put to use to foster economic development? Obviously detection or diagnosis is not enough. What good is it to tell Britain (or India for that matter) that it needs more n Ach, a greater spirit of enterprise? In most such cases, informed observers of the local scene know very well that such a need exists, though they may be slower to discover it than the psychologist hovering over n Ach scores. What is needed is some method of developing n Ach in individuals or nations.

Since about 1960, psychologists in my research group at Harvard have been experimenting with techniques designed to accomplish this goal, chiefly among business executives whose work requires the action characteristics of people with high n Ach. Initially, we had real doubts as to whether we could succeed, partly because like most American psychologists we had been strongly influenced by the psychoanalytic view that basic motives are laid down in childhood and cannot really be changed later, and partly because many studies of intensive psychotherapy and counseling have shown minor if any long-term personality effects. On the other hand we were encouraged by the nonprofessionals; those enthusiasts like Dale Carnegie, the Communist ideologue or the Church missionary, who felt they could change adults and in fact seemed to be doing so. At any rate we ran some brief (7 to 10 days)"total push" training courses for businessmen, designed to increase their *n* Ach.

Four Main Goals

In broad outline the courses had four main goals: (1) They were designed to teach the participants how to think, talk and act like a person with high *n* Ach, based on our knowledge of such people gained through 17 years of research. For instance, men learned how to make up stories that would code high in *n* Ach (i.e., how to think in *n* Ach terms), how to set moderate goals for themselves in the ring toss game (and in life). (2) The courses stimulated the participants to set higher but carefully planned and realistic work goals for themselves over the next two years. Then we checked back with them every six months to see how well they were doing in terms of their own objectives. (3) The courses also utilized techniques for giving the participants knowledge about themselves. For instance, in playing the ring toss game, they could observe that they behaved differently from others — perhaps in refusing to adjust a goal downward after failure. This would then become a matter for group discussion and the man would have to explain what he had in mind in setting such unrealistic goals. Discussion could then lead on to what a man's ultimate goals in life were, how much he cared about actually improving performance v. making a good impression or having many friends. In this way the participants would be freer to realize their achievement goals without being blocked by old habits and attitudes. (4) The courses also usually created a group *esprit de corps* from learning about each other's hopes and fears, successes and failures, and from going through an emotional experience together, away from everyday life, in a retreat setting. This membership in a new group helps a man achieve his goals, partly because he knows he has their sympathy and support and partly because he knows they will be watching to see how well he does. The same effect has been noted in other therapy groups like Alcoholics Anonymous We are not sure which of these course "inputs" is really absolutely essential — that remains a research question — but we were taking no chances at the outset in view of the general pessimism about such efforts, and we wanted to include any and all techniques that were thought to change people.

The courses have been given: to executives in a large American firm, and in several Mexican firms; to underachieving high school boys; and to businessmen in India from Bombay and from a small city — Kakinada in the state of Andhra Pradesh. In every instance save one (the Mexican case), it was possible to demonstrate statistically, some two years later, that the men who took the course had done better (made more money, got promoted faster, expanded their businesses faster) than comparable men who did not take the course or who took some other management course.

Consider the Kakinada results, for example. In the two years preceding the course 9 men, 18 percent of the 52 participants, had shown "unusual" enterprise in their businesses. In the 18 months following the course 25 of the men, in other words nearly 50 percent, were unusually active. And this was not due to a general upturn of business in India. Data from a control city, some forty-five miles away, show the same base rate of "unusually active" men as in Kakinada before the course — namely, about 20 percent. Something clearly happened in Kakinada: the owner of a small radio shop started a chemical plant; a banker was so successful in making commercial loans in an enterprising way that he was promoted to a much larger branch of his bank in Calcutta; the local political leader accomplished his goal (it was set in the course) to get the federal government to deepen the harbor and make it into an all-weather port; plans are far along for establishing a steel rolling mill, etc. All this took place without any substantial capital input from the outside. In fact, the only costs were for our 10-day courses plus some brief follow-up visits every six months. The men are raising their own capital and using their own resources for getting business and industry moving in a city that had been considered stagnant and unenterprising.

The promise of such a method of developing achievement motivation seems very great. It has obvious applications in helping underdeveloped countries, or "pockets of poverty" in the United States, to move faster economically. It has great potential for businesses that need to "turn around" and take a more enterprising approach toward their growth and development. It may even be helpful in developing more *n* Ach among low-income groups. For instance, data show that lower-class Negro Americans have a very low level of *n* Ach. This is not surprising. Society has systematically discouraged and blocked their achievement striving. But as the barriers to upward mobility are broken down, it will be necessary to help stimulate the motivation that will lead them to take advantage of new opportunities opening up.

Extreme Reactions

But a word of caution: Whenever I speak of this research and its great potential, audience reaction tends to go to opposite extremes. Either people remain skeptical and argue that motives can't really be changed, that all we are doing is dressing Dale Carnegie up in fancy "psychologese," or they become converts and want instant course descriptions by return mail to solve their local motivation problems. Either response is unjustified. What I have described here in a few pages has taken 20 years of patient research effort, and hundreds of thousands of dollars in basic research costs. What remains to be done will involve even larger sums and more time for development to turn a promising idea into something of wide practical utility.

Encouragement Needed

To take only one example, we have not yet learned how to develop *n* Ach really well among low-income groups. In our first effort — a summer course for bright underachieving 14-year-olds — we found that boys from the middle class improved steadily in grades in school over a two-year period, but boys from the lower class showed an improvement after the first year followed by a drop back to their beginning low grade average. (See chart.) Why? We speculated that it

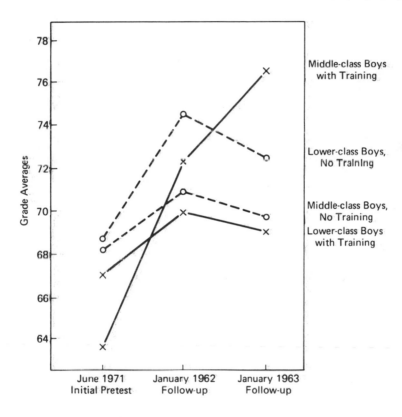

was because they moved back into an environment in which neither parents nor friends encouraged achievement or upward mobility. In other words, it isn't enough to change a man's motivation if the environment in which he lives doesn't support at least to some degree his new efforts. Negroes striving to rise out of the ghetto frequently confront this problem: they are often faced by skepticism at home and suspicion on the job, so that even if their *n* Ach is raised, it can be lowered again by the heavy odds against their success. We must learn not only to raise n Ach but also to find methods of instructing people in how to manage it, to create a favorable environment in which it can flourish.

Many of these training techniques are now only in the pilot testing stage. It will take time and money to perfect them, but society should be willing to invest heavily in them in view of their tremendous potential for contributing to human betterment.

CHARLES N. GREENE

THE SATISFACTION-PERFORMANCE CONTROVERSY

New developments and their implications

Current speculation continues to imply that satisfaction and performance are causally related. While the performance-causes-satisfaction proposition is a more recent development, the contention that satisfaction causes performance remains more widely held. Recent research findings, however, offer only moderate support of the former view and reject the latter. The evidence indicates that the relationship is more complex: rewards constitute a more direct cause of satisfaction than does performance, and rewards based on current performance cause subsequent performance. Thus, the manager who wants to improve his subordinates' performance must, first, provide valued rewards of sufficient magnitude and then establish the necessary contingencies between effort and performance and between performance and rewards. Last, he needs to consider a range of nonmotivational factors.

As Ben walked by smiling on the way to his office, Ben's boss remarked to a friend: "Ben really enjoys his job and that's why he's the best damn worker I ever had. And that's reason enough for me to keep Ben happy." The friend replied: "No, you're wrong! Ben likes his job because he does it so well. If you want to make Ben happy, you ought to do whatever you can to help him further improve his performance."

Four decades after the initial published investigation on the satisfaction-performance relationship, these two opposing views are still the subject of controversy on the part of both practitioners and researchers. Several researchers have concluded, in fact, that "there is no present technique for determining the cause-and-effect of satisfaction and performance." Current speculations, reviewed by Schwab and Cummings, however, still imply at least in theory that satisfaction and performance are causally related although, in some cases, the assumed cause has become the effect, and, in others, the relationship between these two variables is considered to be a function of a third or even additional variables.[1]

THEORY AND EVIDENCE

"Satisfaction Causes Performance"

At least three fundamental theoretical propositions underlie the research and writing in this area. The first and most pervasive stems

1. Initial investigation by A. A. Kornhauser and A. W. Sharp, "Employee Attitudes: Suggestions from a Study in a Factory," *Personnel Journal,* X (May, 1932), pp. 393-401.

First quotation from Robert A. Sutermeister, "Employee Performance and Employee Need Satisfaction—Which Comes First?" *California Management Review,* XIII (Summer, 1971), p. 43.

Second quotation from Donald P. Schwab and Larry L. Cummings, "Theories of Performance and Satisfaction: a Review," *Industrial Relations,* IX (October, 1970), pp. 408-30.

Reprinted by permission of the author and *Business Horizons* from *Business Horizons,* October 1972, pp. 31–41.

from the human relations movement with its emphasis on the well-being of the individual at work. In the years following the investigations at Western Electric, a number of studies were conducted to identify correlates of high and low job satisfaction. The interest in satisfaction, however, came about not so much as a result of concern for the individual as concern with the presumed linkage of satisfaction with performance.

According to this proposition (simply stated and still frequently accepted), the degree of job satisfaction felt by an employee determines his performance, that is, satisfaction causes performance. This proposition has theoretical roots, but it also reflects the popular belief that "a happy worker is a productive worker" and the notion that "all good things go together." It is far more pleasant to increase an employee's happiness than to deal directly with his performance whenever a performance problem exists. Therefore, acceptance of the satisfaction-causes-performance proposition as a solution makes good sense, particularly for the manager because it represents the path of least resistance. Furthermore, high job satisfaction and high performance are both good, and, therefore, they ought to be related to one another.

At the theoretical level, Vroom's valence-force model is a prime example of theory-based support of the satisfaction-causes-performance case.[2] In Vroom's model, job satisfaction reflects the valence (attractiveness) of the job. It follows from his theory that the force exerted on an employee to remain on the job is an increasing function of the valence of the job. Thus, satisfaction should be negatively related to absenteeism and turnover, and, at the empirical level, it is.

Whether or not this valence also leads to higher performance, however, is open to considerable doubt. Vroom's review of twenty-three field studies, which investigated the relationship between satisfaction and performance, revealed an insignificant median static correlation of 0.14, that is, satisfaction explained less than 2 percent of the variance in performance. Thus, the insignificant results and absence of tests of the causality question fail to provide support for this proposition.

"Performance Causes Satisfaction"

More recently, a second theoretical proposition has been advanced. According to this view, best represented by the work of Porter and Lawler, satisfaction is considered not as a cause but as an effect of performance, that is, performance causes satisfaction.[3] Differential performance determines rewards which, in turn, produce variance in satisfaction. In other words, rewards constitute a necessary intervening variable and, thus, satisfaction is considered to be a function of performance-related rewards.

At the empirical level, two recent studies, each utilizing time-lag correlations, lend considerable support to elements of this proposition. Bowen and Siegel, and Greene reported finding relatively strong correlations between performance and satisfaction expressed later (the performance-causes-satisfaction condition), which were significantly higher than the low correlations between satisfaction and performance which occurred during the subsequent period (the "satisfaction-causes-performance" condition).[4]

In the Greene study, significant correlations were obtained between performance

2. Victor H. Vroom, *Work and Motivation* (New York: John Wiley & Sons, Inc., 1964).

3. Lyman W. Porter and Edward E. Lawler, III, *Managerial Attitudes and Performance* (Homewood, Ill.: Richard D. Irwin, Inc., 1968).

4. Donald Bowen and Jacob P. Siegel, "The Relationship Between Satisfaction and Performance: the Question of Causality," paper presented at the annual meeting of the American Psychological Association, Miami Beach, September, 1970.

Charles N. Greene, "A Causal Interpretation of Relationship Among Pay, Performance, and Satisfaction," paper presented at the annual meeting of the Midwest Psychological Association, Cleveland, Ohio, May, 1972.

and rewards granted subsequently and between rewards and subsequent satisfaction. Thus, Porter and Lawler's predictions that differential performance determines rewards and that rewards produce variance in satisfaction were upheld.

"Rewards" as a Causal Factor

Closely related to Porter and Lawler's predictions is a still more recent theoretical position, which considers both satisfaction and performance to be functions of rewards. In this view, rewards cause satisfaction, and rewards that are based on current performance cause affect subsequent performance.

According to this proposition, formulated by Cherrington, Reitz, and Scott from the contributions of reinforcement theorists, there is no inherent relationship between satisfaction and performance.[5] The results of their experimental investigation strongly support their predictions. The rewarded subjects reported significantly greater satisfaction than did the unrewarded subjects. Furthermore, when rewards (monetary bonuses, in this case) were granted on the basis of performance, the subjects' performance was significantly higher than that of subjects whose rewards were unrelated to their performance. For example, they found that when a low performer was not rewarded, he expressed dissatisfaction but that his later performance improved. On the other hand, when a low performer was in fact rewarded for his low performance, he expressed high satisfaction but continued to perform at a low level.

The same pattern of findings was revealed in the case of the high performing subjects with one exception; the high performer who was not rewarded expressed dissatisfaction, as expected, and his performance on the next trial declined significantly. The correlation between satisfaction and subsequent performance, excluding the effects of rewards, was 0.00, that is, satisfaction does *not* cause improved performance.

A recent field study, which investigated the source and direction of causal influence in satisfaction-performance relationships, supports the Cherrington-Reitz-Scott findings.[6] Merit pay was identified as a cause of satisfaction and, contrary to some current beliefs, was found to be a significantly more frequent source of satisfaction than dissatisfaction. The results of this study further revealed equally significant relationships between (1) merit pay and subsequent performance and (2) current performance and subsequent merit pay. Given the Cherrington-Reitz-Scott findings that rewards based on current performance cause improved subsequent performance, these results do suggest the possibility of reciprocal causation.

In other words, merit pay based on current performance probably caused variations in subsequent performance, and the company in this field study evidently was relatively successful in implementing its policy of granting salary increases to an employee on the basis of his performance (as evidenced by the significant relationship found between current performance and subsequent merit pay). The company's use of a fixed (annual) merit increase schedule probably obscured some of the stronger reinforcing effects of merit pay on performance.

Unlike the Cherrington-Reitz-Scott controlled experiment, the fixed merit increase schedule precluded (as it does in

5. David J. Cherrington, H. Joseph Reitz, and William E. Scott, Jr., "Effects of Contingent and Non-contingent Reward on the Relationship Between Satisfaction and Task Performance," *Journal of Applied Psychology*, LV (December, 1971) pp. 531-36.

6. Charles N. Greene, "Source and Direction of Causal Influence in Satisfaction-Performance Relationships," paper presented at the annual meetings of the Eastern Academy of Management, Boston, May, 1972. Also reported in Greene, "Causal Connections Among Managers' Merit Pay, Satisfaction, and Performance," *Journal of Applied Psychology*, 1972 (in press).

"The finding that rewards based on current performance affect subsequent performance does . . . offer a strategy . . . . Unfortunately, it is not the path of least resistance for the manager."

most organizations) giving an employee a monetary reward immediately after he successfully performed a major task. This constraint undoubtedly reduced the magnitude of the relationship between merit pay and subsequent performance.

IMPLICATIONS FOR MANAGEMENT

These findings have several apparent but nonetheless important implications. For the manager who desires to enhance the satisfaction of his subordinates (perhaps for the purpose of reducing turnover), the implication of the finding that "rewards cause satisfaction" is self-evident. If, on the other hand, the manager's interest in his subordinates' satisfaction arises from his desire to increase their performance, the consistent rejection of the satisfaction-causes-performance proposition has an equally clear implication: increasing subordinates' satisfaction will have no effect on their performance.

The finding that rewards based on current performance affect subsequent performance does, however, offer a strategy for increasing subordinates' performance. Unfortunately, it is not the path of least resistance for the manager. Granting differential rewards on the basis of differences in his subordinates' performance will cause his subordinates to express varying degrees of satisfaction or dissatisfaction. The manager, as a result, will soon find himself in the uncomfortable position of having to successfully defend his basis for evaluation or having to put up with dissatisfied subordinates until their performance improves or they leave the organization.

The benefits of this strategy, however, far outweigh its liabilities. In addition to its positive effects on performance, this strategy provides equity since the most satisfied employees are the rewarded high performers and, for the same reason, it also facilitates the organization's efforts to retain its most productive employees.

If these implications are to be considered as prescriptions for managerial behavior, one is tempted at this point to conclude that all a manager need do in order to increase his subordinates' performance is to accurately appraise their work and then reward them accordingly. However, given limited resources for rewards and knowledge of appraisal techniques, it is all too apparent that the manager's task here is not easy.

Moreover, the relationship between rewards and performance is often not as simple or direct as one would think, for at least two reasons. First, there are other causes of performance that may have a more direct bearing on a particular problem. Second is the question of the appropriateness of the reward itself, that is, what is rewarding for one person may not be for another. In short, a manager also needs to consider other potential causes of performance and a range of rewards in coping with any given performance problem.

Nonmotivational Factors

The element of performance that relates most directly to the discussion thus far is effort, that element which links rewards to performance. The employee who works hard usually does so because of the rewards or avoidance of punishment that he associates with good work. He believes that the magnitude of the reward he will receive is contingent on his performance and, further, that his performance is a function of how hard he works. Thus, effort reflects the motivational aspect of performance. There are, however, other nonmotivational considerations that can best be considered prior to examining ways by which a manager can deal with the motivational problem."

Direction—Suppose, for example, that an employee works hard at his job, yet his performance is inadequate. What can his manager do to alleviate the problem? The manager's first action should be to identify the cause. One likely possibility is what can be referred to as a "direction problem."

Several years ago, the Minnesota Vikings' defensive end, Jim Marshall, very alertly gathered up the opponent's fumble and then, with obvious effort and delight, proceeded to carry the ball some fifty yards into the wrong end zone. This is a direction problem in its purest sense. For the employee working under more usual circumstances, a direction problem generally stems from his lack of understanding of what is expected of him or what a job well done looks like. The action indicated to alleviate this problem is to clarify or define in detail for the employee the requirements of his job. The manager's own leadership style may also be a factor. In dealing with an employee with a direction problem, the manager needs to exercise closer supervision and to initiate structure or focus on the task, as opposed to emphasizing consideration or his relations with the employee.[7]

In cases where this style of behavior is repugnant or inconsistent with the manager's own leadership inclinations, an alternative approach is to engage in mutual goal setting or management by objectives techniques with the employee. Here, the necessary structure can be established, but at the subordinate's own initiative, thus creating a more participative atmosphere. This approach, however, is not free of potential problems. The employee is more likely to make additional undetected errors before his performance improves, and the approach is more time consuming than the more direct route.

Ability—What can the manager do if the actions he has taken to resolve the direction problem fail to result in significant improvements in performance? His subordinate still exerts a high level of effort and understands what is expected of him—yet he continues to perform poorly. At this point, the manager may begin, justifiably so, to doubt his subordinate's ability to perform the job. When this doubt does arise, there are three useful questions, suggested by Mager and Pipe, to which the manager should find answers before he treats the problem as an ability deficiency: Could the subordinate do it if he really had to? Could he do it if his life depended on it? Are his present abilities adequate for the desired performance?[8]

If the answers to the first two questions are negative, then the answer to the last question also will be negative, and the obvious conclusion is that an ability deficiency does, in fact, exist. Most managers, upon reaching this conclusion, begin to develop some type of formal training experience for the subordinate. This is unfortunate and frequently wasteful. There is probably a simpler, less expensive solution. Formal training is usually required only when the individual has never

7. For example, a recent study reported finding that relationships between the leader's initiating structure and both subordinate satisfaction and performance were moderated by such variables as role ambiguity, job scope, and task autonomy perceived by the subordinate. See Robert J. House, "A Path Goal Theory of Leader Effectiveness," *Administrative Science Quarterly*, XVI (September, 1971), pp. 321-39.

8. Robert F. Mager and Peter Pipe, *Analyzing Performance Problems* (Belmont, Calif.: Lear Siegler, Inc., 1970), p. 21.

"Once training needs have been identified and the appropriate training technique employed, the manager can profit by asking himself one last question: "Why did the ability deficiency develop in the first place?"

done the particular job in question or when there is no way in which the ability requirement in question can be eliminated from his job.

If the individual formerly used the skill but now uses it only rarely, systematic practice will usually overcome the deficiency without formal training. Alternatively, the job can be changed or simplified so that the impaired ability is no longer crucial to successful performance. If, on the other hand, the individual once had the skill and still rather frequently is able to practice it, the manager should consider providing him greater feedback concerning the outcome of his efforts. The subordinate may not be aware of the deficiency and its effect on his performance, or he may no longer know how to perform the job. For example, elements of his job or the relationship between his job and other jobs may have changed, and he simply is not aware of the change.

Where formal training efforts are indicated, systematic analysis of the job is useful for identifying the specific behaviors and skills that are closely related with successful task performance and that, therefore, need to be learned. Alternatively, if the time and expense associated with job analysis are considered excessive, the critical incidents approach can be employed toward the same end.[9] Once training needs have been identi-

fied and the appropriate training technique employed, the manager can profit by asking himself one last question: "Why did the ability deficiency develop in the first place?"

Ultimately, the answer rests with the selection and placement process. Had a congruent man-job match been attained at the outset, the ability deficiency would have never presented itself as a performance problem.[10]

Performance Obstacles—When inadequate performance is not the result of a lack of effort, direction, or ability, there is still another potential cause that needs attention. There may be obstacles beyond the subordinate's control that interfere with his performance. "I can't do it" is not always an alibi; it may be a real description of the problem. Performance obstacles can take many forms to the extent that their number, independent of a given situation, is almost unlimited.

However, the manager might look initially for some of the more common potential obstacles, such as a lack of time or conflicting demands on the subordinate's time, inadequate work facilities, restrictive policies or "right ways of doing it" that inhibit performance, lack of authority, insufficient information about other activities that affect the job, and lack of cooperation from others with whom he must work.

An additional obstacle, often not apparent to the manager from his face-to-face interaction with a subordinate, is the operation of group goals and norms that run counter to organizational objectives. Where the work group adheres to norms of restricting productivity, for example, the subordinate will similarly restrict his own performance to the extent that he identifies more closely with the group than with management.

9. See, for example, J. D. Folley, Jr., "Determining Training Needs of Department Store Personnel," *Training Development Journal*, XXIII (January, 1969), pp. 24-27, for a discussion of how the critical incidents approach can be employed to identify job skills to be learned in a formal training situation.

10. For a useful discussion of how ability levels can be upgraded by means of training and selection procedures, the reader can refer to Larry L. Cummings and Donald P. Schwab, *Performance in Organizations: Determinants and Appraisal* (Glenview, Ill.: Scott, Foresman & Co., 1972; in press).

Rewards and Effort

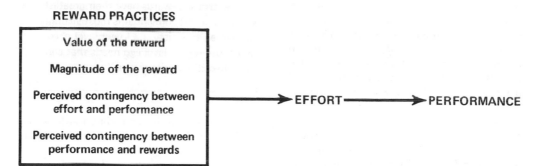

REWARD PRACTICES

Value of the reward

Magnitude of the reward

Perceived contingency between effort and performance

Perceived contingency between performance and rewards

→ EFFORT ────────→ PERFORMANCE

Most performance obstacles can be overcome either by removing the obstacle or by changing the subordinate's job so that the obstacle no longer impinges on his performance. When the obstacle stems from group norms, however, a very different set of actions is required. Here, the actions that should be taken are the same as those that will be considered shortly in coping with lack of effort on the part of the individual. In other words, the potential causes of the group's lack of effort are identical to those that apply to the individual.

The Motivational Problem

Thus far, performance problems have been considered in which effort was not the source of the performance discrepancy. While reward practices constitute the most frequent and direct cause of effort, there are, however, other less direct causes. Direction, ability, and performance obstacles may indirectly affect effort through their direct effects on performance. For example, an individual may perform poorly because of an ability deficiency and, as a result, exert little effort on the job. Here, the ability deficiency produced low performance, and the lack of effort on the individual's part resulted from his expectations of failure. Thus, actions taken to alleviate the ability deficiency should result in

improved performance and, subsequently, in higher effort.

Effort is that element of performance which links rewards to performance. The relationship between rewards and effort is, unfortunately, not a simple one. As indicated in the figure, effort is considered not only as a function of the (1) value and (2) magnitude of reward, but also as a function of the (3) individual's perceptions of the extent to which greater effort on his part will lead to higher performance, and (4) that his high performance, in turn, will lead to rewards. Therefore, a manager who is confronted with a subordinate who exerts little effort must consider these four attributes of reward practices in addition to the more indirect, potential causes of the lack of effort. The key issues in coping with a subordinate's lack of effort—the motivation problem—or in preventing such a problem from arising involve all four of the attributes of rewards just identified.[11]

Appropriateness of the Reward— Regardless of the extent to which the individual believes that hard work determines his performance and subsequent rewards, he will

11. The discussion in this section is based in part on Cummings and Schwab, *Performance in Organizations,* and Lyman W. Porter and Edward E. Lawler, III, "What Job Attitudes Tell About Motivation," *Harvard Business Review,* LXVI (January-February, 1968), pp. 118-26.

obviously put forth little effort unless he *values* those rewards—that is, the rewards must have value in terms of his own need state. An accountant, for example, may value recognition from his boss, an opportunity to increase the scope of his job, or a salary increase; however, it is unlikely that he will place the same value on a ten-year supply of budget forms.

In other words, there must be consistency between the reward and what the individual needs or wants and recognition that there are often significant differences among individuals in what they consider rewarding. Similarly, individuals differ in terms of the *magnitude* of that valued reward they consider to be positively reinforcing. A 7 or 8 percent salary increase may motivate one person but have little or no positive effect on another person at the same salary level. Furthermore, a sizable reward in one situation might be considered small by the same individual in a different set of circumstances.

These individual differences, particularly those concerning what rewards are valued, raise considerable question about the adequacy of current organization reward systems, virtually none of which make any formal recognition of individual differences. Lawler, for example, has suggested that organizations could profit greatly by introducing "cafeteria-style" wage plans.[12] These plans allow an employee to select any combination of cash and fringe benefits he desires. An employee would be assigned "X" amount in compensation, which he may then divide up among a number of fringe benefits and cash. This practice would ensure that employees receive only those fringe benefits they value; from the organization's point of view, it would reduce the waste in funds allocated by the organization to fringe benefits not valued by its members. As a personal strategy, however, the manager could

12. Edward E. Lawler, III, *Pay and Organizational Effectiveness: a Psychological View* (New York: McGraw-Hill Book Company, 1971).

> "... extrinsic rewards have their greatest value when the individual is most strongly motivated to satisfy ... lower level needs ... and those higher level ego needs that can be linked directly to status."

profit even more by extending Lawler's plan to include the entire range of nonmonetary rewards.

Rewards can be classified into two broad categories, extrinsic and intrinsic. Extrinsic rewards are those external to the job or in the context of the job, such as job security, improved working facilities, praise from one's boss, status symbols, and, of course, pay, including fringe benefits. Intrinsic rewards, on the other hand, are rewards that can be associated directly with the "doing of the job," such as a sense of accomplishment after successful performance, opportunities for advancement, increased responsibility, and work itself.

Thus, intrinsic rewards flow immediately and directly from the individual's performance of the job and, as such, may be considered as a form of self-reward. For example, one essentially must decide for himself whether his level of performance is worthy of a feeling of personal achievement. Extrinsic rewards, to the contrary, are administered by the organization; the organization first must identify good performance and then provide the appropriate reward.

Generally speaking, extrinsic rewards have their greatest value when the individual is most strongly motivated to satisfy what Maslow has referred to as lower level needs, basic physiological needs and needs for safety or security, and those higher level ego needs that can be linked directly to status. Pay, for example, may be valued by an individual because he believes it is a determinant of his social position within the community or because it constitutes a means for acquiring status symbols.

Intrinsic rewards are likely to be valued more by the individual after his lower level needs have been largely satisfied. In other words, there must be an adequate level of satisfaction with the extrinsic rewards before intrinsic rewards can be utilized effectively. In order to make the subordinate's job more intrinsically rewarding, the manager may want to consider several actions.

Perhaps most important, the manager needs to provide meaningful work assignments, that is, work with which the subordinate can identify and become personally involved. He should establish challenging yet attainable goals or, in some cases, it may be more advantageous for him to create conditions that greatly enhance the likelihood that his subordinate will succeed, thus increasing the potential for attaining feelings of achievement, advancement, and recognition. The manager may also consider such means as increased delegation and job enlargement for extending the scope and depth of the subordinate's job and thereby increasing the subordinate's sense of responsibility and providing greater opportunity to make the job into something more compatible with his own interests.

In short, the manager should as best he can match the rewards at his disposal, both extrinsic and intrinsic rewards, with what the subordinate indicates he needs or wants. Second, he should, by varying the magnitude and timing of the rewards granted, establish clearly in the subordinate's mind the desired effort-performance-reward contingencies.

Establishing the Contingencies—The contingency between effort and performance (that is, the extent to which the individual believes that by working harder, he will improve his performance) is largely a function of his confidence in his own abilities and his perceptions of the difficulty of the task and absence of obstacles standing in the way of successful task performance. When the effort-performance contingency is not clear for

these reasons, the manager should consider several actions. He can reassign work or modify the task to be more consistent with the individual's perceptions of his own abilities; treat the problem as a "real" ability deficiency; remove the apparent performance obstacles; or simply reassure the individual.

The second contingency, the individual's belief that the rewards he receives reflect his accomplishments, is usually more difficult to establish. Here, two rather vexing predicaments are frequently encountered, both of which stem primarily from administration of extrinsic rewards. First, the instrument (usually a merit evaluation or performance appraisal device) may inaccurately measure the individual's contribution and thus his performance is rewarded in error. Reward schedules constitute the source of the second problem. Given fixed reward schedules (that is, the ubiquitous annual salary increase) adopted by the great majority of organizations, there is more frequently than not a considerable delay between task accomplishment and bestowal of the reward. As a result, the individual may not only fail to perceive the intended contingency but may incorrectly associate the reward with his behavior just prior to being rewarded. In other words, he may perceive a nonexistent contingency, and his subsequent behavior will reflect that contingency and, this time, go unrewarded.

Reward Schedules—The manner in which a given reward, or reinforcer, is scheduled is as strong a determinant of the effectiveness of that reward as is the value of the reward itself, or, for that matter, any other attribute of the reward. In organizations, the only plausible forms of reward schedules are intermittent as opposed to the continuous reward schedule in which the reward or punishment is administered after every behavioral sequence to be conditioned. In the case of the intermittent schedules, the behavior to be conditioned is reinforced only occasionally. There are four schedules of interest to the manager, each with varying effects on performance as a number of investigations in the field of experimental psychology have revealed.

1. *Fixed-interval schedule*—Rewards are bestowed after a fixed period, usually since the last reward was granted. This schedule is equivalent to the annual salary increase schedule in organizations, and its effects on performance are well-known. Typically, the individual "saves up," that is, he exerts a high level of effort just prior to the time of the reinforcement, usually his annual performance review. His performance more than likely will then taper off until the time just prior to his next annual review.

2. *Variable-interval schedule*—Rewards are administered at designated time periods, but the intervals between the periods vary. For example, a reward may be given one day after the last rewarded behavior sequence, then three days later, then one week later, and so on, but only if the behavior to be conditioned actually occurs. This schedule results in fairly consistent rates of performance over long periods of time. Praise or other forms of social reinforcement from one's peers and superior, as an example, usually occur according to a variable-interval schedule, not by intention but simply because they are too involved with their own affairs to provide systematic reinforcement.

3. *Fixed-ratio schedule*—Reinforcement is provided after a fixed number of responses or performances by the individual. Incentive wage plans so frequently utilized in organizations constitute the prime example of this type of schedule. It is characterized by higher rates of effort than the interval schedules unless the ratio is large. When significant delays do occur between rewards, performance, much like in the fixed schedule, declines immediately after the reward is bestowed and improves again as the time for the next reward approaches.

4. *Variable-ratio schedule*—The reward is administered after a series of responses or performances, the number of which varies from the granting of one reward to the next.

For example, an individual on a 15:1 variable-interval schedule might be reinforced after ten responses, then fifteen responses, then twenty responses, then ten responses, and so on, an average of one reinforcement for every fifteen responses. This schedule tends to result in performance that is higher than that of a comparable fixed ratio schedule, and the variation in performance both before and after the occurrence of the reward or reinforcement is considerably less.

Virtually all managers must function within the contraints imposed by a fixed-interval schedule (annual salary schedule) or fixed ratio schedule (wage incentives).

However, this fact should not preclude consideration of the variable schedules, even within the framework of fixed schedules. Given their more positive effects on performance, such consideration is indeed highly desirable. It is conceivable, at least in a sales organization, for example, that monetary rewards (bonuses in this case) could be administered according to a variable-ratio schedule. From a more practical point of view, the entire range of nonmonetary rewards could be more profitably scheduled on a variable-interval basis, assuming that such scheduling was done in a systematic fashion.

CONCLUSIONS

This article has reviewed recent research concerning the relationship between satisfaction and performance and discussed the implications of the results of this research for the practicing manager. As noted at the outset, current speculation on the part of most practitioners and researchers continue to imply that satisfaction and performance are causally related, although confusion exists concerning the exact nature of the relationship. While the performance-causes-satisfaction proposition is a more recent development, the contention that satisfaction causes performance, nonetheless, remains the more widely held of the two beliefs, particularly among practitioners.

The recent research findings, however, offer only moderate support of the former view and conclusively reject the latter. Instead, the evidence provides rather strong indications that the relationship is more complex: (1) rewards constitute a more direct cause of satisfaction than does performance and (2) rewards based on current performance (and not satisfaction) cause subsequent performance.

For the manager who is concerned about the well-being of his subordinates, the implication of the finding that rewards cause satisfaction is self-evident. In order to achieve this end, the manager must provide rewards that have value or utility in terms of the subordinate's own need state and provide them in sufficient magnitude to be perceived as positively reinforcing. The manager whose goal is to increase a subordinate's performance, on the other hand, is faced with a more difficult task for two reasons. First, the relationship between rewards and performance is not a simple one. Second, there are other causes of performance—direction, the subordinate's ability, and existence of performance obstacles standing in the way of successful task performance—which the manager must deal also with.

The relationship between rewards and performance is complex because in reality there is at least one intervening variable and more than one contingency that needs to be established. An employee exerts high level effort usually because of the valued rewards he associates with high performance. Effort, the intervening variable, may be considered a function of the value and magnitude of the reward and the extent to which the individual believes that high effort on his part will lead to high performance and that his high performance, in turn, will lead to rewards.

Therefore, the manager in addition to providing appropriate rewards, must establish contingencies between effort and performance and between performance and rewards. The first contingency, the extent to which the individual believes that "how hard he works" determines his performance, is perhaps the more readily established. This contingency is a function, at least in part, of the individual's confidence in his own abilities, his perceptions of the difficulty of the task, and the presence of performance obstacles. When a problem does arise here, the manager can take those actions indicated earlier in this article to overcome an apparent ability deficiency or performance obstacle. The performance-reward contingency requires the manager, by means of accurate performance appraisals and appropriate reward practices, to clearly establish in the subordinate's mind the belief that his own performance determines the magnitude of the rewards he will receive.

The establishment of this particular contingency, unfortunately, is becoming increasingly difficult as organizations continue to rely more heavily on fixed salary schedules and nonperformance-related factors (for example, seniority) as determinants of salary progression. However, the manager can, as a supplement to organizationally determined rewards, place more emphasis on nonmonetary rewards and both the cafeteria-style reward plans and variable-interval schedules for their administration.

It is apparent that the manager whose objective is to significantly improve his subordinates' performance has assumed difficult but by no means impossible task. The path of least resistance—that is, increasing subordinates' satisfaction—simply will not work.

However, the actions suggested concerning reward practices and, particularly, establishment of appropriate performance-reward contingencies will result in improved performance, assuming that such improvement is not restricted by ability or direction problems or by performance obstacles. The use of differential rewards may require courage on the part of the manager, but failure to use them will have far more negative consequences. A subordinate will repeat that behavior which was rewarded, regardless of whether it resulted in high or low performance. A rewarded low performer, for example, will continue to perform poorly. With knowledge of this inequity, the high performer, in turn, will eventually reduce his own level of performance or seek employment elsewhere.

Arthur Friedman's Outrage: Employees Decide Their Pay

Martin Koughan

One thing for sure, Arthur Friedman will never become the chairman of the board at General Motors.

It is not just because the modish, easygoing Oakland appliance dealer does not look the part — Hush Puppies, loud shirts and denim jackets tend to clash with the sober decor of most executive suites. And it certainly is not because he is an incompetent administrator — the Friedman-Jacobs Co. has prospered during the 15 years of his stewardship.

It is mainly because Art Friedman has some pretty strange ideas about how one runs a business.

Five years ago, he had his most outrageous brainstorm. First he tried it out on his wife Merle and his brother Morris.

"Here he goes again," replied Merle with a sigh of resignation, "Another dumb stunt."

"Oh my God," was all that Morris could muster.

His idea was to allow employees to set their own wages, make their own hours and take their vacations whenever they felt like it.

The end result was that it worked.

Friedman first unleashed his proposal at one of the regular staff meetings. Decide what you are worth, he said, and tell the bookkeeper to put it in your envelope next week. No questions asked. Work any time, any day, any hours you want. Having a bad day? Go home. Hate working Saturdays? No problem. Aunt Ethel from Chicago has dropped in unexpectedly? Well, take a few days off, show her the town. Want to go to Reno for a week, need a rest? Go, go, no need to ask. If you need some money for the slot machines, take it out of petty cash. Just come back when you feel ready to work again.

His speech was received in complete silence. No one cheered, no one laughed, no one said a word.

"It was about a month before anyone asked for a raise," recalls Stan Robinson, 55, the payroll clerk. "And when they did, they asked Art first. But he refused to listen and told them to just tell me what they wanted. I kept going back to him to make sure it was all right, but he wouldn't even talk about it. I finally figured out he was serious."

"It was something that I wanted to do," explains Friedman. "I always said that if you give people what they want, you get what you want. You have to be willing to lose, to stick your neck out. I finally decided that the time had come to practice what I preached."

Soon the path to Stan Robinson's desk was heavily travelled. Friedman's wife Merle was one of the first; she figured that her contribution was worth $1 an hour more. Some asked for $50 more a week, some $60. Delivery truck driver Charles Ryan was more ambitious; he demanded a $100 raise.

In most companies, Ryan would have been laughed out of the office. His work had not been particularly distinguished. His truck usually left in the morning and returned at 5 in the afternoon religiously, just in time for him to punch out. He dragged around the shop, complained constantly and was almost always late for work. Things changed.

"He had been resentful about his prior pay," explains Friedman. "The raise made him a fabulous employee. He started showing up early in the morning and would be back by 3, asking what else had to be done."

Instead of the all-out raid on the company coffers that some businessmen might expect, the 15 employees of the Friedman-Jacobs Co. displayed astonishing restraint and maturity. The wages they demanded were just slightly higher than the scale of the Retail Clerks union to which they all belong (at Friedman's insistence). Some did not even take a raise. One service man who was receiving considerably less than his coworkers was asked why he did not insist on equal pay. "I don't want to work that hard," was the obvious answer.

When the union contract comes across Friedman's desk every other year, he signs it without even reading it. "I don't care what it says," he insists. At first, union officials would drop in to see how things were going, but they would usually end up laughing and shaking their heads, muttering something about being put out of a job. They finally stopped coming by. It was enough to convince George Meany to go out to pasture.

The fact is that Friedman's employees have no need for a union; whatever they want, they take and no one questions it. As a result, they have developed a strong sense of responsibility and an acute sensitivity to the problems that face the American worker in general that would have been impossible under the traditional system.

George Tegner, 59, an employee for 14 years, has like all his coworkers achieved new insight into the mechanics of the free enterprise system. "You have to use common sense; no one wins if you end up closing the business down. If you want more money, you have to produce more. It can't work any other way. Anyway, wages aren't everything. Doing what you want to is more important."

Roger Ryan, 27, has been with the company for five years. "I know about the big inflation in '74, but I haven't taken a raise since '73. I figure if everybody asks for more, then inflation will just get worse. I'll hold out as long as I can."

Payroll clerk Stan Robinson: "I'm single now. I don't take as much as the others, even though I've been here longer, because I don't need as much. The government usually winds up with the extra money anyway."

Elwood Larsen, 65, has been the company's ace service man for 16 years.

When he went into semi-retirement last year, he took a $1.50 cut in pay. Why? Larsen does not think a part timer is worth as much. "I keep working here because I like it. We all know that if the Friedmans make money, we do. You just can't gouge the owner."

In the past five years, there has been no turnover of employees. Friedman estimates that last year his 15 workers took no more than a total of three sick days. It is rare that anyone is late for work and, even then, there is usually a good reason. Work is done on time and employee pilferage is nonexistent.

"We used to hear a lot of grumbling," says Robinson. "Now, everybody smiles."

As part of the new freedom, more people were given keys to the store and the cash box. If they need groceries, or even some beer money, all they have to do is walk into the office, take what they want out of the cash box and leave a voucher. Every effort is made to ensure that no one looks over their shoulder.

There has been only one discrepancy. "Once the petty cash was $10 over," recalls Friedman. "We never could figure out where it came from."

The policy has effected some changes in the way things are done around the store. It used to be open every night and all day Sunday, but no one wanted to work those hours. A problem? Of course not. No more nights and Sundays. ("When I thought about it," confesses Friedman, "I didn't like to work those hours either.")

The store also used to handle TV's and stereos — high-profit items — but they were a hassle for all concerned. The Friedman-Jacobs Co. now deals exclusively in major appliances such as refrigerators, washers and dryers.

Skeptics by now are chuckling to themselves, convinced that if Friedman is not losing money, he is just breaking even. The fact is that net profit has not dropped a cent in the last five years; it has increased. Although volume is considerably less and overhead has increased at what some would consider an unhealthy rate, greater productivity and efficiency have more than made up for it.

None of this concerns Friedman, though. He keeps no charts, does not know how to read cost analysis graphs, and does not have the vaguest idea what cash flow means. As long as he can play golf a couple of times a week, and make money to boot, he could not be happier.

Encouraged by his success, Friedman decided to carry his revolution beyond labor relations. If it worked there, he figured, it should work with customer relations as well. So policy changes resulted in such innovations as the following 'last bill' notice, that dread purveyor of bad tidings:

"For some reasons which we really cannot understand, you have decided not to pay the bill that you owe us.

"This letter officially cancels that bill and you are no longer under any obligation to pay us. We have decided not to give this bill to a collection agency, as our gain would be small compared to your loss.

"We would appreciate it, however, if you would take a moment to tell us why you made the decision not to pay us. It would be very helpful to us and the rest of our customers."

As cute as this may appear, it could hardly be expected to work. But Friedman claims that delinquent accounts are no more frequent today.

"We don't collect any more money than we did before, but we don't collect any less either. The difference is that you learn a lot more about the problem. Anyway, it's a lot more pleasant way of doing business," Friedman says.

Section B:
Leadership

In the first article of this section, Raymond Miles makes the statement that "to many people, management and leadership are synonymous." The leader in an organization has the ultimate authority to make or influence any decision by the nature of his organizational position, but in this section of the book we shall examine leadership only in terms of its behavioral implications. From the behavioral perspective, leadership always involves some relationship between the leader, his subordinates, and the situation. According to this definition, an effective leader achieves some of the organization's behaviorial goals (such as high levels of performance) in his or her areas of responsibility by motivating employees.

In the first selection, Raymond Miles focuses on one leadership dimension, participation of subordinates in decision making. Two variables are crucial in Miles' analysis, consultation and respect. He reports that the highest levels of satisfaction were obtained from managers "who are high in their respect for their subordinates' capabilities and who consult them regularly on departmental issues." Presumably, these higher levels of satisfaction lead to higher levels of motivation, although this is a controversial proposition. Miles goes on to review some characteristics that either strengthen or weaken the possibilities for subordinate participation. Effective participation from this point of view is "most clearly embodied in the notion of joint planning where the skills of both parties are used to their fullest."

In the second article, Robert Tannenbaum and Warren Schmidt expand Miles' concept of participation to include a "continuum" of leader behavior ranging from an autocratic position in which the manager or leader makes all decisions to a completely democratic or participative position in which subordinates make all decisions within reasonable limits. These authors, then, do not agree with Miles that participative leadership is always the best course of action. Rather, they believe, the manager must answer this question: Which of the seven behaviors is suitable for my leadership situation? Tannenbaum and Schmidt answer this question by examining three sets of "forces" that should be considered in choosing a leadership style. These forces are in the manager, in the situation, and in subordinates. In adopting this type of analysis, the authors are in effect suggesting a "contingency" approach to leadership; that is, the leader's style should change from situation to situation.

Fred Fiedler expands these contingency ideas in his famous contingency leadership model. According to Fiedler, three specific situational factors must be considered before a leadership style can be selected. These are the relationships between the leader and his subordinates, the amount of structure inherent in the task itself, and the amount of formal power that the leader possesses as a result of his or her legitimate position in the organization. In summarizing his general results, Fiedler suggests that leaders in relatively good or poor management situations should use a task-oriented style of leadership whereas those in moderately favorable situations should use a relationship-centered style. Fiedler then goes on to discuss aspects of leadership training, including pros and cons of changing the leader's behavior or modifying his or her job to obtain the "match" that his contingency theory suggests. Although Fiedler's work has been criticized in some circles, it is still the most comprehensive series of leadership studies available and remains a basic building block of the contingency theory of management.

Raymond E. Miles

Leadership Styles and Subordinate Responses*

To many people, management and leadership are synonymous. We have argued, particularly in Chapters 1 and 2, that such is not the case. Our contention has been that managers' theories of management are reflected in the way in which they design jobs, structure units, put together communications and control systems, set up appraisal and development efforts, establish and operate reward mechanisms, etc. Our main point has been that these systems and mechanisms are all part of an overall approach, or model of management, within which direct, face-to-face relationships with subordinates are only one aspect.

Thus, we have sought to de-emphasize leadership as it is usually conceived and to indicate that designing a job or establishing a control

*Much of this chapter is drawn from or based on an article, "Participative Management: Quantity vs. Quality," authored by Professor J. B. Ritchie of Brigham Young University and myself, and which appeared in the *California Management Review*, Summer 1971. I appreciate the *Review's* permission to use the material here. I also appreciate Professor Ritchie's willingness to allow me to blend his ideas with mine in this manner.

system is as much an act of leadership as consulting with a subordinate (or not consulting with him) on a matter of departmental business. We have taken this position because we believe that variables other than interpersonal behavior have too frequently been left out of discussions of leadership style. However, in adopting this stance, we may well have swung the pendulum hard to the opposite side, implying that the way the manager interacts with his subordinates is unimportant. If we have done this, the present chapter should serve to erase that implication. For what we hope to show here, by discussion and by examination of research data, is that subordinates' attitudes toward their superior are indeed affected by the manner in which he interacts with them—specifically by the extent to which he consults them regarding departmental issues and by his attitudes concerning this consultation process.

As we noted in Chapter 3, research indicates that most managers today pay at least lip service to the concept of participative management. That is, most would agree that some amount of consultation with subordinates is probably useful. Nevertheless, even though it is widely accepted, managers' responses indicate that a heavy pall of confusion hangs over the whole concept of participation.

We feel that a prime source of the confusion surrounding the concept concerns its *purpose*. Our research suggests that most managers tend to hold at least two "theories" of participation. One of these, which we labeled the human relations concept, viewed participation primarily as a means of obtaining cooperation—a technique which the manager could use to improve morale and reduce subordinate resistance to policies and decisions. The second, which we labeled the human resources approach, recognized the untapped potential of most organization members and advocated participation as a means of achieving direct improvements in individual and therefore organizational performance. Perhaps predictably, managers regarded the human relations model as appropriate for their subordinates although they preferred the human resources model for themselves.

Our recent research draws attention to a closely related and probably equally important source of confusion involving the *process* of participation. Our earlier descriptions of the *purpose* of participation under the human relations and human resources models implied that it is not only the *degree* that is important but also the *nature* of the superior-subordinate interaction. Upon reflection, the notion that both the quality and quantity of participation must be considered seems obvious. Surprisingly, however, the quality variable has been infrequently specified in management theory and even more rarely researched.

The lack of specific focus in theory or research on the quality aspect of the process has led, in our view, to the promulgation of a simple quantity theory of participation, a concept which, whether intended or not, appears to lump all participative acts together in a common category, which is therefore open to much justified criticism. Clearly, a theory which implies only that some participation is better than none, and that more is better than a little, ignores individual and situational differences. It is just such a simplified view that allows its more vitriolic critics to draw caricatures extending the participative process to include a chairman of the board consulting with a janitor concerning issues of capital budgeting—the sort of criticism which brings humor to journal pages but contributes little to our understanding of this managerial mechanism.

Recognizing these key sources of confusion, our current studies have been aimed at increasing our understanding of the process of participation under the human relations and human resources models. Specifically, we have attempted, within a large sample of management teams, to identify and measure (1) the amount of superior-subordinate interaction, and (2) a dimension of the quality of this interaction—the superior's confidence in his subordinate's capabilities. In our theoretical framework both the quantity and quality of participation are important determinants of subordinate satisfaction and performance. For these analyses, we have focused on the impact of these variables, both separately and jointly, on the subordinate's satisfaction with his immediate superior. We believe our findings clarify the role that quality plays and add substance to the human relations–human resources differentiation.

In the following sections we will explore further the concepts of quantity and quality of participation, integrate these into existing theories of participative management, and examine the implications of our research for these theories and for management practice.

THE QUALITY ASPECT OF PARTICIPATIVE MANAGEMENT

A simple, and we believe familiar, example should assist us in firmly integrating the quantity-quality variables into the major theories of participative management and perhaps demonstrate, in part at least, why we are concerned with this dimension. Most of us have had the following experience:

> We receive an invitation to attend an important meeting. (We know it is important because it is carefully specified as such in the telephone call.) A crucial policy decision is to be made and our views and those of our colleagues are, according to the invitation, vital to the decision. Having done our homework, we arrive at the meeting and begin serious and perhaps even

heated discussion. Before too long, however, a light begins to dawn and illuminated in that dawning light is the fact that the crucial decision we had been called together to decide . . .

The typical organization member completes the final sentence in our example with a cynical, knowing smile: ". . . had already been made." It is helpful, however, to push aside the well-remembered frustration of such situations and examine the logic of the executive who called the meeting and the nature of the participative process flowing from his logic.

We can easily imagine—perhaps because we have frequently used the same logic—the executive in our example saying to himself, "I've got this matter pretty well firmed, but it may require a bit of selling. I'd better call in the troops and at least let them express their views." He may even be willing to allow some minor revisions in the policy in order to overcome resistance and generate among his subordinates a feeling of being part of the decision.

Managers' Attitudes and the Purposes of Participation

Clearly defined in our example is the tight bond between the purpose of participation and the quality of involvement which ensues. And underlying the purpose is the executive's set of assumptions about people— particularly his attitudes concerning the capabilities of his subordinates.

Three theoretical frameworks describe this linkage between the manager's basic attitudes toward people and the amount and kind of consultation that he is likely to use with his subordinates. (Two of these were discussed in another context in Chapters 2 and 3 but deserve amplification here.) It is worth a few lines to compare these theoretical systems and to apply them to our example. Listed chronologically, these frameworks are (1) the theory X–theory Y dichotomy described by the late Douglas McGregor, (2) the system I, II, III, and IV continuum defined by Rensis Likert, and (3) our own traditional, human relations, human resources classification.

McGregor's theory X, Likert's system I, and our traditional model describe autocratic leadership behavior coupled with tight, unilateral control, and obviously little or no subordinate participation in the decision process. Theory X and the traditional model explicitly delineate the superior's assumptions that most people, including his subordinates, are basically indolent, self-centered, gullible, and resistant to change and thus have little to contribute to his decision making. Focusing more on descriptive characteristics and less on an explicit set of assumptions, Likert's system I manager is pictured only as having no confidence or trust in his subordinates.

At the other extreme, theory Y, system IV, and the human resources model define a style of behavior which deeply involves subordinates in the decision process and emphasizes high levels of self-direction and self-control. Again, both theory Y and the human resources model make the logic underlying such behavior explicit—that most organization members are capable of contributing more than demanded by their present jobs and thus represent untapped potential for the organization, potential which the capable manager develops and invests in improved performance. A system IV superior is described simply as one having complete confidence and trust in subordinates in all matters.

In between these extremes fall Likert's systems II and III and our human relations model. Systems II and III describe increasing amounts of subordinate participation as their superior's attitudes toward them move from "condescending" to "substantial, but not complete" confidence and trust. Our human relations model views the superior as recognizing his subordinates' desire for involvement but doubting their ability to make meaningful contributions.

Comparing these frameworks to our example, it is clear that the executive calling the above-mentioned meeting was not operating at the theory X, system I, traditional end of the participative continuum. Had he followed the assumptions of these models he would simply have announced his decision and, if a meeting were called, used it openly to explain his views. Similarly, it seems doubtful that our executive was following the theory Y, system IV, or human resources models. Had he been, he would have called the meeting in the belief that his subordinates might well have important contributions to make and that their participation would possibly result in the construction of a better overall policy. He would have had confidence in their ability and willingness to generate and examine alternatives and take action in the best interest of the organization.

Instead, the meeting in our example, as well as many from our own experience, seems to be defined almost to the letter by our human relations logic and the behavior described in Likert's systems II and III. The casual observer, and perhaps even the more naïve participant, unaware of the motives of the executive calling the meeting, might observe a high level of involvement during the session—participation in both quantity and quality. Most of the participants, however, would be much less charitable, particularly about the meaningfulness of the exercise. They would sense, even though the guidance was subtle, that at least the depth of their participation was carefully controlled if not the entire strategy of the meeting itself.

SUBORDINATE SATISFACTION UNDER THE THREE MODELS

Having described various degrees of quantity and quality of participation flowing from alternative theories of management, and having attempted to link to a common experience through our meeting example, it is not difficult to conjecture about the relationships between these variables and subordinate satisfaction. We would expect subordinate satisfaction to move up and down with both the quantity and the quality of participation, and there is already some evidence (with regard to amount of participation, at least) that it does. Thus, we would expect, particularly within the managerial hierarchy, that satisfaction would be lowest when both quantity and quality of participation were lowest, i.e., as the traditional model is approached, and highest when both quantity and quality are high—when participation moves toward the type described in the human resources model.

Predicting satisfaction under the human relations model is less easy. If the superior's behavior is blatantly manipulative, perhaps close to that in our example, one might expect satisfaction to be quite low, even though the amount of participation was high. On the other hand, if the superior's logic were less obvious, even to himself, we might expect his subordinates to be somewhat pleased to be involved, even if their involvement was frequently peripheral.

While we cannot precisely test the impact of these models on subordinate satisfaction, our recent research does provide some evidence with regard to these conjectures, and we will therefore briefly describe the method of our investigation and look at some of our findings.

Research Approach

The findings reported here were drawn from a broader research project conducted among superior-subordinate management teams from five levels in six geographically separate operating divisions of a West Coast firm.

From extensive questionnaire responses, we were able to develop measures of the three variables important to these analyses: (1) quantity of participation, (2) quality of participation, and (3) satisfaction with immediate superiors. Our measure of quantity was drawn from managers' responses to questions concerning how frequently they felt they were consulted by their superior on a number of typical department issues and decisions. This information allowed us to classify managers as high or low (compared to other managers at the same level) in terms of the amount of participation they felt they were allowed. For our measure of quality, we turned to the responses given by each manager's superior. The superior's attitudes toward his subordinates—his evaluation of their capabilities with regard to such factors as judgment, creativity, responsibility, long-range perspective, etc.—were analyzed and categorized as high or low compared to those of other managers at the same level. Finally, our satisfaction measure was taken from a question on which managers indicated, on a scale from very satisfied to very dissatisfied, their reactions to their own immediate superiors.

Findings

The first thing apparent in our findings, as shown in each of the figures discussed below, is that virtually all the subjects in our study appear reasonably well satisfied with their immediate superiors. This is not surprising, particularly since all subjects, both superiors and subordinates, are in managerial positions. Compared to members lower in the hierarchy, managers generally respond positively on job satisfaction scales. Moreover, the organization in which our research was conducted is reputed to be forward looking and well managed. In a similar vein, and supporting the organization's reputation, most participants reported generally high levels of consultation, and superior's scores on confidence in their subordinates were typically higher than the average scores in our broader research.

Nevertheless, differences do exist which, given the restricted range

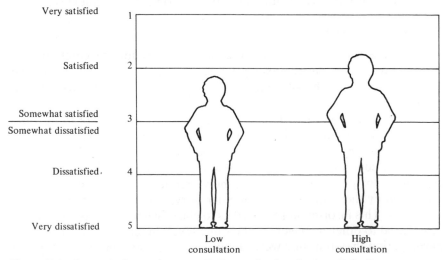

Figure 7-1 Amount of superior consultation and subordinate satisfaction

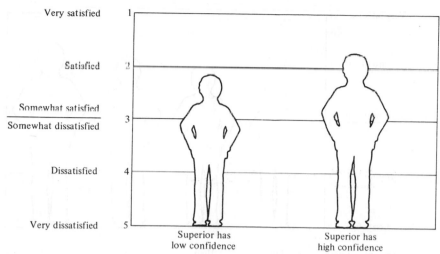

Figure 7-2 Superior's confidence in subordinates and subordinates' satisfaction

of scores, are in most instances highly significant in statistical terms. Moreover, they demonstrate that both the quantity and the quality of participation are related to managers' feelings of satisfaction with their immediate superiors.

As shown in Figure 7-1, the quantity of participation achieved is apparently related to managers' feelings of satisfaction with their superiors. Managers classified as low in terms of the extent to which they are consulted by their superiors are significantly less satisfied than those classified as high. The average score for the low consultation group falls between the satisfied and the so-so (somewhat satisfied–somewhat dissatisfied) categories. For the high consultation group, the score falls between the satisfied and the highly satisfied.

A slightly stronger pattern of results is apparent when managers are regrouped in terms of the amount of confidence their superiors have in them (Figure 7-2). Managers whose superiors have relatively high trust and confidence scores are significantly more satisfied than are their colleagues whose superiors have relatively lower scores on this dimension.

Finally, our results take on their most interesting form when managers are cross-classified on both the quantity and quality dimensions. As shown in Figure 7-3, the progression in satisfaction is consistent with our theoretical formulation. Especially obvious is the comparison between managers classified as low both in amount of consultation received and in the extent to which their superior has confidence in them and managers

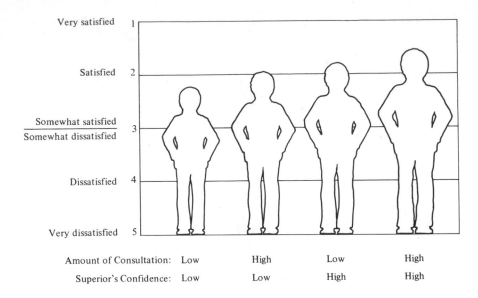

Figure 7-3 Effects of amount of consultation and superior's confidence in subordinates on subordinate satisfaction

who are rated high on both these variables. Interestingly enough, and relevant to our later discussion, managers whose superiors have high confidence in them but who are low in amount of participation appear slightly more satisfied than their counterparts who are high in amount of participation but whose superiors have less confidence in their subordinates.

Linking Findings to Theory

The bulk of our findings, particularly as illustrated in Figure 7-3, appear to support our conjectures. Managers who place the least value in their subordinates' capabilities and who least often seek their contributions on departmental issues have the least-satisfied subordinates. Although it would probably be incorrect to place the traditional (theory X, system I) label on any of the managers in our sample, those who lean closest to these views do so with predictable results in terms of subordinate satisfaction.

Similarly, managers who are high in their respect for their subordinates' capabilities and who consult them regularly on departmental issues also achieve the expected results. Again, although precise labeling is probably inappropriate, managers whose attitudes and behavior are closest to the human resources (theory Y, system IV) model do in fact have the most satisfied subordinates.

Further, those managers who consult their subordinates frequently but who have little confidence in their ability to make decisions, and who thus fall nearest to our human relations model, have subordinates who are more satisfied than those under managers who lean toward the traditional model but are significantly less satisfied than those under human resources managers.

Although the majority of our findings support the major formulations of participative management theory, they also suggest the need for elaboration and clarification. This need is brought to attention by the total pattern of our findings and particularly by the results for one of our categories of managers—those high in superiors' confidence but relatively low in participation. If you recall, although the differences were not large, this group had the second highest average satisfaction score in our sample—the score falling between that of the human relations group (high participation, low superior confidence) and the human resources group (high on both). Moreover, for the two groups characterized by high participation, there is substantially higher satisfaction for those whose superior expresses his confidence in his subordinates. Clearly, any theory which focused on the amount of participation would not predict these results. Rather, for these managers at least, the quality of their relationship with their superiors as indicated by their superiors' attitudes of trust and confidence in them appears to modify the effects of the amount of participation.

Implications for Theory

Although the quality dimension of the theory of participative management has not been fully developed, its outlines are suggested in our own human resources model and in McGregor's theoretical framework. McGregor stressed heavily the importance of managers' basic attitudes and assumptions about their subordinates. Expanding on this point in his more recent writing, he suggested that a manager's assumptions about his subordinates' traits and abilities do not bind him to a single course of action. Rather, he argued that, taking circumstances into account, a range of behaviors is appropriate under theory Y assumptions—i.e., a manager with high trust and confidence in his subordinates could and should take into account a number of situational and personality factors in deciding, among other things, when and how to consult with them. Extending this reasoning, one can even imagine a theory Y or human resources manager actually consulting with his subordinates less often than some of his colleagues. Nevertheless, the nature and quality of participation employed by such a manager, when it occurs, would presumably be deeper and more meaningful, which would be reflected in high levels of subordinate satisfaction and—hopefully—performance.

This view of the superior-subordinate interaction process, emphasizing as it does the quality of the interaction rather than only the amount, can be used to provide an answer to three of the more pervasive criticisms of participative management. These criticisms, each of which is probably most accurately aimed at the simple quantity theory, focus on the inappropriateness of extensive consultation when the superior is constrained by time, technology, and temperament (his own or that of his subordinates). Let us discuss these criticisms further.

The Time Constraint   "In a crisis, you simply do not have time to run around consulting people." This familiar explication is difficult to debate and in fact would receive no challenge from a sophisticated theory of participation. In a real "burning building" crisis, consultation is inappropriate and unnecessary. A crisis of this nature is recognized as such by any well-informed subordinate and his self-controlled cooperation is most likely willingly supplied. The behavior of both superior and subordinate in such a situation is guided by the situation and each may freely turn to the other, or to any available source of expertise, for help in solving the problem at hand.

Many crises, however, do not fit the "burning building" category and in fact may be much more real to one individual or to one level of management than to those below them. Our experience and some very tentative research findings suggest that managers may not be nearly so bound by their constraints as they frequently claim, or at least if they are constrained, these limits are either known in advance or are open to modification if circumstances demand. In many instances it appears that managers employ the "time won't permit" argument primarily to justify autocratic and risk-free behavior—if he succeeds the credit is his; if he fails, he can defend his actions by pointing out that he had no time to explore alternatives.

Such self-defined, or at least self-sustaining, crises are, it seems to us, most frequently used by the manager with a human relations concept of participation—one who views participation primarily as a means of obtaining subordinate cooperation and who focuses mainly on the amount of formal involvement required. The crisis itself can be employed in place of participation as the lever to obtain cooperation, and there is clearly no time for the sort of routine, frequently peripheral consultation in which he most often indulges.

On the other hand, the manager with high trust and confidence in his subordinates' capabilities, the human resources manager, is less likely to use time constraints as a managerial tactic. In real crises, he moves as rapidly as the situation demands. He is, however, more likely, because of his normal practices of sharing information with his subordinates, to have a group which is prepared to join him in a rapid review of alternatives. He is unconcerned with involvement for the sake of involvement, and his consultation activities are penetrating and to the point. His subordinates share his trust and feel free to challenge his views, just as he feels free to openly question their advice and suggestions.

The Technology Barrier "Look, I've got fifteen subordinates scattered all over the building. What do you expect me to do—shut down the plant and call a meeting every time something happens?" This argument is obviously closely linked to the time-constraint argument—technology is a major factor in determining the flow and timing of decisions. Similarly, it too flows from a human relations–quantity-oriented view of participation.

Of course a good manager does not regularly "stop the presses" and call a conference. He has confidence in his subordinates' abilities to handle problems as they appear and to call him in when the problem demands his attention. This confidence is, however, reinforced by joint planning, both one to one and across his group of subordinates, before the operation gets under way. Having agreed in advance on objectives, schedules, priorities, and procedures, involvement on a day-to-day basis may be minimal. The manager in this instance does not seek participation to obtain cooperation with his views. The regularly scheduled work planning and review sessions are viewed as important by both parties because they result in well-considered solutions to real problems.

The Temperament Barrier "I'm simply not the sort who can run around to his subordinates asking them how things are going. It's just not my style." The manager who made this statement (a participant in one of our earlier studies) did so somewhat apologetically. In fact, there was little for him to be apologetic about. He had a high-performing group of subordinates in whom he placed great trust and confidence, and who were in turn highly satisfied with him. Further, while he did not seek their views on a variety of routine departmental matters, and his subordinates did not drop into his office to chat, he freely shared all departmental information with them and, on a regular basis, worked with his subordinates in coordinating departmental plans and schedules. In addition, he practiced a somewhat formal but effective form of management by objectives with each of his subordinates.

This manager and, unfortunately, many of the more outspoken critics of participative management, tend to feel that consultation must be carried out in a gregarious, back-slapping manner. Quite the contrary— joint planning is a decision-making technique and not a personality attribute. Extreme shyness or reserve may be an inhibiting factor, but it is not a complete barrier. Trust and confidence in subordinates can be demonstrated at least as effectively by actions as by words.

Similarly, as suggested earlier, the manager who holds a human resources view of participation acknowledges personality and capability differences among his subordinates. He feels a responsibility to the organization as well as to his subordinates to assist *each* to continuously develop his potential. He recognizes that individuals move toward the free interchange of ideas, suggestions, and criticisms at different paces. However, by demonstrating his own confidence in his subordinates' capabilities, he tends to encourage more rapid growth than other managers.

CONCLUDING REMARKS

Our continuing research on the purpose and process of participative management has, in our view, contributed additional support for the human resources concept of participation. It has emphasized that when the impact on subordinates is considered, the superior's attitudes toward the traits and abilities of his subordinates is at least as important as the amount of consultation in which he engages.

This not-so-startling finding allows expansions and interpretations of modern theories of participation to counter criticisms which may be properly leveled at a simple quantity theory. However, while our findings have obvious implications for both management theory and behavior, they too are open to possible misinterpretation. One can—and some surely will—read into our findings that subordinate consultation may be neglected—that all that matters is that the superior respect his subordinates.

Our findings do not support such a view, and, in fact, it has been tried and regularly found wanting. Such a philosophy is embodied in the frequently heard statement, "All you need to do to be a good manager is to hire a good subordinate and turn him loose to do the job as he sees fit." Such a philosophy, in our view, abdicates the superior's responsibility to guide, develop, and support his subordinates. The most satisfied managers in our sample were those who received high levels of consultation from superiors who valued their capabilities. We feel that effective participation involves neither the "selling" of the superior's ideas nor the blanket approval of all subordinate suggestions. Rather, it is most clearly embodied in the notion of joint planning where the skills of both parties are used to their fullest.

While our findings emphasize the importance of feelings of trust and confidence in subordinates, they do not indicate their source. It is possible of course that those superiors in our sample who reported the highest levels of trust and confidence in their subordinates did so because their subordinates were of higher caliber than those of their colleagues. However, this seems to us a bit unlikely. Rather, within our large sample of managers, several indicators suggested that the capabilities of managers were roughly evenly distributed across levels and divisions within the organization.

Another possible reason for differences in superior attitudes on this dimension is that they are caused by interaction with subordinates in the first place, rather than being a determinate of the nature of this interaction. That is, the manager who attempts consultation which is highly successful increases his confidence in his subordinates and thus develops broader involvement. This explanation seems to us to be a highly plausible one which has implications for management development. In fact, there is growing evidence that managers who experiment with participative techniques over lengthy periods of time do develop both a commitment to such practices and additional trust in their subordinates.

BIBLIOGRAPHY

Bowers, D. G. and Stanley E. Seashore, "Predicting Organizational Effectiveness with a Four-Factor Theory of Leadership," *Administrative Science Quarterly*, vol. 11, pp. 238–263 (September 1966).

Fiedler, Fred E., "Engineer the Job to Fit the Manager," *Harvard Business Review*, vol. 43, pp. 115–122 (September-October 1965).

Heller, Frank A., "Leadership, Decision Making and Contingency Theory," *Industrial Relations*, vol. 12, pp. 183–199 (May 1973).

McGregor, Douglas, *The Professional Manager* (New York: McGraw-Hill, 1969).

Miles, Raymond E. and J. B. Ritchie, "An Analysis of Quantity and Quality of the Participative Decision Making Process," *Personnel Psychology*, vol. 23, pp. 347–359 (Autumn 1970).

Roberts, Karlene, Raymond E. Miles, and L. Vaughn Blankenship, "Organizational Leadership, Satisfaction, and Productivity: A Comparative Analysis," *The Academy of Management Journal*, vol. 11, pp. 401–414 (December 1968).

Strauss, George, "Human Relations—1968 Style," *Industrial Relations*, vol. 7, pp. 262–276 (May 1968).

Vroom, Victor and Philip Yetton, *Leadership and Decision Making* (Pittsburgh: University of Pittsburgh Press, 1973), chaps. 5 and 6.

How to Choose
a Leadership Pattern

Robert Tannenbaum
Warren H. Schmidt

"I put most problems into my group's hands and leave it to them to carry the ball from there. I serve merely as a catalyst, mirroring back the people's thoughts and feelings so that they can better understand them."

"It's foolish to make decisions oneself on matters that affect people. I always talk things over with my subordinates, but I make it clear to them that I'm the one who has to have the final say."

"Once I have decided on a course of action, I do my best to sell my ideas to my employees."

"I'm being paid to lead. If I let a lot of other people make the decisions I should be making, then I'm not worth my salt."

"I believe in getting things done. I can't waste time calling meetings. Someone has to call the shots around here, and I think it should be me."

Each of these statements represents a point of view about "good leadership." Considerable experience, factual data, and theoretical principles could be cited to support each statement, even though they seem to be inconsistent when placed together. Such contradictions point up the dilemma in which the modern manager frequently finds himself.

New Problem

The problem of how the modern manager can be "democratic" in his relations with subordinates and at the same time maintain the necessary authority and control in the organization for which he is responsible has come into focus increasingly in recent years.

Earlier in the century this problem was not so acutely felt. The successful executive was generally pictured as possessing intelligence, imagination, initiative, the capacity to make rapid (and generally wise) decisions, and the ability to inspire subordinates. People tended to think of the world as being divided into "leaders" and "followers."

New Focus

Gradually, however, from the social sciences emerged the concept of "group dynamics" with its focus on *members* of the group rather than solely on the leader. Research efforts of social scientists underscored the importance of employee involvement and participation in decision making. Evidence began to challenge the efficiency of highly directive leadership, and increasing attention was paid to problems of motivation and human relations.

Through training laboratories in group development that sprang up across the country, many of the newer notions of leadership began to exert an impact. These training laboratories were carefully designed to give people a first-hand experience in full participation and decision making. The designated "leaders" deliberately attempted to reduce their own power and to make group members as responsible as possible for setting their own goals and methods within the laboratory experience.

It was perhaps inevitable that some of the people who attended the training laboratories regarded this kind of leadership as being truly "democratic" and went home with the determination to build fully participative decision making into their own organizations. Whenever their bosses made a decision without convening a staff meeting, they tended to perceive this as authoritarian behavior. The true symbol of democratic leadership to some was the meeting — and the less directed from the top, the more democratic it was.

Some of the more enthusiastic alumni of these training laboratories began to get the habit of categorizing leader behavior as "democratic" or "authoritarian." The boss who made too many decisions himself was thought of as an authoritarian, and his directive behavior was often attributed solely to his personality.

New Need

The net result of the research findings and of the human relations training based upon them has been to call into question the stereotype of an effective leader. Consequently, the modern manager often finds himself in an uncomfortable state of mind.

Often he is not quite sure how to behave; there are times when he is torn between exerting "strong" leadership and "permissive" leadership. Sometimes new knowledge pushes him in one direction ("I should really get the group to help make this decision"), but at the same time his experience pushes him in another direction ("I really understand the problem better than the group and therefore I should make the decision"). He is not sure when a group decision is really appropriate or when holding a staff meeting serves merely as a device for avoiding his own decision-making responsibility.

The purpose of our article is to suggest a framework which managers may find useful in grappling with this dilemma. First, we shall look at the different patterns of leadership behavior that the manager can choose from in relating himself to his subordinates. Then, we shall turn to some of the questions suggested by this range of patterns. For instance, how important is it for a manager's subordinates to know what type of leadership he is using in a situation? What factors should he consider in deciding on a leadership pattern? What difference do his long-run objectives make as compared to his immediate objectives?

Range of Behavior

Exhibit I presents the continuum or range of possible leadership behavior available to a manager. Each type of action is related to the degree of authority used by the boss and to the amount of freedom available to his subordinates in reaching decisions. The actions seen on the extreme left characterize the manager who maintains a high degree of control while those seen on the extreme right characterize the manager who releases a high degree of control. Neither extreme is absolute; authority and freedom are never without their limitations.

Now let us look more closely at each of the behavior points occurring along this continuum.

The manager makes the decision and announces it. In this case the boss identifies a problem, considers alternative solutions, chooses one of them, and then reports this decision to his subordinates for implementation. He may or may not give consideration to what he believes his subordinates will think or feel about his decision; in any case, he provides no opportunity for them to participate directly in the decision-making process. Coercion may or may not be used or implied.

The manager "sells" his decision. Here the manager, as before, takes responsibility for identifying the problem and arriving at a decision. However, rather than simply announcing it, he takes the additional step of persuading his subordinates to accept it. In doing so, he recognizes the possibility of some resistance among those who will be faced with the decision, and seeks to reduce this resistance by indicating, for example, what the employees have to gain from his decision.

The manager presents his ideas, invites questions. Here the boss who has arrived at a decision and who seeks acceptance of his ideas provides an opportunity for his subordinates to get a fuller explanation of his thinking and his intentions. After presenting the ideas, he invites questions so that his associates can better understand what he is trying to accomplish. This "give and take" also enables the manager and the subordinates to explore more fully the implications of the decision.

Exhibit I Continuum of leadership behavior

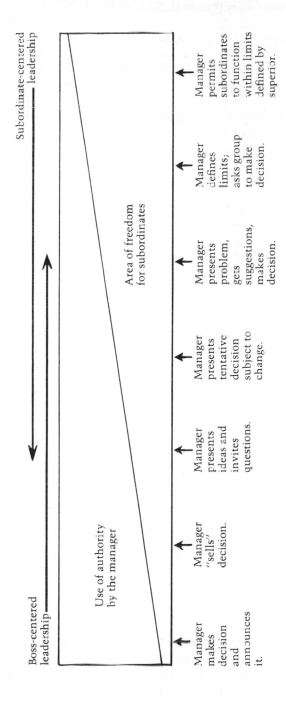

The manager presents a tentative decision subject to change. This kind of behavior permits the subordinates to exert some influence on the decision. The initiative for identifying and diagnosing the problem remains with the boss. Before meeting with his staff, he has thought the problem through and arrived at a decision — but only a tentative one. Before finalizing it, he presents his proposed solution for the reaction of those who will be affected by it. He says in effect, "I'd like to hear what you have to say about this plan that I have developed. I'll appreciate your frank reactions, but will reserve for myself the final decision."

The manager presents the problem, gets suggestions, and then makes his decision. Up to this point the boss has come before the group with a solution of his own. Not so in this case. The subordinates now get the first chance to suggest solutions. The manager's initial role involves identifying the problem. He might, for example, say something of this sort: "We are faced with a number of complaints from newspapers and the general public on our service policy. What is wrong here? What ideas do you have for coming to grips with this problem?"

The function of the group becomes one of increasing the manager's repertory of possible solutions to the problem. The purpose is to capitalize on the knowledge and experience of those who are on the "firing line." From the expanded list of alternatives developed by the manager and his subordinates, the manager then selects the solution that he regards as most promising.[1]

The manager defines the limits and requests the group to make a decision. At this point the manager passes to the group (possibly including himself as a member) the right to make decisions. Before doing so, however, he defines the problem to be solved and the boundaries within which the decision must be made.

An example might be the handling of a parking problem at a plant. The boss decides that this is something that should be worked on by the people involved, so he calls them together and points up the existence of the problem. Then he tells them:

"There is the open field just north of the main plant which has been designated for additional employee parking. We can build underground or surface multilevel facilities as long as the cost does not exceed $100,000. Within these limits we are free to work out whatever solution makes sense to us. After we decide on a specific plan, the company will spend the available money in whatever way we indicate."

The manager permits the group to make decisions within prescribed limits. This represents an extreme degree of group freedom only occasionally encountered in formal organizations, as, for instance, in many research groups. Here the team of managers or engineers undertakes the identification and diagnosis of the problem, develops alternative procedures for solving it, and decides on one or more

---

[1] For a fuller explanation of this approach, see Leo Moore, "Too Much Management, Too Little Change," HBR January–February 1956, p. 41.

of these alternative solutions. The only limits directly imposed on the group by the organization are those specified by the superior of the team's boss. If the boss participates in the decision-making process, he attempts to do so with no more authority than any other member of the group. He commits himself in advance to assist in implementing whatever decision the group makes.

Key Questions

As the continuum in *Exhibit I* demonstrates, there are a number of alternative ways in which a manager can relate himself to the group or individuals he is supervising. At the extreme left of the range, the emphasis is on the manager — on what *he* is interested in, how *he* sees things, how *he* feels about them. As we move toward the subordinate-centered end of the continuum, however, the focus is increasingly on the subordinates — on what *they* are interested in, how *they* look at things, how *they* feel about them.

When business leadership is regarded in this way, a number of questions arise. Let us take four of especial importance:

Can a boss ever relinquish his responsibility by delegating it to someone else? Our view is that the manager must expect to be held responsible by his superior for the quality of the decisions made, even though operationally these decisions may have been made on a group basis. He should, therefore, be ready to accept whatever risk is involved whenever he delegates decision-making power to his subordinates. Delegation is not a way of "passing the buck." Also, it should be emphasized that the amount of freedom the boss gives to his subordinates cannot be greater than the freedom which he himself has been given by his own superior.

Should the manager participate with his subordinates once he has delegated responsibility to them? The manager should carefully think over this question and decide on his role prior to involving the subordinate group. He should ask if his presence will inhibit or facilitate the problem-solving process. There may be some instances when he should leave the group to let it solve the problem for itself. Typically, however, the boss has useful ideas to contribute, and should function as an additional member of the group. In the latter instance, it is important that he indicate clearly to the group that he sees himself in a *member* role rather than in an authority role.

How important is it for the group to recognize what kind of leadership behavior the boss is using? It makes a great deal of difference. Many relationship problems between boss and subordinate occur because the boss fails to make clear how he plans to use his authority. If, for example, he actually intends to make a certain decision himself, but the subordinate group gets the impression that he has delegated this authority, considerable confusion and resentment are likely to follow. Problems may also occur when the boss uses a "democratic" façade to conceal the fact that he has already made a decision which he hopes the group will accept as its own. The attempt to "make them think it was their idea in the first place" is a risky one. We believe that it is highly important for the manager to be honest and clear in describing what authority he is keeping and what role he is asking his subordinates to assume in solving a particular problem.

Can you tell how "democratic" a manager is by the number of decisions his subordinates make? The sheer *number* of decisions is not an accurate index of the amount of freedom that a subordinate group enjoys. More important is the *significance* of the decisions which the boss entrusts to his subordinates. Obviously a decision on how to arrange desks is of an entirely different order from a decision involving the introduction of new electronic data-processing equipment. Even though the widest possible limits are given in dealing with the first issue, the group will sense no particular degree of responsibility. For a boss to permit the group to decide equipment policy, even within rather narrow limits, would reflect a greater degree of confidence in them on his part.

Deciding How to Lead

Now let us turn from the types of leadership which are possible in a company situation to the question of what types are *practical* and *desirable*. What factors or forces should a manager consider in deciding how to manage? Three are of particular importance:

Forces in the manager.
Forces in the subordinates.
Forces in the situation.

We should like briefly to describe these elements and indicate how they might influence a manager's action in a decision-making situation.[2] The strength of each of them will, of course, vary from instance to instance, but the manager who is sensitive to them can better assess the problems which face him and determine which mode of leadership behavior is most appropriate for him.

Forces in the Manager

The manager's behavior in any given instance will be influenced greatly by the many forces operating within his own personality. He will, of course, perceive his leadership problems in a unique way on the basis of his background, knowl-

[2] See also Robert Tannenbaum and Fred Massarik, "Participation by Subordinates in the Managerial Decision-Making Process," *Canadian Journal of Economics and Political Science,* August 1950, p. 413.

edge, and experience. Among the important internal forces affecting him will be the following:

1. *His value system.* How strongly does he feel that individuals should have a share in making the decisions which affect them? Or, how convinced is he that the official who is paid to assume responsibility should personally carry the burden of decision making? The strength of his convictions on questions like these will tend to move the manager to one end or the other of the continuum shown in *Exhibit I.* His behavior will also be influenced by the relative importance that he attaches to organizational efficiency, personal growth of subordinates, and company profits.[3]

2. *His confidence in his subordinates.* Managers differ greatly in the amount of trust they have in other people generally, and this carries over to the particular employees they supervise at a given time. In viewing his particular group of subordinates, the manager is likely to consider their knowledge and competence with respect to the problem. A central question he might ask himself is: "Who is best qualified to deal with this problem?" Often he may, justifiably or not, have more confidence in his own capabilities than in those of his subordinates.

3. *His own leadership inclinations.* There are some managers who seem to function more comfortably and naturally as highly directive leaders. Resolving problems and issuing orders come easily to them. Other managers seem to operate more comfortably in a team role, where they are continually sharing many of their functions with their subordinates.

4. *His feelings of security in an uncertain situation.* The manager who releases control over the decision-making process thereby reduces the predictability of the outcome. Some managers have a greater need than others for predictability and stability in their environment. This "tolerance for ambiguity" is being viewed increasingly by psychologists as a key variable in a person's manner of dealing with problems.

The manager brings these and other highly personal variables to each situation he faces. If he can see them as forces which, consciously or unconsciously, influence his behavior, he can better understand what makes him prefer to act in a given way. And understanding this, he can often make himself more effective.

Forces in the Subordinate

Before deciding how to lead a certain group, the manager will also want to consider a number of forces affecting his subordinates' behavior. He will want to remember that each employee, like himself, is influenced by many personality

---

[3] See Chris Argyris, "Top Management Dilemma: Company Needs vs. Individual Development," *Personnel,* September 1955, pp. 123–134.

variables. In addition, each subordinate has a set of expectations about how the boss should act in relation to him (the phrase "expected behavior" is one we hear more and more often these days at discussions of leadership and teaching). The better the manager understands these factors, the more accurately he can determine what kind of behavior on his part will enable his subordinates to act most effectively.

Generally speaking, the manager can permit his subordinates greater freedom if the following essential conditions exist:

If the subordinates have relatively high needs for independence. (As we all know, people differ greatly in the amount of direction that they desire.)

If the subordinates have a readiness to assume responsibility for decision making. (Some see additional responsibility as a tribute to their ability; others see it as "passing the buck.")

If they have a relatively high tolerance for ambiguity. (Some employees prefer to have clear-cut directives given to them; others prefer a wider area of freedom.)

If they are interested in the problem and feel that it is important.

If they understand and identify with the goals of the organization.

If they have the necessary knowledge and experience to deal with the problem.

If they have learned to expect to share in decision making. (Persons who have come to expect strong leadership and are then suddenly confronted with the request to share more fully in decision making are often upset by this new experience. On the other hand, persons who have enjoyed a considerable amount of freedom resent the boss who begins to make all the decisions himself.)

The manager will probably tend to make fuller use of his own authority if the above conditions do *not* exist; at times there may be no realistic alternative to running a "one-man show."

The restrictive effect of many of the forces will, of course, be greatly modified by the general feeling of confidence which subordinates have in the boss. Where they have learned to respect and trust him, he is free to vary his behavior. He will feel certain that he will not be perceived as an authoritarian boss on those occasions when he makes his decisions by himself. Similarly, he will not be seen as using staff meetings to avoid his decision-making responsibility. In a climate of mutual confidence and respect, people tend to feel less threatened by deviations from normal practice, which in turn makes possible a higher degree of flexibility in the whole relationship.

Forces in the Situation

In addition to the forces which exist in the manager himself and in his subordinates, certain characteristics of the general situation will also affect the manager's behavior. Among the more critical environmental pressures that surround him are those which stem from the organization, the work group, the nature of the problem, and the pressures of time. Let us look briefly at each of these:

Type of organization — Like individuals, organizations have values and traditions which inevitably influence the behavior of the people who work in them. The manager who is a newcomer to a company quickly discovers that certain kinds of behavior are approved while others are not. He also discovers that to deviate radically from what is generally accepted is likely to create problems for him.

These values and traditions are communicated in numerous ways — through job descriptions, policy pronouncements, and public statements by top executives. Some organizations, for example, hold to the notion that the desirable executive is one who is dynamic, imaginative, decisive, and persuasive. Other organizations put more emphasis upon the importance of the executive's ability to work effectively with people — his human relations skills. The fact that his superiors have a defined concept of what the good executive should be will very likely push the manager toward one end or the other of the behavioral range.

In addition to the above, the amount of employee participation is influenced by such variables as the size of the working units, their geographical distribution, and the degree of inter- and intra-organizational security required to attain company goals. For example, the wide geographical dispersion of an organization may preclude a practical system of participative decision making, even though this would otherwise be desirable. Similarly, the size of the working units or the need for keeping plans confidential may make it necessary for the boss to exercise more control than would otherwise be the case. Factors like these may limit considerably the manager's ability to function flexibly on the continuum.

Group effectiveness — Before turning decision-making responsibility over to a subordinate group, the boss should consider how effectively its members work together as a unit.

One of the relevant factors here is the experience the group has had in working together. It can generally be expected that a group which has functioned for some time will have developed habits of cooperation and thus be able to tackle a problem more effectively than a new group. It can also be expected that a group of people with similar backgrounds and interests will work more quickly and easily than people with dissimilar backgrounds, because the communication problems are likely to be less complex.

The degree of confidence that the members have in their ability to solve problems as a group is also a key consideration. Finally, such group variables as cohesiveness, permissiveness, mutual acceptance, and commonality of purpose will exert subtle but powerful influence on the group's functioning.

The problem itself — The nature of the problem may determine what degree of authority should be delegated by the manager to his subordinates. Obviously he will ask himself whether they have the kind of knowledge which is needed. It is possible to do them a real disservice by assigning a problem that their experience does not equip them to handle.

Since the problems faced in large or growing industries increasingly require knowledge of specialists from many different fields, it might be inferred that the more complex a problem, the more anxious a manager will be to get some assistance in solving it. However, this is not always the case. There will be times when the very complexity of the problem calls for one person to work it out. For example, if the manager has most of the background and factual data relevant to a given issue, it may be easier for him to think it through himself than to take the time to fill in his staff on all the pertinent background information.

The key question to ask, of course, is: "Have I heard the ideas of everyone who has the necessary knowledge to make a significant contribution to the solution of this problem?"

The pressure of time — This is perhaps the most clearly felt pressure on the manager (in spite of the fact that it may sometimes be imagined). The more that he feels the need for an immediate decision, the more difficult it is to involve other people. In organizations which are in a constant state of "crisis" and "crash programming" one is likely to find managers personally using a high degree of authority with relatively little delegation to subordinates. When the time pressure is less intense, however, it becomes much more possible to bring subordinates in on the decision-making process.

These, then, are the principal forces that impinge on the manager in any given instance and that tend to determine his tactical behavior in relation to his subordinates. In each case his behavior ideally will be that which makes possible the most effective attainment of his immediate goal within the limits facing him.

Long-run Strategy

As the manager works with his organization on the problems that come up day by day, his choice of a leadership pattern is usually limited. He must take account of the forces just described and, within the restrictions they impose on him, do the best that he can. But as he looks ahead months or even years, he can shift his thinking from tactics to large-scale strategy. No longer need he be fettered by all of the forces mentioned, for he can view many of them as variables over which he has some control. He can, for example, gain new insights or skills for himself, supply training for individual subordinates, and provide participative experiences for his employee group.

In trying to bring about a change in these variables, however, he is faced with a challenging question: At which point along the continuum *should* he act?

Attaining Objectives

The answer depends largely on what he wants to accomplish. Let us suppose that he is interested in the same objectives that most modern managers seek to attain when they can shift their attention from the pressure of immediate assignments:

1. To raise the level of employee motivation.
2. To increase the readiness of subordinates to accept change.
3. To improve the quality of all managerial decisions.
4. To develop teamwork and morale.
5. To further the individual development of employees.

In recent years the manager has been deluged with a flow of advice on how best to achieve these longer-run objectives. It is little wonder that he is often both bewildered and annoyed. However, there are some guidelines which he can usefully follow in making a decision.

Most research and much of the experience of recent years give a strong factual basis to the theory that a fairly high degree of subordinate-centered behavior is associated with the accomplishment of the five purposes mentioned.[4] This does not mean that a manager should always leave all decisions to his assistants. To provide the individual or the group with greater freedom than they are ready for at any given time may very well tend to generate anxieties and therefore inhibit rather than facilitate the attainment of desired objectives. But this should not keep the manager from making a continuing effort to confront his subordinates with the challenge of freedom.

Conclusion

In summary, there are two implications in the basic thesis that we have been developing. The first is that the successful leader is one who is keenly aware of those forces which are most relevant to his behavior at any given time. He accurately understands himself, the individuals and group he is dealing with, and the company and broader social environment in which he operates. And certainly he is able to assess the present readiness for growth of his subordinates.

But this sensitivity or understanding is not enough, which brings us to the second implication. The successful leader is one who is able to behave appropriately in the light of these perceptions. If direction is in order, he is able to

[4] For example, see Warren H. Schmidt and Paul C. Buchanan, *Techniques that Produce Teamwork* (New London, Arthur C. Croft Publications, 1954); and Morris S. Viteles, *Motivation and Morale in Industry* (New York, W. W. Norton & Company, Inc., 1953).

direct; if considerable participative freedom is called for, he is able to provide such freedom.

Thus, the successful manager of men can be primarily characterized neither as a strong leader nor as a permissive one. Rather, he is one who maintains a high batting average in accurately assessing the forces that determine what his most appropriate behavior at any given time should be and in actually being able to behave accordingly. Being both insightful and flexible, he is less likely to see the problems of leadership as a dilemma.

How Do You Make Leaders More Effective?

New Answers to an Old Puzzle

Fred E. Fiedler

et's begin with a basic proposition: The organization that employs the leader is as responsible for his success or failure as the leader himself. Not that this is a new insight —far from it. Terman wrote in 1904 that leadership performance depends on the situation, as well as on the leader. Although this statement would not be questioned by anyone currently working in this area, it also has been widely ignored. Practically all formal training programs attempt to change the individual; many of them assume explicitly or implicitly that there is one style of leadership or one way of acting that will work best under all conditions. Most military academies, for example, attempt to mold the individual into a supposedly ideal leader personality. Others assume that the training should enable the individual to become more flexible or more sensitive to his environment so that he can adapt himself to it.

Before going further let's define a few terms. I will confine my discussion to *task groups* rather than the organization of which the group is a part. Furthermore, we will assume that anyone who is placed in a leadership position will have the requisite technical qualifications for the job. Just as the leader of a surgical team obviously has to have medical training, so a manager must know the essential administrative requirements of his job. We will here talk primarily about training *as a leader* rather than training as a specialist. The effectiveness of the leader will be defined in terms of how well his group or organization performs the primary tasks for which the group exists. We measure the effectiveness of a football coach by how many games his team wins and not by the character he builds, and the excellence of an orchestra conductor by how well his orchestra plays, not by the happiness of his musicians' or his ability as a musicologist. Whether the musicians' job satisfaction or the conductor's musicological expertness do, in fact, contribute to the orchestra's excellence is an interesting question in its own right, but it is not what people pay to hear. Likewise, the performance of a manager is here measured in terms of his department's or

Reprinted by permission of the publisher from *Organizational Dynamics*, Autumn 1972, pp. 3-18. © 1972 by AMACOM, a division of American Management Associations.

group's effectiveness in doing its assigned job. Whether the accomplishment of this job is to be measured after a week or after five years depends, of course, upon the assignment the organization gives the group, and the accomplishments the organization considers important.

When we think of improving leadership, we almost automatically think of training the individual. This training frequently involves giving the man a new perspective on his supervisory responsibilities by means of role playing, discussions, detailed instructions on how to behave toward subordinates, as well as instruction in the technical and administrative skills he will need in his job. A training program might last a few days, a few months, or as in the case of college programs and military academies, as long as four years. What is the hard evidence that this type of training actually increases organizational performance?

Empirical studies to evaluate the effectiveness of various leadership training programs, executive development, and supervisory workshops have been generally disappointing. Certainly, the two field experiments and two studies of ongoing organizations conducted by my associates and me failed to show that training increases organizational performance.

The first experiment in 1966 was conducted at a Belgian naval training center. We chose 244 Belgian recruits and 48 petty officers from a pool of 546 men. These men were assembled into 96 three-men groups: 48 groups had petty officers and 48 groups had recruits as leaders. The recruits ranged in age from 17 to 24, and none had been in the service longer than six weeks. The petty officers ranged in age from 19 to 45 years, and had an average 6f ten years' experience. All petty officers had received a two-year technical and leadership training course at petty officer candidate school. Since most successful graduates enlist for a 20-year term, Belgian petty officers are not only well-trained but they are also truly motivated and committed careermen.

The petty officers were matched with the recruit leaders on intelligence and other relevant scores. Each group worked on four cooperative tasks which were considered fair samples of the type of work petty officers might perform. One task consisted of writing a recruiting letter urging young men to join the Belgian navy as a career; the second and third tasks required the groups to find the shortest route for a convoy first through ten and then through twelve ports; the fourth task required the leader to train his men without using verbal instructions in the disassembling and reassembling of a .45-caliber automatic pistol.

Despite the fact that the recruits had had no leadership experience or training, their groups performed as well as those led by petty officers.

To test whether these results were not simply due to the chance or to a fault in our experimental design, we conducted a second experiment at a leadership training workshop for officers of Canadian military colleges. This study compared the performance of groups led by captains and majors with groups led by enlisted men who had just finished their eight weeks of basic training. All of the officers were, themselves, graduates of a Canadian military college. In addition, the officers had from 5 to 17 years of leadership experience and training after graduation. The 32 enlisted men were basic trainees between 19 and 22 years of age, and their intelligence scores were substantially below those of the officers'. To reduce the possibility that they might feel anxious or inhibited by working with officers, the officers wore casual clothes and the enlisted men were told that they would work with civilian instructors.

The officers and men worked as three-men groups on three different tasks. They were asked to (a) write a fable, (b) find the shortest route for a truck convoy, and (c) draw bar graphs from score distributions that first had to be converted from one scale to another. As in the Belgian study, the tasks were designed so that all three group members had to participate in the work. As in the Belgian study, the groups led by the trained and experienced officers performed no better than the groups led by untrained and inexperienced enlisted men.

It is, of course, possible that experimental tasks do not give realistic results. For this reason we further checked in real-life situations whether the amount of training influenced performance by a study of 171 managers and supervisors in U.S. post offices. The performance of each of these supervisors was rated by two to five of his superiors. Amount of training ranged from zero hours of training to three years, with a median of 45 hours. The number of hours of supervisory training received by these managers was totally unrelated to their rated performance. We also investigated whether the post offices with highly trained supervisors were more effective on such objective post office performance measures as target achievement in number of first-class pieces handled, indirect costs, mail processing, etc. However, 12 of the 15 correlations were slightly *negative;* none was significant. Thus, training apparently did not improve organizational performance.

Another study related the amount of training received by police sergeants with the performance ratings made by their supervisors and other sergeants. Here again, training was unrelated to performance. Thus, neither the two controlled experiments nor the two field studies provide any basis for assuming

that leadership training of the type given in these institutions, or in the training programs taken by postal managers or police sergeants, contributed to organizational performance.

I repeat that these findings are by no means unusual. Empirical studies to determine whether or not leadership training improves organizational performance have generally come up with negative findings. Newport, after surveying 121 large companies, concluded that not *one* of the companies had obtained any scientifically acceptable evidence that the leadership training for their middle management had actually improved performance.

T-group and sensitivity training, which has become fashionable in business and industry, has yielded similarly unsatisfactory results. Reviews of the literature by Campbell and Dunnette and by House found no convincing evidence that this type of training increased organizational effectiveness, and a well-known study at the International Harvester Company by Fleishman, Harris, and Burtt on the effects of supervisory training concluded that the effects of supervisory training in modifying behavior were very short-lived and did not improve performance.

EFFECT OF EXPERIENCE ON LEADERSHIP

Let us now ask whether supervisory experience improves performance. Actually, since leadership experience almost always involves on-the-job training, we are dealing with a closely related phenomenon.

Interestingly enough, the literature actually contains few, if any, studies which attempt to link leadership experience to organizational effectiveness. Yet, there seems to be a firmly held expectation that leadership experience makes a leader more effective. We simply have more trust in experienced leaders. We can infer this, for example, from the many regulations that require time in grade before promotion to the next higher level, as well as the many specifications of prior job in hiring executives for responsible positions.

We have already seen that the experienced petty officers and military academy officers did not perform more effectively than did the inexperienced enlisted men, nor did the more experienced officers or petty officers perform better than the less experienced.

In addition, we also analyzed data from various other groups and organizations. These included directors of research and development teams at a large physical research laboratory, foremen of craftshops, general foremen in a heavy machinery manufacturing company, managers of meat, and of grocery markets in a large supermarket chain as well as post office supervisors and managers, and police sergeants. For all these managers we could obtain reliable performance ratings or objective group effectiveness criteria. None of the correlations was significant in the expected direction. The median correlation relating leadership experience to leadership performance for all groups and organizations was $-.12$—certainly not significant in the positive direction!

To summarize the findings, neither orthodox leadership training nor leadership experience nor sensitivity training appear to contribute across the board to group or organizational effectiveness. It is, therefore, imperative first that we ask why this might be so, and second that we consider alternative methods for improving leadership performance.

The Contingency Model

The "Contingency Model," a recent theory of leadership, holds that the effectiveness of group performance is contingent upon (a) the leader's motivational pattern, and (b) the degree to which the situation gives the leader power and influence. We have worked with a leadership motivation measure called the "Esteem for the Least Preferred Coworker," or LPC for short. The subject is first asked to think of all the people with whom he has ever worked, and then given a simple scale on which he describes the one person in his life with whom he has been able to work *least well*. This "least preferred coworker" may be someone he knows at the time, or it may be someone he has known in the past. It does not have to be a member of his present work group.

In grossly oversimplified terms, the person who describes his least preferred coworker in relatively favorable terms is basically motivated to have close interpersonal relations with others. By contrast, the person who rejects someone with whom he cannot work is basically motivated to accomplish or achieve on the task, and he derives satisfaction from being recognized as having performed well on the task. The task-motivated person thus uses the task to obtain a favorable position and good interpersonal relations.

Classifying Leadership Situations

The statement that some leaders perform better in one kind of situation while some leaders perform better in different situations is begging a question. "What kinds of situations are best suited for which type of leader?" In other words, how can we best classify groups if we wish to predict leadership performance?

We can approach this problem by assuming that leadership is essentially a work relationship involving power and influence. It is easier to be a leader when you have complete control than when your control is weak

Figure 1
Cells or "Octants"

	Very Favorable			Intermediate in Favorableness			Unfavorable	
	1	2	3	4	5	6	7	8
Leader-member relations	Good	Good	Good	Good	Poor	Poor	Poor	Poor
Task structure	High	High	Low	Low	High	High	Low	Low
Position power	Strong	Weak	Strong	Weak	Strong	Weak	Strong	Weak

and dependent on the good will of others. It is easier to be the captain of a ship than the chairman of a volunteer group organized to settle a school bussing dispute. The *job* may be more complex for the navy captain but *being in the leadership role* is easier for him than for the committee chairman. It is, therefore, not unreasonable to classify situations in terms of how much power and influence the situation gives the leader. We call this "situational favorableness." One simple categorization of groups on their situational favorableness classifies leadership situations on the basis of three major dimensions:

1. *Leader-member relations.* Leaders presumably have more power and influence if they have a good relationship with their members than if they have a poor relationship with them, if they are liked, respected, trusted, than if they are not. Research has shown that this is by far the most important single dimension.

2. *Task structure.* Tasks or assignments that are highly structured, spelled out, or programmed give the leader more influence than tasks that are vague, nebulous and unstructured. It is easier, for example, to be a leader whose task it is to set up a sales display according to clearly delineated steps than it is to be a chairman of a committee preparing a new sales campaign.

3. *Position power.* Leaders will have more power and influence if their position is vested with such prerogatives as being able to hire and fire, being able to discipline, to reprimand, and so on. Position power, as it is here used, is determined by how much power the leader has over his subordinates. If the janitor foreman can hire and fire, he has more position power in his own group than the chairman of a board of directors who, frequently, cannot hire or fire—or even reprimand his board members.

Using this classification method we can now roughly order groups as being high or low on each of these three dimensions. This gives us an eight-celled classification (Figure 1). This scheme postulates that it is easier to be a leader in groups that fall into Cell 1 since you are liked, have position power, and have a structured task. It is somewhat more difficult in Cell 2 since you are liked, have a structured task, but little position power, and so on to groups in Cell 8 where the leader is not liked, has a vague, unstructured task, and little position power. A good example of Cell 8 would be the disliked chairman of the volunteer committee we mentioned before.

The critical question is, "What kind of leadership does each of these different group situations call for?" Figure 2 summarizes the results of 63 analyses based on a total of 454 separate groups. These included bomber and tank crews, antiaircraft artillery units, managements of consumer cooperative companies, boards of directors, open-hearth shops, basketball and surveying teams, and various groups involved in creative and problem-solving tasks.

The horizontal axis of the graph indicates the "situational favorableness," namely, the leader's control and influence as defined by the eight-fold classification shown in Figure 1. The vertical axis indicates the relationship between the leader's motivational pattern, as measured by the LPC score, and his group's performance. A median correlation above the midline shows that the relationship-motivated leaders tended to perform better than the task-motivated leaders. A correlation below the midline indicates that the task-motivated leaders performed better than the relationship-

motivated leaders. Figure 3 shows the predictions that the model would make in each of the eight cells.

These findings have two important implications for our understanding of what makes leaders effective. First, Figure 2 tells us that the task-motivated leaders tend to perform better than relationship-motivated leaders in situations that are very favorable and in those that are unfavorable. Relationship-motivated leaders tend to perform better than task-motivated leaders in situations that are intermediate in favorableness. Hence, both the relationship- and the task-motivated leaders perform well under some conditions and not under others. It is, therefore, not correct to speak of any person as generally a good leader or generally a poor leader. Rather, a leader may perform well in one situation but not in another. This is also borne out by the repeated findings that we cannot predict a

Figure 2

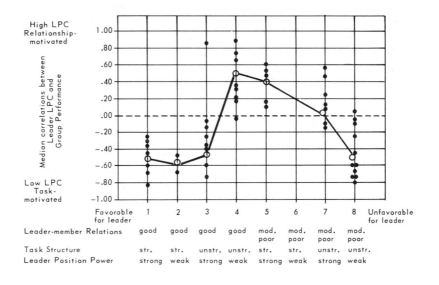

Figure 3

Prediction of the Performance of Relationship- and Task-Motivated Leaders

Relationship-Motivated High LPC				Good	Good	Some-what better	Some-what better	
Task-Motivated Low LPC	Good	Good	Good					Good
	1	2	3	4	5	6	7	8

leader's performance on the basis of his personality traits, or even by knowing how well he performed on a previous task unless that task was similar in situational favorableness.

Second, the graph on Figure 2 shows that the performance of a leader depends as much on the situational favorableness as it does on the individual in the leadership position. Hence, the organization can change leadership performance either by trying to change the individual's personality and motivational pattern or by changing the favorableness of the leader's situation. As we shall see, this is really what training is all about.

Before we go further, we must ask how valid the Contingency Model is. How well does it predict in new situations? There have been at least 25 studies to date that have tested the theory. These validation studies included research on grocery and meat markets, a physical science laboratory, a machinery plant, a hospital, an electronics company, and teams of volunteer public health workers in Central America, as well as various experimentally assembled groups in the laboratory. Of particular importance is a large experiment that used cadets at West Point to test the entire eight cells of the model. This study almost completely reproduced the curve shown on Figure 2. In all studies that were recently reviewed, 35 of the 44 obtained correlations were in the predicted direction—a

finding that could have occurred by chance less than one time in 100. An exception is Cell 2, in which laboratory experiments—but not field studies—have yielded correlations showing the relationship-motivated leaders perform better than task-motivated leaders.

EFFECT OF LEADERSHIP TRAINING?

The main question of this paper is, of course, how we can better utilize leadership training and experience to improve leadership performance. While appropriate leadership training and experience apparently do not increase organizational performance, there is considerable evidence that they do affect the manager's attitudes, behavior, and of course, his technical skills and administrative know-how. These programs teach the leader better methods of getting along with his subordinates, more effective handling of administrative routines, as well as technical background required for the job. In other words, the leader who is trained or experienced will have considerably greater control and influence over his job and his subordinates than one who is untrained and inexperienced.

In contrast, the inexperienced and untrained leader confronts numerous problems that are new to him, and for which he does not have a ready answer. As a result, he

Figure 4

Favorableness of the situation for the
trained or experienced leader

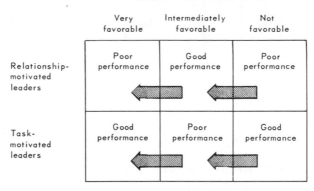

Arrows indicate the predicted effect of experience and training.

cannot give clear and concise instructions to his subordinates. Moreover, since so many situations are novel, he will be more anxious and less sure of himself, which will tend to make him more dependent upon his group and others in the organization. Not even the most detailed manual of operating instructions will enable a new manager to step into his job and behave as if he had been there for years. Thus, situations will be correspondingly less favorable for the untrained and inexperienced leader than for the trained and experienced leader.

What we are really saying here is that leadership training and experience primarily improve the favorableness of the leadership situation. But, if the Contingency Model is right, a more favorable situation requires a different type of leadership than a less favorable situation. Hence, leadership training and experience that will improve the performance of one type of leader *will decrease the performance of the other*. On the average, it will have little or no measurable effect on organizational performance. This is

schematically shown by Figure 4. The arrows indicate that effect of training and experience in improving the favorableness of the leadership situation.

The headings on Figure 4 indicate the situational favorableness for the already trained or experienced leader. The untrained or inexperienced leader obviously would face a correspondingly less favorable situation. Thus, while the situation at the left of the table is very favorable for the trained leader, it is likely to be intermediate for the leader who lacks training and experience. The training or experience, as indicated by the arrow, would then change the untrained leader's situation from one which is intermediate to one which is very favorable. Likewise, if the trained leader's situation is intermediate in favorableness, the untrained leader's situation would be unfavorable. Training would, then, improve the untrained leader's situation from an unfavorable one to a situation which is intermediate in favorableness.

But why should an inexperienced and untrained leader perform better than someone with training and experience? Under certain conditions this is not too difficult to see. An individual who is new on the job is likely to seek good interpersonal relations with his coworkers so that he can enlist their full cooperation. He is not likely to throw his weight around and he will, therefore, be less likely to antagonize his group members. In other words, the proposition is far from absurd, and it is quite compatible with the behavior of the manager who learns to rely on his staff of experts in making various decisions.

The proof of this theoretical pudding lies in various studies that bear out our suppositions.

STUDY OF SCHOOL PRINCIPALS

One study was conducted by McNamara on principals of rural elementary schools and of urban secondary schools in Canada. The performance of elementary principals was evaluated by means of ratings obtained from school superintendents and their staffs. The performance of secondary school principals was measured on the basis of province-wide achievement tests given to all students in the 11th grade. The average test score was used as the measure of the principal's effectiveness.

McNamara divided his group into task- and relationship-motivated principals, and again into inexperienced principals who had been on their job less than two years and those with three or more years of experience.

Let us now consider the favorableness of the leadership situation of elementary school principals. Their position power is reasonably high, and their task is fairly structured. The schools in McNamara's sample were quite small, the curricula of these schools are determined by the authorities of the province and by the school superintendent's office,

and the elementary school principal typically is not called upon to make many policy decisions or innovations. His task is, therefore, structured. Hence, the experienced principal will have a very favorable leadership situation, and we would expect the task-motivated principals to perform better than the relationship-motivated principals.

The inexperienced principal faces a considerably less favorable situation. While his position power is high, he does not know his teachers well, and many of the administrative problems that arise will have to be handled in a manner that is new to him. We would predict that his task is unstructured and that the situation is intermediate. Without much experience the relationship-motivated principals will, therefore, perform better than their task-motivated colleagues. That this is the case is shown on Figure 5.

The secondary principal also has high position power. However, his organization is considerably more complex. In McNamara's sample, the schools had from 25 to 40 teachers who, in turn, were supervised by department heads. Thus, the principal's control over the teachers is less direct. In addition, of course, the curriculum of a high school varies from school to school and the high school principal generally has to make a considerable number of policy decisions about the teaching program, his staff, as well as the activities and disciplinary problems of his students. For this reason, the experienced principals of secondary schools were judged to have a situation of intermediate favorableness. Relationship-motivated principals should perform best. The inexperienced high school principal will have to set new precedents and he will have to think through many of the problems for the first time as they arise. Hence, the situation will be relatively unfavorable. We would predict, therefore, that the task-motivated principals with less than two years' experience will perform best in these situations. Here, again, the data follow the prediction. (See Figure 5.)

It is particularly important to note that the relationship-motivated elementary school principal with longer experience actually performed *less well* than the relationship-motivated elementary school principal with less experience. Likewise, the task-motivated secondary school principal with more experience had significantly *poorer* performance than the task-motivated principal with considerably less experience. Thus, for these particular administrators, the more extensive experience not only failed to improve their performance but actually decreased their effectiveness.

STUDY OF CONSUMER COOPERATIVES

Another study that illustrates the effect of training and experience was conducted some years ago on 32 member companies of a large federation of consumer cooperatives. The federation used two indices for measuring company effectiveness and managerial performance. These were (a) the operating efficiency of the company, that is, roughly the proportion of overhead to total sales, and (b) the proportion of net income to total sales. We used the three-year average of these measures for our study.

In a reanalysis of these data, the managers were divided into those with task- and relationship-motivated leadership patterns, and of these, the ten with the most and the ten with the least years of experience in the organization. Since the federation of the companies maintained a strong management development program, managers with long experience also tended to have the most extensive training.

The leadership situation for the experienced managers was judged to be relatively favorable. They had considerable position power, and their job was relatively structured. As in the case of school administrators, the inexperienced and less well trained managers would, of course, face a larger number of problems that they had not encountered before,

Figure 5

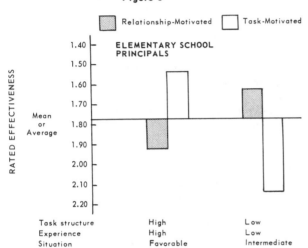

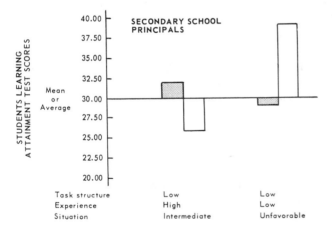

Figure 6

Performance of relationship- and task-motivated managers with relatively high and relatively low levels of experience

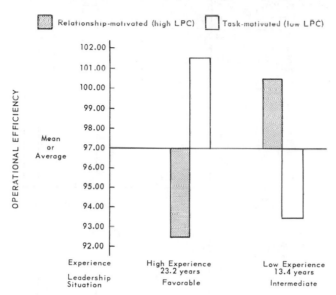

Relationship-motivated (high LPC)   Task-motivated (low LPC)

and the task would, therefore, be correspondingly less structured. Hence, for the inexperienced managers the situation would be intermediate in favorableness.

The Contingency Model would then predict that the experienced managers with task-oriented leadership patterns would perform better, as would the inexperienced managers with relationship-motivated leadership patterns. That this was the case is shown on Figure 6 for operating efficiency. Somewhat weaker results were obtained for the net income criterion. It is again apparent that the experienced and trained relationship motivated managers performed less well than did the relatively inexperienced and untrained managers who are relationship-motivated.

We have also studied the effect of training and experience on the performance

of the post office managers and supervisors, police sergeants, and formal and informal leaders of company boards. These studies have yielded essentially similar results.

New Studies of Military Leadership

Two studies were recently conducted specifically for the purpose of testing the hypothesis on completely new data. These were of field artillery sections and navy aircraft maintenance shops. Training and experience data were available for the noncommissioned officers in charge of these groups. In these studies, groups were assigned to cells 1, 3, 5, and 8 of the model. (See Figure 7.) Just as predicted, the task-motivated leaders performed best in cells 1, 3, and 8, while the relationship-moti-

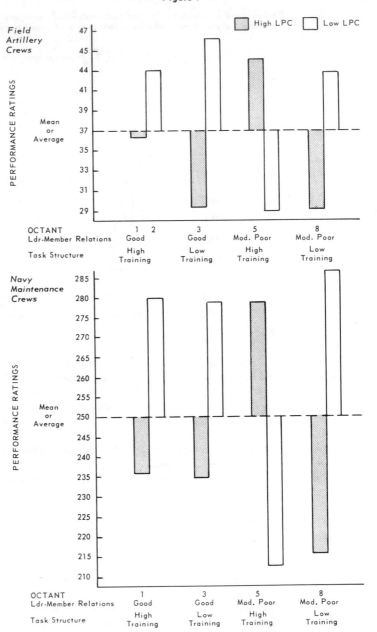

Figure 7

vated leaders performed best in cell 5. All findings were statistically significant.

To Train or Not to Train

What does all this mean for improving managerial performance, and how can we apply the findings that we have described?

In sum, if we want to improve leadership performance, we can either change the leader by training, or we can change his leadership situation. Common sense suggests that it is much easier to change various aspects of a man's job than to change the man. When we talk about leadership behavior, we are talking about fairly deeply ingrained personality factors and habits of interacting with others. These cannot be changed easily, either in a few hours or in a few days. In fact, as we have seen, not even four years of military academy and 5 to 17 years of subsequent experience enable a leader to perform significantly better on different tasks than someone that has had neither training nor experience.

We have seen that a leader's performance depends not only on his personality, but also on the organizational factors that determine the leader's control and influence, that—is, the "situational favorableness." As we have shown, appropriate training and experience improve situational favorableness. Whether or not they improve performance depends upon the match between the leader's motivational pattern and the favorableness of the situation. This means that a training program that improves the leader's control and influence may benefit the relationship-motivated managers, but it will be detrimental to the task-motivated managers, or vice versa, depending upon the situation.

The idea that we can improve a leader's performance by increasing the favorableness of his situation is, of course, far from new. A poorly performing manager may be given more authority, more explicit instructions, more congenial coworkers in the hope that it will help him do a better job. Moreover, decreasing the favorableness of the situation in order to improve a manager's performance is also not quite as unusual as it might appear at first blush. If a man becomes bored, stale, or disinterested in his job, a frequent remedy is to transfer him to a more challenging job. As it turns out, "challenging" is just another way of saying that the job is less structured, has less position power, or requires working with difficult people. It is certainly well known that some men perform best under pressure and that they get into difficulty when life is too calm. These are the trouble shooters who are dispatched to branch offices or departments that need to be bailed out.

What, then, can an organization do to increase managerial performance? As a first step, it is necessary to determine which of the managers are task- and which are relationship-motivated. This can be accomplished by means of a short scale. Second, the organization needs to categorize carefully the situational favorableness of its managerial jobs. (Scales are available in Fiedler, F. E., *A Theory of Leadership Effectiveness*, McGraw-Hill, 1967.) Third, the organization can decide on a number of options in its management of executive personnel.

The least expensive and probably most efficient method is to develop a careful program of managerial rotation that moves some individuals from one job to another at a faster rate than it moves others. For example, it will be recalled that the relationship-motivated elementary school principals on the average became less effective after two years on the job. Moving these men to new jobs probably would have made them more effective than leaving them at the same school for many more years. Likewise, moving the

Dr. Fiedler has published more than one hundred articles and papers on leadership, group processes, and organizational behavior. He is author of Leader Attitudes and Group Effectiveness (*University of Illinois Press, 1958*)*, co-author of* Boards, Management and Company Success (*Interstate Publishers, Danville, Illinois, 1959*)*, and* A Theory of Leadership Effectiveness (*McGraw-Hill, 1967*)*. He has served as consulting editor for* Sociometry *and is currently a consulting editor for* Administrative Science Quarterly *and* The Journal of Applied Social Psychology.

Dr. Fiedler has served as a consultant to numerous governmental and private agencies and business concerns. Among them the U.S. Veterans Administration; the U.S. Naval Research Laboratory; the Walter Reed Army Institute of Research; the U.S. Post Office; the U.S. Military Academy, West Point; the U.S. Naval Academy, Annapolis; the U.S. Civil Service Commission; and the Battelle Northwest Memorial Institute. He has been the principal investigator in a number of large research programs sponsored by the Office of Naval Research, the Office of the Surgeon General of the Army, the Department of Health, Education and Welfare, and the Advanced Research Projects Agency.

Fred E. Fiedler *is professor of psychology and of management and organization and director of the Organization Research Group at the University of Washington. He received his M.A. in 1947 and his Ph.D. in 1949 at the University of Chicago. From 1951 to 1969 he was professor of psychology at the University of Illinois and director of the Group Effectiveness Research Laboratory. In 1958–59 he was appointed Fulbright Research Scholar and Visiting Professor at the University of Amsterdam, and in 1963–1966 he received a Ford Faculty Research Award and served as guest professor at the University of Louvian, Belgium.*

task-motivated secondary school principals after two years probably would have increased their performance. In the case of the consumer cooperatives, it took 15 to 20 years in the organization (as employee and assistant manager, as well as manager) before the relationship-motivated managers began to go stale. How long a man should stay on a particular job must, of course, be determined empirically in each organization.

A second major option is management training. The problem here is whether to train only some people or all those who are eligible: training a task-motivated manager who is accepted by his group and has a structured task is likely to improve his performance; training a relationship-motivated manager for the same job is likely to make him less effective. The organization would, therefore, be better off if it simply did not train relationship-motivated managers for these particular jobs. On the other hand, the relationship-motivated but not the task-motivated managers should be trained for jobs in which the situational favorableness is intermediate.

Leadership training should devote more effort to teaching leaders how to modify their environment and their own job so that they fit their style of leadership. We must get rid of the implicit assumption that the environment and the organization, or a particular leadership position, are constant and unchanging. In addition to changes which occur as the leaders gain experience, they also continuously modify their leadership positions. They often speak of showing their men who is boss, presumably to assert their position power or of "being one of the boys" to deemphasize it; they speak of getting to know their men, presumably to establish better relations with them; they speak of different approaches to their work; they look for certain types of assistants who complement their abilities; they demand more authority, or they play down the authority they already have; they ask for certain types of assignments and try to avoid others. The theory that has here been described merely provides a basis for a more rational modification of the leadership job.

How can we train leaders to determine the conditions under which they are most likely to succeed or fail, and how can they learn to modify their own leadership situation? The frequently negative relationship between leadership experience and leader performance undoubtedly stems in part from the difficulties in obtaining feedback about one's own leadership effectiveness. As research has shown, unless the group fails utterly in its task, most leaders are unable to say with any degree of accuracy how well their group performed in comparison with other groups.

Leadership training away from the organization should provide the prospective leader with a wide range of leadership situations in which he can get immediate feedback on how well he has performed. On the basis of these experiences, he must learn to recognize which situations fit his particular style of leadership and how he can best modify situations so that they will enable him to perform

effectively. This may involve the development of six to eight short leadership tasks and situations, or adequately measured organizational tasks, in which each trainee is required to lead. He must then be given an objective appraisal of how well his group's performance compared with the performance of others under the same conditions.

The closest approximation to the all-around good leader is likely to be the individual who intuitively or through training knows how to manage his environment so that the leadership situation best matches his leadership style.

It may be desirable for various reasons to train all managers of a certain level, especially since being sent to executive training programs has in many organizations become a symbol of success. Men are sent to these training programs not because they need to learn, but because they need to be rewarded. If this is the case, the organization might do well to place the manager who completes the training program into a position that matches his leadership motivation pattern. For example, in the consumer cooperative companies, the relationship motivated managers might have been given staff jobs, or jobs with troubled companies at the conclusion of an extensive training program.

Conclusion

As a consequence of our research, we have both discredited some old myths and learned some new lessons.

The old myths:

• That there is one best leadership style, or that there are leaders who excel under all circumstances.

• That some men are born leaders, and that neither training, experience, or conditions can materially affect leadership skills.

The lessons, while more pedestrian and less dogmatic, are more useful. We know that people differ in how they respond to management situations. Furthermore, we know that almost every manager in an organization can perform effectively, providing that we place him in a situation that matches his personality, providing we know how to match his training and experience to the available jobs—and providing that we take the trouble.

Section C:
Group Behavior

Groups are usually defined according to four criteria:[1] (1) the interaction of two or more individuals on a face-to-face basis; (2) differentiation from other groups or individuals; (3) the members' consciousness of the group and of belonging to it; and (4) the members' perception of the relationships they have with each other as ends in themselves. Two kinds of groups are important for organizations. The first, the formal group, meets the above criteria as a result of its members' formal position in the organization as defined by the organization structure. The second, the informal group, meets the definition of a group, but the relationships of its members lie outside those formally defined by the organization. Both types are equally important to the successful functioning of the organization. Numerous examples of the importance of each, as well as useful guidelines for effective management, are given in the following readings.

In the first reading, Edgar Schein discusses the socialization of the individual into the work group, either formal or informal. Since this happens to some degree in all organizations, it is essential to be aware of and understand the problem. The degree of socialization depends on the individual's initial motivation to join the organization and the organization's "power" to hold the individual during the socialization period. The most interesting basis of class discussion is usually the "basic responses" to socialization, which Schein describes as rebellion, creative individualism, and conformity. The ultimate question is: Which of these is the most desirable for the individual and for the organization, and which organizational practices foster the most desirable outcomes? Since socialization is a fundamental process in all organizations, utilization of organizational socialization to the maximum benefit of both parties should be a desired end product.

In the second reading, Richard Muti provides an excellent review of the informal group literature and guidelines for its management. The incidents presented in the opening paragraphs and the recounting of the bank wiring room experiments from the Hawthorne studies present a vivid picture of the socialization of the individual into the informal group and the negative

[1] B. Berelson and G. Steiner, *Human Behavior* (New York: Harcourt, Brace, and World, 1964), p. 325.

effects it can have both for the individual and for the organization. His guidelines for informal group management although broad, serve as a good starting point for decision making in this area. Respect for group standards and norms, fair treatment of all group members, participation where appropriate, and increasing group responsibility are all essential in using the informal group for positive purposes.

In the final selection, Alan Filley examines three factors in a formal group problem, committee management. The first factor is committee size. Filley recommends a group size of five, since this number provides an optimal balance of task and interpersonal factors. For the second factor, the role of the chairperson in the group, he indicates that, ideally, the chairperson should serve both task and social leadership roles, although this may be "an ideal which is seldom attained, but should be sought." If the ideal cannot be reached, then the leader should at least be directive. Finally, the question of cooperation or competitiveness is discussed. Filley concludes that cooperation among the members of the group is more desirable, since individual motivation is stronger, division of labor is enhanced, intermember communication and friendliness increase, and in general, productivity rises.

Organizational Socialization and the Profession of Management

Edgar H. Schein

This paper was presented as the 1967 Douglas McGregor Memorial Lecture in honor of the late Douglas McGregor, Alfred P. Sloan Professor of Management at the Massachusetts Institute of Technology.

It examines the process of organizational socialization, the process by which a new member learns and adapts to the value system, the norms, and the required behavior patterns of an organization, society, or group. The paper indicates the power of the organizational socialization process and goes on to point out the dangers of either nonconformity or over-conformity to the individual and to the organization. Finally, it presents the relationship between organizational socialization and professional socialization and discusses the impact on this relationship of changes in the practices of both business schools and business organizations.

Introduction Ladies and gentlemen, colleagues and friends. There are few times in one's professional life when one has an opportunity, indeed something of a mandate, to pull together one's thoughts about an area of study and to communicate these to others.

I can define my topic of concern best by reviewing very briefly the kinds of issues upon which I have focused my research over the last several years. In one way or another I have been trying to understand what happens to an individual when he enters and accepts membership in an organization. My interest was originally kindled by studies of the civilian and military prisoners of the Communists during the Korean War. I thought I could discern parallels between the kind of indoctrination to which these prisoners were subjected, and some of the indoctrination which goes on in American corporations when college and business school graduates first go to work for them. My research efforts came to be devoted to learning what sorts of attitudes and values students had when they left school, and what happened to these attitudes and values in the first few years of work. To this end I followed several panels of graduates of the Sloan School into their early career.

When these studies were well under way, it suddenly became quite apparent to me that if I wanted to study the impact of an organization on the attitudes and values of its members, I might as well start closer to home. We have a school through which we put some 200 men per year — undergraduates, regular Master's students, Sloan Fellows, and Senior Executives. Studies of our own students and faculty revealed that not only did the student groups differ from each other in various attitude areas, but that they also differed from the faculty.

From Edgar H. Schein, "Organizational Socialization and the Profession of Management," *Industrial Management Review*, Vol. 9, No. 2, Winter 1968. Reprinted by permission.

For example, if one takes a scale built up of items which deal with the relations of government and business, one finds that the Senior Executives in our program are consistently against any form of government intervention, the Sloans are not as extreme, the Master's students are roughly in the middle, and the faculty are in favor of such intervention. A similar line-up of attitudes can be found with respect to labor-management relations, and with respect to cynicism about how one gets ahead in industry. In case you did not guess, the Senior Executives are least cynical and the faculty are most cynical.

We also found that student attitudes change in many areas during school, and that they change away from business attitudes toward the faculty position. However, a recent study of Sloan Fellows, conducted after their graduation, indicated that most of the changes toward the faculty had reversed themselves to a considerable degree within one year, a finding which is not unfamiliar to us in studies of training programs of all sorts.

The different positions of different groups at different stages of their managerial career and the observed changes during school clearly indicate that attitudes and values change several times during the managerial career. It is the process which brings about these changes which I would like to focus on today — a process which the sociologists would call "occupational socialization," but which I would prefer to call "organizational socialization" in order to keep our focus clearly on the setting in which the process occurs.

Organizational socialization is the process of "learning the ropes," the process of being indoctrinated and trained, the process of being taught what is important in an organization or some subunit thereof. This process occurs in school. It occurs again, and perhaps most dramatically, when the graduate enters an organization on his first job. It occurs again when he switches within the organization from one department to another, or from one rank level to another. It occurs all over again if he leaves one organization and enters another. And it occurs again when he goes back to school, and again when he returns to the organization after school.

Indeed, the process is so ubiquitous and we go through it so often during our total career, that it is all too easy to overlook it. Yet it is a process which can make or break a career, and which can make or break organizational systems of manpower planning. The speed and effectiveness of socialization determine employee loyalty, commitment, productivity, and turnover. The basic stability and effectiveness of organizations therefore depends upon their ability to socialize new members.

Let us see whether we can bring the process of socialization to life by describing how it occurs. I hope to show you the power of this process, particularly as it occurs within industrial organizations. Having done this, I would like to explore a major dilemma which I see at the interface between organizations and graduate management schools. Schools socialize their students toward a concept of a profession, organizations socialize their new members to be effective members. Do the two processes of socialization supplement each other or conflict? If they conflict, what can we do about it in organizations and in the schools?

Some Basic Elements of Organizational Socialization The term socialization has a fairly clear meaning in sociology, but it has been a difficult one to assimilate in the behavioral sciences and in management. To many of my colleagues it implies unnecessary jargon, and to many of my business acquaintances it implies the teaching of socialism — a kiss of death for the concept right there. Yet the concept is most useful because It focuses clearly on the interaction between a stable social system and the new members who enter it. The concept refers to the process by which a new member learns the value system, the norms, and the required behavior patterns of the society, organization, or group which he is entering. It does not include all learning. It includes only the learning of those values, norms, and behavior patterns which, from the organization's point of view or group's point of view, it is necessary for any new member to learn. This learning is defined as the price of membership.

What are such values, norms, and behavior patterns all about? Usually they involve:
1   The basic *goals* of the organization.
2   The preferred *means* by which these goals should be attained.
3   The basic *responsibilities* of the member in the role which is being granted to him by the organization.
4   The *behavior patterns* which are required for effective performance in the role.
5   A set of rules or principles which pertain to the *maintenance of the identity and integrity* of the organization.

The new member must learn not to drive Chevrolets if he is working for Ford, not to criticize the organization in public, not to wear the wrong kind of clothes or be seen in the wrong kinds of places. If the organization is a school, beyond learning the content of what is taught, the student must accept the value of education, he must try to learn without cheating, he must accept the authority of the faculty and behave appropriately to the student role. He must not be rude in the classroom or openly disrespectful to the professor.

By what processes does the novice learn the required values and norms? The answer to this question depends in part upon the degree of prior socialization. If the novice has correctly anticipated the norms of the organization he is joining, the socialization process merely involves a reaffirmation of these norms through various communication channels, the personal example of key people in the organization, and direct instructions from supervisors, trainers, and informal coaches.

If, however, the novice comes to the organization with values and behavior patterns which are in varying degrees out of line with those expected by the organization, then the socialization process first involves a destructive or unfreezing phase. This phase serves the function of detaching the person from his former values, of proving to him that his present self is worthless from the point of view of the organization and that he must redefine himself in terms of the new roles which he is to be granted.

The extremes of this process can be seen in initiation rites or novitiates for religious orders. When the novice enters his training period, his old self is symbolically destroyed by loss of clothing, name, often his hair, titles and other self-defining equipment. These are replaced with uniforms, new names and titles, and other self-defining equipment consonant with the new role he is being trained for.

It may be comforting to think of activities like this as being characteristic only of primitive tribes or total institutions like military basic training camps, academies, and religious orders. But even a little examination of areas closer to home will reveal the same processes both in our graduate schools and in the business organizations to which our graduates go.

Perhaps the commonest version of the process in school is the imposition of a tight schedule, of an impossibly heavy reading program, and of the assignment of problems which are likely to be too difficult for the student to solve. Whether these techniques are deliberate or not, they serve effectively to remind the student that he is not as smart or capable as he may have thought he was, and therefore, that there are still things to be learned. As our Sloan Fellows tell us every year, the first summer in the program pretty well destroys many aspects of their self-image. Homework in statistics appears to enjoy a unique status comparable to having one's head shaved and clothes burned.

Studies of medical schools and our own observations of the Sloan program suggest that the work overload on students leads to the development of a peer culture, a kind of banding together of the students as a defense against the threatening faculty and as a problem-solving device to develop norms of what and how to study. If the group solutions which are developed support the organizational norms, the peer group becomes an effective instrument of socialization. However, from the school's point of view, there is the risk that peer group norms will set up counter-socializing forces and sow the seeds of sabotage, rebellion, or revolution. The positive gains of a supportive peer group generally make it worthwhile to run the risks of rebellion, however, which usually motivates the organization to encourage or actually to facilitate peer group formation.

Many of our Sloan Fellow alumni tell us that one of the most powerful features of the Sloan program is the fact that a group of some 40 men share the same fate of being put through a very tough educational regimen. The peer group ties formed during the year have proven to be one of the most durable end-results of the educational program and, of course, are one of the key supports to the maintaining of some of the values and attitudes learned in school. The power of this kind of socializing force can be appreciated best by pondering a further statement which many alumni have made. They stated that prior to the program they identified themselves primarily with their company. Following the program they identified themselves primarily with the other Sloan Fellows, and such identification has lasted, as far as we can tell, for the rest of their career.

Let me next illustrate the industrial counterpart of these processes. Many of my panel members, when interviewed about the first six months in their new jobs, told stories of what we finally labeled as "upending experiences." Upending experiences are deliberately planned or accidentally created circumstances which dramatically and unequivocally upset or disconfirm some of the major assumptions which the new man holds about himself, his company, or his job.

One class of such experiences is to receive assignments which are so easy or so trivial that they carry the clear message that the new man is not worthy of being given anything important to do. Another class of such experiences is at the other extreme —

assignments which are so difficult that failure is a certainty, thus proving unequivocally to the new man that he may not be as smart as he thought he was. Giving work which is clearly for practice only, asking for reports which are then unread or not acted upon, protracted periods of training during which the person observes others work, all have the same upending effect.

The most vivid example came from an engineering company where a supervisor had a conscious and deliberate strategy for dealing with what he considered to be unwarranted arrogance on the part of engineers whom they hired. He asked each new man to examine and diagnose a particular complex circuit, which happened to violate a number of textbook principles but actually worked very well. The new man would usually announce with confidence, even after an invitation to double-check, that the circuit could not possibly work. At this point the manager would demonstrate the circuit, tell the new man that they had been selling it for several years without customer complaint, and demand that the new man figure out why it did work. None of the men so far tested were able to do it, but all of them were thoroughly chastened and came to the manager anxious to learn where their knowledge was inadequate and needed supplementing. According to this manager, it was much easier from this point on to establish a good give-and-take relationship with his new man.

It should be noted that the success of such socializing techniques depends upon two factors which are not always under the control of the organization. The first factor is the initial motivation of the entrant to join the organization. If his motivation is high, as in the case of a fraternity pledge, he will tolerate all kinds of uncomfortable socialization experiences, even to extremes of hell week. If his motivation for membership is low, he may well decide to leave the organization rather than tolerate uncomfortable initiation rites. If he leaves, the socialization process has obviously failed.

The second factor is the degree to which the organization can hold the new member captive during the period of socialization. His motivation is obviously one element here, but one finds organizations using other forces as well. In the case of basic training there are legal forces to remain. In the case of many schools one must pay one's tuition in advance, in other words, invest one's self materially so that leaving the system becomes expensive. In the case of religious orders one must make strong initial psychological commitments in the form of vows and the severing of relationships outside the religious order. The situation is defined as one in which one will lose face or be humiliated if one leaves the organization.

In the case of business organizations the pressures are more subtle but nevertheless identifiable. New members are encouraged to get financially committed by joining pension plans, stock option plans, and/or house purchasing plans which would mean material loss if the person decided to leave. Even more subtle is the reminder by the boss that it takes a year or so to learn any new business; therefore, if you leave, you will have to start all over again. Why not suffer it out with the hope that things will look more rosy once the initiation period is over.

Several of my panel members told me at the end of one year at work that they were quite dissatisfied, but were not sure they should leave because they had invested a year of learning in that company. Usually their boss encouraged them to think about staying. Whether or not such pressures will work depends, of course, on the labor market and other factors not under the control of the organization.

Let me summarize thus far. Organizations socialize their new members by creating a series of events which serve the function of undoing old values so that the person will be prepared to learn the new values. This process of undoing or unfreezing is often unpleasant and therefore requires either strong motivation to endure it or strong organizational forces to make the person endure it. The formation of a peer group of novices is often a solution to the problem of defense against the powerful organization, and, at the same time, can strongly enhance the socialization process if peer group norms support organizational norms.

Let us look next at the positive side of the socialization process. Given some readiness to learn, how does the novice acquire his new learning? The answer is that he acquires it from multiple sources — the official literature of the organization; the example set by key models in the organization; the instructions given to him directly by his trainer, coach, or boss; the example of peers who have been in the organization longer and thus serve as big brothers; the rewards and punishments which result from his own efforts at problem solving and experimenting with new values and new behavior.

The instructions and guidelines given by senior members of the organization are probably one of the most potent sources. I can illustrate this point best by recalling several incidents from my own socialization into the Sloan School back in 1956. I came here at the invitation of Doug McGregor from a research job. I had no prior teaching experience or knowledge of organizational or managerial matters. Contrary to my expectations, I was told by Doug that knowledge of organizational psychology and management was not important, but that some interest in learning about these matters was.

The first socializing incident occurred in an initial interview with Elting Morison, who was then on our faculty. He said in a completely blunt manner that if I knew what I wanted to do and could go ahead on my own, the Sloan School would be a great place to be. If I wasn't sure and would look to others for guidance, not to bother to come.

The second incident occurred in a conversation with our then Dean, Penn Brooks, a few weeks before the opening of the semester. We were discussing what and how I might teach. Penn said to me that he basically wanted each of his faculty members to find his own approach to management education. I could do whatever I wanted — so long as I did not imitate our sister school up the river. Case discussion leaders need not apply, was the clear message.

The third incident (you see I was a slow learner) occurred a few days later when I was planning my subject in social psychology for our Master's students. I was quite nervous about it and unsure of how to decide what to include in the subject. I went to Doug and innocently asked him to lend me outlines of previous versions of the subject, which had been taught by Alex Bavelas, or at least to give me some advice on what to include and exclude. Doug was very nice and very patient, but also quite firm in his refusal to give me either outlines or advice. He thought there was really no need to rely on history, and expressed confidence that I could probably make up my own mind. I suffered that term but learned a good deal about the value system of the Sloan School, as well as how to organize a subject. I was, in fact, so well socialized by these early experiences that nowadays no one can get me to coordinate anything with anybody else.

Similar kinds of lessons can be learned during the course of training programs, in orientation sessions, and through company literature. But the more subtle kinds of values which the organization holds, which indeed may not even be well understood by the senior people, are often communicated through peers operating as helpful big brothers. They can communicate the subtleties of how the boss wants things done, how higher management feels about things, the kinds of things which are considered heroic in the organization, the kinds of things which are taboo.

Of course, sometimes the values of the immediate group into which a new person is hired are partially out of line with the value system of the organization as a whole. If this is the case, the new person will learn the immediate group's values much more quickly than those of the total organization, often to the chagrin of the higher levels of management. This is best exemplified at the level of hourly workers where fellow employees will have much more socializing power than the boss.

An interesting managerial example of this conflict was provided by one recent graduate who was hired into a group whose purpose was to develop cost reduction systems for a large manufacturing operation. His colleagues on the job, however, showed him how to pad his expense account whenever they traveled together. The end result of this kind of conflict was to accept neither the cost reduction values of the company nor the cost inflation values of the peer group. The man left the company in disgust to start up some businesses of his own.

One of the important functions of organizational socialization is to build commitment and loyalty to the organization. How is this accomplished? One mechanism is to invest much effort and time in the new member and thereby build up expectations of being repaid by loyalty, hard work, and rapid learning. Another mechanism is to get the new member to make a series of small behavioral commitments which can only be justified by him through the acceptance and incorporation of company values. He then becomes his own agent of socialization. Both mechanisms involve the subtle manipulation of guilt.

To illustrate the first mechanism, one of our graduates went to a public relations firm which made it clear to him that he had sufficient knowledge and skill to advance, but that his values and attitudes would have to be evaluated for a couple of years before he would be fully accepted. During the first several months he was frequently invited to join high ranking members of the organization at their luncheon meetings in order to learn more about how they thought about things. He was so flattered by the amount of time they spent on him, that he worked extra hard to learn their values and became highly committed to the organization. He said that he would have felt guilty at the thought of not learning or of leaving the company. Sending people to expensive training programs, giving them extra perquisites, indeed the whole philosophy of paternalism, is built on the assumption that if you invest in the employee he will repay the company with loyalty and hard work. He would feel guilty if he did not.

The second mechanism, that of getting behavioral commitments, was most beautifully illustrated in Communist techniques of coercive persuasion. The Communists made tremendous efforts to elicit a public confession from a prisoner. One of the key functions of such a public confession, even if the prisoner knew he was making a false confession, was that it committed him publicly. Once he made this commitment, he found himself under strong internal and external pressure to justify why he had confessed. For many people it proved easier to justify the confession by coming to believe in their own crimes than to have to face the fact that they were too weak to withstand the captor's pressure.

In organizations, a similar effect can be achieved by promoting a rebellious person into a position of responsibility. The same values which the new member may have criticized and jeered at from his position at the bottom of the hierarchy suddenly look different when he has subordinates of his own whose commitment he must obtain.

Many of my panel members had very strong moral and ethical standards when they first went to work, and these stood up quite well during their first year at work even in the face of less ethical practices by their peers and superiors. But they reported with considerable shock that some of the practices they had condemned in their bosses were quickly adopted by them once they had themselves been promoted and faced the pressures of the new position. As one man put it very poignantly — "my ethical standards changed so gradually over the first five years of work that I hardly noticed it, but it was a great shock to suddenly realize what my feelings had been five years ago and how much they had changed."

Another version of obtaining commitment is to gain the new member's acceptance of very general ideals like "one must work for the good of the company," or "one must meet the competition." Whenever any counter-organizational behavior occurs one can then point out that the ideal is being violated. The engineer who does not come to work on time is reminded that his behavior indicates lack of concern for the good of the company. The employee who wears the wrong kind of clothes, lives in the wrong neighborhood, or associates with the wrong people can be reminded that he is hurting the company image.

One of my panel members on a product research assignment discovered that an additive which was approved by the Food and Drug Administration might in fact be harmful to consumers. He was strongly encouraged to forget about it. His boss told him that it was the F.D.A.'s problem. If the company worried about things like that it might force prices up and thus make it tough to meet the competition.

Many of the upending experiences which new members of organizations endure are justified to them by the unarguable ideal that they should learn how the company really works before expecting a position of real responsibility. Once the new man accepts this ideal it serves to justify all kinds of training and quantities of menial work which others who have been around longer are unwilling to do themselves. This practice is known as "learning the business from the ground up," or "I had to do it when I first joined the company, now it's someone else's turn." There are clear elements of hazing involved not too different from those associated with fraternity initiations and other rites of passage.

The final mechanism to be noted In a socialization process is the transition to full fledged member. The purpose of such transitional events is to help the new member incorporate his new values, attitudes, and norms into his identity so that they become part of him, not merely something to which he pays lip-service. Initiation rites which involve severe tests of the novice serve to prove to him that he is capable of fulfilling the new role — that he now is a man, no longer merely a boy.

Organizations usually signal this transition by giving the new man some important responsibility or a position of power which, if mishandled or misused, could genuinely hurt the organization. With this transition often come titles, symbols of status, extra rights or prerogatives, sharing of confidential information or other things which in one way or another indicate that the new member has earned the trust of the organization. Although such events may not always be visible to the outside observer, they are felt strongly by the new member. He knows when he has finally "been accepted," and feels it when he becomes "identified with the company."

So much for examples of the process of socialization. Let us now look at some of the dilemmas and conflicts which arise within it.

Failures of Socialization — Non-Conformity and Over-Conformity   Most organizations attach differing amounts of importance to different norms and values. Some are *pivotal*. Any member of a business organization who does not believe in the value of getting a job done will not survive long. Other pivotal values in most business organizations might be belief in a reasonable profit, belief in the free enterprise system and competition, belief in a hierarchy of authority as a good way to get things done, and so on.

Other values or norms are what may be called *relevant*. These are norms which it is not absolutely necessary to accept as the price of membership, but which are considered desirable and good to accept. Many of these norms pertain to standards of dress and decorum, not being publicly disloyal to the company, living in the right neighborhood and belonging to the right political party and clubs. In some organizations some of these norms may be pivotal. Organizations vary in this regard. You all know the stereotype of IBM as a company that requires the wearing of white shirts and hats. In some parts of IBM such values are indeed pivotal; in other parts they are only relevant, and in some parts they are quite peripheral. The point is that not all norms to which the new member is exposed are equally important for the organization.

The socialization process operates across the whole range of norms, but the amount of reward and punishment for compliance or non-compliance will vary with the importance of the norm. This variation allows the new member some degrees of freedom in terms of how far to conform and allows the organization some degrees of freedom in how much conformity to demand. The new man can accept none of the values, he can accept only the pivotal values, but carefully remain independent on all those areas not seen as pivotal, or he can accept the whole range of values and norms. He can tune in so completely on what he sees to be the way others are handling themselves that he becomes a carbon-copy and sometimes a caricature of them.

These basic responses to socialization can be labeled as follows:

Type 1   Rebellion
Rejection of all values and norms

Type 2   Creative individualism
Acceptance only of pivotal values and norms; rejection of all others

Type 3   Conformity
Acceptance of all values and norms

Most analyses of conformity deal only with the type 1 and 3 cases, failing to note that both can be viewed as socialization failures. The rebellious individual either is expelled from the organization or turns his energies toward defeating its goals. The conforming individual curbs his creativity and thereby moves the organization toward a sterile form of bureaucracy. The trick for most organizations is to create the type 2 response — acceptance of pivotal values and norms, but rejection of all others, a response which I would like to call "creative individualism."

To remain creatively individualistic in an organization is particularly difficult because of the constant resocialization pressures which come with promotion or lateral transfer. Every time the employee learns part of the value system of the particular group to which he is assigned, he may be laying the groundwork for conflict when he is transferred. The engineer has difficulty accepting the values of the sales department, the staff man has difficulty accepting the high pressure ways of the production department, and the line manager has difficulties accepting the service and helping ethic of a staff group. With each transfer, the forces are great toward either conforming or rebelling. It is difficult to keep focused on what is pivotal and retain one's basic individualism.

Professional Socialization and Organizational Socialization   The issue of how to maintain individualism in the face of organizational socialization pressures brings us to the final and most problematical area of concern. In the traditional professions like medicine, law, and teaching, individualism is supported by a set of professional attitudes which serve to immunize the person against some of the forces of the organization. The questions now to be considered are (1) Is management a profession? (2) If so, do professional attitudes develop in managers? and (3) If so, do these support or conflict with organizational norms and values?

Professionalism can be defined by a number of characteristics:

1   Professional decisions are made by means of general principles. theories, or propositions which are independent of the particular case under consideration. For management this would mean that there are certain principles of how to handle people, money, information, etc., independent of any particular company. The fact that we can

and do teach general subjects in these areas would support management's claim as a profession.

2   Professional decisions imply knowledge in a specific area in which the person is expert, not a generalized body of wisdom. The professional is an expert only in his profession, not an expert at everything. He has no license to be a "wise man." Does management fit by this criterion? I will let you decide.

3   The professional's relations with his clients are objective and independent of particular sentiments about them. The doctor or lawyer makes his decisions independent of his liking or disliking of his patients or clients. On this criterion we have a real difficulty since, in the first place, it is very difficult to specify an appropriate single client for a manager, and, in the second place, it is not at all clear that decisions can or should be made independent of sentiments. What is objectively best for the stockholder may conflict with what is best for the enterprise, which, in turn may conflict with what is best for the customer.

4   A professional achieves his status by accomplishment, not by inherent qualities such as birth order, his relationship to people in power, his race, religion, or color. Industry is increasingly moving toward an acceptance of this principle for managerial selection, but in practice the process of organizational socialization may undermine it by rewarding the conformist and rejecting the individualist whose professional orientation may make him look disloyal to the organization.

5   A professional's decisions are assumed to be on behalf of the client and to be independent of self-interest. Clearly this principle is at best equivocal in manager-customer relations, though again one senses that industry is moving closer to accepting the idea.

6   The professional typically relates to a voluntary association of fellow professionals, and accepts only the authority of these colleagues as a sanction on his own behavior. The manager is least like the professional in this regard, in that he is expected to accept a principle of hierarchical authority. The dilemma is best illustrated by the previous example which I gave of our Sloan Fellow alumni who, after the program, related themselves more to other Sloans than to their company hierarchy. By this criterion they had become truly professionalized.

7   A professional has sometimes been called someone who knows better what is good for his client than the client. The professional's expertness puts the client into a very vulnerable position. This vulnerability has necessitated the development of strong professional codes and ethics which serve to protect the client. Such codes are enforced through the colleague peer group. One sees relatively few attempts to develop codes of ethics for managers or systems of enforcement.

On several bases, then, management is a profession, but on several others it is clearly not yet a profession.

This long description of what is a profession was motivated by the need to make a very crucial point. I believe that management education, particularly in a graduate school like the Sloan School, is increasingly attempting to train professionals, and in this process is socializing the students to a set of professional values which are, in fact, in severe and direct conflict with typical organizational values.

For example, I see us teaching general principles in the behavioral sciences, economics, and quantitative methods. Our applied subjects like marketing, operations management, and finance are also taught as bodies of knowledge governed by general principles which are applicable to a wide variety of situations. Our students are given very broad concepts which apply to the corporation as a whole, and are taught to see the relationship between the corporation, the community, and the society. They are taught to value the long-range health and survival of economic institutions, not the short-range profit of a particular company. They come to appreciate the necessary interrelationships between government, labor, and management rather than to define these as mutually warring camps. They are taught to look at organizations from the perspective of high ranking management, to solve the basic problems of the enterprise rather than the day-to-day practical problems of staff or line management. Finally, they are taught an ethic of pure rationality and emotional neutrality — analyze the problem and make the decisions independent of feelings about people, the product, the company, or the community. All of these are essentially professional values.

Organizations value many of the same things, in principle. But what is valued in principle by the higher ranking and senior people in the organization often is neither supported by their own behavior, nor even valued lower down in the organization. In fact, the value system which the graduates encounter on their first job is in many respects diametrically opposed to the professional values taught in school. The graduate is immediately expected to develop loyalty and concern for a particular company with all of its particular idiosyncrasies. He is expected to recognize the limitation of his general knowledge and to develop the sort of *ad hoc* wisdom which the school has taught him to avoid. He is expected to look to his boss for evaluation rather than to some group of colleagues outside the company.

Whereas the professional training tells him that knowledge is power, the graduate now must learn that knowledge by itself is nothing. It is the ability to sell knowledge to other people which is power. Only by being able to sell an application of knowledge to a highly specific, local situation, can the graduate obtain respect for what he knows. Where his education has taught the graduate principles of how to manage others and to take the corporate point of view, his organizational socialization tries to teach him how to be a good subordinate, how to be influenced, and how to sell ideas from a position of low power.

On the one hand, the organization via its recruiters and senior people tells the graduate that it is counting on him to bring fresh points of view and new techniques to bear on its problems. On the other hand, the man's first boss and peers try to socialize him into their traditional mold.

A man is hired to introduce linear programming into a production department, but once he is there he is told to lay off because if he succeeds he will make the old supervisors and engineers look bad. Another man is hired for his financial analysis skills but is not permitted access to data worth analyzing because the company does not trust him to keep them confidential. A third man is hired into a large group responsible for developing cost reduction programs in a large defense industry, and is told to ignore the fact that the group is overstaffed, inefficient, and willing to pad its expense accounts. A fourth man, hired for his energy and capability, put it this way as an explanation of why he quit to go into private consulting: "They were quite pleased with work that required only two hours per day; I wasn't."

In my panel of 1962 graduates, 73 per cent have already left their first job and many are on their third or fourth. In the class of 1963, the percentage is 67, and in the class of 1964, the percentage is 50. Apparently, most of our graduates are unwilling to be socialized into organizations whose values are incompatible with the ones we teach. Yet these organizations are precisely the ones who may need creative individualists most.

What seems to happen in the early stages of the managerial career is either a kind of postponement of professional socialization while organizational socialization takes precedence, or a rebelling by the graduate against organizational socialization. The young man who submits must first learn to be a good apprentice, a good staff man, a good junior analyst, and perhaps a good low level administrator. He must prove his loyalty to the company by accepting this career path with good graces, before he is trusted enough to be given a position of power. If he has not lost his education by then, he can begin to apply some general principles when he achieves such a position of power.

The businessman wants the school to provide both the professional education and the humility which would make organizational socialization smoother. He is not aware that teaching management concepts of the future precludes justifying the practices of today. Some professional schools clearly do set out to train for the needs of the profession as it is designed today. The Sloan School appears to me to reject this concept. Instead we have a faculty which is looking at the professional manager of five, ten, or 20 years from now, and is training its graduates in management techniques which we believe are coming in the future.

Symptomatic of this approach is the fact that in many of our subjects we are highly critical of the management practices of today, and highly committed to re-educating those managers like Sloan Fellows and Senior Executives who come back to study at M.I.T. We get across in a dozen different ways the belief that most organizations of today are obsolete, conservative, constipated, and ignorant of their own problems. Furthermore, I believe that this point of view is what society and the business community demands of a good professional school.

It would be no solution to abandon our own vision of the manager of the future, and I doubt that those of you in the audience from business and industry would really want us to do this. What you probably want is to have your cake and eat it too — you want us to teach our students the management concepts of tomorrow, and you want us to teach them how to put these concepts into deep freeze while they learn the business of today. Then when they have proven themselves worthy of advancement and have achieved a position of some influence, they should magically resurrect their education and put it to work.

Unfortunately, socialization processes are usually too powerful to permit that solution. If you succeed in socializing your young graduates to your organizations, you will probably also succeed in proving to them that their education was pretty worthless and might as well be put on a permanent rather than temporary shelf. We have research evidence that many well educated graduates do learn to be complacent and to play the organizational game. It is not at all clear whether they later ever resurrect their educational arsenal.

What Is to Be Done about This Situation?   I think we need to accept, at the outset, the reality of organizational socialization phenomena. As my colleague, Leo Moore, so aptly put it, organizations like to put their fingerprints on people, and they have every right to do so. By the same token, graduate schools of business have a right and an obligation to pursue professional socialization to the best of their ability. We must find a way to ameliorate the conflicts at the interface, without, however, concluding that either schools or organizations are to blame and should stop what they are doing.

What the Schools Can Do   The schools, our school in particular, can do several concrete things which would help the situation. First, we can insert into our total curriculum more apprenticeship experience which would bring the realities of organizational life home to the student earlier. But such apprenticeship experiences will not become educational unless we combine them with a second idea, that of providing a practicum on how to change organizations. Such a practicum should draw on each of the course specialties and should be specifically designed to teach a student how to translate his professional knowledge into viable action programs at whatever level of the organization he is working.

Ten years ago we would not have known how to do this. Today there is no excuse for not doing it. Whether the field is operations research, sophisticated quantitative marketing, industrial dynamics, organizational psychology or whatever, we must give our students experience in trying to implement their new ideas, and we must teach them how to make the implementation effective. In effect, we must teach our students to become change-agents, whatever their disciplinary specialty turns out to be. We must teach them how to influence their organizations from low positions of power without sacrificing their professional values in the process. We must teach them how to remain creative individualists in the face of strong organizational socialization pressures.

Combined with these two things, we need to do a third thing. We need to become more involved in the student's efforts at career planning and we need to coordinate our activities more closely with the company recruiters and the university placement officers. At the present I suspect that most of our faculty is quite indifferent to the student's struggles to find the right kind of a job. I suspect that this indifference leaves the door wide open to faulty selection on the part of the student, which can only lead, in the end, to an undermining of the education into which we pour so much effort. We need to work harder to insure that our graduates get jobs in which they can further the values and methods we inculcate.

What the Companies Can Do   Companies can do at least two things. First, they can make a genuine effort to become aware of and understand their own organizational socialization practices. I fear very few higher level executives know what is going on at the bottom of their organization where all the high priced talent they call for is actually employed. At the same time, I suspect that it is their own value system which ultimately determines the socialization activities which occur throughout all segments of the organization. Greater awareness and understanding of these practices should make possible more rational choices as to which practices to encourage and which to de-emphasize. The focus should be on pivotal values only, not on peripheral or irrelevant ones.

I have argued for such training for many years, but still find that most company effort goes into training the graduate rather than his boss. Yet it is the boss who really has the power to create the climate which will lead to rebellion, conformity, or creative individualism. If the companies care whether their new hires use one or the other of these adaptation strategies, they had better start looking at the behavior of the first boss and training him for what the company wants and hopes for. Too many bosses concentrate on teaching too many peripheral values and thus undermine the possibilities for creative individualism and organization improvement.

Conclusion   The essence of management is to understand the forces acting in a situation and to gain control over them. It is high time that some of our managerial knowledge and skill be focused on those forces in the organizational environment which derive from the fact that organizations are social systems who do socialize their new members. If we do not learn to analyze and control the forces of organizational socialization, we are abdicating one of our primary managerial responsibilities. Let us not shrink away from a little bit of social engineering and management in this most important area of the human side of the enterprise.

References

1   Blau, P. M. and Scott, R. W. *Formal Organizations.* San Francisco: Chandler, 1962.

2   Goffman, E. *Asylums.* Garden City, N.Y.: Doubleday Anchor, 1961.

3   Schein, E. H., Schneier, Inge and Barker, C. H. *Coercive Persuasion.* New York: W. W. Norton, 1961.

4   Schein, E. H. "Management Development as a Process of Influence," *Industrial Management Review,* II (1961), 59-77.

5   Schein, E. H. "Forces Which Undermine Management Development," *California Management Review,* Vol. V, Summer, 1963.

6   Schein, E. H. "How to Break in the College Graduate," *Harvard Business Review,* Vol. XLII (1964).

7   Schein, E. H. "Training in Industry: Education or Indoctrination," *Industrial Medicine and Surgery,* Vol. XXXIII (1964).

8   Schein, E. H. *Organizational Psychology.* Englewood Cliffs, N.J.: Prentice-Hall, 1965.

9   Schein, E. H. "The Problem of Moral Education for the Business Manager," *Industrial Management Review,* VIII (1966), 3-14.

10   Schein, E. H. "Attitude Change During Management Education," *Administrative Science Quarterly,* XI (1967), 601-628.

11   Schein, E. H. "The Wall of Misunderstanding on the First Job," *Journal of College Placement,* February/March, 1967.

The Informal Group—What It Is And How It Can Be Controlled

RICHARD S. MUTI

When Jim Simpson reported for his first day of work at the Wilson plant, Harry Eaton, the shop supervisor, introduced him to the ten men he'd be working with in the die shop. After a brief tour of the shop, Simpson settled down at his machine, anxious to begin the day's work. By mid-morning, he had turned out half his day's quota of dies and it seemed a cinch that he'd beat the standard output by at least a hundred. Not bad for the first day on the job, he thought. But he wondered why the standards were set so low. It didn't seem right that a new man should be able to step in on the first day and exceed the output that the company had set for its more seasoned workers. He shrugged it off, and continued to turn out the dies at an even pace.

Just before noon, Ed Morgan, one of his coworkers in the shop, stopped at Simpson's machine.

"Hey, Speedy Gonzales, you got a light," said Morgan, taking a cigarette and offering the pack to Simpson.

Simpson laughed. "Sure," he said. He stopped work and accepted one of the cigarettes, happy for the pause and grateful for Morgan's friendly gesture. After both cigarettes were lit, Morgan spoke first.

"What do you think of Eaton, the supervisor?" Morgan asked.

"He seems like a real nice guy," replied Simpson.

Morgan grunted. "It's all an act, believe me. He'd sooner turn you in than look at you. You've got to watch what you say around him. He's a 'company man' all the way."

"Oh," said Simpson.

"You know, I've been watching you all morning, Joe," said Morgan. "You're going to kill yourself the way you've been working. You ought to slow down and take it easy like the rest of us. Say, you don't own part of this company, do you?"

Simpson laughed. "No," he said, "but I could sure use some of that bonus money they pay for beating the standard."

"We all could use the money, Joe, but don't you see what'll happen? We all start turning in work over the standard and, sure, they'll pay us the bonus for a while, but then what happens. The first thing you know, they go and raise the standard on you. Then where are you— breaking your back, turning out more work for the same money you got in the first place. It doesn't make sense, does it?"

"You know," said Simpson, "I never thought of that before."

"Listen, kid," said Morgan, "You'll be alright around here. Stick with me and I'll teach you the ropes in no time. Say, why don't you come to lunch with me and the guys. We always go to this little place around the corner."

"Say, that'd be great," said Simpson.

"See you later," Morgan said as he walked off, "and remember—*slow down.*"

Simpson turned to his machine and began work again. That Morgan is quite a guy, he thought. He really knows what the score is. He unconsciously settled back into the same, efficient pace, punching out the dies with an easy economy of motion. But after a few minutes, he caught himself, and slowed his pace noticeably. He looked up from his machine at the faces of his coworkers. They were all smiling at him, nodding their heads in approval.

Joe Simpson has just been introduced to an informal group. He has met the group's leader, Ed Morgan, who set him straight on what the group thinks of Harry Eaton, the supervisor, what the group feels is a fair day's work, and where the group likes to eat lunch together. In time, Simpson will be taught all the group's norms and values. The pressures to conform will be great, probably too great for an average man like Simpson to resist.

The situation described above is fictional, of course. There is no "Wilson plant," as such. But the exchange between Simpson and Morgan, with only the names changed, probably takes place many times daily in the plants and factories across the country. A new man joining a small work force is taught the informal group's standards and norms, instructed in the proper attitude to have, and given time to conform, or else. It occurs at every level. Shop space or office space, blue collar or white collar, manager or operator—every echelon of American business is rife with informal groups.

Not every informal group is antagonistic toward management, as was the case in the die shop at the Wilson plant. Indeed, some groups can be extremely cooperative, policing their members with regard to tardiness or absenteeism, or even exceeding managerial demands for output. For example, a group of salesmen might have as its goal high sales, the higher the better. Management might do well to cultivate such a group, to encourage its growth and strength. An informal group can also be neutral, with goals purely social in nature. Caution is necessary in dealing with neutral informal groups. By restricting fulfillment of the group's social needs, management can easily turn a neutral group into an antagonistic group, at odds with the company at every ground.[1]

Origins of the Study of Informal Groups

Not until the early 1900's did management really begin to recognize the existence of informal groups. The problem of restricted output was perceived as early as 1911 by Frederick W. Taylor. He and other scientific managers felt that the problem could be solved by having management, rather than the workers, determine production rates.[2] Time-study men went to work to help management set production standards, but they probably only increased the workers' determination to regulate output, since retiming of a job almost always meant a cut in pay. Workers felt, especially during the depression, that by working slowly, they could make their job last longer. It was, for them, a defensive device to protect them from the whims of management. It indicated a basic distrust between management and the workers.

Henri Fayol, one of the leading proponents of the Universalist school of management, felt that the interests of the company should prevail over the informal group. In 1916, he stated that combating the ignorance, ambition, selfishness, laziness, and weaknesses that cause the interests of the company to be lost sight of is "one of the great difficulties of management." He suggested three ways to effect this subordination of the individual to the company: firmness and good example on the part of superiors, agreements as fair as is possible, and constant supervision.[3]

[1]Robert Dubin, *Human Relations in Administration* (Englewood Cliffs, N. J., 1961), pp. 84-85.

[2]Loren Baritz, *The Servants of Power* (Middleton, Conn., 1960), p. 96.

[3]Henri Fayol, "General Principles of Management—From Division of Work to Esprit de Corps," in *The World of Business,* ed. by Edward C. Bursk, Donald T. Clark, and Ralph W. Hidy (New York, 1962), p. 1691.

Although Taylor and Fayol were among the first to identify informal groups, their studies contributed little to the understanding of group structure and behavior. There were still many unanswered questions. Why did informal groups exist? How were they formed? What factors affected group behavior? The first really definitive study of the informal group was the bank wiring room phase of the Hawthorne

members, and enforced its standards by using ridicule, sarcasm, or "binging"[6] to keep its members in the fold. They also set standards of production. By adjusting production reports, the group effectively circumvented the "bogey"[7] set by management. The workers liked to have some completed work saved up and ready to turn in on days when output was low. Consequently, they reported a consistent output that

In this phase of the Hawthorne Experiments, fourteen male operators in the bank wiring room of the Western Electric Company were observed during the period November, 1931, through May, 1932. An observer, stationed with the group, followed certain rules to gain the group's acceptance. He assumed no formal authority, he tried to be noncommittal in any argument, he respected all confidence, he tried not to be overimposing in gathering information, and he became, through speech and behavior, as much a part of the group as possible.[4]

The observer found that the fourteen workers had an intricate, informal social organization of their own. There were sub groups, cliques, and isolated individuals. The personal relationships of each operator in this informal organization "determined to a large degree his status in the group, the expectations of the other members, and the kinds of satisfactions and expectations he had of himself."[5]

The group set standards of behavior for its

concluded that no direct relationship between performance and ability to perform as determined by dexterity or intelligence tests existed.[9]

The sentiments of the group were: (a) don't be a "rate buster", (b) do your share of the work; don't be a "chiseler", (c) don't be a "squealer", and (d) don't put on airs (i. e., if you are an inspector, don't act like one).[10] At first glance, it would seem that the group was antagonistic toward management. But the researchers point out that, in fact, there was no conscious effort on the part of the workers to oppose management.[11] The workers were not hostile toward management, the Western Electric Company had a reputation of being very fair with its employees. The restriction of output in the bank wiring room could not be blamed on poor management or inefficiency, either actually. The work within Western's bank compared most favorably with similar work of other companies. What, then, caused the regulation of output? The researchers concluded that

[4]F. J. Roethlisberger and William J. Dickson, *Management and the Worker* (Cambridge, Mass., 1956), pp. 388-389.

[5]Baritz, pp. 92-93.

[6]Roethlisberger, p. 421. "Binging" is a physical attempt to control workers who deviated. It was used to regulate the output of the faster workers. The observer in the wire bank room remarked, "one of them walked up to a man and hit him as hard as he could on the upper arm. The one hit made no protest, and it seems that it was his privilege to 'bing' the one who hit him. He was free to retaliate with one blow. One of the objects of the game is

to see who can hit the hardest. But it is also used as a penalty."

[7]Roethlisberger, p. 418. "Bogey" is the standard output as determined by management. Wire bank workers feared that if they consistently met the bogey or exceeded it, management would raise the bogey or cut the piece rate, causing an operator to work harder to make the same pay.

[8]Roethlisberger, p. 420.

[9]Roethlisberger, pp. 442-443.

[10]Roethlisberger, p. 522.

[11]Roethlisberger, p. 535.

"noneconomic motives, interests, and processes, as well as economic, are fundamental in behavior in business."[12]

The findings of the bank wiring room phase of the Hawthorne Experiments created great interest in human relations in industry. It seemed that management had two alternatives—either change the informal group's thinking so that it paralleled management's or neutralize the group's power to control standards. Perhaps a better understanding between management and workers could more closely align the logic and sentiments of the informal organization to the formal organization. By asking for suggestions and criticisms, the workers could have had a more active role in the decisions concerning them. The Hawthorne experimenters, more closely attuned to management policies, failed to adequately explain the informal organization, merely terming the workers' behavior as irrational.

The work of many early human relations experimenters is suspect. Many of them believed that industrial cooperation meant that labor should do as management said. Elton Mayo, the head researcher at Hawthorne, failed to recognize that the informal organizations of workers may have been necessary antidotes to an overbearing management. In fact, the Mayo school barely touched on the idea that management, itself, was filled with informal organizations, that managers, just like workers, could act "emotionally and irrationally." This anti-labor, pro-management attitude of Mayo and his colleagues has caused much of their work to be severely criticized by some social scientists.

Management's reaction to the informal group at odds with formal policy was limited. Either the group had to be destroyed or its thinking changed. The bank wiring experiment showed that the group's power exceeded management's. It seemed that the second alternative—promoting friendly informal groups—would more likely meet with success. Amid cries of manipulation, management sought to encourage groups to think constructively along managerial lines.

Sociometry, the study of personal likes and dislikes, provided a technique for greater understanding of informal associations. In 1934, Jacob L. Moreno introduced this technique of learning about the group through study of its individuals. Using this approach, it became possible to "speak of the degree of cohesiveness of a specific group and to make comparisons between one group and another."[13] Sociometry asked questions of individuals such as: who do you like best, least in your shop? who do you like to work with best, least? A sociometric map or sociogram provided a means of displaying these social choices of the shop workers.

In a further attempt to understand group behavior, several men tried to classify the informal work group. Elton Mayo and George F. F. Lombard formed three classifications. The "natural" group, composed of six or seven members, functioned automatically, unguided by supervision. The "family" group, about thirty members, had a core of regulars that provided an example for the other members. The "organized" group was large and had a direct relationship with management (e.g., the "whole factory" concept).[14]

Leonard R. Sayles probably came closest to a realistic classification of informal work groups. He placed the groups into four basic categories. The *"apathetic"* groups are those least likely to make complaints or to join together to pressure management. They are characterized by a dispersed leadership, not clearly identified or accepted, internal frictions that cause low cohesion, and undercurrent of discontent, but little action to change things. Their jobs are usually in a noisy environment, with little interaction between members.

The *"erratic"* groups are easily incensed over minor, insignificant issues, or can remain inactive when confronted with more important grievances. When they do take action, they are

---

[12]Roethlisberger, p. 557.

[13]Baritz, p. 177.
[14]Dubin, pp. 88-89.

poorly controlled and inconsistent. This type of work group is most susceptible to conversion to good relations with management. They have a strong, independent leadership, but high turnover lessens their cohesiveness. Their jobs consist mainly of crew operations or groups performing similar tasks.

The *"strategic"* groups are the shrewd instigators. They maintain high work standards in their jobs, which usually consist of crew or assembly type operations.

The *"conservative"* groups are composed of highly skilled workers with high status, engaged in individual operations throughout the plant. They are the most stable, most likely to give warning before taking any action. They are least likely to be union participants. Members of the conservative groups are characterized by self-assurance, success, and patience.[15]

Characteristics of the Informal Group

A small group can be defined as two or more people who interact with one another in face-to-face relations over an extended period of time, who differentiate themselves in some way from others around them, who are conscious of belonging to the group, and whose relations with one another are taken as an end in itself.[16] It's impossible to set an upper limit on group membership. The only limiting factor is that all members must have direct personal contact with one another. This would probably necessitate a group no larger than fifteen or twenty members.

Informal groups are formed because they satisfy human needs. Every human being has a need for companionship, for identification. This need to belong is most easily satisfied at one's own level. One needs understanding from one's friends to combat life's frustrations and tensions. The informal group provides answers for its members; it serves as a "guide to correct behavior." It helps solve work problems. Team work can get the job done more easily and enjoyably, and can promote either efficiency or work restriction. Protection for its membership during sabotage of the work.[17]

Satisfying these individual needs of belonging, prestige, recognition, etc., is the primary function of the informal group. The informal group is a natural unit in which work decisions and judgments are reached. It provides an atmosphere for testing new procedures, and creates standards of conduct for its members.

Group standards of behavior pervade the informal social organization. They can take many forms—eating lunch together, following certain customs to make the job easier, and regulating production to attain a few. Management may either benefit or suffer from the group's standards and group pressure to conform. It depends on how close the goals of the group are to the goals of management.

"There are also group standards of attitude—or norms." "This job is good," or, "the foreman should be fired," are examples of what group norms might be. These attitudes could be completely unfounded, but to the group they are real, and management must recognize they exist.

The group member experiences certain pressures to conform to group standards and norms. The individual point of view becomes aligned with the group's point of view, and since the group satisfies the member's social needs, he

[15]Dubin, pp. 96-95.
[16]Bernard Berelson and Gary A. Steiner, *Human Behavior* (New York, 1964), p. 325.
[17]Leonard R. Sayles and George Strauss, *Personnel* (Englewood Cliffs, N. J., 1960), pp. 56-60.
[18]Sayles, p. 65.

accepts the group's goals. He wants to be "well regarded" by the other members. A member who exceeds the group's accepted level of output may find himself ostracized. Any deviation from group standards may cause the member to be isolated, given the "silent treatment." He may be left out of group activities. More direct methods of pressuring the individual to conform include letting management know of the deviant's "mistakes", flooding his desk with work, or even sabotaging his equipment.

The enforcement of group standards and norms is a four phased operation. First the new man is educated. He learns what the group expects of him. Then he is watched by all the group members to see if he conforms. He is bound to make mistakes, and for any deviation, a warning is given, and surveillance continued. Finally, disciplinary or rewarding actions ensue.[19]

The sum total of forces acting on group members, causing them to remain a part of the group, is called group cohesiveness. As cohesiveness increases, so does the power of the group over the individual increase. There is more pressure to conform.[20] Many factors affect group cohesion. Size is one factor. The smaller the group, usually, the more cohesive it will be. Lack of homogeneity will decrease cohesion. There will be a tendency for sub-groups and cliques to form, made up of members with like interests and backgrounds. Easy communications between the members and physical isolation of the group from other groups will both increase cohesion.

Supervisory practices can influence cohesion. For example, if management promotes competition between group members, there will be a lessening of cohesion. Likewise, rewarding team work builds cohesion. Outside pressure is a factor. Threats from outsiders result in increased cohesiveness that tends to remain, even after the danger or inequity is removed. Success-

ful group ventures, which cause the group's status as a unit to increase, also build cohesiveness.[21] Other contributing factors are a high degree of dependency upon the group, stability of the group, the presence of ritual in the daily contacts of the members, and strong leadership.[22]

The group's leader tends to be the member who most closely conforms to the group's standards and norms, or the one who has the most information and skill related to the group's activities. The leader must enable the members to achieve their private goals as well as the group's goals. Consequently, leadership must simultaneously satisfy two conflicting needs of the group—that for initiative and guidance, and that for harmony and mutual acceptance. Often, a leader may begin by satisfying both these needs, but before long, he can effectively assume only one of these roles.[23] "As a result, there are often two leaders: a task or work leader and a social-emotional specialist."[24] When given the choice, most leaders prefer the popular role. The controlling role loses its player popularity.

The informal leader can sometimes mold and change the group's goals and norms. When he speaks, the group listens, and is influenced. But if he tries to change things too fast, he can lose his leadership role.

Informal groups overlap. People belong to a number of informal groups, a fact which sometimes causes conflicts and stress. When an individual is a member of two conflicting groups, he will experience emotional strain, which he will attempt to reduce by resolving the conflict in favor of the group to which he is most closely tied.[25]

Managing the Informal Group

The first step in any scientific method is defining the problem. Managing the informal

[19]Joseph A. Litterer, *The Analysis of Organization* (New York, 1965), pp. 110-111.

[20]Richard P. Calhoon, *Managing Personnel* (New York, 1963), p. 480.

[21]Sayles, pp. 74-76.

[22]Litterer, pp. 92-100.

[23]Berelson, pp. 343-345.

[24]Litterer, p. 116.

[25]Berelson, p. 329.

group begins just as basically. Management must first recognize that informal groups exist. Once this is acknowledged, management should gather as much information as possible about the existing groups. Who belongs to which informal groups? What are the goals of the different groups? Are they opposed to the company's goals? What are the operating techniques ... How ... are they? On-the-

can gain acceptance for decisions. Management seems least willing to give the group decision making powers in production areas. Output standards, production planning, use of equipment, changes in technology. It seems more willing to let the group handle areas like absenteeism, tardiness, health, and discipline. It is most willing to let the group decide in areas where there is a common goal, like accident

sor is the key to good management informal group relations.

The supervisor can gain cooperation only by respecting the group's standards and norms. Supervisors have been characterized as the "men in the middle." They are formal leaders, but must rely on more than the authority of the formal organization to get successful results. They must build acceptance of themselves by the informal group, and, in effect, attain some portion of the role of informal leader. Formal authority alone will not be enough to give the formal leader sufficient influence.

A good supervisor knows what the group expects of him, and adjusts his behavior accordingly. He makes *fair* demands of the group. He must emphasize "getting the job done," rather than use authority for its own sake. Rules imposed on the group should be reasonable. Time honored customs should be respected whenever possible, although there are times when such customs are in direct conflict with managerial desires. At such times, action should be taken to thwart the custom, but perhaps not by frontal assault. Management must weigh the implications carefully before taking a position at odds with the accepted practices of the group.

More positive action would be to give the informal group an opportunity to participate in decision making. Group discussion of problems

right decision. Whether the informal group depends on what management knows about the group. Are they hostile to the company? If this were the case, they certainly wouldn't be given decision making powers in an area as vital as production. But if the group is not openly antagonistic, management would be wise to let the group take an active role in decision making. "The mere fact that the group is given the power to enforce and implement rules makes the group more likely to accept the rules themselves, even rules to which they might otherwise object."[28] If management does give some decision making powers to the informal group, it is most important that the gesture be sincere. The group can readily detect insincerity. Nothing could be more detrimental to promoting good relations with the group than taking a patronizing attitude.

Encouraging group discussion and decision making will help to develop group responsibility. Unimportant and trivial jobs increase the group's feeling of irresponsibility. Management must build group responsibility by making the job more important, or at least, by making the people in the job feel more important. Allocating work assignments at the group level, decentralization, and decreasing specialization will result in added group responsibility, and ulti-

George S. Odiorne, "Put Cliques to Work For You," *Nations Business* (August, 1958), pp. 50-53.

[27]Henry Clay Smith, *Psychology of Industrial Behavior* (New York, 1964), p. 155.
[28]*Ibid.*, p. 167.

mately increase the effectiveness of a cooperative group.

"Leaders of small groups tend to direct the group's activities along lines at which they themselves are proficient and away from those areas where they are less competent."[29] Management should give informal leaders a chance to gain recognition by working with rather than against management. Build good relations with the informal leader—pass information to him, ask his advice, have him train others. But beware of the dangers. It is sometimes hard to identify the group leader. The group spokesman is not necessarily the leader. There may be different leaders for different group functions. A close management-leader relationship may cause the leader to lose status (and eventually, his leadership role) in the group. He could get the reputation of being a "company man." This could happen if the leader were asked to deviate from the group's norms. It is important not to build cooperation so far that it becomes favoritism.

Should management try to build cohesiveness? There is no clear answer to this question. Cohesive groups display teamwork, higher morale, lower turnover and absenteeism, and are easier to supervise. But high cohesive groups may not readily accept new employees. They may not cooperate well with outsiders. Consequently, competition and hard feelings between rival groups can develop. Does high cohesiveness increase productivity? Studies show that a highly cohesive group produces either somewhat higher than the average or somewhat lower, depending on the attitudes of the group. Cohesiveness means that the group members will follow more closely the group's norms, be they beneficial or not to the company.

If the group is cooperative, or even neutral, management should obviously try to encourage cohesion. The use of sociometrics to avoid the formation of sub-groups and cliques is one

tactic. Helping to bring isolated individuals into the group will increase each employee's identification with the group. Stability promotes cohesion, so management might cut down on transfers in and out of the group. When new workers are assigned to the group, a "big brother" type system to help them gain acceptance more quickly would contribute to cohesion. Group piece rates rather than individual piece rates develop teamwork and cohesion.[30]

If management feels that compatibility between informal and formal goals is not possible, it should work toward weakening or destroying the group. This could be accomplished by moving personnel about, particularly the informal leaders. Stressing dealing with individuals rather than the group will lessen cohesiveness. Since group standards will be strengthened in areas where external standards are weak,[31] beefing up company policies and standards may be necessary in some areas.

Resistance to change by the informal group can be disastrous to a company in an industry where change is imperative. "But we've always done it this way," is the cry most often heard. This resistance is natural. We all fear the unknown, and that is basically what change is. Therefore, if it wants to get a change accepted, management must furnish accurate and meaningful information about company plans through either formal or informal channels. The group should be informed why management made a decision that concerns them. Any objections from the group should be cleared up as quickly as possible. A trivial matter unattended to could lead to more deep-seated problems.[32] It is usually more effective to try to influence people as group members rather than as individuals. Even so, it is still difficult to change the group, because of the support members receive from each other.

---

[29]Berelson, p. 343.

[30]Sayles, pp. 178-179.
[31]Berelson, p. 334.
[32]John T. Doutt, "Management Must Manage The Informal Group Too," *Advanced Management* (May, 1959), pp. 26-28.

Conclusions

The existence of informal groups within formal organizations can no longer be ignored. They must be dealt with effectively—on friendly, cooperative terms, if possible, or on decisive, not-so-friendly terms, if necessary. Cooperation between formal and informal organization is desirable. Lower turnover and absenteeism, higher morale, higher production—these are the rewards when a strong, highly cohesive group's goals are closely attuned to managerial goals. If this is the case, management should do all it can to create a permissive atmosphere for the formation of informal groups. If an informal group is antagonistic to the company, management should try its best to change the group's attitude. But failing in that, it should attempt to weaken or destroy the power of the group.

Effective action is impossible without a thor-ough knowledge and understanding of informal groups at all managerial levels. Managers should be trained in group behavior and human relations. This is especially important at the supervisory level, where day to day encounters take place.

Above all, it is important that management, itself, maintain an open-minded realistic attitude about informal groups, and not be led into the trap of thinking that management is always right, the group always wrong. If there is a better way to do something, the group will probably be the first to find it. Informal groups perform necessary functions—they satisfy human needs. Management should help satisfy these human needs whenever possible, thereby encouraging group goals and company goals to coincide. Of course, there will always be a gap between manager and worker. Understanding is the only power that can fill that gap.

A. C. FILLEY

Committee Management: Guidelines from Social Science Research

THE COMMITTEE is one of the most maligned, yet most frequently employed forms of organization structure. Yet despite the criticisms, committees are a fact of organization life. For example, a recent survey of 1,200 respondents revealed that 94 percent of firms with more than 10,000 employees and 64 percent with less than 250 employees reported having formal committees.[1] And, a survey of organization practices in 620 Ohio manufacturing firms showed a similar positive relationship between committee use and plant size.[2] These studies clearly indicate that committees are one of management's important organizational tools.

My thesis is that committee effectiveness can be increased by applying social science findings to answer such questions as:

- What functions do committees serve?
- What size should committees be?
- What is the appropriate style of leadership for committee chairmen?
- What mix of member characteristics makes for effective committee performance?

Committee Purposes and Functions

Committees are set up to pursue economy and efficiency within the enterprise. They do not create direct salable value, nor do they supervise operative employees who create such value.

The functions of the committee have been described by business executives as the exchange of views and information, recommending action, generating ideas, and making major decisions,[3] of which the first may well be the most common. After observing seventy-five conferences (which were also referred to as "committees"), Kriesberg concluded that most were concerned either with communicating information or with aiding an executive's decision process.[4] Executives said they called conferences to "sell" ideas rather than for group decision-making itself. As long as the executive does not manipulate the group covertly, but benefits by its ideas and screening processes, this activity is probably quite legitimate, for members are allowed to influence and to participate, to some extent, in executive decision-making.

Some committees also make specific operating decisions which commit individuals and organization units to prescribed goals and policies. Such is often the province of the general management committee composed of major executive officers. According to one survey, 30.3 percent of the respondents reported that their firms had such a committee and that the committees averaged 8.6 members and met 27 times per year.[5]

Several of the characteristics of committee organization have been the subject of authoritative opinion, or surveys of current practice, and lend themselves to evaluation through inferences from small-group research. Current practice and authoritative opinion are reviewed here, followed by more rigorous studies in which criteria of effectiveness are present. The specific focus is on committee size, membership, and chairmen.

Committee Size

Current Practice and Opinion

The typical committee should be, and is, relatively small. Recommended sizes range from three to nine members, and surveys of actual practice seldom miss these prescriptions by much. Of the 1,658 committees recorded in the Harvard Business Review survey, the average membership was eight. When asked for their preference, the 79 percent who answered suggested an ideal committee size that averaged 4.6 members. Similarly, Kriesberg reported that, for the 75 conferences analyzed, there were typically five or six conferees in the meetings studied.[6]

Committees in the federal government tend to be larger than those in business. In the House of Representatives, Appropriations is the largest standing committee, with fifty members, and the Committee on Un-American Activities is smallest, with nine. Senate committees average thirteen members; the largest, also Appropriations, has twenty-three.[7] The problem of large committee size is overcome by the use of subcommittees and closed executive committee meetings. The larger committees seem to be more collections of subgroups than truly integrated

operating units. In such cases, it would be interesting to know the size of the subcommittees.

Inferences from Small-Group Research

The extent to which a number is "ideal" may be measured in part in terms of the effects that size has on socio-emotional relations among group members and thus the extent to which the group operates as an integrated whole, rather than as fragmented subunits. Another criterion is how size affects the quality of the group's decision and the time required to reach it. Several small experimental group studies have evaluated the effect of size on group process.

Variables related to changes in group size include the individual's capacity to "attend" to differing numbers of objects, the effect of group size on interpersonal relations and communication, its impact on problem-solving functions, and the "feelings" that group members have about proper group size and the nature of group performance. To be sure, the effects of these variables are interrelated.

Attention to the Group.—Each member in a committee attends both to the group as a whole and to each individual as a member of the group. There seem to be limits on a person's ability to perform both of these processes—limits which vary with the size of the group and the time available. For example, summarizing a study by Taves,[8] Hare[9] reports that "Experiments on estimating the number of dots in a visual field with very short-time exposures indicate individual subjects can report the exact number up to and including seven with great confidence and practically no error, but above that number confidence and accuracy drop."

Perhaps for similar reasons, when two observers assessed leadership characteristics in problem-solving groups of college students, the raters reached maximum agreement in groups of six, rather than in two, four, eight, or twelve.[10]

The apparent limits on one's ability to attend both to the group and the individuals within it led Hare to conclude:

The coincidence of these findings suggests that the ability of the observing individual to perceive, keep track of, and judge each member separately in a social interaction situation may not extend much beyond the size of six or seven. If this is true, one would expect members of groups larger than that size to tend to think of other members in terms of subgroups, or "classes" of some kind, and to deal with members of subgroups other than their own by more stereotyped methods of response.[11]

Interpersonal Relations and Communication.— Given a meeting lasting a fixed length of time, the opportunity for each individual to communicate is reduced, and the type of communication becomes differential among group members. Bales *et al.*[12] have shown that in groups of from three to eight members the proportion of infrequent contributors increases at a greater rate than that theoretically predicted from decreased opportunity to communicate. Similarly, in groups of from four to twelve, as reported by Stephen and Mishler,[13] size was related positively to the difference between participation initiated by the most active and the next most active person.

Increasing the group size seems to limit the extent to which individuals want to communicate, as well. For example, Gibb[14] studied idea productivity in forty-eight groups in eight size categories from 1 to 96. His results indicated that as group size increases a steadily increasing proportion of group members report feelings of threat and less willingness to initiate contributions. Similarly, Slater's[15] study of 24 groups of from two to seven men each working on a human relations problem indicated that members of the larger groups felt them to be disorderly and time-consuming, and complained that other members became too pushy, aggressive, and competitive.

Functions and Conflict.— An increase in group size seems to distort the pattern of communication and create stress in some group members, yet a decrease in group size also has dysfunctional effects. In the Slater study check-list responses by members rating smaller groups of 2, 3, or 4 were complimentary, rather than critical, as they had been for larger groups. Yet observer impressions were that small groups engaged in superficial discussion and avoided controversial subjects. Inferences from post hoc analysis suggested that small group members are too tense, passive, tactful, and constrained to work together in a satisfying manner. They are afraid of alienating others. Similar results have been reported in other studies regarding the inhibitions created by small group size, particularly in groups of two.[16]

Groups of three have the problem of an overpowerful majority, since two members can form a coalition against the unsupported third member. Four-member groups provide mutual support when two members oppose the other two, but such groups have higher rates of disagreement and antagonism than odd-numbered groups.[17]

The data reported above are not altogether consistent regarding the reasons for dysfunctional consequences of small groups. The "trying-too-hard-for-agreement" of the Slater study seems at odds with the conflict situations posed in the groups of three and four, yet both agree that for some reason tension is present.

Groups of Five.— While it is always dangerous to generalize about "ideal" numbers (or types, for that matter), there does appear to be logical and empirical support for groups of five members as a suitable size, if the necessary skills are possessed by the five members. In the Slater study, for example, none of the subjects felt that a group of five was too small or too large to carry out the assigned task, though they objected to the other sizes (two, three, four, six, and seven). Slater concluded:

Size five emerged clearly . . . as the size group which from the subjects' viewpoint was most effective in dealing with an intellectual task involving the collection and exchange of information about a situation, the coordination analysis, and evaluation of this information, and a group decision regarding the appropriate administrative action to be taken in the situation. . . .
These findings suggest that maximal group satisfaction is achieved when the group is large enough so that the members feel able to express positive and negative feelings freely, and to make aggressive efforts toward problem solving even at the risk of antagonizing each other, yet small enough so that some regard will be shown for the feelings and needs of others; large enough so that the loss of a member could be tolerated, but small enough so that such a loss could not be altogether ignored.[18]

From this and other studies,[19] it appears that, excluding productivity measures, generally the optimum size of problem-solving groups is five. Considering group performance in terms of quality, speed, efficiency and productivity, the effect of size is less clear. Where problems are complex, relatively larger groups have been shown to produce better quality decisions. For example, in one study, groups of 12 or 13 produced higher quality decisions than groups of 6, 7, or 8.[20] Others have shown no differences among groups in the smaller size categories (2 to 7). Relatively smaller groups are often faster and more productive. For example, Hare found that groups of five take less time to make decisions than groups of 12.[21]

Several studies have also shown that larger groups are able to solve a greater variety of problems because of the variety of skills likely to increase with group size.[22] However, there is a point beyond which committee size should not increase because of diminishing returns. As group size increases coordination of the group tends to become difficult, and thus it becomes harder for members to reach consensus and to develop a spirit of teamwork and cohesiveness.

In general, it would appear that with respect to performance, a task which requires interaction, consensus and modification of opinion requires a relatively small group. On the other hand, where the task is one with clear criteria of correct performance, the addition of more members may increase group performance.

The Chairman

Current Practice and Opinion.—Most people probably serve on some type of committee in the process of participating in church, school, political, or social organizations and while in that capacity have observed the effect of the chairman on group progress. Where the chairman starts the meeting, for example, by saying, "Well, we all know each other here, so we'll dispense with any formality," the group flounders, until someone else takes a forceful, directive role.

If the committee is to be successful, it must have a chairman who understands group process. He must know the objectives of the committee and understand the problem at hand. He should be able to vary decision strategies according to the nature of the task and the feelings of the group members. He needs the acceptance of the group members and their confidence in his personal integrity. And he needs the skill to resist needless debate and to defer discussion upon issues which are not pertinent or where the committee lacks the facts upon which to act.

Surveys of executive opinion support these impressions of the chairman's role. The Harvard Business Review survey stated that "The great majority [of the suggestions from survey respondents] lead to this conclusion: the problem is not so much committees in management as it is the management of committees." This comment by a partner in a large management consulting firm was cited as typical:

Properly used, committees can be most helpful to a company. Most of the criticism I have run into, while probably justified, deals with the way in which committees are run (or committee meetings are run) and not with the principle of working with committees.[23]

A chairman too loose in his control of committee processes is by no means the only difficulty encountered. Indeed, the chronic problem in the federal government has been the domination of committee processes by the chairman. This results from the way in which the chairman is typically selected: he is traditionally the member of the majority party having the longest uninterrupted service on the committee. The dangers in such domination have been described as follows:

If there is a piece of legislation that he does not like, he kills it by declining to schedule a hearing on it. He usually appoints no standing subcommittees and he arranges the special subcommittees in such a way that his personal preferences are taken into account. Often there is no regular agenda at the meetings of his committee—when and if it meets . . . they proceed with an atmosphere of apathy, with junior members, especially, feeling frustrated and left out, like first graders at a seventh grade party.[24]

Inferences from Small Group Research.—The exact nature of the chairman's role is further clarified when we turn to more rigorous studies on group leadership.

We shall confine our discussion here to leader roles and functions, using three approaches. First, we shall discuss the nature of task leadership in the group and the apparent reasons for this role. Then we shall view more specifically the different roles which the leader or leaders of the group may play. Finally, we shall consider the extent to which these more specific roles may be combined in a single individual.

Leader Control.—Studies of leadership in task-oriented, decision-making groups show a functional need for and, indeed, a member preference for directive influence by the chairman. The nature of this direction is illustrated in a study by Schlesinger, Jackson, and Butman.[25] The problem was to examine the influence process among leaders and members of small problem-solving groups when the designated leaders varied on the rated degree of control exerted. One hundred six members of twenty-three management committees participated in the study. As part of an initial investigation, committee members described in a questionnaire the amount of control and regulation which each member exercised when in the role of chairman. Each committee was then given a simulated but realistic problem for 1.5 hours, under controlled conditions and in the presence of three observers.

The questionnaire data showed that individuals seen as high in control were rated as more skillful chairmen and as more valuable contributors to the committee's work.

The study also demonstrated that leadership derives from group acceptance rather than from the unique acts of the chairman. "When the participants do not perceive the designated leader as satisfactorily performing the controlling functions, the participants increase their own attempts to influence their fellow members."[26] The acceptance of the leader was based upon task (good ideas) and chairmanship skills and had little to do with his personal popularity as a group member.

The importance of chairman control in committee action has been similarly demonstrated in several other studies.[27] In his study of 72 management conferences, for example, Berkowitz[28] found that a high degree of "leadership sharing" was related inversely to participant satisfaction and to a measure of output. The norms of these groups sanctioned a "take-charge" chairman. When the chairman failed to meet these expectations, he was rejected and both group satisfaction and group output suffered. These studies do not necessarily suggest that committees less concerned with task goals also prefer a directive chairman. Where the committees are composed of more socially oriented members, the preference for leader control may be less strong.[29]

Leadership Roles.—A second approach to understanding the leadership of committees is to investigate leadership roles in small groups. Pervading the research literature is a basic distinction between group activities directed to one or the other of two types of roles performed by leaders. They are defined by Benne and Sheats[30] as task roles, and as group-building and maintenance roles. Task roles are related to the direct accomplishment of group purpose, such as seeking information, initiating, evaluating, and seeking or giving opinion. The latter roles are concerned with group integration and solidarity through encouraging, harmonizing, compromising, and reducing conflict.

Several empirical investigations of leadership have demonstrated that both roles are usually performed within effective groups.[31] However, these roles are not always performed by the same person. Frequently one member is seen as the "task leader" and another as the "social leader" of the group.

Combined task and social roles.—Can or should these roles be combined in a single leader? The prototypes of the formal and the informal leader which we inherit from classical management lore tend to lead to the conclusion that such a combination is somehow impossible or perhaps undesirable. The research literature occasionally supports this point of view as well.

There is much to be said for a combination of roles. Several studies have shown that outstanding leaders are those who possess both task and social orientations.[32] The study by Borgotta, Couch, and Bales illustrates the point. These researchers assigned leaders high on both characteristics to problem-solving groups. The eleven leaders whom they called "great men" were selected from 126 in an experiment on the basis of high task ability, individual assertiveness, and social acceptability. These men also retained their ratings as "great men" throughout a series of different problem-solving sessions. When led by "great men" the groups achieved a higher rate of suggestion and agreement, a lower rate of "showing tension," and higher rates of showing solidarity and tension release than comparable groups without "great men."

When viewed collectively two conclusions emerge from the above studies. Consistent with existing opinion, the leader who is somewhat assertive and who takes charge and controls group proceedings is performing a valid and necessary role. However, such task leadership is a necessary but not a sufficient condition for effective committee performance. Someone in the group must perform the role of group-builder and maintainer of social relations among the members. Ideally both roles should probably be performed by the designated chairman. When he does not have the necessary skills to perform both roles, he should be the task leader and someone else should perform the social leadership role. Effective committee performance requires both roles to be performed, by a single person or by complementary performance of two or more members.

Committee Membership

The atmosphere of committee operations described in the classic literature is one where all members seem to be cooperating in the achievement of committee purpose. It is unclear, however, if cooperation is necessarily the best method of solving problems, or if competition among members or groups of members might not achieve more satisfactory results. Cooperation also seems to imply a sharing or homogeneity of values. To answer the question we must consider two related problems: the effects of cooperation or competition on committee effectiveness, and the effects of homogeneous or heterogeneous values on committee effectiveness.

Cooperation or Competition.—A number of studies have contrasted the impact of competition and cooperation on group satisfaction and productivity. In some cases the group is given a cooperative or competitive "treatment" through direction or incentive when it is established. In others, competition and cooperation are inferred from measures of groups in which members are operating primarily for personal interest, in contrast with groups in which members are more concerned with group needs. These studies show rather consistently that "group members who have been motivated to cooperate show more positive responses to each other, are more favorable in their perceptions, are more involved in the task, and have greater satisfaction with the task."[33]

The best known study regarding the effects of cooperation and competition was conducted by Deutsch[34] in ten experimental groups of college students, each containing five persons. Each group met for one three-hour period a week for six weeks, working on puzzles and human relations problems. Subjects completed a weekly and post-experimental questionnaire. Observers also recorded interactions and completed over-all rating scales at the end of each problem.

In some groups, a cooperative atmosphere was established by instructing members that the group as a whole would be evaluated in comparison with four similar groups, and that each person's course grade would depend upon the performance of the group itself. In others, a competitive relationship was established by telling the members that each would receive a different grade, depending upon his relative contribution to the group's problem solutions.

The results, as summarized by Hare, show that:

Compared with the competitively organized groups, the cooperative groups had the following characteristics:
(1) Stronger individual motivation to complete the group task and stronger feelings of obligation toward other members.
(2) Greater division of labor both in content and frequency of interaction among members and greater coordination of effort.
(3) More effective inter-member communication. More ideas were verbalized, members were more attentive to one another, and more accepting of and affected by each other's ideas. Members also rated themselves as having fewer difficulties in communicating and understanding others.
(4) More friendliness was expressed in the discussion and members rated themselves higher on strength of desire to win the respect of one another. Members were also more satisfied with the group and its products.
(5) More group productivity. Puzzles were solved faster and the recommendations produced for the human-relations problems were longer and qualitatively better. However, there were no significant differences in the average individual productivity as a result of the two types of group experience nor were there any clear differences in the amounts of individual learning which occurred during the discussions.[35]

Similar evidence was found in the study of 72 decision-making conferences by Fouriezos, Hutt, and Guetzkow.[36] Based on observer ratings of self-oriented need behavior, correlational evidence showed that such self-centered behavior was positively related to participant ratings of high group conflict and negatively related to participant satisfaction, group solidarity, and task productivity.

In general, the findings of these and other studies suggest that groups in which members share in goal attainment, rather than compete privately or otherwise seek personal needs, will be more satisfied and productive.[37]

Homogeneity or Heterogeneity.—The effects of member composition in the committee should also be considered from the standpoint of the homogeneity or heterogeneity of its membership. Homogeneous groups are those in which members are similar in personality, value orientation, attitudes to supervision, or predisposition to accept or reject fellow members. Heterogeneity is induced in the group by creating negative expectations regarding potential contributions by fellow members, by introducing differing personality types into the group, or by creating subgroups which differ in their basis of attraction to the group.

Here the evidence is much less clear. Some homogeneous groups become satisfied and quite unproductive, while others become satisfied and quite productive. Similarly, heterogeneity may be shown to lead to both productive and unproductive conditions. While the answer to this paradox may be related to the different definitions of homogeneity or heterogeneity in the studies, it appears to have greater relevance to the task and interpersonal requirements of the group task.

In some studies, homogeneity clearly leads to more effective group performance. The work of Schutz[38] is illustrative. In his earlier writing, Schutz distinguished between two types of interpersonal relationships: power orientation and personal orientation. The first emphasizes authority symbols. The power-oriented person follows rules and adjusts to external systems of authority. People with personal orientations emphasize interpersonal considerations. They assume that the way a person achieves his goal is by working within a framework of close personal relations, that is, by being a "good guy," by liking others, by getting people to like him. In his later work, Schutz[39] distinguished among three types of needs: *inclusion,* or the need to establish and maintain a satisfactory relation with people with respect to interaction and association; *control,* or the need to establish and maintain a satisfactory relation with people with respect to control and power; and *affection,* or the need to establish and maintain a satisfactory relation with others with respect to love and affection.

Using attitude scales, Schutz established four groups in which people were compatible with respect to high needs for personal relations with others, four whose members were compatible with respect to low personal orientation, and four which contained subgroups differing in these needs. Each of the twelve groups met twelve times over a period of six weeks and participated in a series of different tasks.

The results showed that groups which are compatible, either on a basis of personalness or counterpersonalness, were significantly more productive than groups which had incompatible subgroups. There was no significant difference between the productivity of the two types of compatible groups. As might be expected, the difference in productivity between compatible and incompatible groups was greatest for tasks which required the most interaction and agreement under conditions of high-time pressure.

A similar positive relationship between homogeneity and productivity is reported for groups in which compatibility is established on the basis of prejudice or degree of conservatism, managerial personality traits, congeniality induced by directions from the researcher, or status congruence.[40] In Adams' study, technical performance first increased, then decreased, as status congruence became greater. Group social performance increased continuously with greater homogeneity, however.

The relationship posited above does not always hold, however. In some studies, heterogeneous groups were more productive than homogeneous. For example, Hoffman[41] constructed heterogeneous and homogeneous groups, based on personality profiles, and had them work on two different types of problems. On the first, which required consideration of a wide range of alternatives of a rather specific nature, heterogeneous groups produced significantly superior solutions. On the second problem, which required primarily group consensus and had no objectively "good" solution, the difference between group types was not significant. Ziller[42] also found heterogeneity to be associated with the ability of Air Force crews to judge the number of dots on a card.

Collins and Guetzkow[43] explain these contradictory findings by suggesting that increasing heterogeneity has at least two effects on group interaction: it increases the difficulty of building interpersonal relations, and it increases the problem-solving potential of the group, since errors are eliminated, more alternatives are generated, and wider criticism is possible. Thus, heterogeneity would seem to be valuable where the needs for task facilitation are greater than the need for strong interpersonal relations.

Considering our original question, it appears that, from the standpoint of cooperation versus competition in committees, the cooperative committee is to be preferred. If we look at the effects of homogeneous or heterogeneous committee membership, the deciding factor seems to be the nature of the task and the degree of interpersonal conflict which the committee can tolerate.

Summary and Conclusions

Research findings regarding committee size, leadership, and membership have been reviewed. Evidence has been cited showing that the ideal size is five, when the five members possess the necessary skills to solve the problems facing the committee. Viewed from the standpoint of the committee members' ability to attend to both the group and its members, or from the standpoint of balanced interpersonal needs, it seems safe to suggest that this number has normative value in planning committee operations. For technical problems additional members may be added to ensure the provision of necessary skills.

A second area of investigation concerned the functional separation of the leadership role and the influence of the role on other members. The research reviewed supports the notion that the committee chairman should be directive in his leadership, but a more specific definition of leadership roles makes questionable whether the chairman can or should perform as both the task and the social leader of the group. The evidence regarding the latter indicates that combined task and social leadership is an ideal which is seldom attained, but should be sought.

The final question concerned whether committee membership would be most effective when cooperative or competitive. When evaluated from the standpoint of research on cooperative versus competitive groups, it is clear that cooperative membership is more desirable. Committee operation can probably be enhanced by selecting members whose self-centered needs are of a less intense variety and by directions to the group which strengthen motivations of a cooperative nature. When the proposition is evaluated from the standpoint of heterogeneity or homogeneity of group membership, the conclusion is less clear. Apparently, heterogeneity in a group can produce both ideas and a screening process for evaluating their quality, but the advantage of this process depends upon the negative effects of heterogeneous attitudes upon interpersonal cooperation.

REFERENCES

Based on A. C. Filley and J. Robert House, *Managerial Process and Organizational Behavior* (Glenview, Ill.: Scott-Foresman, 1969).

1. Rollie Tillman, Jr., "Problems in Review: Committees on Trial," *Harvard Business Review*, 38 (May-June 1960), 6-12, 162-172. Firms with 1,001 to 10,000 reported 93 percent use; 250 to 1,000 reported 82 percent use.

2. J. H. Healey, *Executive Coordination and Control*, Monograph No. 78 (Columbus: Bureau of Business Research, The Ohio State University, 1956), p. 185.

3. "Committees," *Management Review*, 46 (October 1957), 4-10; 75-78.

4. M. Kriesberg, "Executives Evaluate Administrative Conferences," *Advanced Management*, 15 (March 1950), 15-17.

5. Tillman, *op. cit.*, p. 12.

6. Kriesberg, *op. cit.*, p. 15

7. "The Committee System—Congress at Work," *Congressional Digest*, 34 (February 1955), 47-49; 64.

8. E. H. Taves, "Two Mechanisms for the Perception of Visual Numerousness," *Archives of Psychology*, 37 (1941), 265.

9. A. Paul Hare, *Handbook of Small Group Research*, (New York: The Free Press of Glencoe, 1962), p. 227.

10. B. M. Bass, and F. M. Norton, "Group Size and Leaderless Discussions," *Journal of Applied Psychology*, 35 (1951), 397-400.

11. Hare, *op. cit.*, p. 228.

12. R. F. Bales, F. L. Strodtbeck, T. M. Mills, and M. E. Roseborough, "Channels of Communication in Small Groups," *American Sociological Review*, 16 (1951), 461-468.

13. F. F. Stephen and E. G. Mishler, "The Distribution of Participation in Small Groups: An Exponential Approximation." *American Sociological Review*, 17 (1952), 598-608.

14. J. R. Gibb, "The Effects of Group Size and of Threat Reduction Upon Creativity in a Problem-Solving Situation," *American Psychologist*, 6 (1951), 324. (Abstract)

15. P. Slater, "Contrasting Correlates of Group Size," *Sociometry*, 21 (1958), 129-139.

16. R. F. Bales, and E. F. Borgotta, "Size of Group as a Factor in the Interaction Profile," in *Small Groups: Studies in Social Interaction*, A. P. Hare, E. F. Borgotta, and R. F. Bales, eds. (New York: Knopf, 1965, rev. ed.), pp. 495-512.

17. *Ibid.*, p. 512.

18. Slater, *op. cit.*, 137-138.

19. R. F. Bales, "In Conference," *Harvard Business Review*, 32 (March-April 1954), 44-50; also A. P. Hare, "A Study of Interaction and Consensus in Different Sized Groups," *American Sociological Review*, 17 (1952), 261-267.

20. D. Fox, I. Lorge, P. Weltz, and K. Herrold, "Comparison of Decisions Written by Large and Small Groups," *American Psychologist*, 8 (1953), 351. (Abstract)

21. A. Paul Hare, "Interaction and Consensus in Different Sized Groups," *American Sociological Review*, 17 (1952), 261-267.

22. C. B. Watson, "Do Groups Think More Efficiently Than Individuals?" *Journal of Abnormal and Social Psychology*, 23, (1928), 328-336; Also D. J. Taylor and W. L. Faust, "Twenty Questions: Efficiency in Problem Solving as a Function of Size of Group," *Jour-*

nal of Experimental Psychology, 44 (1952), 360–368.

23. Tillman, *op. cit.,* **p.** 168.

24. S. L. Udall, "Defense of the Seniority System," *New York Times Magazine* (January 13, 1957), 17.

25. L. Schlesinger, J. M. Jackson, and J. Butman, "Leader-Member Interaction in Management Committees," *Journal of Abnormal and Social Psychology,* 61, No. 3 (1960) 360–364.

26. *Ibid.,* p. 363.

27. L. Berkowitz, "Sharing Leadership in Small Decision-Making Groups," *Journal of Abnormal and Social Psychology,* 48 (1953), 231–238; Also N. T. Fouriezos, M. L. Hutt, and H. Guetzkow, "Measurement of Self-Oriented Needs in Discussion Groups," *Journal of Abnormal and Social Psychology,* 45 (1950), 682–690; also H. P. Shelley, "Status Consensus, Leadership, and Satisfaction with the Group," *Journal of Social Psychology,* 51 (1960), 157–164.

28. Berkowitz, *Ibid.,* p. 237.

29. R. C. Anderson, "Learning in Discussions: A Resume of the Authoritarian-Democratic Studies," *Harvard Education Review,* 29 (1959), 201–214.

30. K. D. Benne, and P. Sheats, "Functional Roles of Group Members," *Journal of Social Issues,* 4 (Spring 1948), 41–49.

31. R. F. Bales, *Interaction Process Analysis* (Cambridge: Addison-Wesley, 1951); Also R. M. Stogdill and A. E. Coons (eds.), *Leader Behavior: Its Description and Measurement,* Monograph No. 88 (Columbus: Bureau of Business Research, The Ohio State University, 1957); Also A. W. Halpin, "The Leadership Behavior and Combat Performance of Airplane Commanders," *Journal of Abnormal and Social Psychology,* 49 (1954), 19–22.

32. E. G. Borgotta, A. S. Couch, and R. F. Bales, "Some Findings Relevant to the Great Man Theory of Leadership," *American Sociological Review,* 19 (1954), 755–759); Also E. A. Fleishman, and E. G. Harris, "Patterns of Leadership Behavior Related to Employee Grievances and Turnover," *Personnel Psychology,* 15, No. 1 (1962), 43–56; Also Stogdill and Coons, *Ibid.;* Also H. Oaklander and E. A. Fleishman, "Patterns of Leadership Related to Organizational Stress in Hospital Settings," *Administrative Science Quarterly,* 8 (March 1964), 520–532.

33. Hare, *Handbook of Small Group Research, op. cit.,* p. 254.

34. M. Deutsch, "The Effects of Cooperation and Competition Upon Group Process," in *Group Dynamics, Research and Theory,* D. Cartwright and A. Zander, eds., (New York: Harper and Row, 1953).

35. Hare, *Handbook of Small Group Research, op. cit.,* p. 263.

36. Fouriezos, Hutt, and Guetzkow, *op. cit.*

37. C. Stendler, D. Damrin and A. Haines, "Studies in Cooperation and Competition: I. The Effects of Working for Group and Individual Rewards on the Social Climate of Children's Groups," *Journal of Genetic Psychology,* 79 (1951), 173–197; Also A. Mintz, "Nonadaptive Group Behavior," *Journal of Abnormal and Social Psychology,* 46 (1951), 150–159; Also M. M. Grossack, "Some Effects of Cooperation and Competition Upon Small Group Behavior," *Journal of Abnormal and Social Psychology,* 49 (1954), 341–348; Also E. Gottheil, "Changes in Social Perceptions Contingent Upon Competing or Cooperating," *Sociometry,* 18 (1955), 132–137; Also A. Zander and D. Wolfe, "Administrative Rewards and Coordination Among Committee Members," *Administrative Science Quarterly,* 9 (June 1964), 50–69.

38. W. C. Schutz, "What Makes Groups Productive?" *Human Relations,* 8 (1955), 429–465.

39. W. C. Schutz, *FIRO: A Three-Dimensional Theory of Interpersonal Behavior,* (New York: Holt, Rinehart and Winston, 1958).

40. I. Altman and E. McGinnies, "Interpersonal Perception and Communication in Discussion Groups of Varied Attitudinal Composition," *Journal of Abnormal and Social Psychology,* 60 (May 1960), 390–393; Also W. A. Haythorn, E. H. Couch, D. Haefner, P. Langham and L. Carter, "The Behavior of Authoritarian and Equalitarian Personalities in Groups," *Human Relations,* 9 (1956), 57–74; Also E. E. Ghiselli and T. M. Lodahl, "Patterns of Managerial Traits and Group Effectiveness," *Journal of Abnormal and Social Psychology,* 57 (1958), 61–66; Also R. V. Exline, "Group Climate as a Factor in the Relevance and Accuracy of Social Perception," *Journal of Abnormal and Social Psychology,* 55 (1957), 382–388; Also S. Adams, "Status Congruency as a Variable in Small Group Performance," *Social Forces,* 32 (1953), 16–22.

41. L. R. Hoffman, "Homogeneity of Member Personality and Its Effect on Group Problem-Solving," *Journal of Abnormal and Social Psychology,* 58 (1959), 27–32.

42. R. C. Ziller, "Scales of Judgment: A Determinant of Accuracy of Group Decisions," *Human Relations,* 8 (1955), 153–164.

43. B. E. Collins and H. Guetzkow, *A Social Psychology of Group Process for Decision-Making,* (New York: John Wiley and Sons, 1965), p. 101.

Section D:
Communication

Every few years a national survey of business executives attempts to uncover their most pressing problems. Communication is always near the top of the list. This result may be interpreted in two ways. The executives may simply be expressing a desire for more pertinent information for the decisions they must make, a task objective. Or, these executives may have difficulty in "relating" to other members of the organization on an interpersonal basis, a behavioral problem. It should be obvious at this point in the text that both of these problems are highly related; it is very difficult to accomplish task objectives without meeting the behavioral needs of organizational members.

Communication in the organizational setting is usually defined as the exchange of information, attitudes, or feelings. Communication can take place on the formal or informal level in the organization, and very often at both levels simultaneously. The two readings in this section apply to both types of communication.

In the first selection, Jack Gibb presents two divergent viewpoints of the relationship of communication to productivity in the organization. The first, the persuasion approach, focuses on communication as an end or goal in itself. "Communication . . . is seen as a basic cause of poor work or problem solving and is worked on directly by altering managerial communications." The second, the problem-solving approach, focuses on communication "as a symptom or indicator of more basic organizational or managerial inadequacy." The problem-solving approach is consistent with several other views of organizational processes that have been discussed earlier in the text. For example, it is very similar to the Blake and Mouton 9,9 managerial style and the adult-adult mode of interaction from transactional analysis. In most organizational settings, this approach is viewed as leading to greater productivity than the persuasion approach. As Gibb states,

> The problem solving manager tends to think more in terms of input. He may ask himself questions such as the following. What information is needed? How do others look at the problem? What other solutions are there to problems that face us? How can we get more data? How can we interpret what information is

available? What cues are we failing to process?... The managerial rewards are presumably very great (from the problem solving approach).

In the second article, Carl Rogers and Richard Farson deal with the "input" problem in communications, effective listening. Active listening, as defined by the authors, is consistent with the problem-solving approach to communication explored by Gibb: "the listener has a very definite responsibility. He does not passively absorb the words which are spoken to him. He actively tries to grasp the facts and the feelings in what he hears, and he tries by his listening, to help the speaker work out his own problems." The successful active listener avoids evaluation in responding to communication and is aware of both the content of the communication and the feelings that accompany this content, or both the task and behavioral aspects of the communication. Rogers and Farson go on to discuss problems in this approach to communication and the relationship between this approach and the common goals of organizations, such as production and creativity. An interesting discussion point is whether the active listening approach is equally applicable to all organizational models or to all hierarchical levels of an organization. For example, is this approach applicable to the bureaucratic model or is it more consistent with the professional employee model of organization?

Communication and Productivity

Jack R. Gibb

Communication is a process of people relating to other people. As people relate to each other in doing work and in solving problems they communicate ideas, feelings and attitudes. If this communication is effective the work gets done better and the problems are solved more efficiently. Thus, in one sense, at this level of abstraction, there is an obvious relationship between communication and productivity.

Work and problem solving can each be viewed as the taking of appropriate roles at appropriate times as the task or problem evolves. Role taking *is* communication. This apparent and real relationship has caused management to take an increasing interest in all phases of communication. Books are written, training courses are devised, and communications specialists are created and demanded. The rapid growth of literature and programs has far out-distanced the relevant research and the clear knowledge that management can use in making decisions about communications programs. The literature is confusing, contradictory and voluminous.

Although in the most global sense it is fairly

Dr. Gibb has had a long interest in group and organizational phenomena. In addition to being an educator, trainer and author, he has kept his research interests alive while teaching at Brigham Young and U. of Colorado, and while holding appointments as Research Professor at the Fels Group Dynamics Ctr., and as Dir. of Research for the National Education Assn.'s National Training Laboratory. Now a consulting psychologist in private practice, part of his time is occupied on a project, sponsored by the Office of Naval Research, to study defensive behavior in small groups.

From *Personnel Administration*, January–February 1964, pp. 8–13, 45. Reprinted by permission of the International Personnel Management Association, 1313 East 60th Street, Chicago, Illinois 60637.

obvious that communication is related to productivity. it is very difficult to find satisfying evidence of clear relationships between specific communicative programs or acts, on the one hand. and measures of productivity, profit or corporate vitality on the other. Most studies of communication are short term in nature and relate aspects of communication to various personal and group variables that are perhaps assumed to be related to productivity in the long run, but whose relationships are tenuous at best.

It is the purpose of this paper to look at the over-all problem from the standpoint of managerial decision making. What does top management or the individual manager do? The paper is organized around 9 fundamental communication issues that confront management in today's corporate world. These issues grow out of research, theory and management experience. While it is true that in both practice and theory there are many and varied legitimate positions on each issue, it is possible to distinguish two clusters of related managerial behaviors that are fairly consistently antithetical on each of the fundamental issues. In Table One are summarized the extreme positions of the conflicting views— the views of the "persuasion manager" and of the "problem-solving manager"—on each of the nine issues. Each issue is stated in more detail at the beginning of each of the nine sections of the paper. The issues are practical, overlapping and in general are worded in the language of management rather than in the language of the specialist.

In general, the *persuasion approach* to communication tends to assume that it is the responsibility of management to regulate the flow of fact and feeling through the organization, to use such regulation as a convenient managerial tool, to build staff roles to work on communication problems, to spend a great deal of time and energy building "communications" programs, and to show a high concern about the information flow in the organization, particularly about verbal and written messages downward.

An alternative approach, designated for convenience as the *problem-solving approach,* is to assume that effective communication is an intrinsic component of effective work and efficient problem solving, that if communications problems exist they are symptoms of aberrant organization or poor line management, that communication is improved by more adequate line man-

agement action and problem solving rather than by staff action, and that by creating a managerial climate in which trust and openness is a norm appropriate facts, attitudes and feelings tend to be spontaneously fed into the process of getting the job done.

In each of the following sections a focus or viewpoint consistent with each of the two above approaches is discussed.

1. Symptom or Cause

Is communication seen primarily as a symptom of more basic organizational processes or as itself a fundamental factor to be manipulated by management in the quest for greater productivity and organizational vitality? Is communication best viewed as a symptom or as a cause?

A manager with what might be termed a persuasion approach to management sees communication primarily as a management tool to be used in getting people to get the job done. When he sees some defect in the work pattern that must be remedied he tends to attempt to manipulate the flow of communications as a remedial action. Communicative distortion is seen as a basic cause of poor work or problem solving and is worked on directly by altering managerial communications.

TABLE ONE

Two Alternative Views of the Communication Processes

A Persuasian Approach— The focus is on:	A Problem-Solving Approach— The focus is on:
1. Remedial programs	1. Diagnosis and etiology
2. Staff responsibility	2. Line responsibility
3. Morale and hygiene	3. Work product and job requirements
4. Persuasion	4. Problem solving
5. Control of communication flow	5. Trust and openness
6. Verbal communication	6. Management action
7. One-way messages	7. Interaction and climate
8. Knowledge and logic	8. Attitudes and feelings
9. Output and telling	9. Input and listening

A manager with what might be termed a problem-solving approach to management tends to see communication primarily as a symptom or indicator of more basic organizational or managerial inadequacy. Information about communicative distortion is used as diagnostic data which will guide the manager in taking new managerial actions, reorganizing work patterns, or achieving new attitudes toward the organization or the people in it.

The evidence is fairly clear that when people are in an effective problem-solving or work relationship with each other they tend to communicate relevant feelings, ideas and perceptions with each other. When there is goal ambiguity, poor supervision or role inadequacy then communicative distortion occurs as a symptom of these more basic problems.

An analog occurs in the concurrently flowering field of human relations. Human relations can be viewed as a symptom or as a cause. The growing awareness of human relations and communications problems is symptomatic of growing feelings of inadequacy on the part of management, and of a growing awareness of basic inadequacies in both management and organization theory and practice. When people have trouble getting along with each other and understanding each other, it is probably an indication that somehow they have been unable to create satisfactory jobs or a satisfying and effective work organization. The way to improve human relations and communications is to evolve new job prescriptions and more adequate work organizations—to change managerial actions. It may be a temporary solution to build human relations training programs and communications workshops—but this is at best a *temporary* or intermediate solution, a step that is getting at symptoms rather than more basic causes, and that is working on the shadow of the problem rather than on the problem itself.

2. Staff or Line

Who is primarily responsible for effective communication—staff or line? The persuasion manager tends to emphasize the staff role in improvement of communications. The problem-solving manager tends to build responsibility for communications and human relations directly into the line functions.

A differentiating characteristic between the persuasion manager and the problem-solving manager is his emphasis upon one of two paths. The persuasion manager tends to build a communications staff with many responsibilities for studying communications, instituting programs, managing information and data flow within the organization, training people to communicate, and using various media to *persuade* people to change behavior or to communicate more adequately.

The problem-solving manager makes the assumption that communication is a direct line responsibility, that communication *must* occur in the process of doing work, solving problems, controlling distribution, or getting the job done. He works directly on the line causes of communicative errors. He works with others towards recomposing work groups, changing organizational patterns, reorganizing work space, or creating more adequate man-job relationships. He tends to change his behavior rather than his speech. He tends to control actions rather than to control talk.

It seems well at this point to call attention to the fact that we are describing two extreme typologies of management. In one sense the two types of managers being considered are hypothetical or "ideal" cases. The pure cases do not exist in the natural state. However, anyone with wide experience on the industrial scene can recognize the *genre*. The intent is to sharpen assumptions and to focus attention upon the implications of communications research for management practices. In practice individual managers tend to show mixtures of the above patterns.

3. Hygiene or Production

If there is a "communications program" is it primarily centered upon the requirements of the job and the product or is it primarily remedial in nature? Is it directed toward morale, hygiene and human relations or is it directed toward work and productivity?

The persuasion manager tends to direct the communication program toward improvement of morale and hygiene around the plant. He fights fires, drops verbal bombs where they are presumed to do the most good, centers upon remedial aspects of the situation, and directs plant and company campaigns toward curing ills such as absenteeism and waste.

The problem-solving manager tends to have no special communications program as such.

When he does create such a program he tends to deal with analyses of job requirements, production schedules, goals of the enterprise, information storage and retrieval, efficiency of work flow, and other aspects of communication flow that are directly relevant to job performance and problem solving.

Hygiene-centered communication programs tend to send out information that is irrelevant, distorted to fit management goals, camouflaged to cover management errors, sent in too great a quantity, irrelevant to the concerns of the moment that *grow out of* task and problem demands or out of spontaneous group maintenance demands. Such programs are often met with suspicion and apathy, and may be seen as propaganda or as attempts to meet management needs rather than work needs or worker needs.

There is some evidence that communication is best when it is in response to natural interaction on the job between people who are learning appropriate trust, when it is in small groups or face-to-face situations, when it is asked for, and when it is between members who do not have too great psychological or hierarchical distance. The most effective communication thus tends to arise spontaneously out of situational demands.

Effective communication tends to be best in work units, where line managers and co-workers are learning a degree of trust appropriate to their relationship, and are learning to send and receive attitudes, feelings and information that are necessary for appropriate job performance. The interrelated assumptions here are that people like to do meaningful work, feel good when they have satisfactory job relationships, have good morale when they do challenging work that is related to their own choices, goals, and abilities, and that effective communication is a residual property of effective work and problem solving.

4. Persuasion or Problem-Solving

Is the communication program focussed upon persuasion of people or upon individual and team problem solving?

The persuasion manager tends to see communication as primarily an influence process through which people can be changed, controlled, guided, or influenced. Communication becomes education, propaganda, leadership, or guidance. Managers try to sell ideas, or to motivate others to work harder, feel better, have higher morale, and be more loyal.

> *If one were to believe the public statements and writings of leading administrators, one could believe that most of them are genuinely anchored in the democratic style. Few will openly admit being autocratic or bureaucratic. After all, this is the age of the enlightened executive who assumes his social responsibility. However, upon close inspection they show a tendency to cling to the democratic theme out of feelings of inadequacy and uncertainty. They are democrats out of fear of public opinion rather than because they genuinely understand the needs and problems of people.*
>
> —Eugene E. Jennings in
> *The Executive—Autocrat,
> Bureaucrat, Democrat, 1962*

The problem-solving manager sees communication primarily as a necessary adjunct of the process of doing work or solving problems. In order to solve the problem or get the job done certain information must be obtained, certain feelings must be expressed, and a certain amount of interpersonal perceptions must be exchanged in order for a team to be a healthy work or problem-solving unit. Job demands or team maintenance demands determine the amount and kind of communication that is necessary. Communication *is* problem solving.

The difference in the two approaches is one of *focus*. Communication is *both* influence and problem solving. The emphasis and the approach are the significant things. Persuasive communication tends to produce resistance, distrust, circumvention, or counter-persuasion. It is seen by the worker or subordinate as "news management", as propaganda, or as an effort to get him to do what he may not want to do. Research has shown persuasion-centered communications programs to be discouragingly ineffective in accomplishing management goals.

Problem-solving communication is subordinate to the demands of the job or the problem. The nature of the job or the problem calls forth certain bits of information, feelings or perceptions that are relevant to job accomplishment or problem solution. In general, the research shows that when conditions are created which produce relevant *emergent* communications out of the work situation, that communications problems are reduced. Thus, face-to-face communications in small groups tend to be superior to other forms of communication because there is a greater likelihood that communications will emerge from interactive job and problem demands.

5. Regulation or Trust

Does one trust the manager and the worker or does one regulate the communication flow?

An increasingly clear body of evidence indicates that communication is related to the trust level in the relationship or in the organization. People who trust each other tend to be more open with each other. With high trust people are free to give information and feelings and to respond spontaneously to questions, are less apt to devise control strategies to manipulate others, are less apt to be closed and devious, are less apt to manufacture rumors or distortions, perhaps have less need to engage in extra communication, and thus they lay the groundwork for higher productivity. With low trust, people use more strategy, filter information, build interpersonal facades, camouflage attitudes, deliberately or unconsciously hold back relevant feelings and information in the process of interpersonal in-fighting, distort feedback upward in the direction of personal motivations, engage in extra communication, and thus indirectly sabotage productivity.

Managers tend to regulate the communication flow when distrust is high and tend to be more spontaneous and open with feelings and information when distrust is low. The persuasion manager tends to regulate communication flow—both in his personal actions and in his managerial policies. The problem-solving manager tends to create trust by allowing communications to follow the demands of the work situation. The openness-trusting stance is antithetical to the persuasion stance. Experimentation indicates that work and problem-solving efficiency is dependent upon the spontaneous flow of information and feelings through the system. Trust and openness are related to productivity.

6. Talk or Action

Does a manager talk or act? Given a choice of where to focus effort, does management spend energies getting the problems solved and the jobs done or deciding what kinds of communications to send to the subordinate and the worker?

With articulate people words can become a fetish. What shall we say to the worker? What can I tell my subordinate? How shall I word the message? Part of this word-focus habit arises from a naive confidence that people will take the words at face value, part of it perhaps from an unconscious protest to one's intuitive understanding that talk will make little difference and that people won't listen at all. Interviews with managers indicate bimodal reactions of naive trust or equally naive cynicism about the effectiveness of words in communication.

Experimental and field studies can be interpreted to show that actions are more significant than words in communication. Gestures, bodily attitudes, empathic postures, and management actions communicate a great deal more than words do. A manager who says verbally that he trusts a subordinate and then proceeds to require detailed and frequent reports, or to make frequent checks on the subordinate's work, usually is *perceived* as distrusting the subordinate. Actions take priority over words in the communication channels.

The persuasion manager tends to ascribe an inordinately high value to words, symbols, pictures, and formal communications. Most people would perhaps agree that both words and actions communicate. The difference in management technologies lies in the relative emphasis in day to day management decision. The problem-solving manager tends to rely upon actions to communicate rather than upon words. He tends to use words more for information than for influence.

7. Traffic or Climate

Is the "communication problem" basically a climate problem or a traffic problem? Do we focus attention upon refining the messages we send or upon creating a climate in which "messages" are decreasingly necessary? Is communication primarily directional or is it an interaction among people doing a job? Is the management problem one of creating a climate for interaction or one of regulating the message traffic?

The persuasion manager tends to be a traffic man, usually centering attention upon the one-way channels down the hierarchy or command channel. Great attention is paid to the mass media, refinement of the message, timing of the presentation, organizing the campaign, hitting at the psychological moment, and devising an appropriate propaganda strategy. Public relations, advertising and visual aids are in great demand. The problem is control of the traffic patterns of communication. Communication is often one-way.

The problem-solving alternative to such action is to focus upon the interactive climate of work, to rely upon face-to-face interaction in line units who are working or solving problems together, to give all relevant information to line managers with maximum openness, to arrange the geography of work in such a way as to optimize relevant interaction, and to encourage questions, criticisms and all forms of informal interaction. Group discussions, small, flexible and overlapping work teams, and open channels are seen as communication tools. The problem is seen as one of creating a climate for work and problem solving. Communication is seen as flowing in a field of interaction, rather than as occurring on a one-way street—or even on a two-way street. Communication is a relationship.

8.   Knowledge or Attitude

Which is more central in determining effective communication—information and logic or attitudes and feelings? If communication is seen as poor does the manager direct his energies toward refining the flow of information or toward changing the attitudes of persons engaged in communicating? Which is a more critical "leverage point" in adequate communication—knowledge and logic or attitudes and feelings?

The persuasion technologist tends to place an emphasis upon information and upon getting the "facts" to the right people. He tends to assume that information will change attitudes and behavior, and that information can be transmitted with acceptably high reliability through formal channels.

The evidence seems to point to the relative importance of attitudinal and motivational factors over informational factors in management and in behavior change. Campaigns to increase information usually accomplish considerably less than management would hope. Information does not necessarily change attitudes, value systems, or even perceptions. People tend to perceive information or reinterpret data in the direction of their motivations and wishes. People hear what they want to hear. They forget what they want

to forget. There are various motivational reasons why people select from available information, ignore posters and pamphlets, overperceive or underperceive the "facts", and in general add their own distortions to the information that they receive.

The communication of intangibles like warmth, acceptance, respect, and trust are complex processes which are poorly correlated with the words people use and the information that is conveyed. The problem-solving manager tends to place emphasis upon feelings and perceptions of people, and to focus upon the work climate which will determine the way information is received and which may make special communication decreasingly necessary.

9.   Output or Input

If something goes wrong does the manager start telling or listening? If a manager wishes to take a diagnostic stance toward the communication problem in his company does he accomplish more by refining the outputs or the inputs? Supposing we knew no other information about the alternatives than the titles of the courses, which management development course would we keep going: "Management Public Speaking" or "Management Listening"?

The persuasion manager tends to think in terms of output. He tends to talk of getting the message across, telling subordinates about the goals of the company, motivating people to work, seeing that people understand what management is trying to do, and putting out the message efficiently and quickly with a minimum of effort.

The problem-solving manager tends to think more in terms of input. He may ask himself such questions as the following. What information is needed? How do others look at the problem? What other solutions are there to problems that face us? How can we get more data? How can we interpret what information is available? What cues are we failing to process?

In examining the above clusters of management behavior we find that tradition and precedent are on the side of the persuasion manager. Most of the scientific evidence where it is available is on the side of the problem-solving approach. The skills and habits of persuasion are readily available. The skills, habits, and attitudes appropriate to the problem-solving approach are less easily acquired. The paths to creative problem solving are unclear. The managerial rewards are presumably very great.

References

1. Gibb, Jack R. "Defensive communication." *J. Commun.*, 1961, 11, 141-148.
2. Gibb, Jack R. "Climate for trust formation," in Bradford, Leland P., Gibb, Jack R., and Benne, Kenneth (Eds.), *T-group theory and laboratory method.* New York: Wiley, 1963.
3. Jackson, Jay M. "The Organization and Its Communication Problems." *J. Commun.*, 1959, 9, 158-167, 189.
4. Johannsen, James R., and Edmunds, Carolyn Y. *Annotated bibliography on communication in organizations.* La Jolla, California: Western Behavioral Sciences Institute, 1962.
5. Mellinger, G. D. "Interpersonal Trust As a Factor In Communication." *J. Abnorm. Soc. Psychol.*, 1956, 52, 304-309.
6. Schutz, William C. Interpersonal Underworld. *Har. Bus. Rev.*, 1958, 36, 123-135.

ACTIVE LISTENING

Carl R. Rogers
Richard E. Farson

THE MEANING OF ACTIVE LISTENING

One basic responsibility of the supervisor or manager is the development, adjustment, and integration of individual employees. He tries to develop employee potential, delegate responsibility, and achieve cooperation. To do so, he must have, among other abilities, the ability to listen intelligently and carefully to those with whom he works.

There are, however, many kinds of listening skills. The lawyer, for example, when questioning a witness, listens for contradictions, irrelevancies, errors, and weaknesses. But this is not the kind of listening skill we are concerned with. The lawyer usually is not listening in order to help the witness adjust, cooperate, or produce. Our emphasis will be on listening skills of the supervisor or manager that will help employees gain a clearer understanding of their situations, take responsibility, and cooperate with each other.

Two Examples

The kind of listening we have in mind is called "active listening." It is called "active" because the listener has a very definite responsibility. He does not passively absorb words which are spoken to him. He actively tries to grasp the facts and the feelings in what he hears, and he tries, by his listening, to help the speaker work out his own problems.

To get a clearer picture of what active listening means, let us consider two different approaches to the same work problem. The example is set in the printing industry, but the behavior of the men could surface in any organization.

Example No. 1:

Foreman: Hey, Al, I don't get this rush order. We can't handle any 50,000 run today. What do they think we are?

Supervisor: But that's the order. So get it out as soon as you can. We're under terrific pressure this week.

F: Don't they know we're behind schedule already because of that press breakdown?

S: Look, Kelly, I don't decide what goes on upstairs. I just have to see that the work gets out and that's what I'm gonna do.

F: The guys aren't gonna like this.

S: That's something you'll have to work out with them, not me.

Example No. 2:

F: Hey, Ross. I don't get this rush order. We can't handle any run of 50,000 today. What do they think we are?

S: They're pushing you pretty hard aren't they Kelly?

F: They sure are and I'm getting sore. We were just about back to schedule after the press breakdown. Now this comes along.

S: As if you didn't have enough work to do, huh?

F: Yeah. I don't know how I'm going to tell the pressman about this.

S: Hate to face him with a rush order now, is that it?

F: I really do. Joe is under a real strain today. Seems like everything we do around here is rush, rush, rush!

S: I guess you feel it's unfair to load anything more on him today.

F: Well, yeah. I know there must be plenty of pressure on everybody to get the work out, but—well, Joe doesn't deserve all the rush orders. But, if that's the way it is—I guess I'd better get the word to him and see how I can rearrange the work flow.

There are obviously many differences between these two examples. The main one, however, is that Ross, the supervisor in the second example is using the active-listening approach. He is listening and responding in a way that makes it clear that he appreciates both the meaning and the feeling behind what Kelly is saying.

Active listening does not necessarily mean long sessions spent listening to grievances, personal or otherwise. It is simply a way of approaching those problems which arise out of the usual day-to-day events of any job.

To be effective, active listening must be firmly grounded in the basic attitudes of the user. We cannot employ it as a technique if our fundamental attitudes are in conflict with its basic concepts. If we try, our behavior will be empty and sterile, and our associates will be quick to recognize such behavior. Until we can demonstrate a spirit which genuinely respects the potential worth of the individual, which considers his rights and trusts his capacity for self-direction, we cannot begin to be effective listeners.

What We Achieve by Listening

Active listening is an important way to bring about changes in people. Despite the popular notion that listening is a passive approach, clinical and research evidence clearly shows that sensitive listening is a most effective agent for individual personality change and group development. Listening brings about changes in people's attitudes toward themselves and others, and also brings about changes in their basic values and personal philosophy. People who have been listened to in this new and special way become more emotionally mature, more open to their experiences, less defensive, more democratic, and less authoritarian.

When people are listened to sensitively, they tend to listen to themselves with more care and make clear exactly what they are feeling and thinking. Group members tend to listen more to each other, become less argumentative, more ready to incorporate other points of view. Because listening reduces the threat of having one's ideas criticized, the person is better able to see them for what they are and is more likely to feel that his contributions are worthwhile.

Not the least important result of listening is the change that takes place within the listener himself. Besides the fact that listening provides more information about people than any other activity, it builds deep, positive relationships and tends to alter constructively the attitudes of the listener. Listening is a growth experience.

HOW TO LISTEN

The goal of active listening is to bring about changes in people. To achieve this end, it relies upon definite techniques —things to do and things to avoid doing. Before discussing these techniques, however, we should first understand why they are effective. To do so, we must understand how the individual personality develops.

The Growth of the Individual

Through all of our lives, from early childhood on, we have learned to think of ourselves in certain, very definite ways. We have built up pictures of ourselves. Sometimes these self-pictures are pretty realistic but at other times they are not. For example, an overage, overweight lady may fancy herself a youthful, ravishing siren, or an awkward teenager regard himself as a star athlete.

All of us have experiences which fit the way we need to think about ourselves. These we accept. But it is much harder to accept experiences which don't fit. And sometimes, if it is very important for us to hang on to this self-picture, we don't accept or admit these experiences at all.

These self-pictures are not necessarily attractive. A man, for example, may regard himself as incompetent and worthless. He may feel that he is doing his job poorly in spite of favorable appraisals by the organization. As long as he has these feelings about himself he must deny any experiences which would seem not to fit this self-picture, in this case any that might indicate to him that he is competent. It is so necessary for him to maintain this self-picture that he is threatened by anything which would tend to change it. Thus, when the organization raises his salary, it may seem to him only additional proof that he is a fraud. He must hold onto this self-picture, because, bad or good, it's the only thing he has by which he can identify himself.

This is why direct attempts to change this individual or change his self-picture are particularly threatening. He is forced to defend himself or to completely deny the experience. This denial of experience and defense of the self-picture tend to bring on rigidity of behavior and create difficulties in personal adjustment.

The active-listening approach, on the other hand, does not present a threat to the individual's self-picture. He does not have to defend it. He is able to explore it, see it for what it is, and make his own decision as to how realistic it is. He is then in a position to change.

If I want to help a man or woman reduce defensiveness and become more adaptive, I must try to remove the threat of myself as a potential changer. As long as the atmosphere is threatening, there can be no effective communication. So I must create a climate which is neither critical, evaluative, nor moralizing. The climate must foster equality and freedom, trust and understanding, acceptance and warmth. In this climate and in this climate only does the individual feel safe enough to incorporate new experiences and new values into his concept of himself. Active listening helps to create this climate.

What to Avoid

When we encounter a person with a problem, our usual response is to try to change his way of looking at things—to get him to see his situation the way we see it, or would like him to see it. We plead, reason, scold, encourage, insult, prod —anything to bring about a change in the desired direction, that is, in the direction we want him to travel. What we seldom realize, however, is that under these circumstances we are usually responding to *our own* needs to see the world in certain ways. It is always difficult for us to tolerate and understand actions which are different from the ways in which *we* believe *we* should act. If, however, we can free ourselves from the need to influence and direct others in our own paths, we enable ourselves to listen with understanding, and thereby employ the most potent available agent of change.

One problem the listener faces is that of responding to demands for decisions, judgments, and evaluations. He is constantly called upon to agree or disagree with someone or something. Yet, as he well knows, the question or challenge frequently is a masked expression of feelings or needs which the speaker is far more anxious to communicate than he is to have the surface questions answered. Because he cannot speak these feelings openly, the speaker must disguise them to himself and to others in an acceptable form. To illustrate, let us examine some typical questions and the type of answers that might best elicit the feeling beneath it.

Employee's Question	*Listener's Answer*
Just who is responsible for getting this job done?	Do you feel that you don't have enough authority?
Don't you think talent should count more than seniority in promotions?	What do you think are the reasons for your opinion?
What does the boss expect us to do about those broken-down machines?	You're tired of working with worn-out equipment, aren't you?
Don't you think my performance has improved since the last review?	Sounds as if you feel your work has picked up over these last few months?

These responses recognize the questions but leave the way open for the employee to say what is really bothering him. They allow the listener to participate in the problem or situation without shouldering all responsibility for decision-making or actions. This is a process of thinking *with* people instead of *for* or *about* them.

Passing judgment, whether critical or favorable, makes free expression difficult. Similarly, advice and information are almost always seen as efforts to change a person and thus serve as barriers to his self-expression and the development of a creative relationship. Moreover, advice is seldom taken and information hardly ever utilized. The eager young trainee probably will not become patient just because he is advised that, "The road to success is a long, difficult one, and you must be patient." And it is no more helpful for him to learn that "only one out of a hundred trainees reach top management positions."

Interestingly, it is a difficult lesson to learn that *positive evaluations* are sometimes as blocking as negative ones. It is almost as destructive to the freedom of a relationship to tell a person that he is good or capable or right, as to tell him otherwise. To evaluate him positively may make it more difficult for him to tell of the faults that distress him or the ways in which he believes he is not competent.

Encouragement also may be seen as an attempt to motivate the speaker in certain directions or hold him off rather than as support. "I'm sure everything will work out O.K." is not a helpful response to the person who is deeply discouraged about a problem.

In other words, most of the techniques and devices common to human relationships are found to be of little use in establishing the type of relationship we are seeking here.

What to Do

Just what does active listening entail, then? Basically, it requires that we get inside the speaker, that we grasp, *from his point of view,* just what it is he is communicating to us. More than that, we must convey to the speaker that we are seeing things from his point of view. To listen actively, then, means that there are several things we must do.

Listen for Total Meaning

Any message a person tries to get across usually has two components: the *content* of the message and the *feeling* or attitude underlying this content. Both are important, both give the message *meaning*. It is this total meaning of the message that we must try to understand. For example, a secretary comes to her boss and says: "I've finished that report." This message has obvious factual content and perhaps calls upon the boss for another work assignment. Suppose, on the other hand, that the secretary says: "Well! I'm finally finished with your damned report!" The factual content is the same, but the total meaning of the message has changed—and changed in an important way for both supervisor and worker. Here sensitive listening can facilitate the work relationship in this office. If the boss were to respond by simply giving his secretary some letters to type, would the secretary feel that she had gotten her total message across? Would she feel free to talk to her boss about the difficulty of her work? Would she feel better about the job, more anxious to do good work on her next assignment?

Now, on the other hand, suppose the supervisor were to respond, "Glad to get that over with, huh?" or "That was a rough one, wasn't it?" or "Guess you don't want another one like that again," or anything that tells the worker that he heard and understands. It doesn't necessarily mean that her next work assignment need be changed or that he must spend an hour listening to the worker complain about the problems she encountered. He may do a number of things differently in the light of the new information he has from the worker—but not necessarily. It's just that extra sensitivity on the part of the supervisor that can transform an average working climate into a good one.

Respond to Feelings

In some instances the content is far less important than the feeling which underlies it. To catch the full flavor or meaning of the message one must respond particularly to the feeling component. If, for instance, our secretary had said, "I'd like to pile up all those carbons and make a bonfire out of them!" responding to content would be obviously absurd. But to respond to her disgust or anger in trying to work with the report recognizes the meaning of this message. There are various shadings of these components in the meaning of any message. Each time the listener must try to remain sensitive to the total meaning the message has to the speaker. What is she trying to tell me? What does this mean to her? How does she see this situation?

Note All Cues

Not all communication is verbal. The speaker's words alone don't tell us everything he is communicating. And hence, truly sensitive listening requires that we become aware of several kinds of communication besides verbal. The way in which a speaker hesitates in his speech can tell us much about his feelings. So too can the inflection of his voice. He may stress certain points loudly and clearly, and he may mumble others. We should also note such things as the person's facial expressions, body posture, hand movements, eye movements, and breathing. All of these help to convey his total message.

What We Communicate by Listening

The first reaction of most people when they consider listening as a possible method for dealing with human beings is that listening cannot be sufficient in itself. Because it is passive, they feel, listening does not communicate anything to the speaker. Actually, nothing could be farther from the truth.

By consistently listening to a speaker you are conveying the idea that: "I'm interested in you as a person, and I think that what you feel is important. I respect your thoughts, and even if I don't agree with them, I know that they are valid for you. I feel sure that you have a contribution to make. I'm not trying to change you or evaluate you. I just want to understand you. I think you're worth listening to, and I want you to know that I'm the kind of a person you can talk to."

The subtle but most important aspect of this is that it is the *demonstration* of the message that works. Although it is most difficult to convince someone that you respect him by *telling* him so, you are much more likely to get this message across by really *behaving* that way—by actually *having* and *demonstrating* respect for this person. Listening does this most effectively.

Like other behavior, listening behavior is contagious. This has implications for all communications problems, whether between two people, or within a large organization. To insure good communication between associates up and down the line, one must first take the responsibility for setting a pattern of listening. Just as one learns that anger is usually met with anger, argument with argument, and deception with deception, one can learn that listening can be met with listening. Every person who feels responsibility in a situation can set the tone of the interaction, and the important lesson in this is that any behavior exhibited by one person will eventually be responded to with similar behavior in the other person.

It is far more difficult to stimulate constructive behavior in another person but far more valuable. Listening is one of these constructive behaviors, but if one's attitude is to "wait out" the speaker rather than really listen to him, it will fail. The one who consistently listens with understanding, however, is the one who eventually is most likely to be listened to. If you really want to be heard and understood by another, you can develop him as a potential listener, ready for new ideas, provided you can first develop yourself in these ways and sincerely listen with understanding and respect.

Testing for Understanding

Because understanding another person is actually far more difficult than it at first seems, it is important to test constantly your ability to see the world in the way the speaker sees it. You can do this by reflecting in your own words what the speaker seems to mean by his words and actions. His response to this will tell you whether or not he feels understood. A good rule of thumb is to assume that one never really understands until he can communicate this understanding to the other's satisfaction.

Here is an experiment to test your skill in listening. The next time you become involved in a lively or controversial discussion with another person, stop for a moment and suggest that you adopt this ground rule for continued discussion. Before either participant in the discussion can make a point or express an opinion of his own, he must first restate aloud the previous point or position of the other person. This restatement must be in his own words (merely parroting the words of another does not prove that one has understood, but only that he has heard the words). The restatement must be accurate enough to satisfy the speaker before the listener can be allowed to speak for himself.

You might find this procedure useful in a meeting where feelings run high and people express themselves on topics of emotional concern to the group. Before another member of the group expresses his own feelings and thought, he must rephrase the *meaning* expressed by the previous speaker to that person's satisfaction. All the members in the group should be alert to the changes in the emotional climate and the quality of the discussion when this approach is used.

PROBLEMS IN ACTIVE LISTENING

Active listening is not an easy skill to acquire. It demands practice. Perhaps more important, it may require changes in our own basic attitudes. These changes come slowly and sometimes with considerable difficulty. Let us look at some of the major problems in active listening and what can be done to overcome them.

The Personal Risk

To be effective in active listening, one must have a sincere interest in the speaker. We all live in glass houses as far as our attitudes are concerned. They always show through. And if we are only making a pretense of interest in the speaker, he will quickly pick this up, either consciously or subconsciously. And once he does, he will no longer express himself freely.

Active listening carries a strong element of personal risk. If we manage to accomplish what we are describing here—to sense the feelings of another person, to understand the meaning his experiences have for him, to see the world as he sees it — we risk being changed ourselves. For example, if we permit ourselves to listen our way into the life of a person we do not know or approve of—to get the meaning that life has for him — we risk coming to see the world as he sees it. We are threatened when we give up, even momentarily, what we believe and start thinking in someone else's terms. It takes a great deal of inner security and courage to be able to risk one's self in understanding another.

For the manager, the courage to take another's point of

view generally means that he must see *himself* through another's eyes—he must be able to see himself as others see him. To do this may sometimes be unpleasant, but it is far more *difficult* than unpleasant. We are so accustomed to viewing ourselves in certain ways—to seeing and hearing only what we want to see and hear—that it is extremely difficult for a person to free himself from the need to see things his way.

Developing an attitude of sincere interest in the speaker is thus no easy task. It can be developed only by being willing to risk seeing the world from the speaker's point of view. If we have a number of such experiences, however, they will shape an attitude which will allow us to be truly genuine in our interest in the speaker.

Hostile Expressions

The listener will often hear negative, hostile expressions directed at himself. Such expressions are always hard to listen to. No one likes to hear hostile words or experience hostility which is directed against them. And it is not easy to get to the point where one is strong enough to permit these attacks without finding it necessary to defend himself or retaliate.

Because we all fear that people will crumble under the attack of genuine negative feelings, we tend to perpetuate an attitude of pseudo-peace. It is as if we cannot tolerate conflict at all for fear of the damage it could do to us, to the situation, to the others involved. But of course the real damage is done by the denial and suppression of negative feelings.

Out-of-Place Expressions

Expressions dealing with behavior that is not usually acceptable in our society also pose problems for the listener. These out-of-place expressions can take the extreme forms that psychotherapists hear—such as homicidal fantasies or expressions of sexual perversity. The listener often blocks out such expressions because of their obvious threatening quality. At less extreme levels, we all find unnatural or inappropriate behavior difficult to handle. Behavior that brings on a problem situation may be anything from telling an "off-color" story in mixed company to seeing a man cry.

In any face-to-face situation, we will find instances of this type which will momentarily, if not permanently, block any communication. In any organization, expressions of weakness or incompetency will generally be regarded as unacceptable and therefore will block good two-way communication. For example, it is difficult to listen to a manager tell of his feelings of failure in being able to "take charge" of a situation in his department because *all* administrators are supposed to be able to "take charge."

Accepting Positive Feelings

It is both interesting and perplexing to note that negative or hostile feelings or expressions are much easier to deal with in any face-to-face relationship than are positive feelings. This is especially true for the manager because the culture expects him to be independent, bold, clever, and aggressive and manifest no feelings of warmth, gentleness, and intimacy. He therefore comes to regard these feelings as soft and inappropriate. But no matter how they are regarded, they remain a human need. The denial of these feelings in himself and his associates does not get the manager out of the problem of dealing with them. The feelings simply become veiled and confused. If recognized they would work for the total effort; unrecognized, they work against it.

Emotional Danger Signals

The listener's own emotions are sometimes a barrier to active listening. When emotions are at their height, when listening is most necessary, it is most difficult to set aside one's own concerns and be understanding. Our emotions are often our own worst enemies when we try to become listeners. The more involved and invested we are in a particular situation or problem, the less we are likely to be willing or able to listen to the feelings and attitudes of others. That is, the more we find it necessary to respond to our own needs, the less we are able to respond to the needs of another. Let us look at some of the main danger signals that warn us that our emotions may be interfering with our listening.

Defensiveness

The points about which one is most vocal and dogmatic, the points which one is most anxious to impose on others—these are always the points one is trying to talk oneself into believing. So one danger signal becomes apparent when you find yourself stressing a point or trying to convince another. It is at these times that you are likely to be less secure and consequently less able to listen.

Resentment of Opposition

It is always easier to listen to an idea which is similar to one of your own than to an opposing view. Sometimes, in order to clear the air, it is helpful to pause for a moment when you feel your ideas and position being challenged, reflect on the situation, and express your concern to the speaker.

Clash of Personalities

Here again, our experience has consistently shown us that the genuine expression of feelings on the part of the listener will be more helpful in developing a sound relationship than the suppression of them. This is so whether the feelings be resentment, hostility, threat, or admiration. A basically honest relationship, whatever the nature of it, is the most productive of all. The other party becomes secure when he learns that the listener can express his feelings honestly and openly to him. We should keep this in mind when we begin to fear a clash of personalities in the listening relationship. Otherwise, fear of our own emotions will choke off full expression of feelings.

Listening to Ourselves

To listen to oneself is a prerequisite to listening to others. And it is often an effective means of dealing with the problems we have outlined above. When we are most aroused, excited, and demanding, we are least able to understand our own feelings and attitudes. Yet, in dealing with the problems of others, it becomes most important to be sure of one's own position, values, and needs.

The ability to recognize and understand the meaning which a particular episode has for you, with all the feelings which it stimulates in you, and the ability to express this meaning when you find it getting in the way of active listening, will clear the air and enable you once again to be free to listen. That is, if some person or situation touches off feelings within you which tend to block your attempts to listen with understanding, begin listening to yourself. It is much more helpful in developing effective relationships to avoid suppressing these feelings. Speak them out as clearly as you can, and try to enlist the other person as a listener to your feelings. A person's listening ability is limited by his ability to listen to himself.

ACTIVE LISTENING AND ORGANIZATION GOALS

"How can listening improve productivity?"

"We're in business, and it is a rugged, fast, competitive affair. How are we going to find time to counsel our employees?"

"We have to concern ourselves with organizational problems first."

"We can't afford to spend all day listening when there is work to do."

"What's morale got to do with service to the public?"

"Sometimes we have to sacrifice an individual for the good of the rest of the people in the organization."

Those of us who are trying to advance the listening approach in organizations hear these comments frequently. And because they are so honest and legitimate, they pose a real problem. Unfortunately, the answers are not so clear-cut as the questions.

Individual Importance

One answer is based on an assumption that is central to the listening approach. That assumption is: the kind of behavior which helps the individual will eventually be the best thing that could be done for the work group. Or saying it another way: the things that are best for the individual are best for the organization. This is a conviction of ours, based on our experience in psychology and education. The research evidence from organizations is still coming in. We find that putting the group first, at the expense of the individual,

besides being an uncomfortable individual experience, does
not unify the group. In fact, it tends to make the group less
a group. The members become anxious and suspicious.

We are not at all sure in just what ways the group does
benefit from a concern demonstrated for an individual, but
we have several strong leads. One is that the group feels more
secure when an individual member is being listened to and
provided for with concern and sensitivity. And we assume
that a secure group will ultimately be a better group. When
each individual feels that he need not fear exposing himself
to the group, he is likely to contribute more freely and spontaneously. When the leader of a group responds to the individual, puts the individual first, the other members of the group
will follow suit, and the group comes to act as a unit in recognizing and responding to the needs of a particular member.
This positive, constructive action seems to be a much more
satisfying experience for a group than the experience of dis-
pensing with a member.

Listening and Productivity

As to whether or not listening or any other activity
designed to better human relations in an organization actually
makes the organization more productive—whether morale has
a definite relationship to performance is not known for sure.
There are some who frankly hold that there is no relationship
to be expected between morale and productivity—that productivity often depends upon the social misfit, the eccentric, or
the isolate. And there are some who simply choose to work in
a climate of cooperation and harmony, in a high-morale group,
quite aside from the question of achievement or productivity.

A report from the survey Research Center[1] at the University of Michigan on research conducted at the Prudential Life
Insurance Company lists seven findings relating to production
and morale. First-line supervisors in high-production work
groups were found to differ from those in low-production
groups in that they:

1. Are under less close supervision from their own supervisors.
2. Place less direct emphasis upon production as the goal.
3. Encourage employee participation in the making of
decisions.

4. Are more employee-centered.
5. Spend more of their time in supervision and less in straight production work.
6. Have a greater feeling of confidence in their supervisory roles.
7. Feel that they know where they stand with the company.

After mentioning that other dimensions of morale, such as identification with the company, intrinsic job satisfaction, and satisfaction with job status, were not found significantly related to productivity, the report goes on to suggest the following psychological interpretation:

> People are more effectively motivated when they are given some degree of freedom in the way in which they do their work than when every action is prescribed in advance. They do better when some degree of decision-making about their jobs is possible than when all decisions are made for them. They respond more adequately when they are treated as personalities than as cogs in a machine. In short if the ego motivations of self-determination, of self-expression, of a sense of personal worth can be tapped, the individual can be more effectively energized. The use of external sanctions, or pressuring for production may work to some degree, but not to the extent that the more internalized motives do. When the individual comes to identify himself with his job and with the work of the his group, human resources are much more fully utilized in the production process.

The Survey Research Center has also conducted studies among workers in other industries. In discussing the results of these studies, Robert L. Kahn writes:

> In the studies of clerical workers, railroad workers, and workers in heavy industry, the supervisors with the better production records gave a larger proportion of their time to supervisory functions, especially to the interpersonal aspects of their jobs. The supervisors of the lower-producing sections were more likely to spend their time in tasks which the men themselves were performing, or in the paper-work aspects of their jobs.[2]

Maximum Creativeness

There may never be enough research evidence to satisfy everyone on this question. But speaking from an organizational point of view, in terms of the problem of developing resources for productivity, the maximum creativeness and productive effort of the human beings in the organization are the richest untapped source of power available. The difference between the maximum productive capacity of people and that output which the organization is now realizing is immense. We simply suggest that this maximum capacity might be closer to realization if we sought to release the motivation that already exists within people rather than try to stimulate them externally.

This releasing of the individual is made possible first of all by listening, with respect and understanding. Listening is a beginning toward making the individual feel himself worthy of making contributions, and this could result in a very dynamic and productive organization. Profit making organizations are never too rugged or too busy to take time to procure the most efficient technological advances or to develop rich sources of raw materials. But technology and materials are but paltry resources in comparison with the resources that are already within the people in the organization.

G. L. Clements, of Jewel Tea Co., Inc., in talking about the collaborative approach to management says:

> We feel that this type of approach recognizes that there is a secret ballot going on at all times among the people in any business. They vote for or against their supervisors. A favorable vote for the supervisor shows up in the cooperation, teamwork, understanding, and production of the group. To win this secret ballot, each supervisor must share the problems of his group and work for them.[3]

The decision to spend time listening to employees is a decision each supervisor or manager has to make for himself. Managers increasingly must deal with people and their relationships rather than turning out goods and services. The minute we take a man from work and make him a supervisor he is removed from the basic production of goods or services and now must begin relating to men and women instead of nuts and bolts. People are different from things, and our supervisor is called upon for a different line of skills completely. These new tasks call for a special kind of person. The development of the supervisor as a listener is a first step in becoming this special person.

Suggested Readings

Borman, Ernest G., Nichols, Ralph G., Howell, William S., and Shapiro, George L. *Interpersonal Communication in the Modern Organization.* Englewood Cliffs, N. J.: Prentice Hall, 1969.

Presents a practical, non-academic treatment of communication in the modern organization. Written by a group of nationally recognized authorities in interpersonal communication.

Burns, Robert K. *The Listening Techniques.* Chicago: Industrial Relations Center, The University of Chicago, 1958.

Presents in outline format various aspects of listening skills concluding with a table displaying key listening techniques, the purpose of each, and how each can be used.

Demers, Robert W. "Are We Listening?" *Supervision,* 35 (December 1973), pp. 3-6.

Describes some of the errors which impair listening and suggests constructive ways to improve and build good listening skills.

Ehat, D. M. and Schnapper, M. "What Your Employees' Non-Verbal Cues are Telling You." *Administrative Management,* 35 (August 1974), pp. 64-66.

Grikscheit, Gary M. and Crissy, William J. E. "Improving Interpersonal Communications Skill," *MSU Business Topics,* 21 (Autumn 1973), pp. 63-68.

Develops the idea that the more adept an individual becomes at attending to incoming signals, the more effective he will become as a communicator.

Leavitt, Harold J. *Managerial Psychology: An Introduction to Individuals, Pairs, and Groups in Organizations.* 2nd ed. Chicago: The University of Chicago Press, 1972. In paperback, 1972.

The second section of this book is concerned with the individual interacting with others. Leavitt's *Readings in Managerial Psychology* serves as a supplement to this text.

Leavitt, Harold J. and Pondy, Louis R., eds. *Readings in Managerial Psychology*. 2nd. ed. Chicago: The University of Chicago Press, 1974. In paperback.

> Contains classic articles by various authorities including A. H. Maslow, Frederick Herzberg, Douglas M. McGregor, and William R. Dill.

Likert, Rensis. *New Patterns of Management.* New York: McGraw Hill, 1961.

> Reports (in Chapters 2-4) of the results of the University of Michigan Survey Research Center's investigation of the relationship between group morale and productivity.

Nierenberg, Gerald I. and Calero, Henry H. "Metatalk: The Art of Deciphering Everyday Conversation," *MBA,* 8 (January 1974), pp. 42-48.

> Discusses how phrases in daily conversation mean much more or much less than the words suggest, a type of conversation which the authors characterize as metatalk.

Turner, Arthur N. and Lombard, George F. F. *Interpersonal Behavior and Administration.* New York: The Free Press, 1969.

> Discusses interpersonal communication in formal organizations and ways of practicing and improving the skill of listening with understanding. Includes cases and explanatory materials as aids in studying the cases; reprints articles by leading behavioral scientists on the process of person-to-person communication.

---

[1] "Productivity, Supervision, and Employee Morale," *Human Relations,* Series 1, Report 1, Survey Research Center, University of Michigan.

[2] Kahn, Robert L., "The Human Factors Underlying Industrial Production," *Michigan Business Review,* November 1952.

[3] Clements, G.L. "Time for 'Democracy in Action' at the Executive Level," An address given before the A.M.A. Personnel Conference, February 28, 1951.

MANAGERIAL
DECISION MAKING

IV

■ No other dimension typifies the role of managerial action in the organization better than decision making. In fact, it is sometimes useful to distinguish managers from nonmanagers by the fact that managers make decisions with the goals of the organization in mind whereas nonmanagers do not. Further, virtually all management writers see decision making as one of the key management process variables. However, they do not all agree on the definition of or the steps in the decision process itself. For example, many writers believe that the rational or objective process is central to decision making. For the most part, they focus on the selection of a "best" alternative. McKenney and Keen, however, see decision making as a somewhat "irrational" decision process that involves, among other variables, the cognitive style of the decision maker.

An obvious first step in decision making is to define the problem. MacCrimmon, in the first selection, views problem definition "as a gap between the decision maker's desired state and his existing state. The desired state consists of the goals and objectives he is trying to attain. The existing state is described by the decision maker's resources at some point in time." Further, the decision problem is influenced by the decision maker's perceptions of the decision environment, his or her motivation to resolve the problem, the factors that are controllable and uncontrollable in the situation, and the degree to which the problem can be solved using current resources.

MacCrimmon focuses on preliminary diagnosis as a crucial step in the resolution of problems. This diagnosis may often involve breaking problems into "smaller pieces" and is a basis for the management by objectives model (See Part II, Section A). The author cautions, however, that this process of breaking up the problem into small sections is useful only if the problem subparts are not highly interrelated.

The second article, by James McKenney and Peter Keen, expands MacCrimmon's introduction to problem solving by examining decision making in terms of "the processes through which individuals organize the information they perceive in their environment, bringing to bear habits and strategies of thinking." Their resultant model of cognitive styles is based on two variables, information gathering and information evaluation. Each variable is associated with two cognitive styles, which results in a four-quadrant model. Perceptive individuals focus on relationships when gathering information, whereas receptive individuals focus on detail. When evaluating information, systematic individuals tend to structure problems according to some method, whereas intuitive individuals are more likely to use trial and error. The cognitive styles are shown to affect not only the type of problems that are selected for solution but also the effectiveness of the problem solver. The authors then go on to examine the cognitive decision styles of management scientists and managers. This approach to decision making is extremely important and represents many of the views of researchers who work in this field today. As the authors point out, there may be no "right" way of solving problems, since the demands of different problem types and the diversity of cognitive styles available in an organization affects not only the results of attempted problem solution but the very nature of problem definition.

The final article, by T. J. Lincoln, focuses on the information needs of managers in a changing environment and represents the important field of management information systems and their increasing effect on the decision maker. Lincoln explores the ramifications of the current inflation problem by reporting the conclusions reached by senior executives from British companies at a recent management conference. Among the more important conclusions reached was the need for flexibility of the information system and flexibility in managerial ability "to examine and analyze cross company data." The key to understanding the article is best expressed by the following passage.

> The traditional systems design approach of asking the users for their requirements becomes increasingly inappropriate when their requirements are changing rapidly and unpredictably. In this case system designers must perform a more fundamental analysis of the critical business functions and establish with the help of senior management which functions are likely to change and in what manner.

This type of fundamental planning effort has an obvious effect on other key management areas examined throughout this text.

Managerial Decision-Making

Kenneth R. MacCrimmon

INTRODUCTION

Choice and the Decision Process

The core of decision-making is *choice*. In order for a decision situation to exist, there must be two or more alternatives to choose among. Choice, however, is only the culmination of earlier parts of the decision process. Choice requires some criteria for selecting one alternative over another. These criteria will be linked to the decision maker's objectives. The criteria are applied to the possible outcomes of alternatives. The possible outcomes depend on the uncertainty in the decision environment and on the actions available to the decision maker. Through search and information acquisition, the decision maker learns about the uncertainties and generates the alternatives. The search and information acquisition are influenced by how the decision problem is recognized and defined. Hence, in this chapter, we shall be concerned with *choice* and the *decision processes* proceeding it.

Decision: Thought and Action

Decision-making is a bridge between thought and action. The decision process itself involves both *thought* and *action*. The process following choice is directed toward implementing the thought and action that preceded it (Simon, 1957a). The intertwining of thought and action are at the heart of management. If management is regarded as functional, then decision-making underlies all the functions; if structural, decision-making infuses the structure. Simon (1960) treats "decision-making" and "management" synonymously.

The terms "problem-solving" and "judgment" imply many of the same thought processes as "decision-making." Perhaps they imply somewhat less of an action orientation, but for the purposes of this chapter we shall not bother distinguishing between them. *Decision-making*, then, will mean

From Joseph W. McGuire, *Contemporary Management: Issues and Viewpoints*, © 1974, pp. 445–451. Reprinted by permission of Prentice-Hall, Inc., Englewood Cliffs, New Jersey.

the processes involving both thought and action that culminate in an act of choice.

A thought-oriented mode would view decision-making in terms of *information* acquisition, processing, and communication. The steps of the process could be described as a widening or narrowing of the decision maker's information set. In contrast, an action-oriented mode would view decision-making in terms of *resource* acquisition, commitment, and allocation. The steps of the process could be described as a widening or narrowing of the decision maker's resource set. Both the information processing and the resource processing modes will be used in this chapter to describe the decision-making process.

Elements of Decision-Making

The main elements of decision-making are a *decision maker* in a *decision environment* (MacCrimmon, 1970). For expositional convenience, in describing basic concepts we shall usually refer to a "decision maker," which can mean either an individual, a group, an organization, or a society. The primary considerations for a decision maker are his *values*, his *beliefs*, and his *resources*. That is, in understanding his decision processes we are interested in what he wants, what he knows, and what he has. The various theories to be considered assume differences in values, beliefs, and resources.

The decision environment can be characterized in many ways but perhaps the most pervasive dimensions are complexity and uncertainty. These are the aspects we shall emphasize in this chapter.

Placing a decision maker in a decision environment leads to a decision-making process, such as that described briefly at the beginning of the chapter. This chapter is organized in terms of the decision-making process. Many listings of the steps in a decision process are available, most of them stemming from Dewey (1933) and Wallas (1926); the one used here seems compatible with most.

In real decision situations, one seldom observes the clear, step-by-step process such as that described here. Steps in the process proceed simultaneously, some steps are skipped, steps are repeated, and so on. There are obvious interactions, feedbacks, and cycles. Also, decision situations intermingle; decisions are imbedded in decisions. All these complications are quite real and usually quite rational. In this chapter we try to allude to them within the linear constraint of chapter topics.

Theories of Decision-Making

The theories of decision-making are of two basic kinds. *Normative* theories describe how decisions *should* be made, whereas *descriptive* theories describe how decisions *are* made (Marschak, 1964). We shall consider both types here but the normative theories that are of most interest are those that can be applied and are based on solid premises. The most interesting descriptive theories are those that describe what effective decision makers do.

The decision maker is subject to information processing and other constraints that limit his rationality (Simon, 1957b). On the other hand, the constraints on effective decision makers are probably not so binding as are those that limit poor decision makers. Hence, we shall consider rational behavior subject to the bounds that a purposeful, careful decision maker would confront.

The theories we consider are drawn from many disciplines, including economics, psychology, philosophy, statistics, mathematics, and management itself. The theories will be introduced at those parts of the decision process in which they have a contribution to make. This approach has the disadvantage of fragmenting the theories, so it may be more difficult, for example, to piece together the subjective probability, utility, risk, and expected utility components of statistical decision theory. On the other hand, the process type of format seems to have the advantage of not emphasizing the existing packaging of the theories and makes more apparent the points at which particular theories make a major, minor, or zero contribution. It also allows an opportunity to bring in some minor theories or techniques that may be useful at only small stages of the process—but useful nevertheless.

Hopefully, this format will allow us to (1) pull together and organize the diverse literature on decision-making, (2) provide a concise summary of the main ideas and results useful to managerial decisions, (3) evaluate the theory and results, and (4) suggest ways that students of decisions or decision makers can piece together those components that would be of most use to them.

PROBLEM DEFINITION

Decision Problems

A decision situation can be viewed as a *gap* between the decision maker's desired state and his existing state. The *desired state* consists of the goals and objectives he is trying to attain. The *existing state* is described by the decision maker's resources at some point in time (Dunker, 1945; Newell, Shaw, and Simon, 1958).

A decision maker's desired state and his existing state (whether current or anticipated) seldom coincide exactly, yet he is not constantly involved in decision-making in all areas of his interests. A gap between desired and existing states, then, is a necessary but not a sufficient condition for decision-making behavior to occur. The conditions that determine a *decision problem* are: (1) a *gap* between desired and existing states, (2) *attention* directed to a particular gap, (3) *motivation* to reduce the gap, and (4) an *ability* to do something about it. We shall consider each of these elements in more detail in the next four subsections.

Gap between Existing and Desired States   In the simplest case, the decision maker's desired state may be described by a single dimension. In the classical theory of the firm, for example, the only objective considered is maximization of profit (Marshall, 1890). Real business firms, however, pursue multiple goals—such as profitability, return on investment, share of market, managerial control, growth, and so on (Drucker, 1954; Johnsen, 1968; Carter, 1971).

There are various ways that gaps between existing and desired states can arise or be altered. The desired state may change while the existing state stays the same; the existing state may change while the desired state stays the same; or both the existing and desired states may change. The first case is characteristic of a revision in goals owing to, say, new survey information about the size of a potential market. These situations would be anticipated *opportunities*. The second case is characteristic of something going wrong in a system, such as production costs soaring. These situations are *threats* to the decision maker. The third case is a combination of the two and may occur, for example, when new product ideas come out of research and development activity (Ansoff, 1965).

Perceiving Decision Problems   The many dimensions of existing and desired states imply many possible gaps. The limited capacity of a decision maker clearly precludes him from dealing with many different things at the same time (Miller, 1956; Simon, 1957). Hence, the gap will have to be above some minimal threshold in order for it to be perceived (Lewin, 1946). Cyert and March (1963) discuss the process by which attention sequentially shifts from one gap to another and how this shift can reduce internal conflict. Drucker (1963) points out that threats are more readily perceived than opportunities and subsequently become an overwhelming concern of inefficient managers.

The information about the gap may come from various sources. The differences resulting from a decision occasion being initiated by a communication from a subordinate versus a superior are discussed by Barnard (1938), along with other practical aspects of decision occasions.

Motivation to Resolve   The motivation on the part of the decision maker to reduce the gap between existing and desired states will depend on the size of the gap and on how important the reduction of such a gap is in achieving further ends. The gap does not merely have to be perceived but must be above some threshold to make its reduction worthwhile (Lewin, 1946).

Controllability and Solvability   Clearly it is not enough to be aware of the existence of the gap and to be motivated to reduce it. In order for a meaningful decision problem to exist, the decision maker must be able to take actions that will reduce the gap. This suggests classifying the factors in a decision situation into those that are *controllable* and those that are *uncontrollable*. Those that are partially controllable can be decomposed into their controllable and uncontrollable components (Howard, 1971). If there are no possibilities for action in the controllable class, there is not much use in the decision maker trying to "solve the problem." For even if he was able to generate a solution, there would be no way to implement it. The elements that are controllable depend on the resources that the decision maker is willing to expend in order to obtain control—and this will be part of the decision problem.

Another consideration is whether the problem is solvable even if there are many controllable elements at the decision maker's command. In the extreme, one might say that any problem is resolvable if the appropriate resources are at hand. In practical decision situations the question to ask is whether the problem can be resolved for a feasible level of resource expenditures.

Influences on the Identification of Problems

Premises and Constraints   In diagnosing problems, the decision maker will bring in various premises. Sometimes these premises may be stated explicitly (e.g., no one is to be fired), whereas at other times, and more frequently, they are held implicitly by the decision maker. The premises may be based on interpretations read into the problem information. Rokeach (1960) has described how people often try to resolve problems based on unjustified implicit premises.

The premises may also be regarded as constraints that the decision maker imposes on the problem. Initially most of the constraints are open but as the decision maker proceeds to identify the problem he begins to close these open constraints (Reitman, 1964). If he proceeds judiciously, he efficiently resolves the problem. The imposition or the closing of inappropriate constraints, however, may eliminate the possibility of resolution.

Set   One basis for unjustified premises and interpretations is when a psychological set has developed and a decision maker sees problems as being identical to ones he has faced in the past. Luchins and Luchins (1959) have discussed the rigidity in behavior and stereotyped response that can arise in such a situation. The business analog to this is the individual who sees all problems he encounters as being of the same type—for example, an operations researcher viewing everything as a linear programming problem no matter what the problem differences and its susceptibility to other methods.

There are cases, obviously, when great efficiencies can be attained by identifying a problem as similar to another and using the techniques that were applied to solve the first. Specialized staff and programs in business firms are testimony to this. Gardner (1967) has given examples of seemingly different problems that are similar to tic-tac-toe.

Problem Types

Well-structured and Ill-structured Problems   Simon (1960) and Minsky (1961) have identified two endpoints on a continuum of decision problems. At one end are the well-structured or programmed problems that are repetitive and routine and for which a definite procedure that will yield a solution has been worked out. At the other end are the ill-structured or unprogrammed problems that are novel and important and for which there are no routine solution procedures.

Polya (1957) has subdivided well-structured problems into "problems to find" and "problems to prove." Reitman (1964) has identified six types of ill-structured problems in terms of what is known about (1) the initial (i.e., existing) state, (2) the terminal (i.e., desired) state, and (3) the solution process. Obviously, in most managerial decision situations we are dealing with ill-structured problems. Both Reitman (1964) and Emmet (1960) discuss practical examples of types of ill-structured (or "open") problems.

Quality-dominant and Acceptance-dominant Problems   Maier (1963) has provided another useful distinction in problem types by considering the need for high quality and the need for high acceptance in a decision situation. If the problem is one for which quality is much more important than acceptance, then a non-participative decision seems appropriate. If, however, acceptance of the decision is more important than quality, then a group decision procedure seems desirable. Decisions that require both high quality and high acceptance are handled by combined procedures.

Diagnoses and Preliminary Steps Toward Resolution

Alternative Diagnoses   Clearly, the way a decision problem is defined can have a considerable effect on the types of alternatives considered and the types of resources utilized to solve it. This is illustrated nicely in a simple experiment of Maier's in which two strings hanging from the ceiling have to be tied together, but holding the end of one and trying to walk to the other does not succeed. Consideration is given to whether the problem is defined as (1) the string is too short, (2) the arm is too short, (3) the string will not stay in the proper place, or (4) the string will not swing over. He shows how the definition influences the use of the available resources (e.g., a pair of pliers) for resolving the problem (Maier, 1931).

Diagnosis of Causes of Disequilibria   The diagnosis of decision situations in which a system is temporarily out of equilibrium requires determining what the difficulty is and the steps to take to restore equilibrium. Kepner and Tregoe, (1965) present a very practical approach for dealing with such cases. The decision maker is advised to first attempt to determine what are the characteristics of the out-of-control part and what are the characteristics of the in-control part. Following such a "what is" and "what is not" determination, an attempt is made to find single *causes* that will explain the "is" part and will discriminate it from the "is not" part. Changes are systematically probed until the equilibrium restoring action can be taken. Although Kepner and Tregoe do not limit the scope of their method to these types of problems, it is difficult to see how it could be used more generally, for example, in problems involving structural changes or in open-ended problems (e.g., controlling inflation).

Working Forward or Working Backward   A decision maker may approach a problem by either trying to work forward or backward. In the terms we have used earlier, he may work (forward) from the existing state to see how it might be transformed into the desired state, or he may work (back) from the desired state to see if a means for arriving at the existing state can be developed (Feldman and Kanter, 1964; Miller, Galanter, and Pribram, 1960; Feldman and Kanter, 1965). Both techniques seem to be used in actual decision-making. Working forward is the most apparent and hence most common tactic, but some techniques, such as dynamic programming, emphasize working backward (Bellman and Dreyfus, 1961).

Means-end factoring   The solution of a problem implies eliminating the gap between the existing state and the desired state. The gap can be reduced by applying appropriate operators (Newell and Simon, 1961). The operators are the "means" to the "end" of reducing the gap. After the operator is applied, there may be a new gap (i.e., end) to be reduced and hence new means may be considered. A computer program, the General Problem Solver, has been constructed to operate in this fashion (Newell, Shaw, and Simon, 1960).

The resolution of most problems involves factoring them into subproblems, which in turn may be factored, and so on. This process leads to a hierarchy of means and ends. Simon (1961) has given an example of a watchmaker who by arranging his assembly in terms of subparts can be much more productive when interrupted than a watchmaker who tries to assemble complete clocks at one time (see also Koestler, 1967). Breaking up a problem into subproblems is only useful if there are not too many interrelationships among the subparts, otherwise the coordination problems would clearly outweigh the decomposition. Simon and Ando (1961) have looked at some of the technical conditions for such a decomposition. Decomposition obviously allows the use of specialization and division of labor when the decision maker's subunits have differential capabilities. It also allows for additional parallelism in resolving the problem; hence, the decision maker's sequential processing abilities (Simon, 1969) can be overcome. Braybrooke and Lindblom (1963) have also emphasized this common form of problem separation with their development of concepts of "disjointedness."

Summary: Problem Definition

As the bibliography at the end of this chapter indicates, the literatures on Gestalt psychology, cognitive processes, and management techniques are most useful in problem definition. Most economic and statistical studies pick up after the problem has been defined and so have little to contribute here. It is popularly asserted that once a problem has been correctly defined, the decision situation is essentially resolved. Either this is tautological (implying that the correct definition involves all the other steps in the decision process) or it is false. It may serve, however, to emphasize that careful attention must be given to defining decision problems. If all decision problems one encounters must be resolved "yesterday," there are obvious pressures against paying much attention to diagnosis before making choices.

How managers' minds work

Studies reveal implications of thinking processes for the implementation of analytic models

James L. McKenney and
Peter G.W. Keen

A number of researchers have pointed to particular aspects of thinking and personality that differ between the people who build models and those who use them. Obviously, management scientists and general managers think differently. In an effort to narrow this gap, the authors discuss their recent research on cognitive style, which provides a means of developing strategies of action for the management scientist and a useful way of focusing on the implementation of analytic models for the general manager.

Mr. McKenney is professor of business administration at the Harvard Business School, where he teaches and studies management information systems. Mr. Keen is assistant professor of organizational psychology and management at the Alfred P. Sloan School of Management, Massachusetts Institute of Technology.

A common topic in management literature over the past few years has been the difference between managers and management scientists, usually in relation to the argument that their association has not been a productive one. For example, a recent article by C. Jackson Grayson, Jr., compares the situation with C.P. Snow's famous notion of the two cultures of science and humanities:

"Managers and management scientists are operating as two separate cultures, each with its own goals, languages, and methods. Effective cooperation—and even communication—between the two is just about minimal." [1]

Perhaps this is an overpessimistic viewpoint, but it is one that is expressed often and by individuals who have substantial experience with the use of analytic methods in management.

Management science techniques have been very successful in such areas of business as logistics planning, resource allocation, financial forecasting, and so forth. It appears that, on the whole, these techniques have found the applications for which they are best suited, and managers make substantial and continued use of them.

However, in other areas of business they have been unable to gain any real foothold. Most obviously, they have had little impact on areas of decision making where the management problems do not lend themselves to explicit formulation, where there are ambiguous or overlapping criteria for action, and where the manager operates through intuition.

1. "Management Science and Business Practice," HBR July-August 1973, p. 41.

The major issue for management science as a discipline now seems to be to get managers in such situations to make use of the formal techniques that can clearly be so helpful to them but have not yet been so in practice. There seem to be two main factors affecting this problem.

One concerns the actual techniques available. Obviously, process chemists use linear programming because it suits the constraints and natures of the problems they deal with.

The primary factor, however, is the differences in approach and behavior between the two cultures. A feature under little control by either manager or scientist is that each has a distinctive style of thinking and problem solving. In its own context, each style is highly effective but not easily communicated to the other. The differences in thinking are neither "good" nor "bad"; they simply exist.

In a way, it is platitudinous to state that managers and scientists are different, but a reason for focusing explicitly on this factor is to examine the argument, maintained by management writers, that to bridge the gap between the two groups each should become a little more like the other. In this view, the differences themselves are the problem, and education is generally recommended as the solution: the manager should be trained in elementary quantitative techniques, and the scientist, in interpersonal and managerial skills.

Yet it is this very differentiation of thinking style that makes each of them successful in his chosen specialization. But the cost of differentiation is the increased difficulty it presents in integration. Therefore, the issue for both manager and scientist is complex: how to communicate with each other; how to complement each other's strengths without sacrificing too much of one's own.

In this article, we are explicitly concerned with these differences in thinking between the two cultures. We shall offer suggestions as to how the manager and the scientist can best work together in the development and use of analytic models and decision aids.

We suggest that such aids must be designed to amplify the user's problem-solving strategies. Thus it seems that the central factor determining whether a manager will use a model to reach a decision is

2. See Jerome S. Bruner, Jacqueline J. Goodnow, and George A. Austin, *A Study of Thinking* (New York, John Wiley & Sons, 1956).

the extent to which it "fits" his style of thinking. The main body of this paper largely defines what we mean by "fit."

Over the past four years, we have developed and tested a model of cognitive style, drawing on the developmental psychology that has in recent years reinvigorated the whole study of thinking and problem solving.[2] Our main aim has been to better understand the cognitive aspects of the decision-making process.

In the first section of this article, we shall provide a statement of our model in terms applicable to problem solving and decision making in general, rather than just to analytic techniques. Next, we shall discuss the experimental data we have gathered in validating the model. Finally, we shall extend our findings to the implications of cognitive style for implementing formal analytic models.

Model of cognitive style

We view problem solving and decision making in terms of the processes through which individuals organize the information they perceive in their environment, bringing to bear habits and strategies of thinking. Our model is based on the dual premise that consistent modes of thought develop through training and experience and that these modes can be classified along two dimensions, information gathering and information evaluation, as shown in *Exhibit I*.

Information gathering relates to the essentially perceptual processes by which the mind organizes the diffuse verbal and visual stimuli it encounters. The resultant "information" is the outcome of a complex coding that is heavily dependent on mental set, memory capacity, and strategies—often unconscious ones—that serve to ease "cognitive strain." Of necessity, information gathering involves rejecting some of the data encountered, and summarizing and categorizing the rest.

Preceptive individuals bring to bear concepts to filter data; they focus on relationships between items and look for deviations from or conformities with their expectations. Their precepts act as cues for both gathering and cataloging the data they find.

Receptive thinkers are more sensitive to the stimulus itself. They focus on detail rather than relationships and try to derive the attributes of the information from direct examination of it instead of from fitting it to their precepts.

Each mode of information gathering has its advantages in specific situations; equally, each includes risks of overlooking the potential meaning of data. The preceptive individual too easily ignores relevant detail, while the receptive thinker may fail to shape detail into a coherent whole. In management positions, the former will be most successful in many marketing or planning roles, and the latter in tasks such as auditing.

Information evaluation refers to processes commonly classified under problem solving. Individuals differ not only in their method of gathering data but also in their sequence of analysis of that data. These differences are most pronounced in relation to formal planning.

Systematic individuals tend to approach a problem by structuring it in terms of some method which, if followed through, leads to a likely solution.

Intuitive thinkers usually avoid committing themselves in this way. Their strategy is more one of solution testing and trial-and-error. They are much more willing to jump from one method to another, to discard information, and to be sensitive to cues that they may not be able to identify verbally.

Here again, each mode of information evaluation has advantages and risks. In tasks such as production management, the systematic thinker can develop a method of procedure that utilizes all his experience and economizes on effort. An intuitive thinker often reinvents the wheel each time he deals with a particular problem. However, the intuitive person is better able to approach ill-structured problems where the volume of data, the criteria for solution, or the nature of the problem itself do not allow the use of any predetermined method.

Focus on problem finding

Most modern theories of the decision process stress "rationality." Mathematical decision theory and game theory, for example, are both mainly concerned with defining the basics of rational behavior. Accounting for the discrepancies between it and observed behavior is only a secondary aim. Other theories, particularly those concerning organizational decision making, include factors of motivation, personality, and social forces but still treat decision making as essentially equivalent to problem solving.

In our model of cognitive style, we focus on problem solving, but our central argument is that decision making is above all situational and, therefore, includes problem finding. The manager scans his environment and organizes what he perceives. His efforts are as much geared to clarifying his values and intents as to dealing with predefined problems.

Obviously, some problems do force themselves on his awareness; this is particularly true in crisis situations. Nonetheless, he generally has some discre-

Exhibit I
Model of cognitive style

tion in the selection of problems to deal with and in the level of aspiration he sets for himself. (His aspiration often determines the extent to which he involves himself in terms of effort and risk.)

The manager's activities are bounded not only by the formal constraints of his job, but also by the more informal traditions and expectations implicit in his role. Because of this, the decision-making activity is strongly influenced by his perception of his position. A decision "situation" exists when he sees some event or cue in his environment that activates him into a search-analyze-evaluate sequence that results in a decision. This sequence is initiated by and depends on his environment assessment.

Our cognitive-style model provides some explanation of the processes affecting the manager's assessment of his environment. It thus includes an important aspect of behavior omitted in most theories on decision making—namely, that of problem finding, problem recognition, and problem definition. Generally, other theories assume that the situation has already been defined; the manager is presented with a neatly packaged problem and instructions on what he should try to do.

Implicit in the focus on problem finding is the concept that particular modes of cognition are better suited to certain contexts than others. As we mentioned earlier, the central argument of our study is that there needs to be a fit between the decision maker's cognitive style and the information-processing constraints of his task. Given this fit, the manager is more likely to gather environmental information that leads to successful (or at least comfortable) problem finding. He should also be able to evaluate that information in a way that facilitates successful problem solving. Perhaps the implications of a misfit are easier to indicate.

We mentioned earlier that a receptive thinker focuses on detail rather than pattern. But a receptive field sales manager who receives a wide range of information may well be flooded by it. He probably cannot examine all the sales reports, orders, phone calls, and so on. Instead, he should try to filter his information and be alert to trends and discrepancies. Thus a combination of the sales pattern in a particular region and a recent salesman's report of several customers' comments may lead him to recognize signs of change in consumer taste.

The preceptive individual is particularly suited to those tasks where he must have a concept of his environment. A preceptive manager would not be very successful in a task such as editing.

Similarly, it is easy to envisage tasks in which the intuitive thinker cannot come to terms with the data that are required in his decision making because he is unable to think in terms of a methodical sequence of analysis.

We have chosen the term "style" rather than the more common one of "structure" to stress the fact that modes of thinking relate more to propensity than to capacity. An individual's style develops out of his experience. For example, there is a tendency, particularly in late high school and college, for a student to increasingly choose courses that build on his strengths. This reinforcing pattern further develops those strengths and perhaps atrophies the skills in which he is less confident.

This suggests not only that tasks exist that are suited to particular cognitive styles, but also that the capable individual will *search out* those tasks that are compatible with his cognitive propensities. In addition, he will generally approach tasks and problems using his most comfortable mode of thinking.

Our model indicates some important differences in the ways in which individuals of particular styles approach problems and data. The accompanying list summarizes the main characteristics of each style:

Systematic thinkers tend to—

. . . look for a method and make a plan for solving a problem.
. . . be very conscious of their approach.
. . . defend the quality of a solution largely in terms of the method.
. . . define the specific constraints of the problem early in the process.
. . . discard alternatives quickly.
. . . move through a process of increasing refinement of analysis.
. . . conduct an ordered search for additional information.
. . . complete any discrete step in analysis that they begin.

Intuitive thinkers tend to—

. . . keep the overall problem continuously in mind.
. . . redefine the problem frequently as they proceed.
. . . rely on unverbalized cues, even hunches.
. . . defend a solution in terms of fit.
. . . consider a number of alternatives and options simultaneously.
. . . jump from one step in analysis or search to another and back again.
. . . explore and abandon alternatives very quickly.

Receptive thinkers tend to—

. . . suspend judgment and avoid preconceptions.
. . . be attentive to detail and to the exact attributes of data.
. . . insist on a complete examination of a data set before deriving conclusions.

Preceptive thinkers tend to—

. . . look for cues in a data set.
. . . focus on relationships.
. . . jump from one section of a data set to another, building a set of explanatory precepts.

Our research supports the concept that particular tasks and roles are more suited to one cognitive style than to another. *Exhibit II* shows careers that seem to be especially compatible with the skills and predispositions implicit in each of the cognitive modes of style.

Experimental results

We have carried out a range of experiments over the past four years aimed at validating the assertions made in the preceding statements.[3] The main

Exhibit II
Tasks and roles compatible with each cognitive style

Production & logistics manager Statistician Financial analyst	Preceptive	Marketing manager Psychologist Historian
Systematic		Intuitive
Auditor Clinical diagnostician	Receptive	Architect Bond salesman

effort in the experiments has been to identify and measure cognitive style. In the spring of 1972, a set of 12 standard reference tests for cognitive factors, developed by the Educational Testing Service, was administered to 107 MBA students. Each test was specifically chosen to fit one particular mode of style. The results confirmed most of the main characteristics of each style summarized earlier.

Initial tests

In our first set of experiments, 70% of the sample showed distinct differences in performance level between the systematic and the intuitive tests or between the receptive and the preceptive. This sup-

3. These experiments are described in detail in Peter G.W. Keen, "The Implications of Cognitive Style for Individual Decision Making," unpublished doctoral dissertation, Harvard Business School, 1973.

ports our basic contention that individuals tend to have a definite style.

We chose a conservative approach for our tests, classifying a subject as "intuitive," "systematic," and so on, only when the scores on tests requiring, say, an intuitive response were substantially different from those measuring capacity for the other mode of style along the same dimension. The comparisons focused on relative, not absolute, performance. The numeric scores were converted to a 1 to 7 scale, with a "1" indicating that the subject scored in the lowest seventh of the sample and a "7" corresponding to the top seventh.

From our main sample of 107 MBA students, we selected 20 whose test results indicated a distinct cognitive style for a follow-up experiment. This made use of a "cafeteria" set of 16 problems from which the subjects were asked to choose any 5 to answer. In individual sessions, which were tape recorded, the subjects were invited, though not required, to talk aloud as they dealt with each problem. The results pointed to distinct differences in the ways in which individuals of particular styles respond to problems.

As expected, the systematic subjects tended to be very concerned with getting into a problem by defining how to solve it. They were conscious of their planning and often commented on the fact that there were other specific ways of answering the problem.

In contrast, the intuitive subjects tended to jump in, try something, and see where it led them. They generally showed a pattern of rapid solution testing, abandoning lines of exploration that did not seem profitable.

More important, each mode of response was effective in solving different kinds of problems. In one instance, which required the decoding of a ciphered message, the intuitive subjects solved the problem—sometimes in a dazzling fashion—while none of the systematics were able to do so. In this particular case, there seemed to be a pattern among the intuitives: a random testing of ideas, followed by a necessary incubation period in which the implications of these tests were assimilated, and then a sudden jump to the answer.

There were often unexplained shifts in the reasoning of the intuitives, who were also much more likely to answer the problems orally. The latter tendency provided some confirmation for the idea that intuitive individuals use their own talking aloud to cue their activities and to alert themselves to possible lines of analysis.

There were distinct differences in the problems chosen by each of the groups, and their ratings of which problems they enjoyed most were remarkably consistent. The systematics preferred program-type problems, while the intuitives liked open-ended ones, especially those that required ingenuity or opinion.

The overall results of the initial experiments provided definite evidence to support both our model of cognitive style and the classification methods we developed through the main-sample test scores. The verbal answers in particular highlighted the degree to which these subjects consistently and distinctively respond to problems. There seems little doubt that, in these extreme cases at least, the individual maps himself onto the problem, rather than matching his behavior to the constraints and demands of the particular task.

Secondary sampling

In another set of tests, again using the main sample of 107 subjects, we examined the relationship between cognitive style and personality. We did this through comparisons of our test results with the Myers-Briggs scales used to classify individuals in relation to Jungian theories of psychological type.[*]

The most striking result of our experiment was that, while the scores on the Myers-Briggs scales showed virtually no correlation with absolute performance on our tests, there was a relationship between cognitive style and those scales. In particular, the systematic subjects were very likely to be of the "thinking" type and the intuitives much more likely to be at the other end of the scale, "feeling." R.O. Mason and I.I. Mitroff provide a useful summary of the difference between the thinking-feeling types:

"A Thinking individual is the type who relies primarily on cognitive processes. His evaluations tend to run along the lines of abstract true/false judgments and are based on formal systems of reasoning. A preference for Feeling, on the other hand, implies the type of individual who relies primarily on affective processes. His evaluations tend to run along personalistic lines of good/bad, pleasant/unpleasant, and like/dislike. Thinking types systematize; feeling types take moral stands and are interested in and concerned with moral judgments." [5]

We found a more modest relationship between systematic style and "introversion" and, similarly, between intuitive style and "extroversion." Thus our findings mesh well with Mason and Mitroff's predictions (they did not report any experimental data) about psychological type and information systems.

Final study

A year after the first two sets of experiments, we examined the relationship between style and career choice, using a sample of 82 MBA students. The results showed consistent differentiations between systematic and intuitive subjects. We compared the career preferences of the two groups and also looked at the test scores of those individuals who showed strong preference for particular careers.

In this experiment, the systematic students were attracted to administrative careers, to the military, and to occupations involving production, planning, control, and supervision. The intuitive group's choices centered around the more open-ended business functions; they preferred careers in psychology, advertising, library science, teaching, and the arts.

The overall result of the three sets of student experiments supports the validity of our conceptual model as a useful and insightful framework for examining the role of cognitive processes in decision making. More important, now that we have established such proof, we plan to extend our research to the study of business managers and especially to model builders and model users.

Analytic models

One of our major conjectures, which partly underlay the whole development of our model, has been that computer systems in general are designed by

4. See Isabel Briggs Myers and Katharine C. Briggs, "The Myers-Briggs Type Indicator," Educational Testing Service, New Jersey, 1957.

5. "A Program for Research on Management Information Systems," *Management Science*, January 1973, p. 475.

6. See "Is TIMS Talking to Itself?" *Management Science*, December 1965, p. B-156.

systematic individuals for systematic users. Although management science has lost its early tones of missionary zeal, of bringing "right" thinking to the ignorant, the implementation of analytic techniques not unreasonably reflects the scientist's own distinctive approach to problem solving.

Model building, from the viewpoint of the management scientist, involves making the causal relationships in a particular situation explicit and articulating the problem until he gets a reasonably predictive model; he will then generally refine that model. He has a faith in his own plan and process, and his specialized style of thinking enables him to literally build a model, shaping ideas and concepts into a methodological whole, and above all articulating relationships that the manager may understand but may not be able to make explicit.

The management scientist's skill is indeed a specialized one; the powerful organizing and systematizing capacity he brings to model building is his special contribution. But, obviously, that can be a vice rather than a virtue in specific situations. What Donald F. Heany calls the "have technique, will travel" [6] banner really amounts to the rigorously systematic individual's preference for a methodical approach to all problems in all contexts.

Fortunately, there are many systematic managers. Our assumption is that most general managers who use management science techniques are likely to be systematic in style. The techniques match their own innate approach to problems, and they gravitate to occupations that are suited to their style.

For example, since inventory control is a task that can be systematized, it will attract systematic managers, and it will therefore be an area in which management science techniques will find fruitful ground.

However, there are just as many management positions not filled by systematic thinkers. For example, advertising, which is not so easily systematized, will attract intuitive people. If management scientists want their techniques used in these more loosely structured business areas, they must try both to make their models less awesome to the intuitive managers they will be working with and to support the managers in their decision-making processes.

This requires understanding the intuitive approach to problem solving in general and developing models which will amplify and complement that approach.

Classes of problems

We have found it useful to categorize tasks—and problems in general—in terms of the problem solver's assessment of his ability to first recognize and then act on relevant information.[7] This process provides four basic classes of problems, as in *Exhibit III*.

The classes are easily illustrated. If, for example, a manager encounters a problem of inventory control in which he feels that he knows both what data are relevant and what mental operations and analysis are required to deal with that data, the problem is one of planning (Type 1 in *Exhibit III*). His whole effort then involves merely arranging the data into a form which can be used as input to a defined sequence of evaluation.

Exhibit III
Classification of tasks and problems

		Information acquisition, perceptual process	
		Known	Unknown
Information manipulation, conceptual process	Known	Planning, Type 1	Intelligence-search, Type 2
	Unknown	Invention, Type 3	Research, Type 4

Another class of problem (Type 2) exists when the required operations and methods are known, but the data involved are not. Price forecasting in complex markets is an example of this situation. Before a forecast can be made, a mass of data on economic, price, and market variables must be organized and sifted. Once this has been done, the forecasting procedure is simple.

A very different state of affairs exists when the individual understands the data but does not know how to manipulate them. Many production-scheduling problems fall into this class, invention (Type 3). The relevant data are known and the problem consists of finding a way to achieve the desired end.

The fourth class of problem exists when both information and operations are unknown. In this situation, there is a conscious search for cues and a

generation of explanatory concepts, together with the development of a method for manipulating the data thus organized. The development of new products is a typical research problem.

Specialized styles

Many management-science projects start as research. For example, modeling a complex environment such as the housing market in order to make industry or demand forecasts generally requires a complicated first step in which two areas of the problem are worked on in parallel: (1) the generation of concepts to "explain" reality and identify the most relevant variables, and (2) the definition of the outputs, aims, and implementation of the model.

Systematic individual

In our cafeteria experiment, the one problem rated most enjoyable by well over half the systematic group was a basic planning task. The systematic management scientist can often take a research problem and shift it to one of planning. The methodological formalization he provides helps translate unknown states of perception and conception into known ones.

However, there is sometimes the danger that he will force the translation; he may insist on some objective function that does not really fit the situation, partly because his preference for planning leaves him unwilling to accept "unknown" states. He needs to make the implicit explicit.

Intuitive manager

Just as the systematic management scientist's specialized style of thinking provides very definite strengths in specialized tasks, so too does the intuitive manager's. It is important to again stress that the intuitive mode is not sloppy or loose; it seems to have an underlying discipline at least as coherent as the systematic mode, but is less apparent because it is largely unverbalized.

There are many situations where the volume of information, the lack of structure in the task, and the uncertainty of the environment defy planning and programming. In such situations the intuitive manager's style can be highly effective.

For example, there is no way for any manager to systematically forecast consumer tastes for furniture

7. See James L. McKenney, "A Taxonomy of Problem Solving," working paper, Harvard Business School, 1973.

styles. He can, however, build a set of cues and flexible premises that may alert him to shifts in taste. He may also use the rapid scanning and testing (the main characteristic of the intuitive) for a sense of fit among disparate items of information. More important, he need never make his concepts and methods explicit.

Unlike the model builder, the intuitive manager can act without making any conscious articulation of his premises. An amusing instance of this fact occurred in many of the early efforts to use process-control computers in paper making. The computer experts "knew" that paper makers knew how to make paper; the experts' only problem was articulating the decision processes that the paper makers used, which turned out to depend mainly upon the

operators' "tasting the broth" and controlling the paper flow.

For a long time, this well-established and highly effective human decision process defied conversion into formal and explicit terms. The operators were not too helpful. They "knew" what worked; they had built up out of their experience a clear but not conscious sense of the process, but this sense often varied with the individual. Thus, when a shift changed, the new crew chief, for example, might reset the valves and modify the whole operation,

asserting that the changes were needed because of the time of day. There was no articulated set of concepts or methods by which this assertion could even be tested.

The decision makers here—and they merit the term, since controlling the paper-making process is a constant series of evaluations, assessments, and actions—were able to act efficiently even though they could not articulate their own procedures. This lack of articulation became a problem only when it was necessary for the computer experts to build a model of that process.

Approach differences

Systematic and intuitive individuals often treat the same project as two entirely different problems. The systematic management scientist may try to structure the problem to reduce the unknowns and to define very explicitly all the constraints in the situation. He aims at a model that is complete and has predictive power, which he can then improve and refine. That, essentially, is how he regards problem solving.

However, consciously or not, the intuitive manager is most concerned with using the model to give him a better sense of the problem. He focuses on and enjoys playing with the unknowns until he gets a feeling for the necessary steps for completion. Then he is ready to delegate the process of dealing with the problem to some individual in his organization who can systematically handle it in a more routine fashion.

The intuitive manager may also approach a task for which a model is to be built not with a need to understand the analytic process, but with a desire to discover what he can trust in order to make useful predictions. This can be of value to the systematic scientist, in that, if he can build a model which "works," the manager may well be ready to use it even though he does not understand it.

The central issue, however, is the validation of the model. The scientist validates his model formally and methodologically; he can test it in relation to known inputs and outputs. In general, he will have faith in his plan and in his own systematic process. The manager will validate the model experientially and test it against some of his own concepts and expectations. He places much less faith in external "authority."

Recommendations for action

If our line of argument is valid, it is clear that the solution to the difficulties intuitive managers and systematic management scientists have in working together will not be obtained by trying to blur the differences. The intuitive manager may learn what network optimization is, but that is unlikely to make him think in the same systematic mode as the management scientist, who, in turn, is unlikely to develop intuitive responses through any form of education.

(This is not to assert that cognitive style is fixed, but to reinforce the point that individuals with very distinctive styles in specialized areas of activity have strengths that are directly related to their styles. It seems unlikely that the cognitive specialist will change easily—or that he should do so in any case.)

The real solution seems to lie in two areas: (1) in defining the model's role within the larger decision-making process of the particular situation, and (2) in determining how to validate the model.

From this, the manager and scientist together can better control both the process of building the model structure and their mutual expectations and actions. At the root of both these areas of concern is the whole question of trust and communication, less in the interpersonal than in the cognitive sense.

Role definition

The management scientist's role can be one of either product or service. It is important that he decide which it is in a particular situation.

On the one hand, if his model will mainly help clarify a manager's sense of the issues and options, then there is no point in the scientist's trying to provide a meticulous and complex simulation. The manager does not intend to use the model as the basis for any decision. In fact, the model may simply help him decide what the problem is and can then be thrown away.

On the other hand, the manager may need a product rather than a service; for example, a financial forecasting model, once validated, may be used by a manager as the main basis for ongoing decisions.

The degree and direction of the scientist's efforts will be very different, depending on how he perceives the manager's needs in the situation. The scientist can only identify those needs by asking questions: How does this manager approach problems? How does he define his problem, given the four different classifications in *Exhibit III*? Does he want the model to further his own learning or to help him make a specific decision?

The answer to each question has distinct consequences. For example, if the manager's response to problems is systematic, the model should explicitly reflect this fact. The scientist should explain to him the underlying assumptions as to method; the two can afford to invest substantial time and discussion on how to deal with the problem. Here, the manager is essentially looking for a technique and the scientist is the expert, with a catalog of methods.

However, if the manager is intuitive in style, the scientist should recognize that the model must allow the manager to range over alternatives and test solutions in the fashion that fits his natural mode of problem solving.

In this context, J.W. Botkin has used the paradigm of cognitive style in designing an interactive computer system for intuitive subjects.[8] He has identified five necessary features for such a model:

1
The user should have the ability to create an arbitrary order of processing; the system should not impose a "logical" or step-by-step sequence on him. In Botkin's words, "This lack of set sequence allows the intuitive user to follow his instinct for developing his ill-defined information plan directly from environmental cues."
2
The user should be able to define, explore, and play out "scenarios" that may either generate cues or test solutions.
3
The user should be able to shift between levels of detail and generality.
4
The user should have some control over the forms of output and should be able to choose visual, verbal, and numeric displays at varying levels of detail.
5
The user should be able to extend his programming, providing input in an irregular and unspecific form (i.e., he should be able to provide commands such as, "Repeat the last step, increasing X by 10%").

Botkin's experiment showed fairly clearly that intuitive and systematic subjects used his model in greatly differing ways. The differences corresponded on the whole to those found in our cafeteria experiment. The intuitive group seemed to learn from the system and to enjoy using it as much as the systematic group.

Even though Botkin's model was a special case, his results suggest that an effort on the part of the model builder to consider how the manager will use the model—in terms of process rather than output—will provide large dividends.

Here again, there is a distinction between service and product. Where the manager is most concerned with the recommendations he can derive from the model, the sort of cognitive amplifiers Botkin provides are unnecessary. However, where the manager wants the model to help him clarify his own understanding of the situation, it may well be essential to build them into the formal structure of the model.

Thus the management scientist needs to consider what a "good" model is. For himself, goodness is largely a quality of predictive power and technical elegance. For the manager, it is more a concern of compatibility and comfort—that is, the fit between how he approaches the problem and how the model allows him to do so.

Model validation

Perhaps even more important than either recognizing the relevance of the user's own problem-solving process or determining how that person will use the model is the whole question of trust. Often, the manager does not get involved in the model itself; he simply asks for the outputs. He may well wish to validate the model by testing out some scenarios for which he has some expectations of the outcome.

However, John S. Hammond suggests that the model builder should recognize that in a large and complex model the user will have neither the desire nor the ability to understand its mechanics. The designer must, therefore, provide the user with some other way of testing out—of building trust in—the model. Hammond recommends, therefore, that the management scientist should aim—

8. "An Intuitive Computer System: A Cognitive Approach to the Management Learning Process," unpublished doctoral dissertation, Harvard Business School, 1973.

"... to get something simple and useful up and running as soon as possible. By skillfully manipulating the resultant model, the management scientist should be able to obtain results that will give great insights about the problem, its nature, and its alternatives to the manager. These insights should cue the mind of the manager and cause him to perceive the problems and alternatives differently, which will in turn affect the priorities and direction of the management science effort. . . .

"Thus the management scientist, too, will learn about the nature of the problem and also about the nature of the manager's perception of it." [9]

This recommendation seems particularly relevant in cases where the manager's cognitive style is highly intuitive. For relatively little effort and minimal commitment to a particular definition and design, the manager can obtain the initial exploration and trial testing that may enable him to articulate his assessments of the problem—or, better, that may enable the scientist to deduce them for him.

Our recommendations are fairly modest. Essentially, they argue that if both manager and scientist alike will look at the process instead of the output the techniques will look after themselves. It seems of central importance for the manager and scientist to recognize that each has a distinctive style of problem solving, and that each should accept the other's difference.

If the management scientist can anticipate the fact that the manager may not use in his decision-making process the conscious planning that is so natural for the scientist himself, he will be less likely to assume that the manager's reluctantly given statement of what the problem is has any permanent force. The intuitive manager can recognize a good plan, if he can validate it at some point on his own terms; the scientist's responsibility is to provide the plan and also the validation.

The manager's responsibility is to make very clear, first to himself and then to the scientist, what he wants the model to do and to be. If he asks for an optimization program for a facilities planning project, he should decide well in advance what he will do with the results. If he knows that he will not make his decision on the basis of the model's out-

put, he should make sure that the design process and the model structure allow him to use the model to amplify his own thinking.

The intuitive manager is very happy to relinquish the mechanics of formal analytic techniques to the expert, but only after he has developed confidence and trust in that expert. It is in this sense that the common recommendation of educating the manager in quantitative skills seems so inadequate. The intuitive manager will learn to make use of these skills supplied by others; but this learning is internal, experiential, and informal.

More than anything, the manager needs to learn how to tell a good model from a bad one. For him, a good model is one that he can, by testing his own scenarios, make sense of. However sloppy this may seem to the systematic scientist, his model will be used only if it allows the manager to make such tests or if the process of designing it has done so on a more ongoing basis.

Concluding note

People in general tend to assume that there is some "right" way of solving problems. Formal logic, for example, is regarded as a correct approach to thinking, but thinking is always a compromise between the demands of comprehensiveness, speed, and accuracy. There is no best way of thinking. If the manager and the management scientist can recognize first that each has a different cognitive style, and thus a different way of solving the same problem, then their dialogue seems more likely to bear fruit.

Our model of cognitive style is not necessarily either complete or precise. We suggest, however, that it does provide a useful way of focusing on the implementation of analytic models for decision making and of developing strategies of action that are much more likely to succeed than those based on concepts of technique, education, and salesmanship.

9. "The Roles of the Manager and Analyst in Successful Implementation," paper presented to the XX International Meeting of the Institute of Management Sciences, Tel Aviv, Israel, 1973.

Impact of the changing business environment on management and their information needs*

T. J. Lincoln

Summary Over the past year or so we have heard much about inflation. Of its effect on society, on government, on industry. We are by now very aware that inflation dramatically affects business, particularly the real value of profits. But apart from hoping that either inflation diminishes or that real growth resumes, what can businessmen do to protect their companies? Will, for example, better information about the business and its environment help? If so, how much should be invested into getting better information — and what is 'better' in this situation?

One country which has been hit particularly hard by inflation recently is Britain. Stresses are developing in British society and business which are possible indicators of things to come elsewhere. It seems therefore appropriate to report on the conclusions of a group of senior executives from primarily British companies who came together recently for three days at the Oxford Centre for Management Studies to consider the impact of the changing business environment on management and their information needs. The meeting was held in an atmosphere of confidentiality and complete frankness. Out of the specific problems and solutions which were discussed, certain conclusions of general validity were drawn. This article attempts to synthesise those points which are of general interest to those businessmen who are suffering, or who are potentially susceptible to, similar problems.

1. Introduction

Over the past 18 months or so, those countries with a free economy have been subjected to a burst of abnormally high inflation. This has hit different countries with different severity but there are many that have experienced double figure inflation for a transient period. It now appears that, with a few well-known exceptions, most countries are managing to bring inflation under control.

During this period it has become apparent that inflation of this magnitude has significant side-effects on society. Redistribution of wealth takes place affecting purchasing and saving patterns. Established markets change in size, dominance and profitability. The balance of political power alters at both national and industrial levels. In short, many of the fundamentals of business undergo a period of rapid, often unpredictable, change. Of course society is changing in ways other than that caused by inflation. Indeed Alvin Toffler in his book *'Future Shock'* has claimed that the overall rate of change in society is currently greater than ever before and is accelerating. If true, the problems faced by businessmen over the last 18 months can not be thought of as merely a transient phenomenon. Even if Toffler's general thesis is not accepted, there seems little doubt that senior managers expect business to grow more complex and to become more difficult to plan and control over the foreseeable future.

Over the past few years many companies have developed sophisticated information systems designed to help them cope with the increasing complexities of business. Indeed some consider management information as a key company resource. The claim has been made that

---

* The author is aware that this general topic has been discussed at recent Diebold research seminars. However these seminars are confidential and the author is unaware of any publications relating to their findings in this context.

business information systems can significantly help management cope with the rate of change that is impacting their business. If this is the case, the obvious implication is that senior managers should increase the investment in the resources used to develop information systems.

However there are two opposing factors to this conclusion which must be considered. The first is that the current economic environment has adversely effected profitability and caused liquidity problems for many companies. In some countries this is likely to remain a problem for some time. So monetary considerations combined with uncertainty about the future argue against increasing investment beyond that thought essential for company survival. The second factor relates to the basis upon which information systems were and are continuing to be developed. Those information systems which are currently operational were developed under certain assumptions of stability of environment which are not now valid. In a number of cases the effect of this has been that the system is not sufficiently responsive to changing user requirements. Although this is now recognised as a problem by management, there are no obvious signs that the designers of information systems have identified a design strategy which will allow greatly enhanced flexibility. It is therefore by no means clear that an increased investment in information systems would produce the required return.

We have therefore the situation in which uncertainty about the future coupled with a high rate of change creates a management need for better, more relevant information while the same circumstances force managers to place a limit on possible investment projects and to question whether the basic assumptions underlying current information systems development are still appropriate. So, while a high rate of change appears on the surface to argue for better information systems, it should be borne in mind that 'better' does not necessarily mean 'more as today'.

Senior management therefore face a dilemma to which there is no obvious clear answer. However, it is possible to gain an insight into the problem by examining three questions:

1. How is the changing business environment affecting the management process?

2. How is the changing business environment affecting management information requirements?

3. Are there changes required in the ways in which information systems are developed and in the facilities provided?

These three questions formed the nucleus of the debate at a recent top management briefing held at the Oxford Centre for Management Studies. This paper is an attempt to capture and synthesise the thoughts of the participants of the briefing. It has been felt to be worth while to capture these thoughts since they are relevant to the business community as a whole and provide a representative, executive view of the impact of the changing business environment on management and their information needs.

2. Top management briefings

The Oxford Centre for Management Studies was established in 1965 with the objective of providing development programmes for senior and middle managers. In addition, the Oxford Centre, from time to time, sponsors a briefing seminar on current issues of key interest. These briefings are specifically designed to allow a small, cross-industry group of senior executives to get together for a period of 2 to 3 days in an atmosphere of complete confidentiality and frankness to discuss, within a general framework laid down by the directors of the briefing, the issues most affecting them and their companies. The briefing which forms the foundation of this paper was the second to be held on the topic of management information. The first of these, held in October 1973, explored the importance of management information as a company resource. Out of this session arose a number of key issues which it was felt should be explored further. Accordingly, at the request of some of the original participants, a follow-on briefing was organised, and held in January 1975, with the objective of examining these key issues. The joint directors of both the briefings on management information were the director of the Oxford Centre, Mr. R. I. Tricker, and the author of this paper. Experience has shown that the optimum size for a top management briefing is about 15. In this case there were 17 participants, all of whom were senior executives with responsibilities in the Finance or Management Services areas. A number of the companies represented were multi nationals and participants were drawn from several nationalities.

Although the briefing was called to discuss the key issues identified 15 months earlier, it became clear from early introductions and session discussions that the participants of the briefing were primarily concerned with the impact of inflation, and the associated rate of change, on business and management. Accordingly the majority of the discussion revolved around these and related issues.

For the purposes of clarity therefore this summary has been prepared not under the headings of the individual sessions, but under the areas which generated most debate. These were:

1. Effect of the changing business environment on the management process.

2. Effect of the changing business environment on management information requirements.

3. Implications for information system development.
4. Implications for information system facilities.

Each of these topics are discussed further below.

3. Effect of the changing business environment on the management process [1]

3a. Management morale

At the heart of the question 'How successfully will management resolve the problem of change?' is of course their willingness to try and find solutions. It was disconcerting to find general agreement that the morale of management was being seriously affected in two different ways.

Firstly it was accepted that the current business uncertainty caused by inflation and (in the UK) changes in the traditional power structure at both the industrial and national political levels, were crushing management confidence and ambition in many of our industries. A number of participants spoke of managers being most unwilling to take any risks for fear of being held responsible, on the one hand, for financial difficulties or industrial unrest, or on the other hand for increasing the threat of political action in the case of oversuccess. In short the traditional guidelines for senior managers have in many cases been removed without alternatives being proposed and confusion and uncertainty is all that remains.

The second effect on morale which most strongly affects middle management in larger companies has been caused by the apparent reduction in career path opportunities within a company which had planned on growth but is now a static or contracting business. Many companies have relied in the past on an expanding operation to provide new opportunities and responsibilities for the management of the company. Some international companies are renowned for continuously moving staff from one post to another for this purpose. A static business reduces the opportunity to create new interesting jobs which allow managers to continue to grow. Thus companies which in the past have created a willingness of its staff and their families to be moved by suggesting that this was the best way for career development, are now facing disillusionment amongst their managers because of the lack of new opportunities.

Although it was felt by all that management morale is currently at a low ebb and that the fundamental problems affecting society show no signs of resolution, it was clear that beneath it all there was quiet optimism about the future. This attitude is very significant because it means that the motivation exists for managers to continue to struggle to find ways of overcoming their problems so that when the light at the end of the tunnel is finally reached, companies will be in a position so seize advantage of the opportunities.

3b. Ability to plan

It was accepted by all participants that the current state of business uncertainty makes it very much more difficult to plan ahead, for even a few months, than was the case previously. It is common to find examples of plans being completely rewritten every 3 months. Indeed a company's very survival may depend on its ability to react to changing circumstances, quickly and flexibly. Unfortunately, the rhythm of decision making within many large companies is geared to a traditional pace determined by a more stable environment. Often the problems caused by a rapid rate of change lie in the inadequacy of the decision making system rather than the information system. Thus in part there is a management behavioural problem to be overcome before information systems can be fully effective.

In general it was felt that short term planning was possible, given that strong control was maintained over the company's operations, while the long term was dealt with by assessing the impact of various plausible scenarios and adjusting investment plans accordingly. The real problem was felt to be middle term planning (3 months — 2 years) where decisions had to be taken urgently to ensure survival but the key options were still felt to be wide open. The only suggestion offered to help cope with this situation was that ways must be found to assist managers react faster to trends by encouraging greater use of probabilistic or uncertain data.

However it is quite clear that industry's problems will not be solved by juggling numbers. In the current situation there is an increased need for the middle management entrepreneur who can successfully react instinctively to changing events. All agreed however that such managers are at a premium. In the absence therefore of alternatives, there seems to be a trend towards strengthened top down planning with an acceptance by senior management that this brought reduced commitment from the lower levels of management.

3c. Management appraisal

As described above, the current environment is producing a situation in which business plans are less rigid and more open to interpretation. In this case, the system of 'Management by Objectives', in which managers are set objectives and subsequently appraised on the results they achieve, becomes meaningless. This has a wider implication than merely for those companies who run a formal 'Management by Objectives' system. For even in more informal companies, the concept of using commitments from managers as a basis for planning is very common. If managers have no confidence in the future,

---

[1] This subject was the theme of the keynote speech at the 1975 British Computer Society 'Data Fair' given by Mr. R. I. Tricker, Director, Oxford Centre for Management Studies.

they will be unwilling to accept objectives or give commitments. Even if objectives are imposed, managers will not struggle as hard as otherwise they might, to meet the commitment. Thus the basis for planning and appraising performance is breaking down and there is great uncertainty as to what should take its place.

4. Effect of the changing business environment on management information requirements

Because of the number of companies which have recently run into financial difficulties, the problem of maintaining tight financial control was very prominent in everybody's mind. Only in this way could the dangers of, for example, overtrading or uneconomic pricing, be avoided. Accepting therefore that there was a general requirement for accurate, up-to-date information on all significant financial items, the interesting feature of the briefing was the identification of those items which were commonly felt to be in urgent need of strengthened control. The key items in this category are listed below:

4a. Current assets

Manufacturing industries are by now well aware of the capital tied up in current assets, but the traditional accounting measures (stock turn-over rate, etc. . . . .) were felt to be increasingly inadequate and better, faster information was required so that realistic trade offs between level of service and capital requirements could be evaluated. Accordingly comprehensive statistics on work-in-progress, inventory levels etc. . . . , were being increasingly required both as actuals and trends so that forecasts could be better prepared and impact on future cash flow closely monitored.

4b. Productivity

In a number of countries, but perhaps particularly in the UK, the utilisation factors of fixed assets were being affected by unpredictable changes in labour productivity. This is being caused not only by strikes, go-slows etc., but also by a changing attitude to work which affect, for example, the amount of overtime staff think is reasonable and the mobility considered acceptable for the sake of the company. Flexible working hours represents one way in which companies are reacting to this problem. Accordingly, productivity can vary by time, by location within a country and across countries and this is forcing companies to closely monitor actual unit output so that they can adjust supply to meet demand. An example was quoted of a company which daily assessed unit output so that world wide distribution of part finished products could be optimised. In addition

to the strengthened operational control thereby achieved, such information enabled better international capital investment programmes to be formulated.

4c. Production costs

Because of the impact of unpredictable cost elements on production costs, it was felt desirable to closely monitor the latter with increased emphasis on actual and projected costs rather than standard. Indeed it was suggested that standard costing systems as run by some companies were breaking down under the impact of the current inflation rates.

A feature of the last 18 months has been the violent changes (both positive and negative) in the commodity markets. Examples of very heavy speculation losses are common. Equally common are examples of companies suffering heavy production losses because of failure to protect their forward supply of essential raw materials. It is therefore not surprising that most industries have now a keen interest in closely monitoring the costs of their essential raw materials to ensure that their prices do not become hopelessly uneconomic. In this sense, control of raw material costs is more important than labour costs because, in many companies, their effect on manufacturing cost is often greater and because the variance between actual and standard (or planned) is likely to be more unpredictable.

4d. Currency parity levels

A feature of the current inflation, which is widely different for different countries, is that parity or exchange rates are continually, often quite rapidly varying. Multinational companies in particular but also those who export or import to a significant degree, must closely monitor current parity levels to ensure that their prices remain profitable. Similarly, parity trend forecasts are required to enable assessments to be made of whether products will remain competitive in the future. A commonly heard complaint was that even specialist economic forecasting groups were no guarantee of accuracy in this respect.

4e. Social data

Business cannot work in a vacuum. Data is required about the environment and about the social characteristics of customers. Traditionally such data has been slowly varying in which case use was made of government statistics supplemented where necessary by market surveys. A feature of the ways in which governments gather and process data is the very long time delays involved. Examples of 5 year processing times are apparently not uncommon. However in a period of high inflation, environment and social data can vary quickly. Mobility and leisure patterns are an example. In this case the government processing times of data are totally inadequate to meet business needs and consequently much needless uncertainty is injected into business decisions. One participant considered this to be a sufficiently serious problem to merit the establishment of an 'Institute of Social Measurement' whose function would be to gather, process and disseminate social and environmental data independently from the government.

5. Implications for information systems development

5a. Management involvement

This paper has emphasised throughout the dilemma that currently faces management. On the one hand they need more information to cope with the uncertain environment while on the other they have less money and time to spend on developing new information systems. The struggle to accommodate this dilemma is seen very clearly when one looks at the extent of management involvement in developing information systems, for there was a clear indication that management are currently reacting in two, apparently contradictory ways, on this issue.

The first is that many managers are insisting on all possible speed of system implementation to provide essential information. There was a general feeling that this was resulting in examples of systems being pressed into service prematurely and without adequate testing. One symptom of this pressure is that many systems were not being so rigorously cost justified as in the past.

The apparently contradictory trend is for management to plead more pressing problems and to withdraw their direct involvement during the development phase thereby removing some of the essential checks and balances on the system designer's enthusiasm and inexperience. Executives talked about the difficulty in capturing the time and attention of the appropriate manager during the critical design phases of a new system even when his absence introduced unnecessary delays in the system development cycle. It appears quite clear that management's lack of involvement and lack of insistence on traditional (but often time consuming) checks and balances, means that systems are now increasingly being implemented as a question of faith, and often hastily formed faith.

5b. System planning [2]

A source of debate for some considerable time has been the question of how much effort should be put into planning information systems on a company-wide basis. [3] Some companies attempt to prepare detailed plans for up to 5 years ahead, others allow their systems to evolve at users' request without an overall framework. Up to recently, there seemed to be a growing consensus that a systems overview plan was an essential planning tool given that the plan was sensitive to the business environment. However recent events appeared to have repolarised the attitude that senior executives have towards systems planning.

One reaction is to respond to inflationary events by re-emphasising the planning effort and frequency. The opposite view is that unpredictable and rapidly changing circumstances make a nonsense of planning more than a few months ahead, and that the management effort required could be better used elsewhere.

These two views were clearly present in the briefing and even after prolonged debate, the holders of one view were generally unconvinced by their opponents. The factors which seemed to determine which view was held were the size and type of company, the history of centralised planning and the severity with which the current crisis is being felt. Quite clearly, there is no unique right way (or perhaps wrong way) to react to the current problems and system designers should be sensitive to the pressures on their management and adjust their expectations accordingly.

However regardless of whether or not an information systems plan was thought practical, there was a strong common feeling that two basic principles should be re-emphasised.

The first principle is that flexibility of new systems should be such that unpredictable demands can be met. Whereas information systems have traditionally often evolved vertically within companies, that is by business function, there was now increased need for horizontal developing enabling managers to bring together and compare cross functional data. This trend for integrating data from all levels of the business can be expected to continue and has certain consequences for systems design. The first is that the flexibility required by particular systems can only be gauged by the nature and characteristics of related systems, existing and planned. Thus even if a systems plan is not formalised, system designers must still consider the requirements of all significant business systems when they are considering how much flexibility can be justified. The second consequence impacts the cost justification of systems. Flexibility is a notoriously difficult benefit to quantify especially in light of unpredictable requirements. This implies an increasing reliance on management judgement explaining perhaps the trend commented on earlier for reduced emphasis on formal cost justification for new systems.

The second fundamental principle commonly agreed on was the necessity to capture basic operational data as fast and as accurately as possible even, if necessary, at the expense of detailed analysis. Particularly stressed was the need for standardised data across the company rather than standard systems. In fact the latter were considered

---

[2] A working conference specially on this subject has recently been held by McKinsey and Co Ltd. See J. V. Soden, 'Pragmatic guidelines for EDP long range planning', *Data Management*, September 1975.

[3] See for example T. J. Lincoln, 'A strategy for information systems development', *Management Datamatics*, Vol. 4, No. 4, August 1975.

to be rarely justified in light of the management problems involved. Thus the policy favoured was to emphasise common data, while allowing local management to develop local systems. As an illustration, one participant from a multi-national company spoke of common systems being developed only to the extent where the company had complete control of the input and output information content and format. Where local conditions required, for legal or other reasons, specialised formats, unique subsystems were developed. One trend discussed in this connection, was the increase of users developing, via time-sharing networks, their own sub-systems to meet local requirements. This had advantages in allowing users to exercise their own priorities and react quicker to their own problems, but such conditions make it more difficult to ensure that the base data remained suitable for cross company communication.

6. Implications for information system facilities

The briefing that forms the background for this paper, did not attempt to formally define the range of facilities that should be provided by an information system. However from the more general discussions arose a consensus view as to which facilities were more important in a time of change than otherwise. Some of these facilities have already been touched on, but they are discussed in more depth below since they provide an indication of the key points of current concern to senior management.

6a. Flexibility
The reasons for, and some of the consequences of, increased flexibility were brought out in Section 5b. These requirements imply a more powerful query facility than possessed by many systems. The trend suggests a move towards data base systems capable of supporting sophisticated data structures and equipped with a powerful query language for ad-hoc inquiries. Systems which required purpose-built programs for query analysis were felt to be too inflexible. However, sophisticated data base systems require sophisticated skills. It is widely recognised that such systems will not realise their full potential unless the appropriate skills and experience are available. Thus the introduction of data base systems implies an investment in training, and perhaps recruitment, which must be carefully considered in the early planning phases.

6b. Company models
One of the more noticeable trends amongst the companies represented was the increased use of company

models to assist with planning. This is a consequence of the increased complexity and unpredictability of the environment. Faced with this situation managers are turning to computer models for assistance but are frequently finding that their help is limited. Summarising the views of those present at the briefing, it was felt that models should be kept as simple as possible to allow users to fully understand and be familiar with the model. It was felt strongly that the model should be structured to allow the examination of many alternatives ('what if?' questions) rather than attempt to produce an optimal solution for a large number of input parameters. Interactive models in which the machine and the manager work in a complementary way are to be preferred to batch operation. The models should be geared towards providing quick, financial results and in particular providing forward cash flow analysis.

6c. Data analysis
In those organisations which deal with very large amounts of data (banks, local government, multinational companies, etc.) it was felt that the current rate of change required increased emphasis on sampling and statistical techniques compared with complete analysis of the data base. Behind this point lies the recognition that in uncertain times, decisions often have to be taken quickly and with inadequate information. The analysis of the information requirements of a decision shows that usually there is a noise factor associated with information so that for example the result of a decision will not be affected by small variances in the information content. This should be recognised by information system designers who should provide facilities to enable managers to balance the cost of the information and that of associated time delays against the value of the decision, thereby providing criteria to allow the system to abstract, sample or summarise the information in a more satisfactory way. This problem has existed for some time, especially in connection with environmental data where cost and time delays associated with data collection can be very high. However inflation has accentuated the problem which now gives cause for concern at a wider level.

6d. Data communications
Coupled with the increased requirement for data base systems comes also the requirement for fast collection and analysis of data. Thus there was greater acceptance of the need for on-line systems operating in, as one participant put it, real-enough time. It was stressed a number of times that the increased requirement for fast, accurate data made the cost justification of on-line systems very much easier now than in the past. One participant stated that this had led over the past year to his company putting all their key operating systems on-line with the result that they now felt they were far better equipped to deal with sudden, unexpected changes

in the business than previously. This trend also has significant consequences on the skills and experience required by the systems and programming groups which companies cannot afford to ignore.

7. Conclusions

This paper has attempted to describe the current feelings and conclusions of a group of senior managers, all of whom are directly involved with the management of the information resource within their company, about the impact of business uncertainty on management and their information needs. Within the limits of the size of group and industries represented, these conclusions are probably representative of business as a whole, although wider evidence would be needed before such a claim could be substantiated. Because of the confidentiality agreement relating to specific comments made in a top management briefing, this paper is concerned with trends and consensus views rather than case studies.

The main difference between this briefing and its predecessor is that senior management's attention is now more sharply focussed on the practical, current problems rather than those of the longer term. Managers are aware of the value of information systems in assisting with the complexities of the current environment. This awareness is being demonstrated by their reluctance to cut back system development budgets as much as might be expected and the renewed emphasis on establishing systems for control of the vital elements of the business. The urge to standardise data across business functions and to increase usage of company models is further evidence of this attitude. The system facilities required to support these requirements are available now in some advanced systems but not perhaps in the majority of cases. In such cases the development of inexpensive, reliable, flexible data base systems is an urgent requirement as also is the extension of data communications facilities.

The key to success for the future appears to be flexibility, not only in terms of software but particularly with regard to the ability of managers to examine and analyse cross company data. Flexibility in this sense must be designed into the system from the start whereas too many current systems are using today's technology with yesterday's concepts. The traditional systems design approach of asking the users for their requirements becomes increasingly inappropriate when their requirements are changing rapidly and unpredictably. In this case system designers must perform a more fundamental analysis of the critical business functions and establish with the help of senior management which functions are likely to change and in what manner. In this way flexibility can be constructed at the basic level of information content rather than, as is usually the case, be considered solely in terms of software. In common with many of the advanced techniques however, the success of this approach depends on the skills of the systems analysts and on management time being available for consultation and guidance.

The main worrying, if understandable, trend is for senior managers to become less, rather than more, involved in the critical design phases of a new system. Associated with this appears to be the reduced emphasis on cost justification of new systems. One of the therapeutic consequences of a crisis is that it encourages the stripping away of the inefficient deadwood within a business, leaving it healthier and better able to take advantage of future opportunities. Information systems will aid future recovery only if they themselves are soundly designed and if managers are prepared to use them. Experience has shown that it is often difficult to change an existing business system and introduce an alternative. The inertia involved can frequently only be overcome by a clear lead from the top of the company. Accordingly senior managers, however difficult it may be, must play their full role in ensuring that systems designed today are not regarded in the future as unfortunate legacies of the past.

On the whole, it appears that companies are at the least protecting their information systems development plans from the cut-backs faced by other departments. Some companies are responding more positively to the situation and are, for example, actively placing their operational systems on an on-line basis. The difference in attitude between companies appears to be determined by the skills and experience of their systems analysts and the willingness of their senior management to get involved. So the consensus view appears to be that in times of socio-economic change, relevant information systems, if by no means the ultimate answer, at least offer the manager more obvious assistance with decision making than do other techniques. The key seems to be that in times of great uncertainty the potential opportunity loss associated with wrong decisions is greater and therefore information systems become easier to cost justify and, because their advantages are more obvious, there is less managerial resistance to their introduction. The fortunate companies are those who have the necessary skills, experience and confidence to take advantage of this situation.

MANAGERIAL CAREERS
AND ORIENTATIONS

V

■ Managers view the world in a distinctive fashion. Their problems and concerns are quite different from those of nonmanagers. As Henry Mintzberg's research has demonstrated, managers tend to work long hours at an unrelenting pace, and their activities are fragmented and varied.[1] Mintzberg's viewpoint is consistent with the model of management proposed in this book.

This section focuses on some of these distinctive managerial activities. The emphasis is on managerial careers and orientations, including entrepreneurship, the manager's career problems, and some issues the manager must understand in order to function effectively in his or her current job and in future positions.

[1] Henry Mintzberg, *The Nature of Managerial Work* (New York: Harper and Row, 1973).

Section A:
Entrepreneurship

An entrepreneur is usually defined as an individual who founds, owns, and manages his or her own company. Entrepreneurs differ from professional managers in that they do not assume "detached" responsibility for a company that someone else has organized and brought to its present state. Entrepreneurship has become the focus for a great deal of study during the last several years. Some researchers are interested in discovering the factors that lead to effective entrepreneurial behavior. For example, much of the work of David McClelland (see "That Urge to Achieve," Part III, Section A) has focused on the entrepreneur as the classical high achiever who "selects" this profession since it best meets his or her psychological or motivational needs, including immediate feedback (Did we make a profit this month?) and personal responsibility for decision making. Others, including both psychologists and business school professors, are interested in helping individuals to adopt the entrepreneurial life-style, primarily because of the obvious economic benefits entrepreneurs bring to a society.

The three articles presented here are intended to provide a feeling for entrepreneurs and what makes them "tick" and an understanding of the inherent risks in starting one's own business.

In the first article, Ernest Dale explores the extremely interesting career of Ernest Tener Weir, one of the most successful entrepreneurs of the past century. Beginning with a $3-a-week job, Weir rose to a prominent position in national industrial and political life. Although the story of his career is highly entertaining reading, the ingredients of Weir's success as analyzed by Dale at the conclusion of the article provide the most useful insights into entrepreneurial behavior. The personal qualifications for success, including consistency, innovativeness, and clear goals, especially seem to typify the entrepreneur. Finally, Weir's attention to the managerial details of planning, control, and flexibility in selecting the means to reach goals provides essential discussion points for analyzing his success in terms of the key managerial dimensions discussed previously in this text.

In the second article, *Forbes Magazine* provides some insight into entrepreneurial thought through interviews with several successful entrepreneurs. (Interestingly enough, research has shown that only about 10 percent of all entrepreneurs fit this category.) The interviews reveal some characteristics common to most successful entrepreneurs: (1) They are more interested in creating companies than in making money; (2) They disdain the idea of growing large through acquisition of other companies; and (3) "building a business from scratch" seems to be a predominant life-style for these people. An interesting point of emphasis in the article is the importance entrepreneurs place on supplementing their own skills with those of others, which certainly contradicts the stereotype of the entrepreneur as someone who "does it all" himself.

Finally, Lawrence Lamont analyzes characteristics of second-generation entrepreneurs (those starting their second enterprises), in an attempt to provide some learning experiences for those who wish to start their own company or for those who might invest in such a venture. His conclusions are very revealing. First, second-generation firms appear to be more successful than their first-time counterparts; there is a learning curve involved. Second, entrepreneurs appear to learn from their experience that market planning, financial planning, and a balanced managerial team lead to improved performance. Entrepreneurs seem to share the common experience with "professional" managers, then, that integration of the basic management dimensions into the framework of the organization is essential for success.

ERNEST DALE,

Ernest Tener Weir:
Iconoclast of Management[1]

There are some ways in which I might begin life
with hardly any outlay, and yet begin with a good
hope of getting on by resolution and exertion...
and a head to plan.

CHARLES DICKENS, *David Copperfield*

The fundamental qualities for good execution of
a plan are, first, naturally, intelligence; then dis-
cernment and judgment, which enable one to
recognize the best methods to attain it; then
singleness of purpose; and, lastly, what is most
essential of all, will—stubborn will.

MARSHAL FOCH

[1] The author had the privilege of working on this analysis with E. T. Weir on
a number of occasions, discussing his life's thoughts and plans. E. T. Weir
went over several versions of the draft of this chapter. Many of Weir's personal papers and speeches were studied and drawn upon. A number of visits
were made to Weirton. The charts were conceived and executed by R. S.
Weinberg, manager of market research of IBM. The author alone is responsible for the accuracy of the facts and their interpretation.

Most of the great organizers of American business have been the successors to the founders of the great corporations rather than the founders themselves. The entrepreneurial genius who seizes a unique

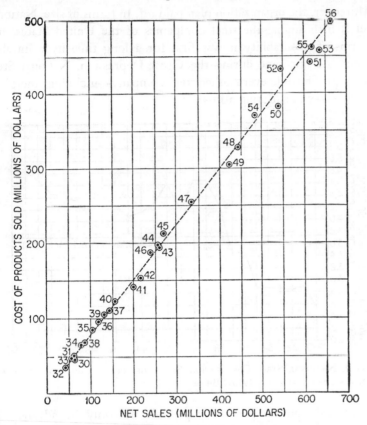

CHART 1. NATIONAL STEEL CORPORATION COSTS OF PRODUCTS SOLD AND NET SALES, 1931–1956

opportunity and builds an empire around it seldom has either the time or the inclination to plan in detail very far in advance.

Ernest Tener Weir, founder of the National Steel Corporation, was an exception to this rule. From the very first he planned his company in its entirety, and it grew according to his plan. When the physical plant consisted only of a run-down tin-plate mill, he had already envisioned a completely integrated steel company—self-sufficient even to ore sources—and had created the nucleus of an organization that could grow as the company grew without major restructuring.

Moreover, the organization plan paid off. In terms of size, National Steel is fifth among the steel companies of the United States, but in terms of profitability it was first for a long time by a number of tests. At one time during the Great Depression, National Steel made a profit while every other steel company—including the giant U.S. Steel—was suffering a loss.

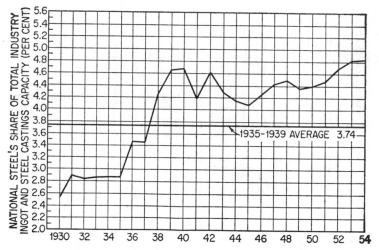

CHART 2. NATIONAL STEEL CORPORATION SHARE OF TOTAL INDUSTRY INGOT AND STEEL CASTINGS CAPACITY, 1930–1954

This profit picture was made possible not only by advances in sales that continued with remarkable steadiness, but by close control of costs, which were held strictly in line with sales. On the few occasions when sales dropped, costs were held absolutely in line. For example, when sales dropped more than $50 million from 1937 to 1938, there was an almost equal drop in cost. Similarly, when sales dipped after World War II, in 1946, 1949, and 1954, there were correspondingly lower costs; in 1949, in fact, the decrease in costs was greater than the decrease in sales. This remarkable correspondence is indicated by Chart 1.

In addition, the company's annual steel-ingot capacity rose more

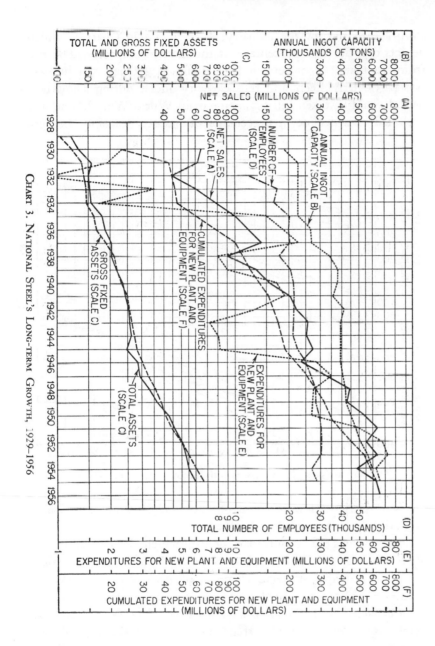

CHART 3. NATIONAL STEEL'S LONG-TERM GROWTH, 1929–1956

steeply than that of the industry, as is shown in Chart 2, which depicts capacity as a percentage of the industry capacity. The rise from less than 2.9 per cent in 1935 to almost 4.7 per cent in 1940 was particularly steep, and thus capacity added during a low-cost period could be taken full advantage of in World War II. The war itself led to a decline in percentage of industry capacity because

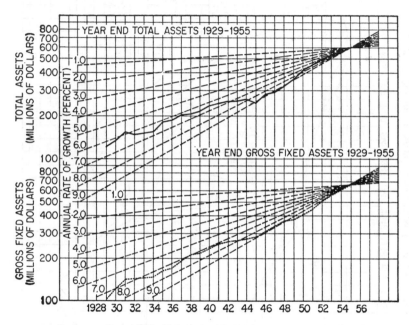

CHART 4. GROSS FIXED ASSETS AND TOTAL ASSETS, 1929–1955

the war restrictions were based on the 1935–1939 average, which in National's case was 3.74 per cent.

Chart 3 shows the extraordinary control which "E. T." had during his 27 years as chief executive at National. This is clearly evident from the principal strategic elements of his company's development. Lines show the development of net sales (scale A), annual ingot capacity (scale B), gross fixed assets and total assets (scale C), number of employees (index trend numbers scale D), expenditures for new plant and equipment (scale E), and cumulated expenditures for new plant and equipment (scale F). At the right and left of the chart (A) relates to scale A, (B) to scale B, and so on.

Charts 4 and 5 show the extraordinary regularity of increase, year by year almost, of capital investment expenditures which are so often subject to violent fluctuations, especially in the steel industry. Chart 4 shows total assets and gross fixed assets from 1929 to 1956 at their annual percentage rate of growth. The growth rate

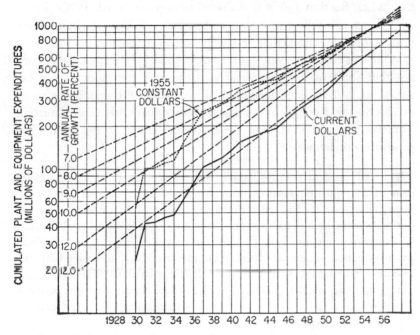

CHART 5. CUMULATED PLANT AND EQUIPMENT EXPENDITURES, 1930–1956

of the former fluctuated between 6 and 9 per cent, that of the latter between 7 and 9 per cent per annum, and this includes the Great Depression years.

Chart 5 shows the cumulated plant and equipment expenditures from 1930 to 1956 in current dollars. These grew steadily at about 12 per cent per annum. Even in terms of "constant dollars," that is, current dollars deflated in terms of 1955 dollars, the fluctuations remain between 7 and 12 per cent per annum.

While there are some breaks in the upward trend of the lines, on the whole there is a remarkable upward consistency, even in the darkest years, in an industry subject to considerable fluctuations.

Weir first became nationally famous—infamous to some—in the 1930's, when he fought unionization more intransigently than his fellow industrialists. He defied government officials in the matter of a union election under the old National Recovery Act—and won his case when Section 7-A was declared unconstitutional. When President Roosevelt talked of "economic royalists," Weir picked up the phrase and announced that he was proud to be one.

Weir was not, however, entirely or even largely the arch-reactionary that some of his words and actions make him appear. For example, in 1932 he developed an analysis of the discrepancy between production and consumption that sounds remarkably like Thorstein Veblen's, though Weir had never read Veblen at the time (and probably not later):

The only reason for production is consumption demand, and there must be a balance between them. If the producer expects his goods consumed, he must do his share in having the consumer's income on an equitable basis. If the producer's profit is excessive, it must be taken from the consumer, and slowly but surely the power of consumption declines and production is not absorbed. Also the trouble is intensified by the producer from his excess share of earnings, using them to increase his plant and equipment, and his production. Thus there results a chasm between the requisites of prosperity—production and consumption—that eventually brings the collapse.

And these words, uttered in 1934, are hardly those of a reactionary: "If there had been some power which could have, by a stroke of the pen, taken some per cent from capital and given it to labor ten years ago, we might have had no depression. The over-expansion of industry would have been curtailed by this mythical reduction in the return to capital, and the purchasing power of wage earners would have been greater by reason of this increase to labor."

Moreover, to a large extent, Weir practiced what he preached. True, he went further than U.S. Steel in reducing wages after 1929, but in 1933 he notified the American Iron and Steel Institute that he was raising wages 15 per cent and forced the rest of the industry to follow suit. "Steel manufacturers," he said, "are not justified in even considering any further liquidation of labor. We have gone, if anything, too far along those lines."

In 1935 he criticized other companies for raising wages, saying the increase was economically unwise, but in 1941 he again forced a rise in industry rates. U.S. Steel, the pace setter for the industry, had not yet settled its union contracts, but Weir knew that the projected profit statements from the industry would show ability to pay and believed that haggling and delay were not justified. As the bickering went on, he told his associates: "It isn't enough—seven cents. When profit reports come later they'll make 'poor mouth' claims look ridiculous. And it will cost a lot of labor confidence." Then suddenly he stopped pacing up and down and called in his public relations man John Ubinger: "You can put out the word that we are raising ten cents an hour—no need to elaborate. We've told our workers."

The announcement dropped like a bomb on the bargaining table where Big Steel and the union leaders were arguing. In a few minutes their long disagreement was dissolved and all steel wages went up ten cents an hour. Weir said: "We felt ten cents the proper figure in view of the industry's earnings. We felt the men should share in that improvement."

Some time later, Weir opposed U.S. Steel's plan to hike prices, supported a wartime price freeze, and marched out of the American Iron and Steel Institute in token of his disagreement.

These contradictions have suggested to some observers that Weir might simply be an "old-fashioned nineteenth-century liberal" who believed that it would be possible to convince businessmen that it would be to their ultimate interest to pay higher wages and hold them to that course by moral suasion.

Certainly his basic philosophy was that of the liberal period in which he grew up, close to John Stuart Mill's principle of "framing the plan of our life so as to suit our character; of doing as we like, subject to such consequences as may follow; without impediment from our fellow-creatures so long as what we do does not harm them, even though they should think our conduct foolish, perverse and wrong." If he was harming his workers by fighting tooth and nail to keep the national unions out of his mills, Weir was not conscious of it, and he seems eventually to have won over the workers themselves to his point of view. (In 1950, when the NLRB held an election in his company, the independent union that had been organized in the meantime won hands down.)

All his life Weir drove his own way, though many of his fellow creatures of varying shades of opinion thought his conduct foolish, perverse, and wrong. In his fight against the unions he was clinging tenaciously to the past, but the ways in which he was ahead of his time are more significant. For it was by violating conservative traditions that he achieved his success.

YOUNG MAN WITH A PLAN

Basic in Weir's career were a lifetime plan and the goal of freedom of action, economic as well as political, social as well as personal. He never forgot his own experience of dependency. He never forgot the dependence of his father, a livery stablekeeper, on the whims of the wealthy who hired the horses. After his father's death, his mother and younger brother were dependent on his own meager earnings, which meant that he himself was dependent on his superiors. From his fear of dependency arose a desire for an integrated operation that would not remain in business "only at the sufferance of someone else."

(Weir's opposition to unions seems to have stemmed from the same cause, more so than from the simple fear that unionization would cost him money. He gained no profit advantage from forcing the industry to raise wages more than it had planned on doing in 1941. Nothing would have been easier for him than to wait for the rest of the industry to settle and then meet the same terms.)

Weir was born in 1875, and began his business career in 1890 when his father died and he had to go to work to help support

his mother and his younger brother. He started as an office boy at
$3 a week and worked 10 to 14 hours a day to make that much.
According to his own account, the family was so poor at this time
that once he was almost unable to get to work because he lacked a
penny for the toll bridge he had to cross on the way. (Just as he
was later to talk bankers into lending him money for his business
ventures, he talked the tollkeeper into lending it to him.)

Weir remained with his first employer, the Braddock Wire
Company, only two years. When he was seventeen he moved to a
clerical job with the Oliver Wire Company and managed to progress
rapidly, acquiring considerable experience in several departments of
the business during the seven years he remained there. In 1898, he
left for the Monongahela Tin Plate Company, which was sold shortly
after to the American Tin Plate Company. By the time he was
twenty-five, he was an assistant manager. In this position his new
superior was James R. Phillips, who, though he was a little older
than Weir, became his friend and later his partner.

In 1901 the United States Steel Corporation took over the American Tin Plate Company, but even in the disruption that generally
attends such an event Weir managed to land on his feet. In that
same year he was placed in charge of the original Monongahela mill
on the south side of Pittsburgh; and in 1903 he became manager
of American's Monessen plant, largest in the Pittsburgh district.

The employee period of his life Weir regarded merely as a
preparation. In preparation for his future career, he systematically
acquired the necessary experience by studying various phases of the
steel business and identifying the steps by which he would progress.
He learned all he could about steelmaking technology, established
important connections, and made himself known as a young man of
high promise.

Also, he checked regularly on the progress of his plans. Even as
a boy of fifteen at Braddock he had figured out that his company
was making enough wire each year to stretch a line to the moon—
about 239,000 miles. He doubted there was need in the world for
that much wire and told his mother, "I guess I'd better look for
another job. There's no future in this one." But his mother could

not afford to lose his weekly income and persuaded him to stay.

Ownership and independence were his ultimate goals, and in this he was entirely in conformity with the ideals of his time. Thus William Miller writes:

> In that era...young men, whether professionally trained or not, who had no prospect of inheriting a business and yet clung to salary jobs... merited as little regard in the business community as spinsters of the same age did at home. Roles of a sort, of course, were prescribed for both spinsters and employees, but for the latter at least, these were likely still to be such as cramp the spirit and cloud over the blue sky of aspiration.[2]

It was in the methods he used to achieve these goals that Weir differed from the majority. The industry was concentrated in Pittsburgh; Weir moved away from it. During the thirties, when the industry was holding up prices and operating at 17 per cent of capacity, Weir cut his prices and kept up volume. He adopted new processes before the rest of the industry considered them feasible, and at a time when large companies were hardening into bureaucracies, he allowed his managers an unprecedented degree of freedom.

Both Weir and his boss at U.S. Steel, Phillips, felt they could have no real future in so large an organization and constantly discussed establishing their own company, even though neither one of them had been able to save much money as yet. "We felt we would do much better in a business in which we would have a substantial share of ownership." But with the trusts gobbling up as much control as possible, it was not until 1905 that Weir and Phillips heard of a small tin-plate mill in Clarksburg, West Virginia, that could be bought at a comparatively low price, especially since its plant was poorly designed, had inefficient machinery, and, as Weir described it, was "horribly congested."

That they themselves had not a tenth of the money needed did not bother them. Phillips was able to get one bank loan, and Weir

[2] "The Business Elite in Business Bureaucracies" in William Miller (ed.), *Men in Business: Essays in the History of Entrepreneurship*, Harvard University Press, Cambridge, Mass., 1952.

went to the Farmer's Bank and talked the president into lending him $10,000 without any collateral, the stipulation being that his father-in-law, who had no collateral either, cosign the note. Because of their reputations as up-and-coming young men, Weir and Phillips were also able to convince others, including the head of the Bank of Pittsburgh, the president of the Fidelity Trust Company, and ten prominent Pittsburghers, each of whom had built his own business, that it would be profitable to put up money for the new firm.

The company had 250 employees and was capitalized at $250,000, $190,000 of which went for the purchase of the plant. Phillips, who became president, died shortly afterwards in a railroad accident near Harrisburg, and the investing group elected Weir to fill the vacant position.

Though the company made money almost from the start, its position was insecure for a long time. Since it was too small to issue bonds or sell common stock, each step toward expansion was marked by a new bank loan. As Weir put it:

> We could have continued on a comfortable basis if we had been content with small operations and small profits. But that was never our idea. From our start, it was our intention to build a successful big company.... Our backs were against the wall many times in those early days. We operated on a shoestring budget. Too many mistakes, one big mistake, or even some accident beyond our control could have broken us.

Early in his career at Clarksburg, one event beyond his control nearly did break him. Weir solved the problem in the characteristically original and slightly ruthless manner that befitted a classical entrepreneur.

Weir had constructed a dam in the West Fork River near the plant, and under ordinary circumstances it would have ensured an adequate water supply for the plant processes. But in the summer and fall of 1908, an unprecedented drought hit West Virginia. No rain fell for months, and the water behind the dam sank dangerously low. The company used the same pickling solutions so many times that the packing on the pumps had to be replaced every day because it was eaten away by the acid. Weir got portable pumping equipment and started pumping out pools left upstream by the drying river, but as the drought dragged on, this source became more and more inadequate.

Finally, Weir cast his eyes on a reservoir commonly supposed to be owned by a nearby chemical company. Though it was pretty much of a forlorn hope, he took the trouble to investigate the title. He discovered that the chemical company actually owned only half of the reservoir. The other half belonged to a local farmer who was perfectly willing to sell. Weir bought the half interest and started pumping that night.

Next morning he got a call from the president of the chemical company in Cleveland. Employees had hastily notified headquarters when they arrived on the scene in the morning.

"I'm just pumping out my half of the water," Weir said innocently. "I bought it yesterday. By the time you can get here, I'll have my half."

The chemical company president called his attorney, John W. Davis, later Democratic candidate for the Presidency, whose birthplace was Clarksburg. Davis agreed that Weir was entitled to his half of the water, but suggested that cooperation in finding other sources might be more profitable than fighting over the division of the scarcity. Weir was willing enough to settle on this basis, and the two companies joined forces to prospect for supplies. By surveying the country for miles around, they found enough pools to carry them through until the drought finally broke early in December.

Meanwhile, in the sales field, Weir was bucking U.S. Steel. Instead of trying to beat the giant corporation on its own terms, he sought gaps in its sales efforts. He used a different price and discount policy and stressed personal attention to customers, providing a good deal of it himself. Gradually he acquired a number of small customers and became their personal friend. Later on, a strike at U.S. Steel's competitive tin-plate mills helped him to gain a larger foothold. From then on Weir took a leading role in selling, either personal or inspirational, following the Carnegie maxim: "Give me a market and I give you a mill."

EXPANSION AND INTEGRATION

The first large expansion movement was planned as a means of protecting the independence of the company. Weir bought his sheet-bar semifinished steel from the U.S. Steel Corporation, as did almost all the other independent tin-plate producers. But this principal supplier was also a competitor in the sale of tin plate, and he knew that the corporation had the power to put him out of business. So he went to Judge Gary, head of the corporation, and told him: "You can break me. You can close me out if you cut the price of plate and keep the price of sheet up or if you decide not to sell me sheet bar. I must know where I stand."

Judge Gary admitted that what Weir said was true. But as of that moment, he said, the corporation had no idea of doing any of the things Weir had mentioned. Then he added: "I cannot give you any guarantee against it. As I say, young man, we haven't any such moves in mind now. But who knows about the future?"

Weir did not choose to remain in business "only by the sufferance of someone else," even though the worst never happened. (In the end, U.S. Steel tried to "join" rather than "fight" Weir and offered him the presidency and an annual salary of $1 million, which he refused.) To assure himself a supply of sheet, he had to be his own supplier, "have a 'Little Steel' fashioned after 'Big Steel,' where you provided everything for yourself. For this reason we had to have an integrated steel operation from the very beginning."

So Weir borrowed another $300,000 and, after careful considera-- tion of alternatives, purchased 105 acres of apple orchard and wheat- fields at Crawford Crossing, West Virginia, and called it Weirton.

The choice of the new location, away from the obvious spot, Pittsburgh, is an example of Weir's unorthodox approach. In Pittsburgh he would not have had to build up an entirely new community from scratch and there would have been certain "external economies"—suppliers and legal, financial, and accounting services would have been readily available.

Weir did not choose the conventional way because, as he put it, we had something else important in mind besides building an integrated plant. We knew that our location would become the main location for our company. We were convinced that the principles and process on which we operated our business would make a basis of peace and harmony possible if we could establish our own environment. Naturally, we could not do that in an existing industrial center. In such a center we would have to share the existing environment, including the attitudes, prejudices, and antagonisms that had built up during its entire previous history.

In order to get harmony and goodwill we were entirely willing to undertake the double burden of building a new community at the same time as we were building our new plant and to undergo the growing pains that such a venture involved. And that is why Weirton did not come into being through accident . . . it was deliberately selected and consciously planned as the location for both a steel plant and a community.[3]

In selecting this spot, Weir, who had no formal training in economics, could not have followed the dictates of the complex economic theory of location more closely if he had worked with a textbook in his hand. The site was close to coal resources, and the coal could be transported by river. Ore would also be transported cheaply, by water to the lower Great Lakes ports and then by rail transshipment. Heavy finished products could be delivered to customers along water routes at a relatively low cost as well as by rail. A "windfall revenue" could be obtained from some customers in the immediate vicinity of Weirton, since, under the old basing-point system, they paid Pittsburgh prices plus the freight rate to Weirton, though this was counterbalanced to some extent by freight cost to customers east of Pittsburgh. The new site was also advantageously near markets—half the population of the United States was within a 500-mile radius. There was adequate water supply; the plant location was free from the floods that threatened so many other sites; and, above all, there was plenty of room for expansion.

Weir built the first tin-plate plant at the lower line of the valley but close to the hills. If it had been his intention to build a finishing plant alone, this move would have been uneconomical. It was logical only in terms of a fully integrated steel plant.

[3] "Some Aspects of Our Personal History," speech given on Feb. 24, 1955.

The first plant, costing about a million dollars and necessitating further loans, was in operation before the end of 1909 and consisted of ten mills. Another ten mills were added in 1910, twelve more in 1911 (through the purchase of the Pope Tin Plate Company of Steubenville, Ohio), four more in 1914, two in 1915. In a few years the company had fifty mills: twenty-six at Weirton, twelve at Steubenville, and twelve at Clarksburg. It was the largest producer of tin plate in the country outside of U.S. Steel. The process of integration was furthered by World War I, which provided an opportunity to set up steel mills and blast furnaces, and in 1920 an up-to-date steel plant was completed. Prior to and during this time Weir purchased iron-ore properties in the Great Lakes region and acquired coal lands in Pennsylvania and West Virginia. Weirton Steel then had more than 5,000 workers and sales of more than $50 million annually. The growth of the company proceeded with remarkable steadiness over its first twenty years.

A real community to support and benefit the commercial venture was planned at the time Weirton property was purchased. Weir said many years later:

As we were walking over the vacant fields and looking over the land, if someone then could have opened a door to the future and made us see the panorama of mills, houses, churches, schools, stores and everything else that goes to make up the Weirton of today, naturally we would have been highly pleased—but I cannot say honestly that we would have been greatly surprised. Because when we came here, it was already a settled matter that we would build a completely integrated steel plant and the community to support it.

The original community, called The Cove, consisted of a few houses. Today Weirton has a population of 30,000, an area of 18 square miles, and 6,400 houses. The physical equipment of the city compares in quality and quantity with the best in the country.

Weir organized the town, as well as the company, according to his own ideas; much of the actual plan was conceived and carried out by Thomas Millsop, Weir's protegé and then president of Weirton Steel. There are only a few city employees; and the cost of running the city is said to be lower per head than that of any other city in the United States, and real estate taxes per head are among the lowest. Most services are contracted for on the basis of bids. All expenses—including postage—are published, so that the administration of all city affairs is indeed a "public" affair. Each householder undertook to pay for paving his part of the street and constructing part of sewers, and the city notes financing the payments were largely paid off on presentation. Ninety-five per cent of Weirton's employed population own their own homes.

Some of the community's feelings may be indicated by the fact that the man who succeeded Weir as president of the company, Thomas E. Millsop, was elected and reelected mayor, though the town is heavily Democratic in national elections and he is a Republican.

By 1929 Weirton Steel was almost twenty-five years old, an established company and an extremely profitable one. And it was still closely held in undisputed control by those who founded it.

But it had one vulnerable point. Though Weir had acquired coal and ore holdings before Weirton was ten years old, the company was far from self-sufficient in raw material. Fifty per cent of the Superior ore reserves, which at that time supplied four-fifths of the steel industry, were owned by U.S. Steel, and other large steel producers had bought up most of the remainder.

One of the few remaining independents was the M. A. Hanna Company, which possessed large reserves of ore, mostly in the Mesabi range. Under the competent direction of George M. Humphrey, later U.S. Secretary of the Treasury, who had helped to reorganize it in 1922, Hanna operated as an independent selling to independents, of whom Weir was one.

But there was a possibility that Weir might lose this source. Cyrus Eaton was then attempting to put together the country's second largest steel company, and it was not improbable that he, or someone else with the same idea, might come to dominate Weir's major independent source of supply. Weir decided that his investment would be better protected if he were "Mr. Humphrey's partner rather than Mr. Humphrey's customer." Humphrey, sensing the difficult years ahead, preferred assured markets to the insecurity of independence.

Weir was also anxious to expand his steel production facilities. Dependence on a single product (tin plate) seemed too dangerous. And he foresaw that the great markets of the future would be the Middle West in general and the automobile industry in particular. So he directed his attention to the Great Lakes Steel Corporation, at Ecorse, a suburb of Detroit.

Great Lakes Steel was itself something of a maverick in the industry. At that time the steel industry had an inhibition about construction in the Detroit area. To open a plant there was something that "just wasn't done." The company was the brain child of George R. Fink, who had sold sheet steel to the automobile industry and had good connections with it. Though a large steel company was said to have offered him a good position if he would desist from opening a plant near the big auto companies, he went ahead on a small scale. Then by 1929 he had done so well that he decided to expand, and selected a site on the Detroit River for a larger plant. Although he was able to raise $20 million, he needed more new capital, and this he could get from Weirton while still preserving the company's identity, which might have been lost had he merged it with a large concern. In becoming a part of the more diversified enterprise, he became less completely dependent on the automobile industry, and the ore resources and nearby blast furnaces of M. A. Hanna assured him of supplies and saved further heavy investments.

Agreement of the merger was reached just before the stock market crash in 1929, and the accord was formally ratified just after the break. Weir got a 50 per cent interest in the newly formed company, which was named the National Steel Corporation, and became its chief executive and chairman of the board. Fink got a 25 per cent interest and became president, and Humphrey got the remaining 25 per cent and became a member of National's Board and chairman of its executive committee. The M. A. Hanna Company did not itself go into the merger. Instead, it maintained its identity as an affiliated company and contributed the ore, the Detroit blast furnaces, and the freighters.

Weir brought in not only Humphrey's assets, but also one of the country's best business brains. As chairman of its executive committee, Humphrey took a prominent part in the company's affairs from the very beginning of his association with it. He became chairman of the board in 1957 after leaving his post as Secretary of the Treasury in order to smooth the changes caused by Weir's death that year. One of Humphrey's important planning contributions was his exploration of related investments and discovery of aggressive managements, which he very successfully combined with M. A. Hanna's investments, such as the Pittsburgh Consolidated Coal Company and the Iron Ore Company of Canada.

There was no new equity financing in the consolidation, no "water," and no promoter's profits. Weir asked banks for a promissory note of $40 million ("it was like asking for the National Debt at that time") and got it with no collateral other than his promise to repay and to issue bonds later as conditions might warrant.

INGREDIENTS OF SUCCESS

Born at the outset of the Great Depression, National Steel might have been expected to collapse almost immediately; from Hanna, Weir got no advantages competitors did not already have, and Great Lakes was handicapped by the worst automobile depression in the history of the industry. Instead, National Steel produced at 62 per cent of capacity while competitors were down to 25 per cent and below. In 1932 Weir made a profit while the rest of the industry was losing money. In 1933 he made a greater profit than all the rest of the industry. How was this possible?

1. National Steel's finishing capacity was considerably in excess of its furnace capacity. Hence it could adapt production to falling demand by the inexpensive method of shutting down a strip mill rather than by the costly process of shutting down a blast furnace.

2. Great Lakes Steel could supply large quantities of steel at low selling and transportation expense; even small quantities could be sold at a profit and supplied in a hurry. "This 'grocery store' busi-

ness did not make anyone rich but it kept Fink from becoming poor."

3. The world had to continue to eat, and much of the food it needed had to be conserved in tin.

4. Finally, the techniques of production were highly efficient, and though it was unostentatious and largely unpublicized, National's management was one of the most competent in America.

Technical innovations included the four-high continuous mill— Weir acquired the patents and built the mills in 1927 before anyone else in the steel industry had introduced the process, though he had to borrow $7 million to finance the construction. This converted a job that had taken a whole day into a three-minute operation. He was also one of the pioneers in another revolutionary technical advance, the electrolytic tinning of steel, building an experimental line in 1938 and going into production in the spring of 1943. In World War II his second-in-command, Thomas Millsop, undertook to roll brass on large steel equipment—a feat never before attempted and for technical reasons considered impossible. In a month's time, Weirton became the country's largest producer of rolled brass and was responsible for breaking a procurement bottleneck. Later the company devised methods of rolling magnesium sheets. In the production of an essential atomic-bomb material, Weirton solved problems that producers in other fields had refused even to tackle.

In the field of organization, Weir built a logical structure from the very first, observing—though he had never heard of them—two of the classical rules of organization: unity of command and authority commensurate with responsibility.

Though he was never much concerned with organization charts and manuals, and in fact operated for a long time without even a chart, he early laid out the broad outlines of the principal jobs, dividing the work logically so that the profitability of the various functions could be gauged.

At the very first, he did transgress the rule that authority should be delegated along with responsibility, but because—unlike many business geniuses—he permitted subordinates to disagree with him, he corrected this fault at the instance of one of the salesmen he hired when he found that he could no longer handle both the sales function and the job of chief executive.

Moreover, he introduced some ideas that organization planners in other companies began to approach cautiously only in very recent times; for example, he delegated both responsibility and authority as far down the line as possible, with control exercised through profit and loss statements rather than through rules regarding set ways of doing things.

From an engineering viewpoint, the individual mill was of optimum size for management; similarly, the optimum unit in marketing was a group of customers for certain specialties or a particular territory. In each case, the "middle manager," who was managing a unit just about large enough for one man to comprehend all the details, was charged with the basic decision making and stood or fell on results.

Weir went much further in this than do many companies that believe they have "decentralized decision making" today. A superintendent of a nearby company once commented:

I have never been able to understand why we do not have financial authority commensurate with responsibility. I have friends at a competitive company [Weirton] and I know that when they write a good order, they get what they need. They don't have to sit around writing justifications and explain why they need it to everybody. They are responsible people holding responsible jobs and they know it is up to them to make a good showing cost-wise, and everybody knows that they don't order things unless they are aboslutely needed. But when they say they want it, they get it immediately. A general superintendent [in our company] can make a mistake that will cost the company half a million dollars, yet he cannot authorize the purchase of a $5,000 tractor.

And middle management did not hesitate to insist on its prerogatives. One new higher-echelon executive who persisted in checking too closely on a lesser member of the management team was frankly told: "This is not the way we do things here. I am not a flunky. If you want to know how I'm doing, take a look at the profit and loss statement." The underling not only got away with it, but also won his point and was free from further interference.

Weir's strong belief in maximum freedom of operation for all managers, including foremen, is one explanation for his stubborn refusal to recognize international unions. He thereby avoided their severe restrictions on work assignment and change of assignments and so increased his supervisors' powers to meet company goals.

Moreover, Weir did not allow the staff men to proliferate as they have often done in other companies. Headquarters staff was kept small, and staff work was supplied where it was most needed, in the field helping with day-to-day problems. Staff men were flexible and could be easily and quickly shifted to new assignments. Central activities were confined to financing, purchasing, and coordinated control.

Since Weir delegated so much real authority, he had time to keep up personal contacts with his executives and through his own leadership imbue them with the company policies that had meant success: first-class personal service to all customers, punctuality (telegrams, even from overseas, were answered within a half-hour of receipt and the answers were equivalent to contracts), acceptable or more than acceptable prices, etc.

Putting together the resources of Hanna, Great Lakes, and Weirton was perhaps the most important of Weir's organization feats. It fitted perfectly into the natural tendencies and development of the steel industry

Weir thought little of formal management training and appraisal forms. The very real delegation of authority and responsibility, combined with the full exercise of accountability, he believed, provides enough training and affords the logical means of appraisal through results.

In this, and in his view that the top manager needs considerable knowledge of all the technical specialties (a training he systematically acquired in his employee days), Weir may appear to have been lagging behind the times. Actually, he may have been ahead of them. The view that management is a "skill in itself" which exists independently of technological knowledge may have been somewhat overdone in recent years. Perhaps it has led to overdependence on certain types of staffs and consequently to growth in overhead. Undoubtedly, technical skill—in metallurgy, or sales, for example—may exist without the ability to plan and coordinate that is the essence of the management job. But the man who plans and co-ordinates, no matter how logically, is at a distinct disadvantage if he has no real knowledge of the things he is planning and co-ordinating.

Weir knew production, he knew financing, and he knew sales and sales problems; in fact, he continued personal selling to some extent almost to the end of his life.

Since Weir was a substantial stockholder himself, he placed prime emphasis on the best use of his and other stockholders' investment. The principal method of control was through a profit and loss system for the main organization units (Weirton, Great Lakes, etc.) and through regular examination of controllable sales costs for the units that were not so large. Much of the detailed control was exercised by the small "management company," which occupied only half a floor in Pittsburgh's Grant Building and contained few but extremely able minds in general management, law, and finance. Finally, banks played an important part in his controls. Weir was continuously in debt, and as soon as one loan was paid off, he entered upon an even larger one: "We've always been in debt and I hope we always will be. It keeps us working harder." Surplus was kept in inventories and fixed assets. "A big cash balance is a terrible thing. It encourages the idea that the company is rich."

It must be noted also that there were important elements of luck in Weir's success. He got into the tin-plate business (where food canning made for a stable or rising demand) more or less by acci-dent. He was raised to the presidency of his new company by the premature death of Phillips. And he was enabled to gather in new customers by a strike against his competitors in tin plate. Later, his company grew with the rising demand for steel from the auto-mobile companies.

But subtracting these nonrepetitive factors, the other ingredients of Weir's success may be instructive.

PERSONAL QUALIFICATIONS FOR SUCCESS

The achievement of Weir's plan was, of course, a highly complex affair, and an outside analyst can, at best, trace only some of the elements.

First among the elements were his own personal qualifications, consisting partly of traits often characteristic of other great founders and organizers, but to some extent underplayed in the selection and development of higher executives today.

Weir had a highly logical mind. He clearly recognized the basic and essential aspects in the business situations that confronted him, and he organized to meet them. His selection of the site at Clarksburg and the fitting together of the logical combination of National Steel were two examples. Another was his successful move in keeping up volume by cutting prices during the Great Depression.

Weir had an innovating disposition and the ability to face risk. He was an innovator in all phases of the business, not only in technical advances but in the location of his plant away from the steel centers, and in building his own community from scratch. He never "played it safe" by waiting to see what the rest of the industry would do. Instead, he obtained new bank loans and went ahead.

He had an absolute will to succeed and few and uncomplicated goals. He sought only business success in the nineteenth-century tradition in which he grew up and complete independence.

Weir possessed great technical knowledge. In his employee period, he systematically acquired knowledge of as many phases of the business as possible, including the technical advances. For this reason he was on surer ground in introducing his innovations than he would have been if he had had to depend entirely on the advice of others, however competent.

Weir's physical energy was prodigious. In his younger days he could work around the clock for several days together, or drive himself steadily for months at a time. Even in his old age he would sometimes have appointments all day in one city, fly home, and then have a long dinner conference on an urgent issue.

His words and deeds were consistent with each other. Although Weir possessed in great measure the ability to make friends and deal diplomatically with others (when he thought it necessary) and to impress others (notably hard-headed bankers) with his own competence, he was not "cooperative" in the usual business sense today; that is, he was not a compromiser willing to water down his views to make them more acceptable, to impress others, or to avoid offending.

One strange quirk in Weir's nature was an extraordinary devotion to the book *David Copperfield*. He once said he had read it a hundred times and would continue to reread it. He kept a copy at each of his five homes and a supply to give away. Did he see in Copperfield's early hardships a parallel with his own early life? Was he warned by the example of Micawber against shiftlessness? Or was there a streak of nineteenth-century sentimentality in him that was warmed by Dickens' occasional mawkishness? Or did Dickens provide him with an escape from the everyday material world?

It is impossible to say. But this strange love for a single book seems to be one way in which he differed from the classic type of entrepreneur—the single-minded innovator and risk taker who concentrates almost entirely on business. His other choices of reading matter were very wide. He preferred the lasting to the ephemeral: books on world affairs, biographies, and history, though he also read detective stories. He read extremely fast and had an extraordinarily retentive memory.

MECHANICS OF SUCCESS

The methods Weir utilized in achieving his success may be summed up under a few headings:

A lifetime plan. Once Weir decided to quit U.S. Steel, he clearly established the goal of building one of the largest integrated steel companies in the country. The Clarksburg tin-plate mill was a stopgap to contribute the necessary funds. He deliberately planned the location of Weirton to make possible an integrated company.

In making, disseminating, and checking on his plans, Weir did not use forms, charts, high-powered machines, and pyrotechnical presentations so dear to the organization man. He focused his mind on the basic questions separating the primary from the secondary, or "details," as he put it. He would draw on his experience and memory, his travels and personal visits and interviews, and use one or at most a few outstanding fact finders. In this way he would assemble something like 85 per cent of the facts obtainable and apply his penetrating analysis to the essentials, conceive the plan, tell his associates about it, and follow it up himself.

Flexibility. Though Weir held tenaciously to his basic objective, he was unusually flexible in the ways in which he sought his ends. Consistency was not a trait he sought to display. He would change his policy violently if he could thereby serve the end, as when he changed his pricing drastically at the outset of the Great Depression and reverted from bulk selling to hand-to-mouth peddling during the great automobile slump. He also rapidly reversed his wage policies when economic conditions changed or when an increase became necessary to ensure that no international union gained a foothold in his mills.

His internal company organization was highly flexible. It was motivated by high rewards, emphasis on the survival of the fittest, and a degree of independence for subordinate managers unusual in industry. He placed no emphasis on formal organization or formal development of individuals. (The latter omission may have been somewhat unwise since at one point the company hastily had to hire executives from other steel companies.)

Conformity in objectives, nonconformity in reaching them. Weir always accepted the basic values of the society in which he grew up. His main objective was frankly the accumulation of wealth, plus independence and freedom to maneuver. He was unorthodox only in his methods of reaching his goals, and that probably because no orthodox ways were open to him.

The fact that he was willing to act differently from competition was his chief strength. If everyone had cut prices when he did, there would hardly have been a larger volume for all. But because he was willing to run away from the crowd, he profited. Similarly, because no one else had thought to move steel mills away from Pittsburgh, he gained advantages of location. He utilized "the power of being a positive stinker" by doing things that were distinctly "not done" in the industry.

Ruthless execution of plans. Weir's long-range goal was broken down into annual rates of increase in what he considered to be the major measures of growth. Assets, investment in plant and equipment were to grow by more or less steady increments regardless of general steel contractions. And expenses for wages and salaries and maintenance were not to get out of line. Through "responsibility accounting" he held each executive rigidly accountable for results both quantitatively and qualitatively. He enforced a Draconian adherence to his plans, even in the depths of depression, on himself as well as on his associates. Financing through bank loans, he said, "keeps us working harder."

Personal inspection and hard work. Though he allowed his executives more freedom than other top managers often do, he did not separate himself entirely from the details of the business. He kept in touch by frequent telephone calls and visits to the various locations. And to avoid corruption from success, Weir liked to quote Einstein: "The only way to escape personal corruption of praise is to go on working. One is tempted to stop and listen to it. The only thing is to turn away and go on working. Work. There is nothing else."

An egalitarian top structure. Weir was deeply conscious of the need for a small oligarchy that could discuss all matters freely. He paid salaries equal to his to the top men, believing they made equal contributions to the company, and preferred to have a group of outstanding top men rather than the biddable nonentities many of the corporate founders surround themselves with.

If much of Weir's later nonconformity turned into rebellion, it may in fact be explained by his clinging to the value structure and goals of his youth when those of his society, and increasingly those of many of his competitors, were changing. As Weir was fond of saying, "There was much that was good in the good old days." It was this that brought Weir into conflict with the New Deal and with many of his business friends (e.g., U.S. Steel and later Ford, after the latter's recognition of CIO unions and the grant of the union shop). Not even Walter Teagle, late president of Standard Oil Company of New Jersey, was able to ease his continued disagreement with the labor boards of the Roosevelt administration (Hugh Johnson threatened to jail him, and his interviews with FDR were mostly cat-and-mouse games).

When Weir had won his battles in a formal way, he became less negative regarding the changing value structure of his time and turned to what might be called constructive nonconformity in the last part of his life. During World War II he fully cooperated in the American war effort, even to the extent of undertaking some seemingly impossible jobs—for example, the rolling of brass on large steel equipment.

THE LATER YEARS

After World War II Weir became convinced that complete refusal to accept the changing values of his society was fruitless and frustrating. Consequently, he actively tried to help shape the values and to persuade others to do the same and to support their beliefs by political action. His basic belief in freedom of economic opportunity and freedom of action did not change appreciably. He still attempted to reduce the scope of governmental intervention. But here, unlike the large majority of businessmen, he attempted to strike at the heart of the government's base for intervention, namely, what he considered to be the excessive amount of international tension and armament. If it could be reduced, then a greater area of freedom for economic and political action would be assured. It was the negative action by governments all over the world that he tried to counter by being positive.

Weir liked to quote Lord Attlee's observation on how to make progress on big, seemingly unresolvable issues: "When the logs are jammed in the river, one must begin by extricating one or two, in the hope that thereby the whole mess might move." And beyond that Weir felt—again unlike many businessmen—that he and his confreres should participate in politics to help legislate a type of government intervention which provides for opportunity or at least does not hinder it.

Toward this end, he wrote annually several papers and speeches, reviving the art of pamphleteering and carrying it to a high level of effectiveness. The Weir tracts were requested by hundreds of thousands of write-ins to the company, even though there was hardly any newspaper or other publicity. As involved in what he considered to be the big international issues as he was in his own affairs, he attempted to be supremely rational in an irrational world. Writing with persuasiveness and forcefulness, he anticipated Ambassador Kennan and Senator Fulbright by almost a decade in his proposals which were designed to halt rising military budgets and the abysmal decline of professional diplomacy, to promote rising living standards and the good life. To this Weir devoted the last ten years of his life. It was the one issue he had not resolved at his death.

The Incurables

Forbes Magazine

A good many Americans dream about starting their own companies, but most of them never get beyond dreaming. They're simply not entrepreneurs. There are others, however, a handful, so thoroughly entrepreneurial they're not satisfied with starting one company and spending the rest of their lives running it. They start company after company. For these people, entrepreneur-ing is a way of life.

Neison and Irving Harris of Chicago built the Toni Company from scratch, then sold it to Gillette for $20 million. That was in 1948, when $20 million was as good as $30 million is today. And what did the Harris brothers do? Retire? No, they bought an old corporate shell and turned it into a $64-million-a-year industrial products maker called Pittway Corp. At that point, more money was the last thing they needed, yet they kept going. "Retire?" snorts Neison Harris. "I just don't know what the hell I'd do in the morning if I couldn't go to work."

The Harris brothers are not unique. In recent weeks, *Forbes* reporter Alex Block has talked with others like them, outstanding examples of the entrepreneurial breed, individuals who have started not one but two or more successful enterprises. He found them a diverse lot. Some were born to wealth; others rose from poverty. Some were salesmen, some technicians, some plain businessmen. They operated in widely diverse fields, from pet foods to jet aircraft, from publishing to transistors. But they had, he found, certain things in common:

They were not interested primarily in money but in creating and building companies. In several cases, when they sold a company they had started, they received so much stock for it they could have taken over control of the company to which they sold it. They didn't, because that wouldn't have been any fun; they would be running something that somebody else created. They would be managers, not entrepreneurs.

The companies they created and built were substantial and profitable but hardly in the billion-dollar class. They did have the base on which to build a billion-dollar conglomerate, but, again, that would have meant taking over businesses established by others. That's not for them. They have an ill-disguised disdain for the men who put together conglomerates. Such men are not creators.

Ask them why they refused to retire, and the usual answer given is, "How would I spend my time?" That obviously is not the real answer, because there are dozens of ways in which a retired man can spend his time — in public service, in politics, by going into Wall Street, by going fishing. To the born entrepreneur, building a business from scratch is a way of life. It's not only his occupation; it is also his vocation and his relaxation.

Reprinted by permission of *Forbes* Magazine from the July 1, 1969 issue, pp. 21–23, 60. **365**

The classic example of the entrepreneurial breed probably is Sherman Fairchild. His father was a founder and the largest shareholder of International Business Machines. Obviously, every door at IBM was open to Sherman. He turned his back on the company. It was not that he scorned his father's money, but IBM was his father's baby, already grown to manhood. He wanted to build something he could proudly call his own. He founded Fairchild Camera & Instrument, the Fairchild Hiller Corp., then Fairchild Recording Equipment. Money? What did he need money for, especially after his father's death, when he became IBM's biggest stockholder? He had an urge to create that has grown stronger with the years. He says: "The truth is that the man who just thinks of making money usually doesn't make much money. You've got to have your eye not on the money but on the job. I've never met a real entrepreneur for whom getting wealthy was the sole object."

Superficially, no one could seem more different from Fairchild than Jeno Paulucci. Yet, basically, they are alike. Jeno Paulucci, son of an immigrant iron miner, is by his own estimate worth about $100 million at the age of 51. In 1966 he sold Chun King to Reynolds Tobacco for $63 million and began building a corporate shell he had held for several years into a brand-new food business, Jeno's, Inc. He gets to his Duluth, Minn. office at 6 A.M. and often works seven days a week. Paulucci says an entrepreneur is a man "who sacrifices everything to his work," not just for money, but for a burning desire to meet a challenge. The money's just a way to measure how successful you are.

William Lear comes from a very different background. A school dropout in the eighth grade, Lear started out as an airplane mechanic for the U.S. Airmail base at Grant Park in Chicago. But he agrees with Paulucci that the entrepreneur can do things no big company can.

"I want to be in a position where I can put an idea into effect," Lear says. "I don't want to have to sell it to four or five different levels of people. If my idea loses *I* lose. If it wins I win. You can't do that in many big corporations."

Says Jeno Paulucci, echoing Lear's dislike of depending on others: "I can't wait even a few days to convince people that what I'm doing is right. I'm in a hurry even when I may be wrong."

William Lear founded Lear, Inc., a manufacturer of aviation electronics; sold the company to Siegler and founded Lear Jet; sold that to Gates Rubber and now runs Lear Motors. His background is just as different from Paulucci's as Paulucci's is from Fairchild's. But he agrees with Paulucci that money is secondary. "I think I'd work even harder if I had a *trillion dollars*," says Bill Lear. "When I see a good thing that needs doing I want to do it. Like the thing I'm working on now, steam power plants for automobiles."

For a while Lear headed a good-sized public company, Lear, Inc. But he quit in frustration when his board of directors refused to let him build his now-famed Lear jet. "Why I might as well have been the janitor there," he says. "At least the janitor could decide on his own where he wanted to sweep."

Jack Kent Cooke, a Canadian, sold his interests in radio and publishing in

1959 when he was 47 and came to Los Angeles to retire. "I found I missed the fun and hurly burly of business," he says, "and in 1965 I went back to work." Cooke is president and owner of the L.A. Lakers basketball team, the L.A. Kings pro hockey team and the Forum, a new $16-million sports arena.

With a personal wealth estimated at nearly $40 million, Cooke could easily have bought control of a large business and tried to make it bigger. But that wasn't what he was after. "I need the feeling that I'm in effective control of the business. That's what makes me different from the professional managers. I guess it isn't fair to call them mercenaries, but their attitude is different from the entrepreneur's."

"They Are Stooges"

German-born Max Ries, 68, has started successful companies on both sides of the Atlantic. In 1940 he fled from Hitler. "I had to make a living here," he says, "and so I started peddling cheese from store to store from my car." Before he was finished, Ries had built his company, Reese Foods, into a $7.5-million-a-year seller of specialty food items. He sold it to Pet Inc. in 1964. Two years later he was back in business, partly because he was bored and partly because he disapproved of what the new owners were doing with his old company. "These big companies," he says in his German accent, "they are very funny. They are stooges. They're more interested in showing what *can't* be done than in what can be done." Ries is now in the snuff business. He says: "All the kids in England are using it, soon they will be here also."

Richard Rich, 38, got a degree in business administration from NYU before entering advertising. After bouncing around several agencies he helped found the now-famous Wells, Rich, Greene advertising agency which he left this past April. Rich, who still holds several hundred thousand shares of Wells, Rich, Greene stock valued at over $3 million, is now starting his own advertising consulting service. Work for someone else or be part of a big agency? "Would you ask Howard Huges that? I've been at the very top of the most glamorous agency ever to hit Madison Avenue. I couldn't see myself working for someone else." Says Jeno Paulucci: "As soon as Reynolds acquired my company and put me on salary I felt inhibited. So I left."

Eduard Baruch sold his Heli-Coil to Topps Industries in 1956 and bought it back 13 months later. Since then he has built its sales from $2 million to $20 million. "These big company people," he says, "are good to move into an organization that already has been created. But they haven't had the exposure to run on their own. They learn about business in graduate school but they haven't actually been out on their own. They should get out and work on the factory floor and get out in the field and sell and find out how people think — what motivates them."

Max Geffen ... has started two successful magazines and several companies and sold them to bigger companies, including McGraw-Hill where he is one of the biggest shareowners. He [recently launched] a new magazine, *Family Health*. Geffen is worth maybe $50 million and, at 73, needs another business like a hole in the head. But he says, "Working is so much more fun than sitting around."

Geffen, too, scorns the idea that money is the main motive for the successful entrepreneur. "I always start a publication when I think it can perform a public service. That's the only kind that makes money. If you're doing a good job, then somebody wants it. Otherwise you're just forcing it on the public, and that's no damned good.

"I never started anything to make money. I've been wealthier than I want to be for 20 years. I don't want to be Charlie Allen or Howard Hughes. I know some of these really rich men and they haven't got anything I can't have. I play golf with a man who is worth about $1 billion and I walk down the fairway with him and he hasn't got a thing I haven't got. In fact, I have to give him strokes."

Dreamer vs. Doer

What are the qualities that an entrepreneur needs? Perhaps these people aren't the most objective observers but we asked them all the same.

"They have to have vision," says Sherman Fairchild. "As contrasted with just having a dream. We have lots of dreamers. Not so many entrepreneurs. The dreamer figures, 'Wouldn't it be nice to have so-and-so.' But he doesn't have any idea how he is going to accomplish this. Real talent has organized vision. The fellow who says, 'Wouldn't it be nice to have an automobile that ran on half the amount of gas? Think of all the money it could make' is a dreamer. I say to him, 'Come up with an idea how you are going to accomplish this.' "

Bill Lear says: "I'm not a good manager. I have an enormous distaste for management. Every minute I spend on it makes me just much less useful at what I am good at.

"What I'm good at is interphasing. That's not the same as being an inventor. An inventor thinks of things that have never been done before. An interphaser is a guy who puts things together that already exist and makes new and better combinations." Lear regards his Lear jet as an example of interphasing. "I wanted to make it so bad I could taste it," he says, explaining why he quit the chairmanship of Lear, Inc. when the board of directors refused to let him go ahead with the project.

Jeno Paulucci says much the same thing in different words. "It's not just a question of long hours and hard work. It's guts. You have to go at it with sheer determination. Otherwise the pitfalls will put you off.

"This is why big companies have to go out and acquire smaller ones. There is a quality in starting a business that only an entrepreneur can provide. My accolades to Reynolds for what they've done since they took over Chun King. But no big company can do as good a job as the individual entrepreneur."

Expensive Is Cheap

Another trait these brilliantly successful entrepreneurs share is a belief in the importance of supplementing their own talents with those of others. They know their limitations. Self-confident though they are, they don't regard themselves as gods. "The most important thing in business," says Neison Harris, "is having people work with you, not for you." Even Lear, who has a reputation for being a lone wolf, emphasizes people. "The greatest mistake I ever made was hiring the second-best man for the job. You pay a terrible penalty for that. No matter what it costs, it's cheaper than hiring the second-best man."

"The most important thing in any business," says Max Geffen, "is attaching the right people to you. The people below you. The people next to you. And the people above you."

Sherman Fairchild waxes eloquent on the subject of getting the best people. Fairchild says that as an entrepreneur he gets as much kick out of devising new organizational tools as out of inventing such things as the aerial camera. New ways to get and keep top-notch people, for example.

"One thing I try to do is regard my executives as partners. My father used to tell me, 'Son, don't worry about how much money you're going to make. Get the right guy in and make *him* a lot of money and that's all you'll need.' I've always followed that advice."

In getting Dr. C. Lester Hogan to leave Motorola and come to Fairchild . . . , Fairchild found a new way to follow his father's advice. He lent Hogan $5 million, interest free, to buy Fairchild stock. "This was a very new thing," Fairchild says, "but a very logical thing. I didn't get him on the basis of 'Look, I'm going to pay you more money.' I talked with him, found out what he wanted in life. I put myself in his place. I asked what would attract him. That's when I came up with the restricted options and interest-free loan."

Fairchild has thought a good deal about the characteristics he wants in his executives. "I look for the ability to study a situation and not be blinded by a lot of past statistics that say it can't be done. Sure it's going to be tough. If it wasn't some dope would have done it already. The man I want thinks the thing through. He thinks what are the factors that have to be put together. You can't decide this on an accountant's report. There are too many factors that just don't show up in the figures.

"What I want is to surround myself with entrepreneurs. A foreman in a shop can be an entrepreneur if he takes existing things and puts them together in a new way. That guy usually ends up being head of the company."

"Bah!"

Perhaps it's the generation gap, but many of the entrepreneurs *Forbes* interviewed professed scorn for today's younger conglomerators. Eduard Baruch says: "I wouldn't give you a dime for some of these hotshot boys who are forming con-glomerates. They're financial manipulators, pure and simple." Sherman Fairchild criticizes a good deal of today's acquisition-mindedness. "Too many of these people are just not entrepreneurial. They pay through the nose for acquisitions instead of trying to put small things together into bigger, better things." Max Ries says: "They give people watered stock. It's a swindle. Bah!"

However, at least two of these men singled out Dan Lufkin, chairman of Wall Street's Donaldson, Lufkin & Jenrette, as being a true entrepreneur of the younger school. They admire his refusal to allow New York Stock Exchange rules to pre-vent his firm from going public. Max Geffen calls him "the most brilliant young man I know today." Eduard Baruch also singled out Lufkin, saying: "He sees opportunities and he moves ahead."

Sherman Fairchild, perhaps because he runs bigger companies than the others, disagrees with the general idea that big companies always smother the entrepre-neurial spirit. "They don't at IBM," he says. "They don't buy things outside. They start them themselves. They're their own entrepreneurs. They avoid the costly business of having to buy a going organization and product acceptance."

Max Ries has some advice for executives who work for big companies and want to preserve their entrepreneurial spirit: "Be true to yourself. Do not crawl to the president or kiss the chairman's shoes. Do whatever you think you should do and if they won't let you, then leave. That's the only way."

WHAT ENTREPRENEURS LEARN FROM EXPERIENCE

by Lawrence M. Lamont

Introduction

There is an old saying that practice makes perfect. Applied to business, it means that a task can always be performed more effectively the second time it is attempted. Surprisingly, the same principle applies to technical entrepreneurship. Entrepreneurs with previous experience in founding and developing a company exhibit substantial learning when they start another business. More often than not, their experience is reflected in superior corporate performance.

The importance of prior experience becomes meaningful when one examines the self-generating nature of the entrepreneurship process.[1] The creation of a technology-based enterprise (called a "spin-off") occurs when an entrepreneur starts a business to commercialize technology transferred from his previous source of employment. As the new firm develops, it in turn becomes a source of technology and entrepreneurs for a second generation spin-off and so on. Entrepreneurial learning becomes apparent when the principal of a first generation spin-off leaves to start another

Dr. Lamont is assistant professor of marketing at the University of Colorado. He was formerly associated with Dow Corning Corporation as a technical sales representative, and subsequently as a research associate at the Institute of Science and Technology at the University of Michigan, where he was a consultant to technology-based firms in the Ann Arbor area. His research and publication activities include the fields of industrial marketing, small business management, corporate responses to consumerism, and consumer purchase behavior for durable goods.

technology-based firm. Arnold Cooper's recent research on technical enterprise formation in the Palo Alto area summarizes the pattern:

> Past entrepreneurship also generates experienced entrepreneurs. Some of these men stay with their firms as they grow. However, many of the firms are acquired and many of the founding teams break up. After the merger or after the fight with the co-founder, what does the former entrepreneur do? Often he turns to entrepreneurship again.
>
> Eight of the 30 companies studied intensively in the Palo Alto area were founded by men who previously had been in the founding groups of other companies. One man was starting his fourth new business. Without exception these men stated that it was easier to start a company the second time, both in regard to making the decision psychologically and in knowing what was involved in launching a firm.[2]

What does the technical entrepreneur do differently when he participates in the formation of a second generation spin-off? Why does his technology-based firm typically perform in a superior manner? These questions are examined in the present article. The answers are of interest to existing and potential entrepreneurs because they can shorten the learning process and improve their chances for success. Venture capital firms, private investors, and businesses interested in acquiring technology-based companies will also find this article useful because it provides insight into the decision to invest in a small business.

My comments are based on an empirical study of a matched sample of 24 technology-based enterprises located in a major scientific complex. Twelve of the

[1] Dean C. Coddington and James F. Mahar, "The Scientific Complex—Proceed with Caution," *Harvard Business Review,* XLIII (January-February, 1965), pp. 141-44.

[2] Arnold C. Cooper, "Entrepreneurial Environment," *Industrial Research,* XII (September, 1970), p. 75.

firms are first generation spin-offs founded by individuals without previous entrepreneurial experience. The balance of the sample consists of 12 second generation spin-offs founded by technical entrepreneurs who had been previously involved in the formation and management of a technology-based enterprise.

Aside from differences in the business experience of the entrepreneurs, the firms were similar in many respects. New businesses having less than $100,000 of sales were included as well as firms with annual sales of several million dollars. Both groups ranged in age between 1 and 11 years and averaged 3.5 years of business operations. The firms were also involved in similar technologies, primarily electronics and optics.

Comparative Performance

Part of the entrepreneur's ability to perform more effectively the second time is reflected in the various measures of corporate performance. Several were examined, including sales growth, profitability, and financial strength. Comparative sales performance shows that the second generation firm experiences a greater rate of sales growth. This is reflected in Table 1 where first year sales are shown for each group of firms.

Over 91 percent of the first generation firms reported sales in the range of $0-100,000 during the first complete year of operations. By comparison, 75 percent

of the second generation enterprises reported sales over $100,000 during a similar period. The differences in sales performance were not a short-run phenomenon. After each group of firms had completed an average of 3.5 years of business, 83 percent of the second generation firms reported sales over $100,000 compared to 58 percent of the first generation spin-offs.

Profitability data confirms the superior performance of the second generation firms during their latest year of business. Over 60 percent of these firms reported profitable operations, while only 25 percent of the first generation spin-offs earned profits. The second generation firms also achieved profitability earlier in their life cycle, were financially stronger and had better credit ratings as reported by a leading business information service.

What Do Entrepreneurs Learn?

During the formation of a second enterprise, the entrepreneur has an opportunity to apply his previous small business experience. Typically it is reflected in a firm having a product orientation, a higher level of capitalization and a better balance of essential business skills.

A product orientation. Technology-based firms can engage in a variety of different business activities. They include consulting, research and development, engineering, and manufacturing on a

Table 1

First Year Sales Performance

Sales	First Generation Spin-off Firms		Second Generation Spin-off Firms	
$0-100,000	11	91.7	3	25.0
Over $100,000	1	8.3	9	75.0
Total Firms	12	100.0%	12	100.0%

contract basis and the provision of proprietary products. Table 2 indicates that first generation firms were performing contract activities during their first year of business, while the second generation spin-offs were usually involved in the development and marketing of proprietary products.

What accounts for the significant variation in business orientation? Most of the difference can be attributed to the entrepreneur's previous small business experience. He has learned that contract-oriented businesses are highly unstable and that products are needed to maintain a profitable level of operations. The point is illustrated by the comments of a first generation entrepreneur. After several years of business his contract engineering firm decided to develop and market an industrial control instrument. He remarked:

> The development of products is a natural extension of our contract capability. These developments give us an opportunity to share on a continuing basis the things we have been doing for other companies on an hourly basis.

The comment illustrates another important characteristic of the technology-based enterprise. As the firms mature, their development is marked by dramatic changes in the nature of their business. Several development patterns are possible, but generally contract-oriented firms move toward a product orientation. A first generation spin-off included in the study illustrates this common pattern.

The firm began business in contract research and development performing environmental studies for the government space program. Two years after formation, two electronic measuring instruments were developed using technology transferred from the government research. In a short period, the first generation spin-off's business had changed from a research and development orientation to a product orientation.

This type of change was quite evident in the sample of firms studied. In the latest year of business operations reported, 33 percent of the first generation spin-offs had achieved a product orientation and 75 percent of the secondary spin-offs had completed the transition. Obviously, the second generation firm has a head-start on the product development.

How does the experienced entrepreneur assure a product orientation for his new firm? To form the technical base for the business he transfers technology from his previous source of employment. Usually this technology includes information related to the development and manufacture of specific products. The entrepreneur takes advantage of the product knowledge the first firm may have taken years to develop.[3] A case in point: One second generation entrepreneur interviewed developed nine products during the first year of business. Prior to starting operations he had completed the design and engineering for these products so that

[3]Victor J. Danilov, "The Spin-Off," *Industrial Research,* XI (May, 1969), p. 58.

Table 2
First Year Business Activities*

Type of Business Activity	First Generation Spin-off Firms		Second Generation Spin-off Firms	
Contract	11	91.7	5	41.7
Product	1	8.3	7	58.3
Total Firms	12	100.0%	12	100.0%

*Firms are classified as product or contract oriented on the basis of sales data and the major focus of their business.

most of the first year of operations was devoted to developing a manufacturing capability and organizing a distribution network. All of the products were improved versions of those marketed in the first business he was associated with. To a large degree, the product orientation of the entrepreneur's second firm accounts for the superior sales performance.

Adequate initial financing. The significance of financing to new technical firms is confirmed by the research of Dr. Edward B. Roberts, Associate Professor of Management, Massachusetts Institute of Technology. He notes that one of the essential characteristics of successful spin-off firms is "large initial capitalization, preferably $25,000 to $50,000."[4] However, obtaining the capital to initially finance the technology-based company is a difficult problem according to Kenneth G. Germeshausen, a first generation entrepreneur and board chairman of EG&G.

> The principal problem is the convincing of financial sources that the idea really is a good one and in obtaining the required financial support without losing control or too much of the equity.[5]

Many of the technology-based firms in the study were undercapitalized at the time of formation and throughout the early stages of development. Again, the second generation entrepreneurs' experience was worthwhile. Their firms had an average initial capitalization of $33,700 compared to the first generation spinoff's average of $19,600. Part of this difference reflects the business orientation of the second generation firms. Product oriented firms simply require higher levels of initial capitalization to finance the product development and the requirements for plant and equipment,

inventory, and labor. Much of the difference, however, is the result of the experienced entrepreneur's knowledge of sources of venture capital, his ability to make a convincing presentation to potential investors and the lower level of risk involved in a business having a tangible product

A balance of business skills. The majority of first generation spin-offs are founded by scientists and engineers having only a casual interest in the business activities required to successfully operate a business. In many firms the situation is perpetuated by hiring only technical personnel whose interests are compatible with those of the original entrepreneurs. The entrepreneur of the second generation firm usually realizes the need for help in management, production, and the other functional areas of business. When it is financially possible, he carefully selects his employees to complement the existing technical and business skills present in the firm.

As shown in Table 3, all firms reported that either a principal founder or employee had research and development or engineering experience at the time of founding. This was expected because the technical experience of the personnel is the primary basis for the firm's creation. However, when the presence of various business skills is considered, the second generation firms clearly have an advantage. They are more inclined to have production, general management, and marketing initially present in their organization.

The difference is due not only to the learning that occurs during the process of entrepreneurship, but it is also the result of a need for a broader range of business skills to successfully operate a product-oriented business. This explains the higher percentage of second generation firms reporting production experience in their business. The contrast in the percentage of firms having marketing and general management experience is a reflection of

---

[4] Edward B. Roberts, "Influences Upon Performance of New Technical Enterprises," A paper presented at the Symposium on Technical Entrepreneurship, Co-sponsored by the Krannert School of Industrial Administration, Purdue University, and the Center for Venture Management, Milwaukee, Wisconsin, October 7-8, 1970, at Purdue University.

[5] Danilov, *op. cit., p. 58*

Table 3

Business Experience Present at the Time of Founding*
(Percent of Firms Reporting Each Type of Experience)

Type of Experience	First Generation Spin-off Firms		Second Generation Spin-off Firms	
Research, Development and Engineering	12	100.0%	12	100.0%
Production	1	8.3	10	83.3
General Management	1	8.3	9	75.0
Accounting or Finance	6	50.0	4	33.0
Marketing or Sales	3	25.0	7	58.3
Total Firms	12		12	

*Percentage total exceeds 100.00% because of multiple response.

the fact that first generation spin-offs are frequently weak in marketing and less concerned about the personnel and project management aspects of the business. Experienced entrepreneurs recognize the significance of marketing and management skills and are more willing to hire specialists to handle the business functions.

Taking Advantage of Experience

The fact that learning occurs in technical entrepreneurship implies that existing and potential entrepreneurs can improve their business skills by taking advantage of the experiences of successful entrepreneurs. However, understanding what entrepreneurs learn and do differently does not automatically lead to concepts that can be applied in a small business setting. In the following sections are discussed some specific ways in which a new enterprise may benefit from the previous entrepreneural experience of its founder.

Market planning. Entrepreneurs with previous small business experience are able to transfer important market knowledge to their new firms. They are usually aware of specific business opportunities and know in advance where their sales are going to come from. Without the benefit of experience, extensive market planning

must be performed to focus the company's product and marketing strategy. More specifically, the plan must define market opportunities, product requirements, potential customers and competition. It also specifies the sales techniques needed to penetrate potential markets, sales goals by product and market, and a detailed marketing budget.

Most experienced entrepreneurs have completed the market planning phase when they begin operations. Even though the approach may have been informal, it helps to direct the operations and maximize the efficient use of the firm's financial and technical resources. By comparison, first time entrepreneurs usually begin business without clear corporate goals and fail to define the scope of their technical and marketing effort. Only after several unsuccessful projects does the entrepreneur begin to realize the necessity for market planning.

Financial planning. A well prepared marketing plan specifies the financial requirements of the business. Experienced entrepreneurs recognize this and carefully project working capital needs to finance the marketing program, product development, inventory, and work (products and contracts) in process. These financing needs are then matched with sources of funds including proprietary product sales and progress payments from contracts. The difference must be made up from external sources—namely profits, loans from private investors, sales of stock, lines of credit from financial institutions, and short term trade credit

The financial and market plans become the basis for a formal presentation to the financial community—including individuals, venture capital firms, SBIC's and other financial institutions. A well prepared presentation emphasizing a marketable product, financial control, and management depth usually enables the entrepreneur to obtain the financing needed to assure a successful start for the business. Experienced entrepreneurs are typically able to secure the necessary financing prior to starting business. The first generation entrepreneur is often in business a year or more before he begins to perceive the need for additional funds. The failure to prepare a financial plan usually means that the firm will be undercapitalized and highly susceptible to a cash flow crisis.

A balanced management team. First-time entrepreneurs admit that technical experience alone is not sufficient to manage and develop a new business. Weaknesses in marketing and management and inexperience in the methods of conducting business spell failure for many new firms. In putting together a management team, the experienced entrepreneur usually recognizes the importance of business experience and the need to interact with the business community. Multiple founders are typically used to provide a balance of business skills and part of the financing. Operating management is hired with emphasis on selecting individuals experienced in project and production management. The experienced entrepreneur surrounds himself with good people and delegates authority. The first

generation entrepreneur too often tries to manage everything himself and is labeled as a poor manager.

Interaction with the business community is made possible by having outside members on the board of directors or an executive committee made up of corporate management and outside advisors such as a C.P.A., lawyer, venture capitalist, consultant, etc. This latter technique works well as a method of bringing outside expertise to bear on the company's problems because the committee can meet informally and with greater frequency than a board. Some venture capital firms are making the establishment of an executive committee a requirement in all firms they finance. Most entrepreneurs welcome the idea because the outside individuals provide an excellent sounding board for new ideas.

Conclusions

Learning is a property of almost all business activity. Applied to technical entrepreneurship it means that experienced entrepreneurs exhibit substantial learning when they form a second technology-based enterprise. Usually their experience is reflected in a business having a product orientation, substantial initial financing and a balance of essential business skills.

Market and financial planning are key factors in the experienced entrepreneurs' performance. Entrepreneurs should strive to begin business with a market plan that focuses the technical activity and gives the firm a head start on the required product development. Careful financial planning is also necessary. Investors are reluctant to provide capital for a business venture when the requirements are uncertain. When these tools are combined with an experienced management team, the business has a sense of direction and a high probability of success.

Section B:
The Individual
and His Career

Since all individuals, especially those enrolled in business programs, have some achievement motivation, the "paths to success" in the business world tend to stimulate a great deal of interest. The articles in this section present two divergent viewpoints of these paths. The first, by Craig Waters, emphasizes the entrepreneurial route to millionaire status. Although his "rules" are general, they draw on a great deal of experience from people who have reached this milestone. On the other hand, Ross Webber enumerates "thirteen career commandments" for success in a large organization that are intended for the professional rather than the entrepreneurial manager. Striking differences are apparent in the two lists. As one obvious example, Waters emphasizes working for oneself whereas Webber adopts the high intraorganizational visibility platform. A further comparison of the two lists provides a good base for discussions of aspirations and future career paths for aspiring managers.

Twenty-five Ways
to Make a Million

Craig Waters

1. Get involved in something you enjoy — you'll be spending a great deal of time doing it, so it had better seem like fun. If it doesn't, you won't be willing to invest the time to make it a success.
2. Work for yourself. You'll never make a fortune by sweating for someone else. The employer is interested in minimizing his expenses, and that means minimizing salaries. He is not in the business of producing rich employees.
3. Provide a utilitarian service or a tangible product. Your chances of becoming a millionaire by writing, painting, or composing music are infinitesimally small. Your chances of making a million in construction, real estate, or manufacturing are good. Remember: Publishers earn more than authors.
4. If you insist on working in a creative area, choose show business. It is one of the few artistic mediums in which fortunes can be made, frequently quite quickly. Rock music and television are the best bets.
5. Whether you are an entertainer or a businessman, maximize your audience. The vocalist who sings in a small cafe does not earn as much as the one who records for RCA. The manufacturer who sells his product in the east does not earn as much as the one who distributes it internationally.
6. Identify a need and fill it. As society becomes increasingly complex, people want more goods and services. The first person to recognize and fulfill those needs profits most; close behind him in the profit category is the individual who can improve on goods or services already being offered.
7. Don't hesitate to do things differently — new approaches and new products make new fortunes. But make sure your new way improves upon the old. It should increase the appeal, efficiency, quality, or convenience of the old, or reduce its cost.
8. If you have had a specialized education or a special expertise, make use of it. If you're a master chef, it would be foolish to begin laying bricks.
9. Before you start any undertaking, research the area thoroughly. A wealth of information is available from government agencies and public libraries. Research will save you time and money, and may prevent you from duplicating someone else's effort. This is particularly true in the area of invention.
10. Don't think about making a fortune. Think instead about ways you can improve the efficiency or effectiveness of your business. A question you should ask yourself constantly: "How can I improve this operation?" If the business runs well, the fortune will be forthcoming.

11. If possible, organize a family business. This approach minimizes overhead; maximizes incentive; provides for an uncomplicated pooling of funds; facilitates effective use of profits; and makes it easier to retain control of all facets of the operation.

12. Minimize your expenses, but don't sacrifice quality. If you do, you are dealing in schlock, and your business will never prosper as fully as it might if you were selling a good product.

13. Cultivate friendships with people in the business — they may be helpful.

14. Spend as much time as possible with your business. Twelve hours a day, six days a week, is the minimum. Days fourteen to eighteen hours long are average, and the seven-day work week is ideal. You will be forced to sacrifice family and social relationships until your business is solidly on its feet; then, and only then, can you begin to delegate responsibilities.

15. Don't be afraid to make your own decisions. Get the advice of experts or people experienced in your field. Listen to compliments and criticism but make your own decisions.

16. Don't be afraid to speak your piece. Time spent beating around the bush is wasted time. Say what you think, and say it as directly and as succinctly as possible.

17. Don't be afraid to admit you've been wrong. Making a mistake is not a crime; perpetuating it is.

18. Don't be deterred by your failures. They are inevitable, and invaluable. From them you learn how to proceed the right way.

19. Don't waste time with losers. As soon as you realize that an idea is not a good one, discard it. There are an infinite number of ideas, and time wasted on an unworkable concept cannot be replaced.

20. Do not risk more capital than you can afford to lose. If you lose $100,000, but can afford to, you can move on to another project if the first one fails. If, however, you lose $5,000 you cannot afford, you are stuck.

21. Reinvest. Don't let your profits stagnate — they should circulate constantly, ideally into other businesses or projects you control. Your profits profit you several times that way.

22. Retain a good attorney — he will save you time and more money than he'll ever charge.

23. Retain a good accountant. You do your own accounting at first, but unless you're a CPA you'll eventually want to hire one. A good accountant may spell the difference between disaster and success — he is worth his weight in gold.

24. Have your taxes prepared by professionals. As President Nixon can attest, a good tax attorney can turn a rich man into a millionaire. And, as President Nixon can also attest, a poor one can get a millionaire into a lot of trouble.

25. Guard your health and your peace of mind — without them, wealth is nothing.

Ross A. Webber

13 Career Commandments

Advising MBAs on how to manage their careers is a risky proposition. It depends upon the individual's objectives and his or her definition of success: Climbing to the top? Maintaining integrity? Keeping job and home separate? Happiness? Now, these are not all mutually exclusive, but they can be competitive.

Assuming that one of your objectives is to climb to higher managerial ranks, the following suggestions have been culled from a wide range of experienced managers:

1. Good performance that pleases your superiors is the basic foundation of success. Recognize, however, that not all good performance is easily measured. Determine the real criteria by which you are evaluated and be rigorously honest in evaluating your own performance against these criteria.

2. Manage your career; be active in influencing decisions about you. Good effort is not necessarily rewarded.

3. Strive for positions that have high visibility and exposure where your heroic deeds can be observed by higher officials. Check to see that the organization has a formal system of keeping track of young people. Remember that high-risk line jobs tend to offer more visibility than staff positions such as corporate planning or personnel, but also that visibility can sometimes be achieved through community activities.

4. Develop relations with a senior executive who can be your sponsor. Become a complementary, crucial subordinate with different skills from your superior.

5. Learn your job as quickly as possible and train a replacement so you can be available to move and broaden your background in different functions.

6. Nominate yourself for other positions; modesty is not necessarily a virtue. However, change jobs for more power and influence, not primarily status or pay. The latter could be a substitute for real opportunity.

7. Before taking a position, rigorously assess your strengths and weaknesses, what you like and don't like. Don't accept a promotion if it draws on your weaknesses and entails mainly activities that you don't like.

8. Leave at your convenience, but on good terms, without parting criticism of the organization. Do not remain under a superior who is not promoted in three to five years.

9. Don't be trapped by formal, narrow job descriptions. Move outside them and probe the limits of your influence.

10. Accept the fact that responsibility will always somewhat exceed authority and that organizational politics are inevitable. Establish alliances and fight necessary battles, minimizing battles with superiors to very important issues.

11. Get out of management if you can't stand being dependent on others and having them dependent on you.

12. Recognize that you will face ethical dilemmas no matter how moral you try to be. No evidence exists that unethical managers are more successful than ethical ones, but it may well be that those who move faster are less socially conscious. Therefore, from time to time you must examine your personal values and question how much you will sacrifice for the organization.

13. Don't automatically accept all tales of managerial perversity. Attributing others' success to unethical behavior is often an excuse for one's own personal inadequacies. Most of all, don't commit an act that you know to be wrong in the hope that your superior will see it as loyalty and reward you for it. Sometimes he will, but he may also sacrifice you when the organization is criticized.

Section C:

The Current and Future State of Management

The final section of the text covers several trends in the future of the management profession. Although forecasting future events in such a diverse area as management is risky, to say the least, there have been some discernible trends that are likely to continue for a number of years. Among these are the spread of the Japanese management system to other parts of the globe and the emphasis on the development of moral education for future managers.

The first three readings present a comprehensive view of the Japanese management system and its application in the United States. The reputation of this system has been largely based on the tremendous productivity, employee motivation and loyalty, and informality of the management system. Certainly, the economic condition of Japan today is testimony of its success. In the first reading, Shigeru Kobayashi describes the system as it operates in the Sony Corporation. He explains the success in terms of a number of managerial actions, including deemphasis of the power structure, participation in decision making, and use of the team concept. In summarizing the success of the system, he states:

> It has become clear to us that organizations supported by free flowing information and by responsible judgment and actions on the part of every one of their members are lively organizations, without any confusion or chaos to disturb their order. They represent genuinely creative organizations firmly based on effective communication and identification with the company through the self-realization it affords.

In the second selection, Tai K. Oh is not so positive about the application of this system. The reading is an excellent review of some of the external societal factors that influence the success of the Nenko system, factors which have been largely neglected in the literature. Among these are the relative rarity of the system in Japan, the limitation of the system to large firms, and the discrepancies between wages and fringe benefits. Oh concludes that "Japanese managerial effectiveness cannot be understood (in the United States) and probably cannot be duplicated outside the context of the Japanese industrial relations system."

Jack Egan describes such a duplication attempt, in which the Japanese system is used in Georgia. Although not all aspects of the system are carried through to the United States plants, job security, participation, and employee ownership of the company are included. Taken together, these three articles present a vivid picture of the relationship between the particular culture of a country and the management system that is most successful in this environment. On the other hand, it can be argued that certain factors will lead to increased employee morale and motivation regardless of the culture.

Recently, the business community has come under increased public suspicion and scrutiny because of certain "immoral" practices, such as bribing of officials of foreign countries and price "gouging" at the expense of customers. The fourth article in this section, by Edgar Schein, explores the ramifications of this problem in inducing moral values in the manager of the future. Schein feels that a professional is someone who knows what is good for the client. If managers are to become professionals, it is imperative to define their moral standards in terms of the needs and characteristics of the client. However, because the professional manager serves so many clients (consumers, stockholders, the community, the enterprise itself, the subordinate, the peer or the boss, and the profession of management) it becomes exceedingly difficult to specify a *single* set of moral behaviors for the manager. In Schein's words, "We must know the *frame of reference* within which the behavior occurred in order to judge it." Further, Schein points out that it is difficult to judge the amount of benefit or harm of immoral actions, the intentions of the professional manager, and the legal and moral obligations of the manager in a given situation. Schein ends with a comparison of several alternatives for instilling moral values in this difficult but vital area.

John Mee, one of the most qualified management historians, describes "the manager of the future" in the final selection. According to Mee's forecast, the future manager will be classified as a public manager, "a business institutional leader who will manage enterprise for the best balanced interests of the state and the nation to preserve and maintain our private enterprise system." Mee sees the future death of the centralized management system and the ultimate diffusion of power throughout all levels of the organization. This role change is partly due to the increasing educational levels of employees who will come to expect better utilization of their talents and increased participation in the management process. Mee describes a number of environmental changes which require the public manager ". . . to achieve the prestige and the recognition that managers have earned but not received on the basis of [their] contribution to society."

The Creative Organization—
A Japanese Experiment

By SHIGERU KOBAYASHI

STARTING virtually from scratch, Sony Corporation had grown into a company of 5,000 employees within the short span of 15 years when the author became manager of its Atsugi plant in 1961. A company almost always reaches a turning point after its rapid early development, because the very quality of vitality that enabled it to grow has a tendency to be weakened as increasingly larger numbers of people are employed. Those who joined during the start-up period were fighters, who staked their future on a company that might turn out to be a failure or a success, but those who come in after the company is solidly established are inclined to "ride" with it, counting on the stability it has achieved.

Moreover, as a rule when a firm grows in size, it increasingly demands a well-defined organization structure, but Sony has always been opposed to a rigid structure, preferring to be a stage on which people, uncoerced, could display their talents for creativity and independent activity. This freedom assured Sony of its initial dynamism and flexibility; as it grew, though, it could no longer maintain control without any form of organization, and the result was the establishment of departments, sections, subsec-

Reprinted by permission of the publisher from *Personnel,* November–December 1970, pp. 8–17. © 1970 by American Management Association, Inc.

ganization were adopted that took away people's planning and controlling functions.

Sony's aspirations to "do away with organization" notwithstanding, there can, of course, be no large-scale company without some form of organization; human dynamism and vitality alone cannot support such a firm. It therefore became necessary for us to organize in such a way as to permit the transformation of this human dynamism and vitality into company dynamism. A type of organization that would be conducive to this approach demanded that we base our effort on creative teamwork and excise the static and dehumanizing aspects of traditional organization patterns. Meeting these specifications called for formulating a pattern through trial and error. Above all, we had to avoid the stabilization of a structure through organization charts and rules based on the concept that organization is a vehicle for directive management, authority, and status. Teamwork is possible only in small groups, so we had to redesign our large organization as a collection of interlocking small groups.

Changing the Power Structure

Here I shall describe, first, how we set about breaking down the concept of organization as a means of ensuring authority and power.

At Sony, top management didn't have a speck of power-conscious-

tions, and what-not, all leading to smaller and smaller subdivisions and to a management hierarchy of department managers, section chiefs, subsection chiefs, and so on, with detailed rules and regulations for all jobs.

The ideals expressed in the letters of intent leading to the establishment of Sony presupposed a company in which uncoerced people saw their own well-being in the well-being of the company and in which everyone could work freely to achieve personal satisfaction and develop himself to his fullest potential. Thus, a glaring contradiction was apparent when principles of or-ness, but the other people, contrary to the philosophy of its top management, did subscribe to the generally accepted notion that superiors do their jobs by using their subordinates. Management based on power-consciousness became less evident as time went by, but one obstacle in the way of improvement was clear—hierarchical position as found in the traditional delineation of jobs.

Our plant organization comprises the crew (at the lowest level), which has about six members; the group, which includes several crews; the section, which includes several groups; and the department, which includes several sections. The first difficulty arose in connection with the titles given to the individuals in charge of these various units. Department superior (*ka-choh* in Japanese), section superior (*kakari-choh*), group supervisor (*kumi-choh*), and crew su-

---

SHIGERU KOBAYASHI *is managing director of Sony Corporation, Japan, in charge of the office for management development. He is also chairman of the Sony manpower committee and board chairman and principal of Sony High School. A graduate of the Tokyo Advanced Industrial Arts School, Mr. Kobayashi previously served as managing director of Sanseido, Ltd. and of Kyodo Printing and as manager of the Sony Atsugi plant. He is the author of* Sony Makes People Live *and of the forthcoming AMA book* Creative Management, *from which this article is drawn.*

pervisor (*han-choh*) all reminded both managers and workers of the old superior-subordinate relationship. We therefore decided to discontinue the use of the suffix *choh*, meaning superior, head, or chief. The department superior and section superior were to be called simply manager (*shunin*). We also decided to use the English words for titles—for instance, leader, in the case of the crew, and chief, in the case of the group. In addition, we encouraged people to address a man with a managerial position not as Mr. Department Manager, for example, but simply by his last name.

A related obstacle was the fact that titles like department superior or section superior represented social status as well as company position. To move a person under any circumstances from the position of department superior to a section superior's job would have been considered a demotion in both job and social standing.

We therefore decided to change our job-assignment policies when we changed our titles. People who are not yet considered eligible for such elevated status are, nevertheless, sometimes made department managers, and people who *are* eligible for more responsibility are sometimes made section managers. In short, our practice became flexible. A man could be appointed department manager and, immediately thereafter, could be reappointed section manager, and vice versa. This new practice, once established, virtually eradicated status-consciousness due to hierarchical position.

Participative Decision Making

The organization climate in which people must be accorded status because they are "somebody" and are expected to exercise the authority of their position to use people was gradually eliminated. But how are managers to do their jobs if they are not to use people to get the work out? I believe they should *assist* people to carry out the necessary tasks voluntarily. When managers use people to do their jobs, orders are called for, but when managers assume a role in which they assist people, they need only explain the general situation and the relevant policies. Then all they have to do is teach people how to *act*.

Since they are not ordered to do anything, it is now the employees' responsibility to question, discuss, and even oppose any explanation or instruction they may receive from their managers. On the other hand, managers should never allow themselves to close their minds to conflicting ideas or opinions from their workers; if they do, it means that they are still harboring power-consciousness—they feel their prerogatives are being attacked. Managers who are unwilling to take any responsibility for an employee's

ideas, once adopted and implemented, are not truly and seriously taking responsibility for much else, either.

The worst kind of manager is the one who blames his people in case of a fiasco, yet who wants to exercise his power and authority by taking credit for their successes. A manager who will not allow himself to dodge any responsibility has no other course but to trust his people, and when he shows this spirit, it kindles a similar spirit in those people and assures their voluntary cooperation. Here we have the real basis of leadership.

"The Rule Is Everything"

Almost as damaging as the concept justifying managers' using their men is the one that makes manuals and rules all-important. In Japanese companies one often finds a kind of thinking that defines organizing as drawing up detailed charts, precise job descriptions, and careful statements of job authority. Employees who don't obey such rules and regulations to the letter are regarded as organization dropouts.

Nothing could be sillier. Rules and regulations are stipulated to aid efficient administration under a certain set of prevailing conditions. Even if we could arrive at perfect rules and regulations, some of them would almost immediately be made impractical by the inexorable change of circumstances.

It is a gross mistake to assume that order will suffer if rules and regulations are not enforced. For instance, we have no company made rules and regulations in our dormitories, yet strict order prevails. People who are spellbound by normative dogmatism can hardly be blamed for believing, upon looking into our dorms, that they are managed like prisons without bars and that the workers who live in them must be suffering severe deprivation of freedom. Such is the degree of order we enjoy without rules or regulations.

Defining Job Duties

Texas Instruments Incorporated maintains a highly commendable position on rules and regulations. On an annual basis, managers define their own duties to best serve the company's interests under the generally prevailing conditions. Therefore, their statements of job duties are not static but are reviewed, revised, and adjusted as the need arises, depending on the requirements of the company during a particular fiscal year. By coincidence, we at Sony follow exactly the same practice.

For instance, suppose that I am appointing a man to be manager of our general affairs department. I ask him to write down what he thinks the problems of the department are and how he anticipates solving them. We then discuss what he has written. I don't force my ideas upon him; I simply let him do whatever he seriously considers must be done. If, after a while, he wants to revise his plan, we hold further discussions. Moreover, when the present manager of the general affairs department is replaced, the definition of the job is bound to change as well. Even the same man may define the same job in a different way, once he has gained new experience or finds his situation altered. Not only is he perfectly free to do so; he is obligated to do so.

As was mentioned earlier, during the initial phase of management innovation in our plant, we decided that small-group organization was necessary to motivate people and ensure voluntary action on their part and to enable every member to strive for the achievement of common goals. We began by breaking down production functions on the basis of crews—teams made up of two to a maximum of 20 people. Those who work in the same process in the manufacture of transistors are grouped together, and we may have one, two, or even three crews, depending on the number of workers in a process.

Secret of Small-Group Success

What is the difference between such a team and the equivalent unit in the traditional organization? First, the leaders of our teams are not supervisors who get the work out by using subordinates. Most of the leaders in our plant are girls 18 to 19 years old; there is practically no age difference between leaders and operators, although we also have some older housewives in the ranks of both leaders and operators. Since our leaders are free of status-consciousness, they assume and resign leadership quite freely.

Until the crew system was established, the first-line supervisors—called group chiefs—had managed every process in the plant. Under the new setup, however, the crews were created within the old groupings and each was assigned to a single work process. Operators in each crew selected a leader from among themselves. The initial task of the crews was to record and control attendance after time clocks were taken out. With such an important control function delegated to the crews, the result was an immediate demonstration of teamwork. Autonomous checking and control over attendance led naturally to autonomy in production control at crew level.

Second, it should be kept in mind that a team is managed chiefly through meetings of its members. Herein lies the basic difference between the team and the traditional work group, in which superiors give instructions individually to their subordinates without holding any meetings.

Rensis Likert writes in his *New Patterns of Management* that management will make full use of the potential capacities of its human resources only when each person in an organization is a member of one or more effectively functioning work groups that have a high degree of group loyalty, effective skills of interaction, and high performance goals.

All our experience testifies to the truth of what he says. The large, traditional organization fails to take advantage of the aggregate power of small groups that enables them to deliver superior performance, sometimes exceeding the most optimistic hopes.

Linking of Teams

It is our goal to reach the point where the full range of our activity is based on teamwork. Each team is necessarily small in size, whereas the plant is large, but we resolved this conflict with the establishment of a cell type of organization, linking small teams with each other, as in a living organism, to make up a single larger body. This structuring did not call for any changes in the way the plant was then organized —the various groupings could remain as they were, and so could the managers at the various levels. The only things that had to be changed were management style and management attitudes.

First, the monthly meeting—in which it is intended that every manager participate—clearly brought out the management style and attitudes of the plant manager, an opponent of power-consciousness. Gradually, then, the new climate came to be understood and percolated down through the entire plant with the help of talks, the way in which those talks were handled, and a succession of new policies implemented one by one. Everybody came to welcome the feeling that grew out of working in an atmosphere of mutual trust, as exemplified by the elimination of time clocks and the introduction of a cafeteria without attendants.

Then there was our practice of holding a meeting for the department managers every morning. Any matters pertaining to the plant as a whole were reported and discussed in this meeting and the resulting decisions were then implemented. The participants—the plant manager and the entire department manager group—formed a team in themselves. Thus, the top team was formed simultaneously with the teams at lower levels, and these teams at the top and bottom led to the formation of intermediary teams, like a chain reaction.

With the number of plant employees exceeding 3,000, the number of departments standing at 20-odd, and our lines of business diversified, we seemed to have reached a stage where we could no longer manage and control our affairs unless we established divisions, but I was reluctant to increase the layers of management. We solved the problem by dividing the weekly morning meeting into four sessions: general meeting, meeting for general affairs, meeting for semiconductors, and meeting for calculators.

The plant manager attends all these meetings of top management, as do the lower-level plant managers who assist him and act in his stead in the absence of the plant manager. The regular participants in the divisional meetings are, of course, the managers of various departments, but no clear line is drawn as to which meeting any one manager is to attend. It is entirely possible, depending on the nature of his business, for one man to attend two or three such meetings.

A divisional meeting is similar in its function to a meeting held within a single department, but it is more flexible than its departmental counterpart, and the plant manager participates in it personally. The general meeting also differs from a departmental meeting in that it is attended not only by department managers but by section chiefs. Thus, the plant manager establishes direct contact with both.

The general meeting, because of its very nature, draws many attendees and therefore inhibits any detailed discussion. In a divisional meeting, the discussion is likely to explore in detail information supplied by the lower organization levels, whereas in the general meeting, top management makes overall plant information available, and discussion follows on that basis.

As a result of all this, from the plant manager down no one is involved in more than three layers of meetings. Communications have thereby been reduced proportionately, but the results show that the merits of the new arrangement far outweigh its drawbacks.

The Pair System

To return to organization by teams, an important role in team development is played by our pair system, a combination of two workers whose relations on the job are like those of a man and his wife in the Japanese home. The fundamental difference between team formation (including the pair system) and the authoritarian, directive type of organization lies in the fact that the latter results in human relations based on the ruler-and-ruled dichotomy, whereas the former bases human relations on partnership. In this partnership one member, it is true, is the leader and the other is a follower, but this is not the relationship between the ruler and the ruled.

A pair must necessarily be composed of two individuals with different characteristics. Man and woman, teacher and pupil, senior worker and junior worker, worker on the morning shift and worker on the afternoon shift, manager and secretary, scientist and technician, two professionals with different academic disciplines and skills, two men with different personalities —all lend themselves to pair formation. The requirements are that the two individuals be heterogeneous, that they be performing the same job to achieve an identical goal, and that they assume joint responsibility for their work.

The pair system concept is not new in Japan. Professor Jiro Kamijima, of St. Paul University in Tokyo, has mentioned, in commenting on old Japanese social organizations and their underlying mental attitudes, that a sort of pair system carried a certain significance even during ancient times. Referring to his comments, I suggested at one of our morning meetings that we should perhaps introduce the pair system as a micro-unit within the crew on the strength of the success of the chief and subchief system with which we had already experimented. Hearing of what I had said, the workers at some stations expressed interest in the idea and started to develop a pair system of their own volition.

We always try to approach organizational matters in this manner. Neither I nor any member of my staff dictates to people how they should proceed with a particular organizing job. Rather, a certain idea seems to emerge informally and workers who are interested in it begin implementing it in their own way. As a result, our pair system differs from one work station to another in both method of operation and timing of application. To this day we have work stations that are using systems that have yet to be set up on an organized basis like the one I have cited.

The prime requisite in developing basic organizational patterns and systems is never to force any particular method upon people across the board. It is only when a pattern or system is created by the individuals who will be required to function within it that we arrive at a means of motivating and stimulating people, instead of stifling them. The pair system in particular could never work smoothly if people were required to form pairs.

Communications Support

Most important to organization by team is reliable information, since the employees are not individually directed or commanded to perform tasks expected of them. Each team member does his own sizing up of a given situation, makes his decision, and takes action in accordance with the facts. Obviously, unless each member understands the information that comes to him from above, below, and around him, the sum total of the action will not be properly coordinated.

Communication that supports the team type of organization depends not only on providing access to information, but also on an atmosphere of mutual respect. No one will take communication seriously if it comes from a person whom he holds in contempt, and vice versa. Nor will communication serve to establish reliable information unless both parties are free from prejudice and favoritism.

Communication cannot be accomplished simply by recording, reproducing, and transmitting messages to company levels above or below the speaker or sidewise, to other departments, as with a tape recorder. Communication has to be established among live human beings and make possible the creation of new ideas based on useful, detailed data derived from a combination of our own and others' information and judgment.

Changes in the context of information during the transmission process create no harm so long as the intermediaries try to transmit the facts in a creative way—that is, so long as the climate favors their being able to think subjectively about the information in question, grasp its true meaning, and convey this meaning on their own responsibility as if the information were their own. It is this creative interpretation that is indispensable to truly effective communication.

The establishment of a climate conducive to *creative* communication may bring astounding changes. For instance, operators' casual remarks about a certain circumstance observed on the job—remarks the operators themselves are not sure have any importance—are transmitted to staff specialists; a significant engineering discovery results, and profits are handsome. It is not too much to say that this kind of information is coming to be an important basis for technological innovation in our semiconductor industry.

At Sony we have formal reports presented at weekly meetings, monthly reports by all personnel above the level of leader, and published media, including a *Management Memo* and companywide magazines, *Sony News,* published monthly, and *Weekly Reports.* At our Atsugi plant we have *Atsugi Topics,* published every other day, and the monthly *Home News,* directed to employees' families. We also have many publications issued by dormitory residents and by members of various work stations.

However, much depends on the unrestricted flow of informal information. A case in point is the Sony "Dial 2000." Any Sony employee can dial this number directly and get or give information through the personnel who respond to his call. All are encouraged to "dial 2000" for these purposes:

• To confirm the validity of rumors being circulated or of "tips" from other employees.

• To get information on whom to approach about problems having to do with their jobs, to find out more on topics they are concerned about, or to get helpful ideas about certain problems.

• To get information as to which groups or people within Sony are trying to do or are already doing things they are planning to do in their own jobs.

• To find out who should receive information, proposals, or opinions that employees think will be helpful to Sony.

In simple terms, each person has access to a source where he can easily obtain the information he needs and discuss it with someone well informed. When it seems appropriate, he can even circumvent his immediate manager, but he has to exercise his judgment and plan a course of action on his own responsibility. And if he does act on the advice of his immediate manager, he cannot and should not be permitted to pass the buck to that manager in the event of failure.

It has become clear to us that organizations supported by free-flowing information and by responsible judgment and actions on the part of everyone of their members are lively organizations, without any confusion or chaos to disturb their order. They represent genuinely creative organizations firmly based on effective communication and identification with the company through the self-realization it affords.

Japanese Management — A Critical Review [1]

TAI K. OH

One must look beyond the behavioral aspects of the Japanese management system to the economic conditions which support the system to understand fully its contribution to Japan's economic recovery. Permanent employment (Nenko) has created a highly efficient dual wage and labor market system but it excludes two-thirds of the Japanese labor force from its benefits.

The startling economic recovery of Japan since the end of World War II has been widely attributed to the effectiveness of Japanese management. American management scholars and practitioners have been particularly impressed with the way in which the permanent employment system, known as Nenko, gives employees job security and promotes strong corporate loyalty, high motivation and group effectiveness while still maintaining the flexibility to meet fluctuations in demand for labor and new developments in technology. It has been seriously suggested that U. S. managers might apply some of the principles underlying the Nenko system (7).

The way in which Japanese cultural behavior patterns and value orientations have affected the organizational behavior characteristic of Nenko has been widely discussed in management literature and is fairly well understood (2, 3, 7, 20, 21, 25, 37). The dynamics of Nenko managerial behavior have been described, examined and discussed in great detail, and Nenko management's role in Japan's remarkable economic achievements has been duly identified and properly appreciated. But the time has now come to look beyond the behavioral aspects of the Japanese management system for a more complete set of answers to the question of how and why the system works so well.

Tai K. Oh (Ph.D. — University of Wisconsin, Madison) is Associate Professor of Management at California State University, Fullerton, Fullerton, California.

[1] The author wishes to acknowledge the generous cooperation and support of Dean Jack W. Coleman of the School of Business Administration and Economics, California State University, Fullerton, in obtaining funds for the collection and acquisition of the data on which this article is based, both in Japan and in the U. S. The author also gratefully acknowledges the generous cooperation and support for this study from Professor Shunichiro Umetani, Japan Institute of Labor.

Portions of this paper were presented at the Thirty-Fifth Annual Meeting of the Academy of Management, New Orleans, Louisiana, August, 1975.

There are several critical economic factors essential to the existence of the Japanese management system which might well be necessary preconditions for the successful application of Nenko principles to U. S. operations. Japan's economic history and the peculiar structure of its industrial sector and labor market bear a large measure of responsibility for the development of and continued effectiveness of the Nenko system. In exploring Japan's permanent employment system in its proper context as an interdependent part of the socio-economic structure of Japanese industry, some unexamined social and economic costs of the system will receive long overdue attention. In this perspective, the applicability of Nenko principles to U. S. operations must be reconsidered.

The Nenko System — A Brief Description and History

The Nenko system of management has attracted widespread discussion among American management scholars and practitioners ever since James Abegglen introduced the system to the U. S. (1).

The basic features of the system are simple: an employee enters a large firm after junior high, high school, or college graduation, receives in-company training, and remains an employee until retirement at age 55.

The practice of payment according to length of service reinforces and maintains the permanence of employment among the workers within a firm. Usually only young, recent graduates can afford to enter such a system at beginning wages, and older workers cannot afford the loss of earnings a change of employer would entail. As a result, inter-firm mobility is severely limited, and the vast majority of employees in Nenko firms remain with the same employers throughout their careers. This makes extensive in-company training a profitable investment, and ties to the employer are often further reinforced by the employee's acquisition of enterprise-specific skills.

Japanese employees have reacted to the permanence of employment under Nenko by developing the strong group loyalty and system of shared obligations, heavy dependence on powerful superiors, and intense competitive drive that have come to be associated with Japanese management in the minds of American businessmen and businesswomen. Among members of a Nenko group, who are associated more by location and situation than by any other common factor, such cohesiveness, coordination and effectiveness is accomplished by several powerful behavioral control mechanisms—a rigid, hierarchical structure based on seniority; intense emotional involvement in the life of the group; early indoctrination into the group ethos; total fulfillment of security needs; and economic interdependence. Yet within the framework of this system, there are areas in which competition is intense and highly motivating. There is competition among different firms within an industry, competition among separate work groups within a single firm, and individual competition for promotion within classes of employees who join a firm in the same year. In the last case, precise measurement of individual performance in terms of work function is not very feasible in the Japanese corporate management system; other criteria such as flexibility, group support, and corporate loyalty are employed to determine promotability (24, 34).

One of the most widespread misconceptions about Nenko is that it pervades the management of Japanese industrial concerns. Actually, the Nenko system is seldom operative in any but the larger Japanese firms (which form only a tiny minority of all firms in Japanese industry) and applies to a minority of Japanese workers. According to an estimate made by Solomon Levine in the early 1960's, the Nenko system applies to less than 30 percent of the nonagricultural labor force (18). Unfortunately, this limitation of Nenko protection and benefits to a minority of Japanese workers appears to be essential to the continued survival of the Nenko system, and is probably its greatest cost to Japanese society.

The best foundation for understanding Nenko and its position in the socio-economic system of Japanese industry today is a knowledge of its development from its inception to the present.

Nenko After World War I

Although the roots of Nenko can be traced back to the 1920's and even earlier (19, 26, 37), the Nenko system became firmly established consequent to World War I (28). During the boom which occurred at that time, Japanese industry expanded rapidly. The rapid growth of the factory system required an immediate expansion of the labor force, and so the need to recruit and retain large numbers of factory workers became a major concern of management. At the Mitsubishi-Nagasaki shipyard, for example,

> the ratio of resigning workers to staying workers was as high as 52.0%. The situation hit the machinery and metal industries so hard that they lost ¾ of their workers because the latter moved to other industries (27, pp. 145-146).

Japanese employers attacked the problem of employee turnover on two fronts, and the practices they initiated to deal with it can be easily recognized as basic elements of the Nenko system today. First, companies began to recruit labor directly from the farm population and educational institutions and to provide intra-enterprise training for several years. The result was usually workers with highly specialized skills useful only to a specific industry. This worked to reduce interfirm mobility. Second, the principle of using length of service as the principal wage determinant was initiated to create a further barrier to separation. During the first half of their working life, employees under the Nenko system are underpaid for the work they have performed, so in order to collect all their rightful wages, they must work until retirement, during which time overpayment for work performed will compensate for prior underpayment (8). This delayed compensation adds a significant hidden value to beginning wages offered by Nenko employers.

Of course, length of service is not the only determinant of wage increases. The Japanese wage is a highly complex value composed of many allowances and benefits, few of which have any connection with individual work performance. The basic starting wage, determined by the labor market and the educational level of the new employee, is a minor part of the total wage. Numerous small allowances for commuting, housing, dependents, etc., are added according to employee need, but by far the most important determinant of wage increase is length of service. Rewards for individual performance account for a very small range of variation on the wage increase curve (16, 19, 30). Since age and length of service theoretically reflect degree of skill acquired through occupational progression, payment by length of service does not deviate too drastically from value of work performed. When regular workers are recruited upon graduation, whether from junior high school, high school or college, their training program increases their value to their firm as they progress through occupations with increasing skill requirements and become more proficient at their work (30).

These two management policies of highly specialized training and payment according to length of service were introduced effectively to meet the economic objective of preventing workers from moving to other places of employment. Employers tended to reinforce the permanence of employment in these firms by their reluctance to hire other than new school graduates, who represented a savings in wage costs and were the most adaptable to a system which values long-term commitments (26). Thus there tended to be little shopping around for labor on the open market or from other firms unless the supply of new graduates was nearly exhausted (19). As a behavioral consequence of these policies, Nenko workers came to be involved in a closed system which fostered a strong sense of loyalty to the firms for which they worked.

Although Japanese employers were careful to discourage interfirm mobility, they had not yet reached the point prior to World War II where they actually guaranteed continued em-

TABLE 1. Model Wage Pattern for Employees Beginning Service With a Firm in the Same Year Under the Pre-World War II Nenko System

Year of Employment	No. of Employees	Wage per Employee	Employer's Total Wage
10	1	10	10
9	2	9	18
8	3	8	24
7	4	7	28
6	5	6	30
5	6	5	30
4	7	4	28
3	8	3	24
2	9	2	18
1	10	1	10
			220

Source: Wakao Fujida. *Labor Organization and Activities (Rodo Kumiai no Soshiki to undo)* (Kyoto: Minerva, 1962), p. 278.

ployment to their workers until retirement. They practiced performance evaluation, and employees who performed poorly had to leave the enterprise because of explicit and implicit discrimination against them. During recessions, there was widespread discharge of employees.

This gave Japanese employers considerable control over their labor costs. Although individual wages increased with time, a group of employees hired during any particular year would decline in number as time went by, so that the total wage outlay for that group remained rather stable. Fujida's model, shown in Table 1, illustrates this wage pattern clearly.

Nenko also worked behaviorally to keep wages down. Workers with the same length of service in a firm competed for increased wages by competing for retention, leaving the actual rate of wage increase unaffected. Nenko employers were limited in the area of wage increase since length-of-service, the main determinant of wages, is an inflexible factor. Therefore, emphasis was placed on increasing welfare benefits and rewards in order not to conflict with the wage and length of service status structure among workers (17, 18). The costs to the firm of such rewards and benefits are not easy to evaluate because until recently, few Japanese enterprises bothered with precise accounting of such bene-

fits, considering them "social overhead". Such costs probably represent an asset to the firm because they involve substantial tax advantages. Investment in non-cash welfare services is facilitated by generous government and bank loans, especially when real estate is involved, because it represents a good investment (4).

Nenko After World War II

One of the most significant developments in Japanese industry after World War II was the unionization of the big Japanese industries where Nenko is pervasive. This put an end to the old system of employee discharge. Nenko workers' employment with a company is now guaranteed until retirement at age 55, and companies no longer discharge them unless there are serious economic conditions endangering the existence of the firm. Employees are not laid off during ordinary recessions.

The resulting employment security has intensified cohesiveness and group consciousness among Nenko workers and has been an important factor in the stabilization which the large enterprises require for rational economic planning in the face of rapid technological change and economic growth. But if large Japanese industrial employers had not countered with certain restrictions on the Nenko system, their total wage payments would have gone out of control

TABLE 2. Hypothetical Model of Wage Pattern for Employees Beginning Service with a Firm in the Same Year Under the Post World War II Nenko System With All Employees Being Given Guaranteed Employment

Years of Employment	No. of Employees	Wage per Employee	Employer's Total Wage
10	10	10	100
9	10	9	90
8	10	8	80
7	10	7	70
6	10	6	60
5	10	5	50
4	10	4	40
3	10	3	30
2	10	2	20
1	10	1	10
			550

Source: Wakao Fujida, *Labor Organization and Activities (Rodo Kumiai no Soshiki to undo)* (Kyoto: Minerva, 1962), p. 320.

(8). Fujida's model, shown in Table 2, illustrates this dilemma. The solution was to limit the number of new Nenko recruits, as illustrated by Fujida in Table 3, and to compensate for the decrease in number of permanent employees by extensive use of temporary, subcontract, daily, and retired workers. This limited the number of permanent employees to a cyclically justifiable minimum (29) and set the pattern for what has come to be known as the dual wage structure and dual labor market of Japan. This pattern as it operates today will be examined in detail

TABLE 3. Model of Wage Pattern for Employees Beginning Service With a Firm in the Same Year Under the Post World War II Nenko System, With Limited Recruitment of Employees and Guaranteed Employment

Year of Employment	No. of Employees	Wage per Employee	Employer's Total Wage
10	5	10	50
9	5	9	45
8	5	8	40
7	5	7	35
6	5	6	30
5	5	5	25
4	5	4	20
3	5	3	15
2	5	2	10
1	5	1	5
			275

Source: Wakao Fujida *Labor Organization and Activities (Rodo Kumiai no Soshiki to undo)* (Kyoto: Minerva, 1962), p. 321.

Nenko and Non-Nenko Firms and Employees: A "Dual" System

Japanese industrial firms range in size from huge corporations with 1,000 or more employees to tiny household enterprises. The labor force employed in these firms is composed of permanent employees in big enterprises, retired workers, temporary workers, and subcontract and daily workers. The dual wage and labor market structure is formed by the interrelationships of these firms and employee groups.

Size Distribution of Industrial Firms

Large industrial firms with 300 or more employees, in which the Nenko system is in widespread use, account for less than one percent of the total number of firms enumerated, and this ratio has remained virtually unchanged for over a decade. Medium-small firms, in contrast, comprise over 99 percent of all the enterprises in Japanese industry (11, 1965, 1973).

Distribution of Labor Force by Size of Firm

From 1962 to 1970, a little over 25 percent of the labor force was employed by small firms of less than 20 employees, from 40 to 45 percent was employed by medium-sized firms of from 20-299 employees, and 30 to 33 percent was employed in firms of 300 or more employees (11, 1973). Since the Nenko system seldom applied to workers in medium-small enterprises, the statistics support Levine's estimate that only about a third of the labor force is employed in Nenko firms, and that Nenko coverage has not expanded significantly over the past decade.

Wage and Benefit Differences by Size of Firm

Compensation paid by Japanese industry is of two kinds: standard wages and fringe benefits. There are substantial differences in both types of compensation by size of firm.

The Standard Wage and its Determinants — The standard wage covers the minimum cost of living of the wage earner and is composed primarily of the basic wage, the hierarchy (length of service) allowance, and various family and living allowances. It is determined by such factors as education, length of service, performance evaluation, and cost of living. For regular workers who are hired directly from an educational institution without skill or experience, the level of education and the labor market determine the level of the starting wage. The average high school graduate, 16 years old, a juvenile and unskilled, receives no family allowance or hierarchical allowance but is paid as if still a member of an original family unit with no dependents. As a result, the starting wage is extremely low. In 1972, the monthly starting salary of college graduates was $179, for high school graduates $142, and for junior high graduates $114 (Y280 = $1.00) (13). The standard wage then increases primarily in relation to workers' length of service but also according to the needs of their age group, their education, and perhaps to a small degree their performance appraisal. The cost of living is also considered when the worker is the sole supporter of his or her family.

In the large firms where Nenko is in effect, there is a much stronger and more consistent correlation between wages and length of service than among small firms where Nenko is not practiced (10). Because job classification plays little or no role in the determination of wages in these firms, they usually evidence very little occupational structure (18). (Simple and unitary group participation in the achievement of work objectives is another reason for the absence of clearly differentiated occupational roles and structure (23).) There are some indications that length of service could become a somewhat less important wage determinant among Nenko firms in the future; large Japanese firms have talked increasingly of establishing some sort of job evaluation and merit rating system which would tie compensation directly to occupation and skill. Nevertheless, the basic structure of the Nenko system remains as yet one of permanent employees in large establishments who are paid largely on the basis of length of service (19).

Differentials in the Standard Wage by Size of Firm — There are substantial wage differences between large Nenko and small, non-Nenko firms in the Japanese manufacturing industry. In 1970, workers in medium-small industry still made slightly less than two-thirds the wages of workers in large enterprises, and workers employed by firms with from one to three employees, who constitute 14 percent of all workers in the manufacturing industry (11, 1973), received wages little more than one-tenth as high as the wages of workers in large enterprises (13).

From these statistics (summarized in Table 4), an outline of the dual wage structure of the Japanese labor market begins to emerge.

Prospects for Erosion of Wage Differentials — It has been suggested that, because of the labor shortage resulting from economic expansion and a low birth rate, the wage gap between large and small firms has begun to narrow (36). There has been considerable narrowing, but it seems to be confined largely to young workers. Since wage

increases for workers in smaller firms do not keep pace with wage increases in large firms, the significance of the narrowing is limited. Overall, the trend does not appear strong enough to suggest that the dual wage structure will be phased out in the forseeable future (22).

Fringe Benefits

It is the practice of Japanese employers to make semi-annual bonus payments based on workers' current wages. Table 5 shows the size of the bonuses paid to employees in the manufacturing industry by size of firm for 1960—1972 and reveals a clear positive correlation between size of firm and size of bonus (11, 1973).

Another striking feature of firms under the Nenko system is their distinctly well-equipped welfare facilities for workers. Their welfare benefits include company dormitories, housing facilities, summer resorts, loans, and so on (1). In con-

TABLE 4. Selected Characteristics of Japanese Manufacturing Firms and Employees, by Size of Firm

Size of firm by no. of employees	Percent Distribution by size, 1969	Percent Distribution of workers, 1970	Wage Indices, 1970 [a]
1-19		27.0	
1-3			13
4-9			47
10-19			63
20-299		40.0	
20-99			70
100-299			77
1-299	99.4	67.0	
300 or more	.6	33.0	100

[a] Wages of workers in firms of 300 or more employees = 100.

Source: Japan Medium-Small Enterprise Agency (Chusho Kigyo Cho), *White Paper on Medium-Small Enterprise* (1973), Appendices 2, 6 and 10.

TABLE 5. Semi-Annual Bonuses Paid in the Japanese Manufacturing
Industry, by Size of Firm, 1960-1972[a]

Year	Size of Firm (Number of Employees)		
	500 or more	100-499	30-99
1960	3.36	2.76	1.75
1962	3.52	3.01	2.02
1964	3.60	3.00	2.10
1966	3.62	3.20	2.22
1968	3.91	3.57	2.68
1970	4.40	4.02	3.04
1972	4.29	3.96	3.05

[a] In terms of monthly wage.

Source: Japan, Ministry of Labor, *White Paper on Labor (Rodo Hakusho)* (Tokyo, 1973), p. 393.

trast, medium and small enterprises have few such welfare facilities. Retirement payments are another advantage enjoyed only by employees of large scale enterprises.

Other Differences

Employment in small enterprises has some other disadvantages not clearly shown by wage and benefit statistics alone. First, while wages in smaller firms are lower, the hours required to earn them are longer (13). Second, employment security is constantly jeopardized due to the fact that medium-small enterprises frequently go bankrupt while larger enterprises are not permitted to go bankrupt (5). Third, employment by small firms is relatively dangerous. According to a Japanese government report, "In the manufacturing industry, the accident rate among firms of 30-99 employees is 6 times higher than that of firms with 1,000 or more employees" (12, p. 30).

Temporary, Subcontract, Daily, and Retired Workers — Their Role and Their Wages

Simplified methods of production made possible by technological change have enabled Japanese employers to rely to a great extent on workers other than their regular employees. The extensive use of temporary, subcontract, daily, and retired workers gives employers the needed labor force flexibility to deal with fluctuations in the economy. Unfortunately, little substantive data concerning these types of workers are available (35).

Temporary Workers — Temporary workers are hired by management for specific time periods when expansion of the work force is required by the business cycle. Most of the time they function as regular workers in terms of skills and work content, but they are paid less—often 50 percent less — than regular workers (21), and the wide variety of fringe benefits enjoyed by Nenko workers are not available to them (15). Their jobs are not guaranteed, since their tenure depends on the current business cycle.

The use of temporary workers has been a growing trend. Statistics on the automotive industry between 1954 and 1960 show that by 1961 the proportion of temporary workers among 11 firms had risen from 5.5 percent in 1954 to more than one-third of the total work force (32).

Subcontract and Daily Workers — Frequently, big firms will contract with smaller firms to supply labor for them. The workers supplied by these firms have an even lower status and more casual attachment to their employers than

TABLE 6. Wage Indices for Daily Workers in the Japanese Manufacturing Industry, by Size of Firm, 1960 - 1972

Year	All Sizes	Size of Firm		
		500 or more employees	100-499 employees	30-99 employees
1960	45.0	37.0	50.5	57.1
1962	48.5	41.8	54.1	56.5
1964	50.5	40.5	54.1	64.1
1966	45.0	39.5	49.2	52.1
1968	44.5	38.7	45.9	56.3
1970	43.6	38.1	46.2	52.7
1972	41.9	35.0	46.6	49.7

Note: Wage of regular employees = 100.

Source: Japan, Ministry of Labor, *White Paper on Labor (Rodo Hakusho)* (Tokyo, 1973), p. 391.

temporary workers (19). Usually, they perform unskilled tasks, but occasionally are found doing the same work as permanently employed workers. Like temporary workers they receive no fringe benefits and depend on the business cycle for employment, but their compensation tends to be even lower than that of temporary workers. Table 6 shows the wage ratio between daily workers and regular workers [2] in the manufacturing industry by size of firm for 1966 — 1972. Subcontract workers are even more economical because management is not responsible for them directly and saves the expense of direct hiring. The utilization of these workers varies from industry to industry, but the shipbuilding industry utilizes especially large numbers of them.

Retired Workers — Most Japanese firms, especially firms under the Nenko system, make retirement at age 55 mandatory (12). Since wages increase by length of service, this permits employers to terminate employees at the point at which their wages become excessively costly (19).

[2] Whether Nenko or non-Nenko can only be deduced approximately from these statistics by size of firm; i.e., regular workers in firms of 500 or more employees are usually under the Nenko system while those employed in firms of 30-99 employees are rarely if ever under the Nenko system. Regular employees of firms of 100-499 employees might be under the Nenko system.

The firms from which workers retire still consider them as a source of labor, often designating them as "special employees" and hiring them at reduced wages under yearly contracts. In this capacity they provide their employers with yet another source of labor force flexibility—one which is especially valuable since the "special employees" have acquired a lifetime of training in the skills required for work in those firms.

Nenko retirement benefits beyond such supplementary employment are: (a) generous lump-sum retirement benefits based on the last monthly wage multiplied by the number of years of service, plus an additional factor that increases them by as much as 30 percent (33) and/or (b) in a small but growing number of cases, monthly pensions (19). Nevertheless the retirement years of the ordinary non-executive worker can be difficult, as public pension payments are severely inadequate (c $65 per month at age 60) and access to company housing is cut off by compulsory retirement (33).

The Subcontracting System

There are many types of inter-firm relationships involved in the subcontracting system in Japanese industry. In one type of subcontract arrangement, the master company invests directly in the smaller company and controls and regulates its management. In other cases, the arrangement may simply be that an independent smaller establishment delivers almost all of its output to the master company. The affiliates may produce component parts for completion in the large firm, or may manufacture finished products which are marketed in the master distribution system.

Subcontract relationships are often more than simple two-level arrangements. They frequently involve a pyramidal chain of relationships with a large master firm at the top subcontracting with a group of smaller firms who may in turn subcontract with a group of even smaller firms. In the automotive industry, there are 14 auto makers. Below those are 350 parts makers, and below the 350 parts makers are about 8,000 even smaller subcontract firms. Likewise, manufacturers of electrical parts contract out much of their minor cutting and initial assembly work to small firms and these small firms in turn subcontract some of their work to household enterprises (26).

This pyramidal structure of the manufacturing industry had its origins in the economic conditions peculiar to Japan at the beginning of its economic expansion period. Cheap surplus labor was widely available, but large Japanese firms lacked the capital necessary for accelerated industrialization. To make up for this lack of capital, they utilized the output of already established smaller enterprises whenever possible. Today there are several technological and other reasons for subcontracting. Not all subcontracting arrangements in the Japanese manufacturing industry are exploitative in nature. Nevertheless, some firms in the subcontracting system still do serve the purpose of providing large firms with a valuable cushion against fluctuations in the business cycle, enabling them to make higher profits by manufacturing goods at lower cost. Conversely, these types of small subcontract firms depend on the market provided by the larger firms and must resist the trend toward higher wages in order to produce at a price their larger partners are willing to pay (9, 19).

Labor Unions and the Nenko System

At present, union membership in Japan numbers about 12 million workers distributed among more than 56,000 unit unions (the closest equivalent to local unions in the United States) (19).

Japanese labor unions characteristically include manual as well as non-manual workers and are organized on an enterprise basis. The enterprise-wide union typically includes all branches and plants of a single firm, whether production includes single or multiple lines and whether one or several industries are involved. The union usually reflects the structure of the enterprise entity (17).

Japanese unions are found primarily in the larger public and private enterprises. Nearly 70 percent of all organized workers are employed by firms with 500 or more employees, while firms with less than 30 employees account for less than one percent of all union membership. Only about 34.4 percent of the wage and salary earners eligible to become union members are organized (13). In other words, very few workers outside the Nenko system belong to a labor union.

Naturally, Japanese unions tend to resist changes which appear to threaten job security, wages, or benefits. Within the firms they represent, they have tended to resist the introduction of job evaluation and merit-rating systems which link compensation directly to occupational skills because they want to protect the middle-aged and older employees who benefit from the present system and are most likely to be hurt by the changes.

Because the system of payment by length of service still prevails in Nenko firms, there are substantial differences in reward between workers in their 20s and workers in their 40s regardless of the nature of their performance or the work they perform. This has given rise to some dissatisfactions and frustrations among younger workers. Management has tended to cultivate such natural grievances in order to prevent younger employees from unifying with older ones to oppose management (15).

Thus, unions, in protecting the wages and benefits of older Nenko workers, find themselves in the ironic position of siding with management in support of a policy which is intended to keep labor down. Since the benefits the unions have secured for their firms are supported to some degree by the dual wage structure, they also find themselves opposed to the betterment of wages, benefits, and security among unorganized workers in medium and small industries who suffer from the burden the dual wage structure imposes (16). Tsuru summarizes the dilemma of the Japanese labor movement:

> Here is a paradoxical situation of organized workers in large firms sharing in the productivity rise with the monopoly capitalists who tend to exploit their small subsidiary firms, which in turn can survive only by exploiting their non-union workers to the utmost (31, p. 96).

Thus the major effect of the Japanese labor movement appears to be to reinforce Nenko and the dual wage and labor market system.

Summary and Conclusions.

Much has been said about the effectiveness and efficiency of Japanese management practices. On-the-job training, security, and employee loyalty and motivation have been particularly admired. Behaviorally speaking, the question of whether these practices would be compatible with American behavior patterns and value orientations should not be overlooked. Clearly the question of adapting Nenko principles to U. S. management operations is much larger and involves the possibility that a Nenko-type management system might require the stability of permanent employment, which seems to require for its existence a kind of supporting labor market and wage structure which does not exist in the United States. Japanese managerial effectiveness cannot be understood and probably cannot be duplicated outside the context of the Japanese industrial relations system.

Robert Cole's view of the Japanese and U. S. management systems as "generalized functional alternatives which are compatible with the demands of advanced industrial technologies" (6, p. 630) illustrates how U. S. and Japanese management function within the context of two radically different industrial relations systems. In the context of Cole's concept, the Japanese alternative to the demands of advanced industrial technology has been to place great value on employee commitment among key workers in large firms as a resource, and to encourage it by a system of deferred rewards combined with guaranteed lifetime employment, while maintaining a large pool of untenured and underpaid workers to deal with changing business conditions. The American alternative has been to provide flexibility to meet business fluctuations and the need for external sources of trained labor on short notice by maintaining high rates of interfirm mobility. The sacrifice has been in "high turnover rates, poor returns on training costs, high cost of recruitment and termination, and seemingly high levels of alienation" (6, p. 628).

In terms of the cost-benefit tradeoff involved, it seems unlikely that U. S. employees would welcome the Japanese system. One would not expect employees of medium-small firms in the United States to willingly accept the role and wages of their Japanese counterparts. Even though unemployment is quite high among U. S. youth, it seems unlikely that the beginning wages offered Japanese youth would appeal to them, especially when only a third could expect to receive Nenko-type wage increases and benefits as compensation. Furthermore, it is questionable whether U. S. employees would be willing to accept mandatory retirement at age 55, without an adequate pension, and then to work on yearly contracts at reduced wages until disability or death.

If the assertion is correct that the stability of permanent employment and all it entails is a necessary precondition for the successful adaptation of Nenko principles to U. S. management operations, American management scholars and practitioners who have been interested in such adaptation may want to take a long, careful second look at the idea.

REFERENCES

1. Abegglen, James. *The Japanese Factory* (Glencoe, Illinois: Free Press, 1958).
2. Abegglen, James C. *Management and Worker: The Japanese Solution* (Tokyo: Sophia University, 1973).
3. Bairy, Maurice. "Motivational Forces in Japanese Life," in Robert J. Ballon (Ed.), *The Japanese Employee* (Tokyo: Sophia University, 1969), Chapter 2.
4. Ballon, Robert J. "Lifelong Remuneration System," in Robert J. Ballon (Ed.), *The Japanese Employee* (Tokyo: Sophia University, 1969), Chapter 6.
5. Ballon, Robert J. "Participative Employment," in Robert J. Ballon (Ed.), *The Japanese Employee* (Tokyo: Sophia University, 1969), Chapter 3.
6. Cole, Robert E. "Permanent Employment in Japan: Facts and Fantasies," *Industrial and Labor Relations Review*, Vol. 26, No. 1 (1972).
7. Drucker, Peter. "What We Can Learn From Japanese Management," *Harvard Business Review*, Vol. 49, No. 2 (1971).
8. Fujida, Wakao. *Labor Union Organization and Activities (Rodo Kumiai no soshiki to undo)* (Kyoto: Minerva, 1962).
9. Ito, Taikichi. *The High Growth of the Japanese Economy and the Problems of Small Enterprises* (Tokyo: Keio University Institute of Management and Labour Studies, Reprint Series, March 1964).
10. Japan, Institute of Labor. *Japan Labor Statistics* (Tokyo: 1970).
11. Japan, Medium-Small Enterprise Agency (Chusho Kigyo Cho). *White Paper on Medium-Small Enterprise (Chusho Kigyo Hakusho)*, (Tokyo, 1965, 1973).
12. Japan, Ministry of Labor. *Analysis of Labor Economics (Rodo Keizai no Bunseki)* (Tokyo, 1969).
13. Japan, Ministry of Labor. *White Paper on Labor (Rodo Hakusho)* (Tokyo, 1973).
14. Johnson, Richard Tanner, and William G. Ouchi. "Made in America (Under Japanese Management)," *Harvard Business Review*, Vol. 52, No. 5 (1974).
15. Kato, Tsunefumi. *Socialistic Salaryman (Shakaishugiteki Salaryman)* (Tokyo: Kobunsha, 1967).
16. Kawada, H. "Japanese Industrial Relations System: A Model for Developing Nations." Paper prepared for the University of Wisconsin Seminar on Comparative Labor Movements, Washington, D.C., April 1967.
17. Levine, Solomon B. *Industrial Relations in Postwar Japan* (Urbana: University of Illinois Press, 1958).
18. Levine, Solomon B. "Labor Markets and Collective Bargaining in Japan," in William Lockwood (Ed.), *The State and Economic Enterprise in Japan* (Princeton, N.J.: Princeton University Press, 1965).
19. Levine, Solomon B., and Gerald G. Somers. "Youth Employment and Wages in Japan." *IRRI Reprint No. 132* (Madison, Wisconsin: Industrial Relations Research Institute), reprinted from *Youth Unemployment and Minimum Wages* (1970), Chapter 11.
20. Nakane, Chie. *Japanese Society* (Berkeley: University of California Press, 1970).
21. Nakayama, Saburo. "Management by Participation in Japan," *Management Japan*, Vol. 6, No. 4, and Vol. 7, No. 1 (1973).
22. Oh, Tai K. "Characteristics of the Japanese Labor Market" (unpublished ms.), 1966.
23. Oh, Tai K. "Understanding Japanese Management" (California State University, Fullerton, 1975). Mimeographed.
24. Ratcliffe, Charles Tait. "Japan's Employment System in the 1970's," in Mainichi Newspapers, *How to Succeed in Japan; a Guide for the Foreign Businessman* (Tokyo: Japan External Trade Organization (Jetro), 1974).
25. Shuichi, Kato. "Reconstruction of the Japanese Group," *Japan Quarterly*, Vol. 21 (Jan.-March 1974).
26. Somers, Gerald G., and Masumi Tsuda. "Job Vacancies and Structural Change in Japanese Labor Markets." Paper presented for the Conference on Job Vacancy Research, National Bureau of Economic Research, New York, Feb. 11-13, 1965.
27. Sumiya, Mikio. *Social Impact of Industrialization in Japan* (Tokyo: Japanese National Commission for UNESCO, 1963).
28. Sumiya, Mikio. "The Impact of Technological Change on Industrial Relations in Japan," in *The Changing Patterns of Industrial Relations: Proceedings of the International Conference on Industrial Relations*, Japan Institute of Labor (Tokyo, 1965).
29. Taira, Koji. "Characteristics of Japanese Labor Markets," *Economic Development and Cultural Change*, Vol. 10 (January 1962).
30. Tsuda, Masumi. "Japanese Wage Structure and Its Significance for International Comparisons," *British Journal of Industrial Relations* (July 1965).
31. Tsuru, Shigeto. "Survey of Economic Research in Postwar Japan; Major Issues of Theory and Public Policy Arising Out of Postwar Economic Problems," *American Economic Review*, Vol. 54, No. 4, Pt. 2 suppl. (June 1964), 96-97.
32. Umetani, Shunichiro. "Statistics Prepared from a Lecture Given by Iwakoshi at the University of Tokyo." Nissan Motor Co., Ltd., 1972 (mimeographed).
33. Umetani, Schunichiro. "The Life of the Japanese Worker," *Japan Labor Bulletin* (Jan. 1, 1974).
34. Umetani, Shunichiro. "Man and Organization in Japan," *Japan Labor Bulletin* (Oct. 1, 1974).
35. Yamamoto, Kiyoshi. "Labor Market for Temporary and Subcontract Workers," in Rodomondai Bunken Kenkyukai (Ed.), *Bunken Kenkyu, Nihon no rodo mondai* (Tokyo, 1966).
36. Yamamura, Kozo. "Wage Structure and Economic Growth in Postwar Japan," *Industrial and Labor Relations Review* (October 1965).
37. Yoshino, M. Y. *Japan's Managerial System; Tradition and Innovation* (Cambridge, Mass.: MIT Press, 1968).

Work Ethics Transplant

Jack Egan

Backed by an aggressive state and local campaign to lure foreign investment, this central Georgia town of 150,000 [Macon] has become the unlikely setting for an experiment in transplanting the Japanese style of business management to American soil.

Japan's YKK Industries Inc., the world's largest zipper manufacturer, last year opened a $15 million plant in a new industrial park on the outskirts of Macon. YKK now employs nearly 100 American workers (in addition to a dozen native Japanese) and plans to eventually bring this number to 500.

In its nearly one year of operations, YKK has tried to imbue its American workers with the Japanese corporate values of strong company loyalty and identification, pride in quality work and high productivity that have made that country's industries the envy of many U.S. managers.

To achieve this, YKK promises its workers an unusual degree of job security, a daily feeling of participation in how the factory is run and, eventually, part-ownership in the company.

Another traditional Japanese work incentive, the twice-yearly bonus, also has been used to cement worker morale and boost output. The bonus is calculated on the basis of productivity and absenteeism as well as a percentage of salary.

"Of course, money is important," says Yoshinori Kitano, president of the Macon YKK plant. But the worker also needs to feel that the "company is his family" and that he has "another home here," he adds.

The hard-working Kitano in turn feels a special responsibility to the workers: "I protect everyone, I'm working for employees — not myself. I forget my wife, my children. I love 110 people. Even sleeping, I worry about them."

As part of the enthusiastic Kitano's open management style, he has no office. His desk is close to YKK's main reception area, out in the open, and is freely accessible to the employees.

Constantly wearing the company's uniform, a gray windbreaker with zippers everywhere, Kitano spends about two hours each day on the factory floor. He personally checks each department and works at various machines. Kitano also participates in the mandatory five-minute afternoon factory cleanup.

"Everybody is management, everybody operator, everybody repairman, everybody sweeper," he says, summarizing his management philosophy.

Although it is still early to tell, workers appear to be responding favorably to the system.

"The hours are long, the work is hard, but you seem not to mind that because of better feelings, a better attitude," says Bennie Shelton, 24, and in charge of two separate departments at YKK's highly automated factory.

"It's a more exciting system," he adds. The Japanese "have something over the Americans in handling people."

Jim MacDonald, who said he left Coca-Cola Bottling Co. because they bothered him about his long hair, says "the Japanese don't care about things like that as long as you are a hard worker and productive. . . . The more work you do, the better off you are."

Alex Gregory says working for YKK has required "divorcing myself from the American way of thinking and constantly watching the clock."

Gregory, 26, was the first American hired by Kitano. A graduate of Georgia Tech in textile engineering, Gregory spent three months at YKK's headquarters in Ikuji, Japan, living in a company dormitory and learning the company's operations.

He works between 65 and 70 hours a week as supervisor of the 282 weaving machines that each spew out a yard of zipper material every minute. "But rather than a sacrifice, I consider it an investment," he says. "If and when the factory makes money, I know I will share in the profits."

Even among Japanese corporations, YKK is unique. Founded in 1934 by Tadao Yoshida, who still is its president, YKK operates under an elaborate enterprise philosophy called "the Cycle of Goodness" that has given Japanese workers 80 per cent ownership of the company.

Supposedly inspired by the writings of Andrew Carnegie, the steel magnate and philanthropist, "the Cycle of Goodness" amounts to an ethical justification for capitalism and also serves as a practical source of internal financing for YKK's continuous and spectacular rate of growth.

Specifically, the phrase refers to a system of forced savings by YKK employees in Japan which gives them ownership shares in the company. Each employee is required to deposit at least 10 per cent of his monthly salary and living allowances with YKK and 50 per cent of his bonuses.

YKK pays dividends on the money — currently 18 per cent, which is in line with other Japanese lending rates — and uses the funds for capital expansion. The shares are not publicly traded, remain at a fixed price and must be returned to the company in the infrequent circumstance of an employee's departure.

"In this manner, business income directly affects the prosperity of society," Yoshida explained last year, "for businesses are not mere seekers after profit, but vital instruments for the improvement of society.

"The cycle enriches our free society and contributes to the happiness of those who work within it. The perpetual working of this cycle produces perpetual prosperity for all."

Although "the Cycle of Goodness" slogan appears throughout the Macon YKK plant, the plan itself has not yet been put into effect there or at any other YKK plants in the U.S.

It is questionable whether American workers would be willing to go along with such a required expropriation of a significant portion of their salaries, although Kitano said the plan is "under consideration."

For YKK, however, the system has catapulted the company from a $170 investment in 1934 to a $600 million investment in 1974 with 34 factories in 30 countries and enough annual zipper production to reach to the moon and back and corner 25 per cent of the world market for slide fasteners.

The company's success, in fact, has aroused suspicion among competitors in the U.S., Canada and Europe that YKK has dumped zippers on foreign markets at below production costs to undercut other manufacturers and carve out market shares. The charge has been upheld only in Canada.

The motivation for YKK's construction of the Macon plant and its other international ventures is based in part, at least, on problems the company has had in marketing its products abroad.

A 25 per cent inflation rate in Japan, the rising cost of plant sites there, the relative appreciation of the yen against the dollar, duties on shipments to the U.S. and the constant threat of import quotas on textile items have combined to make it more profitable for Japanese firms to build factories in the U.S. to supply the American market.

Across the way from YKK in the same industrial park, Texprint, Inc. — a joint venture of two Japanese companies and a Hawaiian-based American firm — has constructed a sophisticated $10 million fabric printing plant for many of these same reasons.

Marshall Cooley, the president of Texprint who has spent the last 20 years in Honolulu and Japan, says the goal was to "bring Japanese printing expertise here and produce in a dollar-controlled area."

He says the company chose the South because "the southern worker is not as transient as workers elsewhere" and "traditionally displays a greater loyalty to his employer."

William Durrett, the head of the Macon-Bibb County Industrial Authority, which played a large role in bringing YKK and Texprint to Macon, says there has been no discernible citizen reaction against foreign investment in the local area.

The Problem of
Moral Education
for the
Business Manager *

Edgar H. Schein

When we refer to the moral[1] education of the business manager, we may have one of three different concepts in mind: 1) education for general character which would reflect itself in moral behavior in any occupation; 2) morality in the *process* of education itself—that is, an educational process that *exemplifies* the moral values to be taught; and 3) the teaching of a particular value system as part of the general preparation of a candidate for a particular occupational role. This paper will focus on the third of these concepts.

I have chosen this focus deliberately, in order to stimulate research on moral education in the business realm. Such research has been carried out in medicine, dentistry, and law, but is lacking in the business area. I suspect that one reason for this is the difficulty in elucidating what may be moral questions and moral solutions for business managers. My attempt here will be to provide some clarifying categories drawn from a socio-psychological frame of reference which, I hope, will make it possible to select research questions and testable hypotheses that are relevant to the moral

* Paper prepared for the Seventeenth Conference on Science, Philosophy and Religion, Chicago, August, 1966.
[1] For purpose of this discussion I will not distinguish between concepts of "ethical" and concepts of "moral." The two words will be used interchangeably.

problem, whether we are talking about the behavior of practicing managers or the teaching of management.

Some Categories for Classifying Moral Values

Moral or ethical behavior and the values from which such behavior derives are often believed to be generalizable across all kinds of situations and all kinds of human relationships. Yet most research on such behavior consistently finds that people apply different standards to different situations. For example, killing is wrong, yet we may do it in wartime or in self-defense. Stealing is wrong, yet a prisoner of war may steal from his captor. Lying is wrong, yet we may and are supposed to lie if we must do so to protect someone's self-esteem. In the recent cases of price-fixing in the electrical industry, this point came out in the defense argument that the forces at work in the particular situation offered the executives no choice but to collude, just as the soldier has no choice but to try to kill the enemy.

If we accept the argument that one must analyze values and moral standards in reference to *particular* situations or relationships, we can next ask: What kinds of categories would help us to classify such situations?

 From Edgar H. Schein, "The Problem of Moral Education for the Business Manager," *Sloan Management Review,* Vol. 8, No. 1, Fall 1970. Reprinted by permission.

My major classifying principle will be to consider who is involved in the relationship I shall ask: With respect to whom is the behavior being judged as moral or immoral? Following a detailed discussion of this classification, I will discuss briefly some additional issues, such as who benefits vs. who gets hurt, the closeness of the behavior to the consequences thereof, the reversibility of the behavior, the problem of intentions vs. effects, and sins of commission vs. sins of omission.

Who Is Involved? The Multiple Clients of the Manager

There are a number of ways of defining a profession. One of my favorites comes from the sociologist Everett Hughes,[2] who has stated the simple proposition that a professional is someone who knows better what is good for his client than the client himself does. This definition includes the more usual definition that the professional has had extensive training in a body of knowledge and skills which he exercises on behalf of his clients.

If we examine this definition in reference to the well-established professions of medicine and law, we find that the value or moral issues of the profession tend to be defined around the relationship with the client. Both doctor and lawyer receive moral training in how to exercise responsibility in their relationship with clients, and in how to work for the client's welfare—even if this means the sacrifice of self-interest or the compromising of some other value. Doctors are expected to make economic sacrifices if the patient's welfare demands it, to ignore the welfare of their own family if midnight calls require their services, to lie to their patients about their conditions, and so on. Perhaps the best example comes from the prisoner of war camp where the doctor's oath required him to treat enemy officers in clear violation of the patriotic standards of the POWs who were witness to the behavior and who viewed it as traitorous.

If we accept this definition of professionalism—knowing better what is good for the client than the client himself—we may speculate that it is the *vulnerability of the client* which has necessitated the develop-

ment of moral and ethical codes surrounding the relationship. The client must be protected from exploitation in a situation in which he is unable to protect himself because he lacks the relevant knowledge to do so.

In recent years we have tended to view the business man and industrial manager as becoming increasingly professionalized. There is a broader base of technical knowledge and skills required to be a manager, a longer period of training for managerial responsibility, and a greater tendency for managers to be able to move from one type of organization to another, implying that managerial skills are quite general. If, then, the manager is becoming a professional, who is his client? With respect to whom is he exercising his expert knowledge and skills? Who needs protection against the possible mis-use of these skills?

The Consumer as Client. Business generates products and services that are purchased by various types of consumers, thus raising the obvious possibility of exploitation of the consumer. Traditional economic theory minimized this problem by assuming that the marketplace was an automatic arbiter of prices and quality, hence the businessman enjoyed no special power relative to the consumer. *Caveat emptor,* let the buyer beware, was a not-so-gentle reminder to the consumer to exercise what power he had to prevent himself from being exploited. This assumption in turn legitimized any practice that any manager may have wished to engage in vis-à-vis the consumer, and thereby bypassed the moral issues altogether.

The point is well made by the story of the storekeeper whose son asked him what it meant to be in moral conflict. The father replied: "If a customer comes into the store and looks at some material, and asks how much it costs, and I tell him it is $1.00 per yard, and he asks for one yard, and pays me the dollar, and as he is leaving the store I discover that there are two one-dollar bills stuck together—then I face the moral conflict—do I tell my partner about it or just keep the extra dollar."

Many economists argue persuasively that the traditional economic assumptions have never been validated by experience; that the marketplace has not been able to

[2] Hughes, E. C. [1]

curb the power of the businessman vis-à-vis the consumer; that the consumer has not been in a position to know what he was buying and hence was, in fact, in a relatively vulnerable position. Thus we have seen the development of formal codes, laws, and informal ethical standards pertaining to cleanliness in production processes, weights and measures in packaging, truthfulness in stating contents of products and in making advertising claims, rights of consumers to sue businesses for the return of their money if they have been cheated, and so on.

Clearly then, one whole area of values deals with the relationship between the manager and consumers, and one area of moral training for the individual manager concerns the development in him of a sense of responsibility to his customers. Whether graduate schools of management actually attempt to inculcate a sense of responsibility to the consumer is an important question for empirical research. Our own school, if it touches the area at all, does so implicitly. Courses in marketing tend to focus heavily on the technical issues, not on the moral ones. I would hypothesize that most of our faculty would assume that the requisite set of responsible feelings and values are already "built into" our students, hence do not have to be a subject of concern in graduate courses.

The Stockholder as Client. The consumer is a client of the manager only in a very limited sense. Most managers do not deal directly with customers, and only a small percentage of their decisions have anything to do with the final consumer relationship. Instead, one often hears the assertion that the manager's only responsibility is to the stockholder.

According to this concept, the manager is a person who uses his expert knowledge and skills to bring to fruition some ideas about how to build or develop a product or service for profit, to implement these ideas, and actually to generate a reasonable rate of return on the investment of the stockholders. The client-professional relationship is here defined as primarily an economic one, and the vulnerability of the client lies in the possibility that the manager may misuse, misallocate, steal, or otherwise mishandle the economic resources entrusted to him.

Deriving from this concept is a second area of potential moral training, having to do with embezzlement, misappropriation of funds, not taking advantage of inside financial information, nepotism, and a variety of other behaviors which have in common that they reduce the profitability of the enterprise and thus take advantage of the stockholders. The power of the stockholder to protect himself is greater than that of the consumer, however. He has a potential organization in the form of the annual meeting and his representative body, the Board of Directors. He can and often does demand more direct surveillance of the financial activities of the managers to supplement those of regulatory agencies such as the Security Exchange Commission.

The Community as Client. A third client of the manager is the community, viewed broadly as the individuals and other organizations who are in some way interdependent with the business enterprise. The individuals in the community who depend upon the company for jobs are vulnerable to discriminatory hiring policies, the suppliers are vulnerable to discrimination, exploitation, and bribery, and the community as a whole is highly vulnerable to economic loss if the business moves or conducts its affairs in such a way as to minimize the economic return to the community. The company can bring in its own labor force, refuse to buy supplies or raw materials from local vendors, fail to support community activities, and so on.

It is interesting to note that in this value area, as in the others, the legal sanctions tend to be applied where vulnerability is at a maximum, such as in the case of discriminatory hiring practices, or of minimum wages for employment.[3] The more difficult moral decisions occur, however, where ambiguity is greater, as in the process of defining the economic responsibilities of a company if it is the sole employer in a community.

---

[3] One might hypothesize that legal sanctions tend to develop when a) vulnerability is at a maximum, b) there is a specific identifiable target who is potentially vulnerable, c) the manager's behavior is potentially observable and unambiguous, and d) there are immediate or short-run consequences of the managerial behavior.

A special case of the community as client results when businesses have overseas subsidiaries and the managers become not only representatives of the particular organization vis-à-vis the local foreign community, but become representatives of the United States as a nation with a certain kind of value system. In this situation it is often not clear who is more vulnerable—the local community, the business enterprise, or the United States in having its image tarnished. Do we expect the overseas manager to uphold the values of service and community development, the values of efficiency and economic growth for the business, the values of democracy and free enterprise, or the values of nationalism, patriotism, and allegiance to the United States? These values can and often do come into conflict with each other. What is best for the local community, for the business, and for the United States are often not the same things.

We have had to face this issue in the Sloan School when we were selecting candidates for our Fellows in Africa and Fellows in South America programs. In each case our graduate was expected to become an employee of the local government and to convince it that he could be trusted. He had to have a value system that would permit him to work on behalf of his employer, even if this meant short-run disregard of United States interests, as in the case of planning a local development program that might draw most of its financial and technical resources from the Soviet Union if these were more accessible than their U.S. equivalent. In our selection we were clear about one thing: We could not afford to send super-patriots or individuals whose prime motivation was to export their own concept of American values to another culture. Whether our Fellows faced such conflicts, and how they handled them if they did, constitutes an important research question which we are currently trying to answer.

The Enterprise as Client. A fourth client is the enterprise itself—the organization that employs the manager.[4] With the increasing

[4] Since the organization is an abstraction, can one view it as a client? I believe we can treat it as an "object" in the same sense in which clubs, fraternal organizations, political parties, and countries exist as objects to which we give loyalty and attention and from which we obtain material and symbolic rewards.

tendency to analyze business organizations as complex social systems comes an increasing tendency for the manager to view himself as being basically responsible to the system as a whole. He is responsible for its efficiency, maintenance, effectiveness, and growth. He is expected to make decisions on behalf of these values even if they run counter to the short-run interests of consumers, stockholders, and the community.

The important value referent becomes the organization as a whole, and the assumption is made that in the long run what is good for the organization will be good for the consumer, the stockholder, and the community. Considerations of profit, consumer benefits, and community involvement are subordinated to the ethic or values of efficiency and growth, based on criteria of the "health" of the organizational system. What is required of the manager is commitment and dedication to organizational goals.

Thus, whether the manager decides to hire only certain kinds of employees at certain very low wages is based not on moral considerations in the usual sense but on considerations of what is required to produce the product efficiently. I know of one industry that has solved this dilemma by moving to countries where labor was cheap and no legal sanctions existed concerning hiring practices.

Teaching the importance of commitment and loyalty to the enterprise as values may be particularly important because the enterprise, being an abstraction, is not in a good position to control such behavior. It is highly vulnerable to low commitment, indifference, disloyalty, apathy, sabotage, and treason. Business organizations cannot apply legal sanctions against such behaviors as easily as nations can and do through their governments. Businesses can only fire the apathetic person, but if apathy is widely spread through managerial ranks there may be a tendency not only to condone such behavior but to develop practices of concealing it from top management, the Board of Directors, and the stockholders.

Most of the technical courses in a business school probably take the values of enterprise efficiency and growth for granted. Organizational goals are accepted as given; the only problem is how best to achieve them. If ethical or moral dilemmas are in-

412   Edgar H. Schein

volved in the choice of means, they are either ignored or settled by considering whether the means are in fact illegal. If the survival of the organization depends upon it, even illegal means are sometimes condoned with the argument that the law is not fair in the first place.

The Subordinate as Client. A fifth type of client of the business manager is his subordinate-employee. Many kinds of managerial behaviors labelled as immoral or unethical deal with aspects of the superior-subordinate relationship—starvation wages, excessive working hours, unsafe working conditions, withholding a promotion or raise to enforce subordination, and arbitrary lay-offs. Employees as clients have been so vulnerable to these kinds of behavior on the part of their managers that they have had to band together and, through unions and the passage of protective legislation, reinforce their own position.

Thus, much behavior formerly labelled immoral is now defined as illegal, but the issue remains unsettled in that a more subtle counterpart of each of the above kinds of behaviors is possible. Bosses can still threaten their employees with the withholding of rewards or with subtle punishments; they can still exercise arbitrary and unfair authority; they can play favorites, fail to give credit where credit is due, persecute someone until he quits, steal their subordinates' suggestions, or fail to recommend their best subordinates for promotions.[5]

As one story puts the issue, a company wanted to institute a new benefit program more favorable to employees. All employees signed up except one older clerk who held up the entire proceedings by refusing to sign. His boss told him of the great benefits, but to no avail. The boss asked the Vice-President to try, but no amount of persuasion could get the old employee to sign. After several more futile attempts to get the man to understand the benefits, the President himself was told about the case. The President called the old man in, sat him down at the desk, put the paper in front of him, and said, "Listen you S.O.B.

Sign that paper right now or you're fired." The old man signed. The President, somewhat puzzled, asked him why he signed so readily when others had had such difficulty getting him to sign. The old man said, "Well, sir, you were the first one who really explained the program to me."

The values implied by traditional management theory have always held that the boss is the boss and should only do that which is good for the enterprise. The argument has been that no special obligations or responsibilities accrue to workers and/or managerial subordinates beyond those specified by the contract or law. On the other hand, the human relations movement has usually been viewed as an attempt to reverse this trend and to argue that managers are responsible to their subordinates, should consider their needs, should treat them as human beings and not merely as interchangeable economic resources, and that they should do this because it is right in and of itself in a democratic society.

A third argument, which many human relationists/behavioral scientists claim for themselves, is that managers should consider the needs of their subordinates not because it is basically immoral not to do so but because it will in fact lead to greater economic and productive efficiency on the part of the enterprise. Since commitment, loyalty, and energy are desirable in employees for good organizational performance, it is argued that these qualities are most easily obtainable by treating people fairly, by considering their needs, and by attempting to enhance rather than weaken their sense of individuality and contribution to the organization.

We have here an area where values and science overlap to an unknown degree since the evidence is not yet clearcut whether in fact people will generally perform better if trusted and treated well, or whether this happens only under certain special conditions. If the latter is the more accurate statement of where our scientific knowledge lies, the manager is in the difficult position of having to be a diagnostician in an area where it is not at all clear whether the issues are scientific or moral ones.

What we then teach in a school of management may well be a function of whether

---

[5] William Evan points out that in organizational life employees do not have the protection of due process of law and a system of appeals as they do in the larger society. [2]

the teacher is an economist who leans toward traditional assumptions about economic man or a behavioral scientist who leans toward assumptions of a complex man capable of a variety of involvements in organizations.[6] In our school we teach both positions.

The Peer and/or Boss as Client. A sixth type of client for the manager is his peer and/or boss. I am assuming that the manager is by definition a part of an organized enterprise, and that any organized enterprise depends on the coordinated behavior of all its members. The nature of organized effort thus makes the members of the organization highly interdependent, and therefore highly vulnerable to certain kinds of behaviors vis-à-vis each other. For example, the boss is highly vulnerable to having his subordinates lie to him about what is going on in those portions of the organization which he cannot check on directly. Peers are very vulnerable to having negative information about themselves passed on to their boss, which is one aspect of the set of activities generally referred to as "playing politics."

Where departments of a single organization are arrayed competitively with each other, the manager of each may be motivated to exaggerate the virtues of his own group and devalue the other group, and may implement the motive by falsifying figures, by failing to pass on key information, by subtle distortions, and the like. All the pathology of intergroup conflict in society and community can play itself out inside the organization, with managers being tempted into various kinds of questionable behavior in regard to their peers and superiors.

Part of the value dilemma in this area is that we do not have clear ethical or moral standards pertaining to collaboration-competition. Not only is it unclear in our society how far one should go in defining the game as being a competitive one, but it is not clear how far one can go in bending or breaking rules in the process of trying to win. We say that free enterprise is by definition a competitive game and that competition is good for all the various enterprises engaging in it, yet we

find that competition breeds behavior that is clearly harmful, and against which society must protect itself. For example, for a company to win over a competitor may mean reducing its costs by cutting its labor force, compromising on quality of product, making untrue advertising claims, or sabotaging the competitor, to the point where government intervention becomes necessary to redefine the rules of the game.

Most companies assume that the productivity of individuals as well as departments within their organization can be enhanced by having them compete with each other. Rarely do they observe until too late some of the costs of such competition—in the amount of distortion of information, hiding of failures, falsification of figures, empire building, and mutual mistrust among managers presumably working for the same enterprise. Are these managers immoral, or does competition stimulate certain kinds of behavior which are well within the rules of the *competitive* game? It is only in the context of persons attempting to work together that some of these behaviors look questionable.

I would state the hypothesis that most schools of management start with the values of individualism and competition, rarely examining the consequences of these values inside the enterprise. Group effort, collaboration, and cooperative coordination tend to be viewed as fuzzy inventions of the behavioral scientists, not as concepts to be taken seriously. The only group in our faculty that believes in the effectiveness of *group* incentives (which force cooperation among workers) is the labor-relations—organizational psychology group. The economists, mathematicians, marketers, and others are clearly in favor of individual effort and individual incentives and, by implication, the ethic of competition.[7]

The Profession as Client. A final type of client can be thought of as the profession with which the person identifies and to which he belongs. To the extent that management has become a mature profession with clear standards, the individual manager can judge his own behavior against those standards, regardless of the requirements of the various other client systems.

---

[6] Schein, E. H. [3]

[7] Schein, E. H. [4]

In a sense the manager then becomes his own client in that he protects his own self-esteem and his professional identity at the same time that he upholds the profession. However, the profession as client may not solve the problem of identifying moral standards in that the professional standard may merely be to try to serve the various other client systems as well as possible.

Summary and Implications. The various *clients* of the manager are represented in Figure 1. The manager as a professional has obligations and responsibilities to each of these clients. This very fact has a number of implications:

● The managerial role, in contrast to many other professional roles, tends to be defined in terms of a system of *multiple clients*. It is not yet clear in the profession which clients, if any, are to be considered the primary ones.

● Because the values which underlie the different manager-client relationships differ from each other, creating potential conflict situations, and, because we have not yet defined primary client responsibil-

ities for the managerial role, *we cannot specify a single set of values and moral behaviors for the manager*. The search for such a single value system is doomed to failure until we define to whom we ultimately want the manager to be responsible.

● The responsibilities with respect to one client system often require the compromising of responsibilities to another client system. Just as members of organizations have often been found to suffer from role conflict because of the multiple links they have to others, so they suffer from potential *value conflict* or *moral conflict* because of the conflicting responsibilities to different client systems.

● Because of the potential value conflicts which the manager faces, we cannot glibly label his behavior as moral or immoral in any particular situation. We must know the *frame of reference* within which the behavior occurred in order to judge it. In other words we must know which of several values the individual was trying to implement before we praise or condemn him.

● By classifying types of behavior in terms

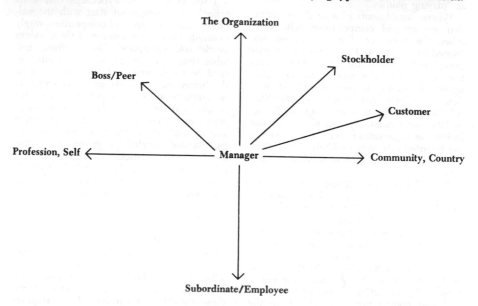

Figure 1 Various client systems toward which the manager has responsibilities. Each arrow defines one area of values and moral behavior.

of the client relationship involved, we can study empirically the kinds of values managers hold, and how these vary as a function of other variables such as rank, type of job in the organization, age, prior experience, and so on. It would be extremely valuable to know, for example, whether managers are more likely to view as immoral, behavior that hurts a consumer rather than behavior that hurts a subordinate. At present we have no value theory which would be able to make any predictions about this sort of question.

● The nearest thing to a superordinate value is the assertion that the manager is ultimately responsible to the enterprise. Much of the teaching in our school seems to be based on this premise, and most often when managers are under attack they seem to retreat to this as the ultimate defense: What is good for the company is ultimately good.

● If indeed we are moving toward an organizational ethic of the type implied above, it becomes essential to study carefully the implications of this "ultimate" value position. If managers are taught primarily to respond to the needs of the organization, will this undermine or subvert other important values, or are the needs of the organization indeed compatible with the needs of the consumer, the employee, and the community?

Who Gets Hurt and Who Benefits?

A second way of classifying moral value questions is according to the criterion of whether the immoral behavior involved is defined as immoral because it unfairly benefits the person doing it, or unfairly hurts one or more others who are affected by it. To exemplify the distinction, discriminatory hiring practices or personal prejudice leading to unfair treatment of an employee are immoral because they are unduly harmful to the recipient of the behavior. Embezzlement on a small scale, theft of company office supplies, financial gain due to inside information, accepting bribes or kickbacks from suppliers, etc. are immoral because they are unduly beneficial to the person committing the deed. The latter type of behavior may in fact be doing no one any visible harm in the short run. But it implies that there are certain categories of rewards to which people are not entitled or

certain means of obtaining benefits which are not sanctioned regardless of whether anyone else is harmed or not.

A closely related issue concerns whether the potential harm from an immoral action is directed at a particular individual or small group, or whether it is widely distributed among an anonymous mass. I would conjecture that we tend to label behavior as immoral much more readily if the harm is directed at particular persons.[8] Thus, to cheat a customer in a face-to-face relationship is considered more immoral than to cheat an anonymous mass of customers by mislabeling a package. To fire twenty particular men from a hundred-man work force is considered more immoral than to order an arbitrary 20 percent reduction in the labor force and draw names out of a hat. Stealing office supplies, tools, and materials from the "company" is not as immoral as stealing a single tool from a fellow worker which may make his job more difficult to perform.

The double standard we use in this regard is illustrated by the story of the man whose son came home from school complaining that a friend had taken his pencil. The father told his boy that it was probably accidental, not to worry about it, and gave him another pencil. The next day the boy reported that the friend had again taken his pencil. Once more the father played the issue down and gave his son another pencil. When the behavior was repeated a third and fourth day, the father finally got mad, called the friend's father and said, "Look Fred, my boy tells me that your boy has been taking his pencils. I want you to see that this stops. It is the principle of the thing which is bothering me, not the pencils. I can get plenty of those at the office."

It is not clear whether the tendency to condone cheating or stealing with respect to a large anonymous mass like a company comes about because of the belief that the anonymous mass can somehow afford it, and that it is not really hurt, or whether it is simply easier to commit hurtful deeds when the hurt party is not there to re-

---

8 Both "helping" and "hurting" are *interpersonal* concepts with limited meaning when applied merely as a trait like "helpful" or "mean". They become meaningful as we specify *who* is hurt or *who* is helped.

proach or induce guilt. The latter position would lead to the proposition that the greater the physical or psychological distance between the manager and the client, the easier it would be for him to commit irresponsible hurtful acts toward the client.

Some recent experiments by Milgram[9] support the idea that morality is easier to give up as psychological distance builds up between the person hurting and the person hurt. In Milgram's experiments, subjects are asked to give extremely painful electric shocks to a partner whenever he makes an incorrect response on a learning problem. In fact there is no partner, but the subject believes that there is one. Not only did Milgram find that a surprisingly high number of people will give extreme shocks to partners in this situation if ordered to do so by the experimenter, but that they are more likely to do so if they cannot see, hear, or feel the reactions of the partner. In other words, fewer subjects will obey the experimenter if they can hear moans whenever they give a shock, and still fewer will obey if the "partner" holds hands with the subject and clenches the hand strongly every time the presumed shock is delivered. Apparently we *do* find it easier to be cruel if we *don't* have to witness the effect of our cruelty.

If this phenomenon is general, one might suppose that the manager is most likely to be moral with his immediate subordinates, peers, and superiors, and least likely to be moral with customers (unless he is in sales), the community (unless he is in public relations), and stockholders (unless he is a large one himself or the treasurer who must report to them). It suggests also that one of the most effective means of curbing immoral behavior or training for morality is to maintain close contact between the manager and those clients toward whom one wants him to be particularly responsible. In conflict situations, one might predict that the person will choose behavior which will be least hurtful to those clients (including the person himself) who are psychologically closest to him.[10,11]

A further hypothesis would be that we tend to view either self-enhancement or hurting as more immoral if the person is viewed to be acting on his own behalf rather than as an agent or representative of some group. One of the commonest defenses against charges of immoral behavior is that the person was only carrying out orders (as in the Milgram experiment and the Nuremberg trials) or was only representing the best interests of some other client system with which he is identified.[12]

If this last hypothesis is supportable, it has implications for the way in which we train members of any profession. To the extent that we teach them to identify with groups, to allow themselves to become representatives, and to develop loyalties, to that extent we are encouraging them to abdicate more personal concepts of responsibility. Perhaps one of the functions of professional associations is to "drain off" the belongingness needs of the individual professional lest he join a group that will bias his moral judgments.

Reversibility, Sins of Omission, and Intentions vs. Consequences

When we consider society's judgments with respect to certain categories of immoral behavior, it appears clear that not only is the amount of harm and the fairness of the deed considered, but that irreversible harms are more severely judged than reversible ones. Thus, killing is most severely punished because it is most harmful and totally irreversible. Rape, maiming, and other physical insults fall under this same umbrella. Do they have a counterpart in the realm of managerial behavior?

Blacklisting a fired employee and thus depriving him of a livelihood, driving someone out of business by unfair means, ruining a colleague's career by a whispering campaign that destroys his reputation, and stealing a patent all have a certain

---

[9] Milgram, S. [5]

[10] One might speculate that the *motivation* to help or not hurt comes from the *feelings* of compassion, fear, or guilt, not from a *rational* assessment of need or vulnerability. We are more likely to give something

to a beggar who confronts us than a starving country which may need our help more but which arouses no direct feeling in us. In any case this is an hypothesis worth testing.

[11] Robert Kahn has suggested the further implication of organizing our enterprise as small units, possibly federated into larger ones, to insure a maximum of close contacts among managers and their various clients. [6]

[12] I am indebted to John Thomas for this point.

quality of irreversibility, but the judgment is not too easy to make in many cases. It is easier to identify the clearly reversible cases such as those which involve cheating a customer (wherein the customer can recover his money), fraud (wherein the injured party can sue for damages), or accepting a bribe (which the person can be forced to return).

The most difficult judgments arise in situations where it is not easy to determine what harm was done. Suppose a supervisor deliberately gives low ratings to an employee whom he dislikes even though the employee's performance is excellent. If the low ratings cause the employee to be passed over for promotion, he has clearly been harmed, but neither he nor the boss may know whether this has actually occurred. As was noted previously, employees in organizations do not have the protection of anything comparable to due process of law. The manager, especially, is highly vulnerable with respect to higher levels of management, and has few channels of appeal in most organizations. Hence, even if immoral behavior were reversible in principle, it often would not be in practice.

In discussion with Robert Kahn another dimension was identified which poses difficult judgment problems. This dimension concerns essentially the distinction between sins of commission vs. sins of omission. Most of my discussion so far has taken its examples from sins of commission—some clear behavior which was irresponsible with respect to some client. Yet many kinds of situations become unduly hurtful or beneficial only if the manager does *not* do certain things.

For example, the manager may not transmit his positive evaluation of a subordinate and thus undermine the subordinate's chance for promotion. He may fail to report to the production manager information received from customers pertaining to defects in a product, and thus make the production department more vulnerable to criticism. He may allow slipshod practices in the organization to continue rather than correct them, thus weakening the competitive position of the company. He may fail to report a potential problem in a product to the customer, thus endangering the customer. Failing to inform car buyers of possible safety hazards

in certain models or failing to notify NASA of weak spots in a missile system or booster would be extreme examples of this sort.[13]

How do we tend to judge this category of "sins of omission"? Two criteria that appear to be involved are 1) the amount of potential harm that can result from the omission, and 2) whether the manager knew that he was withholding behavior and knew of the potential consequences. In the case of commission we generally hold the person responsible for the consequences whether or not he knew what he was doing. "Ignorance of the law is no excuse." But in the case of sins of omission, ignorance or good intentions appear to be sounder defenses. If this hypothesis is supportable, it suggests that specific training in thinking through the consequences both of acting and not acting becomes an important part of professional training, particularly for the manager.

It is my impression that such training is indeed heavily emphasized in graduate school. Without stating specific value criteria for the student, we emphasize being able to think through various courses of action and accurately assessing consequences in order that the person should learn how to implement those values that he holds.

Concluding Remarks

I have tried to clarify the issue of moral education for the manager by pointing out the inherent difficulty of classifying for this emerging profession what is moral and what is not. Not only is it not clear to which client the manager is ultimately responsible, but it is difficult to judge the amount of benefit or harm, the effect of psychological distance from the client, intentions within a given frame of reference and the obligations of the manager to do more than avoid illegal or clearly immoral actions. All of these difficulties should make us cautious in glibly labeling particular managerial acts as moral or immoral.

On the other hand, the issue cannot be dismissed merely because it is difficult. We should vigorously pursue empirical research to clarify the conditions under which dif-

---

[13] The obvious, more general case is the passive behavior of the witness to a crime, as in recent cases in New York City, i.e., failing to help where help is needed.

ferent kinds of behavior will in fact occur and how various groups in our society judge these behaviors. We should determine what kinds of value positions are held in our professional schools of management and how these jibe with values in business and in the larger community. And we should stimulate inquiry among students themselves to begin investigation of the educative process on the part of its recipients.

Until we have more data, we should attempt to discern what the trends are in our present educative process. I would like to conclude this paper by pulling together some of these trends, as I see them from the perspective of our own Sloan School.

● Most faculty members tend to avoid the value issues, concentrating instead on what they call "analytical approaches" to problem-solving. This means that goals are taken as given and the focus of the course is on how best to achieve the goals. The emphasis is on means and how to choose among competing means in terms of criteria of efficiency. A corollary emphasis is to "know the consequences of your own behavior" and choose means appropriately in terms of rationally assessed consequences.

● If the faculty member is pushed on the value issue or asked what are the ultimate goals toward which the means are to be used, he would most often choose the enterprise as the relevant client. The goals are to maximize the economic performance of the enterprise or to insure the survival and growth of the enterprise as a social system. The values are efficiency and effectiveness. I am not aware that any course seriously questions whether any given enterprise should in fact exist or not. Such questions are treated as being outside the realm of most of our courses.

● If asked about other clients such as consumers, employees, and community, the faculty member would tend to respond that "other courses" worry about these unless it happens to fall squarely within his own area. Thus, obligations to employees are the concern of psychology or labor relations courses, not economics or mathematics. Within the area, emphasis on the pragmatic means tends to be maintained. Speaking for my own area of organizational psychology, I would tend to justify moral behavior toward employees, colleagues, and superiors on the pragmatic basis that such

behavior insures better organizational performance, thus seemingly removing the question from the moral realm.

● A recent survey of the beliefs and values of our faculty revealed that in a number of areas there were considerable differences, as a function of teaching area. If these findings are reliable, they suggest that even though, as individual teachers, we may try to de-emphasize the value questions, in fact we do feel differently about certain basic issues; and students probably are well aware of this. I have evidence also that students definitely are influenced by faculty beliefs and values. But, since we differ as a function of teaching area, we influence the student differentially as a function of the courses he takes.[11]

● If we have within the school a kind of pluralism with respect to values, the ultimate responsibility for value choice seems to fall to the student himself. Either we force him through a pattern of required courses exposing him to a variety of positions which he must then integrate, or we let him choose his own courses and thus force him to make value choices during the process of education itself, or some of both. In the Sloan School I believe we do both, but we do not provide a clear forum during the student's second year of education for integrating the diverse points of view or forcing an examination of value issues. The fact that such integrative courses have been difficult to design and to teach may well reflect the difficult value questions with which they would have to deal.

References

1 Hughes, E. C., *Men and Their Work*, Glencoe, Illinois: Free Press, 1958.
2 Evan, W. M., "Due Process of Law in Military and Industrial Organizations," *Administrative Science Quarterly*, 1962, 7, 187-207.
3 Schein, E. H., *Organizational Psychology*, Englewood Cliffs, New Jersey: Prentice Hall, 1965.
4 Schein, E. H., "Attitude Change During Management Education: A Study of Organizational Influences on Student Attitudes," *Administrative Science Quarterly*, 1967, in press.
5 Milgram, Stanley, "Some Conditions of Obedience and Disobedience to Authority," in *Current Studies in Social Psychology*, edited by I. D. Steiner and M. Fishbein, New York:

[11] See Schein, 1967, *Op. cit.*

Holt, Rinehart and Winston, Inc., 1965, 243-262.

6 Kahn, R. L., Personal communication.

Edgar H. Schein, Ph.D., *Professor of Organizational Psychology and Management, Sloan School of Management, Massachusetts Institute of Technology.* Formerly Research Psychologist, Walter Reed Army Institute of Research. Author of *Organizational Psychology*, Prentice Hall, 1965; Coauthor of *Interpersonal Dynamics*, Dorsey, 1964, and of *Personal and Organizational Change Through Group Methods*, Wiley, 1965.

JOHN F. MEE

PROFILES OF THE FUTURE

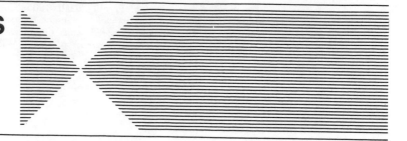

The manager of the future

John F. Mee is Mead Johnson Professor of Management and dean of the Division of General and Technical Studies, Indiana University.

Coming events cast their shadows before—if we study those shadows, we can observe the forces and factors that are shaping the manager of the future.

There will be managers in the future. The pathologists can predict with certainty that bleeding will always stop; managers can predict with certainty that the future will eventually involve them. Their concern is whether or not they are prepared for the changing social, economic, technological, and political environments that emerge as the future unfolds.

MANAGERS OF THE PAST

Managers of the past can be described and classified in relation to the environments in which they operated. The antecedents of the managers in our English-influenced culture can be recognized in sixteenth century Tudor England. They were the office-holders in the royal household, in the major departments of state, and in the army and the navy. They were men to whom administration and management was a professional life commitment, and their function was to administer the affairs of the state and the economy within the rules of the social order.

After the separation of the United States from England, our constitution provided that individuals might own private property. Our government, founded on the concept of government by law rather than government by men, established an environment of opportunity for the owner-manager in a private enterprise economy. For over a century, the owner-managers of small enterprises flourished, managing by right of ownership rather than by birthright in a predominantly agricultural society.

Some of those owner-managers thrived with the changing environment at the turn of the century, and, using their authority of ownership, developed our basic industries and promoted our industrial society. Facing death

 Reprinted by permission from the author and *Business Horizons* from *Business Horizons,* June 1973, pp. 5–14.

from the impact of the Sherman Act they resorted to corporate forms of business organizations to perpetuate their firms. The growth of large and complex organizations with the capability of generating a trillion dollar gross national product originated with these "captains of industry."

They were followed by a new breed of managers who are now classified as corporate speculators and exploiters. These managers, who had financial or legal backgrounds, gained control of the business organizations that they managed for corporate share owners. The era of the speculators and exploiters was rather short. They met with an ignominious end in the decade of the 1930s because they were unable to manage business organizations for the benefit of society through the intelligent use of human and capital resources.

During that decade the federal government set about helping managers with legislative guidelines and regulations. The health of the economy was deemed too important to trust to capricious managers with improper human values and undesirable social ethics. The flow of legislation regulating business activities and the pressures for social responsibilities and objectives of business were initiated by the failures of these managers.

Following the debacle of the thirties, a class of managers known as professional managers appeared; most operating managers of business enterprise today are in this category. The term professional managers is used because these men manage for pay and do not own any significant share of the enterprises they manage. They profess to have the knowledge, the skills, and the value systems suitable for setting objectives and then attaining them through the utilization of other people's money, talents, and physical facilities. Some of them acquire professional manager citations from their professional associations to reinforce their image.

Evaluated by their records of economic progress and the creation of material wealth, our American managers have the best perfor-

mance records in the history of the world. U.S. resources include 6 percent of the world's population and 7 percent of the land area of the world; with these, our managers have generated over half of the wealth of the world and about 35 percent of the world's annual income. They have achieved the world's first trillion dollar gross national product. The combined efforts of Russia, Japan, West Germany, and the United Kingdom—with double the population of the United States—would be required to equal that figure.

That is a formidable record of managerial achievement; why, then, are managers experiencing so much dissatisfaction with their performance? Why are today's professional managers, working on the objectives established for the decade of the sizzling sixties, absorbing attacks for matters that previously have not been considered germane to operating businesses? Despite the most outstanding performance of managers in all history, they are criticized and attacked by:

Consumer groups and regulatory agencies
Aroused antipollutionists who often press for hasty, costly, or sometimes unavailable solutions
Ecologists who are more concerned with preserving the wilderness than creating employment opportunities
Civil rights activists who demand more jobs for minority groups from top to bottom ranks
Naive and well-meaning activists who clamor for democracy on boards of directors
Employees who want relief from boring and monotonous work assignments.

Recognizing merit in some of the criticism, perhaps too many well-meaning people are finding themselves influenced by the extremists and activists who can proclaim without responsibility. James Roche of General Motors Corporation has tried to bring the extremist view into perspective: "Profits are the incentives, the driving force behind economic expansion and rising employment. It takes about $25,000 investment to create one new job opportunity. Just to keep pace with the rising labor force each year requires an opening of about 1.75 million new jobs."

Obviously, the managers of the future

must be mindful of several worthwhile corporate objectives, but they had better not lose sight of the primary objective of a business, that of staying in business. No profits, no business. Survival is the first priority of managing.

Managers in the future will be expected to create wealth, generate profits, and provide employment for the fulfillment of the public policy outlined in the Employment Act of 1946. Furthermore, they will be expected to utilize the human resources of the nation in accordance with the spirit of equal economic opportunity, civil rights, equal employment opportunity, and, at the same time, adhere to the clean air and clean water guidelines of the Environmental Protection Agency within the Occupational Health and Safety Act standards. Managers will be challenged to create almost 2 million new employment opportunities a year with people working fewer hours per week. The four-day work week is on the horizon with "gliding work time" a probability. A 28-hour work week has been predicted for the turn of the century, compared with 37.3 hours in 1970, 49 hours in 1930, 57 hours in 1900, 70 hours in 1850, and 84 hours in 1800.

Future managers will be expected to create more goods and services with more profits and more employment, and to deal with employees' demands for more leisure, more services, and more conveniences in a technological economy in a scientific society. The role of future managers will be complicated further by energy and power shortages and pressure to guard the environment from damage.

Some of the most obvious and pressing factors and forces in the changing economic, social, and political situation have been cited to illustrate that managers of the future will be operating in an environment different from that in which managers of the past operated. The question of managerial concern is now posed. What knowledge, skills, and values will be required for the future manager's survival and success?

MANAGERS OF THE FUTURE

According to the time schedule, a new type of manager should now be emerging to cope with the complexity of factors and forces in a society that is struggling to adapt to changing human values and rapid technological advances. It is probable that the manager of the future will be classified as a "public manager" or a "public oriented executive." Harlan Cleveland, in his recent book *The Future Executive,* predicts the role of the future public executive and gives reasons for his or her emergence.

Today's professional manager will modify his style and begin the transition towards the era of the public manager; the potential managers among the some 8 million students in the universities today will complete the transition during the last portion of the century. The manager will develop from a hired man for private corporation shareholders into a business institutional leader who will manage enterprise for the best balanced interests of the state and the nation to preserve and maintain our private enterprise system. This development could be changed, of course, in the event of war, epidemic, depression, or some other unforeseen catastrophe.

The environmental factors and forces at work, such as changing human values along with the growing size and complexity of organizational patterns, are blurring the traditional lines between what is private and what is public. The future managers of private enterprise—profit or nonprofit—will gravitate toward the concept that they are responsible for people in general and reluctantly accept the government as a monitor of business affairs. Concurrently, the government will contract to the private sector of the economy a growing proportion of public business because public managers will be better qualified to achieve the results desired by the body politic.

The National Aeronautics and Space Administration is a prime example of this method of operation. No large business organization, whatever its formal ownership, will be able to escape social and public responsibility. Public managers will be faced with the major responsibility for merging human values with the potential from technological advances to conserve human energy in the creation and distribution of goods and services for improved life styles.

For the managers of the future, policies for the conduct of their firms will be formulated mostly by their sense of direction as modified by negotiation with their colleagues and peers. Private enterprise will prevail, but managers will be sensitive to the need to satisfy multiple claimants for the benefits flowing from national and multinational corporations.

Actually, it is the success of past managers that has developed this trend toward the concept of the public manager. The managers of our corporate enterprises have succeeded in creating most of the wealth of the nation; they also have attracted most of the nation's competent personnel into the work force of the corporations. Corporations, therefore, have the greatest capability of achieving state and national goals for economic and social progress. If the managers of private enterprise do not adopt the public manager concept, the alternative would not be acceptable to the advocates of the private enterprise system that has been the foundation of the American dream.

Future Managerial Situation

The first priority for managers of the future will be the survival of the companies that they manage and their own survival as managers. If present professional managers could send a scout into the future, receive reports, and ensure their survival by being prepared, such reports probably would include subject areas that already are discernible. The public manager in the future will perform functions with resources that may have names the same

as or similar to present ones, but they will change in concept and nature in response to changing human values and environmental conditions.

The manager of the future will deal with highly complex organizations. The organizational vehicle will not be the hierarchical pyramid in which decisions are centralized and most of the planning and control are done at the top. The future manager's organizational mechanism will be in the nature of systems that will have interlaced webs of tension with loose control; power will be diffused among plural centers of decision. Decision making will become an increasingly intricate process of multilateral brokerage both inside and outside the organization.

As organizations become more horizontal and less vertical in structure, the style by which they will be governed will be more consensual, collegial, and consultive. The more challenging the objective and the more

---

"If the managers of private enterprise do not adopt the public manager concept, the alternative would not be acceptable to the advocates of the private enterprise system. . . ."

---

formidable the problems to be resolved, the more authority and power will be diffused so that a larger number of capable people can work toward achievement and problem solving. Collective leadership is not for the expression of democratic feelings; it is an imperative of size and complexity. The manager of the future must manage more complexity for survival.

Evidence of the increasing complexity of organizations is easily observable in the growth and influence of multinational firms, bank holding companies, and conglomerate corporations. Multinational firms already dominate much of the production of the world, and they are growing at a rate double the purely domestic companies. Some of

"The manager of the future will realize that employees will be more inclined to take authority from agreed-upon objectives and the nature of the work than from the dictation of an authoritarian boss. More than one mode of thinking can be utilized. The future manager will be a multiplier of the work of others . . . ."

them exert great influence on the world's financial affairs and have grown in economic size beyond all but the wealthiest nations. They are creating an economic and social movement that rivals the impact of the industrial revolution. Bank holding companies, as of mid-1972, held nearly 40 percent of all commercial banks in the nation with 58 percent of all deposits and 60 percent of all U.S. assets. The responsibilities of the managers of these complex organizations are greater than those faced by previous managers; the consequences of error and mismanagement could have serious negative impacts on the world economy.

Managers of these organizations have the opportunity to influence the peace of the world and the living standards and life styles of the peoples of less developed nations because the influence of their operations can transcend national boundaries more readily than that of governments or religious orders. However, they can only achieve their potential by managing with the concept and style of a public oriented manager. J. J. Servan-Schreiber, in his book *The American Challenge* paid tribute to the genius and viability of American managers: "American industry spills out across the world primarily because of the energy released by the American system—by the opportunity for individual initiative, by the innovative knack of teams, by the flexibility of business structure and by the decentralization of business decision."

The manager of the future will encounter an accelerating growth in the size and complexity of organizational systems that seem destined to move away from formal, authoritarian, and hierarchical managing. The trend is toward more informal, fluid ways of bargaining, brokerage, advice, and consent. Management will be practiced less as a system of authority and more as a resource in an organizational system to achieve desired results.

The view of William Blackie, the past chariman of Caterpillar Tractor Company, reflects the changing concept: "Insofar as authority has meant the power to order or command, its definition will be modified by the addition of some such qualification as 'but expect or deserve to be obeyed or followed only if you can satisfy those being ordered or led'." According to Blackie, the boss-man relationship will prevail and embrace both a superior and a subordinate. The gap will be narrowed, however, because of the rapidity with which the well-educated subordinate is acquiring skill and experience. The essential requirement is that both parties understand and appreciate the basic nature of their respective responsibilities.

The manager of the future will realize that employees will be more inclined to take authority from agreed-upon objectives and the nature of the work than from the dictation of an authoritarian boss. More than one mode of thinking can be utilized. The future manager will be a multiplier of the work of others; in the more complex organizations of the future, he will find it necessary to utilize the knowledge and skills that others possess. He will be responsible for results and for "getting it all together," rather than for preoccupying himself with individual processes.

Authority as used by the future manager

will be modified by the changing values and motivations of university students as they populate the organizations of business. By 1985, college graduates will outnumber those without a high school education in the U.S. work force, and managers will have as a resource the most highly educated personnel in the history of the world. Employees will regard themselves as partners in management and expect to have their talents utilized for self-esteem and self-realization. The better educated young people today, especially those in the so-called new culture or counter culture, tend to demand their rights, resist authority and regimentation that try to put them into an organizational harness too tight for comfort, and search for their own identity instead of allowing themselves to be "house-broken" by endless procedures and processes.

Before anyone makes a quick decision that universities are subversive places and our young people have revolutionary ideas, it might be enlightening to read *The Unanimous Declaration of the Thirteen United States of America*. In this document, popularly known as the Declaration of Independence, one will find written:

> We hold these truths to be self-evident, that all men are created equal, that they are endowed by their Creator with certain unalienable Rights, that among these are Life, Liberty, and the pursuit of Happiness—That to secure these rights, governments are instituted among Men, deriving their just powers from the consent of the governed—That whenever any form of government becomes destructive of these ends, it is the Right of the People to alter or to abolish it, and to institute new government, laying its foundation on such principles, and organizing its powers in such form, as to them shall seem most likely to effect their Safety and Happiness.

If a substitution of the words "management" for "government" and "employees" for "people" is made in the reading of that document, one can better understand why there is a trend in the concept of management by the consent of those managed. Of course, there is no reference to women. The proposed 27th amendment to the constitution might remedy this original writing. Some thirty states have ratified the amendment with thirty-eight required to provide equal rights for women by the enactment of an Equal Rights Act. Depending upon one's point of view, an equal rights act may be necessary to enlarge opportunities for women. With few exceptions, most professions and trades employed about the same percentage of women in 1970 as in 1950, twenty years previously.

Henry B. Schacht, commenting on the changing trend in organizational design and the use of human resources, has stated that managers must learn to handle both the underprivileged and the bright young people, especially those who are calling for a change [*Business Horizons*, August, 1970, pp. 29-34]. He adds:

> What this means is shorter, flatter organizations; it means responsive management; it means a true willingness to allow people to participate in setting their own destiny; it means that the militaristically-oriented hierarchy that has characterized societies and most business enterprises is a thing of the past, and the quicker we recognize it the better. . . . all organizations will have to think of their key assets in terms of people and knowledge. People can be the most flexible of all assets; knowledge is the one thing that will give us insight into change and the consequences of change. Many companies say that people are its most important resource, but few believe it. Many people say that they live or die with their people but then spend all of their time analyzing balance sheets and income statements.

Current professional managers who make the transition to public oriented managers will master the methods required to achieve objectives in organizations with more complex and decentralized relationships; they will develop the skills to use a modified concept of authority that will enable personnel to exercise self-commitment and self-control for the achievement of agreed upon results instead of emphasizing processes.

For the realization of high motivation and performance of personnel in more complex organizational relationships, authority must be applied with the consent and cooperation of those managed. Future managers will cope with the challenge of generating purposeful action while more and more employees demand the satisfaction of getting into the act.

Future External Forces on Managers

All organizations exist and operate in an environment of some kind. External forces and factors in the environment will complicate the work of future managers. Before the end of the present decade, for example, managers of all organizations in the United States will be faced with the problem of adapting their operations to the metric system of weights and measurements. (The meter unit of measurement was determined by measuring the distance from the North Pole to the equator and then dividing by 10 million. The meter is 3.3 feet or 1.1 yards in the English system.) At present, the United States and Burma are the only major nations still using the English system. Because of the world trend, Congress asked in 1968 for a sweeping investigation of the question. This investigation involved public hearings and surveys on almost every activity in our society—from education, manufacturing, and the consumer to international trade and national security. The recommendation of the Secretary of Commerce was that the United States should adopt the metric through a nationally coordinated program.

This conversion will affect all managers of business enterprise, especially the manufacturers. Temperature will be measured by Celsius instead of Fahrenheit; length will be computed by centimeters and kilometers rather than by inches and miles; mass weight will change from ounces and pounds to grams and kilograms; area will be determined by square meters and square kilometers instead of by square feet and square miles; hectares will replace acres; and volume will be measured by milliliters and liters.

Present managers are planning for the costs of conversion, which will be relatively greater in the manufacturing industry. The greatest burden of costs will be in production and industrial educational programs, particularly in the machine tool and automotive industries. The conversion will entail considerable costs for manufacturers during a time when costs will be increasing for pollution and environmental damage control.

The material wealth of the nation, measured by either the metric system or the passing English system, stems from the managerial use of the basic factors of production, land, labor, and capital. The manager of the future will be more restricted in his use of land than his predecessors. Managers of the past have enjoyed freedom of decision in the use of private land, regardless of whether or not it was devoted to its highest and best use. The market system prevailed. The future manager, however, will be confined to operating within federal and state land-use policy. A bill now in Congress (S. 268) will give grants to states for the development of plans for private land use.

J. Irwin Miller, a prominent Indiana industrialist, in a recent issue of *U.S. News and World Report,* expressed his views concerning corporate survival by serving effectively and well some real current need of society. He wrote:

> We have a fixed amount of land in the continental United States. Contained in that fixed amount of land is a fixed amount of natural resources. On the fixed amount of land, then, with a finite quantity of resources, there exists a growing population of human beings. By the end of the century there will be somewhere between 50 and 100 million more people in this country. . . . Growing demand for a shrinking supply of land and materials can prudently be expected only to accelerate the rise in cost of capital construction despite the miracles that need performing in labor costs, regulations and design.

Land-use policy for the guidelines of the future manager stems from the growing population that requires more land for living, domestic and foreign consumption, recreation, and energy sources. Future managers will be expected to create the equivalent of a new city for a million people about every four months during the remainder of the century. They will also be expected to produce for a per capita consumption of some 700 British thermal units of energy by the year 2000, in comparison with 377 in 1970, and at the same time protect the environment from water and air pollution and trash.

Proposed legislation in Congress (S.1283) will create a new federal agency with authority to relieve the fuel shortage. The legislation will create five "government-industry" corporations to develop technology to turn coal into gas, extract oil from shale rock, and harness geothermal energy. Soon legislation may be passed for the control of trash pollution in addition to water and air pollution. Currently we are producing enough trash annually to fill the Panama Canal four times over with a disposal cost of some $5 billion a year. This cost is exceeded only by that for schools and roads in the public services. Our trash volume will triple in the next decade to harass the future manager as increased demands will be made for the discharge of his social responsibilities.

Although the land resource is considered fixed for the future manager, he will have an increasing supply of labor flowing from the enlarging population. However, this labor resource will be different from that of the past and will require a different style of managing. This style must recognize the consent of the managed with an orientation around results rather than activities in more viable organizations. The members of the labor force of the future will be the best educated in history with knowledge and skills that many managers will need but will not possess. Furthermore, employees' expectations and value systems will be different.

Over 80 percent will be high school and college graduates who will expect managers to utilize their talents and abilities in interesting and challenging work opportunities with a minimum of boredom and monotony. Their work styles and life styles may be as important to them as their pay scales. They will resist being used as impersonal "inputs" in complex organizations under authoritarian supervisors. They will be products of the new knowledge industry that may account for half of the GNP by the end of the century, and they will expect managers to fulfill their responsibilities for both economic and social objectives.

In the future labor force, some will be specialists, others technologists, and many humanists. Some will have broad preparation, such as the proposed "poly-socio-econo-politico-technologist" background that has been conceived by Simon Ramo, vice-chairman of TRW, Inc. The manager of the future will be expected to utilize intelligently this highly competent labor force and avoid underemploying or wasting human resources. The wealth of the state and the nation will be measured more by the productivity of the labor force than by gold bullion, and future managers may be evaluated more on their abilities to skilfully utilize a growing labor force than to use capital equipment. The human asset will appear on the balance sheet of the future. Advancing technology will aid the future manager in his use of resources, but he will need to arrange a satisfactory combination of ethical human values with the flow of science and technology.

The capital resources available to managers in the future should be adequate if inflation can be controlled. National personal income in the United States has passed the lofty mark of a trillion dollars per annum for another historical first. No other nation has come close to this annual flow of personal income from wages, salaries (with fringe benefits), interest, rent, dividends, and social welfare, and the income to business proprietors and professional personnel. Reasonable savings and investment of a portion of this personal income can provide adequate capital resources for future managers to combine with land and labor resources for the maintenance of a healthy economy.

The public managers of the future will

differ more in their values and attitudes than in their knowledge and skills. One can already discern in the United States that the line between public and private is narrowing because all private enterprise has some degree of public responsibility. The larger and more complex the enterprise, the more public responsibility it is expected to carry. Regardless of their personal values, more managers in private enterprise are serving more and more as public managers or executives.

If the manager of the future makes the transition from the firm-oriented professional manager of today to the public oriented manager, the business foundation of democracy and private enterprise can be maintained with managerial freedom to set objectives and policies for the best balanced interests of the economy. Furthermore, the future public manager can be recognized for making contributions to society as beneficial as those made by doctors, lawyers, ministers, engineers, educators, and scientists.

The public manager of the future can lessen the credibility gap in management that has widened since 1965. It is ironic today that our citizens want business to become more active in public leadership, yet believe that business is doing less than before, according to a recent Louis Harris survey. The future public manager will perform the essential managerial functions in society in a manner that will enhance his credibility. Alec Mackenzie, in his recent book *The Credibility Gap in Management,* states that "credibility is that quality, state, or condition that produces believability or trustworthiness." He comments that credibility depends more upon relationships with people than upon systems. Somehow, the public is inclined to believe that business is out of phase with current expectations and demands. It is not the capability and competence of business managers that are being questioned, it is their sense of priorities and good faith.

At a time when the public is crying for a new leadership style, some managers are retreating into fixed behavior patterns. They are charged with proclaiming a modern managerial theory but continuing to execute in antiquated managerial practices. Unless the manager of the future assumes a role similar to the public manager concept, there looms the possibility of the establishment of a public management commission because of the importance of managers in our economy and to prevent serious management failures in essential corporations that affect the public interest.

If governmental commissions are considered essential for the proper utilization of the resources of land, labor, and capital, it is not inconceivable that public pressures could develop for monitoring the application of the management resource in our society. Without the resource of management to utilize other resources, little is accomplished. Managers who learn to manage with a public orientation will obviate any need for a public management commission. Their value systems will embrace the service of multiple claimants in society by the setting and the achievement of both the economic and the social objectives of their firms.

The public manager of the future has the opportunity to achieve the prestige and the recognition that managers have earned but not received on the basis of contributions to society. Congress or a state legislature can recognize the importance of the future public managers by establishing a national or a state Management Day. For the contributions that managers make to economic and social progress, it would be suitable to have two holidays in one week, Labor Day on Monday and Management Day on Tuesday. This would focus attention on the relationship of both segments of our private enterprise society. Together they have produced the biggest national output, the highest personal income, and the highest standard of living in the world.

Readings Cross-Reference Matrix

The cross-reference matrix presented below shows the relationship between the articles in this reader and chapters in selected management texts. The corresponding chapters are listed below the text titles.

Readings in Management: An Organizational Perspective Contents	Albanese, Management: Toward Accountability for Performance, 1975	Donnelly, Gibson, and Ivancevich, Fundamentals of Management: Functions Behavior Models, 1975	Duncan, Essentials of Management, 1975
I. Organization Design			
A. Organizational Models	1, 4, 8	1, 2, 4	1, 2, 13
B. Technology and Environmental Uncertainty	9, 10, 11	10	3, 14
II. Guiding and Monitoring The Organization			
A. Planning	2, 3, 6	3	10, 11, 12*
B. Control	7	5	15
C. Organization Change and Development	12	11	16
III. Behavior in Organizations			
A. Motivation	13, 14, 15, 16	6, 7	11
B. Leadership	17	9	8
C. Group Behavior	19	8	13
D. Communication	18		
IV. Managerial Decision Making	5	12, 13, 14, 15, 16	6
V. Managerial Careers and Orientations			
A. Entrepreneurship			
B. The Individual and His Career			4
C. The Current and Future State of Management			

Contents	Filley, House, and Kerr, *Managerial Process and Organizational Behavior*, 1976	Flippo and Munsinger, *Management*, 1975	Fulmer, *The New Management*, 1974
I. Organization Design			
A. Organizational Models	1, 2, 3, 16, 18	1, 7, 8	1, 2, 3, 4
B. Technology and Environmental Uncertainty	13, 15	2, 11	10
II. Guiding and Monitoring The Organization			
A. Planning	14, 19	4	8
B. Control		16, 17	12
C. Organization Change and Development	20, 21	18	19
III. Behavior in Organizations			
A. Motivation	4, 5, 6, 10	5, 6, 13, 14	5, 16, 17, 18
B. Leadership	11, 12	12	13, 15
C. Group Behavior	8, 9	9, 10	6, 7, 11
D. Communication		15	14
IV. Managerial Decision Making	7	3, 19, 20, 21, 22, 23	9
V. Managerial Careers and Orientations			
A. Entrepreneurship			
B. The Individual and His Career	17		
C. The Current and Future State of Management	22	24	20, 21, 22, 23

Gannon, Management: An Organizational Perspective, 1977	Haiman and Scott, Management in the Modern Organization, 1974	Haynes Massie, and Wallace, Management: Analysis, Concepts, and Cases, 1975	Hellriegel and Slocum, Management: A Contingency Approach, 1974
1, 2, 3	1, 2, 3, 9, 10, 11, 12, 13	1, 2, 4, 23, 24	1, 3, 4
4	9, 10, 11, 12, 13	3	2, 5
5	5, 6, 7, 8	9, 10	8
6	28, 29, 30, 31	11, 12	9
7	29	14, 15	
8	24, 25	5, 6, 8	11
9		7	12
10	14, 15, 16, 26, 27	7	13
11	23	7	12
12, 13	4	13, 17, 18, 19, 20, 21, 22	6, 7
14, 15			
16	17, 18, 19, 20, 21, 22		10
17		25, 26, 27, 28	19

431

Contents	Hodgetts, Management: Theory, Process, and Practice, 1975	Kast and Rosenzweig, Organization and Management: A Systems Approach, 1974	Koontz and O'Donnell, A Systems and Contingency Analysis of Managerial Functions, 1976
I. Organization Design			
A. Organizational Models	1, 2, 3, 4, 5	1, 2, 3, 4, 9	1, 2, 3, 12, 13, 14, 15
B. Technology and Environmental Uncertainty	6, 17, 18	5, 6, 7, 8, 19	4, 5
II. Guiding and Monitoring The Organization			
A. Planning	7, 8, 19	17	6, 7, 8, 11
B. Control	9	18	27, 28, 29, 30
C. Organization Change and Development		22	19, 20, 21, 22
III. Behavior in Organizations			
A. Motivation	13	10	24
B. Leadership	14	13	23, 25
C. Group Behavior		11, 12	16, 17, 18
D. Communication			26
IV. Managerial Decision Making	10, 11, 16	14, 15, 16	9, 10
V. Managerial Careers and Orientations			
A. Entrepreneurship			
B. The Individual and His Career			
C. The Current and Future State of Management	15, 20, 21, 22	20, 21, 23	

432

Longenecker, *Principles of Management and Organizational Behavior*, 1973	Hellriegel and Slocum, *Management: Contingencies Structure and Process*, 1976	Trewatha and Newport, *Management: Functions and Behavior*, 1976	Webber, *Management*, 1975
1, 9	1, 2	2, 13, 14, 15	1, 3, 17, 18, 20
2, 3	6, 7		19
4, 5, 6	10	5, 6, 7, 8	12, 13, 16
24, 25, 26		9, 10, 11, 12	14, 15
14	17, 18	21	24, 25, 26, 27, 28, 29
	5	17, 18	4, 5, 6, 7
10, 11, 12, 19, 21, 23	8	19	8, 9, 10, 11
13, 15, 17	4	16	21, 22, 23
22		20	
7, 8	9, 11, 12, 13, 14, 15, 16	3, 4	2
18, 20	3		30
16, 27	19	1, 22	

DATE DUE

DEC 0 5 2007		
MAY 0 1 2006		